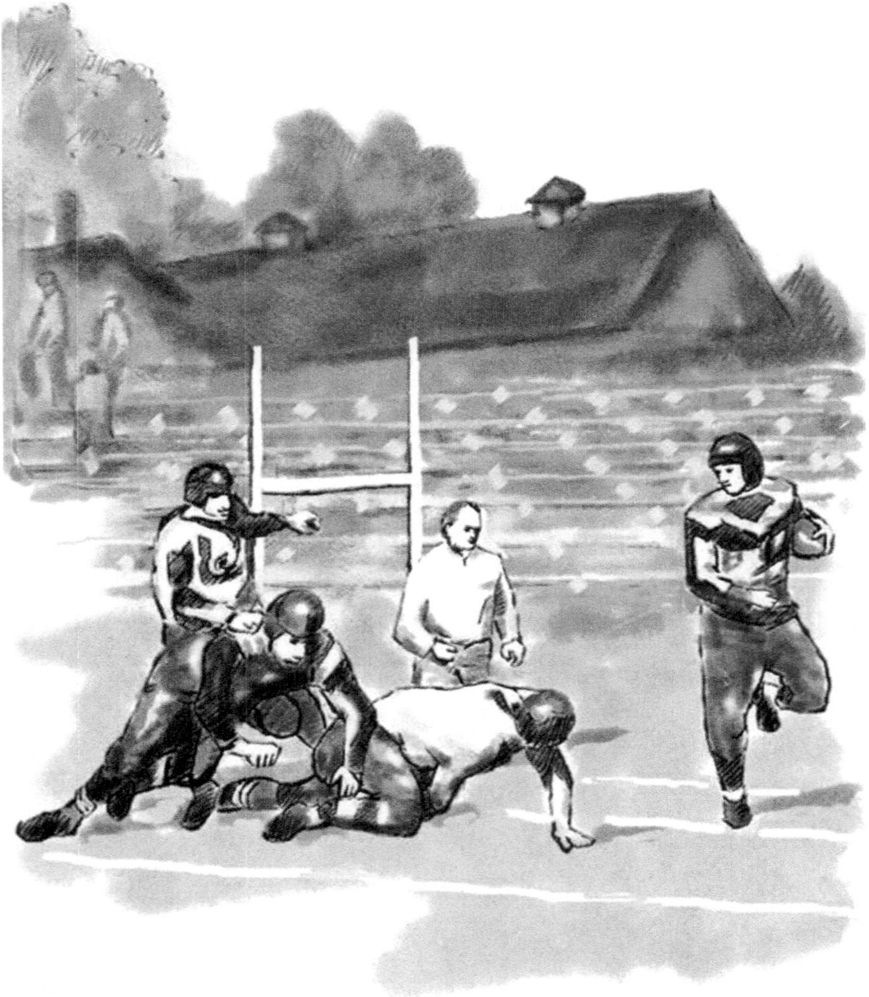

Border Boys

How Americans from Border Colleges
Helped Western Canada
to Win a Football Championship

R. C. Christiansen

borderboysbook.com

Copyright © 2022 by Ryan Cornell Christiansen

All Rights Reserved. Published in the United States by Ryan Cornell Christiansen.

Edited by Dustin Mohagen and Ryan Cornell Christiansen with additional edits by Jodi Christiansen

Cover photo from NDSU Archives, Fargo, N.D. (AF067 Folio)

Author photo by Star-Ann Schank, Copyright © 2013 Ryan Cornell Christiansen

Illustrations by Xian Mao, Copyright © 2021 Ryan Cornell Christiansen

Book design by Ryan Cornell Christiansen

www.borderboysbook.com

For the boys.

We're sorry it took so long to tell your story.

Table of Contents

Preface i

A Note on Sports Teams Nicknames iii

Introduction v

Chapter 1 - Maroon and Gold (1931) 1

Chapter 2 - Yellow and Green (1932) 33

Chapter 3 - Blue and Gold (1933) 95

Chapter 4 - Brown and Gold (1934) 177

Chapter 5 - Grey (1935) 269

Afterword 333

Appendix – Season Records 343

Research Notes 347

Bibliography 351

About the Author 383

"Have you ever heard the name 'Fritz Hanson'?"

-Perham Enterprise-Bulletin, December 12, 1935

PREFACE

On September 21, 2018, I took my family to Investors Group Field in Winnipeg, Manitoba, to watch the Winnipeg Blue Bombers play the Montreal Alouettes in a Canadian Football League (CFL) regular season game. At halftime, the Bombers posthumously inducted a player into their Ring of Honour, a guy named Fritz Hanson who had played college football at North Dakota State University in Fargo, North Dakota. His visage graces the cover of this book.

After the game, I searched through old newspapers to find out more. I quickly discovered that many more players, including more players from Fargo and from Moorhead, Minnesota, contributed to the story of Canadian football in the early 1930s, and that Canadian fans both celebrated and disapproved of the presence of these "imports" on the field.

This is their story.

-R. C. Christiansen, January 1, 2022, Fargo, North Dakota

A NOTE ON SPORTS TEAMS NICKNAMES

In the 1930s, two rival North Dakota colleges adopted the nicknames Bison and Sioux. Long before the colleges or the people who built them walked the Northern Plains, the Lakota Sioux ruled the land and the trade routes on horseback. Great herds of Bison provided food, clothing, and shelter for the Lakota Sioux, but not without struggle. The Sioux culled the weakest Bison from the herd, which kept the herd strong.

The Lakota did not *choose* the name Sioux. Their rivals, the Ojibwa, used a form of the word, which meant "enemies," when they described the Lakota to French traders. The name stuck.

In 1930, students and faculty at the University of North Dakota pushed to change the school's name from the benign Flickertails (ground squirrel, a.k.a. prairie dog) to Sioux, "a good exterminating agent for the Bison... warlike, of fine physique and bearing," wrote professor emeritus Alvin Austin in a letter to the student newspaper, *Dakota Student*. "The Sioux and the Bison," reported the *Student* in 1933, "[were] natural enemies of the plains long before either represented a football team."

Fans did not honor the Sioux name, however. In newspapers, particularly in the *Student*, articles used language that portrayed the athletes as cartoon versions of the Sioux people who exacted cartoon-like violence against opponents. Fans portrayed Fighting Sioux victories as bloodbaths instead of noble triumphs.

For historical accuracy, this book will sometimes use the Sioux nickname and other deprecated nicknames to reference sports teams from the era.

INTRODUCTION

In the 1930s, both the American and Canadian versions of gridiron football matured to more closely resemble the game as it is played today. To fully understand the magnitude of this development, it is important to know more about the origin of the game and about how the Canadian and American systems progressed and intersected during the first several decades.

* *

Both the Canadian and American varieties of football grew out of English rugby. Canadians first modified the English game and then passed on those modifications to Americans. Over the years, both varieties of the game have influenced one another and have evolved into what we now know as Canadian football and American football.

Although variations of football had existed for centuries, not until 1845 did the Rugby School in Warwickshire, England, establish the rules for the game known as rugby, named after the school. Just two years earlier, in 1843, the University of Cambridge in Cambridgeshire, England, first codified the rules for "association football," now known in the United States and Canada as "soccer," slang for as(soc)iation football as opposed to "rugger," slang for (rug)by.

Both rugby and association football found their way to North America. In 1865, English officers played rugby on Canadian soil against players from McGill College of Montreal, Quebec. Over the next decade, the rules for playing rugby at McGill evolved.

When the McGill team traveled to Cambridge, Massachusetts, to play Harvard College in May of 1874, the Canadians introduced their style of rugby to their American counterparts. At the time, McGill played using a ball that looked more like today's football while Harvard played using a ball that looked more like today's soccer ball. Under McGill's rules, a player could kick or pick up the ball and run with it at any time, but Harvard played "the Boston game," a version of association football in which a ball-handler could only pick up the ball and throw it or run with

Introduction

it if he were being pursued by an opposing player. At the time, teams at American universities each played their own version of modified soccer, and when they met to play one another, they determined the rules to be used for each game. The McGill and Harvard teams first played a game with Harvard's rules, and the next day they played with McGill's rules. The Harvard students who watched the games expressed the opinion that they much better enjoyed the game played with McGill's rules. Harvard adopted McGill's rules, modified them further, and traveled to Montreal the following autumn to play McGill at the Montreal Cricket Grounds.

In 1875, Harvard challenged Yale College in New Haven, Connecticut, to play football with the modified rugby rules.

One year later, representatives from Columbia College in New York City, Harvard, the College of New Jersey (now Princeton University), and Yale formed the American Intercollegiate Football Association to play football by the same rules.

*

Since 1876, the American version of football has been played on a field that is 53 1/3 yards wide, while the Canadian version of football has been played on a field that is 65 yards wide. This disparity arguably led the American game to diverge from the Canadian game.

The Canadian game has always included an artifact from early Canadian rugby football called the "rouge," in which the kicking team scores a point when an opponent doesn't return a kick or punt that has been kicked beyond the goal line.

*

In 1880, Walter Camp at Yale replaced the rugby scrummage with a line of scrimmage, and from that "developed the set play, series of plays, and all the aspects of strategy which characterize the modern game," observed the *Yale Daily News*. "It was probably the most important single invention in the history of football." That same year, Camp reduced the number of players on each side from 15 to 11.

In 1882, Camp established a rule that required the offense to gain 5 yards on three plays or lose possession of the ball.

Introduction

By the end of the nineteenth century, American universities played a version of what we would consider to be American football instead of modified rugby or soccer.

*

In Canada, communities formed organizations called "unions" to govern how teams played football in their communities. Member teams of the Quebec Rugby Football Union (QRFU), which included McGill University, along with the Ontario Rugby Football Union (ORFU), led the development of the Canadian version of football. After fits and starts and disagreements over rules, in 1894, the QRFU and ORFU, under the auspices of a national body, the Canadian Rugby Union (CRU), a union of unions, agreed to operate under the same code, but then a third union, the Canadian Intercollegiate Rugby Football Union (CIRFU) formed and joined the CRU. New disagreements arose, mainly driven by those who wanted to play the game more like English rugby and those who wanted to change the game. At the time, teams played with one of four sets of rules that ranged from true English rugby on one end of the spectrum to the Burnside Rules on the other. University of Toronto rugby football team captain John Meldrum "Thrift" Burnside had developed rules for the ORFU, and those rules resembled the rules Americans used at the time. Burnside reduced each team to 12 men, allowed only six to play on the line, and teams used the snap-back (instead of the "heel-back") from center. Unlike the American game, however, the offense needed to gain 10 yards (instead of 5) on three downs.

One of the key differences between the Canadian and American codes at the time is that none of the Canadian versions of the rules allowed for players to block defenders away from the ball-carrier. To combat this, teams would run an "extension" play, which was essentially an option or double-option run play. Without blockers, if the lead runners timed their lateral passes well, those lead runners would become de facto blockers by nature of their position on the field between the defender and subsequent ball-carrier. Teams that played with 12 men per side instead of 14 or 15 men found more success with these "extension" end runs.

*

Introduction

In October 1905, the dramatic rise in injuries and death in American college football led U.S. President Theodore Roosevelt to meet with college officials. He demanded they reform the game to make it less violent. Two months later, representatives from 62 colleges and universities met to appoint members to a rules committee, and in March 1906 the group formally established the Intercollegiate Athletic Association of the United States (IAAUS), later named the National Collegiate Athletic Association (NCAA).

For the 1906 season, college football teams in the United States changed the rules of American football to make it less brutal. Going forward:

- The offense could no longer run a "massed play," the primary play before the rules change, in which backfielders as a group would smash the middle of the line and inch and punch their way forward.
- The offense had to move the ball 10 yards (instead of 5) on three downs, similar to the Canadian Burnside Rules. This reduced the effectiveness of continually smashing the middle of the line. Offenses would need to consider running the ball off tackle or around the end.
- Linemen on either side of the ball would have to begin in a down position and would have to play more nimbly so they could block or tackle across the length of the line.
- To facilitate more nimble play, the rules required opposing linemen to begin play 1 foot further apart than before.
- On offense, the rules imposed restrictions on the use of hands for blocking.
- On defense, tacklers could not tackle below the knee.
- Ball-carriers could no longer hurdle opponents.
- In addition, backfielders could attempt a forward pass thrown from the offense's side of the line of scrimmage, within 5 yards of either side of the center.

Introduction

- A backfielder could throw the ball no more than 20 yards to anywhere on the field of play, but not to within 5 yards of the center over the line of scrimmage, and not over the goal line.
- If a pass receiver bobbled the pass and it fell incomplete, the offense suffered a 15-yard penalty.
- If a pass fell incomplete without touching a player, the play resulted in a turnover at the spot where the ball hit the ground.
- The offense could only attempt one forward pass per play and only backfielders or ends could catch the ball.
- The field of play remained 110 yards long, but with intersecting 5-yard marks to help officials identify legal forward passes.
- Because the offense had to move the ball a full 10 yards on three downs, the offense would need to punt more often. The rules considered a punted ball a live ball that anyone could recover after it touched the ground.
- To protect against outside runs, the forward pass, and short kicks, backfielders on defense would need to stand further back from the line, thereby effectively reducing the number of players in any part of the field.
- The rules gave teams three time outs per half.

"Under the new rules the game will be more open and spectacular," reported the *New York Daily Tribune*. "There will certainly be a great deal more kicking, flukes, passing, tricks, open field running and general hurry scurry."

Meanwhile, it would be decades before the Canadian game would adopt the forward pass.

*

In 1907, the four strongest teams from the QRFU and ORFU—Montreal, Ottawa, Hamilton, and Ontario—formed the Interprovincial Rugby Football Union (IRFU). This new conference would shape the direction of the Canadian game until the late 1920s.

*

In 1909, the IAAUS continued to look for ways to make the American game safer for players. To assist in the effort, the *New York Herald* invited

Introduction

the Ottawa Rough Riders and Hamilton Tigers to demonstrate the Canadian game at Van Cortland Park in New York City. More than 12,000 fans attended the event on December 11, 1909.

Afterward, the *New York Times* suggested the Canadian game had proven to be even more violent than the American version. The Canadian rules would "make a field a charnel house" the newspaper said, and "to return to the game from which the American college game was evolved would entail a bigger hospital list, and possibly more fatalities every year than is now the case in five seasons of our brand of football." The *Times* haughtily observed that the Canadians tackled "all around the waist," which appeared to be less effective than American tackling techniques, which we now understand to be more violent.

*

In 1912, American football rules diverged again from Canadian rules. The updated rules:

- Gave the offense four downs to achieve 10 yards.
- Increased the points value of a touchdown to six points.
- Allowed passers to throw across the goal line.
- Established a 10-yard end zone beyond the goal line (to accommodate passing).
- Shortened the playing field to 100 yards in length (to accommodate the end zones).
- Removed the 20-yard maximum distance that a forward pass could be thrown and caught.

*

In 1914, the Alberta Rugby Football Union (ARFU) adopted many of the Burnside rules, and in 1914 and 1919 respectively, the CIRFU and IRFU legalized blocking. Players could block but only on plays from scrimmage and no more than 3 yards past the line of scrimmage.

In 1921, the remaining western unions followed Alberta in adopting many of the Burnside rules, and then so did the CRU. The CRU established a minimum of five men on the line of scrimmage. At the time, McGill's coach, Frank "Shag" Shaughnessy, a Notre Dame alum who had previously coached at Clemson Agricultural College of South Carolina, suggested Canadian football should adopt the forward pass as the American intercollegiate game had done 15 years prior. The CRU disregarded the suggestion.

Similar to hockey, Canadian football included a "penalty box," an artifact of English rugby, where officials sent players to sit out the game for a minimum of three minutes for rough play. By 1923, players on Canadian teams had learned to use legal blocking to rough up their opponents, and defenders responded with more vicious tackles. The CRU increased the minimum penalty for rough play to 10 minutes in the penalty box.

*

Despite an increased focus in American football on the forward pass, the Canadian game had been slow to follow suit, and by 1929, Canadian football games offered fans low-scoring affairs. However, some teams in Canada demanded the CRU should open up the game, and McGill led the charge. In June 1929, the CRU decided that teams throughout Western Canada and also junior intercollegiate teams in the East could use the forward pass, and that teams could also use the play in the Grey Cup championship game. Players could pass the ball, with restrictions:

- A player could throw the ball only on first or second down from a point 5 yards behind the line of scrimmage.
- Six specific positional players (the backs and ends) were eligible to catch the ball.
- A player could run more than 3 yards beyond the line of scrimmage only if he intended to catch a pass.
- Receivers had to catch passes beyond the line of scrimmage.
- Receivers could only catch passes within the 60-yard span between the 25-yard lines.
- An incomplete pass would result in a turnover, which could be returned by a defender in the same manner as a punt return.

To facilitate the pass, the CRU lengthened the size of a regulation ball by one-quarter of an inch.

Introduction

On September 22, 1929, in a game between the Calgary Tigers and Edmonton Eskimos, fans "waited impatiently to see the forward pass tried" in a game, reported the *Calgary Herald*. Neither Calgary nor Edmonton tried the experiment until the third quarter when Calgary's Jerry Seiberling, an American halfback from Drake University in Des Moines, Iowa, completed the first forward pass in a Canadian football game. After Seiberling completed the pass, "the value of it from a spectator's standpoint was demonstrated," the *Herald* said. Seiberling completed 4 of his 5 pass attempts, which "were all like bullets headed towards a bull's eye. They were beautifully executed and thrilled the crowd. Cheers greeted each one, even from the hostile Edmonton crowd."

Before the game, ARFU executives had held a special session where the union struck down "clause six" of the CRU code, which said an incomplete pass would result in a turnover that could be returned by a defender in the same manner as a punt return, "[thus] making effective the West's intention" of having an American-style passing game, the *Herald* said. A few days later, the ARFU received its official printed copy of the new Canadian football code and said they would adhere to the letter of the law going forward.

Throughout the 1929 season, both players and spectators expressed enthusiasm about the rules changes. Western officials reported that fans in prairie cities showed more interest in football than they had displayed in years. In the 1929 Grey Cup game, Regina completed 8 of 11 pass attempts for 40 yards against Hamilton, which had trouble defending the pass. Hamilton won, anyway, 14-3. The *Manitoba Free Press* observed, "Their extravagant use of the forward pass, which they had scarcely used back home, was one of the chief reasons why [the Roughriders] managed to put up the finest fight of any western team in the Canadian final."

Perhaps embarrassed by Hamilton's unpreparedness, the CRU, which held preference for the East, afterward ruled that in the 1930 Grey Cup final, a team could only use the forward pass if it had been used in the unions of both competing teams.

But then in February 1930, the CRU announced that teams would *not* be allowed to use the forward pass in 1930 after all. "The decision came like a bolt from the blue," reported the *Winnipeg Tribune*. It meant that Western Canada Rugby Football Union (WCRFU) teams, if they continued to use the forward pass, would play a much different game than teams in the East. Some teams in the West felt the WCRFU should break away from competition with Eastern teams or that they should adopt American rules altogether.

Within days, the Western Intercollegiate Rugby Football Union (WCIRFU) expressed strong opposition to the CRU's decision. The WCIRFU also lambasted the CRU's decision-making process, because the rules committee had failed to consult the various unions that fell under the CRU's umbrella. Other unions quickly followed the WCIRFU's opposition, and by July, the CRU adopted a new forward pass rule that included more restrictions. Under the new rule:

- A forward pass could no longer cross the line of scrimmage.
- A forward pass could only be thrown within a 30-yard span between the 40-yard lines.
- Only four different positional players (the backs) could receive the ball.

This new "forward pass," combined with existing rules for the lateral pass, effectively allowed players to complete an "onside pass." In other words, near midfield, a player could toss the ball forward or backward, but only if the receiver caught the ball behind the line of scrimmage.

The incremental rules change satisfied the WCRFU, but by October, the Hamilton Tigers—after a seven-game tour through Western Canada—said they remained opposed to the forward pass, not because they couldn't stop it, but because they said it had been proven ineffective. A month later, Walter Gilhooly, a former player and coach for the Ottawa club, called for more use of the forward pass to open up the game. He criticized the nativistic impulse to reject the play. He wrote, "The objections to the play, where not inspired by prejudice, are totally unsound, the principal one of them being that its origin is American." In December, Ottawa convinced the IRFU, the "Big Four" teams of Montreal, Hamilton, Ottawa, and Toronto, to pass a resolution in favor

Introduction

of the forward pass. The CRU would take up the resolution for consideration in 1931.

*

By the early 1930s, because Canadian football had grown to resemble the American game, many people in Western Canada began to use the term "football" while newspapers in the area continued to use the word "rugby." In fact, newspapers would sometimes refer to the results of American football games as "rugby" results. Farther west, in British Columbia, they called the game "Canadian football" and they referred to English rugby as simply "rugby." In Eastern Canada, they used the term "Canadian rugby" to distinguish the game from "English rugby." Throughout Canada, people had adopted the name "soccer" for association football, but many still called that game "football," too.

As for the positions on the field, Canadian football used its own terms for equivalent positions in the American game. On the line, Canadians called the end an outside wing, the tackle a middle wing, the guard an inside wing, and the center a snap back. In the backfield, Canadians used left halfback, right halfback, and quarterback the same as in the American game, but they called the fullback the center halfback. They called the 12th man in the game the flying wing. Over time, American terminology crept into terms used by Canadians for positions on the field.

In the 1930s, Canadian football scoring still resembled rugby in many ways. In Canada, a "major score" (a touchdown) was worth 5 points. Teams could score 3 points by kicking the ball through the uprights using a drop-kick on the run from anywhere on the field or on a placekick from behind the line of scrimmage. A safety scored 2 points while a point-after-touchdown scored 1 point. The rouge scored 1 point.

* *

In 1879, the original Winnipeg Rugby Football Club formed in Winnipeg, and by 1888, the St. John's Rugby Football Club and the Royal School of Infantry, 90th Regiment, also known as the Royal Winnipeg Rifles, had joined with the Winnipeg club to form the Manitoba Rugby League.

Introduction

In 1892, the *Manitoba Free Press* noted that "many old football players from Eastern Canada and the old country" had moved to Manitoba, "and it is hoped that they will help to keep the ball going now that it has been 'kicked off' by forming clubs." That year, the Royal Canadian Mounted Rifle Corps joined the others to form the Manitoba Rugby Football Union (MRFU), and they decided the union would play under the rules of the CRU. The CRU subsequently granted the MRFU honorary membership.

As early as 1903, Winnipeg football teams began challenging American football teams from across the border. That year, the MRFU champion Winnipeg Shamrocks negotiated a special rate with the Great Northern Railway to have the team transported by train to Grand Forks. They invited fans to join them and watch them play against the University of North Dakota under American rules. Prior to the contest, the Winnipeg team had tried to convince North Dakota to play by American rules in the first half and by Canadian rules in the second half, but North Dakota resisted, and so Winnipeg practiced for the contest using American rules. But the way North Dakota played the game proved a foreign concept to the Winnipeg team. Within the MRFU, the Shamrocks played a modified form of English rugby known as the Quebec rules. The Shamrocks normally fielded 14 players instead of the traditional rugby 15, but they employed a system of downs, with the offense required to gain 5 yards on three downs.

The North Dakota team had other advantages. Their players were "padded up from head to foot" while the Shamrocks wore "plain duck suits without even a head pad." In all, North Dakota players weighed heavier and had professional coaches. They played the entire game by rules more familiar to the Americans, and North Dakota beat the Shamrocks 57-0.

A year later, North Dakota challenged the then-Winnipeg Rugby Club to a game. Winnipeg accepted the challenge and invited North Dakota to come north to Winnipeg to play the game on the first Saturday in November, after the completion of the MRFU season, and later, Winnipeg would travel to Grand Forks and also to Fargo to play games against North Dakota and assumedly North Dakota Agricultural College. The contests did not happen, however, because North Dakota insisted they should play the games by American rules. Winnipeg had offered to play by American rules in Winnipeg and Canadian rules in Grand Forks.

*

Football followed western expansion through North America. Settlers from eastern Canada and the United States emigrated to Alberta and Saskatchewan and they brought along an interest in Canadian and American football. Teams proliferated, and in 1905 the ARFU and the Saskatchewan Rugby Football Union (SRFU) joined in a confederation. Two years later, they would join the CRU.

*

Eager for a rematch, the Shamrocks, who scraped the bottom of the MRFU standings, challenged North Dakota again in 1905 to play two games, one in Winnipeg by Canadian rules, and another in Grand Forks by American rules. For the contest, the Shamrocks assembled an all-star team of players from their own squad and from the Winnipeg Rowing Club, Winnipeg Football Club, and St. John's. They later amended the challenge to play by American rules in Winnipeg and by Canadian rules in Grand Forks. Once again, the cross-border contest never happened, this time because the Shamrocks couldn't raise the funds necessary to cover North Dakota's requested guarantee on gate receipts.

*

In 1911, the MRFU joined the ARFU and SRFU to form another union of unions, the Western Canada Rugby Football Union (WCRFU), to govern and determine a champion for the West. The major teams included clubs in Winnipeg in Manitoba, Moose Jaw, Regina, and Saskatoon in Saskatchewan, and Edmonton and Calgary in Alberta. Hugo Ross, a Winnipeg businessman and longtime fan of amateur sports, paid to have a trophy made to be kept by the winner in western competition each year. Shortly thereafter, Ross left for Europe. He died on his return trip aboard the R.M.S. Titanic when it sank in the North Atlantic Ocean. He never saw the trophy he paid for.

The WCRFU accepted the British Columbia Rugby Football Union (BCRFU) as a member in 1926 and established a playoff system whereby the ARFU champion would play the BCRFU champion and the SRFU champion would play the MRFU champion.

Introduction

In 1927, colleges in the West formed the WCIRFU. That same year, North Dakota played an exhibition game against the University of Manitoba in Winnipeg. To prepare for the match-up, the universities sent representatives from their schools to teach their opponents how to play by opposition rules, and former University of Saskatchewan rugby star Ross Paisley traveled to Grand Forks to teach the North Dakota football squad how to play by Canadian rules.

Manitoba sold more than 600 tickets for the contest, which the teams played on September 24, 1927. North Dakota scored 28 points in the first half played under American rules, and scored 5 points in the second half under Canadian rules, to shutout Manitoba 33-0. A year later, North Dakota beat Manitoba 64-4, and in 1929, North Dakota won 27-1.

In 1930, during a meeting of the MRFU, Leland "Tote" Mitchell officially changed the name of the Winnipeg Tammany Tigers club to the Winnipeg Rugby Club. He adopted the nickname Winnipegs and adorned the team in green and white. A World War I veteran, Mitchell had managed the Tammany Tigers when the team played the Ottawa Senators for the Grey Cup in 1925. He hoped to spark new interest in the game in Winnipeg, and in 1931, he would seek help from a promoter.

* *

By the late 1920s, during a decade of widespread prosperity known as the Roaring Twenties, Canadians and Americans who lived near the border between Manitoba or Ontario with Minnesota intermingled in increasing numbers. By September 18, 1929, more than 328,000 people in automobiles had checked in and out of the U.S. and Canada at the Pigeon River and International Falls customs offices, an increase of 200,000 over the number who had traversed the port of entries in 1928.

And then, the U.S. stock market crashed, on October 29, 1929. The event wiped out billions in assets and thrust the industrialized world into an economic depression. Throughout North America, farmers experienced drought and low grain prices. Crops failed, and grasshoppers devoured the yields that managed to survive. Thousands of farmers who had taken out loans to buy more land and farm implements during World

Introduction

War I abandoned their property. Ranchers reduced their herds by selling off animals. More beasts died from dust in their lungs and stomachs or from a lack of feed.

Workers had a hard time finding employment. Thousands depended on handouts to survive or took jobs created by the government. Young men and women, fresh out of high school, risked being seen as idle, and many became transient. As a result, more young adults sought out an education. In fact, in 1930, nearly 50 percent of adults aged 18-20 in the Fargo, North Dakota, and Moorhead, Minnesota, urbanized area attended school at Concordia College, North Dakota Agricultural College (North Dakota State), or Moorhead State Teachers College. At the schools, amateur athletics thrived as a form of cheap entertainment for the community.

In this context, four individuals—Bob Fritz, Bud Marquardt, Fritz Hanson, and Herb Peschel—stood among the many young men who furthered their education and who played college football in Fargo-Moorhead. All four played with or against one another, with Fritz at Concordia and Marquardt, Hanson, and Peschel at North Dakota State. After college, these four men would attain gridiron glory together at the highest level of the sport, in Canada.

CHAPTER 1 - MAROON AND GOLD (1931)

In 1931, Concordia College would field a powerful fullback who would help the Cobbers chase a conference title. Meanwhile, a speedy little halfback on the North Dakota State freshman team would generate excitement for the future of Bison football. And in Winnipeg, a new football team manager would begin to promote the game in that city with the goal of someday toppling the most dominant club in all of Western Canada. And throughout Canada, football teams would settle into using forward pass rules that finally resembled rules used in the American game.

*　　*

In Moorhead, Minnesota, Concordia College athletic director and football coach Frank Cleve looked over the young men who had assembled on the athletic field southwest of Old Main. The wannabe varsity players displayed enthusiasm, but many had never touched a football before college. In 10 days, the Cobbers would play the North Dakota State Bison across the river at Dacotah Field in Fargo, on the big stage, under the floodlights. For Cleve, the summertime pursuits of fishing, golfing, or sharing ice cream with his sweetheart would have to wait another year. He had a team to coach up.

Born in Minneapolis, Minnesota, Frank Irving Cleve had attended Minneapolis South High school where he excelled in sports, including football. After prep school, he attended St. Olaf College in Northfield, Minnesota, where he lettered in football, basketball, and baseball. Those who had watched him play football remembered Cleve as an excellent passer.

While still in college, but during the summertime, Cleve used his arm to play rookie-level Class D professional baseball on the dusty prairie, first in the Dakota League in 1921 for the Aberdeen Grays. In 1922, he enjoyed a batting average above .300 as he helped the Sioux Falls Soos chase a pennant, but the league folded mid-season. In 1923, Cleve joined the Lincoln Links in the Nebraska State League, where the *Lincoln Sunday Star* said he was "rated as an infielder of high class." In 1924, Cleve returned to Sioux Falls to play with the Canaries in the Tri-State League.

Throughout his college years, Cleve risked losing his eligibility to play college sports, but at the time, many college players routinely broke the rule against professionalism.

After he graduated from St. Olaf in 1925, Cleve took a summer course at the University of Minnesota and then moved west to coach football at Spokane College in Spokane, Washington. In 1926, Cleve returned to Minnesota, and in Moorhead, he took the job of athletic director and football coach for Concordia.

Cleve's assistant, Louis Arthur "Louie" Benson, had played football at Carleton College in Northfield. He then coached high school football in Two Harbors, Minnesota, where his football teams lost only two games in three seasons. Benson, too, had enjoyed a career in professional baseball. He played shortstop for the Aberdeen Grays in the Dakota League in 1922, one year after Cleve had played for the Grays. Benson went on to play for the Cedar Rapids Bunnies in the Mississippi Valley League and for the Sioux City Cardinals in the Tri-State League in 1924. He played for the Fort Smith Twins in the Western Association in 1925, for Fort Smith and the Syracuse Stars in the International League in 1926, and for Syracuse again in 1927. He closed out his baseball career with the Houston Buffaloes in the Texas League in 1929.

When Cleve arrived at Concordia in 1926, he took over a program that had joined the Minnesota Intercollegiate Athletic Conference (MIAC) just six years earlier in 1920. The school itself began operations in 1891 when the Northwestern Lutheran College Association purchased the former Bishop Whipple Academy building in Moorhead to establish a new Norwegian Lutheran school. A Concordia professor, Alfred "Pop" Sattre, started the football team in 1916, but then during World War I, the school suspended football until 1919. The school had played football continuously only seven years when Cleve took over. Under Cleve, the Cobbers had played the Bison four times and Concordia lost all four contests, the last two by a single touchdown. Cleve and Benson knew that if any team from Moorhead could topple the more-established Bison in Fargo, everyone on the Minnesota side of the Red River would celebrate.

Frank Cleve

For Concordia's first practice on September 8, 1931, a hot prairie day, 20 men came out for football, including local favorites Earl Moran, Pat Hilde, and Cliff Hamrast who had played together at Moorhead High School. The squad included Robert Fritz, a 22-year-old sophomore from International Falls, Minnesota, who had played for Concordia's freshman football and basketball squads in 1929. Fritz had taken a year off, but Cleve could see the young man had come back bigger and stronger. He would need Fritz on a team that returned only four letter-winners. Maybe more would return, but the Depression had hit everyone hard. Concordia, the furthest school from Minneapolis and St. Paul, Minnesota, had suffered the most within the conference due to the cost of travel. A lack of funds had forced the school to drop plans for a new gymnasium. Cleve had to work with what he had.

For Fritz, a return to Moorhead meant he no longer had to hear the whine and grind of blades in the sawmill where, during his year away from Concordia, he worked as a spare hand, but he never forgot about football. He remembered his first college football practice at Concordia in September 1929 when he scrimmaged with the second team led by Benson against the first team led by Cleve. At the time, Fritz watched as the older players proceeded through a signal drill with no mistakes or delays. That year, Cleve had Fritz carry the ball at fullback, but under a new rule for freshmen, Fritz could only play in non-conference games, such as against the West Central School of Agriculture, a residential high school in Morris, Minnesota, and against an alumni team from Moorhead High. Fritz served as a valuable asset on the varsity practice squad where he played the opposition against the starters.

Despite Fritz's limited playing time in 1929, sportswriters that year had taken notice. The school newspaper, the *Concordian*, said Fritz was "a typical lumberman type [of] the pile driving variety and this Fritz hits plenty hard." The *Minneapolis Star* described his work in the defensive secondary as "outstanding" as Fritz frequently stopped plays, and on offense, he "gave promise of developing into a strong backfield candidate." For a young man from a border town, an appearance in a big city newspaper must have felt grand, but Fritz had a long way to go to gain fame and notoriety on the gridiron.

Maroon and Gold (1931)

*

Robert Francis "Bob" Fritz was born July 29, 1909, near the shores of Fall Lake near Winton, Minnesota, about four miles northeast of Ely, to Bridget (McDonald) Fritz, a Canadian-born woman of Irish descent, and Robert Fritz Sr., a first-generation American, born in Wisconsin, of German descent. At the time, Bob was the only son in the family, with two older sisters, Vivian, two years his senior, Arvella, six years older, and a twin sister, Roberta Frances. When Bob was two years old, he welcomed a little brother, John.

By the time Bob reached 10 years old, the family had moved to International Falls where his father worked at a sawmill and rose to the position of superintendent. While in high school, Fritz stood out as an athlete. During the 1924-25 school year, his junior year, Fritz played alongside "Broncho" Nagurski and Howard Kroll. Broncho, born Bronislaw, better known as "Bronko" Nagurski, was one year older than Fritz. Both Nagurski and Kroll went on to play football at the University of Minnesota. Another classmate, a speedy little halfback named Harold Kerry had played with Fritz at Concordia in 1929 and then moved on to Minnesota, too. Nagurski, especially, had made a name for himself. His picture donned the *Minneapolis Sunday Tribune* after a big win over the University of Wisconsin in November 1928. He had gone on to play professional football for the Chicago Bears in 1930. In just about any newspaper with a sports page, Fritz could read about Nagurski's adventures on the gridiron.

*

After a few days of practice, the Concordia football roster swelled to 39 players, and Cleve realized he had assembled the best squad he had ever worked with. Yes, they were inexperienced, but every one of them worked hard and showed a willingness to learn. He believed that even a defeat against the Bison would harden and prepare them for success against conference opponents. The future looked bright.

On the night before the big game, Concordia practiced under the floodlights at Dacotah Field to get accustomed to playing football at night. During that hour-long nighttime practice, Cleve finalized his personnel decisions as he watched Fritz carry the ball out of the fullback position.

Bob Fritz and Bronko Nagurski

The *Moorhead Daily News* declared Fritz, "who made things tough for the varsity when he played as a freshman," to be one of the team's "Four Norsemen"—a play on the "Four Horsemen" nickname for the 1924 University of Notre Dame backfield. The *Daily News* ignored the fact Fritz came from German and Irish stock.

On the afternoon of the contest, fans from both sides of the river filled downtown Broadway for a big parade. Players and coaches from both teams mounted automobiles and drove down the main thoroughfare to rouse cheers from their respective fans dressed in or waving Bison green and yellow or Cobber maroon and gold.

In the evening, Dacotah Field drew a festive crowd, and as twilight set in, the lighted windows of Ceres Hall, the women's dormitory southeast of the gridiron, winked as curious co-eds peered out across the lawn toward the athletic field. The sweet smell of cattle manure rode the breeze from the dairy building to the west and from farm buildings to the northwest. On the playing field and on the sidelines, players flexed their muscles and ruminated over past and future triumphs.

Cleve knew the oddsmakers favored the Bison by at least one touchdown. The North Dakota State eleven had a passing attack that featured left halfback Paul Bunt throwing to right halfback Vivian McKay, and the team's captain, quarterback Cy Longsbrough, could dash through the open field or push his way into the end zone with the best of them. Cleve loved the role of the underdog, however, and he reminded his men about the opportunity that stood before them. He hoped that his veteran halfback, Cliff Hamrast, might provide the shiftiness on the run and the passing arm necessary to keep the Bison defense from keying Fritz as the young fullback plunged the line in his first varsity game. And yet, at 22 years old, Fritz wasn't young, only inexperienced. He looked like a senior and a full-grown man.

Cleve had three more years' experience coaching college boys than his rival, North Dakota State Coach Casey Finnegan, but Finnegan had bigger fish to fry. He hoped a tough game against Concordia would prepare his men to face Minnesota eight days later. Finnegan knew that even though his Bison players had started practice earlier in the season than Concordia, he could expect mistakes in the first game. Yes, the Bison outweighed the

Cobbers, but it would come down to resolve. Concordia had kept the score close in their last two meetings.

As excitement grew, Concordia fans broke out in song and yelled, "Stand up and cheer, stand up and cheer for old Concordia, for today we raise the maroon and gold above the rest!..." North Dakota State fans responded, "Green and yellow, colors bright, to them we will be true!..." and "Up with the yellow and green!..."

By the time the clock tower in Old Main struck eight o'clock on September 18, 1931, the largest crowd that had ever assembled for a game between North Dakota State and Concordia covered the grandstands. Those who knew him waved to Halsey Hall, the field judge and a sportswriter for the *Minneapolis Journal*.

After the kickoff, in a back-and-forth affair, both teams worked from a limited playbook. Bison tackle Walter "Dolly" Schoenfelder thrilled the crowd when he returned a punt 40 yards. The team captain, Lonsbrough, broke the Cobber line to score.

In the second half, Concordia pushed the Bison back on their heels, but the Cobbers failed to score. Lonsbrough scored a second touchdown for the Bison and Bunt connected with McKay on a pass for a third. In the end, North Dakota State beat Concordia 19-0.

The *Concordian* noted Fritz "was the most effective in both ground gaining and on defense. His line smashes counted for many yards gained by the Cobber clan. His hard tackling, while backing up the line, was superb." Sports editor Tony Tulip asked rhetorically, "Can he hit?" And answered, "Give him a ball and try to stop him."

* *

Over 200 miles north of Fargo, along the same Red River of the North in Winnipeg, Manitoba, a new, unpaid manager had taken over operations for the Winnipeg Rugby Club, the "Winnipegs." Joseph B. "Joe" Ryan, a University of Manitoba law school dropout from Starbuck, Manitoba, believed Winnipeg and all of Canada deserved something more—that *he* deserved something more—than the style of Canadian rugby football he watched from the grandstands each fall. Ryan had worked as a

Concordia College (Moorhead, Minnesota)

bookkeeper for his mother's cousin in a logging camp in northern Wisconsin during the early 1920s, where he also moonlighted as a hockey referee. In 1924, he fell in love with football after he attended a game at Notre Dame.

Ryan returned to Winnipeg in 1927 to work as a bookkeeper at the Grain Exchange, but while he worked, his mind wandered to football—American intercollegiate football—in all its pageantry and excitement. The Winnipegs, and other clubs in the city, played the closest thing to what he'd witnessed at Notre Dame, and Ryan hoped to recapture that feeling in Winnipeg. With a rye whiskey-and-water in his hand and with a cigarette between his lips, Ryan agreed to take over as manager for the Winnipeg club in 1931.

Fans in Western Canada had grown increasingly interested in Canadian football, but rugby football in Winnipeg needed a boost, despite its long history. Fan interest instead pointed toward Saskatchewan, where the Regina Roughriders had dominated the game in the West. Regina had appeared in the Grey Cup three years in a row in 1928, 1929, and 1930, and it appeared the Roughriders would dominate the West for years to come.

In an effort to generate more interest in Winnipeg teams, Ryan led an effort to form a new Winnipeg Senior League with the Winnipegs, the St. John's Rugby Football Club, which had its roots at St. John's College in Winnipeg, and the University of Manitoba Bisons (a.k.a. "Varsity") as members.

St. John's, the Saints, had won the Manitoba Rugby Football Union (MRFU) title in five of the past seven years, including in 1928, 1929, and 1930, but this year they would play without their star, Eddie James, a Winnipeg native now at left halfback for Regina. Meanwhile, the Manitoba Bisons hadn't won an intercollegiate rugby game in two years.

Ryan scheduled a total of five games between the teams in the league to be played at Wesley Stadium. The Winnipegs would play in four of the contests. But no amount of football would excite the fans, Ryan knew, without an emphasis on the forward pass.

*

Maroon and Gold (1931)

During the CRU's annual meeting in March 1931, late into the evening, the executive committee weighed all arguments from all affiliated unions and decided to adopt the forward pass as a permanent part of the Canadian football code, and not just as an experiment. The CRU decided Canadian football should have a distinctly Canadian forward pass, and the executives resolved to hammer out the details in the coming weeks. Nearly lost in the shuffle, the CRU also decided to adopt a rule which allowed for a place kick, not just a drop kick or a run or a pass, to earn the point after a touchdown.

In May 1931, the CRU announced details for the updated Canadian forward pass, which would resemble its American counterpart in most respects, except:

- Passes thrown into the end zone from outside an opponent's 25-yard line—in other words, from within the middle 60 yards of the field—would have to be caught for a touchdown or the result would be a turnover.
- Any incomplete pass thrown from inside an opponent's 25-yard line—between the 25-yard line and the goal line—would have to be caught or the result would be a turnover.
- In the case of a turnover due to a misstep with the forward pass, the opposing team would start with the ball at their own 25-yard line.
- Within the middle 60 yards of the field—between the 25-yard lines—two consecutive incomplete passes would result in a 10-yard penalty.
- Unlike in the American game, defenders could only interfere with receivers within 1 yard of the line of scrimmage.

Some voices continued to argue the forward pass should be dropped from Canadian football altogether because teams not well-versed in the pass felt demoralized when they spent five times as much effort to gain the same yardage as an opponent with a well-executed passing game. The most conservative voices wished to turn back the clock and employ much older versions of rugby.

Joe Ryan

Except for obvious differences (a 110-yard field, 12 men instead of 11, three downs instead of four), for spectators, the Canadian game would more clearly resemble the American game in most respects. "Teams in eastern Canada will take their first taste of the overhead variety of football in the autumn campaign," reported the *Saskatoon Star-Phoenix*, "but prairie and Pacific coast league squads will merely welcome it as a better play than the one they have used for two years" since 1929 when the CRU first experimented with the play.

* *

North Dakota State freshman team football coach Fay Smith also coached the Bison boxing team. He knew a thing or two about conditioning. And as a Lieutenant in the U.S. Army, he knew a thing or two about how to tackle and bring down an opponent, because he had taught jiu-jitsu to military policemen at Camp Perry, Ohio. Now, in the fall of 1931, he taught the "Baby Bison" the ins and outs of college-level play on the gridiron.

Smith and his assistants, former Bison footballers Joe Blakeslee and Steve Gergen, had a hard time holding back their smiles. They had nine all-state selections from North Dakota and Minnesota high schools to run through their paces, "the most promising group of freshman players in the history of the school, in the opinion of many who have watched the yearlings work out," swooned the student newspaper, *The Spectrum*.

On the field, Fritz Hanson, Bud Marquardt, and Herb Peschel strove to stand out in the herd. Only 5-foot-7 and short of 150 pounds, "Speedy" Hanson competed in a field of 20 freshmen for a position in the backfield, which included a former teammate from Perham, Art Stege. At 6-foot-3 and 165 pounds, Marquardt counted among the big boys for the line at end. And Peschel earned a mention in the newspaper as a lineman that plays "with a style that is pleasing to the coaches." As freshmen, they would provide a worthy opponent to the varsity squad during practice. Off the field, Hanson studied Physical Education, Marquardt studied Science and Mathematics, and Peschel studied Education.

*

Maroon and Gold (1931)

Melvin Lester "Fritz" Hanson was born July 13, 1912, in Perham, Minnesota, to Bertha (Foerstner) Hanson, a first-generation American born in Minnesota to immigrant parents of German and Russian Polish origin, and to Oscar Hanson, a first-generation American born in Wisconsin to Norwegian immigrants. At the time, the family lived in Corliss Township, where Bertha grew up, and where Oscar farmed the land, 8 miles northeast of Perham. Melvin was the couple's third child after his older brother, Elmer, and older sister, Florence.

By the time Melvin was 8 years old his father had become the proprietor of a confectionary and later, a café, in Perham. The family grew to include Melvin's younger sister, Esther.

Both Elmer and Melvin wanted to play football, but their father wanted them to work at the family businesses after school and on weekends. Perhaps their mother convinced their father to allow them to take turns at practice and at the store, but eventually, Elmer recognized his little brother had a knack for the game, and so Elmer volunteered to work during football season so that Melvin could attend all practices and games.

One source suggests Fritz Hanson once scored 11 touchdowns in a high school game, a plausible number for the phenom. Another report says Hanson and the Perham High School football team once beat Detroit Lakes in Perham by the score of 53-0. In 1930, with Hanson carrying the ball, Perham scored 277 points in eight games. That season, Perham beat the Moorhead High School Spuds 19-6 during a Saturday dirt storm, the Spuds' first defeat to another Minnesota team in six years. The *Moorhead Daily News* declared the Perham team to be a "darkhorse threat" and Hanson a "speedy halfback" with "lightning footwork." His future Bison teammate, Marquardt, played for the Moorhead squad at the time.

Before college, in the spring of 1931, Hanson competed in the Minnesota state high school track meet and won the 100-yard dash in 10.1 seconds, one-tenth of a second short of the state record at the time. He made the front page of the sports section in the *Minneapolis Sunday Tribune*, which declared Hanson had "established himself as sprint champion of the state by superb and decisive victories… Had there been anything like secure footing this young marvel might have equaled or bettered the state mark of 10 seconds flat [in the 100-yard dash.] As it was, he flashed down the path through a downpour of rain." At some point in 1931, Hanson ran the 220-yard dash in 22.02 seconds, according to state records.

After the May Festival track meet at North Dakota State in 1931, Hanson had visited with Bison football coach Casey Finnegan at the Alpha Kappa Phi house near campus.

*

Wilbur Paul "Bud" Marquardt was born December 15, 1913, in Hettinger County, North Dakota, to Alma (Grabinski) Marquardt, a second-generation American born in South Dakota to German immigrants, and to Leonard Marquardt, a first-generation American born in Minnesota to German immigrants. Wilbur was a middle child with two older brothers, Marlin and Robert, a younger sister, Alma, and two younger brothers, John and James.

By the time Wilbur entered grade school, the family had moved to Moorhead. It was during high school when Wilbur insisted on being called by his nickname, Bud. A shy kid, his mother urged him to try out for football. As a sophomore in 1929, he earned a starting position on the line and lettered for the Spuds.

Bud, however, preferred basketball. As a sophomore, he found his way onto the Spuds varsity basketball team. Moorhead coach Glenn Hanna quickly moved the lanky kid to center to play post, but he was "so young, tall, and thin that Hanna fears he cannot depend on him for an entire game just yet," said the *Moorhead Daily News*. Marquardt earned a spot in the rotation, and the Spuds secured their second state basketball title in two years when they beat Red Wing 20-16 in overtime. Afterward, Moorhead went on to compete in a national high school basketball tournament in Chicago. Over the summer, Marquardt played American Legion baseball under Hanna.

During the 1929-1930 basketball season, the team reached the state title game again but lost 23-13 to St. Paul Mechanic Arts. Afterward, the team elected Marquardt captain of the basketball team for the 1930-1931 season.

As a senior, Marquardt led the Spuds to their fourth consecutive state basketball tournament berth, but Buffalo, Minnesota, stunned Moorhead

Maroon and Gold (1931)

22-20 in the first round. Nevertheless, the tournament named Marquardt All-State at center.

In track and field events, Marquardt competed in and consistently won the 120-yard high hurdles and won or placed in the 220-yard low hurdles, high jump, and pole vault. At state, Marquardt finished third in the 120-yard high hurdles and second in the 220-yard low hurdles.

*

Herbert Alfred "Herb" Peschel was born September 2, 1913, in Wahpeton, North Dakota, to Mary (Zanzinger) Peschel, a first-generation American born in Wisconsin to German immigrants, and to Marcus Peschel, a first-generation American born in Minnesota to Austrian immigrants. Herb was the first-born child and grew up in Wahpeton, where his father worked as a salesman for a wholesaler. Herb would welcome seven siblings, including Frank, Ben, Billy, Amy, Mark, Mary, and Jean.

While in high school, Herb played football and basketball. In his senior year, he competed in track and field events. He played tackle on the gridiron team, and the undefeated Wahpeton Wops won the unofficial North Dakota state football championship in 1930. They outscored opponents 267-18. The school yearbook quipped, "Herby was never forced to play for any length of time. A couple of plays, and that many losses, forced the opposition to look elsewhere for their yards."

*

After the varsity Bison beat the Cobbers, Hanson, Marquardt, and Peschel pledged to fraternities. Hanson pledged to Theta Chi, while Marquardt and Peschel pledged to Alpha Kappa Phi. And the young men continued to practice hard against the varsity squad, but perhaps too hard, because during practice, Hanson suffered a torn ligament in his shoulder, and it appeared he would have to sit out the remainder of the season.

* *

In 1931, Hibbing Junior College in Hibbing, Minnesota, christened a new football field. The school and community treated the event as a celebration of the team's success in the Little Ten Conference. During

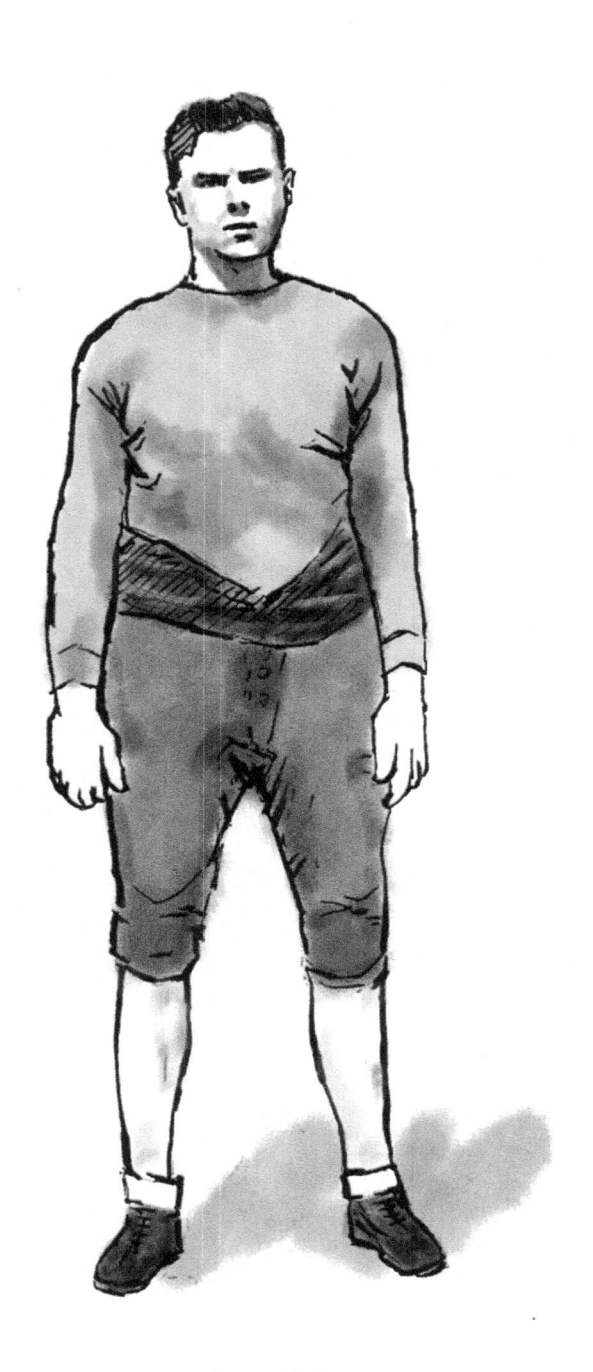

Herb Peschel

seven seasons, Hibbing coach Frank "Doc" Savage had led his men to five conference championships.

Born in St. Paul, Savage had played quarterback for Minneapolis South High School. After graduation, he attended the University of Nebraska, but he did not participate in athletics there. After college, he worked as the cafeteria manager at Rochester High School in Rochester, Minnesota, where school administrators asked Savage to fill in as the school's football and basketball coach. Three years later, Savage took the job of physical education director at the Young Men's Christian Association (YMCA) in Two Harbors, but a year later he decided he missed living in Rochester. He returned to work in the restaurant business and to coach football.

In 1921, Eveleth Junior College in Eveleth, Minnesota, hired Savage to be their full-time coach. After the team lost only three games in three years, nearby Hibbing lured Savage away to coach its teams. He promptly led Hibbing to a conference championship.

Concordia Coach Frank Cleve figured Savage and his Rangers would provide stiff competition, which would help prepare the Cobbers for conference play. On October 3, 1931, Cleve took his men to play Hibbing on their new grid.

Hibbing proved a solid opponent, though at first it looked as if the Cobbers might have an easy time. In the first quarter, Earl Moran scored first for the Cobbers on a drive that began at Concordia's 40-yard line. Hibbing stiffened, however, and neither side scored again until the third quarter when Hibbing blocked a punt and recovered the ball on Concordia's 22-yard line. After three attempts to thrust through the line, Hibbing connected on an 18-yard touchdown pass to score. Two minutes later, Concordia used a series of line plunges to move the ball 48 yards near to Hibbing's end zone. Bob Fritz hit the line but did not succeed, and so on the next play he ran wide for the score. On the run, Fritz had scored his first-ever touchdown for the varsity Cobbers. He also hit the line for the extra point.

For the remainder of the game, Hibbing struggled and Concordia intercepted passes. Fritz scored a second touchdown. The game ended Concordia 26, Hibbing 6.

*

Maroon and Gold (1931)

The Macalester College Scots finished their early season games 2-0 in non-conference play while Concordia stood at 1-1. Nevertheless, the Macalester student newspaper, *The Mac Weekly*, prepared its student body for defeat: The Cobbers would bring a fast backfield behind a strong, heavy line, and even though Concordia had lost its game with North Dakota State, those same Bison had lost to the Minnesota Golden Gophers by only one touchdown. Even without a conference game under their belts, the Cobbers carried credibility.

Cleve would face Macalester head coach Al Gowans for the second time since Gowans had taken over the Scots in 1930 when Macalester had beaten the Cobbers by a slim margin, 7-6. In college, Gowans had played guard for the Cornell College Rams in Mount Vernon, Iowa, where he earned all-conference honors in 1921 and 1922 and where he captained the football team in 1922. After college, he coached the Ottawa University Braves in Ottawa, Kansas, in 1925, and the Des Moines University Tigers in Des Moines, Iowa, from 1926 to 1928.

When the Cobbers stepped onto the gridiron at Shaw Field at Macalaster in St. Paul on Saturday, October 10, 1931, they smelled rain. Clouds had swelled overhead and blocked the sun. No matter what the weather had in store, Fritz knew he had arrived on a bigger stage, and he would do his best to impress. Sure, North Dakota State was a big venue—in North Dakota—but St. Paul boasted a quarter million residents. Macalester had been MIAC champions in 1925. Meanwhile, Concordia had yet to win a conference title.

Immediately after kickoff, the Cobbers ran into a wall. Through most of the first quarter, Macalester prevented Concordia runners from reaching their own line of scrimmage. Fritz and the Cobber backfield persevered, however, and late in the period, they managed to reach first downs with some trickery. They had decided to use the spinner play.

In the 1920s, the Carnegie Institute of Technology Tartans football team in Pittsburgh, Pennsylvania, led by fullback Dwight Beede, introduced the spinner play onto the national scene. On a spinner play, the fullback receives the snap out of an unbalanced line formation, with two men on one side of center and four men on the other side. At first, the play looks like a reverse, but the fullback doesn't actually toss the ball

At Macalester College (St. Paul, Minnesota)

to the right or left halfback for a reverse run to the weak side of the formation. Instead, the fullback fakes the toss, spins around, and runs with the ball away from the defensive pursuit to the halfback on the fake reverse. The play depends on having a fast reverse runner to draw the defense away from the strong side of the formation.

The Cobbers leveraged the spinner play and wore down the Scots. They also moved the ball on off-tackle slants, end runs, and short passes across the middle of the field. Fritz hit the line for successive gains of 15, 11, and 12 yards, and then completed a 55-yard drive with an off-tackle lunge into the end zone for a touchdown. In a photo of the game in the *Concordian*, courtesy the *St. Paul Dispatch*, Fritz plunges through the line without a helmet, one of the few men on the field without one. By the end of the first half, Concordia had covered 132 yards on the ground.

As the game progressed, the sky darkened and dropped light showers.

In the second half, unable to move the ball on the run, Macalester switched to the passing game, but to no avail. The Cobbers intercepted passes and scored touchdowns while Macalester spent the entire game in their own territory. The Macalester student newspaper said the Concordia line proved "impenetrable."

In the fourth quarter, a downpour chased fans from the grandstands into the balcony of the nearby gymnasium. The game ended under a torrent of rain with the final score Concordia 18, Macalester 0.

Afterward, the *Minneapolis Sunday Tribune* opined, "It appears as though the Cobbers will be a real factor in the state conference" and that they must be ranked as one of the favorites to win the title. Fritz had emerged as Concordia's main offensive weapon.

* *

In 1931, the Joe Ryan-managed Winnipeg Rugby Club suffered at the hands of the St. John's Rugby Football Club, but the Winnipegs beat the Manitoba Bisons in league play. Under Ryan, the Winnipegs emphasized the relatively new forward pass.

Just two years before, on September 21, 1929, at Wesley Park, Norm McLeod of the St. John's club attempted the first-ever legal forward pass

Maroon and Gold (1931)

in senior-level play in Winnipeg. It fell into and out of the hands of Winnipeg Tammany Tigers defender Ronnie Gay. Later in the game, McLeod *completed* the first-ever legal forward pass in local history when he connected with a St. John's player with the last name Christensen who caught the ball but then fumbled and lost it to the Tigers.

Now in 1931, the Winnipegs featured Arni Coulter, a Manitoba alum who had tossed his first forward passes for that same Tammany Tigers team in 1929. Coulter continued to play side games in 1931, with the Manitoba "Old Boys" alumni squad, where he also tossed the ball. Fans in Winnipeg showed excitement when Coulter attempted passes, even though he rarely completed them. On Thanksgiving Day in Canada, on October 12, 1931, the Winnipegs featured the forward pass with 25 pass attempts, but completed only 3.

St. John's captured the MRFU title in 1931, and the Saints requested to use Coulter in the Western Canada Rugby Football Union (WCRFU) semifinal game against the Roughriders in Regina. The WCRFU approved, and St. John's decided to use Coulter at halfback and also to move an end, Herb Mobberley, to halfback, in an attempt to increase the Saints' offensive attack.

*   *

Fritz Hanson nursed his injury as he stood near the sideline to watch his teammates play on October 16, 1931. The Baby Bison had traveled to Memorial Stadium in Grand Forks to play North Dakota's freshman team, the "Sioux Papooses." The 46 freshmen on North Dakota's sideline had already played one game. Hanson watched while Marquardt, at end, and Peschel, at tackle, played on the line, and he wished he could run through the holes they created against North Dakota's defense. When Bison fullback George May stiff-armed, dodged, and broke free on a fake punt for a 55-yard touchdown run , the Bison freshman sideline erupted in joy. They had secured a 7-6 victory over North Dakota—the first time the Bison yearlings had ever beaten the Sioux first-years in Grand Forks. Afterward, Hanson thought maybe his shoulder had started to feel a little better. Perhaps he would play in the upcoming rematch.

Maroon and Gold (1931)

* *

With a conference victory under their belts, the maroon- and gold-clad Concordia Cobbers prepared to face another local nemesis: The crimson-and-white Moorhead State Dragons. The Dragons led the rivalry with an overall 5-4-4 record, with all four ties scoreless in 1923, 1924, 1925, and 1930. This year, they would play the game at Concordia, and the Cobbers had their 175-pound fullback, Bob Fritz.

At Moorhead State, Alex J. "Sliv" Nemzek, Jr., served as the school's athletic director, physical education instructor, football, basketball, track, and baseball coach, and he was a member of the Minnesota State Athletic Commission. He ran a coaching school for high school and college coaches from surrounding states.

While in college, Nemzek had captained the North Dakota State Bison football team in 1916. He then starred on the 1st North Dakota Infantry service football team when the unit was stationed in Mercedes, Texas, during the Mexican Border War. After the Army redesignated the unit to the 164th Infantry Regiment for World War I, Nemzek played for that unit's service team. After the war, Nemzek continued to serve as a captain in Company F in the Moorhead unit of the Minnesota National Guard.

During Nemzek's tenure, Moorhead State built a new physical education building with a spacious basketball court, which opened in 1931, and the school enjoyed a new athletic field surrounded by a quarter-mile track. The gridiron offered the best turf of any field in the Fargo-Moorhead community. The school competed in the Interstate Athletic Conference (IAC), which otherwise included teachers colleges across North Dakota. Over eight years, the Dragons had accumulated a 24-4-3 overall record in the IAC and had won five titles, including four titles in a row, and shared one.

Concordia had beaten Moorhead State twice during the past three seasons, but during those years the Dragons had otherwise played strong with 5-1-1, 5-2, and 4-1-1 records overall. Now in 1931, the Dragons had just vanquished Jamestown College of Jamestown, North Dakota, 54-0. Conventional wisdom said the Dragons might be overconfident against the Cobbers, but Nemzek knew how to lead and motivate men. As game day approached, both teams announced their starting lineups, and Concordia had a clear weight advantage. The average Cobber weighed 175 pounds compared to the average Dragon at 166.

Ahead of the game, Cleve and Nemzek met in the studio at KGFK Radio in the Comstock Hotel on Center Avenue in Moorhead. The radio station had invited the coaches to promote the game and to give an assessment of their opponents. The *Moorhead Daily News* reprinted their soliloquies on the sports page.

Nemzek spoke first. "The 1931 game ought to be the most interesting in the history of athletic competition between the two schools," he said. "The systems of play vary enough to offer entertainment beyond that offered in the average football game. Coach Cleve has selected a style of play that suits his individual fancy and I have done likewise. Personally, I have built my own formations without recourse to the diagrams of the plays of other coaches. These formations resemble to some extent the so-called Warner system of offense. Cleve seems to favor the so-called Notre Dame offense. Hence a contrast in offensive play is in store for enthusiasts who will witness the game."

Cleve replied. "The late Coach Rockne of Notre Dame has boasted the fact that no team using a Warner system of play had ever conquered Notre Dame," he said. "As we are using the Rockne system, we hope to uphold this record." Only two years prior, Cleve had named Warner the "greatest of all football coaches" when the *Concordian* surveyed him for the student newspaper. Meanwhile, North Dakota, which used the Warner system, had dominated North Dakota State, which used the Rockne system, in recent years.

*

By the 1930s, the majority of American college football teams used some form of one of three offensive systems:

- The Warner system, pioneered by Glenn Scobey "Pop" Warner at the Carlisle Indian Industrial School in Carlisle, Pennsylvania.

Sliv Nemzek

- The Rockne system, created by Knute Rockne at Notre Dame near South Bend, Indiana.
- The Yost system, engineered by Fielding Yost at the University of Michigan in Ann Arbor, Michigan.

Warner, Rockne, and Yost each had modified Walter Camp's T Formation, the oldest offensive formation in American football. The T Formation employs a balanced line, with a guard, tackle, and end, in that order, to the right and to the left of center, and with the ends split wide from the tackles. The formation begins with backfielders in a pattern that resembles the letter "T". The quarterback stands behind center, and farther back, the fullback stands directly behind the quarterback. Two halfbacks, the left halfback and the right halfback, stand on either side of the fullback.

In the T Formation, the fullback must be big and able to block or crush through the line. He tends to carry the ball between the ends. The halfbacks might carry the ball anywhere, especially around the ends, and often leave the backfield as receivers. The ends, too, can leave the line to receive the ball. The quarterback calls the signals. The center then snaps the ball to the quarterback who may run, pass, or hand-off the ball to one of the other backs. The quarterback in the T Formation tends not to block anyone, but any of the other backs might need to block on a play.

Warner based his Single Wing and Double Wing formations on the T Formation. The Single Wing is a "shift" formation that begins in the traditional T, but before the snap, the quarterback signals which side will serve as the strong side of the formation. A tackle or guard then moves from one side of the formation to the other to form an unbalanced line with two men on one side of center and four men on the other side. Meanwhile, the backfielders move to different positions to form a wing-shaped alignment behind the strong side of the formation. The strong side halfback converts to a wingback position and starts outside, inside, or behind the end. The center might snap the ball to any backfielder within his field of vision. The offense will run most plays to the strong side of the formation, but trickery enables the offense to take advantage of the weak side, too.

The Double Wing also uses an unbalanced line, with a wingback on each side and a tailback who can run, pass, or kick the ball. With two wingbacks, the Double Wing effectively provides a nine-man offensive line. The wingbacks participate in reverses, fakes, and passes that require flawless execution and timing. Most runs hit the line off tackle or around the end.

By contrast, the Notre Dame Shift, made popular by Rockne, uses the traditional balanced line. The shift begins in the traditional T formation, but before the snap, the quarterback signals which side will serve as the strong side of the formation. The line then maintains its balanced strength while the backfielders move to different positions in the backfield to strengthen one side of the formation. The backfielders often form a square- or "box"-shaped alignment in the backfield. The center might snap the ball to any backfielder within his field of vision.

The Short Punt, developed by Yost, also uses a balanced line like the T. The halfbacks covert to wingbacks and stand behind the line between the guards and tackles. The fullback stands farther back behind a guard to create a strong side to the formation. The tailback stands directly behind center but farther back than the tailback does in the Double Wing. Offenses typically use the Short Punt formation to throw a pass for a chunk of yardage instead of using multiple runs to reach the same distance. The tailback can also choose to punt on an early down to send the ball deep into an opponent's territory unexpectedly.

In any of the systems, a team might run a play from the initial T formation or shift into the new formation before the snap.

Because most offenses in the 1930s relied upon a strong running game to move the ball, most defenses employed a seven-man line but would convert to a six-man line to add another backfielder to cover the pass.

*

While a strong south wind blew across the Concordia gridiron on October 17, 1931, Cleve jawed his chewing gum with rhythmic precision as the Cobbers and Dragons lined up for the long-awaited opening kickoff. Moorhead State returned 17 lettermen to the field against Concordia, including John Ingersoll, the team captain, who also coached the freshman football team. Meanwhile, Cleve returned only five

At Concordia Field (Moorhead, Minnesota0

lettermen to the grid, and he had two reserves who had played freshman football with the Dragons in 1930.

Bob Fritz plunged the line repeatedly on offense. He ran on spinner plays and off tackle. He played impenetrable pass defense and helped to defend against Moorhead's end-run strategy. Neither team made much progress, however. And even though Concordia rushed for 134 yards and 7 first downs, the Cobbers didn't make it past Moorhead State's 8-yard line. Neither team completed a forward pass. Cleve kept his best 11 men in the game and didn't rest one of them for a single play. At the end of the game, Cleve and Nemzek shook hands in a moment that felt like déjà vu as both teams tallied a scoreless tie for the fifth time in nine years.

*

After their melee with the Dragons, Fritz and his teammates looked forward to some time to recover, with Concordia's homecoming game against St. John's University still two weeks away. In the meantime, one player stopped shaving above his upper lip, and soon most of the Cobbers grew mustaches.

Coach Cleve, meanwhile, used the open date on the schedule to travel to Collegeville, Minnesota, to watch a game between two undefeated teams, St. John's and St. Olaf. He watched as the Johnnies' big, plunging fullback, Auggie "Gus" Luckemeyer, led a 65-yard crushing drive behind a powerful line that ended when Luckemeyer scored the touchdown and kicked the extra point. When St. John's chose to pass, they succeeded, but Cleve could see the Johnnies lacked speed around the ends. "St. John's is a one-man team," he told the *Moorhead Daily News*. "If we can stop Luckemeyer, we'll stop St. John's." Cleve didn't know that Luckemeyer had been ill but played anyway. In all, St. John's made 21 first downs against St. Olaf and the Johnnies beat the Oles 13-0.

When word of the game results circulated, the *Moorhead Daily News* suggested Fritz would contend against Luckemeyer for all-conference honors. The newspaper framed the game as a duel between the two men. The *Minneapolis Star* described Luckemeyer as a "hard-driving Johnnie star [who] came into his own against the Oles last week and gives promise of developing into one of the leading line-plungers of the conference. His rival Robert Fritz, is a big 190-pound sophomore boasting exceptional

Maroon and Gold (1931)

driving power." The *Concordian* played up the forthcoming duel as a game between the "crashing, line-smashing" Luckemeyer and the "locomotive" Fritz.

Just days before the game, a cold rain pelted the field, and so Cleve took his men inside where they practiced assignments and signal drills. He also promoted bigger men from the reserves to add power to the line. The Cobbers plugged up the middle and Fritz practiced as the main run-stopper on defense.

Cleve watched the skies with frustration. Because his Cobbers had more speed than the Johnnies, he knew his men would have the advantage with end runs on a dry field. But it appeared the teams would play beneath overcast skies and on a wet, soggy grid. He imagined neither team would move the ball except on punts. He feared the Cobbers might suffer another scoreless tie. Three seasons ago, a tie with St. John's had ended Concordia's hopes for a conference title.

Cleve's opponent, Coach Joe Benda, had taken over the St. John's football program in 1930. The Johnnies finished 0-3-1 in the conference that year, which continued the St. John's tradition of losing seasons since the school resumed football in 1920. But now the Johnnies, in cardinal and blue, looked much improved. Benda had played end for Rockne at Notre Dame he who knew the system Cleve now employed.

The Cobbers-Johnnies contest took place as part of Concordia's homecoming celebration on October 31, 1931, exactly 40 years since Norwegian settlers had founded the school. A record crowd of Concordia fans, alumni, administrators, faculty, and students assembled for the game, and they sat or stood in the freezing air as they waited for the players to take the field. Only an exciting game would keep them warm, but Cleve had his doubts on All Hallows' Eve.

During the first 20 minutes of game time, the Johnnies stymied the Cobbers, and vice-versa, as the field turned to mud. Fritz proved ineffective in plunges against the big Johnny line, and in the same way "Galloping Gus" Luckemeyer made no progress against the disciplined Cobber wall.

In the middle of the second quarter, Cleve took out his bag of tricks and had Fritz run around the ends, instead. With 8 minutes remaining in the half, on fourth down, and after three line plunges against a goal-line stand, Fritz circled his left end for a touchdown.

After the ensuing kickoff, the Johnnies fumbled the snap, and the Cobbers recovered on St. John's 15-yard line. Concordia scored again.

Concordia held the momentum. The Johnnies fumbled and incurred a safety when Cobbers captain and end Lloyd "Pinkey" Falgren tackled a man in the end zone.

The Johnnies appeared to give up as Earl Moran ran 50 yards and Fritz ran 64 yards for touchdowns. The Cobbers beat the Johnnies 29-0.

The St. John's student newspaper, *St. John's Record*, blamed field conditions at Concordia. Luckemeyer had been "immediately impeded by the adhesive sod, being unused to that type of footing," the *Record* said.

Despite the slippery conditions, Fritz showed he could stretch his legs on the open field. He didn't always have to bruise his way through the line.

Bad blood between the two teams led officials to penalize the Cobbers 105 yards during the game, mostly for unnecessary roughness. The Johnnies quarterback and halfback both suffered injuries.

Later that evening, Cleve attended the second annual Concordia letterman's reunion, where he received congratulations from at least three dozen men, most of whom had lettered in football or basketball at Concordia. The Cobbers now stood atop the conference tied with the College of St. Thomas for the title.

* *

Three weeks had passed since the North Dakota State freshmen had beaten the North Dakota freshmen in Grand Forks. Multiple times the schools had to postpone a rematch due to poor weather. The Baby Bison itched to defend their dominance over the Sioux first-years. During a scrimmage, George May had strained his back, while Fritz Hanson had healed enough to carry the pigskin again. The *Spectrum* rejoiced in the expected return of Hanson and referred to him as the "Blond Speed Boy" and the "Viking Speedster." Hanson would not disappoint.

Maroon and Gold (1931)

North Dakota brought two complete squads and 26 players to Dacotah Field on November 6, 1931. In the first quarter, Hanson displayed both speed and elusiveness when he returned a punt 80 yards for a touchdown. He didn't gain much ground from scrimmage, however, until the second quarter, when Bud Marquardt entered the game as a substitution at end. "His entry and a sudden power developed by the Baby Bison forward wall were simultaneous," observed the *Moorhead Daily News*. With Marquardt, the "elongated Moorhead youth," on the line at left end, Hanson, the "Perham Flash," managed to slip inside his left tackle and zig-zag through the defense toward daylight to complete a 63-yard run for a score, which stirred the crowd to give him "a great ovation."

Hanson and Marquardt set up a double threat. While the defense looked to stop Hanson around the ends, Marquardt "snared passes for huge gains and a touchdown, he broke up interference, [and] he turned attempted end runs into line smashes." The Baby Bisons' main passer, Wendell "Wendy" Schollander, a stocky, compact, and fast freshman, connected with Marquardt on a touchdown pass in the third quarter. In the fourth quarter, the Baby Bison scored a final touchdown on a 33-yard interception return. The North Dakota State freshmen finished the game with a 26-6 victory over North Dakota's yearlings.

The *Dakota Student* said Hanson "demoralized the Nodak yearlings" with his "dazzling runs" in the open field on punt returns and from scrimmage,

The day filled Hanson with confidence. Not only did he get to play and play well, but his father, Oscar, had watched the game from the stands. Afterward, the elder Hanson stayed with his son at the Theta Chi fraternity house and helped him to celebrate the victory.

"It is not often that a high school player lives up to the prowess claimed of him upon entrance in college. Too often a touted prep star fizzles when facing college competition. Not so Fritz Hanson," observed the *Spectrum*. The newspaper already looked ahead to the next varsity season when Hanson and Marquardt would be eligible to play against Army at West Point. In the *Bison* school yearbook, editors remembered that Hanson's "long, twisting end runs were the delight of the crowd." The annual applauded how the freshman team had twice beaten rival North Dakota.

Fritz Hanson

Hanson, Herb Peschel, and Marquardt all received numerals for the freshman season.

* *

In 1909, when all the various unions in Canada finally played under basically the same rules, Albert Grey, the Governor General of Canada, donated the Grey Cup trophy to the CRU, to be presented each year to the top rugby football team in Canada.

In 1921, teams from Western Canada began to challenge teams in the East for the Cup. The Edmonton Eskimos played for the trophy in 1921 and again with the nickname Elks in 1922. The Regina Roughriders competed in 1923, 1928, 1929, and 1930. The Winnipeg Tammany Tigers competed in 1925. No team from the West had ever returned home with a victory.

In 1931, the Regina Roughriders, "The Monarchs of Western Canada Rugby," once again marched toward the Grey Cup contest, but first they had to beat the St. John's Rugby Football Club in Winnipeg. The rivalry between Saskatchewan and Manitoba trailed back to 1890 when a team from the North West Mounted Police played and lost a game in Winnipeg. At the time, the *Manitoba Free Press* used the nickname "Roughriders" to describe the Mounties. Now in 1931, the Regina club would play the venerable black-and-yellow Saints, a club that traced its lineage back to the original St. John's College Football Club in 1887.

When the Roughriders arrived in Winnipeg for the WCRFU semifinal, they had forgotten their uniforms. They dispatched an airplane to bring the uniforms east from Regina, but by game time on November 7, 1931, the airplane still hadn't arrived. Instead, the normally red-and-black Roughriders wore the green-and-white uniforms of the Winnipeg Rugby Club.

At Wesley Park, on a field hard as concrete, the Roughriders played in unfamiliar boots, but with Curt Schave and Eddie James in Regina's backfield, it didn't seem to matter. James, the former St. John's player, contributed to 2 touchdowns while Schave scored 3 on his own. Schave, who had lettered in football in 1928 and 1930 at North Dakota, had also

Maroon and Gold (1931)

earned a spot on the North Central Conference (NCC) all-conference team at quarterback in 1930. He arrived in Regina in 1931.

In front of 3,500 fans, and while more fans watched from the windows in the buildings at nearby Wesley College, the Roughriders beat the Saints 47-5. Regina reached first down 26 times and scored 8 touchdowns in all. St. John's had Arni Coulter in the backfield for this game, but he made no difference. The Saints completed only 1 of 2 pass attempts, while the Roughriders completed 3 of 5 passes.

Never before had the Roughriders scored as many points in a league contest, and to add insult to injury, the team did it while they wore the Winnipegs uniforms. When their red-and-black sweaters finally arrived at halftime, they left them in their trunk, but they changed into their right-sized boots for the second half.

The Roughriders once again made it to the Grey Cup, where they lost to the Montreal Amateur Athletic Association Winged Wheelers, a team that featured Warren Stevens, a native New Yorker and Syracuse University football player who had used his arm to lead Montreal to an undefeated season. To attract Stevens, the Winged Wheelers had given him a Christmas present of $100 and had arranged a job for him with an oil company. Against the Roughriders for the Cup, he completed the first-ever touchdown pass in a Grey Cup game, and for the first time a team outside of Ontario had taken home the trophy.

*   *

Bob Fritz gripped the pigskin and launched his anger into a pass. Earl Moran, the left halfback and the team's primary passing back, had injured his leg in the game against St. John's. Coach Frank Cleve had asked Fritz and the other backs to practice passing, and Fritz appeared annoyed about how the other men kept dropping the ball. They seemed to put little effort into the workout.

Cleve recognized how only Fritz seemed to take things seriously. The players acted overconfident after their big win over the Johnnies, and they behaved as if they had already beaten their next opponent, Gustavus Adolphus College of St. Peter, Minnesota.

Maroon and Gold (1931)

To guarantee a conference title victory, the Cobbers would need to win all three of their remaining games. Gustavus stood 2-2 in conference games and had lost to St. Olaf and St. Thomas, but in the history of the rivalry, the Cobbers had never defeated the Golden Gusties. "The Gusties have always proved the jinx in some manner for the Cobs," despaired the *Concordian*.

At the helm of the Gustavus program stood George Myrum. In high school, Myrum had coached, played quarterback, and captained his team in Virginia, Minnesota, to a state title in 1919. In college, he played for the Golden Gophers. Myrum took over the Gustavus program in 1926 and led the team to two straight conference titles in 1926 and 1927. His men went undefeated that first year, but during the past three seasons, things had cooled a bit for the Gusties as they took on multiple losses.

The last time they met, the Gusties beat the Cobbers with a strong passing game, but so far in 1931, Concordia had played well against the pass. Cleve knew if his men could defend against Gustavus's aerial attack they should defend well against St. Thomas and St. Olaf later on. The Cobbers also needed to counter Myrum's new offensive tactics. "Gustavus will introduce a new type of shift to sports fans of this territory," reported the *Moorhead Daily News*. "It is patterned after New York University's style, in which the forward wall lines up a yard back of the center during which signals are called. The line then shifts into an unbalanced position with the backfield behind the strong side." Cleve prepared his men for uncertainty.

To help attract a sizable crowd for Concordia's homestand on November 7, 1931, Cleve reduced the price of admission to 75 cents. Fans got their money's worth.

Two minutes into the game, Fritz ran around left end and raced 25 yards for a touchdown. Later in the same quarter, Fritz completed a 32-yard touchdown pass to Pinkey Falgren over the middle of the field. And in the second quarter, at the end of a long drive, and with the Cobbers bucking the line and completing passes, Fritz scored again on a 6-yard, off-tackle plunge over the left side of the formation.

After Fritz had scored three touchdowns, Pat Hilde took over. First, Hilde busted off tackle for the score. Then he threw a touchdown pass to

Falgren, the end's second on the day, and Hilde scored yet another as a pass receiver. The Cobbers also scored on a safety, the result of a blocked punt.

On both sides of the ball, the Cobbers opened large holes in the Gustavus line. They held the Gusties and their new, fancy New York offense to just 6 completions on 23 pass attempts with 4 interceptions.

Meanwhile, with Moran out with an injury, Fritz and the other backs, especially Hilde, picked up the slack in the passing attack. The Cobber backfield completed 7 of 13 pass attempts with 1 interception.

Cleve made frequent substitutions throughout the game. He used 24 different men. In the end, Concordia beat Gustavus 41-6 and for the first time since they first played in 1923.

When the dust settled, the Cobbers learned that both St. John's and St. Thomas had lost their games that day, which opened the door for Concordia to win the conference title. With two games left on the schedule, Concordia stood atop the conference at 3-0 in conference play, tied with St. Thomas. Both teams sat one game ahead of St. Olaf at 2-1. The Cobbers would face both opponents before the end of the season, but the first of the two—St. Thomas, in the Tommies' last game of the season—would be the conference championship game, because even though Concordia had one conference game left to play after St. Thomas, a win over the Tommies would ensure the Cobbers the highest win percentage in the MIAC.

Thus far, Concordia had beaten three conference opponents by a total score of 98-6.

*

The Cobbers participated in only light workouts and practiced punting, passing, and placekicking in the lead up to their game against St. Thomas. North Dakota, a much heavier team, had battered the Tommies in their last game, and Cleve wanted his men more well-rested than the opposition. If Concordia could wear down St. Thomas, they stood to break the Tommies' confidence after a 36-6 loss to the Sioux.

Coach Joe Boland led the St. Thomas football program, and he understood the importance of endurance. Boland had played 57 minutes as a tackle for Notre Dame against Leland Stanford Junior University in the 1925 Rose Bowl. Against the Pop Warner-coached Cardinals, Boland helped the Fighting Irish stop Stanford backfielder Ernie Nevers from scoring that day. The Irish finished their perfect season and earned a consensus national championship.

Boland took over as coach for St. Thomas in 1929 when the team tied St. Olaf with a 4-2 conference record for the title. In 1930, the Tommies won the title outright with a 5-0 conference record. Cleve knew St. Thomas would carry the air of confidence that goes along with winning two consecutive titles. The Cobbers would play the Tommies in St. Paul.

The Cobbers started the 1931 season young and green, but Cleve saw how his men had grown. They had benefitted from their games against St. John's and Gustavus, which together offered the styles of running and passing that St. Thomas would employ. Nevertheless, Cleve made sure his men practiced against the pass. Unfortunately, the Cobber reserves posed no challenge for the starters. Fritz performed particularly well in blocking pass attempts.

*

In a Pullman train car with brass-framed windows, well-dressed men and women moved from observation car to dining car to smoking rooms to play cards, listen to the radio, and enjoy the soda fountain. The Cobbers, enroute to St. Paul to play St. Thomas, had traveled to the capital city once already in 1931 to play Macalester, and the team would take the train again a week later to Northfield to play St. Olaf, but this trip meant more than the others.

Cleve, Louie Benson, and 22 Cobbers left Moorhead at 4:15 p.m. on Friday before the game. They arrived in Minneapolis late in the day and long after dark. Somewhere in the six-story Andrews Hotel on Hennepin Avenue, beds with freshly laundered sheets waited for them, but they knew they wouldn't sleep well. If they won this game, Concordia would be conference champions for the very first time. They yearned to play.

*

After breakfast on November 14, 1931, Coach Cleve assembled his men in the lobby of the hotel. After a brisk walk together and an early lunch, they took a bus to St. Paul. When they arrived at the field off Cretin

Avenue near campus, a slight breeze blew a light rain from sideline to sideline. The first of 4,000 fans had already started to assemble.

Back home in Moorhead, students gathered inside the Concordia chapel to follow the play-by-play of the game. A Concordia professor at St. Thomas would relay the game's progress through a system of runners, telephones, and the telegraph system to the chapel where Concordia Dean Paul Rasmussen would announce the results.

Beneath overcast skies and in a drizzling rain, the game began on a wet, soggy field. The Tommies wore purple and gray and the Cobbers wore maroon and gold, but soon all the players found themselves encased in shades of brown.

From the start, both teams stuck to the ground game. St. Thomas moved the ball no further than Concordia's 37-yard line while the Cobbers only managed to move the ball beyond their own 20, just once. The teams struggled and exchanged punts. Late in the first half, Fritz fumbled and lost the ball on the Concordia 15-yard line. The Tommies then moved the ball to the 6-yard line, but Concordia held and punted away. The half ended in a 0-0 tie.

As the game progressed, Concordia improved. Out of desperation, St. Thomas began to pass more, but the slippery, wet ball and field made passing difficult. The Tommies threatened to score, but the Cobbers played strong defense; they intercepted a pass and returned the ball 85 yards for the score. Concordia won the game 7-0 and walked away conference champions.

A large delegation, including Moorhead Mayor C.I. Evenson, Dean Rasmussen, and Concordia student body President Victor Boe, greeted the Cobbers at the train station in Moorhead when they arrived at 2:40 p.m. Sunday afternoon. The three executives delivered speeches and the students led the crowd in cheers. The players then filled taxicabs for the trip back to campus.

Still stiff from Saturday's competition, the Cobbers rose early Monday morning to join fans in the college chapel to celebrate the conference title victory. The school president, the board of directors, Mayor Evenson, alumni, professors, and students all spoke, as did team captains. The pep band played to rouse the crowd and Benson recounted the game from a coach's perspective. Cleve finished the celebration with an inspired speech. The whole crowd sang the school song to close the 85-minute event.

*

In their last game against St. Olaf, Concordia still had something to play for: an undefeated season. In 1930, St. Olaf had shared the title with St. Thomas, and this season the Oles had beaten St. Mary's College of Winona, Minnesota, by a 20-point margin. Meanwhile, St. Mary's had played the Tommies to a scoreless tie.

For Cleve, the game felt personal. He had played football alongside Ade Christenson, the coach for the Oles, and together they had led St. Olaf to a 5-0-1 record and a conference title in 1922. Christenson had coached the Oles since 1927, and every season the team had improved.

St. Olaf played with speed in the running game, which presented a new challenge for Concordia. The Oles featured two fast backs, including a tall and heavy halfback, Sylvan Leon "Slippery Syl" Saumer.

Throughout the season, Fritz had played an important role in the Cobbers' run-stop defense, but during the title game against St. Thomas, he had suffered a leg injury. Now during scrimmages, he only watched as the team practiced stopping a wide-open running game. Without Fritz, the starters had trouble stopping the reserves. But during the final practice for the week, Fritz resumed his position at fullback. He ran through some plays, but Cleve felt uncertain about whether Fritz should actually play or whether he should just suit him up and have him stand in reserve.

When the Cobbers arrived at St. Olaf on Saturday, November 21, 1931, they met 38-degree temperatures and a dry field beneath overcast skies. The Oles received the opening kickoff, and Fritz started on defense. In the St. Olaf backfield at right halfback stood Al Droen, a menacing figure who wore a form-fitting facemask hammered out of metal that covered his entire face. With their masked man in the backfield, the inspired Oles put together an 80-yard scoring drive that included four first downs. Droen scored the extra point on an end run. In short order, the Oles scored 3 touchdowns and 3 extra points on three successive drives. The St. Olaf student newspaper, the *Manitou Messenger*, attributed the team's success to "spectacular fake maneuvering." The scoring drives featured runs of 35 and 40 yards and a long pass.

In the second half, after some words from Cleve, the Cobbers prevented the Oles from scoring again, but the Oles won the field position battle with punts and kicks of at least 50 yards each time. Eventually, the Cobbers scored a touchdown of their own, but in the end the Oles beat the champs 21-6. The Cobbers finished their championship season with one conference loss.

*

As the 1931 college football season came to a close, news organizations published their all-conference teams. They picked Bob Fritz, who led in scoring in conference games with 5 touchdowns and 2 extra points, as a consensus first-team starter. The *Minneapolis Star*, which named Fritz to its first team at fullback, exclaimed, "Bob Fritz, 190-pound sophomore of Concordia, proved the outstanding fullback of the year. Possessing a powerful build, hard drive and strong defensive ability." The United Press named Fritz to their first team at right halfback. The Northwest News Bureau's coaches' poll named Fritz, "the main threat on the championship aggregation" and an "excellent defensive player, both for line plays and forward pass attacks," to their first team at fullback. The *Minneapolis Journal* and *St. Paul Pioneer Press and Dispatch* both named Fritz to their first teams. At the postseason banquet, Fritz received a letterman's sweater and his first letter, as well as a gold football for the championship.

Bob Fritz

CHAPTER 2 - YELLOW AND GREEN (1932)

In 1932, Joe Ryan would convince football clubs in Winnipeg that they, too, needed to defy amateurism in favor of underhanded professionalism, and that they needed to do even more to promote and expand football in Winnipeg. Meanwhile, at North Dakota State, Fritz Hanson, Bud Marquardt, and Herb Peschel would join the varsity ranks and help the Bison to pursue a conference title and national prominence. And at Concordia College, Bob Fritz and the Cobbers would attempt to shrug off injuries in pursuit of a second conference championship.

* *

In the aftermath of the St. John's Rugby Football Club's defeat to the Regina Roughriders and their American backfielder, Curt Schave—and after Regina's subsequent defeat to the Montreal Winged Wheelers and their American backfielder, Warren Stevens—football promoters in Winnipeg realized that if they wanted to put together a team that could compete, they would have to rely more on professional players, including Americans, instead of amateurs. The Roughriders had recruited players from long distances and had paid them well, which meant they could also expect them to practice the game to perfection. Winnipeg needed to do the same. Winnipeg's rugby enthusiasts also complained that Winnipeg teams didn't play physical football to the same level as Regina. And they blamed local officials for their harsh application of the rules. Ultimately, they argued, teams in Winnipeg needed to combine into one organization.

*

In 1896, the CRU ruled that "no player shall be eligible to play in any match under the auspices of the Union who is not an amateur in good standing [with the Amateur Athletic Union of Canada (AAUC)]." The AAUC defined an amateur as "one who has never competed for money prize or staked bet, or with or against a professional for any prize, or who has never taught, pursued, or assisted in the practice of athletic exercise as a means of obtaining a livelihood or who has never entered any competition under a name other than his own."

Yellow and Green (1932)

In fact, the Grey Cup itself includes an engraved inscription that says, "Presented by His Excellency Earl Grey for the *Amateur* Rugby Football Championship of Canada" [emphasis added]. As early as 1910, just one year after the first Grey Cup championship game, accusations of professionalism emerged in the Interprovincial Rugby Football Union (IRFU), the "Big Four," but the CRU never dealt with the issue. Meanwhile, CRU bylaws included a residency rule, which required players in clubs to be residents of the city or town they represented. The rule required players at universities to be students and academically qualified to study.

In 1912, Ottawa hired an American, "Doc" Galvin, to coach the team, while McGill University hired Shag Shaughnessy. Shaughnessy, a former professional baseball player with a total of 37 major league plate appearances for the Washington Senators and Philadelphia Athletics, also managed the Ottawa baseball team in the Canadian League. At McGill, he employed innovations in Canadian football that annoyed his opponents. For example, on defense, most teams placed their men on the line of scrimmage with only a few backs standing 10 or more yards behind the line. As a result, if a running back broke through, he typically ran for a long gain. To resolve this issue, Shaughnessy employed line backers. And on offense, he employed shifts and unbalanced lines. His opponents accused him of employing "American tactics."

Meanwhile, in the West, an American born in Sheridan, Illionis, by the name of William "Deacon" White from Northwestern University in Evanston, Illinois, coached the Edmonton team, which included three Americans on its roster. And Saskatoon fielded three Americans while Regina fielded two.

In 1921, Queen's University at Kingston in Ontario began to admit players as older-than-average students who enrolled in preliminary level courses. That same year, with Americans Jimmy Enright from Northwestern and Curly Dorman from the University of Southern California in Los Angeles, the Edmonton Eskimos made it to the Grey Cup only to lose 23-0 to the Lionel Conacher-led Toronto Argonauts. Considered Canada's greatest athlete, Lionel "Big Train" Conacher had excelled in football, lacrosse, baseball, boxing, wrestling, hockey, and track and field in high school. He went on to win a Canadian boxing championship as a light heavyweight and later boxed against world heavyweight champion Jack Dempsey in an exhibition bout. He joined the ranks of professional hockey in 1925 and played for the New York Americans, Chicago Black Hawks, and Montreal Maroons. In 1932, he still played for the Maroons.

In 1925, Regina hired an American coach, "Doc" Blackwood, from the University of Chicago. That same year, *Maclean's* magazine said what everyone else was thinking when they published a series of articles about the hypocrisy of amateurism in Canadian sport and about the need to either clean up or accept professionalism. That same season, Shaughnessy introduced a simplified play-calling nomenclature, and his players called plays in a huddle. Opponents complained about Shaughnessy's tactics as an abuse of the rules, mostly because they could no longer hear play calls at the line of scrimmage. A year later, Shaughnessy began to send representatives to scout opponents. His competitors labeled the practice unsportsmanlike.

In 1926, the WCRFU accepted the British Columbia Rugby Football Union (BCRFU) as a member, and the expansion increased travel expenses for western teams. Players had difficulty getting time off from work to travel long distances to play semifinal and championship games. To increase revenue, teams in the West sometimes staged a series of games instead of a single game for the championship, but still the western champion sometimes declined to travel east to play for the Grey Cup due to the expenses involved.

The most successful teams practiced more, and while collegiate teams could find time to practice during daylight hours, club teams depended on employers to allow players to leave work early so they could practice in the Canadian twilight. Meanwhile, "arclight fiends," teams without supportive employers, practiced in the dark, sometimes by the light of the moon. Nevertheless, by 1927, club teams dominated collegiate teams.

By 1930, in the throes of the Depression, players in Canada often moved to bigger cities to look for work. This caused some teams to question the eligibility of certain players under the residency rule. Meanwhile, inflation took its toll on rugby. In 1930, the Toronto club estimated it cost $60 per man to outfit the team. Meanwhile, players demanded more in-kind payments in the form of everyday necessities.

With the forward pass a legal play in 1931, some club and collegiate teams in the East imported Americans to coach their teams in the use of the play. The importation of Americans for this purpose raised some hackles. The *Hamilton Herald* suggested the CRU had intended the pass "[to] be learned by Canadians and developed in this country without the aid of exponents of it from across the border." Some rugby officials suggested the CRU should bar Americans from the game because they took away Canadian jobs.

After the 1931 season, member teams in the Winnipeg Senior League took steps to increase the quality of their product and to promote football in Winnipeg. They added a fourth team to the league, Garrison, a squad of soldiers from Fort Osborne with experience in English rugby. The league would continue to play at Wesley Park, the home of the Winnipeg Amateur Senior Baseball League, where a new grandstand, bleachers, sound system, and floodlights had been installed. They would play night games. At a league meeting, St. John's asked for permission to play home games at the newly built Osborne Stadium, which also had floodlights and which had been built for football, but the rest of the league insisted that all league games must be played at Wesley.

Both the Winnipeg Rugby Club and St. John's acquired American player-coaches to lead their teams. After the Saints announced that Russ Rebholz, a Big Ten Conference player from the University of Wisconsin, would coach their squad, nearly 40 players showed up for tryouts. Rebholz had been a lead scorer at Wisconsin with 48 points as a junior. After the 1931 college football season, he played in the East-West Shrine Game. He would teach St. John's players how to play out of the Double Wing formation. He only needed to figure out what to do with the 12th man.

Meanwhile, Joe Ryan, the Fighting Irish devotee, announced the Winnipegs had acquired Carl "Stumpy" Cronin, a 5-foot-7, 165-pound quarterback and right halfback from Notre Dame. In 1931, Cronin had started against both Drake and West Point, but he spent most of his time on the second and third squads. He could block and tackle well and he persisted as a runner. Against Indiana University, he broke free and sprinted 35 yards for a touchdown. He scored another touchdown against the University of Pennsylvania of Philadelphia.

*   *

When North Dakota Agricultural College (NDAC) opened its doors in Fargo in 1890, a botanist by the name of Henry L. Bolley joined the faculty. He paid a visit to the University of North Dakota in Grand Forks where he met with a fellow botanist, Melvin A. Brannon. Bolley and Brannon had played football against each other when Bolley played for Purdue University in West Lafayatte, Indiana, and Brannon played for Wabash College in Crawfordsville, Indiana. The two men suggested their institutions should field football teams and play each other, and so Bolley and Brannon each recruited men to play. Three years later, in 1893, they had gathered enough men to scrimmage, mostly students who had worked on farms. A year later, in 1894, NDAC played North Dakota in their first game. Bolley's NDAC men won. With few options for opponents within a reasonable distance from Fargo or Grand Forks, Bolley and Brannon agreed the teams would play two games each year, one on each campus.

The men who scrimmaged for Bolley in 1893 continued to attend homecoming games into the 1930s. The men included former left halfback Claude Nugent, secretary of the college who later joined the Magill & Company seed company and then managed the Western Adjustment and Inspection bureau in Minneapolis; right halfback Ralph Ward, a farmer and rancher near Leeds, North Dakota; quarterback and captain Robert Reed, a farmer in the Red River Valley with 12,000 acres; reserve player Fred Loomis, who owned the Fargo Laundry and who later opened Loomis and Loomis dry cleaning; and right tackle O.A. Thompson, who took over the North Dakota Agricultural Experiment Station in Edgeley, North Dakota. All of these men would say they had played for NDAC, for the "Aggies."

The Constitution of North Dakota established there must be an "agricultural college" in Fargo. Since 1890, North Dakota Agricultural College had stood as the official name of the institution, but in 1919 the

Yellow and Green (1932)

Student Commission at the school rallied to change the name of the school to North Dakota State College. The request fell on deaf ears. In 1922, the commission successfully petitioned the college post office to change the address of the school to be "State College, N. Dak." The students believed the address change would be the first volley in an attempt to urge the state legislature to change the name. In practice, students, the community, and the media largely referred to the institution as North Dakota State (with or without the word "College"), even though the school's official name remained unchanged. That same year, shortly after the school joined the newly formed North Central Conference (NCC), the lettermen voted to drop the use of the "Fighting Aggies" nickname. Instead, they called the team the Bison.

The fight continued. In 1926, students presented a petition with 500 student signatures to the State Board of Administration to request the name change. The Alumni and Former Student Association followed up with a poll of former students, and 251 of 314 replies stood in favor of changing the name to North Dakota State College, or perhaps the North Dakota State College of Agriculture and Mechanic Arts. Still, the North Dakota legislature took no action on the matter. In the early 1930s, Bison athletes officially played for North Dakota Agricultural College, but they would have said they played for North Dakota State.

*

Charles Carroll "Casey" Finnegan took over the North Dakota State football program in 1928. Born in Richmond, Wisconsin, he graduated from Ripon College in Ripon in 1913 and attended graduate school at the University of Wisconsin. He taught science and high school athletics in Oconto, Wisconsin, from 1913-1915 and then took a similar position in Grafton, North Dakota, in 1915.

During World War I, Finnegan served as a second lieutenant and spent 20 months overseas, from January 1918 to August 1919. The Army awarded him two Silver Stars for gallantry in action, first for his leadership at the command of a machine gun company in the Meuse-Argonne offensive in October 1918, where he "placed himself at the front of his platoon and was first to enter the barrage. His good judgment... placed the platoon through the barrage without the loss of a man." And second

North Dakota State (Fargo, North Dakota)

for leading a platoon safely through a "shell-swept field" in the same battle.

After the war, Finnegan returned to teach and coach in Grafton, where his Grey Devils football teams finished runners-up four times for the state title. Finnegan had laid claim to inventing the huddle, which offered his opponents less information about the upcoming play. He also served as the superintendent of schools in Grafton from 1922-1928.

Now in 1932, as the athletic director, football coach, and professor of physical education at North Dakota State, Finnegan continued to serve as a captain in the North Dakota National Guard and as adjutant of the 164th infantry. His assistant, Robert Allen "Bob" Lowe, also fought in World War I. He served as a private in the 35th Division. In the Argonne in September 1918, shrapnel struck him in the head and he was gassed. He laid in the hospital for six weeks.

*

In the spring of 1932, a soggy field meant Finnegan would have to wait another week before spring workouts could begin. The players had already checked out their football equipment, and in less than a month the Bison would play Moorhead State in a spring charity game. Finnegan planned 20 sessions of drills and scrimmages, and he wanted to get a closer look at Fritz Hanson, the freshman who had performed so well for the yearling team. He also needed to get a good look at every lineman to see who could step up to fill holes left by graduating seniors.

Because fall semester would not begin until September 14, fall practices would also begin late, on September 10. Finnegan figured a good spring workout could help prepare his men mentally for the autumn football grind and a challenging schedule that included games against Oklahoma City University, which had won 12 consecutive games in 1931. They would also play rival North Dakota. And at the end of the season, they would take a trip east to play Army at West Point, New York, and George Washington University in Washington, D.C. In the NCC town of Sioux Falls, South Dakota, the *Daily Argus-Leader* called the timetable the most "pretentious" grid schedule under Finnegan to date, even more difficult than the 1931 lineup, which had included games against two Big Ten teams.

Yellow and Green (1932)

In the middle of the Depression, some people in the community questioned whether the school should finance an expensive East Coast trip for the football team. The *Spectrum* addressed the concern in an editorial and argued that "although frowned on in some sections as being 'brutal' and 'overemphasized,' football continues to be a very effective means of advertising an institution throughout the country... Athletics have the instant appeal to draw the interests of many to institutions, which interest usually results in a more careful observance of the advantages, educational and intellectual, which the institution has." Finnegan knew he faced scrutiny, but he also knew the fans needed something to cheer for.

*

Across the river at Concordia, Coach Frank Cleve looked over the letter he had received from Bob Fritz. The star fullback had dropped out of school but promised to return in the fall. But even if Fritz did not rejoin the team for the 1932 season, Cleve felt confident he could put together a winning program. On the heels of Concordia's first conference championship, interest in Cobber football remained high. Several new students expressed interest in trying out for the team.

In 1932, the Cobbers would play their toughest schedule since Cleve had taken over. St. Thomas would be the team to beat, but in their first conference game, the Cobbers would match up with St. Olaf, the only team that outplayed Concordia in 1931. In light of these matchups, Cleve felt like the underdog, not the reigning champion, and like Finnegan, he itched to get his players onto the spring practice field. However, poor field conditions meant he would have to start with only chalk talks and walk-throughs.

*

During the offseason, the NCAA instituted several major rules changes intended to make college football safer for players. The changes outlawed the Flying Wedge formation on kick returns, in which teams would amass all of their blockers in front of the returner, and the new rules forbid defensive players from using their hands to strike opponents in the head or neck. The changes also declared that a ball-carrier would be down when any part of his body other than his hands or feet touched the ground, to

Casey Finnegan

prevent piling on by the defense. Coaches could also substitute a player who had already played, once per quarter.

Finnegan needed spring football and the charity game against the Dragons to give his men time to practice the new rules so they could avoid mental mistakes. Cleve, too, needed to discuss the rules changes with his men, but without official guidance from the MIAC, he felt hesitant to change how his players might practice. He hoped he wouldn't have to make many changes at all. At the conference's annual meeting in the Twin Cities, Cleve protested the new rule that restricted the use of hands on defense. He felt confident the other coaches in the conference would join him and reject the rule, too, and he hoped they would reject all the new rules.

*

Spring practices for both North Dakota State and Concordia began April 11, 1932, a week later than desired.

At Concordia, after two weeks of chalk talks, Cleve had 40 men, including 11 lettermen on the field for outdoor practices in perfect weather. His seniors took on coaching roles, and even without Fritz in the lineup, Cleve had a variety of backs at his disposal. On the last day of spring drills, two players wrenched their knees and another broke his finger. Cleve canceled practice early.

At North Dakota State, Hanson competed for a position in the backfield with five other freshmen, including former Perham teammate Art Stege who had sat out a portion of the 1931 season with a broken rib. Hanson's primary competitor his first year, George May, sat out with injuries. On the line, Bud Marquardt competed with six other players for a position at end. He rose above the competition on both offense and defense. Early on, Herb Peschel sat out with injuries, but when he got back into the scrum, he showed promise at tackle.

After a week of blocking, tackling, and learning new plays, the Bison began a week of scrimmages between the Green and Yellow teams to prepare for the spring game against the Dragons.

*

To raise money to help fund the 1932 Olympic Games that would open July 30 in Los Angeles, California, adults paid 35 cents and students paid

Yellow and Green (1932)

15 cents each on Friday, April 29, 1932, to watch the Bison play the Dragons at Dacotah Field. The teams played the game with quarters 12 minutes in duration instead of 15.

When the Bison kicked off at 4:00 p.m., Finnegan chose to have his kicker punt the ball instead of using a place kick. In a defensive struggle, neither team scored until the fourth quarter when Bill "Shifty" Gove caught a 37-yard pass for the Bison. On the next play, he ran 2 yards off tackle for the touchdown. The Bison beat the Dragons 6-0.

Hanson, who had suffered an injury during practice earlier in the week, found himself on the sidelines again while another Bison excelled in the backfield. Meanwhile, both Peschel and Marquardt got into the game. On offense, Marquardt stood out in line play and in pass-catching. On defense, he kept runners from gaining ground around the end. On punts, he showed good speed when he ran down the return man and tackled him with his long arms.

After the game, Finnegan felt good about what he had seen on the field. "We expect to have one of the strongest football teams in the country during the 1932 season," he told the *Spectrum*.

*   *

In August, while on a tour of Shea's Winnipeg Brewery, Winnipeg Rugby Club Coach Carl Cronin watched as a big, tall worker moved barrels around the premises. Cronin attempted to pick up one of the barrels himself but discovered he couldn't budge any of them. He inquired about the employee who carried the barrels and learned the man played goalie for the local Irish soccer team. Cronin attended the team's practice and there in the goal stood his man, Lou Mogul [born Louis Mogulovsky, a Jewish athlete]. Cronin recruited the 203-pound mountain of muscle to play for the Winnipegs. The *Winnipeg Free Press* observed, "When [Mogul] is arrayed in shoulder harness, padded moleskins, and all the official accoutrements, he looks and acts like a ten-ton truck with a yen for manslaughter." Cronin groomed Mogul to play on the line.

In addition, St John's Rugby Football Club attracted Eddie James to return from Regina. He brought four players with him, including a

Yellow and Green (1932)

lineman named Johnny Patrick to shore up an already strong squad that featured Herb Mobberley, former Native Sons junior player Eric Law, Bill Ceretti, and former Young Men's Hebrew Association (YMHA) junior player Eddie Kushner.

To kick off the league season, St. John's would host Regina in a rematch of their 1931 playoff game. The Winnipeg Senior League drummed up publicity. "Winnipeg opens a bigger and better fall show featuring two new ringmasters and several new performers," wrote the *Winnipeg Tribune*. "These teams are expected to make serious efforts to bring the Dominion honors to Winnipeg."

The *Star-Phoenix* in Saskatoon, Saskatchewan, clearly stated the football situation in the West when it wrote, "Year after year, rugby is becoming more of a business proposition than ever before. To ensure teams [that] will be attractive to the fans and consequently benefit the clubs' finances, it has become necessary to import players from across the line. All of which leads to the conclusion that if the other cities in the West wish to stay on the rugby map, they will have to follow the example set by their opponents. This season, Calgary, Moose Jaw, and Saskatoon are about the only cities in the West which have no Americans on their lineups."

In the East, both Montreal and Ottawa fielded American players. Montreal's roster included Hal Baysinger and Lew Newton, both from Syracuse University, and Ottawa's roster included Wally Masters and Rolf Carlsen, both from Pennsylvania. As concerns about professionalism rose in the East, some officials called for the AAUC to allow professionals and amateurs to play together, which would settle the matter once and for all, but the AAUC took no action.

*

St. John's kicked off the 1932 season with a two-game, Labor Day weekend series of exhibition games played Saturday, September 3, and Monday, September 5, 1932, against the Regina Roughriders in Winnipeg. The teams played at Osborne Stadium under newly installed floodlights, and officials declared the games to be the first-ever games in Western Canada to be played at night under artificial light. To promote the event, St. John's invited boys 16 years old and under to attend for a nickel with a chance to win a free football. The team also invited Winnipeg

Yellow and Green (1932)

middleweight boxer Frankie Battaglia to perform the ceremonial kickoff. The venue featured a new 126-square-foot scoreboard and a loudspeaker system for the announcer. The Capitol Theatre in Winnipeg planned to film the game.

Led by Russ Rebholz, St. John's featured five former Roughriders on its roster, while the Roughriders included a new American player, Bill "Whitey" Mjogdalen, who had lettered in football in 1928, 1929, and 1930 at North Dakota. He was a first-team all-conference selection at guard in 1929 and 1930. Mjogdalen, a husky fellow, played end, and with his blond hair he stood out on the field. The Roughriders also added Pinkey Falgren, the three-year letterman from Concordia College who had captained the team in 1931 and who had earned all-conference honors at end. A former Saskatoon Quakers player, Cliff Roseborough, also joined the squad.

In the first game, the Roughriders completed four passes for long gains until Curt Schave injured his shoulder. Meanwhile, the Saints moved the ball on option runs from Rebholz to James. St. John's beat Regina 4-0 on 2 rouge kicks and a safety to become the first Winnipeg team to beat the Roughriders since 1925.

In the second game, Eddie James turned up the heat against Regina with long runs for 45 and 60 yards. He scored 2 touchdowns and St. John's beat Regina 26-6.

Meanwhile, Manitoba, the collegiate entry in the Winnipeg Senior League, announced it had signed a new coach, John Ingersoll, the former captain and a four-year letterman from Moorhead State. Ingersoll had moved to Winnipeg to study for a master's degree in political science. He would coach a team that included second-year varsity player Dick Lane and first-year player Chauncey Dagg, who had played as captain for the Native Sons junior team in 1931. Lane played for the Bisons when the team won the WCIRFU title in 1931. However, two days later the WCIRFU announced it had suspended the season due to financial difficulties at member schools. As a result, Manitoba withdrew from the Winnipeg Senior League and decided instead to compete in football at the junior level where the Winnipeg Rugby Club had taken over management of the Shamrock Rugby Club. The Winnipegs renamed that club the junior Winnipegs, with Cronin as coach, and positioned the juniors as the development team for the Winnipegs. Meanwhile, so many players had turned out to play for the Saints and the Winnipegs that the clubs suggested the city needed an intermediate league to give everyone a chance to play.

*

With Manitoba out of the Senior League, the three remaining teams agreed to fill out the league schedule at Wesley Park. The venue had installed a new, 500-seat grandstand for reserved seating on the west side of the field, and with 4,000 general admission seats available on the east side and 1,500 seats available in the north bleachers, the venue could accommodate up to 6,000 fans. The league continued to offer nickel seats and the promise of free footballs to kids.

In the first game of the season on September 17, 1932, the defending champion Saints played the Winnipegs. The new Cronin-led 'Pegs had absorbed a few Manitoba varsity players, including Lane, to complement the Winnipegs squad that included Lou "Rosy" Adelman, Arni Coulter, Lou Mogul, and Johnny Christie. Adelman had played with the Winnipeg Tammany Tigers in their Grey Cup runner-up finish in 1925 and Christie had played for the Winnipeg club since 1930.

The Winnipegs had also acquired the services of "Toots" Wiggins who had played at St. Rita of Cascia High School in Chicago. In front of a sellout crowd, Rebholz and James proved elusive runners and they used the option run to their advantage, which included a 55-yard touchdown run by James. Cronin and Coulter on the Winnipegs used the forward pass to connect with Wiggins. The Saints beat the Winnipegs 15-1.

*

With a gap in their early season schedule, the Roughriders scheduled a two-game series with a team in Minot, North Dakota, 250 miles southeast of Regina. The team, dubbed the Minot Panthers, played as an independent semi-professional team. It wouldn't be the first time a Canadian or American football team crossed the border to play an opponent, but rules differences meant at least one team might play at a disadvantage.

The Minot Panthers first played as the Minot All-Stars in 1931 when former college and high school football players living in Minot formed a

Yellow and Green (1932)

team to play an Armistice Day exhibition game against the Minot State Teachers College Beavers, to raise money for the Lions Club and its children's shoe fund. The All-Stars included Glenn L. "Red" Jarrett, a Grand Forks Central High School star athlete who had gone on to play at North Dakota from 1928 through 1930, where he "upset the defens[ive] plans of many an NCC opponent by twisting his way thru entire teams for touchdowns," reported the *Minot Daily News*. As a member of the North Dakota football team, Jarrett scored a touchdown in 17 consecutive games. The NCC named him All-Conference in 1929 and 1930. When Jarrett captained the team in 1930, the *New York News* named him to its first team of All-Americans at halfback. He received All-American honorable mentions from the Associated Press, United Press, and the Newspaper Enterprise Association. That same year, the *New York Herald Tribune* named Jarrett "Back of the Year," and after he scored the only touchdown that Army allowed on its way to a national championship in 1930, the New York press gave Jarrett the nickname "The Red Rabbit of the Prairie."

The All-Stars, 26 men in total, also featured former North Dakota players John Booty (1924-1926), Irwin Dunnell (1927), Harlow Samuelson (1924-1925), and Vern Smith (1927, 1929-1930), as well as Harley Robertson from Jamestown, a man with the last name Pierce from Columbus College in Sioux Falls, and players with some freshman-level collegiate football experience, and also a handful of former Minot High School players. H.R. "Caesar" Murphy, a venerable North Dakota player (1913-1914), coached the team.

In Minot in 1931, Jarret had just finished his first season as the Minot High School Magicians football coach, and for the All-Stars, he used a classroom at the school for chalk talks. The men worked out in the high school gymnasium and practiced on the gridiron at Roosevelt Park. They moved to the college gridiron for final practices. For the charity game, the officials donated their services and the college donated use of the field and floodlights. Children 14 years old and under watched the game for free.

On loose turf, the Beavers beat the All Stars 6-0 on Armistice Day in 1931. Jarrett ran 20 yards off tackle and crossed the goal line for the All-

Stars, but officials called his touchdown back on a penalty for holding. Jarrett also had a 30-yard carry in the game. The event attracted 1,500 fans and raised just over $400 for the charity, which hoped to purchased 500 pairs of shoes. The day after the game, the *Ward County Independent* noted, "The All Stars, while all capable players at one time, were not all in the best of condition today. Most of them are limping around a bit due to the hard running and knocks they got in the hard-fought game."

Now in 1932, the All-Stars re-emerged as the Minot Panthers, with new equipment but without Jarrett. The team started workouts in late August and added "Big" Bill Hilts, a former North Dakota State player nicknamed "The Bowbells Bone-crusher," to the team. Hilts graduated from North Dakota State in 1931 and then took a year off from football while he circled the globe playing saxophone as a member of the orchestra on an ocean liner. Hilts had started his college career at North Dakota but then transferred to North Dakota State. He also boxed with the Bison team and won the NCC championship at heavyweight with 2 knockouts.

In advance of their games against the Panthers, the Roughriders advertised that for the first time in Regina, teams would play with American football rules, and for the first time in Saskatchewan, teams would play an evening game under floodlights. The teams would play half of each game with American rules, the other half with Canadian rules. The Roughrider squad had recently acquired the services of Austin "Phat" DeFrate from the Montana College of Agriculture and Mechanic Arts in Bozeman, Montana, another husky fellow but with open-field running skills. DeFrate's mother lived in Minot.

The *Leader-Post* said the Minot team featured "a flock of big boys." Schave, one of Regina's Americans, said the Panthers were "a strong team and one that will provide all kinds of thrills." The newspaper noted that "the forward-passing of the Americans is also recognized to be far superior to that of Canadian teams." The Panthers were said to feature a diminutive, left-handed quarterback by the name of "Ding" Bowlby, a former Minot High School player. In fact, the Panthers roster featured a majority of former Minot High School players, at least nine of whom had played on the 1931 All-Stars. Most of the college players from the All-Stars did not appear on the Panthers roster. The Roughriders billed the

Yellow and Green (1932)

game as an "international rugby" competition. The Panthers squad of 18 players drove eight hours in four vehicles, "radio equipped and all," to Saskatchewan.

In their first game on September 22, 1932, approximately 2,000 fans attended the game at the Exhibition Grounds in Regina. The teams played with a white-painted ball at night under the lights. Under American rules, the Roughriders scored first in the first half when DeFrate threw a touchdown pass. The Panthers responded with a 45-yard end run near to the goal line and then scored on the next play.

In the second half, Whitey Mjogdalen blocked a Panthers kick, and three times Regina scored a rouge under Canadian rules to win the game 10-7.

To the disappointment of fans, the Panthers played without the advertised Bowlby at quarterback and they tried only 3 passes and failed to complete any of them. Meanwhile, the Roughriders entertained fans in the second half when they tried out new formations that included "wheel" moves in the backfield, originally a Montreal club innovation.

Two days later on September 24, 1932, the Roughriders and Panthers played their second night game. DeFrate scored a touchdown in the first half and scored again in the fourth quarter on an interception. In the second quarter, a Regina player intercepted a pass and started to run the ball the wrong way before he turned around and ran instead for a 35-yard gain. The Roughriders and the Panthers combined for 19 pass attempts, but only Minot completed 1, a 40-yard reception to put the team in position to score a field goal as time expired. The Roughriders beat the Panthers 13-3.

Afterward, the Minot squad arranged a second game with undefeated Minot State. Bowlby, the southpaw quarterback who had skipped the game against Regina, played against the Beavers and completed a touchdown pass, but the Panthers lost 14-7. The Panthers lineup that day included a former Navy player named Bertram.

* *

Before North Dakota State's 1932 season began, the *Daily Argus-Leader* declared Fritz Hanson, Bud Marquardt, and Herb Peschel among the best sophomores in the history of North Dakota State football. In particular, the newspaper said Hanson "bids fair to become a gridiron hero before a diploma terminates his athletic career."

Hanson reported early for fall practices on September 7, alongside the other sophomore backs, which included Art Stege and George May. Coach Casey Finnegan wanted to get a good look at his horses. Five days later, when the remainder of the North Dakota State men reported for workouts, Finnegan had his choice of 16 men in competition for a position in the backfield. The team captain and all-conference tackle, Dolly Schoenfelder, insisted that he, too, should be considered for a backfield position. Schoenfelder had spent the entire summer on a farm in rural Aberdeen, South Dakota, and he had lost 20 pounds. He felt like a ball-carrier. "Schoenfelder, despite his weight, is unusually fast," confirmed the *Bismarck Tribune*. "He always was the first out of the line and down under punts. In practice he has shown an aptitude for catching passes and he also has demonstrated his ball-carrying ability in active combat." Finnegan had six returning lettermen on the line, but he felt he needed linemen more than he needed backs, and only Schoenfelder had played tackle before. "He has been so outstanding for two seasons at his position that Finnegan figures he might have an excellent chance of gaining All-American recognition," reported the *Bismarck Tribune*. Schoenfelder recanted and took his place at tackle.

Bison practices continued in three-a-days, with morning drills at 9:30 a.m., chalk talks at 2:30 p.m., and field drills at 4:00 p.m. Peschel competed with eight other men at the tackle position while Marquardt stood among six others at end. The local media held high expectations for Marquardt. "Bud is well known for his basketball ability," wrote the *Fargo Forum* and it "comes in handy playing end. He can get up in the air and pick off passes like nobody's business. He also is strong defensively, having an uncanny ability to diagnose the play of the opposition, and then getting in the right position to upset plans."

*

Yellow and Green (1932)

Coach Frank Cleve called his Concordia men to practice on September 7. Twenty-five men reported that first day. On day two, 35 men suited up for two-a-day workouts, including 12 returning lettermen. Among them stood Bob Fritz.

Cleve had a returning letterman at every position except end. Meanwhile, Fritz, "the husky International Falls battering ram," whom the *Minneapolis Tribune* declared a "bone crusher," had proven himself good at both blocking and tackling. Cleve placed Fritz at end. Amenable, Fritz told the *Moorhead Daily News* that he felt fine with whatever Coach Cleve decided and that, yes, he liked carrying the ball, but he also liked tackling, too.

Cleve's two-a-day practices ended after just a week. Concordia students attending classes earlier than students at North Dakota State. After the first day of school, more players reported, and Cleve had 54 men out for football, including 35 varsity-eligible upperclassmen. With so many more men to choose from, Cleve returned Fritz to fullback.

*

Finnegan, meanwhile, enjoyed three more days of full practices. He had his men scrimmage in the evenings at Dacotah Field, and during one of those scrimmages Hanson "outshone the floodlights" when he returned a punt 48 yards for a score. The Bison line struggled with blocking, and yet Hanson rushed for a 30-yard run off tackle. He juked three potential tacklers on the play.

With the local matchup only a week away, both coaches spoke to the media. Finnegan said he would start all of his lettermen for the game and that he would sit his shiny, new sophomores. The 143-pound Hanson, whom the *Moorhead Daily News* dubbed "The Perham Phantom," would not see the field until perhaps the fourth quarter, Finnegan said. Marquardt, meanwhile, had been "scrapping so hard for an end position that it will be almost impossible to keep him out of the game," insisted the *Daily News*.

Finnegan admitted the Cobbers had always played strong on defense against the Bison, and this year, he expected Concordia to field a strong offense, too. Finnegan suggested the Cobbers may force the Bison to pass to succeed. "We may have to show everything we know to beat them," he said. He moved Vivian McKay from right halfback to fullback and Johnny Fisher took over at right halfback. Wendy Schollander would play as the team's primary passing back from the left halfback position.

When the Cobbers practiced under the lights at Dacotah Field, Cleve moved Fritz to right halfback.

On game day September 23, 1932, fans from Moorhead had a lot to root for, with three Moorhead High School graduates in the game. Earl Moran and Pat Hilde played in the backfield for Concordia while Marquardt played end for the Bison. Like Marquardt, Peschel would play in his first varsity game, but Hanson would watch the game from the sideline. He had broken his right index finger while catching punts during the final practice before the game. Finnegan called on the services of George May, instead.

In the first quarter, Schollander connected on a pass to McKay who raced into the end zone with the white-painted football. Officials called it back, however, and penalized North Dakota State for offsides.

In the second quarter, the Bison reached the end zone on a pass from Schollander to right end Milton Jacobson. Schoenfelder attempted the extra point but the Cobbers blocked the kick.

In the fourth quarter, the Cobbers made a valiant push from their own 48-yard line. The drive, which included four first downs, featured the passing combination of Moran to Fritz. Fritz also carried the ball. Together, they moved the pigskin to the 1-foot line. The Cobbers faced "a quaking band of Bison digging their cleats into the sod behind their own goal line," said the *Moorhead Daily News*. On fourth-and-goal, Fritz blocked around right end for left halfback Eddie Dahl, but the Bison held the line and forced a turnover on downs.

Later in the fourth quarter, the Cobbers launched a passing attack. Moran connected again with Fritz, who charged across the broken field to the end zone. Once again, officials reversed a score and declared the Cobbers offsides on the play. The Bison won 6-0. The *Moorhead Daily News* declared the Cobbers had lost the game by "12 inches and one offside."

As promised, none of the Bison sophomores had started the game, but both Marquardt and Peschel substituted and saw action. The *Spectrum*

Yellow and Green (1932)

noted how Marquardt "sailed in under those punts in a hurry, his long legs pumping rhythmically except for an occasional sidestep and hurdle."

Despite the win, the school's yearbook later said the Bison displayed a "neophytic lack of fineness and balance" across "four disappointing quarters" in their first game of the season.

In diners and at dinner tables, Bison and Cobbers fans argued about which team had played better football. Cobbers fans hoped the team would repeat a conference title run while apologists felt the Bison only narrowly won the game because Finnegan had experimented to find out who should play in the backfield during North Dakota State's first conference game against South Dakota. Overall, the Cobbers looked better at executing plays, while the Bison line exhibited "spotty blocking."

*   *

In the second Winnipeg Senior League game on September 24, 1932, the Winnipeg Rugby Club played Garrison, the soldiers from Fort Osborne. Lyman Van Vliet, who had played rugby for Manitoba, the Winnipeg Victoria Club, and the Winnipeg Tammany Tigers, coached Garrison. Before the game, the Winnipegs acquired another player, Walter Scott, whom the Winnipegs said had played at Washington State College in Pullman, Washington. In flaming red sweaters, the Garrison soldiers looked sharp but played poorly and the Winnipegs won the game 26-6.

Four days later, on September 28, 1932, the tired and sore Garrison soldiers played the St. John's Rugby Football Club in the third Senior League game of the season. Eddie James scored 5 touchdowns to give St. John's a 36-1 victory over Garrison.

Before the second game, St. John's had added Robert Ellis Jackson, an American from the southern United States to the Saints roster. A 25-year-old black athlete, Jackson had played for the Roughriders in 1930 as well as in the Grey Cup game that year while he worked as a porter for the Canadian National Railway. Jackson carried the nickname "Stonewall," a clear reference to the Confederate general in the U.S. Civil War. Newspapers and others may have used "Stonewall" as a double entendre. It's not clear whether Jackson accepted his nickname.

At Dacotah Field (Fargo, North Dakota)

When he played for the Roughriders, Jackson worked as a porter in the team's Pullman car during the trip east to play for the Grey Cup. Jackson carried the team's bags. In a 1930 team photo, he wore his porter's uniform, or something like it but without a hat, alongside his football-uniformed Roughriders teammates.

During the 1930 season, Jackson pulled off a 45-yard run for Regina against Moose Jaw, and in the western final against St. John's, the crowd chanted, "We Want Jackson," which encouraged Roughriders coach Al Ritchie to put him into the game. To the crowd's delight, on an end run attempt Jackson tackled Eddie James who then played with St. John's.

In 1931, Jackson played for the Saskatoon Quakers. The *Star-Phoenix* newspaper in Saskatoon assured readers that Jackson "is taking the game seriously and promises to be a valuable addition to the club," a clear subtextual reference to a racial stereotype.

* *

When the University of South Dakota needed a new athletic director and head football coach in 1931, they turned to their professor of military science and tactics, U.S. Army Capt. Stanley Backman, who had both athletic and military experience. At Ohio State University, Backman had captained the football and baseball teams, and after graduation, he took a position as an associate football coach at the University of Cincinnati. In 1917, he joined the Army and served in France during World War I as an officer in the engineering corps. When he returned, he served as a Reserve Officer Training Corps (ROTC) instructor and freshman football coach at the University of Georgia. During an eight-year stretch, Backman served as the athletic director in charge of intramural athletics in various army camps, for as many as 2,500 men at a time.

Backman coached like he led in the military, but many of South Dakota's players disliked his methods. Nevertheless, to start the 1932 season Backman coached a sophomore squad behind a heavy, veteran line to two shutout home victories, including a 25-0 win over Dakota Wesleyan University of Mitchell, South Dakota, and a 20-0 victory over Yankton College of Yankton, South Dakota.

Yellow and Green (1932)

In 1931, the Bison had beaten the Coyotes at Inman Field in Vermillion, South Dakota, where alumni had paid for and erected massive concrete sections with seating for 3,300 spectators. Dacotah Field in Fargo lacked the same, big-school atmosphere, but Bison fans knew how to fill the stands. In 1932, they rabidly sought to see Fritz Hanson carry the ball. Those who watched the Bison closely had seen what he could do on the freshman team and the school needed a great running back to get to the next level. Under Casey Finnegan, the Bison had lost three times to their nemesis, North Dakota. But all three times the Sioux had a "getaway man" on their squad, first in Red Jarrett and later in Ralph Pierce. Bison fans set their hopes on Hanson to be *their* getaway man. As the *Spectrum* observed, "[Hanson] has all the color and allure of a sensational gate attraction. Whether he makes gains or not the fans will be there so they can say they saw it if he uncorks one of those spectacular runs for which he is rapidly becoming famed."

In the lead up to the game against South Dakota, Finnegan focused on blocking and tackling. He had his backs run through a gauntlet of three linemen. Hanson, however, did not practice. Finnegan said Hanson would not start but would play with his broken finger encased in a metal splint. Johnny Fisher, who had played well against the Coyotes in the Bison victory the year before, would get the start at right halfback.

The night before the game, Backman led his 26 men through signal drills for over an hour at Dacotah Field. According to newspaper reports, Backman's men appeared heavier than they did the previous season. Backman reminded the media that the two schools had a non-scouting agreement, but it's hard to imagine *no one* with Bison football connections took a look at the Coyotes.

On the night of the game on September 30, 1932, fans with automobiles parked on the north side of the field. Season ticket holders entered through the northeast gate, while general admission ticket purchasers entered through the main gate on the south side. Finnegan had invited North Dakota and western Minnesota high school football teams to attend the game, and coaches from 26 schools had accepted the invitation.

Meanwhile, in Vermillion, fans paid for a play-by-play account of the game by telegraph.

Early in the game, the Coyotes had the Bison backed up to their own end zone. The Bison attempted a punt from behind their own goal line, but the right side of the Coyotes' defensive line blocked the kick and recovered the ball in the end zone. Concerned about momentum, on the next possession Finnegan sent in Hanson to play right halfback, "which proved to be what the crowd was waiting for," reported the *Spectrum*. "When this 143-pound halfback came onto the field the attitude of the team seemed to change and every man seemed to be working for him."

In the second quarter, with Hanson as the primary ball-carrier, the Bison reached scoring position four times. On two occasions, Hanson needed to escape just one more tackler before he would have found daylight and a path to the end zone, but three times the Bison turned the ball over on downs due to poor blocking. Before the quarter ended, however, Hanson scored a touchdown on an 8-yard run around right end. On the right side of the formation, in substitution, Herb Peschel played tackle and Bud Marquardt played end.

In the fourth quarter, Hanson led the Bison on another scoring drive. "It was Hanson's individual brilliance which pulled the Bison out of a serious situation," the *Fargo Forum* extolled. On fourth down and inches, he "weaved and squirmed" through defenders; he slid off left tackle and then moved back to the right side of the field to gain 15 yards for the score. The Bison won 18-8.

The Bison defense held the Coyotes to just 1 first down while Hanson provided the pyrotechnics with exciting end runs and broken-field gymnastics on punt returns. The *Bison* yearbook said the Bison won because they had "just a little more power, a little more deception, and a little more Fritz Hanson." Everett Wallum, the sports editor for the *Spectrum*, quipped, "If Fritz [Hanson] can play that well with a broken finger, we think we'll give each of the other players a smart rap on the digit before the University [of North Dakota] game."

*   *

Yellow and Green (1932)

> *In its lair on Memorial Field sits a ferocious Dragon,*
> *straining impatiently at its leash*
> *and casting menacing glances out over the campus*
> *in anticipation of the approach of the Concordia Cobbers.*
>
> – *The Western MiSTiC*, September 30, 1932.

The student newspaper at Moorhead State, the *Western MiSTiC*, reminded readers that the school's upcoming game against Concordia would include bands and a pep squad and suggested that "a multitude of citizens from the two cities [of Moorhead and Fargo]" would "overflow the bleachers to witness what they hope will be the decisive battle for the city football championship."

In reality, the heated rivalry between the Dragons and the Cobbers had grown a bit stale for football fans. Five of the last nine times the colleges had met, the games ended in scoreless ties, including in the past two seasons. The *Moorhead Daily News* hoped the matchup would feature more of the passing game that the Cobbers had displayed against the Bison and that this year, there would be a winner.

With Bob Fritz at right halfback and Earl Moran at left halfback, the Cobbers had a passing game at those positions, but Coach Frank Cleve needed more. He needed help with his ends, and so he turned to Pinkey Falgren who had recently returned from Regina. Injuries had forced him to bid farewell to the Roughriders and return home. As an assistant coach, Falgren would help the team to stretch out its passing game. And because the Cobbers would face two of the fastest halfbacks Moorhead State had ever brought against Concordia, Cleve also needed Falgren to coach the ends on stopping the run.

Cleve expressed concern that the excitement for the game within the student body might mentally drain his players ahead of all-important conference stints against St. Olaf and St. Thomas. At Moorhead State, Coach Sliv Nemzek wanted his men to rebound from their 25-0 loss to North Dakota and to play well against the Cobbers so that they might regain their confidence. After Concordia, the Dragons would play their first game in a new conference, the newly formed Northern Teachers

Moorhead State Dragons

Yellow and Green (1932)

Athletic Conference (NTAC), a loop of teachers colleges throughout Minnesota.

Early in the week, both teams practiced indoors to keep out of a downpour. When they finally moved outside they focused on executing and defending the pass, which raised hopes amongst fans that one of the teams might generate enough offense to break the deadlock.

On a hot, muggy day at Memorial Field, on October 1, 1932, Coach Nemzek's nephew, Johnny Nemzek, took the field to call signals at quarterback for the Dragons. The players perspired heavily in the humid air, and the Cobbers got hot in the first quarter when "Elusive Earl" Moran returned a punt 67 yards to the 13-yard line. "Stinging" Bob Fritz then carried the ball to the 10-yard line where he dove the final 3 yards through a big hole over left tackle for a touchdown.

At halftime, the Moorhead State marching band played Concordia's anthem and the crowd applauded the school's sportsmanship.

Throughout most of the game, the Dragons shut down the Cobber passing attack, which forced Concordia to rely on power running plays led by Fritz. In the fourth quarter, however, Concordia's aerial attack finally kicked in, and Fritz scored a second touchdown. Moran brought the crowd to its feet when he ran the ball 52 yards on a punt return, and Eddie Dahl made the final score for the Cobbers.

The Dragons refused to hand their rivals a shutout, however. Late in the game, Moorhead State scored a touchdown on a spectacular 80-yard forward-lateral pass play, but in the end Concordia broke the string of scoreless ties with a 20-6 victory.

* *

In the fourth game of the Winnipeg Senior League season on October 1, 1932, the tired and sore St. John's Rugby Football Club played against the Winnipeg Rugby Club, and the Saints put on a show when Russ Rebholz scored the first touchdown on a forward pass. Late in the game, Rebholz carried the ball twice to move the ball 75 yards with "reeling, shifting tactics, a change of pace and piston-like straight arm, that sent his would-be tacklers off his path like fodder falling before the keen edge of a scythe," described the *Winnipeg Tribune*. The Saints beat the Winnipegs 26-0.

*   *

North Dakota State Coach Casey Finnegan had seen enough to know that the South Dakota State College Jackrabbits played like a brick wall against the run. He had watched the Jackrabbits play the Golden Gophers at Memorial Stadium in Minneapolis, where South Dakota State held Minnesota to just 2 touchdowns. Finnegan had also scouted the Jackrabbits when they played Northern Normal and Industrial School in Aberdeen, South Dakota, in late September.

Finnegan expected his backs would have a tough time moving the ball on the inside run against the Jackrabbits' defense, and so he would have to rely on the passing game and the speed of Fritz Hanson to score. On defense, the Bison would face a Jackrabbit runner named Roy Michaelson, a Glencoe, Minnesota, athlete who had transferred from Notre Dame where Rockne had high hopes for the young man until he lost his eligibility to play due to "scholastic difficulties." Michaelson could kick, pass, and run the ball well, and Coach Cy Kasper, a Notre Dame alum, invited him to play for the Jackrabbits.

Thomas C. "Cy" Kasper, a product of Shattuck Military Academy in Faribault, Minnesota, served as a lieutenant during World War I and then played football under Rockne at Notre Dame in 1919-1920. Before he took the coaching job at South Dakota State in 1928, Kasper had coached football and administered athletics at a high school and at small, private colleges, including Alfred University in Alfred, New York, and Columbus College in Sioux Falls. Along the way, he played one year of professional football in 1923 for the 0-4 Rochester Jeffersons in Rochester, New York, which tied for last place in a field of 20 teams in the National Football League (NFL). At South Dakota State, Kasper succeeded Jack West who went on to coach at North Dakota, a conference opponent. In Kasper's first three seasons as coach, the Jackrabbits finished 6-5-1 in conference play.

Michaelson didn't offer the only threat out of the Jackrabbits backfield, however. The rumor mill foretold the Jackrabbits had moved their heavier back, Jap Pofahl, to fullback during practices. Pofahl had played well against Minnesota's heavy line.

Sophomores on both teams would play at skill positions on offense, and the young players held no ill will for their opponents. The older players, however, expected a grudge match. In 1931, the Jackrabbits had downed the Bison in North Dakota State's homecoming game in Fargo. Both Finnegan and Kasey expected passions would rise amongst the veterans in the trenches.

In advance of the game, Kasey sent a scout to Fargo to watch the Bison play. When the scout returned, he said about Hanson, "give him the ball, and honest, coach, you never saw anything like him in all your life."

Although Kasey had played for Rockne, he now employed the Warner system of offense. To prepare, Finnegan first taught Jackrabbit formations and plays to his reserves and then had them run those plays against the freshman team. Two days before the big game, when he felt confident the reserves had learned South Dakota State's offense, he pitted those reserves against the starters. Meanwhile, he tried out some fresh legs in the backfield and at end, which increased competition for playing time for both Hanson and Bud Marquardt. Finnegan walked away from the scrimmage pleased with the work of his line.

The Bison departed Fargo early Friday morning, and on Saturday, October 8, 1932, the team took the field in front of a crowd of shivering spectators at Memorial Field in Brookings, South Dakota.

To keep the Jackrabbits' running game in check, Finnegan employed a seven-man line throughout the first half. Twice the Jackrabbits threatened to score, first from the Bison 5-yard line and then from the 3-yard line, but the Bison held. Meanwhile, even though the Bison had started the game with a strong wind at their backs, they failed to move the ball. But with only seconds remaining in the first half, from the Bison 21-yard line, Hanson completed a pass to Vivian McKay to score a touchdown.

In the second half, South Dakota State figured out how to penetrate the Bison seven-man front to gain good yardage. Finnegan responded with a six-man line, instead, but with a guard positioned as a line backer.

Yellow and Green (1932)

Kasey countered with the passing game, and after Bison right halfback Wendy Schollander fumbled and lost the ball, the Jackrabbits reached the end zone on a long pass followed by an end run. On the very next play, Bison captain Dolly Schoenfelder wrenched his left knee and ankle while preventing the Jackrabbits from scoring the extra point. He had to be carried off on the shoulders of his fellow players.

In the fourth quarter, perhaps in retribution for the loss of their captain, the Bison gave the Jackrabbits a "terrific pounding" that sent five South Dakota State players to the clinic. The Bison managed to do the dirty deed without penalties for unnecessary roughness.

To make up for his earlier mistake, Schollander moved the ball through the air for the Bison and gained five successive first downs on five consecutive plays to the Jackrabbits' 1-yard line, where McKay ran for his second touchdown of the day.

Late in the fourth quarter, Michaelson mimicked Schollander and threatened to score on a passing drive, but Hanson, on defense, intercepted Michaelson's heave to put the game away, and North Dakota State beat South Dakota State 12-6.

To beat the Jackrabbits, the Bison had used multiple backs for passing and multiple backs and the ends for receiving. Afterward, Finnegan shared that he had "secretly thought the boys would have done well had they held the Bunnies to a tie," but North Dakota State had prevailed.

Hanson, whom the *Minneapolis Tribune* dubbed "The Bison Dynamo," had led North Dakota State to victory. The Jackrabbits had keyed on him and kept him largely in check but he found a way to put the Bison over the top. On defense, Herb Peschel had played a key role on the line by plugging up the Jackrabbits rushing attack.

Both team captains had departed the game injured. After the game, Finnegan had Schoenfelder's leg x-rayed in Brookings, which revealed season-ending injuries, including a broken ankle and a splintered tibia in his lower leg that would require surgery and for him to be off the leg for six weeks.

* *

Yellow and Green (1932)

Against St. Olaf, the Cobbers would face both a quick halfback and a hard-driving fullback, and to win, the Cobbers would need great performances from Bob Fritz and the other backs. To rest and recover after playing the Dragons under the hot sun Coach Frank Cleve had his Cobbers take some extra time. When workouts resumed, the Cobbers practiced their passing attack. Cleve said he would "shoot the works, if necessary" and use his entire playbook against St. Olaf, because a loss in the first conference game might eliminate Concordia from title contention. The Oles had already enjoyed a 14-12 victory over St. Thomas.

The day before the game, Cleve supervised as workers set up extra bleachers. Only Concordia had scheduled a home game in Fargo-Moorhead for the upcoming weekend and Cleve expected more than 1,000 fans would turn out and pay 75 cents each to watch the game versus St. Olaf.

Overcast skies portended rain, and Cleve hoped it would. A wet field would prevent the Oles' sprinting halfback Harry Newby from digging in and gaining speed. Under the new rule, if he were to slip and fall, he would be down. Meanwhile, Cleve's own men, led by Fritz, would have no problem running the ball with power and in pushing the Oles back on their heels.

But Cleve knew he couldn't depend on the weather, and his men needed to stop Newby no matter what. Most observers regarded Newby as the fastest ball-carrier in the conference. The Oles tended to run the quick halfback around their own right flank, which meant Cleve needed to find the best man to stop him there. The end position continued to be the weakest link in the Concordia line and Cleve leaned on Pinkey Falgren to help strengthen that position through instruction.

In chilly air, the Cobbers met the Oles on October 8, 1932. In the first quarter, the Oles scored on a 60-yard touchdown pass to go ahead 7-0. The Cobbers didn't come to life until the second quarter when Fritz provided interference and paved the way for Ralph Miller to score a touchdown over left guard.

In the third quarter, St. Olaf reached Concordia's 6-yard line. On second down, the Oles executed a lateral to Newby who ran toward the

Yellow and Green (1932)

sideline but met three Cobbers at the goal line. They stopped Newby 6 inches short of a score. On third down, the Oles tried a line smash but again the ball rested 6 inches from the goal line. Again on fourth down again the Oles couldn't break the 6-inch barrier.

Both teams exchanged punts until the middle of the fourth quarter when Fritz led the Cobbers into Ole territory. Earl Moran ran around right end for a score.

In the closing minutes, the Oles unleashed a passing attack, which brought fans to their feet. The Cobbers played good pass defense, however, and the game ended with St. Olaf on Concordia's 35-yard line. The Cobbers beat the Oles 13-7.

The weather never did give the Cobbers an advantage, but despite a dry field, the Cobbers had managed to stymie Newby. St. Olaf never made a substitution. The Oles starters played valiantly and only allowed the Cobbers to reach inside the 20-yard line twice, but Concordia scored both times.

Three games into the 1932 season, the 5-foot-11, 181-pound Fritz had caught the attention of sportswriters. "[Fritz] has the strange ability to throw passes with either hand as well as to kick punts with either foot... frequently he will flip a short pass over the line with either hand, depending on which direction the play is going," reported the *Minneapolis Tribune*. And "Fritz can bust the line and sweep around end better than a majority of the backs in the conference." When the newspaper asked Fritz about being moved to halfback from fullback, Fritz responded, "It doesn't make any difference to me, just so that I can carry the ball," and he said, "The more plays I get in the less tired I am."

*   *

In the second half of the Winnipeg Senior League season in a rematch on October 10, 1932, Thanksgiving Day, the Garrison soldiers played the Winnipeg Rugby Club in the league's fifth game. With improved tackling, and with the Winnipegs' Rosy Adelman sidelined with an injured foot, Garrison held a lead at halftime. In the second half, Carl Cronin completed a 30-yard drop-kick to put the Winnipegs ahead, and on their next drive, Cronin led an aerial attack to secure Winnipeg a 14-7 victory.

* *

With all-conference tackle and team captain Dolly Schoenfelder out for the season, Herb Peschel stepped onto the practice field with a renewed sense of urgency. The Bison needed a replacement, and even though Peschel was only a sophomore, he braced himself to fill that spot. He only needed to convince Coach Casey Finnegan that he should be the man to fill Schoenfelder's shoes. The city and student newspapers suggested Peschel should be the lead candidate for the vacancy, but Finnegan had other ideas. First, he tried fullback Shifty Gove in Schoenfelder's spot, but Gove proved ineffective. He then tried Merlyn Jahr, Kenneth Pirnie, and Roy Platt, but none of them were as effective as Herb Peschel, the nephew of Cy Peschel, the former Bison quarterback and captain who had graduated the year before Finnegan took over as coach. Finnegan wouldn't allow Herb to take the job on his name alone, and he didn't. He'd earned it. But was he ready?

Would any of the Bison be ready?

The Oklahoma City Goldbugs starters averaged over 200 pounds per player. The backs alone averaged 176 pounds per man. Most of the players were veterans of the team that finished 12-0 in 1931, with wins over the University of Oklahoma Sooners, the Oklahoma Agricultural and Mechanical College Cowboys, and the Haskell Institute Fighting Indians. The Goldbugs would be one of the heaviest squads ever to play on Dacotah Field as of 1932.

Oklahoma City Coach Vivian Julius "Vee" Green took the job in 1928. In college, he had played center for Bob Zuppke at the University of Illinois in Champaign and Urbana, Illinois, in 1922 and 1923. A few years later, in 1926, he played left tackle for the 0-4-0 Louisville Colonels professional football team, which tied for 21st out of 22 teams in the NFL.

At Illinois, Green had played alongside Harold Edward "Red" Grange, who in 1932 was still one of the most famous football players ever to play

Yellow and Green (1932)

in the United States. Grange had attained popularity for his long runs out of the backfield and on kick returns. In 1924, he ran for 5 touchdowns and completed a touchdown pass, all in one game. He dropped out of school in 1925 to play professional football and as of 1932 he still played for the Chicago Bears in the NFL.

As a coach, Green used what Zuppke had taught him at Illinois. The Goldbugs offensive attack, with an unbalanced line, featured reverses, spinners, laterals, and passes. While Zuppke had used both a version of the T formation as well as an unbalanced line formation, Green preferred the latter. Zuppke's unbalanced line offense appeared similar to Warner's Single Wing except the offense would use the formation to run a series of "angle plays" where the tailback would receive the snap and run or pass the ball.

Green took an offensive-minded approach to the game. He believed an aggressive offense would beat a strong defense every time. "My boys will make their share of first downs," he told the *Fargo Forum*. "We always work hard for our touchdowns, but we usually get them." Green responded to the scouting report he had received about the Bison for the game in Brookings. "We'll depend on concerted marches to cross the goal line—no long, flashy touchdown runs," he said. "We've got a lot of drive in our backfield but it's not especially fast. We haven't anyone nearly as speedy as your [Fritz] Hanson, but we should make some of our plays click. I hope, mind you, I say hope, we can deceive the Bison defense occasionally.

"I'm not afraid of quick kicks," he added, "because I want to impress on the other team we'll take that ball anytime they want to give it to us."

And while Green's passion flowed from his offense, his boys did play well on defense. In 1931, the squad had allowed the Sooners only 1 first down.

As for the Bison, "Casey Finnegan's team is deceptive," Green said. "It's passing game is particularly effective and the Bison line certainly hits hard."

To prepare for the Goldbugs, Finnegan emphasized the passing game during practices, with Wendy Schollander, Vivian McKay, and Hanson all

Herb Peschel

throwing the ball. Finnegan had the reserves run Zuppke-style angle plays against the starters, but the Bison had trouble defending them.

The Goldbugs arrived in Fargo the day before the game. That afternoon, they held an unannounced practice at Moorhead State. In the evening, they worked out under the lights at Dacotah Field. At the five-story Graver Hotel in downtown Fargo, a 250-pound Goldbugs tackle complained to the night clerk about the accommodations. "I can't even sleep crosswise on your beds," he said.

The next day, Coach Green addressed the issue with the *Fargo Forum*. "They sure grow them big in Oklahoma," he quipped. "I've about ten or twelve freshman boys coming up, all more than six feet tall who average about 215 pounds, all from Oklahoma City high schools."

Neither coach divulged probable starting lineups to the newspapers.

In this game, the Bison would play the first football team from the southwestern United States "ever to set foot on North Dakota soil" declared the *Fargo Forum*, and the Goldbugs would play "to uphold the football prestige of the oil fields." North Dakota State had only ever played one other team from below the Mason-Dixon Line when the Bison had traveled to Elkins, West Virginia, in 1930, to play the Davis & Elkins College Senators.

Reserved seats for the game had already sold out and so North Dakota State erected additional bleachers for the overflow crowd. On the day of the game, the girls drum corps from Alexandria, Minnesota, led a procession of Bison fans as they paraded from Ceres Hall on campus through downtown on Broadway.

On October 14, 1932, on the sidelines and in a special section of the grandstand at Dacotah Field sat the knothole gang. Finnegan had decided to follow the example of St. Louis Cardinals owner Branch Rickey: He simply gave away free seats to children under 13 in an attempt to prevent young kids from sneaking in to watch the games.

After the opening kickoff when the Bison offense took the field, fans expressed amazement when they saw Coach Finnegan had started the game with seven sophomores in the lineup. Bud Marquardt and Peschel started side-by-side on the left side of the line. On a sustained drive that featured perfect execution, a constellation of different backs carried the ball out of the Bison backfield. George May, at right halfback, scored the first touchdown on a 17-yard run over right tackle.

Hanson did not start the game with the others. Finnegan preferred to unleash his rising star only after the opposing team had begun to show signs of feeling winded. Hanson did return kicks, however, and eventually he got into the game on offense and ran 16 yards for a touchdown around the left side of the line. In the fourth quarter, after a long drive, Hanson dove 6 yards over left tackle for his second touchdown. Late in the game, he scored a third touchdown on a 35-yard run when he "took the ball around right end, pivoted and sidestepped his way through a mass of tacklers and outran three pursuers to the last white line," described the *Moorhead Daily News*. Simply put, "The Bison running game was too speedy for the Bugs." The crowd gave Hanson an ovation as he left the field after his final score. The Bison beat the Goldbugs 27-7.

The *Bison* yearbook declared the Goldbugs "bewildered by the electrifying speed of Hanson" and the Oklahoma City University student newspaper concurred: "Everybody tackled at him but he seemed unstoppable." The Goldbugs weight advantage had turned into a disadvantage against the speedy Bison.

Alongside Peschel, Marquardt played outstanding at end and had performed well as a gunner on punt and kick coverages. He played the entire game.

* *

Because Macalaster College had a heavy, hard-charging line that could open holes, Concordia's varsity squad needed to practice tackling. During workouts, Coach Frank Cleve turned his freshman ball-carriers loose like rabbits while Bob Fritz, a good tackler, watched from the sidelines. Fritz needed a rest and didn't suit up for practice. He watched as the freshman boys eluded the varsity men more often than not.

On October 14, 1932, Cleve and 21 players boarded the North Coast Limited at 4:35 p.m. bound for St. Paul. Before they departed, Cleve warned Dick Hackenberg at the *Moorhead Daily News* against misusing the word "overconfidence." Cleve told Hackenberg that confidence is a good thing and that you can never have too much. Instead, Cleve said, he feared "doggyness, laziness, or staleness." Perhaps the poor tackling he observed during practice weighed heavily on his mind.

Meanwhile, the Macalester student newspaper calculated that the Scots, who had enjoyed a bye week, would have had time to "store up energy" for their contest against the Cobbers, and that they would need it. "Allow the Cobbers to get within 30 yards of the goal and they will score," *The Mac Weekly* warned. "They are big, hard-fighting boys."

The Cobbers stepped onto Shaw Field on October 15, 1932, ready for a grind. In the first half, both teams spent most of their time in a struggle on Macalester's side of the 50-yard line. The Scots repeatedly punted the ball from deep within their own territory to gain field position. Neither team scored until early in the second half when Pat Hilde returned an interception 25 yards for a touchdown. Earl Moran kicked the extra point to put the Cobbers ahead 7-0. Macalester, too, scored in the third quarter to reach an even 7-7.

Late in the fourth quarter, the Cobbers repeatedly fought to reach the goal line. In their most dramatic attempt, Bob Fritz caught a 27-yard pass and then later carried the ball to Macalester's 3-yard line. With first down and goal to go, four times Concordia attempted to plunge across the line, but the Scots held the Cobbers to within a yard of the score. When the final gun sounded, Concordia and Macalester finished in a 7-7 tie.

* *

On the evening of October 15, 1932, the Winnipeg Rugby Club played a rematch against the St. John's Rugby Football Club, in the sixth game of the Winnipeg Senior League season. This time, the Winnipegs put the Saints back on their heels. Carl Cronin scored twice on two 40-yard, drop-kicked field goals while Russ Rebholz caught a 15-yard forward pass for a touchdown. They finished in a 6-6 tie.

In the seventh game of the season, on October 19, 1932, St. John's played Garrison in a rematch. In mud and sleet and in front of a paltry 100 fans, Eddie James rushed for long gains of 20, 30, and 50 yards. The Saints and soldiers walked off the field encased in mud as St. John's captured the league title for the sixth year in a row on an 18-5 win. But the soldiers had crossed the Saints' goal line, a feat no other team had accomplished so far in 1932.

* *

A renewed sense of gridiron urgency converged upon the Fargo-Moorhead community in late October 1932. Both North Dakota State and Concordia hoped to win their respective conference titles but they would have to defend their home turf during homecoming celebrations, on the same day.

While Fargoans saw North Dakota as the juggernaut in the ten-year-old NCC, fans who followed the conference more broadly knew that the Sioux coach, Charles Aaron "Jack" West, had proven to be the real steamroller in the loop. West had coached South Dakota State from 1919 to 1927 where he led the Jackrabbits to three conference titles in 1922, 1924, and 1926. His 1926 team finished the regular season undefeated and traveled to Honolulu, Hawaii, to beat the University of Hawaii in the Pineapple Bowl on Christmas Day 1927, which featured Rockne himself as the referee.

Coach West moved to Grand Forks in 1928 to take over the reins of the North Dakota football program, and from 1928 to 1931, his teams played undefeated and untied in conference play and earned NCC titles all four years. Rivalry aside, Finnegan and the Bison wanted to unseat West and the Sioux.

Born in Cherokee, Iowa, West attended Coe College in Cedar Rapids, Iowa, where he played football on the undefeated 1913 Kohawks team. After he graduated in 1914, he took a high school coaching job at Mason City, Iowa, where his 1917 team set a national scoring record, 524-7. His Mason City boys twice defeated high school championship teams from Chicago.

West and Finnegan both took over their respective programs in 1928, and Finnegan's teams had never beaten North Dakota. The Bison and Sioux had played one another in football 38 times, for nearly 40 years, and the Bison had won 11 of those games, and tied once, but lately, Bison fans

Jack West

and alumni had come to believe the Bison had suffered a jinx. The Sioux had beaten the Bison in every contest since 1926, and the Bison had not won a homecoming contest since 1924. But North Dakota State had started to gain some respect. Under Finnegan, the team played well against Michigan State in 1930 and went toe-to-toe with Wisconsin and Minnesota in 1931. Now in 1932, the Bison executed plays faster and better than ever before, made apparent by the fact fans had a hard time knowing which backfielder carried the ball. And even though Fritz Hanson stood out above the rest, all of the backfielders played well. After the Bison sophomores' great performance against Oklahoma City, Everett Wallum at the *Spectrum* declared, "Pick your own starting lineup for the Bison."

Bison fans questioned, "Can the Sioux stop Hanson?" For hopeful fans, the question was a rhetorical one. They answered, "No, not unless they want to allow the other boys to reach the end zone, instead." The locals compared Hanson to Claude Miller, the running back who had led the charge for the Bison in their last victory over the Sioux in 1925. Miller, who led the Bison to their first NCC championship (split with Creighton College of Omaha, Nebraska) in 1925 earned All-American honors when the Bill Evans All-Western Honor Roll selected him in 1926. Miller also received honorable mentions to All-American teams in 1924 and 1925. The Mandan Sioux Indian Tribe conferred Miller the honorary title of Chief Seize the Bear in 1926.

*

The Cobbers, meanwhile, faced a different kind of challenge. At 1-0-1, Concordia sat tied with St. John's at 3-0-0 for the conference title, but to win the championship, the Cobbers would have to win their final three games against St. Thomas, St. John's, and Gustavus. Yes, the Johnnies stood in their way, but first the Cobbers needed to beat the Tommies. St. Thomas had lost to St. Olaf by only 2 points, and the Oles had been a handful for the Cobbers. Now, Concordia faced an uphill battle, but it would begin in front of a partisan homecoming crowd.

*

The newspapers billed the Bison-Sioux game as Fritz Hanson, "the white-headed Nordic flash," versus Ralph Pierce, "the most dangerous scoring threat in the northwest." The *Dakota Student* suggested Dolly Schoenfelder's season-ending injury had weakened the Bison considerably in the face of Pierce's off-tackle runs and "thus far, Coach Finnegan has found no performers capable of filling [in]." The Sioux writers had yet to learn about Herb Peschel.

The loss of Schoenfelder aside, the *Student* said the expected soft, muddy field would play into North Dakota's advantage because the Sioux had a heavy backfield while the Bison backfield played light and fast. Hanson "will undoubtedly be slowed up considerably by a slippery field and will likely find it difficult to get beyond the line of scrimmage," the *Student* suggested. The previous Saturday, an injured Pierce had watched as Sioux tailback Rip Dablow carried the ball 32 times for 139 yards in North Dakota's game against Howard College from Birmingham, Alabama. Dablow had also completed 4 of 6 passes, each of them for over 30 yards.

North Dakota used Warner's Double Wing formation in 1932, with Pierce at left wingback and Larry Knauf at right wingback. To prepare for the Sioux, Finnegan held his scrimmages behind closed gates. The weather and field conditions forced his players to handle a slippery ball in a slight drizzle, and Finnegan expected they might have a similar experience during the game.

On offense, the varsity squad practiced passing, including Hanson, whose broken finger had healed enough to throw accurate passes. As a freshman, Hanson had thrown short passes into the flat while on the run. He had also delivered and received lateral passes and caught forward passes, too. Finnegan wanted to involve Hanson more in the passing game as both a passer and a pass-catcher. During practice, Hanson displayed his athletic ability when he completed two long passes on the run.

During their final scrimmage of the week, the Bison players had to stay off the Dacotah Field grid, which was too wet.

In Grand Forks, West closed Memorial Stadium to the public while the team scrimmaged and focused on stopping the pass. Reports suggested North Dakota had not performed well on defense in their pre-conference schedule wins against Howard, Moorhead State, and St. Thomas. West played his sophomores in the second half against Howard as he continued to break in young reserves due to injuries at almost every position. On offense, his backs ran with speed, even in the mud, and the team employed powerful blocking. Pierce, with his bruised foot, did not participate in scrimmages. But despite the team's early season travails, West expressed confidence in his men. "For the first time this year it looks as though we have a chance to win a conference football game," he said. He suggested the team's young right tackle, Ted Meinhover, might be all-conference material.

By midweek, West halted scrimmages to keep his men from getting injured. Two days of rain had soaked the outdoor practice and playing fields and so he took his players out onto the university golf course for practice on the tackling and blocking dummies. The team also practiced east of the stadium where West had attempted to grow new turf in 1930 but it had come in mostly weeds. The strangled turf gave the team good footing for practice. Eventually, West moved practices indoors.

The Bison, too, filled their final practices with dummies, walk-throughs, and chalk talks. Finnegan sat his men down for a serious discussion, a "tiger talk," about what they wanted to get out of football and what they needed to sacrifice to obtain it. By Friday, the weatherman predicted fair conditions for Saturday's game, which meant Hanson might get to run at top speed.

*

Inclement weather forced the Cobbers indoors, too. Coach Frank Cleve didn't want to take the chance his players might injure themselves on the slippery field. Instead, he stood at the chalkboard and read dire predictions from the newspapers: The Tommies featured a heavy, powerful line, with two players who ran fast, evaded tackles, passed, and kicked, and they relieved one another through substitutions. St. Thomas felt so confident in its running game, the Tommies focused on their passing attack during practices. St. Thomas had the edge, too, in terms of reserve strength for substitutions, and they would bring 33 players to Moorhead from St. Paul.

Cleve's motivational tactics worked. During practice, the Cobber varsity team had an easy time countering the reserve team and the

Yellow and Green (1932)

Tommies' offensive plays. Afterward, Hackenberg at the *Moorhead Daily News* reported that assistant football coach Louie Benson, whose vocabulary about the team usually included the word "lousy," professed the Cobbers looked *good* in practice. The men had displayed a work ethic and spirit that impressed both coaches, and to Cleve that meant the players had bounced back mentally from their tie with St. Olaf. He said he believed that if his squad could stop St. Thomas's passing game, they should be able to stop them in the ground game, too. Both coaches hoped their heavier Cobber backfield could handle the likes of "Wee" Willie Walsh on the Tommies. The media, meanwhile, suggested the teams would take to the air.

*

On Friday night, college kids attended the freshman football contest, gathered around the bonfire, or danced at the Casino ballroom to Rollie Chesney and his Radiolians while high school football fans from both cities gathered at Moorhead State to watch the Moorhead High School Spuds defend their turf against the Fargo Central High School Midgets. The Spuds won. Meanwhile, North Dakota held a pep rally in the Dakota Theater in Grand Forks.

On game day, the colleges celebrated homecoming on both sides of the Red River. A gridiron buzz filled both cities. Grins covered the faces of football fans all around Moorhead. Everyone expected high attendance at the games, with Concordia defending its conference championship in Moorhead, and with two undefeated rivals from the same state contending in Fargo. North Dakota State had already sold all of its reserved seating, including all they had allocated for sale at the Club cigar store in downtown Grand Forks, and so they opened up additional seats. Concordia, too, made arrangements for an overflow crowd and erected temporary bleachers that would accommodate an additional 1,000 fans. Around town, professional gamblers took bets that favored the Sioux by 3 points over the Bison.

In Grand Forks, the University chartered a train with Great Northern to carry the football team, band, and students, over 250 people in all, to Fargo. The train departed University Station at 9:00 a.m. and students paid $2 each for a roundtrip ticket, with the return train scheduled to depart at

10:00 p.m. after the game. Wes Meyer, editor for the *Dakota Student*, predicted more than 300 students would make the trip to watch and root for the Sioux. The *Grand Forks Herald* reported the number of people who caravanned to Fargo totaled upwards of 1,000.

The North Dakota State homecoming parade included the Gold Star Marching Band and automobiles and floats sponsored by students, faculty, and alumni, as well as the Greek organizations and ROTC units. The procession departed campus at 10:30 a.m. and marched downtown to the Great Northern Depot where, at 11:00 a.m., they met the 96-member University of North Dakota Concert Band dressed in military style uniforms. The Sioux bandmembers joined the parade as they disembarked from the train. A crowd-pleaser, the Sioux musicians had performed monthly concerts on the radio. The parade returned to campus at noon.

*

On the sideline before the game, Schoenfelder looked across the width of the field at the 35 Sioux players and their coaches. He told the *Fargo Forum* "he'd give his left leg" (the injured one) to be in the game and fulfill his dream of beating the Sioux. Finnegan said Schoenfelder was "without argument, the best tackle in the North Central Conference." And in 1932, on both offense and defense, many considered tackle the most important position on the field. Most tackles played both ways. Most often, the biggest, toughest, most stable, and smartest man on the team played tackle, and more than anyone else, he took and meted out punishment. Everyone hoped Schoenfelder's absence from the gridiron would not dash the team's hopes for victory. At 190 pounds and smaller than Schoenfelder, Peschel started at left tackle for the Bison.

On October 22, 1932, under beautiful, warm weather conditions, shoe leather met pigskin on both sides of the river to kick off homecoming games at Concordia and North Dakota State. In front of rabid fans, the North Dakota and North Dakota State bands competed for musical supremacy while Bison and Sioux leatherheads found themselves entrenched in the first quarter near midfield or in Bison territory. The teams participated in a punting duel. When they switched sides to begin the second quarter, the Bison blocked a Sioux punt to gain possession in

Yellow and Green (1932)

North Dakota territory. Finnegan sent in Hanson who then fumbled and lost the ball on a sweep around left end. The Sioux recovered on their own 45-yard line. On the ensuing drive, Knauf ran 15 yards and two plays later, Pierce ran off right tackle, evaded all four tacklers in the Bison secondary, and ran 24 yards for the opening score. Knauf missed the extra point attempt and the Sioux took a 6-0 lead.

Near the end of the first half, Knauf attempted to run around his left end, but a vicious group of Bison tacklers met him there and the ball shot from his arms into the hands of defensive halfback Wendy Schollander. The Bison didn't break his stride and advanced the ball 57 yards for a touchdown. When the Bison split the goalposts for the extra point, "the pandemonium became downright bedlam" recalled the *Bison* annual. The Sioux found themselves down 6-7 at the half.

At halftime, the North Dakota band marched and assembled into the letters "NDS" and "UND" on the field. The students at North Dakota State then crowned homecoming royalty and the alumni presented a genuine buffalo robe to a graduate from Northampton, Massachusetts, the alum who had traveled the furthest to watch the game.

*

Meanwhile, in Moorhead, the Cobbers allowed "Wee" Willie Walsh to run wild around the ends. The St. Thomas whirlwind shook off three Concordia tacklers and crossed the goal line to wake up the scoreboard. The Cobbers answered by sending Bob Fritz around right end for a 54-yard race to the end zone. As the clock wore down the first half, St. Thomas fumbled a punt return on their own 5-yard line and on the next play, Earl Moran connected with Fritz on a pass for another touchdown.

*

During the second half, North Dakota State worked hard to maintain its lead. Finnegan made no substitutions on the line. The Sioux defense keyed on Hanson and used seven men on the line, which subjected him to punishment at the hands of tacklers. And yet, he performed well enough in the second half to keep the Bison in good field position. Meanwhile, the Sioux couldn't get past the Bison secondary. When the final gun sounded, it "blast[ed] a jinx that has hovered over State teams for years," declared the *Bison* yearbook. The Bison beat the Sioux 7-6 and simultaneously clinched the conference title and prevented the Sioux from nabbing their fifth straight. Most North Dakota fans blamed Knauf for fumbling the ball that Schollander returned for a score and for missing a kick for a point after.

For North Dakota, Pierce carried the ball 15 times for 93 yards while Knauf ran the ball 16 times for 73 yards. For North Dakota State, Hanson "was a constant threat," reported the *Grand Forks Herald*, "and every time he took the ball there was considerable scrambling before he was located." Hanson ran the ball 17 times for 65 yards, with a long run of 26 yards.

*

When play resumed in Moorhead, St. Thomas scored quickly on a drive that started from midfield. The Tommies missed the extra point but tied the game 12-12.

Late in the third quarter, Walsh found open field around the Tommies' right end and ran 33 yards for a touchdown. After a missed extra point attempt, St. Thomas led 18-12 and the Cobbers failed to score again.

*

After the Bison homecoming celebration, the State Theater on Northern Pacific Avenue in Fargo announced that, for the first time in "moving pictures," the theater would replay the Homecoming parade and game. Intrigued North Dakota State students, alumni, and fans looked forward to watching their college festivities projected onto the silver screen beneath a domed ceiling with blinking star-lights and cottony clouds, perhaps with a musical selection played by an accompanist on the pipe organ. However, due to faulty development of the film, the theater canceled the show.

* *

On October 23, 1932, the St. John's Rugby Football Club and the Winnipeg Rugby Club closed out the Winnipeg Senior League season with a rematch. Approximately 2,500 fans watched Eddie James score 2 touchdowns while Russ Rebholz ran in a third to lead the Saints to a 21-0 victory over the Winnipegs and the MRFU title.

Yellow and Green (1932)

Because the Saints had captured the title undefeated in eight games, the league canceled its final Winnipeg vs. Garrison and St. John's vs. Winnipeg games to give the Saints time to prepare for the WCRFU semifinal.

* *

After the Bison victory over the Sioux, the Associated Press started to track undefeated schools and included North Dakota State on that list. The win opened the door for the Bison to win the NCC title and they could secure that top spot with a win over Morningside College in Sioux City, Iowa, on Thanksgiving Day.

Meanwhile, sports pages in Grand Forks tried to console North Dakota fans. The streak of wins over the Bison had to end *sometime*, they said, and so did the Sioux's string of conference championships. What better than to have another North Dakota team atop the conference? The *Dakota Student*, however, refused to concede victory. The game against the Bison had "proved that the Nodaks are once again the best outfit in the conference," wrote columnist Bob Schonberger. "In total yardage, first downs, and individual play, the Sioux piled up a big edge, and only a bad break prevented the boys from starting off on another championship jaunt." He blamed Larry Knauf's fumble into Wendy Schollander's arms on poor Bison sportsmanship. "The loss of the ball," he wrote, "which gave the A.C. their seven points, cannot be called a fumble. Those Bison are taught to tackle the ball instead of the carrier."

The victory effort had taken its toll on the Bison. The following Monday, Coach Casey Finnegan excused the men who had played from workouts because he felt his starters needed to play against Moorhead State. His team's readiness might suffer from a layoff followed by days of travel to the Atlantic Seaboard to play George Washington and Army. They needed to keep their head in the game because they knew very little about the Colonials or Cadets. They could not prepare strategically. Instead, they would have to rely on fundamentals and instincts.

At Moorhead State, Coach Sliv Nemzek indicated he would play his reserves and save his starters for the Dragons' homecoming game against

Yellow and Green (1932)

Northern Normal the following week. With a roster full of injuries and with underclassmen in the ranks, the Dragons had experienced some tough breaks. But for Moorhead State fans, Nemzek knew how to make lemonade out of lemons. He promised to play three freshman graduates of Moorhead High School against the Bison.

On Tuesday, all the Bison players dressed for practice, but Finnegan didn't ask the 14 men who had played against North Dakota to do much during scrimmage. He promised he would play both the starters and the reserves each for half the game against the Dragons.

On Wednesday, both teams worked out indoors. With a steady rain outside, Nemzek ran through plays in the gymnasium while Finnegan had his players run around the indoor track in the basement of the school's new physical education building.

On Thursday, the Bison practiced outside, but off the gridiron. The backs and ends practiced passing and defending the pass with a wet ball. In scrimmage, they practiced using both six-man and seven-man defensive lines. Finnegan expected a muddy game.

On October 29, 1932, fans assembled at Dacotah Field to watch the Bison and Dragons start in the snow and finish in slop. After several days of rain, snow flurries, and melting snow, the combination had softened the turf. The teams found the snowy field treacherous and in no time their cleats turned the gridiron in an ocean of ooze.

With mostly sophomores in the starting lineup, North Dakota State halfback Johnny Fisher scored the first touchdown. The Bison scored 2 safeties when twice the Dragons attempted to punt but fumbled the ball behind their own goal line. The Bison scored twice more, first on a plunge by Shifty Gove and second on a 70-yard punt return by George May to give the Bison a 24-0 win over the Dragons.

Against his own pregame logic, Finnegan had played his reserves most of the game. Wendy Schollander dislocated his shoulder and Earl Thomas, the backup center, broke his femur. And someone stepped on Fritz Hanson's hand, which led fans to believe he had broken bones. Afterward, Hackenberg at the *Moorhead Daily News* criticized Finnegan for putting Hanson "the greatest backfield threat to grace a Bison team since 1926" into the game on "a bitter cold day; a wet, sloppy, soggy field;

uncertain footing; no control over momentum, no possible coordination between mind and muscle because of a slippery underpinning."

It turned out Hanson had only suffered a terrible bruise, and Finnegan responded to questions about his decision. He said Hanson needed contact work to stay in game shape, the same as all the other players. Hackenberg then doubled down on his contention that Finnegan should not have played Hanson. He said the Bison should have depended on a "hard, plunging battering ram" of a fullback, instead.

The Dragons, too, suffered broken bones and twisted ankles on top of injuries sustained in the game against Concordia. Fans suggested Concordia and Moorhead State should play their annual contest later each season, due to the prospect of injuries. Cobbers Coach Frank Cleve came out against the idea, however, because he felt his players got distracted by the hype that led up to the game, and he would rather get the hysteria out of the way at the start of the season.

* *

In the WCRFU semifinal, St. John's Rugby Football Club would play the Saskatchewan Rugby Football Union (SRFU) champion, but first the Saints intended to play the North Dakota freshman football team in an exhibition game scheduled for October 29, 1932. The Senior League had originally planned to have the Saints play an all-star team from the other teams in the league, but always on the lookout for a way to better promote the game, league executives insisted St. John's needed a bigger challenge because they fully expected to face the Regina Roughriders again in the WCRFU semifinal. St. John's needed to overcome the "jinx" the Roughriders held over teams in Manitoba. The Sioux freshmen fielded a good team with four wins on the season and besides, if they brought the Americans up to Winnipeg they would provide "an eye-pleasing grid spectacle for fans," suggested the *Winnipeg Tribune*. The Saints would play the Sioux Papooses at Wesley Park in a split format, with half the game by Canadian rules, and half by American rules. The Sioux planned to send 24 freshman players to Winnipeg for the contest.

At the last minute, however, due to weather and poor conditions at Wesley Park, St. John's called off the game. The Sioux Papooses turned in their uniforms for the season.

* *

On the same weekend, the Cobbers fell to the Tommies and St. John's clinched the MIAC title with a victory over Augsburg Seminary. Concordia now found itself in a four-way tie for second place with St. Olaf, Gustavus, and St. Thomas. And yet, Concordia had something to play for. They could score against the Johnnies who had outscored opponents 71-0 and hand St. John's their only defeat. Nevertheless, with the conference title out of reach, Coach Frank Cleve eased up on his Cobbers during practices. He and 22 men left at noon on Friday on the eastbound train for St. Cloud, Minnesota, to play their game in nearby Collegeville on Saturday.

On Parents Day at St. John's, on October 29, 1932, and on a wet field under gray skies, the Cobbers refused to let the Johnnies impress. During the first quarter, the rivals spent most of their time on Concordia's end of the grid. The Johnnies repeatedly drove but ground to a halt while the Cobbers punted the ball away to gain field position. Late in the period, however, and into the second quarter, Concordia managed to gain four consecutive first downs to reach St. John's 28-yard line. The Johnnies held, and when Concordia fumbled on fourth down, the Johnnies recovered. The teams spent the remainder of the first half in an exchange of punts and neither team came within 25 yards of their opponent's goal line.

In the third quarter, Gus Luckemeyer and the Johnnies reached the Cobber 1-foot mark, but Concordia held. With only 3 minutes remaining on the game clock, the Cobbers drove 65 yards from their own 4-yard line, and after a 15-yard penalty against the Johnnies, Concordia found itself on St. John's 15-yard line. But then the Johnnies intercepted a pass and raced back to Concordia's 44-yard line where Bob Fritz ran the player down and tackled him. On the very next play, Fritz intercepted a pass attempt, which ended the game in a scoreless tie.

From the left halfback position, Fritz led all Cobbers rushers, but he also displayed his value as a defensive player against both the run and the pass.

In the final calculus, the Johnnies walked away undefeated in conference play and did not allow a conference opponent to cross their goal line the entire season.

* *

After the Bison beat the Sioux, a handful of North Dakota State alumni who had attended the game contributed to the team's travel expense fund so that the injured Dolly Schoenfelder might also make the trip east for the team's games against George Washington and West Point. Alumni and fans expressed hope for the Bison, and the *Moorhead Daily News* proclaimed "the Bison are taking with them into the East a prestige worthy of an intersectional conflict." Coach Casey Finnegan expected a tough haul, however. The 4-2-0 Colonials had just beaten the University of Iowa 21-6, and as for Army, they always stood as clear favorites.

In 1930, George Washington had played South Dakota to a scoreless tie. A year later, on Thanksgiving Day 1931, the buff-and-blue Colonials played the Sioux to a 6-6 tie. The *University Hatchet*, George Washington's student newspaper, suggested the Bison "are probably the strongest of all these eleven." Newspapers in Fargo and Moorhead suggested the Bison had a chance to beat the Colonials but oddsmakers predicted otherwise. As for the game at West Point, just about everyone conceded that Army would come out on top.

George Washington Coach James Ebenezer "Possum Jim" Pixlee had played fullback in college at the University of Missouri. He graduated in 1913. At 5-foot-9 and 190 pounds, Pixlee went on to play one season at right end for the Multnomah Amateur Athletic Club Winged M's in Portland, Oregon, before he signed on to coach at Missouri Wesleyan College in Cameron, Missouri, in 1914. During World War I, he served as a captain in the 36th Division and as the athletic director at Camp Bowie, Texas, until that Division went overseas. He oversaw the unit's boxing and wrestling programs as well as physical examinations for officer candidates, and he taught self-defense. After the war, he took the job of head football coach and athletic director at Oklahoma A&M in Stillwater, Oklahoma, for the 1919, 1920, and 1921 football seasons. After A&M's disastrous 1921 season, he resigned just before the holidays. He went on to coach at Westminster College in Fulton, Missouri, where his teams compiled a 32-19-4 record from 1922 to 1928. In 1929, he took over as coach and athletic director at George Washington.

Finnegan knew little about Pixlee's offensive strategy or the strengths of the George Washington offense, but before he headed east, he received some intelligence from Iowa about the formations the Colonials had used against the Hawkeyes. Finnegan assembled his men inside the new physical education building and they walked through what they might encounter. Finnegan figured his men could stop the Colonials' passing game, but they needed more work on stopping the run. He figured he would use the same starting line he had used against North Dakota, which included Herb Peschel at tackle. Fritz Hanson would suit up and play but he might not get the start. Sportswriter Eugene Fitzgerald at the *Fargo Forum* suggested Bud Marquardt might be Finnegan's "secret weapon" for their games in the East. "Marquardt is an exceptional pass receiver," he wrote, "although most of his ability in this respect has been demonstrated in practice sessions. Marquardt has been virtually unstoppable."

*

At the train depot, students gathered to give the Bison football team a sendoff. However, before they departed on their 1,600-mile trip east, nine players of voting age walked from the depot to the Cass County Auditor's Office to cast absentee ballots for the general election, which included the presidential race between incumbent president Herbert Hoover and challenger Franklin D. Roosevelt.

On the train, Finnegan filled his men's time with study periods and chalk talks, and when they switched trains in Chicago, they limbered up on the platform. When they arrived in D.C., the team showed the strain that results from a two-day train ride. Hanson lamented he could not run on the train, and he felt out of shape. Thankfully, Schoenfelder helped to lift their spirits as he walked now with a cane instead of crutches. Later, at the stadium, Finnegan led the team through a short walkthrough of

Yellow and Green (1932)

plays, then ordered supper and an early bedtime. He hoped his men just needed some rest. They would play the next day.

*

On November 4, 1932, at Griffith Stadium, the home of baseball's Washington Senators in the American League, the Bison got ready in the visitors locker room. A worker at the stadium told Vivian McKay that Babe Ruth used his locker when the New York Yankees came to town, which put things in perspective for the entire team.

That evening, in front of 13,000 fans, the Bison offense stepped onto the grid. Peschel started at left tackle while Hanson started at right halfback. The breeze carried the smell of Wonder Bread baking in a nearby factory.

Throughout the opening period, the Bison outplayed the Colonials, and in the second quarter fans watched a punting duel between the two teams. Late in the first half, George Washington reached near to the Bison end zone, but with a line that averaged 190 pounds per man, North Dakota State held off repeated rushing attempts from inside the 10-yard line. After two offside penalties against the Bison, the Colonials tried an off-tackle run on fourth down with just inches to go and scored on the last play of the half.

In the third quarter, both teams tried passing, which led to an interception for each side. Early in the fourth quarter, Hanson, the "Platinum Blond Speedster," raced 80 yards as he zig-zagged past the Colonials and crossed the goal line, but officials called the play back because they said Hanson had stepped out of bounds at the Bison 26-yard line. Later, he ran back a punt from the goal line 52 yards to George Washington's 48-yard line. Coach Pixlee substituted frequently and the Colonials managed to stop the Bison advance at or behind the line of scrimmage. The Colonials blocked a Bison punt and after they recovered the ball at North Dakota State's 15-yard line, instead of plunging against the Herd's superior line, the Colonials opened up the game with a sensational passing attack. The easterners used some razzle dazzle to move the ball and then scored on a 2-yard run up the middle. The Colonials scored a final touchdown on a 16-yard zig-zag run at the end of

At Griffith Stadium (Washington, D.C.)

a 62-yard drive. In the end, George Washington beat North Dakota State 20-0.

As reported by the *University Hatchet*, "The game ended with North Dakota State still attempting in vain to shake Hanson loose." Hanson broke into the open several times throughout the game, but couldn't score. "In Fritz Hanson, the Bisons offered a ball-carrier who single-handedly threatened the Colonials' composure on frequent occasions," the *Hatchet* said. "Bearing the title of one of the dreaded 'jackrabbit' backs, this fragile-looking lad lived up to the reputation of his colleagues by breaking away several times for long runs and proving to be a constant menace all evening."

Over the next three days, and before they left for West Point, the Bison enjoyed a banquet, reception, and dance with North Dakota State alumni at the Roosevelt Hotel. They also toured D.C. and the White House and visited the U.S. Naval Academy in Annapolis, Maryland.

* *

At the Exhibition Grounds in Regina, Saskatchewan, on November 4, 1932, approximately 4,500 spectators showed up with large, red poppies in their buttonholes to remember those lost in war. Remembrance Day was still a week away, but on this day they assembled to *forget* the Depression while they watched St. John's Rugby Football Club play the Regina Roughriders in a WCRFU semifinal game under clear skies.

Earlier in the day, workers had scraped ice and snow from the playing surface, and now as the Regina Rifles band played festive music the ground sat nearly dry as both teams in red and black color schemes took the field.

Once again, American imports helped to define a western playoff game. The visitors, led by Russ Rebholz, included seven former Roughriders. On the Regina team, former rivals—one Bison and two Sioux—played side-by-side. A relative newcomer to the team, Big Bill Hilts, the former Bison whom the Roughriders had met when the team played the Minot Panthers earlier in the season, now played end for Regina opposite Whitey Mjogdalen, the former Sioux, and in front of

Yellow and Green (1932)

backfielder Curt Schave, also a former Sioux. When the band played, "O Canada," to put everyone in the proper mood, one might wonder whether *all* the players sang along or even knew the words.

For St. John's, the mood changed quickly. On the first play of the game, the Saints fumbled, and the Roughriders fell on the ball at the St. John's 12-yard line. A few plays later, the Saints stopped Cliff Roseborough on a plunge and St. John's forced a field goal attempt. Schave split the uprights from an obtuse angle to put the Roughriders up 3-0.

Ten minutes later, Eddie James fumbled a bad pass and then dove for it in competition with three Regina players. On his first touch of the ball, he broke his arm. The Roughriders recovered on St. John's 35-yard line and then Schave faked a field goal attempt and completed a 20-yard pass, which set up a touchdown and extra point. The quarter ended with the Roughriders up 9-0.

During the remaining three quarters, neither team achieved a major score, but the players filled the game with injuries, fights, and penalties, likely due to the bad blood the teams had generated during the exhibition season when St. John's had beaten Regina twice. In the end, St. John's only managed to score a rouge on a missed field goal attempt when the ball sailed past the deadline, and Regina won its seventh consecutive WCRFU title in a 9-1 victory.

*   *

After their scoreless tie with St. John's University, the Cobbers failed to exhibit their usual spirit and determination during practice sessions. Not even the chance to ruin Gustavus's homecoming shook the team from their malaise. Meanwhile, Coach Frank Cleve knew the Gusties would provide a challenge because Gustavus had beaten St. Olaf 3-0 and had lost to St. John's by only one touchdown.

On November 5, 1932, the maroon-and-gold Cobbers took the field in St. Peter to face off against the ebony- and gold-clad Golden Gusties. In the second quarter, Gustavus intercepted a pass intended for Bob Fritz and ran it back 88 yards to the 7-yard line. Gustavus failed to score, however, and the Cobbers punted it away. In the third quarter, on an end run to the left, Fritz cut back inside and carried the ball through the open field 28 yards for a touchdown, only to have it called back for holding. In the fourth quarter, Concordia won the time of possession battle due to Gustavus's multiple fumbles, and the Cobbers reached near the goal line on three separate drives, but still the Cobbers didn't score. The game ended in a scoreless tie.

Fritz, at right halfback, was "the outstanding back on the field, as he drove through for consistent gains and snagged passes," wrote the student newspaper, *Gustavian Weekly*. But Concordia had tallied its third tie in an "unimpressive grid season"—harsh words from the *Concordian*.

* *

The Roughriders had eliminated St. John's Rugby Football Club, the MRFU champion, from the playoffs, but that didn't stop Joe Ryan from continuing to promote football. Ryan convinced St. John's and North Dakota to reschedule their canceled bout and to play a double-header on Remembrance Day weekend at 2:30 p.m. each day Friday and Saturday, November 11-12, at Wesley Park. This time the Winnipegs would be in the mix. In both games, St. John's would play in the first half against the Sioux under Canadian rules, and in the second half, the Winnipegs would play under American rules. In Grand Forks, North Dakota's equipment manager handed out uniforms again to the Sioux players.

Ryan made arrangements to prepare the grounds at Wesley Park. Workers scraped and rolled and filled the bad spots with sand and dust. If Mother Nature did not bring snow or rain to Winnipeg, the players would find a dry field ready for football. Ryan placed ads in the *Winnipeg Tribune* to announce the game, with the cost of admission at 75 cents for reserved seats, 50 cents for general admission, and 10 cents for children.

Meanwhile, while Russ Rebholz and the Saints practiced outdoors at Osborne Stadium, Carl Cronin got to work teaching the Winnipegs how to play 11-man football by American intercollegiate rules. Because of the poor weather, Cronin worked out his men indoors at the Winnipeg rink. He focused on teaching his men legal blocking, because unlike in Canadian football, the Americans could block for their ball-carriers

Yellow and Green (1932)

anywhere on the playing field, and new rules prohibited blockers from leaving their feet and prohibited defenders from using flying tackles. The Winnipegs would continue to use their familiar formations but they would have to drop the position of flying wing with one less backfielder in the game.

In a letter from North Dakota Coach Jack West to Johnny Buss at the *Winnipeg Tribune*, Coach West suggested North Dakota and Winnipeg might establish a perennial home-and-home affair. "Forecasts for this weekend indicate that splendid football weather will prevail," promised the *Winnipeg Free Press*.

But this time, North Dakota canceled the contest. The team had departed Grand Forks for Winnipeg on November 10, the day before the first game, but because of the weather, the team couldn't get through to Winnipeg and they were forced to turn back.

* *

Concordia scheduled a final, non-conference game at home against Hibbing for November 11, 1932, on the Moorhead State grid. Coach Frank Cleve planned to start several of his freshmen in that game and to keep them in for as long as possible. However, as an abrupt storm forced the team indoors to practice signals in the gymnasium, he had little opportunity to prepare the yearlings. The poor weather continued, and on Friday morning, the schools canceled the contest.

*

For the 1932 season, the Associated Press sportswriters and coaches poll for the MIAC named Bob Fritz to the all-conference first team at right halfback. The AP report noted that "Fritz was shifted to halfback this year and did his share of all carrying in addition to paving the way with strong blocking." *St. Paul Daily News* sportswriter Bill Haman named Fritz to his first team at right halfback, the second time he had named Fritz to the all-conference team. "Fritz was one of the Cobbers' chief defensive men and was also their leading ball carrier," Haman said. In addition, the *Minneapolis Journal*, *St. Paul Dispatch*, and *Pioneer Press* each named Fritz to their all-conference teams at right halfback. The *Pioneer*

Press observed, "Fritz is big, likes the rough going, and can run, pass, or block as the occasion demands. Incidentally he can pass with either hand." Two student newspapers within the conference also named Fritz to their all-conference teams. *Mac Weekly* placed Fritz at right halfback while *St. John's Record* placed him at left halfback.

During the Cobbers' postseason banquet, Cleve revealed that Fritz had broken his hand during Concordia's game against St. Olaf and that he had played through the last four games with injury, which required heavy taping. The injury had made it difficult for Fritz to handle the ball and to catch passes with the hand, but as noted previously, Fritz was ambidextrous.

* *

The Regina Roughriders played the Calgary Altomah Athletic Association Indians in the WCRFU championship in front of 5,000 fans in Calgary on November 11, 1932. Curt Schave opened the game with a 50-yard kickoff return for the Roughriders. The former Sioux played a key role in both the running and passing game for Regina and his performance included a 65-yard touchdown run. Meanwhile, Phat DeFrate from Montana also played a central role in the passing game for the Roughriders. Another former Sioux, Whitey Mjogdalen, ran the ball up the middle for Regina and once carried tacklers 30 yards on a carry.

With 7 minutes still remaining in the game, Regina had snuffed Calgary so definitely that the home crowd started to leave and crossed the field to exit, which delayed the contest. In the end, the visiting Roughriders beat the Indians 30-2 and captured their seventh WCRFU title in a row.

* *

The Bison departed D.C. by train. They arrived and unloaded in New Jersey, where they transferred their luggage and gear to a ferry boat. The travelers then rode up and across the Hudson River and took in New York City's nighttime skyline. They docked in Manhattan and found their way to the Hotel Pennsylvania, a 27-floor building that opened as the

Yellow and Green (1932)

world's largest hotel in 1919 with 2,200 rooms and baths that surrounded four courtyards, with offices, lobbies, dining rooms, cafes, and galleries on the first four floors. North Dakota State alumni greeted the boys at their accommodations, and the next day paid for the team to view the city aboard a sightseeing tour bus. They also supplied the players with tickets to watch films at two of the largest Paramount-owned theaters in Manhattan.

All the while, Coach Casey Finnegan's thoughts stayed close to the team's next challenge: the West Point Cadets, which had already beaten Harvard University 46-0. Back home, newspapers didn't hold out much hope that North Dakota State might beat Army, but they did hope the Bison might perform better than Harvard. Finnegan played along when he told the *Fargo Forum* staff correspondent, "Army may expect a harder game than they had against Harvard last week."

Meanwhile, Major Ralph Sasse, the coach for the Cadets since 1930, saw the game against North Dakota State as a warm-up for West Point's games against Notre Dame and Navy. Sasse had graduated from the academy himself in 1916 and had attended calvary school in Fort Wayne, Kansas, and general staff school at Fort Leavenworth. During World War I, while he served in the U.S. cavalry, Maj. Sasse commanded the 301st heavy tank battalion during the allied assault on the Hindenburg Line. For courage under fire, the British awarded him the Distinguished Service Order. A few years after the war, in 1924, Sasse returned to West Point to serve as a mathematics instructor. He assumed the duties of assistant coach for the Cadets in 1929 and then head coach in 1930. Under his leadership, Army had posted a 9-1-1 record in 1930 and an 8-2-1 tally in 1931.

Finnegan hoped the Bison would have more energy to play against the Cadets. Already, West Point had defeated Furman University of Greenville, South Carolina, as well as Carleton, Yale University, The College of William & Mary in Williamsburg, Virginia, and Harvard by a combined score of 169-0. Only the University of Pittsburgh had defeated the Cadets 18-13.

Finnegan arranged for his team to lodge in the barracks at West Point, to eat in the same mess hall, and to enjoy four days practice on the academy grounds, overall a much better setup than the team had before they played George Washington. Finnegan also expected Wendy Schollander and his passing arm would be healthy enough to play.

After they reached West Point on November 8, 1932, the Bison practiced while their counterparts continued their military training, in addition to football practice. After they suffered injuries in riding accidents, two Cadets, the left tackle and the reserve quarterback, checked into the infirmary. Still, Army stood as a heavy favorite to win, but that didn't keep fans away from the ticket office. The staff correspondent for the *Forum* learned that "Fritz Hanson, whose running took Washington critics by storm last week, is the reason for a larger anticipated crowd than usual. Army ticket officials say thousands who would not otherwise attend want to see him in action." And even though the Bison would play on a bigger stage, Finnegan said his men exhibited confidence. "Our task will be to make openings for Hanson," he said. "We hope to put up a stubborn defense, and we will concentrate on getting [Hanson] into the clear. If we succeed in this, I think we can cross Army's goal line."

In the days before the game, the weather brought a steady drizzle to West Point. On the night before the game, the conditions forced the Cadets to practice with a slippery ball in the mud.

On game day morning, November 12, 1932, the skies opened up, but by the kickoff, fans in the stands sat in chilly air beneath an overcast sky. On the Army sideline, with mixed emotions stood Harold Johnson, the equipment manager for the football team who was a fourth-year student from Grafton, North Dakota.

Both Peschel and Hanson made the starting lineup for the Bison.

The Bison defense played in a seven-man line and the Cadets consistently tossed passes over center to gain field position. They then used the running game to push through the line for a score. In reply, Hanson spun off a nice 25-yard run, but the Bison fumbled before they could finish the drive. Again, Army scored, and Maj. Ralph Sasse put in his reserves.

In the second quarter, West Point charged down the field on a series of forward passes and end runs to reach the end zone. As halftime approached, the Bison moved the ball well with runs up the middle,

Yellow and Green (1932)

around the end, and through the air, but Hanson limped off with a leg injury. "With his departure from the game, the much-vaunted Bison attack faltered and stopped," reported the *Howitzer*, the academy's yearbook.

At the top of the second half, with North Dakota State down 0-26, Sasse put in his starters. The Bison received the kickoff and on the first drive, Hanson reeled off a 25-yard run to the 50-yard line. He had only one man to beat, but his opponent slowed him up enough so that other Cadets could catch him. The Bison eventually reached the 22-yard line before the drive fizzled out. When Hanson limped off again he received "one of the biggest ovations given any player from either team who was forced to leave the field," reported the *Spectrum*.

Sasse kept his starters in the game until late in the fourth quarter and only put in his reserves after the Cadets had scored 46 points. Over 300 North Dakota State fans sat together in the stands at Michie Stadium, and "even though they were backing a lost cause" they "cheer[ed] noisily throughout" the game, reported the *Forum*. The Army reserves scored a final touchdown to trample the Bison 52-0. West Point had scored in every quarter of the game and tallied more points than they had scored against Harvard.

After the game, Finnegan walked away impressed by Army's passing game. The Cadets had exhibited perfect timing and the backs had completed nearly every pass they attempted. With two complete squads available to Sasse, West Point simply wore out North Dakota State. Meanwhile, Sasse confessed to Finnegan that his scouts had told him Hanson was the best ball-carrier they had observed all season, and the scouts had looked at Pittsburgh, Harvard, Yale, Notre Dame, Ohio State, and smaller schools. Finnegan said Hanson could have returned to the game, but he had kept him out to avoid a more serious injury.

Afterward, Finnegan received word that due to snow, South Dakota had canceled its game against North Dakota, which secured the NCC championship title for North Dakota State. Finnegan and his men could relax and enjoy the trip home.

*

At West Point

Yellow and Green (1932)

Upon their return to Fargo on November 13, 1932, Finnegan gave his NCC champion North Dakota State Bison football team two days off from practice so that they could catch up on their studies. The Bison still had to play the Morningside Maroons in Sioux City on Thanksgiving Day, a traditional game day for Morningside. North Dakota State needed to win to remove any doubt that the Bison deserved to be conference champions.

Head coach and athletic director Jason M. "Saundy" Saunderson led Morningside, which sat winless in conference play. Born in Rockville, Ontario, Canada, Saunderson had played high school sports in Indianapolis, Indiana, and Lansing, Michigan, before he attended and played quarterback at Albion College in Albion, Michigan. He captained the Britons during his senior year in 1907 and was named to the All-Michigan team. After college in 1909, Saunderson coached at South Dakota State where he compiled a 5-5-2 record in two seasons. He took a position at the University of the South in Sewanee, Tennessee, in 1911. Saunderson took over the Morningside eleven in 1912. The Maroons had achieved a 14-29-1 record in NCC play under his guidance. Morningside had last won the NCC title in 1923 and the team had last enjoyed a winning season in 1926.

The Bison needed to stay in game shape, both mentally and physically, but on their first day back to practice on Wednesday, the weather forced the team into the basement of the physical education building. Finnegan had the players wear rubber-soled shoes and they participated in a non-contact scrimmage, but not everyone participated because some students had fallen too far behind on classwork and needed to catch up. Finnegan found it necessary to schedule a practice for Saturday, too.

On Thursday, the team continued to practice indoors, where they worked on spinner plays and reverses, but Finnegan found he needed to cut practice short because some players still found themselves behind in coursework. Afterward, the team put away their field equipment for the season and departed Fargo for Sioux City. The day before the game, the Bison enjoyed their first outdoor practice in two weeks. Farther south in Sioux City, the weather remained tolerable, and Finnegan had his men

Yellow and Green (1932)

practice more than an hour at Bass Field, but with no sod, the field muddied beneath their cleats in mild weather.

The next day on November 24, 1932, Finnegan and the Bison traveled to Stock Yards Park near the city center where crews had cleared snow from the grass for the Thanksgiving Day matchup. In a light wind, North Dakota State faced a nimble Morningside line, which managed to keep the Bison running game in check. The rusty Bison missed many blocking assignments. Morningside forced the Bison to punt. Bud Marquardt, who started at left end, sped downfield to cover the return man but then he was clipped. The officials awarded the Bison the ball at Morningside's 40-yard line. On the very next play, Schollander took to the air and connected with George May on a 40-yard touchdown pass.

Finnegan substituted frequently and used all 24 of his men, while the shorthanded Maroons made only one substitution.

Morningside opened the second half with a dropkick kickoff to North Dakota State's 8-yard line where Hanson, the "Midget Towhead," caught the ball and ran behind his blockers. He cut to the left, broke free, and outran the Maroons 92 yards along the sideline for the score. Once again Hanson left fans stupefied to see someone return a kickoff the length of the field for a score.

In the fourth quarter, Schollander intercepted a pass and returned it to Morningside's 40-yard line. The Bison then reached the 26-yard line where Hanson ran off left tackle, cut back to the right, and scampered across the goal line for a touchdown. The Bison took home the win 20-0.

*

At the end of the season, the Associated Press named Fritz Hanson to its second team all-conference at right halfback. Hanson, Bud Marquardt, and Herb Peschel each received letters in football.

During the conference's annual meeting in Chicago in late November, the NCC decided that member teams should be allowed to play each other twice in a season, which would allow for easier scheduling and for longer schedules.

*   *

Yellow and Green (1932)

The Canadian Press named four Americans on the Regina Roughriders to the 1932 Western All-Star team, including Curt Schave at flying wing, Phat DeFrate at quarterback, Whitey Mjogdalen at inside lineman, and Big Bill Hilts at outside lineman.

On December 3, 1932, the Roughriders played the Hamilton Tigers in front of 7,000 fans in Hamilton, Ontario, for the Grey Cup. Schave and DeFrate thrilled the crowd with the forward pass, but DeFrate threw 3 interceptions, including one the Tigers returned for a touchdown. DeFrate also fumbled a punt return, which the Tigers picked up and advanced for the score. Hamilton scored yet another touchdown on a fumbled kickoff return by Schave. By the end of the game, Tiger tacklers had torn Schave's sweater to pieces, and DeFrate scored the only Regina touchdown on a line plunge. Mjogdalen joined Cliff Roseborough in the backfield for runs against the line, but in the end Hamilton beat Regina 25-6 for the trophy and the Roughriders' fifth consecutive Grey Cup loss.

Sportswriters and fans alike blamed American imports for the loss. Former Saskatchewan *Star-Phoenix* sportswriter Vern DeGeer commented, "Not within memory or reading experience of this writer has there been such a display of gridiron dumbness... As a result, the arguments of certain eastern Canada critics against the importation of former college players to this side, has gained a point... [the imports] were guilty of errors in judgment that would make even the most humble of high school players blush for shame. And strangely enough these former American players did their poorest work with a weapon that they should be expert with—the forward pass—and for which they were drawn to Regina."

Earlier in the season, A.F. "Biddy" Barr, a former coach for the University of Toronto, had written a long editorial asking fans to have patience with the forward pass in Canadian football. He noted how the forward pass had been in use for 26 years in the American game, but still the Americans considered the play undeveloped. The big colleges in the Eastern United States, he said, largely ignored the pass, but years later, teams in the Midwest, "in the more radical air of their region broke away from the conservation of the east and began to develop the pass as a real scoring threat." He predicted that, in the American game, players would

Yellow and Green (1932)

begin to complete passes for longer distances and "the use of the pass will be developed a great deal faster in Canada than in the States because we have had the advantage in taking it up at a time when all the experimental stages have been ironed out."

In Regina, *Leader-Post* sportswriters had to endure complaints they had somehow influenced "uncalled for publicity" for the American Roughriders players and that homegrown talent had been given "second place," which had, in effect, canceled any growing unity in the sport between East and West. The real stars, they insisted, had all been homegrown talent, not the "unsavory" imports.

Eastern sportswriters gloated over Hamilton's victory. "The East's football stronghold was as secure today after the ninth western assault as it ever was—a grim fortification scarcely scratched from the futile battering that started back in 1921," wrote Elmer Dulmage in the *Windsor Star*.

Meanwhile, the tug-of-war escalated between those who desired professionalism in Canadian football and those who wished for the game to remain amateur. Officially, Canadian football continued to call itself an amateur sport and in the IRFU in the East, the Big Four teams continued to enforce amateurism, at least on the surface. Elsewhere in Canada, however, football teams practiced "synthetic amateurism"—they outright paid athletes or extolled benefits upon them to play, and many Canadians felt that professionalism in the sport should be allowed.

In December 1932, preeminent Canadian athlete Lionel Conacher decided to call the IRFU's bluff. Earlier that year, the IRFU had expelled two Ottawa rugby players because they had played professional baseball. Conacher, a professional hockey player, had decided Eastern Canada should have outright professional football teams and that he should manage, coach, and play on a professional team in Toronto. He suggested he had enlisted others to form teams and that they would compete for fans in IRFU cities. Conacher stated, "Professional football is going ahead by leaps and bounds in the United States and we intend to have a shot at it."

CHAPTER 3 - BLUE AND GOLD (1933)

In 1933, the Cobbers would escape a serious setback in their pursuit of another conference title, while the Bison would learn to deal with injuries and adversity. Up north, Joe Ryan and the Winnipegs would watch football in their city crumble, but the club would rebound to win the hearts of fans in more than just Winnipeg. Meanwhile, in Eastern Canada, a Canadian sports hero and major promoters would set out to prove that football, like hockey, should be a professional sport for Canadian clubs.

* *

In January 1933, NCAA President Maj. John L. Griffith reported on the economic state of college football in the depths of the Depression. He said in 1932, attendance at college football games had decreased remarkably, but gate receipts still covered the operational costs of varsity college football, and very few of the 1,000 or so colleges across the United States had chosen to abandon varsity football. However, colleges had begun to cut other sports, including freshman and lower-level football offerings. Griffith noted that many college athletes had a difficult time paying for college.

* *

In a shocking turn of events, the *Moorhead Daily News* reported that Concordia fullback Bob Fritz planned to transfer to Moorhead State to play football for Coach Sliv Nemzek and the Cobbers' intracity rival, the Dragons. In a letter to the *Daily News* from International Falls, the two-time MIAC all-conference Fritz said he planned to enroll at Moorhead State by March 4 for spring quarter, which would make him eligible to play football in the fall. Fritz said he made the decision because he had experienced financial difficulties that prevented him from registering for spring semester courses at Concordia. If he missed spring semester, he would miss out on required courses that would affect his ability to continue at Concordia in the fall. In 1929, 1931, and 1932, Fritz had

Blue and Gold (1933)

attended Concordia only during fall semesters when he also played football. Fritz made it clear in his letter that Nemzek did not recruit him to attend Moorhead State and that he only arrived at the decision out of necessity. He expressed angst at being "completely at the mercy of Concordia as far as my continuing at that institution was concerned" and "the only alternative I had was to go to some other school." Fritz said his decision largely hinged on remaining eligible to play football again during the 1933 season. He said Moorhead State told him he could play for the Dragons both in 1933 and 1934.

After the Moorhead newspaper published the report, Dick Hackenberg, *Daily News* sportswriter, said Coach Frank Cleve scorned Fritz. However, within a fortnight, the situation reversed itself. Fritz spent three days with administrators at both schools and ended up re-enrolling at Concordia. Concordia's dean assured the *Daily News* that "what is being done for Fritz to allow him to continue his school at Concordia would be done for anyone regardless of their athletic ability."

* *

For the 1933 season, NCAA adopted new regulations that would help to open up the game even further. First, the rules committee established a new rule against clipping in any circumstance. Previously, a player could block an opponent by hitting him in the back above the waist, but the new rule eliminated blocking from behind entirely.

Second, the committee established that the football field should have hash marks in a line running 10 yards inside of and parallel to each sideline. Previously, only when a ball carrier went *out of bounds*, officials would place the ball in line with hash marks 15 yards inside of each sideline. But if officials declared the ball down *inbounds*, the offense would start with the ball at exactly that point on the field—even if the ball stood just inches from the sideline. The committee studied the issue and found that offenses in a game collectively wasted an average of 14 downs per game just trying to move the ball away from the sidelines to gain better field position. Under the new rule for 1933, whenever officials declared the ball down anywhere within the newly established 10-yard zones between the hash marks and the sidelines, officials would place the ball in line with the hash marks, instead.

Meanwhile, the NFL broke from college rules when it announced it would allow players to pass the ball from anywhere behind the line of scrimmage. The NFL made this change because, during a playoff game between the Chicago Bears and the Portsmouth Spartans in 1932, Bronko Nagurski faked a run toward the line of scrimmage and then instead tossed a touchdown pass to Red Grange. It's not clear whether Nagurski had thrown the ball from at least 5 yards behind the line of scrimmage, which had been the requirement like in the college game. The Spartans had argued for a penalty, but officials allowed the touchdown and the Bears won the game. Afterward, the Spartans argued for a rules change that would allow a passer to throw the ball from anywhere behind the line of scrimmage because, Spartans Coach George "Potsy" Clark declared, "Nagurski will do it anyway."

* *

Eager to have his men ready for spring practices, Concordia Coach Frank Cleve distributed uniforms to his players on March 27. The team would lose three lettermen to graduation and Cleve wanted to make the most of his four weeks of practice and the intrasquad game that would cap it all off. But Cleve would have bad news for Bob Fritz. During the MIAC annual meeting at the Nicollet Hotel in Minneapolis, conference members had discussed eligibility. Under MIAC rules, players could play four years, including their freshman year, which meant 1933 would be Fritz's last season of eligibility. The conference later clarified that a player could play four years of varsity football, but only if the player never played freshman ball. Fritz had played as a freshman in 1929, which meant 1933 would be his fourth year of football.

Cleve and Louie Benson had upwards of 30 men tossing the ball around outdoors on April 3, and Cleve had Pinkey Falgren, who now lived in East Grand Forks, Minnesota, at his side again as an assistant coach for the ends. The seniors, too, helped with coaching. Fritz stood out from the crowd as he wore a pair of tailored football pants.

Blue and Gold (1933)

Even with seniors excluded from drills, Cleve could see he would have veterans at every position except tackle and center. And he would have a heavier team than in 1932. To inspire his players to compete, Cleve decided to follow the lead of other college football programs and announced he would give awards to the best tackler, blocker, and pass receiver at the conclusion of spring practices.

Heavy snows overnight April 3 forced the team indoors for the rest of the week.

*

Across the river, Coach Casey Finnegan didn't start North Dakota State spring football until April 17. As many as 40 players turned out for practices, where Finnegan explained the itinerary for 20 days of training with an intrasquad game between a Yellow and a Green team at the end of it all. He had scheduled eight games for 1933 and was still working to schedule a ninth. The itinerary included Moorhead State during Moorhead's homecoming.

As the players assembled on the practice field behind the new physical education building, Finnegan saw in stark relief how he would lose four seniors, including Dolly Schoenfelder, on the line for 1933. Herb Peschel, who suffered from a bad knee, would compete for a starting position at tackle. Finnegan figured he might have to move his veteran ends to other positions, which would give Bud Marquardt the start on the flank. He needed Wendy Schollander to move to quarterback, which meant Fritz Hanson needed to improve his passing skills at right halfback.

*

In short order, North Dakota Coach Jack West stole Falgren away from Concordia to coach the Sioux ends, which meant Falgren could work near his home and could watch his brother, Fritz Falgren, practice at right halfback for the Sioux. With Falgren lost to North Dakota, Cleve faced a bigger challenge when it came time to switch from the Rockne system to the Warner system and to introduce the Double Wing formation to his Cobbers. However, when spring ball wrapped up on May 5, Cleve felt good about what his players had accomplished. "The tackling drills and practices have been absolutely of the vicious type," he said, "and that means a group well-drilled," he told the *Moorhead Daily News*. Fritz had begun spring football recovered from his autumn injuries, but they returned during the last week of practice, which forced him to sit out. He had practiced enough, though, for Cleve to award him a bronze medal for his blocking and tackling.

*   *

During the MRFU annual meeting in April 1933, Joe Ryan and the Winnipeg Senior League pushed the MRFU to abandon Canadian football rules and instead adopt American intercollegiate rules. Ryan argued that games played under the American rules would attract more interest and fans. Some teams in the Alberta Rugby Football Union (ARFU) and SRFU backed the proposal, but the Regina Roughriders wished to continue to pursue an elusive Grey Cup victory under current rules. During a lengthy discussion, representatives from the junior, juvenile, and school leagues objected to the wholesale adoption of American rules because they felt they lacked the training facilities necessary to get their players in physical condition "to withstand the bumps of the American interference game." In a compromise, MRFU membership drafted proposed rules changes that eliminated the rouge and made pass interference legal from 5 yards beyond the line of scrimmage to the end zone, which would bring football in Western Canada more in line with American rules. The MRFU submitted the proposed changes to the WCRFU, which in turn requested permission from the CRU to deviate from the CRU football code for games played in the West. Competition for the Grey Cup would still be played using the CRU football code.

The effort failed. The CRU expressed a desire for football rules in Canada to be uniform throughout the dominion and therefore rejected the proposed changes. The CRU did adopt one rule change, however, which required potential tacklers to give a punt returner a five-yard berth until he catches the ball.

Meanwhile, as the forward pass increased in popularity, several teams painted their helmets for the first time to help passers identify their receivers.

Blue and Gold (1933)

*   *

Even though Bud Marquardt had spent the entire spring football regimen training to compete in the low and high hurdles and the pole vault for the North Dakota State track team, Coach Casey Finnegan confirmed that Marquardt, with his "remarkable ability to intercept and receive passes" would start at end in 1933. "His long legs serve him to cover a good deal of territory in a hurry and his ability to ground punts came into prominence [in 1932]," the *Spectrum* observed.

Fritz Hanson, too, trained to compete for the track team in the 100- and 220-yard dash as well as the broad jump. During a meet in Moorhead, he took first place in both events and finished the 100-yard dash in 10.0 seconds and the 220-yard dash in 22.6 seconds. The *Spectrum* heaped praise on the rising star:

> "During last year's football season, Fritz Hanson probably gained more recognition for the Bison than anyone else in the backfield. This was mainly due to Fritz's work at skirting the ends at dazzling speed and covering the ground faster than anyone else behind the line. It was due to this speed that he placed the Bison into scoring position in many of the games last year. Although Fritz weighs but 147 pounds, an opponent must be doubly sure that he is going to stop Fritz squarely because, like Claudie Miller, former Bison backfield star, with a quick pivot or side step Fritz is streaking down the gridiron again. Unlike many light and fast backfield men, Fritz can 'take them' as was evident in last year's game with the University. For that reason he is doubly valuable as a backfield player."

Due to rainy weather, Finnegan and his players lost several days of training before the May 17 spring game, where Finnegan assigned Herb Peschel, Marquardt, and Hanson to play together on the Yellow team against the Green. The boys played the game under a blazing hot sun.

Bud Marquardt

With practice time to burn, and with North Dakota in the same situation, Finnegan and West gained approval from the NCC to schedule a spring game between the two teams to be played at Memorial Stadium in Grand Forks on May 23. The state legislature had cut the athletics budgets at both schools drastically, and the athletic directors needed the game to raise money for their 1933 budgets. Under the arrangement, the coaches would give the younger players most of the playing time and graduating seniors could not play.

With the price of admission set at 40 cents, the teams hoped for a capacity crowd. The game kicked off at 8:00 p.m. Neither Peschel, Marquardt, or Hanson started the game, and the Sioux backfield averaged 20 pounds heavier at 185 pounds than the Bison at 165 pounds. The players found a slippery field, but the Bison didn't bring along cleats suitable for mud. North Dakota beat North Dakota State 19-7 and saw the victory as "partial revenge" for the Sioux's regular season loss to the Bison during the 1932 season. Fritz Falgren scored for North Dakota while Wendy Schollander scored for the Bison when he advanced a fumble 47 yards to the end zone.

* *

When the Winnipeg Senior League called for the city's football club representatives to meet in the Wheat Pool building in Winnipeg in June 1933, only Garrison sent a representative to meet with the Winnipeg Rugby Club head. Apparently a dispute had arisen within the St. John's Rugby Football Club organization and nobody showed up to represent the club.

Meanwhile, the athletic director at Manitoba declared there would be no varsity Bisons football team in 1933 due to budget cuts. "The University of Manitoba is peculiarly unfortunate in that its isolation here in the middle of the continent raises the cost of Inter-Collegiate activities to a high figure," explained the student newspaper, the *Winnipeg Manitoban*, in an editorial. "We have no near neighbors and transportation costs for the various teams reach alarming totals. In depression years athletic trips become impossible. Another factor bearing upon Inter-

Blue and Gold (1933)

Collegiate sport is that Winnipeg is not an athletic-minded city. Considerable difficulty is experienced in creating a proper enthusiasm and gate receipts are always precarious." Instead, the school would maintain its junior football team with plans to develop a regulation football field at Fort Garry.

The Winnipeg Senior League decided to operate without the varsity Bisons and, if necessary, without St. John's, the oldest football organization in the city, but the league would not outright drop the Saints. Winnipegs manager Joe Ryan, who was involved in the grounds and scheduling committees for the league, indicated the Winnipegs and Garrison would have to attract outside competitors to Winnipeg to fill out a schedule. Therefore, the league would seek to schedule games with college teams in the "Swede Belt" of northern Minnesota and the Dakotas, which would not only provide strong competition for the Winnipeg clubs but would also serve as a gate attraction.

Because only soldiers could play for Garrison, the *Winnipeg Free Press* speculated the Winnipeg Rugby Club might absorb top talent from St. John's, including the club's American imports. The *Free Press* also predicted that the Garrison team would bolster its ranks with new arrivals from Camp Borden and the Royal Military College in Ontario.

Russ Rebholz, the coach for the Saints, attended the meeting as an "interested party." Rebholz had stayed in Winnipeg over the winter to play with the Canadian national champion Winnipeg Toilers basketball team. Fortunately for Rebholz, he had not traveled with the Toilers to Tulsa, Oklahoma, when the team's plane crashed near Neodesha, Kansas, on the return trip. The tragic event took the lives of several Toilers players.

* *

In July 1933, Lionel Conacher announced that promoters in both Toronto, Ontario, and Montreal, Quebec, had put together teams to play in his new professional football league and the league would seek to include American teams as members. Toronto would play its games at Maple Leaf Baseball Stadium and Conacher hoped to stage a Labor Day game in Ottawa, Ontario. Conacher said fans felt starved for the professional game in Canada and he pointed to the 10,000 fans who had paid to watch Red Grange play professional football in Toronto in 1926 with his New York Yankees in the American Football League (AFL). Conacher indicated he intended to recruit from the ranks of Canadian professional hockey players.

In Montreal, Joe Cattarinich led efforts to field a professional football team there. The Québécois referred to Cattarinich and his business partners, H.A. "Louie" Letourneau and Leo Dandurand, as the "Three Musketeers" of sports promotion in the province. Together they owned and operated Montreal's Club de Hockey Les Canadiens (i.e. Montreal Canadiens), among other sports assets. Letourneau handled the financial side of the partnership while Dandurand handled operations and Cattarinich handled promotions. They sought to recruit American college football players and professional wrestlers for Montreal's entry into professional football.

Under threat from Conacher in 1933, the Big Four reversed its view about American imports. Toronto hired an American, Lew Hayman, to be its coach and included two Americans, Frank Tindall and Andy Mullan from Syracuse University, as players. Montreal rostered three Americans while Ottawa slated five. Complaints about professionalism soon followed. The AAUC suggested some teams should lose their amateur standing, but officials on those teams said the AAUC had no jurisdiction over the activities of the Big Four.

In his column in the *Calgary Herald*, sportswriter Ralph Wilson suggested the uproar about the amateur status of Americans on teams in the Big Four would only lead to increased attention and attendance. "There will be no shortage of funds," he quipped, for paying the American imports, either directly or indirectly. To help pay for the rising cost of including Americans in their ranks, the Big Four would eventually schedule a revenue-raising, two-game series to determine the IRFU champion.

* *

Blue and Gold (1933)

In July 1933, Red Grange served as master of ceremonies for the College Days Revue at the Northwest Fair in Minot, North Dakota. During the event, Grange wore his football uniform and kicked a ball over the grandstands. He inflated new footballs and passed them into the grandstands, which incited a mad scramble to gain possession of the pigskins because they served as backstage passes to meet personally with Grange who would then autograph them. Fritz Hanson attended the fair, and although he didn't catch a pigskin, he did manage to meet Grange to talk about football, and Grange offered advice about how to be effective in the passing game.

* *

The Winnipeg Rugby Club announced it had acquired the services of Greg Kabat, an American import from the University of Wisconsin and a three-time, first-team All-Big Ten selection at lineman. Kabat had captained the Badgers in 1932 and he also played in the East-West Shrine Game that year. Now with Kabat, the Winnipegs promised to field a team that included three Americans, with the acquisition of Russ Rebholz from St. John's and with the return of Carl Cronin to lead the Winnipegs. The *Winnipeg Tribune* expressed hope that the combination would be "capable of ending at last the prairie dynasty of the Regina Roughriders." Boosters in Winnipeg had grown weary of the Roughriders' dominance in the WCRFU.

The Canadian talent the Winnipegs had absorbed from St. John's included Bill Ceretti and Eddie Kushner, but also Eric Law, Herb Mobberley, and Johnny Patrick who had played for Regina as well as St. John's.

The Winnipeg Senior League announced its nine-game schedule, which included a third team, the Shamrocks, which would play against the Winnipegs and Garrison and that would also serve as a developmental team for the Winnipegs. To separate themselves from the Shamrocks, Joe Ryan, the Notre Dame fan, decided the Winnipegs should wear Fighting Irish-reminiscent blue and gold instead of green and white. The league schedule included games versus North Dakota, Mayville State Teachers

College, South Dakota, and Concordia. The Winnipegs alone would play North Dakota and South Dakota while an all-star squad from all three teams in the league would play Mayville and Concordia.

In late August, for the first time, the league offered advanced ticket sales and the league posited the tickets as a booster program and "a means of getting sufficient money to carry out the elaborate program that has been mapped out," reported the *Winnipeg Tribune*. "The Winnipeg club has mustered a squad that appears to have an excellent chance of knocking Regina off the Western Canada pinnacle, but local athletes need hard struggles to get them ready, and to provide them, the local league has arranged for four American college teams to play here this fall. It requires considerable money to bring the Americans here." In 1933, the MRFU and SRFU champions would play the WCRFU semifinal in Winnipeg, which would also require funds to operate.

* *

During the summer of 1933, Concordia Coach Frank Cleve unfolded his baseball pants and took the field at second base for the Fargo-Moorhead Twins. Nine years had passed since Cleve last played professional baseball in his last stint with the Sioux Falls Canaries in the Tri-State League, but now his adopted community of Fargo-Moorhead fielded a team in the Northern League with games played in Moorhead. The unaffiliated Twins finished dead last in the upstart Class D league, but Cleve enjoyed traveling with his fellow batsmen to play teams in Minnesota, Wisconsin, North Dakota, and Manitoba, where the Winnipeg Maroons attracted as many as 108,000 fans during the season and took home the league pennant.

When officials finished their tally of statistical records for the 1933 Northern League season, Cleve finished with 231 at-bats in 60 games and with 71 hits for a .307 batting average, including 16 doubles and 1 home run. He tied for the best batting average on the Twins. At second base, Cleve managed 190 assists and 130 putouts with 11 errors.

When September rolled around, Cleve had to give up baseball. Concordia fall practices began September 5, four days before freshman registration, and one week before classes would begin September 12. A record 35 men turned out for workouts, one less than had showed up for spring football. Cleve expected the numbers might swell to more than 40 by the time classes began. With so many players on the roster, Cleve hoped to give his freshmen plenty of snaps in early, non-conference games. The Cobbers enjoyed two workouts per day in cool weather but only one per day in warm weather, and Cleve found that overall, the line weighed lighter than in past years, and he needed a center. Bob Fritz slightly injured his left knee during practice, but Cleve had plenty of backs to fill in for him as the Cobber ranks swelled to more than 40.

*

Meanwhile, North Dakota State Coach Casey Finnegan fully expected 25 to 30 men to show up when workouts began September 11, but he found that many of the players had worked summer jobs and instead, they arrived in waves. Early on, Finnegan only had 20 players work out twice a day, which limited practices to fundamentals. During the offseason, the Bison had lost eight players to graduation, including their signal-calling quarterback. Finnegan soon learned he had lost his replacement for that position, too, due to illness, and that he had lost a starter at end to law school. When Finnegan finally managed to field a full squad on each side of the ball, he practiced Wendy Schollander at quarterback. As expected, Herb Peschel would get the start at tackle, Bud Marquardt at end, and Fritz Hanson at halfback. Finnegan assigned George May to the other halfback position and Shifty Gove to fullback. The old coach focused his players' attention on the passing game and had all four backfielders throwing or catching the ball on various plays.

With Marquardt new to the starting lineup, the *Moorhead Daily News* focused on his prospects. "Marquardt is a deadly tackler, that's sure," wrote sports editor Dick Hackenberg. "He gets down under punts and he can snare passes anywhere within 10 feet of himself. Tall and gangling, Bud is nevertheless wiry and tough. He can 'take it.'"

In Hackenberg's opinion, for the first time ever the Cobber-Bison game would be a toss-up, in part because Cleve had such a strong turnout for football while Finnegan had such a low early turnout, and the Cobbers had enjoyed several more days of practice than the Bison. Besides, the

Cobbers sought their first win against the cross-town rivals. During the week before the game, while Cleve had his men play touch football as they healed their bumps and bruises from earlier practices, Finnegan started to ramp up contact for the first time to get his late-comers used to the fray.

* *

The Winnipeg Rugby Club opened its 1933 season with two-hour practices in the evenings at Osborne Stadium. And even though the St. John's Rugby Football Club team had folded, the Winnipegs had a hard time filling both their own roster and a roster for their new, lighter developmental team, the Shamrocks. Coach Carl Cronin put out the call for more men to come out for football while the Garrison team managed to attract 40 soldiers to practices.

More men did come out for football, but by the time the first game of the Winnipeg Senior League season rolled around on September 18, 1933, Cronin had to ask Lou Mogul, Herb Mobberley, and Arni Coulter from the Winnipegs to play for the Shamrocks, too. After Manitoba Premier John Bracken performed the ceremonial opening kick, and while the band of Princess Patricia's Canadian Light Infantry, also known as the Princess Pats, played for a small opening day crowd of 1,000 fans, Shamrocks halfback Dan "Sterno" Renix thrilled the spectators. He led the green-and-white Shamrocks under-squad to victory over Garrison when he intercepted a forward pass on the Shamrocks' 53-yard line and skirted two tacklers to run 57 yards for the score. The Shamrocks beat Garrison 8-6.

* *

Tragedy struck the Bison during Coach Casey Finnegan's full-contact scrimmage. On an off-tackle plunge, fullback Shifty Gove twisted his leg into an unnatural position and the weight of several men fell on him. He broke both bones in his lower leg and an ambulance carried him to a local hospital.

Blue and Gold (1933)

With Gove lost for the season, Finnegan knew opposing defenses would be less likely to cover inside runs. Instead, they would play their tackles and ends wider on the line and watch for Fritz Hanson to run outside. They would also miss Gove as a line backer. On the same day Gove fell injured, Concordia Coach Frank Cleve found he had 47 men available to play against the Bison.

In the *Fargo Forum*, Moorhead State Coach Sliv Nemzek weighed in on the Bison situation. "I think it is the toughest break they could get," he said. "It should be an incentive for the rest of the squad to fight harder and go beyond themselves for the rest of the season." Finnegan admitted to the *Moorhead Daily News* that he wished North Dakota State's game against Concordia had been scheduled for later in the season. To remedy the situation, Finnegan worked out several men to find a replacement. His eyes fell on Moorhead High School product Erling Schranz, who had recently added weight. The former Spud, now a junior at North Dakota State, hadn't played varsity football as a sophomore, not with Vivian McKay and Gove ahead of him in the depth chart. He also did not play because he had experienced lingering complications from a broken hand.

Because Schranz could not ably fill Gove's shoes on defense, Finnegan used his last practice the day before the game to try different men in Gove's former position as a line backer.

The night before the game, Cleve had his men practice plays on Dacotah Field. Cleve said his biggest concern was catching Hanson if he reached the open field.

Two years earlier, when Concordia and North Dakota State faced off to start the 1931 season, Bob Fritz had played for the varsity Cobbers but Hanson, Bud Marquardt, and Herb Peschel had watched from the sidelines with all the other players on the Baby Bison freshman team. In 1932, Hanson had sat out the game with a broken finger while Marquardt and Peschel only saw action in substitution. Now in 1933, for the first time, the probable starting lineups listed Fritz at right halfback for the Cobbers and Hanson at right halfback, Marquardt at left end, and Peschel at right tackle for the Bison. Hackenberg billed the game as a "battle of backfields," and on the day of the game, the *Spectrum* featured a picture of

Bob Fritz

Fritz Hanson

Bud Marquardt

Herb Peschel

opposing Cobbers halfback Fritz while the *Concordian* featured a picture of opposing Bison halfback Hanson.

At a pep rally to kick off Concordia's fall season, Fritz gave a speech on "student loyalty" to athletics. Given the hype leading up to the game, Fritz had given a superfluous homily. Meanwhile, the Horton-Scott Company, an electrical store in Fargo, donated a radio so that Gove could listen to the broadcast of the game from his hospital bed.

On September 22, 1933, the Cobbers played the Bison in a night game at Dacotah Field. In the first quarter, North Dakota State reached Concordia's 2-yard line, but after three unsuccessful line plunges, the Bison dropped a pass in the end zone. Meanwhile, Hanson limped off with a bad ankle sprain. In the second quarter, the Bison reached Concordia's 16-yard line, but once again a Bison player dropped Wendy Schollander's pass past the goal line.

In the second half, the teams looked evenly matched as they punted the ball back and forth to gain field position. In the fourth quarter, Hanson returned to the lineup for five more plays, for a minute or two, and at the end of the game, the Bison reached Concordia's 9-yard line but turned the ball over on downs. The game ended in a scoreless tie.

In past meetings, all losses for Concordia, the Cobbers had always finished the game down by at least a touchdown. They could now brag they equaled their cross-town rivals. Yes, the game featured "no sustained drives, no long runs, no thrilling spearing of passes," observed Dick Hackenberg in the *Moorhead Daily News*, but for Concordia fans, he said, the game was "uninteresting from an offensive standpoint yet thrilling in the Cobbers' stubborn defense of their goal line."

For their part, the Bison held back the Cobbers when it counted. Concordia consistently gained 4 or 5 yards on line plunges, cutbacks, and reverses, but only near midfield. The Bison line held strong when the Cobbers moved the ball into Bison territory or on third down.

As predicted, the game featured a battle of backfields. "Bob Fritz, crashing halfback of the Cobbers, gave the Concordians an advantage in power, while the flying feet of Fritz Hanson carried the speed threat for the Bison," observed the *Fargo Forum*. Several times ball-carriers on both sides dropped the ball and, most often, a teammate fell on it or the ball-carriers recovered it by themselves.

After the game, Hanson took his injured ankle to his family home in Perham, Minnesota.

*   *

To prepare his men for a home stand against George Washington, North Dakota Coach Jack West scheduled an early game against the Winnipeg Rugby Club in Winnipeg. With only two weeks of practice to prepare for the Winnipegs, West worked his men hard in scrimmages. Multiple starters had either graduated or didn't return to school and so West had to figure out which players could fill seven vacancies on the starting squad. Wingback Ralph Pierce showed off his speed with runs of 20 and 35 yards against the reserves and halfback Fritz Falgren showed great ability with a 15-yard run. However, many players suffered from bruises. Even big Ted Meinhover, the team's right tackle, sought comfort and wore a special pad over a bruised shoulder.

West told his charges that because the Canadians had added the forward pass to their football code, he expected they would use it a lot in the same way Canadian footballers make frequent use of the lateral pass on option run plays.

Thirty-one varsity football players, two coaches, two administrators, and the student newspaper editor climbed into automobiles and departed Grand Forks at 3:30 p.m. Friday, September 22, bound for Winnipeg and the St. Regis Hotel. Amongst the travelers sat West, his assistant, C.L. "Buck" Starbeck, and Pierce, the team captain and left halfback who held NCC records in the 100- and 220-yard dash.

The Winnipegs, with Americans Carl Cronin, Russ Rebholz, and Greg Kabat, anxiously awaited their foes, but perhaps not as much as their manager, Joe Ryan, who encouraged the community to welcome the Sioux as worthy opponents, as "a bunch of athletes who are thoroughly trained and capable of giving any team in the United States a stubborn battle," reported the *Winnipeg Free Press*. Without enough time to prepare the Winnipegs to pass effectively against the Americans, Cronin instead focused on developing an effective running attack. *Winnipeg Tribune* sportswriters suggested the Winnipegs were too light and would need to resort to passing.

The Sioux, meanwhile, had never practiced using Canadian football rules. Instead, West had his men focus on the passing game, which is something the Canadian crowd salivated to observe. He would go over what he knew about Canadian football when the team practiced at Osborne Stadium the evening before the game.

On September 23, 1933, the Winnipegs and Sioux stood on the sidelines ready to play the first half of a game under American rules and the second half with the Canadian code. In the stands sat a scout sent by George Washington to watch the game. The fans could see the Sioux weighed heavier at every position, especially on the line where the players averaged 196 pounds, about 20 pounds heavier per man than the Winnipegs. But perhaps that number seemed a little skewed because Meinhover didn't stand among the collegians. He had stayed in Grand Forks to nurse his shoulder. Meinhover's absence stood out because Ryan had promoted the big man's presence as a reason to come watch the game. Football historian Parke H. Davis had declared Meinhover the largest player ever to play football at six feet and seven inches tall and between 245 and 250 pounds.

Before kickoff, the Winnipeg Light Infantry band performed for the crowd and both Manitoba Premier John Bracken and American consul general P. Stewart Heintzleman about the relationship between the United States and Canada.

With Starbeck at referee and Irving Kupcinet, a Sioux halfback with an injured wrist, at umpire for the first half under American rules, the teams lined up on a dirt field for the afternoon kickoff. In the first quarter, the Winnipegs displayed their ignorance of American rules when the team committed an offsides penalty and Pierce ran 60 yards uninhibited with a still-live ball for a touchdown. In the second quarter, the Sioux engineered a scoring drive that included a 20-yard run around right end by Pierce. Later, the Winnipegs forced North Dakota to attempt six runs at the line in a set of downs that included two penalties, but the Sioux scored again.

Blue and Gold (1933)

In the second half, under Canadian rules, Cronin tallied 2 points on rouge kicks and the Winnipegs scored 4 more on 2 safeties. The Sioux also scored on a rouge. Throughout the half, Sioux players could not stop themselves from blocking for their ball-carriers and officials penalized the Americans frequently. In the fourth quarter, the Winnipegs used the option run, which confused the Sioux and forced North Dakota to defend its own territory for most of the quarter. Late in the game, the Winnipegs blocked a Sioux punt in the end zone and Bill Ceretti recovered the ball for a Winnipeg touchdown. Kabat played superior defense in this game even though he experienced a severe charley horse. But the Winnipegs couldn't catch up and North Dakota beat Winnipeg 20-12.

After the game, Ryan threw a banquet at the St. Regis Hotel for 80 guests, with the entire North Dakota and Winnipeg teams present. Premier Bracken spoke once more and Coach West gave a speech where he said he hoped the event might become an annual affair. "The Canadian game of kicking at any time combined with forward and lateral passes was just the thing to put a team on edge," he said. In his own speech, Cronin agreed with West that the teams should play again.

After the banquet, the Sioux drove home to Grand Forks. In his column in the *Dakota Student*, Kupcinet wrote, "in rugby, a player tackling around the neck is termed a 'scragger' and is sent to the penalty box for five minutes. The first play of the second half found one of the Sioux violating this rule and ordered off the field." The concept of timed penalties and the penalty box bewildered the Sioux.

* *

Four days later, when the Winnipegs played Garrison on the evening of September 27, 1933, boys 14 and older paid a nickel or exchanged a bundle of old clothes for admission. The Winnipegs donated the clothing to the Back-to-the-Land Assistance Association.

The Garrison soldiers featured Bryce Gillis, a triple threat athlete from the Royal Military College in Kingston, Ontario. Gillis could run, pass, and kick the ball well, but one man does not make a team. During this game, Gillis attempted long passes, but he didn't have the receivers to pull

At Osborne Stadium (Winnipeg, Manitoba)

in the ball. The Winnipegs scored their first touchdown when tackle Eddie Kushner blocked Gillis' punt attempt and the Winnipegs recovered the ball past the goal line for the score. Meanwhile, Russ Rebholz, Carl Cronin, and Herb Mobberley combined on excellent backfield play that included 5 completions on 12 pass attempts that carried the Winnipegs to a 33-6 victory over the soldiers. At one point, Rebholz faked a punt and completed a 35-yard pass to Cronin to move the ball deep into Garrison territory. Rebholz scored twice, once on a pass and again on a run. Cronin scored on 2 touchdown runs and Shamrocks star, Sterno Renix, scored a touchdown on a run. Garrison, too, scored a lone touchdown at the end of the game.

* *

High off a 7-0 win over Morningside, St. Thomas would bring a squad full of veterans to Dacotah Field, including "Wee" Willie Wash, the fast little halfback who had dashed Concordia's championship hopes in 1932. To counter Walsh, North Dakota State Coach Casey Finnegan hoped Fritz Hanson would recover from his ankle injury in time for the game.

Finnegan needed a fullback to fill in for Shifty Gove, and he chose Neville Reiners. He then moved Herb Peschel to guard to replace Reiners. To test Peschel's ability to stop the run on short yardage plays, Finnegan placed the ball at the 1-yard line and had the varsity squad practice stopping the plunge against the freshmen. To practice pass defense, Finnegan had his assistant, Bob Lowe, a southpaw, stand in to imitate the Tommies' left-handed passing threat.

Against St. Thomas, Finnegan would face off against a new coach. The previous Tommies coach, Joe Boland, had resigned in the spring to become a sports announcer for WCCO Radio in Minneapolis with a 6:15 p.m. Saturday evening show. In his place stood Wilbur Eaton who had played right end for Rockne at Notre Dame in 1923 and 1924 and then coached the Fighting Irish freshman team in 1925. In 1926, he assumed the position of head football coach at Mount Saint Charles College, in Helena, Montana. He lead the team there to the Montana intercollegiate championship in 1928. In 1931, Eaton moved to Alabama to coach the

Blue and Gold (1933)

Howard College football team in Birmingham while he studied medicine at the University of Alabama. Now he studied medicine at Minnesota. Several players from Montana chose to attend St. Thomas when they heard Eaton would coach at the school.

Eaton had 25 players on the St. Thomas sideline on September 29, 1933, when they faced off against North Dakota State at Dacotah Field. Throughout the first quarter, the teams participated in a punting duel within St. Thomas territory. At the end of the period, the Bison scored on a 4-yard off-tackle run by Erling Schranz.

In the fourth quarter, Tommies southpaw quarterback Frank Haider ran to his left and threw a pass to Walsh who had run a crossing route from right to left into open territory. Walsh pulled in the ball and carried it into the end zone to tie the game. The game ended 7-7, the second tie in a row for North Dakota State.

Bud Marquardt started at left end and pulled down 1 catch in this game. Peschel substituted at right guard and Hanson did not play. The *Fargo Forum* listed Cub Buck, the former University of Wisconsin, Canton Bulldogs, and Green Bay Packers football player as the referee for the game.

* *

Mayville State Teachers College Coach Lewy Lee understood how to make his team's visit to Winnipeg an event. Despite the fact his Comets had only practiced for a week before they traveled to Winnipeg to play a game, he bragged to the Canadians about his players' athletic abilities. "My boys have speed to burn and play a game that pleases the crowd," he told the *Winnipeg Tribune*. "We use an attack similar to Michigan [with the Short Punt formation], only we do more running than they do." Lee said he had several good broken field runners and also Ed Rorvig, the fullback, the team's heaviest player at 195 pounds. "He hits the line hard and is shifty in the open," Lee told the *Winnipeg Free Press*. And Lee complimented the Winnipegs. "Winnipeg must have a good team to make such a great showing against the Nodaks [the Sioux]," he said, "but I expect my boys to provide stubborn competition and a style of play that will please the crowd." Lee had coached at Mayville since 1930. He played and lettered in football at North Dakota from 1926 through the 1928 seasons. Joe Ryan couldn't have found a better promoter, and the newspapers played along. They reported that Lee used an open game with his light team and "a passing and kicking game makes for sensational running plays and that's what jerks the fans out of their seats," said the *Winnipeg Tribune.*

On Friday night before the game, Coach Lee arrived with 20 players and stayed at the St. Regis Hotel. The Winnipegs would play the Mayville boys under American rules through the first half while Garrison would play with the Canadian code through the second half.

On the afternoon of September 30, 1933, Mayville and the Winnipegs held each other scoreless until Russ Rebholz fired up the aerial game for Winnipeg. He evaded two tacklers in the backfield and completed a 30-yard pass to Herb Mobberley to move within scoring distance, and then Rebholz ran over left tackle for the touchdown. Later, the Comets threw an interception, and on the subsequent drive, Rebholz scored another touchdown around his right end.

Just before halftime, the Comets partially blocked a punt. A penalty moved the ball into Winnipeg territory where Rorvig crashed the line for the score.

In the second half, on their first drive, Garrison used only four plays, including a 50-yard run by a fleet-footed 200-pound soldier, to move the ball from their own 15-yard line to the other end of the field for a touchdown. On their next possession, Garrison ran back a punt 75 yards to the Mayville 12-yard line, but then fumbled and lost the ball.

In the fourth quarter, Mayville's passing attack moved the team within scoring distance but they failed to run the ball through the Garrison line. The Comets settled for a field goal attempt, but Garrison blocked it and responded with a 55-yard run that included a lateral pass for the score. Garrison completed a 45-yard pass for the final touchdown and the game ended Mayville 7, Winnipeg 31.

Garrison's "inspired scarlet-clad soldiers did pretty well as they pleased" against the Comets, said the *Winnipeg Free Press.* Carl Cronin and several starting linemen sat out the game, and so did Greg Kabat, who suffered from a lingering leg injury.

Blue and Gold (1933)

* *

Football fans in Moorhead needed a win and they hoped the upcoming game between Concordia and Moorhead State would satisfy that itch. Both Concordia and Moorhead State had tied their first opponents of the season. While the Cobbers had held off the Bison in a scoreless struggle, the Dragons rallied in the final 40 seconds to tie the Duluth State Teachers College Bulldogs 7-7.

Moorhead State's backfield featured Lyle Glass, the "Dark Mahnomen Speedster" from Mahnomen, Minnesota, and the White Earth Indian Reservation. The *Moorhead Daily News* reported Glass had once competed against Fritz Hanson in the 100-yard dash in a high school, district-level competition, where Glass and Hanson broke the tape simultaneously. After the judges conferred, they awarded the victory to Hanson.

Both Moorhead coaches closed their practices to observers. Because Duluth State had scored against Moorhead State on two successive long passes of 35 and 30 yards, Dragons Coach Sliv Nemzek focused on defending the pass while Cobbers Coach Frank Cleve focused on completing passes. Because the Cobbers outweighed the Dragons by an average of 10 pounds per player, Nemzek had his men practice blocking assignments while Cleve had his men scrimmage against trick plays, including a spread offense and open formations, which Nemzek sometimes used. Cleve also had his backfielders practice the shift to avoid the offside and in-motion penalties that had killed Concordia's momentum against North Dakota State.

The night before the game, the new Moorhead State Pep Squad, dressed in white and crimson, led a pep fest in the auditorium at Weld Hall. The event featured an illustrated speech that explained the game of football to freshmen unfamiliar with the game.

The next day, on September 30, 1933, the Moorhead crowd watched as the schools engaged in a punting duel. Late in the second quarter, on first down at Moorhead State's 34-yard line, the Dragons intercepted a Bob Fritz pass attempt in the Cobbers backfield. The Dragon end raced toward daylight but Fritz ran him down and knocked him off balance.

The ball-carrier fell at the 20-yard line just as the gun sounded to end the half.

In the second half, still unable to move the ball on the ground, both teams took to the air. Moorhead State completed 6 of 12 pass attempts for 71 yards with 2 interceptions while Concordia completed 7 of 18 pass attempts for 75 yards with 2 interceptions. Both sides spent the majority of their time on offense within their own territories. In a valiant effort, the Cobbers reached the Dragon 19-yard line as the gun sounded to end the contest 0-0. The game would join the majority, with six of the last 11 games between the two schools ending in a scoreless tie.

Two games into the season, all three colleges in Fargo-Moorhead found themselves undefeated and winless.

* *

To fill a bye week in their schedule, the Regina Roughriders arranged to play a game on October 2, 1933, in Minot, North Dakota, against the Minot Panthers. The Panthers once again featured Red Jarrett. The teams played the first half of the game under American rules and the second half under Canadian rules in front of approximately 800 fans.

In the first quarter, Minot scored a touchdown on a line buck over the goal line. The yellow-sweatered Panthers scored a safety when they blocked a punt attempt by Phat DeFrate. And late in the first half, Jarrett completed a forward pass for a touchdown.

In the second half, Regina crashed the line for a touchdown, but then Jarrett completed a second touchdown pass for Minot. Regina twice scored on rouges and then tallied a second touchdown, but in the end the Panthers beat the Roughriders 20-13.

Jarrett played 45 game minutes, and while he completed 2 passes for touchdowns, for the first time in four years of football he did not score with his own legs.

* *

Blue and Gold (1933)

The Monday after their draw with St. Thomas, many varsity Bison players missed practice while tied up in fraternity rush activities. Those upperclassmen who did show up ran through aerial drills while Coach Casey Finnegan taught the freshman squad passing plays he expected Morningside would use against them on Saturday. Finnegan and Morningside Maroons Coach Saundy Saunderson had a non-scouting agreement, but the teams were old conference foes and Finnegan had a good idea about Saundy's grid strategy. However, the old Maroons coach had a new weapon in sophomore quarterback Denton Dean. Against the Augustana College Vikings the previous weekend, Dean had scored two touchdowns late in the game to lead the Maroons to a 13-7 victory. Saundy had pulled his own son, Jason, from the game and replaced him with Dean.

Because football fans in Fargo desired to travel to Grand Forks on Friday night to watch North Dakota defend its home turf against George Washington, Finnegan felt obliged to reschedule the Bison game to Saturday night. The extra day meant a day off from practice for the Bison on Friday. Meanwhile, Saundy and his 22 Maroons departed Sioux City for Fargo at their scheduled time on Thursday afternoon.

When the Bison and Maroons met on October 7, 1933, at Dacotah Field, both teams sought their first conference win of the season. Morningside hoped to gain its first win since 1931. Herb Peschel started the game at right tackle while Bud Marquardt played the game in substitution at left end.

In the opening minutes of the second quarter, after Fritz Hanson substituted for Erling Schranz at right halfback, George May, quarterback for the Bison, launched a long pass toward Hanson, but Dean, defensive left halfback for the Maroons, leapt in front of Hanson to block the catch. Hanson reached over Dean's shoulder and caught the ball. When he landed on the ground, Hanson spun around and raced toward the goal line to score a touchdown. The "rabbit-like" and "speedy, rhythmic towhead halfback" for the Bison looked "even more brilliant than the floodlights [that] cast his flying shadow on the ground," reported the *Bismarck Tribune*.

Throughout the game, both teams drove deep into opposing territory, but the Bison made the Maroons work the hardest for yardage as May dropped multiple punts out of bounds within Morningside's 10-yard line. In the first, third, and fourth quarters, the Maroons reached near to the Bison goal line, but North Dakota State held, and the Bison won 7-0.

For halftime entertainment, the Fargo Chamber of Commerce sponsored another appearance by the 30-member Alexandria High School girls' drum corps. The percussion team had traveled over 2,000 miles during the summer months to play at events throughout the United States.

* *

Several Winnipeg Rugby Club players nursed injuries. Nevertheless, 29 players continued to work out for the Winnipegs and for their under-squad, the Shamrocks. Over the Thanksgiving Day holiday weekend, the Shamrocks would play Garrison on Saturday and the Winnipegs would play Garrison on Monday.

Once again, the Winnipeg Senior League did its best to attract young boys—future football players—to its games when it offered 5 cents admission to boys 17 and under with the promise of the chance at a free football. Those kids who showed up in time for the opening kickoff on October 7, 1933, got their money's worth. On the first play of the game from their own 30-yard line, the Shamrocks took to the air and Sterno Renix ran 30 yards, pulled down a pass, and raced 40 more yards through the open field for a touchdown. The play switched on an aerial circus. "Both teams used the forward pass freely," noted the *Winnipeg Tribune*. "Its constant use led to a thrilling affray, with the threat of sudden extinction constantly hanging over both squads. The long and accurate flips" of the Shamrocks "were an ever-present source of danger to the Soldiers." On the ground, "the shifty [Arni] Coulter, in particular, proved a difficult problem for Garrison tacklers." The Shamrocks won 6-1, a low score despite the aerial assault.

* *

Blue and Gold (1933)

Because Concordia had played both North Dakota State and Moorhead State to scoreless ties, the student newspaper at Gustavus suggested the Golden Gusties would play the role of underdog in their upcoming game against the Cobbers. Concordia Coach Frank Cleve refused to believe the suggestion. The "Shrouds," as the *Gustavian Weekly* liked to call the Gusties, were "a big, heavy, rangy squad." They carried themselves like executioners decked out in black uniforms, black helmets, black socks, and black shoes. "This sombre garb makes them look all the bigger to their opponents," suggested Dick Hackenberg in the *Moorhead Daily News*. In fact, the Gusties *were* big, and Cleve admitted to the *Fargo Forum* that he was "scared to death" of the "Galloping Gusties" because they stood bigger than they did the year before when the Cobbers played them to a scoreless tie. Cleve suggested that even with big, line-plunging Bob Fritz in the game, the Cobbers should pass the ball or run around the ends. Louie Benson, the line coach, said he hoped the Cobbers would at least finish in a tie. Against Carleton and behind a heavy line the Gusties had rushed for big gains with Earl Witty, a backfielder and full-grown adult who had just returned to school after an absence of several years. During the week, to get his mind off the game, Cleve participated in and won the 72-hole Moorhead Golf Club medal score tournament by four strokes in a field of 22 golfers to take home the Leo Johnson loving cup.

On October 7, 1933, the Cobbers and Gusties stepped onto a dust-covered Concordia field. Cleve started Ralph Miller instead of Fritz at halfback. In the first half, the Cobbers tried but failed to gain yardage with Miller around the ends, and so Cleve replaced Miller with Fritz. Late in the second quarter, the Cobbers drove to the Gusties 20-yard line on runs by Fritz and Pat Hilde, but Gustavus held and forced a turnover on downs. On the very next play, the Gusties fumbled and the Cobbers recovered. Concordia then used a passing attack to reach near the goal line, but Hilde dropped a pass from Fritz in the end zone and the Gusties took over.

During the entire second half, both teams maintained possession within the middle 40 yards of the grid. The Gusties rushed up the middle or off tackle while the Cobbers took to the air instead of pounding the ground.

In all, the Cobbers threw 24 pass attempts and completed 8 for 102 yards but with 3 interceptions, and when the final gun sounded, the game ended in a scoreless tie. The teams combined for 135 yards in penalties, mostly for offsides or unnecessary roughness.

Cleve felt good about the result. He said his men played better than in previous games. "We'll never meet a line as tough as that one for the remainder of the season," Cleve told the *Moorhead Daily News*. "That Gustavus outfit was a tarter and I'm glad we're by them with something as good as a scoreless tie." In fact, the result stood as Concordia's fifth straight scoreless tie, a streak that began against St. John's late in 1932. "It's taking on the proportions of the well-known jinx," suggested Hackenberg. He opined the scoreless-but-undefeated Cobbers had focused too much on scoring touchdowns and that the "foot" had been severed from 'foot'-ball. "The field goal," he wrote, "either dropkick or placekick, is becoming as rare as a peaceful day in Cuba." Both Gustavus and Concordia had had opportunities to attempt field goals, but they did not.

* *

The Winnipeg Rugby Club played teams from south of the border in 1933, but only games they played against other Winnipeg Senior League teams counted toward winning the MRFU title. Technically, only two teams contended for the title—the Winnipegs and Garrison—because the Shamrocks had served as the practice squad for the Winnipegs.

On October 9, 1933, Thanksgiving Day in Canada, the Winnipegs played Garrison for the MRFU title. Greg Kabat, who had injured his leg against North Dakota, returned to the lineup, as did other linemen who had experienced injuries earlier in the season. The *Winnipeg Tribune* predicted the tired soldiers, who had taken a beating from the Shamrocks just two days earlier, would lose by at least seven touchdowns. Sometimes sports pundits get it right.

Blue and Gold (1933)

In front of a holiday crowd, Russ Rebholz and the Winnipegs "cut loose with the most spectacular passing attack ever seen on a local gridiron," said the *Tribune*. Rebholz completed 8 passes for an average of 25 yards per catch, including a 45-yard pass to Carl Cronin and "kept the hapless Soldiers in a state of constant bewilderment." The Winnipegs moved the ball on option runs and through the air to beat the soldiers 39-0. Rebholz scored 3 touchdowns on the ground and 1 as a passer. Cronin and Greg Kabat each scored 1 rushing touchdown.

The Winnipegs still had more exhibition games to play, but already on October 9 they had captured the MRFU title.

* *

Several years after he last played Canadian rugby football, multi-sport athlete extraordinaire and professional hockey player Lionel Conacher would return to the gridiron to lead Canada's first-ever unabashedly professional football team against a team from Rochester, New York, at Maple Leaf Stadium in Toronto, Ontario. The teams would play the game under Canadian rules, with 12 men and 3 downs to gain 10 yards, but Conacher had modified the rules to allow blocking 10 yards from the line of scrimmage and also on kick returns. The Crosse and Blackwell foods brand sponsored Conacher's team, the Chefs, while the Rochester Packing Co., Inc., in Rochester, New York, sponsored the opponent—the Rochester Arpeakos—named after the packing company's brand of meat products.

In addition to Conacher as a player, coach, and manager, the Toronto team featured "Jumping" Joe Savoldi who had played fullback at Notre Dame on the undefeated teams of 1929 and 1930. After an undisclosed marriage and divorce scandal had forced him from the Fighting Irish roster in 1930, Savoldi finished the season playing for the Chicago Bears. "Jumping Joe" then went on to become a professional wrestler.

Conacher's team also featured former Haskell Institute backfielder named Mayes "Chief" McLain, a 230-pound fullback of Cherokee and Irish heritage who had played in the NFL for the Portsmouth Spartans and Staten Island Stapletons in 1930-31. The roster also included Lionel's brother, Charlie, also a professional hockey player.

The Arpeakos, contenders in the New York State Football League, featured Gregg Swarthout, a former end at Dartmouth College in Hanover, New Hampshire.

The teams met on October 9, 1933, in a game played in front of upwards of 13,000 fans. Conacher "carried 90 per cent of the Chefs' offensive burden, ran back kicks, rammed the line for consistent gains, caught forward passes and punted well," wrote the *Ottawa Citizen*. In the first quarter, the 200-pound Conacher intercepted a pass and returned it 30 yards to the 18-yard line. Two plays later, he ran a sweep around left end for 12 yards and the touchdown. On the ensuing extra point attempt, the Chefs fumbled the ball, and an Arpeakos player picked it up and returned it for a touchdown. The Arpeakos later scored a rouge on a punt by Swarthout. Late in the first half, McLain lateraled to Conacher who streaked 65 yards down the sideline for a touchdown.

In the third quarter, the Arpeakos started at midfield and used several long runs to score a touchdown and later scored a third touchdown on a 70-yard drive. On the final play of the game, Charlie Conacher tossed a lateral pass to Lionel who forced his way 30 yards through multiple tacklers before he passed the ball to a teammate who raced 30 yards for the score. In the end, despite Conacher's outstanding performance, the Arpeakos won 18-15.

* *

The Cobber varsity football squad had so flawlessly executed plays and blocked opponents to open up holes during practice that Coach Frank Cleve so much as guaranteed Concordia would beat Macalester. He told Hank Hurley, the sportswriter for the *Fargo Forum*, "We were hitting so hard in that practice [that] three freshmen were carried from the field," he said, "the result of being hit hard by varsity men." Cleve unloaded on *Moorhead Daily News* sportswriter Dick Hackenberg, too. "We'll whip 'em," he told Hackenberg. "If they ever get going, it's going to be too bad for somebody." Hackenberg observed, "[Bob] Fritz has shown a

Blue and Gold (1933)

complete rejuvenation in practice this week and may launch a bid for his third successive all-state honor in tomorrow's contest." The sportswriter's observation proved prescient.

The Cobbers and the Scots met on October 13, 1933, at Concordia. Because the Cobbers had failed to score in several games, Cleve decided to start Fritz at his old position at fullback and the Cobbers would use both passes and end runs to open up the middle of the line for Fritz. In the first quarter, the teams appeared equal, but late in the second quarter, the Cobbers returned a punt to Macalester's 17-yard line. Two plays later, Fritz completed a 12-yard touchdown pass to Pat Hilde. The fans gave the Cobbers a standing ovation because Concordia had scored its first touchdown since mid-season 1932. Students and alum together sang "Stand Up and Cheer" for the first time in a year.

In the third quarter, Fritz hit the line six times on a drive that moved the ball to Macalester's 30-yard line, and then Hilde connected with Fritz on a 27-yard pass to the 3-yard line. Fritz, the "International Falls Pile Driver" then charged over left guard for the score. Fritz crossed the goal line twice more in the fourth quarter, first on a drive where he fielded a 30-yard pass from Hilde, and second on a drive that ended when he burrowed past his left guard over the goal line. In the end, in extreme heat and on a dusty field, Concordia's reserves finished the game against the tired Scots. When the final gun sounded, Concordia had beaten Macalester 26-0. No opponent had crossed the Cobber goal line in six straight games.

Concordia backfielders had tossed accurate passes, but on the receiving end, pass-catchers bobbled and dropped the ball 4 times. Concordia completed only 9 of 23 pass attempts with 4 interceptions but scored all of their touchdowns on drives where the pass played a key role. Because Concordia had played strong against the run, they forced Macalester, too, to take to the air. Macalester completed 8 of 21 pass attempts with 4 interceptions.

* *

After a highly successful turnout for an exciting game in Toronto, Lionel Conacher took his Crosse and Blackwell Chefs to Rochester, New York, for a night game against the Rochester Arpeakos at Red Wing Stadium. The local American Legion sponsored the matchup. Because Conacher had filled his roster with professional wrestlers who had scheduled bouts elsewhere, he recruited Len Macaluso, the former fullback from Colgate University in Hamilton, New York, who had led the Raiders to a 23-5 record during his career. Macaluso also led U.S. college players in scoring with 144 points in 1930.

After a successful draw at the gate for the game in Toronto, Conacher carried high hopes to Rochester. The *Democrat and Chronicle* suggested local fans had expressed interest in watching football played under modified Canadian football rules that resulted in a "wide-open contest" in Toronto. "The free scoring went over big with the Toronto fans," the newspaper said. "The new rules invite more open play with passing and long distance kicking at a premium." However, when the teams took the field in Rochester, only 1,000 fans watched from the stands.

In the first half, the Arpeakos scored the first touchdown on a diving pass catch. Later, Lionel Conacher booted a high arcing punt that bounced off a player in the end zone and the Chefs recovered the ball for a touchdown. Conacher booted several sky-high punts during the game and more than one kick traveled 60 yards through the air.

In the second half, Macaluso rushed for significant gains for the Chefs, but the Arpeakos scored again on a drive that included two consecutive long passes followed by a 4-yard off-tackle run by Arpeakos backfielder Gregg Swarthout. The Arpeakos won the game 12-6 as well as the series.

Afterward, the *Chronicle* declared the Canadian game more violent than its American counterpart. "The game as played under Canadian rules (*sic*) does not allow blocking after a man has gone 10 yards, and this resulted in some vicious tackling especially on the part of the Canadians. Time and again two and three tacklers would crash a ball carrier bringing him down to earth with a thud."

* *

Blue and Gold (1933)

With so many injuries on the North Dakota State Bison varsity football squad, "it is even dangerous for the scribes to lurk in the Bison camp," joked *Fargo Forum* sportswriter Eugene Fitzgerald. "You can't tell what night you might be recruited to scrimmage as a halfback."

On Monday after the game against Morningside, the Bison reserve players scrimmaged against the freshmen while many of the starters sat out. Fritz Hanson remained questionable after reinjuring his ankle in the game against the Maroons. Meanwhile, doctors ordered Wendy Schollander and starting tackle Roy Platt to sit out the remainder of the season. Schollander suffered from a skin infection while Platt lay in the hospital with a bout of inoperable appendicitis. Erling Schranz, too, sat out with an injured hip. Coach Casey Finnegan dreaded having his men scrimmage during practice for fear the team might not finish out the varsity schedule. He moved Herb Peschel from guard to tackle, the same position Peschel had filled when the Bison lost Dolly Schoenfelder for the season in 1932. "Fortunately, the Bison had a capable performer in Peschel, a sophomore," Fitzgerald wrote about the situation. "Peschel upheld his duties... and the Bison got along splendidly. Now Peschel is needed as a tackle almost for full time."

After holding Minnesota to a 19-6 victory, South Dakota State would play the Bison with two weeks rest. The Jackrabbits and Gophers had entered the last 5 minutes of their matchup in a 6-6 tie but Minnesota had found a way to win.

The Jackrabbits, too, suffered from debilitations. The team captain, Dale Palmer, lay in the hospital with pernicious anemia. And the team's star halfback, Cleo Terry, looked weak in practice after he had given blood in a transfusion for Palmer.

Hanson returned to the field on Tuesday and scrimmaged against the freshman team. He "showed no signs of injury," Fitzgerald reported, and he "heaved long passes to Bud Marquardt, elongated flanker, who took nearly everything the Perham towhead got near him. The [freshmen] had trouble breaking up the attack, even though it was apparent what was coming." Hanson's resurgence changed the overall calculation for oddsmakers. Without him in the contest, the Jackrabbits had stood as favorites.

The night before the game, the homecoming committee held a bonfire and pep rally behind Festival Hall. Before the rally, the committee had scolded the student body and in a declaration wrote, "The school spirit at past games has been negligible, and since this is an essential element in the backing of the team, a big improvement is desired." It's not clear why students had neglected the pep rally in the recent past, but at least one columnist in the *Spectrum* noted that students had celebrated homecoming as an "alcoholiday" despite prohibition prior to 1933.

The next day, units in the homecoming parade lined up on campus, and at 10:00 a.m. they headed south on 13th Street North [now University Drive], east onto 11th Avenue North to Broadway, and south on Broadway to Front Street. The Fargo police led the parade on motorcycle, followed by automobiles with the chief of police, members of the city commission, the college president, members of the board of administration and state budget board, and Governor William Langer. Within the mix rode the homecoming queen as she held a bouquet of yellow chrysanthemums bordered by read autumn leaves. The Gold Star Band, 108 members strong, and members of the ROTC led the remainder of the procession, which included decorated automobiles and floats driven by student organizations, fraternities, and sororities at the school.

Before the Bison took the field, Finnegan gave a rousing speech to his men. They stood as the underdog in the game, he said, and so they must pour everything they've got into fighting South Dakota State.

On a hot, sunny day, October 14, 1933, the Bison met the Jackrabbits at Dacotah Field. This year, the homecoming game did not include a section of free seats for a "knothole gang" of youngsters. Instead, North Dakota State required grade-schoolers to pay 15 cents while high-schoolers paid 25 cents for admission.

Immediately after the opening kickoff, South Dakota State failed to move the ball, and so they chose to punt on third down. With Herb Peschel at right tackle and Bud Marquardt at left end the Bison crashed through the line and blocked Jackrabbit star Paul Miller's kick. The ball fell at the 10-yard line and after a mad scramble, Peschel fell on the ball in the end zone for a touchdown.

Blue and Gold (1933)

On the next Bison possession, the drive ended on a bad snap out of punt formation. The Jackrabbits recovered the ball at North Dakota State's 16-yard line. Two plays later, South Dakota State tied the game when Miller pushed his way across the line.

After an exchange of punts, the Jackrabbits regained possession. They used only three plays to move the pigskin from their own 37-yard line into the end zone for another score.

At halftime, the Gold Star Band entertained the crowd while marching in letter formation. The student body provided a military escort and an arch of sabers for the homecoming queen to proceed to her coronation.

During the entire second half, both teams played in a stalemate. Late in the game, the Bison suffered another bad snap that resulted in a change of possession. The Jackrabbits won 13-7.

Throughout the game, South Dakota State Coach Cy Kasper had frequently substituted the Jackrabbit backfield. All of his backs found success through holes in the offensive line. Kasper had used four ends, three tackles, five guards, two centers, and two full backfields to outgain the Bison in yardage, while Hanson reached only negligible distances.

After the game, with little to celebrate, the fraternities and sororities on the Fargo campus opened their houses. In the evening, students and alumni gathered in the physical education building where the homecoming committee had erected a bandstand along the center of the east wall.

* *

After North Dakota had trampled South Dakota 41-0 in Grand Forks on Friday night, October 13, 1933, the reserve squad for the Coyotes traveled north overnight to Winnipeg to play a game against the Winnipeg Rugby Club. The exhausted South Dakota collegians, high on adrenaline for the international contest, arrived in Winnipeg at 8:15 a.m. At 2:30 p.m., just six hours after they had arrived, five seniors, five juniors, and a sophomore took the field at Osborne Stadium. They would play the opening half under American rules, which by now had grown familiar to the Winnipegs who had already played two halves across two games with the American code.

In the opening period, the Winnipegs threatened to score when Russ Rebholz returned a punt from midfield to the 25-yard line. On the next play, he raced another 20 yards on a run around right end. From the 5-yard line, Greg Kabat wormed his way to the 1-yard line, but then the Coyotes held on three successive plunge attempts to force a turnover on downs. On a long scamper, the Coyotes reached Winnipeg's 10-yard line, but the Winnipegs held off their attackers. The half ended with the score tied 0-0.

In the second half, under Canadian rules, the Winnipegs turned on the scoring machine. Winnipeg's first score came in the third quarter after a mistake by South Dakota when the Coyotes fumbled and lost the ball at the 3-yard line on a mishandled lateral pass. Kabat recovered the ball and two plays later, he dove into the end zone for the score. Late in the third quarter, Rosy Adelman raced downfield and recovered a kicked ball to score a touchdown for Winnipeg.

In the fourth quarter, the Coyotes marched downfield and scored a field goal on a drop-kick from 32 yards by one of their star players, Lowell "Chappie" O'Connor. Later, Kabat took advantage of Coyote confusion when he kicked the ball 50 yards on the run. He raced downfield to pick up the ball and ran it 15 yards for a touchdown. Late in the game, the Coyotes scored a safety on a kickoff when the Winnipeg return man touched the ball and it rolled back over the goal line where the Winnipegs downed it. In the end, the Winnipegs beat the Coyotes 21-5.

Despite the victory, the Winnipeg offensive line had played poorly against the Coyote defensive attack. South Dakota had blocked 3 Winnipeg punts, sacked the passer 4 times, and stopped Winnipeg backfielders for losses multiple times.

* *

While Toronto's foray into professional football featured a premier Canadian athlete in Lionel Conacher, Montreal's endeavor to field a professional football team leaned on a roster filled with mostly New

Englanders, including former college and professional football players who also wrestled professionally, and the lineup included former Olympic athletes Earl McCready, John "Jack" Spellman, and Charlie Strack.

McCready, a Canadian-born athlete, had been a three-time U.S. collegiate heavyweight wrestling champion for Oklahoma A&M. He represented Canada in the 1928 Olympic Games.

Spellman had captained the Brown University football team in Providence, Rhode Island. He won a gold medal in the light heavyweight freestyle wrestling division in the 1924 Olympic Games. He later played professional football in the NFL for the Providence Steam Roller from 1925-1931 and finished with the Boston Braves in 1932.

Strack, the coach for the Mount Royals, had competed in the light heavyweight freestyle wrestling division of the 1924 Olympic Games. He played football at Colgate and then transferred to Oklahoma A&M where he finished as the U.S. collegiate heavyweight wrestling champion in 1926. He later played one year of professional football with the Chicago Cardinals of the NFL in 1928.

Other Mount Royal roster standouts included Tony Siano, who had played college football at Fordham University in New York City. He later played alongside Strack in Boston in the NFL in 1932; Jim Wallis, who had played at the College of the Holy Cross in Worcester, Massachusetts, and also for the Boston Bulldogs of Red Grange's AFL in 1926; and Robert "Bibber" McCoy, a New England heavyweight wrestling champion in the 1920s who had attended Holy Cross.

Shag Shaughnessy, the head football coach at McGill, served as the general manager for the Mount Royals. Shaughnessy also ran the Montreal Royals minor league baseball team at the time. Before the football season began, he had lights installed at De Lorimier Stadium in Montreal to accommodate night baseball. The Mount Royals would play under those same lights with an American-sized football field laid out along the third base line into left field. However, instead of Canadian rules or American collegiate rules, the team would play their games using NFL rules in their entirety but including the Canadian rouge.

Most of the players on the Mount Royals team lived in Boston, and so they practiced in Boston. Strack wired quotes to the *Gazette* in Montreal.

Blue and Gold (1933)

"We'll show Montrealers a brand of football that will top anything they've seen before around here," he told the newspaper.

For their first game, the Mount Royals would play the Portland Arrows out of Maine, which claimed to have lost only one game per year during the past three seasons. Composed of former college players from schools along the Eastern Seaboard, most players on the team had played together for the past couple of years. Both teams had to travel to Montreal. The Mount Royals wore the colors of the Montreal flag with cardinal red pants, white socks, and white jerseys emblazed with a red diamond over the heart and with black numerals. Shaughnessy and others involved in Canadian football organizations in Montreal served as officials for the game.

Five thousand dubious spectators filled the stands on October 15, 1933, to watch the Royals play the Arrows. After a stalemate first quarter, the Royals used an aerial attack with passes to McCoy. They reached near to the Arrows' goal line where Wallis ran through the line for the score. Later in the same period, the Royals completed a 40-yard pass, and a few runs later, Montreal scored a second touchdown.

In the second half, the Royals, who outweighed their opponents by an average of 30 pounds per man, began to slow down, and the lighter Arrows threatened but failed to score. Montreal beat Portland 14-0.

Afterward, the *Gazette* gave the event mixed reviews. While the paper expressed satisfaction that the pro wrestlers had left the "showmanship of the wrestling mat behind them in the dressing room," the crowd never did invest into the outcome of the game. And while the Royals lacked teamwork, they exhibited "brilliantly skillful individual play," especially with the forward pass and with blocking, but the backfield lacked speed, and "the crowd was frankly skeptical," noted the *Gazette*. "The spectacle met with a mixed reception... The game was played entirely under the United States professional rules and for this reason it was somewhat mystifying to most of those in attendance." The paper observed the fans did not align themselves with either team and mostly cheered the forward passing of both teams as well as the offensive blocking allowed anywhere on the field.

Blue and Gold (1933)

Meanwhile, in the United States, newspapers compared Montreal's efforts to field a team of wrestlers to the 1932 film *Rackety Rax* wherein a gambler creates a fake college team made up of wrestlers who play the game like pro wrestlers in the theater of the ring. Gangsters in the film purchase intelligence about the opposition's plays and even shoot a football with a gun before it can reach between the goal posts. *Philadelphia Inquirer* sportswriter Stan Baumgartner first previewed the ring theatrics of all the pro wrestlers on Montreal's roster and then shared the *Montreal Daily Herald* report on the game, which made fun of McCoy placekicking the ball with his big belly and bosom obscuring the ball from his own vision. "He kicks by instinct," the *Herald* scoffed, and then reportedly suggested one of the giant wrestlers on the team had simply sauntered through the line and brushed tacklers aside, suggesting the team did, in fact, put on a show instead of a legitimate football contest. Four days after the game, Baumgartner ran into Strack in Camden, New Jersey. Baumgartner said he chided Strack about the team, and Strack responded by saying, "It's no joke. We have a great team. I am trying to secure a game with the [Philadelphia] Eagles right now. We drew 5,000 people to that tilt in Montreal. And say, football is just ping-pong compared to wrestling."

The Eagles never did play "ping-pong" with the Mount Royals.

* *

At first, Coach Casey Finnegan thought his Bison had escaped the Jackrabbits relatively unscathed, but then the starting center, Earl Thomas, didn't report to practice due to a leg injury. Meanwhile, the Bison backfield continued to play with lingering enervations, including Fritz Hanson with his ankle. Apprehensive, the otherwise contact-makes-you-stronger Finnegan decided his backfielders should not participate in contact during practice. His assistant, Bob Lowe, taught the reserves how to execute the plays Superior State Teachers College might run using the Warner offensive system. Afterward, those reserves ran all over the starters. The team continued their simulations through Wednesday. The

Blue and Gold (1933)

team had to leave for Superior, Wisconsin, by train Thursday afternoon. Meanwhile, Finnegan tried out Bud Marquardt as a punter.

The Superior Yellowjackets, in black and gold, answered to coach Edward "Ted" Whereatt, a young leader and native to the Wisconsin city. Whereatt had served as captain of the Superior Central High School football team where he played alongside future Stanford phenom Ernie Nevers who went on to play in the NFL for the Duluth Eskimos. After high school, Whereatt stayed home and played college ball in Superior. After graduation, he coached high school football in Mellen, Wisconsin, where his teams won two conference championships. The coach for the Yellowjackets since 1930, Whereatt had managed to turn the team around with winning seasons. Earlier in the 1933 season, Superior had beaten St. Olaf in Northfield.

Twenty-seven Bison players, including Wendy Schollander who had only watched practices in a sweat suit, left for Superior. The doctors decided Schollander had recovered well enough to play. Finnegan needed Schollander's passing ability.

When the Bison and Yellowjackets took the field on October 20, 1933, they played in front of the smallest turnout in Superior so far in the season with 1,731 fans in the stands. Marquardt started at left end while Herb Peschel started at right tackle. Both offenses appeared anemic and finished the first half in a 0-0 tie. In the second half, a cold drizzle began to fall and both sides had a difficult time on the run.

Superior suffered from a poor punting game. In the fourth quarter, the Bison managed to reach Superior's 22-yard line only to have the Yellowjackets close down the drive with an interception. Later in the quarter Hanson, "Bison Speed Merchant Extraordinary," came in as a substitute and ran 28 yards on a sweep to reach the Superior's 48-yard line. Hanson then helped to move the ball to the 30-yard line but Superior intercepted another pass.

Schollander played one cold, wet quarter against the Yellowjackets. North Dakota State threw 2 interceptions and fumbled and lost the ball three times. Neither team reached inside its opponent's 20-yard line and the game ended in a 0-0 tie.

Blue and Gold (1933)

*   *

Less than a week before his team would play the Winnipeg Rugby Club, Concordia Coach Frank Cleve admitted he knew "little or nothing" about the rules of Canadian football. "And the kids know less," he said, "but we'll get along," he told the *Fargo Forum*. "I'm going to get myself a rule book and the kids and I will go into a huddle and learn the book from Page 1 to the end."

Moorhead Daily News sportswriter Dick Hackenberg exposed his American naïveté when he decided to visit the Moorhead Public Library to learn more about rugby—the English game—and then wrote about its rules in his newspaper column, as if the Cobbers would field 15 men, kick the ball around like a soccer ball, and scrummage. He admitted, "there are variations in nearly every British province" and suggested that "Canadian Rugby may have its own characteristics, too."

On the Monday after the Macalaster game, Cleve gave his men the day off from practice, but then on Tuesday he placed assistant coach Louie Benson in charge of teaching the reserves how to play Canadian football. Benson would also coach the team while in Winnipeg. Cleve instructed Benson to play the Cobber starters under American rules and the reserves and the freshmen under Canadian rules. Cleve told Hackenberg, "Both Louie and I are more or less ignorant of the game of rugby as it is now played, but we have a rule book now and it's much easier. It looks like an interesting game, at that."

It's not clear which set of rules Cleve and Benson had managed to obtain, but Benson had played centre back on an English rugby team in Toronto, Ontario, during the three years he had played International League baseball for the Syracuse Stars in Syracuse, New York. Cleve and Benson also consulted with former Cobber and Regina Roughrider Pinkey Falgren, now the assistant coach at North Dakota, about how the Sioux had played in their game against Winnipeg earlier in the season.

By the end of the week, after Hackenberg had watched Benson run his men through their paces, the sportswriter appeared to come to his senses when he wrote,

> "This game of rugby, as she is played in Canada, seems to be a hybrid between English rugby and American football... Coach Louie Benson has 12 men to a team instead of 15, forward passes are allowed as well as backwards and laterals. The big difference between the Canadian and the American, however, is that no blocking is tolerated up north. The game looks tricky, with players following their ball-carrier instead of massing before him, so that he can flip the ball to one of them, and so on, when tackled. The line is made up of seven forwards in the identical football formation but there are five backs. Forward passing is tough because of this additional man."

Cleve admitted he held no expectation his reserves would play well against the Winnipegs under the Canadian code, but he expected his starters to have their way with the Winnipegs during the American half of the game. In his view, the entire weekend would serve as a sort of vacation for the team with some interesting game-play mixed in. For his part, Cleve would spend the weekend on a scouting expedition of future opponents in central and southern Minnesota where he would watch St. Olaf play Carleton in Northfield and St. John's play St. Mary's in Collegeville. In their final three games, in order, Concordia would face St. John's, St. Mary's, and St. Olaf.

When asked to describe the Cobbers for the *Winnipeg Tribune*, Hackenberg sent the following dispatch:

> "Concordia is a well balanced team. [They] have a flashy passing attack, some good power plays in which Bob Fritz and Ralph Miller figure, and some end sweeps in which Earl Moran, Pat Hilde or Eddie Dahl are the stars. Virtually the entire backfield can toss passes. Moran and Hilde do the kicking and the latter the place kicking. They have a super star in Fritz."

Blue and Gold (1933)

In Winnipeg, the *Winnipeg Free Press* introduced Bob Fritz as the "Red Grange of the Northwest" and "almost unstoppable at times." The *Tribune*, too, sized up Fritz:

> "Local fans will see a great backfield player when Bob Fritz trots onto the field tomorrow afternoon," the *Tribune* reported. "Weighing between 175 and 180, he was placed two years on all-Minnesota college elevens at fullback; and he was unanimously chosen. Fritz is a hard driver, tireless pounder of lines, adept at running the ends and is an exceptionally accurate passer. At times he is well nigh unstoppable and the morale of the team is highest when he is in action."

When asked about Fritz, Benson didn't hold back. He told the *Free Press*, "I really have a great ball player in Bob Fritz," he said. "He is brilliant defensively, can toss or take a pass, great blocker and hits the ball like a cannon. He is unquestionably the 'Red Grange' of our section." He told the *Tribune*, "I have a well balanced machine but it all pivots around Fritz and you will see today just how good that boy is. He is good every way you take him; he is just as good defensively as offensively... He hits the line low and hard and takes and tosses passes equally well. He is a ball player." As for the rest of the team, they are a "husky and large squad of athletes," noted the *Free Press*.

Like the other coaches before him, Benson understood how Concordia had a role in helping to promote football in Winnipeg. He told the *Tribune*, "I expect a tough game today and who wouldn't when going against a team having such well known players as Cronin, Rebholz, and Kabat. They're enough to make any team tremble." The Winnipeg newsmen noted how Concordia would arrive undefeated and unscored against in their last several games, and they promised an exciting game. "Both the Cobbers and locals have had several games under their belts and have reached the peak of form," said the *Tribune*.

South of the border, the *Concordian* defined the Winnipegs as "an independent amateur team which plays both American style football and rugby." The Winnipegs had gained a reputation for being a hybrid team that straddled the international playing codes. The newspaper described the Canadian game as "made up mostly of kicking, lateral and forward passing and spinner plays."

When Benson, his 28 men, and a trainer arrived in Winnipeg late Friday afternoon, they checked into the Marlborough Hotel, a nine-story, concrete-and-steel, Late Gothic Revival-style hotel with 24-foot ceilings, English stained glass, and carved, heavy oak beams and walnut wainscoting, with light fixtures in wrought iron by Tiffany of New York. The Winnipegs provided the Cobbers with free theater passes for their evening entertainment and on Saturday morning, the day of the game, the Winnipegs chartered a bus to give the Cobbers a sightseeing tour of the city.

An overnight rain had left pools of water on the field at Osborne Stadium, and as the Cobbers met the Winnipegs on the afternoon of October 21, 1933, they knew the game would be a mud bowl. Only a few hundred fans watched from the stands as they shivered in bone-chilling temperatures. Within the first 5 minutes of the first quarter, under American rules, Concordia recovered a blocked kick on Winnipeg's 35-yard line. The Cobbers then completed a long pass to the 3-yard line and Fritz, who started at right halfback, skirted the right end for a touchdown. Fritz kicked the extra point to put the Cobbers ahead.

On Concordia's next possession, Ralph Miller fumbled and lost the ball on Concordia's 40-yard line. Winnipeg's Carl Cronin then ran 20 yards around right end, completed a 17-yard pass to Herb Mobberley, and ran around the end again to score a 3-yard touchdown. Greg Kabat completed a pass to Cronin for the extra point to tie the game. Early in the second quarter, the Winnipegs fumbled and lost the ball at their own 27-yard line. After a series of line plunges, Pat Hilde bucked the line and scored a touchdown for Concordia.

In the second half, officials penalized Concordia 10 yards per play for six straight plays because they attempted to block for their backs. Later, officials forced a Cobbers player to sit out 5 minutes of the game in the penalty box for tackling around the neck. On the next play, the officials sat out yet another Cobbers player for the same reason, and so the

Blue and Gold (1933)

Cobbers played with only 10 men on the field under Canadian rules. Concordia did manage to regain possession of the ball but then found themselves without their center who sat in the penalty box, and so Coach Benson moved a guard to center. Later, Winnipeg had the ball and tried an end run, but just before the Cobbers could force the runner out of bounds he drop-kicked the ball from behind the line of scrimmage 60 yards downfield. The Cobbers didn't realize the ball was live and so they just watched as the Winnipegs raced downfield to recover it.

In the third quarter, under Canadian rules, Kabat completed a pass to Concordia's 28-yard line and then Russ Rebholz, who had intended to sit out the game while he nursed a cold, entered the fray for the first time. The "Wisconsin Wraith" proceeded to "outguess" the Cobbers. On a run, at least four Concordia players stood in his path, but Rebholz avoided them all, as well as the mud, and raced 28 yards for a touchdown in a clean uniform. The Winnipegs failed to score the extra point and the game sat tied.

In the final quarter, three times Winnipeg failed to score on rouge attempts from between Concordia's 10- and 20-yard line. The field had turned to muddy clay, which stuck to the ball, weighed it down, and made it difficult to punt far enough to score a rouge. After several attempts and with 2 minutes remaining in the game, officials gave the Winnipegs a dry ball and Kabat finally scored the rouge from the 27-yard line. In the final seconds, Concordia attempted to move the ball with a passing attack but fell short. Winnipeg won the game by the rouge 14-13.

Despite the Cobbers' weight advantage of 180 pounds per man to Winnipeg's 173, the Winnipegs had managed to cross Concordia's goal line—the first team to do so in several games.

Afterward, the Winnipegs treated the Cobbers to another round of theater tickets.

During the week after the game, Hackenberg met up with Benson at the lunch counter at the Bluebird Cafe on Center Avenue in Moorhead where Benson sat drinking a cherry Coke. Benson told Hackenberg, "That's the craziest cockeyed game I ever saw. Talk about nightmares. That second half was a whole herd of wild ones." Benson said several times he wanted to walk out and question a call the officials had made, but each time the Cobbers players would mob the officials with questions and Benson didn't want to compete with them. He said the officials eventually gave up trying to explain their rulings. Benson questioned whether Concordia had really lost the game. Canadian officials had scored the game 14-13 in favor of Winnipeg. Yes, Concordia had led 13-7 at the half under American rules, where a touchdown is 6 points and a kicked point after is worth 1 point. But in the second half, played under Canadian rules—where a touchdown is worth 5 points—the Canadian officials awarded the Winnipegs 6 points, instead. The Winnipegs missed the extra point but later scored a rouge. The final score should have been a 13-13 tie. The officials had erred in the same manner during previous contests between the Winnipegs and American colleges and they would continue to make the same mistake during future contests.

* *

The Montreal Mount Royals had scheduled a second game at De Lorimier Stadium with the Pere Marquette Knights of Columbus of Boston, a club that had a history of playing future, current, and former NFL teams, including the Hartford Blues (in 1925), New York Giants (1927), Providence Steam Roller (1928), Frankford Yellow Jackets (1928), Cleveland Indians (1931), and Orange A.C. Tornadoes (1931), but recent changes in the Boston-based fraternal organization had led the club to cancel its game with the Royals. The *Gazette* in Montreal claimed Marquette had "backed down after reports of the powerful showing of the Montreal eleven in its opening game" and that "the Marquette team is lighter than most professional football squads and officials declared they did not want to take chances of having any of their men injured by the husky Montreal front rank." More likely the Pere Marquettes felt a little disorganized with the recent resignations of their coach of seven years, manager of 17 years, and the loss of their home field at C.J. Lee Park in South Boston. Instead, the Mount Royals invited a 17-member team dubbed the Philadelphia Trojans up for a game. The *Gazette* reported the Trojans featured all former collegians from Southern California,

Blue and Gold (1933)

Alabama, Brown, Penn, and especially Purdue, and that the team's line averaged 220 pounds to the man.

In the meantime, Royals coach Charlie Strack signed a fullback, Pat Ryan, from the Portland Arrows, the Royals' first opponent. Ryan had played at New York University. Strack also signed Ben Langmard, the 6-foot-3, 200-pound former captain of the Williams College team in Williamstown, Massachusetts, for right halfback. In advance of the game, Strack worked on the team's passing game with Ryan on the throwing end.

On October 21, 1933, approximately 1,000 fans at De Lorimier Stadium in Montreal watched the game in a steady rain with the field under inches of water. In the first quarter, the Mount Royals reached the Trojans' 30-yard line when Bibber McCoy caught a 30-yard pass and crossed the goal line "with two Trojan tacklers clinging to his sturdy form," reported the *Gazette*. In the same period, Jack Spellman caught a 15-yard pass for the Royals and fell across the goal line for the score. In the second quarter, the Mount Royals scored a rouge on a punt from the Trojans' 40-yard line.

In the second half, which officials shortened due to the fading light of the evening downpour, the Mount Royals approached the Trojan goal line twice more but failed to score They fumbled and lost the ball on the first drive and threw an interception on the second drive.

A few days after the game, Louis Letourneau and Lucien Riopel, directors for the Mount Royals, announced the club would play in an eight-team international professional football league beginning in August 1934 that would include teams from New York, Boston, Brooklyn, Albany, Providence, and Philadelphia, as well as Montreal, with possible teams in Ottawa and Newark. The announcement conspicuously excluded Toronto because, reported the *Gazette*, "the failure of Lionel Conacher's Chefs to agree to meet the Mount Royals this season has prejudiced the local club against the inclusion of a Toronto team." The very next day, the team announced it would play the remainder of its 1933 schedule south of the border. The team cited poor weather, "snow and cold," and low gate receipts in Montreal, as well as "large guarantees for games" as the impetus for the decision. The report in the *Gazette* said the team would play its next game in Boston against a team dubbed the Saints, and then the Providence Steam Rollers, the Staten Island Stapletons, and the final two games in Atlantic City indoors in the Atlantic City Auditorium. The team would continue to organize the international pro league for next year.

It was all a lie, or high hopes. Instead, the "Three Musketeers" sent their professional wrestling-cum-football operation back to the United States to fend for themselves. It's not clear whether the team ever played the Steam Rollers, the Stapletons, or in Atlantic City, or even the Saints of Boston. The team did, however, play at least two more games under the wrestling-appropriate nickname Bone Crushers.

In a carnival tone, the *Lowell Sun* in Lowell, Massachusetts, reported on a game played in November 1933 between the Bone Crushers and the semi-professional Lowell Indians at Laurier Park, where several hundred spectators showed up to watch the wrestlers, led by "Masked Marvel" at quarterback, play the local boys in the snow. The Bone Crushers continued to wear their Mount Royals uniforms but instead of straight football, they put on a pro wrestling style show. At halftime, the Bone Crushers donned skates and skis, which led to a choreographed heated argument between Strack and the referee. The theatrical Bone Crushers beat the Indians 12-0.

Meanwhile, back in Canada, the manager of the Chicago Black Hawks, Tommy Gorman, announced he would field a professional football team in Ottawa in 1934 with Wally Masters of the Big Four's Ottawa Rough Riders as coach. The team would recruit college players from the Chicago area and be part of *les trois mousquetaires* proposed International Professional Football League. The *Gazette* reported, "Gorman, Lionel Conacher and Leo Dandurand yesterday conferred at the Canadien Hockey Club's headquarters and discussed football. The result was a set of ambitious plans for 1934." Ambitious, but scaled back. The proposed league had shrunk to six cities, with teams in Montreal, Ottawa, Toronto, Buffalo, Rochester, and Niagara Falls. "The Montreal team, backed by Canadiens, will be distinct from the Mount Royals," the *Gazette* reported. Clearly, the Canadian operation had divorced itself from the Mount Royals.

Blue and Gold (1933)

When the Bone Crushers played a game against the Medford Athletic Association at Fulton Street Playground in Boston on the Sunday of Thanksgiving Day weekend, the team had fully adopted the Bone Crushers moniker. The *Boston Globe* reported on the game but made no mention of the Mount Royals.

* *

While the Mount Royals had staged their final game in Montreal before heading south to become the Bone Crushers, Lionel Conacher and his Crosse & Blackwell Chefs took the field one last time in Toronto to play a team dubbed the Buffalo Bison. It's not clear whether the Buffalo squad otherwise played football.

In advance of the game, Conacher hired Gregg Swarthout, the top athlete for the Rochester Arpeakos, to play in the backfield for the Chefs. He also hired two linemen with the last names Cahill and Siebold from the Arpeakos to join the Toronto squad.

When the Chefs met the Bison in Toronto on October 21, 1933, intermittent heavy rains muddied up the field and in short order, nobody could tell the teams apart as the muck-covered players battled in the mire. In the first quarter, Buffalo drove to Toronto's 10-yard line, where the Bison battled near the goal line, but the Chefs forced a turnover on downs at the 3-yard line. On Toronto's next possession, Conacher scored a rouge with a kick to the deadline. When Buffalo later failed to return the ball out of the end zone, the Chefs scored another rouge. Later in the same period, Toronto scored its first touchdown on an option run with laterals from Charlie Conacher to Swarthout and from Swarthout to Lionel Conacher, with Lionel finishing the final 20 yards for the score. In the second quarter, Lionel Conacher intercepted a Buffalo pass and returned it 40 yards for a touchdown.

In the second half, Toronto blocked a Buffalo kick and fell on the ball in the end zone for a touchdown. In the final period, Buffalo started to open holes in the line, but when Conacher intercepted another pass attempt, the Chefs reached the Toronto 8-yard line. When Buffalo regained the ball, they took to the air, but the slippery ball led to a circus of fumbles. Late in the game, Swarthout made a 50-yard dash through the line, and then Nick Zellars, who had carried the ball many times on line plunges for the Chefs, took off on a long run. He reached the 1-yard line when the gun sounded and Toronto won the game 18-0.

*   *

By 1933, North Dakota State and North Dakota had cultivated a rivalry that stood on 40 separate battles between the two colleges and their football teams. As the *Grand Forks Herald* observed, "Interest in the event does not depend on the caliber of the teams anymore. Rivalry has become so intense supporters of neither team will make concessions no matter what the apparent outcome."

While North Dakota State used the Rockne system on offense, North Dakota employed the Warner system. South Dakota State had beaten them both but scored fewer points against the Bison. This meant the Bison stood as favorites and the Sioux would motivate themselves to play hard against their rivals. This is the logic North Dakota State Coach Casey Finnegan employed as he prepared his men to play the Sioux in Grand Forks during North Dakota's homecoming celebration. Neither team could hope for an NCC title, but the rivalry game would determine North Dakota's champion for 1933. The Sioux would also celebrate Ralph Pierce Day, named for the team's star backfielder in his final appearance on the home field. Pierce, a LaMoure, North Dakota, native had been the lead back for North Dakota and the lead punter in the conference. He held NCC records in the 100-yard dash (9.8 seconds) and 220-yard dash (21.8 seconds). Multiple newspapers repeated the idea that while North Dakota State enjoyed a superstar in Fritz Hanson, Pierce stood above the Perham Flash in running ability.

Despite the fact both Hanson and Pierce suffered lingering injuries, newspapers suggested their performances would decide the outcome of the game. The *Dakota Student* figured if the turf remained frozen Hanson would "get good footing to send him off on some of his long journeys toward the goal." *Dakota Student* sports columnist Irving Kupcinet, himself a Sioux halfback but with an injured wrist, suggested, "As long as

Blue and Gold (1933)

Fritz Hanson is able to run, the Bison will always have a threat, for 'little Fritzie' is the type of ball carrier who might break away at any time." North Dakota Coach Jack West believed if his team could stop Hanson, they could stop the Bison. The *Dakota Student* also talked up Bud Marquardt, "the A.C.'s star left end [who] has been known to snare passes that look far out of this rangy boy's reach."

Finnegan and assistant Bob Lowe had scouted the Sioux during North Dakota's 18-2 loss to South Dakota State in Brookings, and now the Bison practiced in secret, indoors until twilight, outdoors until dark, behind closed gates at Dacotah Field. The Bison didn't practice on the actual gridiron, however. Finnegan had ordered the field to be plowed under and made smooth for reseeding. The move had forced Fargo High School to move its home game against Moorhead High School to the grid at Moorhead State. The only alternative to Dacotah Field in Fargo remained the old Fargo College stadium south of Island Park. The college had closed its doors in 1922, its buildings now occupied by the Good Samaritan Institute, a Lutheran hospital, home, and school for "normal minded cripples." Fargo High preferred the Moorhead venue.

During a week of practices, the *Fargo Forum* reported that Finnegan focused on working out his linemen and a couple of sophomores had challenged Marquardt and Herb Peschel for starting positions. By the end of the week, however, Peschel had impressed Finnegan on both offense and defense.

Both the Bison and Sioux had suffered uncertain rosters throughout the season and now fielded young, injured squads depleted in part by players who hadn't returned to school. In fact, compared to 1932, the Bison now played a new man at every position on the line. At 180 pounds per man, the Bison front had reached its lowest weight in five years. Meanwhile, the Sioux had two sophomore ends who weighed less than 150 pounds apiece.

While North Dakota State had managed to survive its game in Superior with no serious new injuries, the Bison remained hobbled at multiple positions. North Dakota found itself in a similar state. Sioux players suffered from infections, injured knees, broken feet, broken wrists, torn ligaments, pulled muscles, and "charley horses." Worst of all, Pierce remained infirm. He had pulled a muscle in the game against Winnipeg and the injury lingered. Nevertheless, Coach West had played Pierce against South Dakota State "simply to bolster the morale," he said, and now he regretted that decision. And yet, West wanted Pierce on the field for the kickoff against the Bison for the same reason. West said it had been North Dakota's worst year for injuries and "our only hope is improvement among the cripples." He resorted to chalk talks and walk-throughs to allow his players to heal. West did have his linemen practice blocking, but with Memorial Field in Grand Forks covered in 6 inches of snow, the Sioux worked out inside beneath the stadium where they only had enough room for the offense or the defense to line up in formation, but not both. The chalk talks may have been the correct prescription for the Sioux, after all, as West blamed "stupid football" on North Dakota's loss to South Dakota State.

With the Sioux huddled indoors, the *Grand Forks Herald* waxed melodramatic. "The stadium was a bleak and cheerless sight," the paper said, "as the October gloom of late afternoon settled over a gridiron covered with 6 inches of snow, and a chilly northwest wind broke the silence with mournful notes as it swept around the corners of the huge pile of brick and concrete." West decided to wait until Friday to clear any snow from the field, with the hope that it might melt.

North Dakota's homecoming committee held a pep fest at the campus armory in Grand Forks on Thursday night, but then the temperature dropped, and for that reason and because they wanted the field to be in good condition for the varsity game, Finnegan and West agreed to call off the freshman game scheduled for Friday night. In its place, the homecoming committee rescheduled the annual Friday night bonfire to begin three hours early on the corner of Columbia Road and University Avenue, with 5,000 cubic feet of debris stacked 35-feet high near the stadium. Streetcars would carry rooters and the band downtown to "Hotel Corners" for the continued pep rally and snake dance.

The next morning, on October 28, 1933, the day of the game, a chartered train left Fargo at 9:00 a.m. filled with fans and the North Dakota State Gold Star Band. The band had raised money for the trip by selling tickets to a benefit concert held Thursday night in Festival Hall.

Blue and Gold (1933)

In Grand Forks, the school's freshmen and sophomores rose early or had stayed awake to participate in the traditional freshmen versus sophomores tug-of-war at 9:30 a.m. at the English Coulee. At 11:00 a.m., the school celebrated with a homecoming parade through the snow-covered streets of downtown Grand Forks and also East Grand Forks on the other side of the Red River. Thirty fans from Pierce's hometown of LaMoure, North Dakota, honored him in a ceremony where they presented him with a shotgun.

Snow fell Saturday morning, but workers cleared the field. Only 5,000 fans, less than half the projected figure, sat in the stands with Governor William Langer and with everyone in furs, blankets, and overshoes as the teams lined up for the kickoff. On slippery turf, Pierce took the field for the opening boot. Peschel started at left tackle while Hanson started at right halfback.

Throughout the game, both sides punted frequently to gain field position on the slippery field. The teams didn't wait until fourth down to punt and many times punted on second down. In the first quarter, the Bison stumbled to gain field position, even on punts, as a stiff wind blew the ball back toward the line of scrimmage.

After the Sioux recovered a Bison fumble at North Dakota State's 20-yard line, the Sioux drove to the goal line, but the Bison held and forced a turnover on downs. North Dakota State then punted out of its own end zone but a North Dakota player got his hand on the ball and it fell at the 8-yard line. Two plays later, the Sioux used a double reverse run to their reserve right halfback who scored over left end. Ralph Pierce came in to kick the extra point and the Sioux led 7-0.

In the second quarter, Fritz Hanson led the Bison on a long drive deep into North Dakota territory, but the Sioux held. On the ensuing drive, Wendy Schollander intercepted a Sioux pass and returned it to North Dakota's 41-yard line. Schollander carried the ball three times to gain 3 yards and on fourth down he completed a long pass to Hanson 21 yards through the air and beyond the Sioux defensive backs. Hanson scampered 20 yards down the sideline and outran Fritz Falgren for the score. Schollander kicked the extra point to tie up the score 7-7.

At North Dakota (Grand Forks, North Dakota)

Near the end of the first half, the Bison threatened to score again when Schollander stretched out a 20-yard run to North Dakota's 32-yard line. The Sioux dug in and held off the Bison drive.

At halftime, the 108-member Gold Star Band joined the 100-member North Dakota Concert Band band on the field for entertainment. The crowd also observed a 30-second period of silence to observe the death of Mike Geston, the team's 1927 football captain who had died Thursday from injuries suffered in an automobile accident.

In the third quarter, Hanson returned a punt 38 yards before Pierce managed to tackle him. Later in the quarter, the Sioux drove to the Bison 30-yard line where they fumbled and lost the ball. In the fourth quarter, North Dakota State intercepted a North Dakota pass and returned the ball to the Sioux 38-yard line. Two plays later, the Bison reached the 12-yard line and after the Sioux dug in and allowed only six more yards on the ground, Schollander reached Bud Marquardt on a pass in the end zone. The ball hit the tips of Marquardt's fingers but a Sioux player knocked the ball away and North Dakota took possession. In the final minutes, Falgren intercepted a Bison pass and the Sioux tried a desperate passing game until the game ended. The teams finished in a 7-7 tie, their first draw since 1905. Throughout the game, snowball fights between Sioux and Bison fans erupted in the stands, but like the game itself, the fights ended in a draw.

Peschel played an outstanding game at tackle while Leo Gerteis, the substitute fullback for the Bison and the former Fargo football star who worked the night shift full-time while he attended North Dakota State, called signals in the game for the first time. When George May had left the game injured, Marquardt filled in at punter and performed well, despite the wind. Hanson had left the game injured in the third quarter. Until his injury, Hanson had been "the outstanding back on the field," wrote *Fargo Forum* sportswriter Eugene Fitzgerald, "scintillating with brilliant runs even though he was deprived of his greatest offensive weapon, wide end runs, and handicapped by treacherous underfooting." Pierce remained ineffective throughout the game.

After the game, alumni from both North Dakota and North Dakota State gathered at the campus armory for the homecoming dance. Because

Blue and Gold (1933)

the game had ended in a draw, the attendees left their partisan feelings at the door.

In the *Dakota Student*, Kupcinet criticized his team's use of the Warner system. He said the offensive scheme "is almost useless on an icy field" while "the double wing back system is a total failure. It is almost impossible for the halfback to come around behind the line, get the ball from the fullback, and then run up the designated spot of attack... The conditions of the field were more favorable to the A.C. than to the U; and we make that comment not from a biased point of view, but merely from what is known in football circles. On a dry field, the Sioux attack would have been given much more opportunity to operate." It's not clear whether Kupcinet criticized or parroted Coach West in his remarks.

* *

When Earl Jackson made the trip to Moorhead from Fergus Falls, Minnesota, in late October, he may have had little or no idea about the hostility that stood between Concordia and St. John's in athletics. Jackson had only been the football and basketball coach in Fergus Falls for several weeks, and when Concordia athletic director Frank Cleve asked if Jackson could referee the upcoming football game in Moorhead between the two schools, Jackson agreed. After all, Jackson had officiated in that area before, for a game between North Dakota State and North Dakota.

A member of the Illinois association of officials, Jackson had lettered in football while attending Lawrence College in Appleton, Wisconsin. He went on to coach four different championship track teams at Carleton before he took a job in Galesburg, Illinois, where he coached various athletic teams at Knox College for 10 years. In 1929, he took over the Prairie Fire football program at Knox and led the team to a 7-1 record. The following spring, he took a leave of absence to study and learn more about football, track, and physical training at Stanford. When he returned, he led the Prairie Fire to records of 5-2-1, 3-5-1, and 0-8 from 1930 to 1932. It's not clear whether the alumni chased him out of Galesburg or if he escaped.

Blue and Gold (1933)

Historically, Concordia had been the goliath in the contest with the Johnnies. Concordia had either tied or beaten St. John's in every contest since 1927. But now, the Johnnies would travel to Moorhead as the reigning MIAC champions and no opponent had crossed their goal line in 12 consecutive games. Only Concordia had made St. John's sweat in 1932 when the Cobbers played the Johnnies to a scoreless tie. Now in 1933, the Johnnies had finished their first two conference games in disappointing ties against Hamline University of St. Paul and St. Mary's. Teams in the MIAC had collectively tallied six ties in conference games thus far in 1933, which left five teams undefeated and in contention for the conference title.

Cleve had watched St. Mary's play at St. John's in Collegeville. He found St. Mary's fielded a tough defense but couldn't gain ground on offense against St. John's. The Johnnies had a big line that averaged 183 pounds per man with the heaviest player, a tackle, at 201 pounds. Collectively, the team weighed just over one ton at 2,017 pounds. They had two first-team and two second-team all-conference players on the line as well as all-conference Gus Luckemeyer at fullback. Reserve halfbacks Joe Marx and Walt Johnson had run 100-yard dashes in the 10-second range. Cleve had observed how the Johnnies offense executed plays with precision, but still St. Mary's held them at bay. The Johnnies, Cleve surmised, might be Concordia's toughest opponent in their quest for a conference title. He spelled out one simple goal for his men: Cross the Johnnies' goal line.

While the Cobbers had escaped serious injury in their game in Winnipeg, Cleve remained doubtful whether Earl Moran, the triple-threat quarterback from Moorhead High School, had healed enough to play. Moran had suffered a knee injury against Macalester, so Cleve played Moran's Moorhead Spuds teammate Pat Hilde at quarterback instead. Hilde suffered from a "trick knee," too, but handled it better than Moran. Homecoming presented the final opportunity for Moran and Hilde, both seniors, to play football in front of the home crowd, but "I absolutely will not use Moran unless all the other backs break their legs," Cleve said. He held out hope Moran might recover for the later games against St. Mary's and St. Olaf. Meanwhile, Cleve worked out Hilde in the passing game.

Blue and Gold (1933)

On October 28, 1933, the Concordia choir opened homecoming festivities with a concert in Concordia's chapel. Afterward, alumni and friends gathered in the dining halls for lunch before they walked to the parade. At 1:00 p.m., the procession wound its way through downtown Moorhead and over the river onto Front Street [now Main Street] in Fargo and then up Broadway. The only game in town, Concordia's homecoming contest attracted 1,800 fans. Bob Fritz started at fullback.

In the first quarter, St. John's drove to the Concordia 18-yard line where the Cobbers forced a field goal attempt. Luckemeyer, who suffered a concussion on the drive, attempted the field goal kick but the ball sailed short and wide and slid toward the sideline. Luckemeyer later said he had no memory of the kick.

Later that same period, St. John's reached Concordia's 2-yard line and on the next play, the Johnnies rushed over the goal line. The head linesman signaled a touchdown but then reversed his decision and said the runner had stopped in front of the goal line, which forced a turnover on downs. Hilde then punted the ball out of the end zone for field position. The Johnnies returned the ball to Concordia's 7-yard line, but officials called a penalty against St. John's and forced a re-kick.

In the second half, Hilde returned the opening kickoff 74 yards to St. John's 18-yard line. On the next play, Concordia fumbled but kept the ball for a 2-yard loss. In the scramble for the ball a Johnnies player threw himself on top of the downed Cobbers ball-holder and the Johnnies drew a penalty for unnecessary roughness for piling on, which put the Cobbers on St. John's 3-yard line. Hilde ran the ball again to the 1-foot line, and then the Johnnies stopped "Dynamiting Bob Fritz" for no gain. Officials penalized both teams for offsides and so play continued with a repeat of second down. On the next play, Fritz plunged again and gained 6 inches, and on third down he charged to reach the 1-inch line. On fourth down, Fritz plunged again. In the *Moorhead Daily News*, Dick Hackenberg described what happened next:

> "Fritz blasted into those stalwart defenders with all the drive at his command. The Johnnies massed for the plunge. There was a pileup over Fritz's body. The whistle

blew. Referee Earl Jackson began to untangle the players. On the bottom of the pile the ball rested solidly on the line, its tip projecting a bare 2 inches over."

The Cobbers failed to score the extra point, but an opponent had crossed St. John's goal line for the first time in more than a dozen games, and the Johnnies found themselves down 0-6.

After the score, both teams engaged in a punting duel. The Johnnies sagged on offense while the Cobbers knocked down or intercepted passes to keep St. John's in its own territory. Late in the game, the Cobbers reached St. John's 18-yard line but Hilde missed on a field goal attempt and the Cobbers beat the Johnnies 6-0.

Afterward, Hackenberg said the Cobbers owed their victory to the "demon defensive work of Bob Fritz who gave as beautiful an exhibition of backing up a line as spectators will see all year. He was in every play [and] made countless tackles all afternoon." The loss all but assured St. John's could not repeat as conference champions.

After the game, Cleve shared that St. John's Coach Joe Benda had told him the Johnnies had "played their best game of the year," which only increased Concordia's accomplishment in Cleve's eyes.

And then, "like a bolt out of a clear blue sky," he said, Cleve received notice that the St. John's athletic board had severed athletic relations with Concordia, for all sports, including scheduled basketball games, for an indefinite period. The noticed stated, "As a player and a coach, you know the cause of this rupture," but the notice did not give a specific reason. Many St. John's fans blamed the officials for the outcome of the game, and because Cleve had selected the officials, St. John's opted for divorce. A United Press report said Coach Benda claimed he hadn't been consulted when choosing the officials, but Cleve had written Benda to inform him about the officials, with no reply.

Throughout the game, Jackson, the referee, had entered into frequent arguments with the umpire, head linesman, and the captains of the rival teams over rules and penalties.

Concordia president J.N. Brown sent a letter to St. John's and demanded specific reasons for the severed relationship. Newspaper reports out of Collegeville hinted St. John's had felt suspicious about officials in several past athletic contests played at Concordia. Cleve responded to the accusations and told the *Fargo Forum*, "We have always used highly recommended officials for all our home games," he said. "We always have tried to be fair in the selection of our officials and it was for that reason, so there would be no arguments, that I went out of Fargo and Moorhead to get a referee for the game Saturday with St. John's." He continued, "Jackson used to officiate in the University of North Dakota-North Dakota Agricultural College games and was satisfactory. To my mind that is one of the hardest games in which to officiate and if Jackson was good enough for those games he should be good enough to work in our games.

"I cannot understand the action of St. John's," Cleve continued. "I distinctly remember losing a one-point decision in basketball to St. John's in 1930. The game was to decide the conference title and was played in Moorhead. We lost and that was all there was to it. There were no alibis forthcoming from us."

Hackenberg suggested St. John's had exhibited a history of poor sportsmanship. "We have it on good authority," he wrote, "that St. John's hasn't been on speaking terms with St. Olaf ever since the Oles drubbed the Johnnies by an excessive score some years back."

Jackson issued his own statement on the officiating team's work. "Penalties were numerous in that game," he said, "but if the penalties are totaled for each team, I think you will find Concordia lost the most yardage because of them." The umpire for the game, P.E Mickelson, and the head linesman, Don Gates, both of Fargo, backed up Jackson's statement. Moorhead State Coach Sliv Nemzek and North Dakota State Coach Casey Finnegan confirmed they had never had a problem with the work of the officials, whom had officiated games throughout the area during the season.

* *

To keep the team fresh, and in an attempt to earn more gate receipts, the Winnipeg Rugby Club scheduled an "Appreciation Day" exhibition game against the Manitoba and YMHA junior-level teams. When fans turned out for "booster rugby" on October 28, 1933, the MRFU champion Winnipegs played weak. In advance of the club's pending WCRFU semifinal game against the Regina Roughriders, Americans Carl Cronin and Greg Kabat did not play, and neither did local veteran Rosy Adelman. Coach Cronin had flown to Regina to scout their future opponent.

In the first half, the collegians held the Winnipegs to a 2-0 lead. In the second half, the Winnipegs outplayed YMHA and won the game 9-0. Russ Rebholz did most of the work out of the backfield for the Winnipegs. However, despite the fact the Winnipegs fielded the best of both the Winnipegs and the Shamrocks on their starting line, the team provided little support for Rebholz's efforts. The performance did little to fire up the small crowd that watched from the stands at Osborne Stadium.

* *

With so many injuries in the Bison backfield and with Fritz Hanson still hobbled by an ankle sprain, Moorhead State football coach Sliv Nemzek did not fear North Dakota State's ground game. So far in 1933, the Bison had largely used an aerial attack, with Hanson on the receiving end, to move the ball. Twice those passes had led Hanson to race for a touchdown. Meanwhile, the Dragons had not allowed a rushing touchdown yet in 1933, and the Bison had not scored more than one offensive touchdown in any one game. To get ready for the Bison, the Dragons needed to prepare to defend against the pass.

Long after darkness fell, the Moorhead State Dragons practiced by moonlight. Nemzek had his starters scrimmage against the reserves, and Nemzek himself played the role of Bison quarterback Wendy Schollander in North Dakota State's offensive scheme. Nemzek, who could toss fast, accurate passes, ran through each player's assignments on defense over and over again, and he showed them how to match up against an offense with a proficient passing game. Afterward, they broke for a late dinner. Nemzek knew his men still needed more work, so he told them to return to the gymnasium for chalk talks and dummy drills. Nemzek had a long

Blue and Gold (1933)

list of items to focus on during practice. They needed to block better. They needed to clear holes on wide runs for their star runner, Lyle Glass. His halfbacks needed to learn how to protect the punter. And his ends needed to learn how to race downfield to get under kicked balls. Nemzek had *played* for North Dakota State. He treated the game as a personal matter.

Meanwhile, Dragons fans, students, faculty, and alumni had done their math homework. In their minds, it didn't look good for the Bison. Already in 1933, Moorhead State had played Concordia to a scoreless tie, and Concordia had played North Dakota State to a scoreless tie. South Dakota State had beaten North Dakota State and also Northern Normal. Moorhead State beat Northern Normal. Fans in Moorhead believed they had good reason to look forward to the school's homecoming celebration when the Dragons would defend their lair against the Bison.

But Moorhead State fielded a young team. Winless in three games, they had just come off a 2-0 loss to the Bemidji State Teachers College Beavers in Bemidji, where they had to climb a snowbank to reach the football field, and where the locals had used a horse-drawn snow plow to clear the gridiron. Wintry conditions had delayed the arrival of an official from Duluth and so the Dragons and Beavers waited an extra hour before kickoff. To finish the game before dark, officials reduced the length of the game to 12 minutes per period. They played in sleet and wind and in ankle-deep snow.

Temperatures fell in Moorhead. While Nemzek continued to work on defending the pass, North Dakota State Coach Casey Finnegan had his quarterback, Schollander, throwing passes.

New injuries plagued both teams. Bison backfielder George May walked on crutches. Bud Marquardt's brother, Bob, who played center for the Dragons, had suffered a broken nose, but expected to play. Hanson, with his limp, reported for practice late in the week.

For homecoming, over 200 alumni returned to the Moorhead State campus, where a new dragon lit in neon hung over the doorway of MacLean Hall. A large crimson dragon protected the gates to the campus, while two smaller dragons breathed fire nearby. The light posts on campus fluttered with crimson and white pennants and their lamps cast red light through red cellophane-covered globes.

By midday Friday, so much snow had fallen that both the Fargo and Moorhead high schools and the Bison freshman teams had to cancel their games due to poor travel conditions. Only the Dragons and Bison varsity teams committed to play in a potential blizzard.

On a cold and snowy Friday night, Moorhead State partisans attended the coronation of the homecoming queen in Weld Hall. They walked in a torchlight parade through soft, falling snow to the gates on 11th Street and stood by a bonfire to watch fireworks shoot skyward as the snow fell earthward.

Overnight, more than 6 inches of snow accumulated and continued to fall on Saturday morning, November 4, 1933, when the homecoming parade began on time at 10:15 a.m. Meanwhile, snow plows cleared the gridiron for the game.

In the afternoon, fans crunched through quiet snow to Memorial Field. Students from North Dakota State showed their registration cards to gain free admission, which Finnegan had arranged for, and everyone sat while the brand-new public address system announced the lineups for both sides. The field remained slippery and snow-covered. Nemzek expected they would play with a wet ball that would take away the Bison passing game.

The Bison ran. In the first quarter, Erling Schranz carried the ball 48 yards on a drive to Moorhead State's 5-yard line, but the Dragons dug in to prevent an early score. In the second quarter, Hanson returned a punt 48 yards to the end zone but officials penalized the Bison for clipping and called the play back. With only 15 seconds remaining in the half, on fourth down with 8 yards to go from the Dragon 22-yard line, the Bison called a forward-lateral play. Schollander completed a short pass to end Acey Olson, who then tossed it back to Hanson, who then streaked 15 yards down the sideline and juked several tacklers to reach the end zone for a touchdown.

At halftime, both the Moorhead State band and the Gold Star Band, together over 160 members strong, took the field and marched in combined letter formations.

Blue and Gold (1933)

In third quarter, the Dragons punted from their own end zone, but it fell short at their own 12-yard line. On the ensuing drive, Schollander completed an 8-yard pass to Marquardt for the score. Early in the fourth quarter, Schollander kept the ball for himself and carried several Dragon tacklers with him as he ran the ball 12 yards behind his tackle for a third touchdown. After North Dakota State got the ball back, the Bison fumbled and lost the ball on their own 27-yard line. Moorhead State halfback Lyle Glass then ran the ball 11 yards for a first down, but on the next play, he fumbled and lost the ball. When the desperate Dragons got the ball back, they launched an aerial attack and moved into scoring territory, but Glass fumbled and lost the ball again. The game ended with the Bison beating the Dragons 20-0.

Overall, the Bison exhibited superior blocking and Herb Peschel played an outstanding game at tackle to help Schranz to gain on runs of 48 and 23 yards around the end. The Dragons did not gain a single first down until the fourth quarter when Finnegan put in his reserves.

After the game, the downtrodden Dragons attended a banquet in Comstock Hall followed by the homecoming dance in the gymnasium.

* *

When Winnipeg Rugby Club Coach Carl Cronin had traveled to Regina to watch the Roughriders play in the SRFU final, he saw the Roughriders earn their 16th title in that region that day, with an 11-0 victory over the Moose Jaw Millers. As a result, and as expected, the MRFU champion Winnipegs would host the Roughriders for the WCRFU semifinal. Just about anyone with any common sense favored Regina to win. The Roughriders had won the WCRFU semifinal for the past seven seasons and had competed for the Grey Cup during the past five. The 1925 season featured the last and only time an MRFU winner had won the WCRFU semifinal and gone on to compete for the Grey Cup, back when the Winnipeg Rugby Club had been the Winnipeg Tammany Tigers. Because the Roughriders dominated football in Western Canada, the *Winnipeg Free Press* dubbed the Roughriders "The Perennial Champions of the West." Fans in Winnipeg needed their team to break the "Regina Jinx."

Cronin had a plan. During his return trip to Winnipeg, he organized an arduous four days of practice for his men. They would drill through offensive and defensive plays for hours until they could execute them with precision. And they would practice protecting the pass and the kick. He had 30 men to choose from for a game-day roster of 20, but he wouldn't choose the finalists until the last minute.

Cronin moved the club's practices and upcoming game from Osborne Stadium to Carruthers Park, the soccer field in Winnipeg's north end, because the turf at Osborne Stadium remained in rough condition. To make up for the venue change, Joe Ryan put Osborne Stadium officials in charge of ticket sales throughout the city. No local radio station planned to broadcast the game, perhaps due to the venue change, and fans turned out in droves for advanced tickets. Adults paid $1.00 for a reserved seat or 75 cents for general admission, with a 25-cent charge for parking. Children could attend for 25 cents. In response to high demand, the Winnipegs offered standing room only tickets for 25 cents each. On the day of the game, November 4, 1933, Barry Bain, president of the Winnipeg club, expressed the hope of Winnipegers when he said, "We have a deep down hunch today that the lengthy Roughrider reign will be terminated."

Winnipegers had reason to hope. As *Winnipeg Free Press* columnist W.G. Allen pointed out, the Winnipegs fielded more talent in 1933 than in previous years with the addition of Greg Kabat and also former members of the St. John's Rugby Football Club. Allen failed to mention, however, that the University of Manitoba had placed its athletic programs in stasis in 1933 and so the Winnipegs had absorbed interested players from that organization, too. At least seven Manitoba Bisons alumni and one undergraduate student played with the team in 1933. Allen pointed out that the Winnipegs had not experienced a serious injury, and he noted, "Against United States college teams of no mean calibre, the Winnipegs have shown both power on defense and versatility in attack." The Canadians fielded Americans, and they had played against Americans.

On the day of the game, the Roughriders arrived in Winnipeg at 8:00 a.m. via the Canadian National Railroad. Curt Schave, the team's backfield leader, limped his way to the Fort Garry hotel where the maitre d' Alfred

Blue and Gold (1933)

Banyon, known as "The Great Zanzig," greeted the team with his magician's flair. The Roughriders took a nap and ate a meal, but with a return train scheduled for 9:00 p.m., the Roughriders planned to remain in Winnipeg a total of 13 hours.

Carruthers Park greeted the teams and their fans with a snow-covered field in a blizzard. In the first quarter, the Winnipegs kicked off against a headwind. The teams held a punting duel until the Roughriders threatened to score but then settled for a rouge by Phat DeFrate. Later that same period, the Winnipegs punted into the end zone. The Roughriders tried but failed to return the kick, and so the Winnipegs scored a rouge to tie the game. Kabat later scored yet another rouge. At the end of the first quarter, Cronin completed a 25-yard pass and on the next play, he ran around right end and carried three tacklers with him to reach the 20-yard line. Kabat then kicked another rouge.

In the second half, Cronin kicked a rouge. Unable to gain ground rushing, the Roughriders switched to passing and completed two pass attempts for 27 yards, but the drive stalled. The Winnipegs then drove into Roughrider territory where Kabat scored another rouge as the quarter ended.

In the fourth quarter, when the Winnipegs had the Roughriders pinned back at Regina's 8-yard line, DeFrate kicked the ball to midfield. Russ Rebholz, who had sat out injured, entered the game. He ran 35 yards off the left side of the formation and slipped and skidded his way past tacklers until a handful of Roughriders brought him down at the 17-yard line. Rebholz suffered reinjury on the play and left the game. When Regina gained the ball back, they punted to midfield, and Kabat punted it right back. Winnipeg then blocked Regina's answer kick at the 10-yard line and on the next play, Cronin ran 9 yards through a big hole to reach the 1-yard line. On his next attempt, he leapt over the linemen for the score. In the late minutes, the Roughriders continued their aerial attack but completed only 2 of 5 pass attempts and threw 2 interceptions. When the final gun sounded, the Winnipegs had beaten Regina 11-1. They had dispelled the "Regina Jinx" and won the WCRFU semifinal match. "The cheer that went up as the final gun sounded must have been heard [140 miles away] in Brandon," wrote Dave Dryburgh in the *Leader-Post*. "Winnipeg had saved up that cheer for eight years."

Despite the change of venue, the players had experienced poor footing on the snow-covered field, and the Winnipegs held the Roughriders to just 4 yards rushing the entire game. Schave did not play while De Frate completed 5 of 12 pass attempts for Regina. Winnipeg blocked 3 Roughrider kicks. Coach Cronin didn't call any trick plays in the game and the Winnipegs won with near-perfect play execution and with Cronin the main ground-gainer. As Dryburgh observed, "[Cronin] could hold his feet, while others slid around, taking short strides and pivoting and squirming to break tackle after tackle." The *Leader-Post* summed up the game in a staff editorial that read, "Four measly yards just once. Every other buck was smothered on the spot, and end runs, well, they might have done better on skates, which is no alibi. If Winnipeg players could stay on their feet there was no excuse for the Roughriders."

* *

The Cobbers had escaped serious injuries in their game against St. John's, except for Carroll "Shorty" Malvey, who had walked away from the scrum with his faced scratched up pretty bad. More than anything, Coach Frank Cleve felt his backfielders could have blocked better against the Johnnies.

In advance of Concordia's game against St. Mary's, Earl Moran returned to the practice field but Coach Cleve made him sit out offensive drills to protect him from tackles. Moran had missed two games after he wrenched his knee against Macalester. But then Cleve allowed Moran to play defensive halfback, and when Moran planted his foot to make a turn to cover a pass receiver, he twisted his knee once again. Moran collapsed in pain and his teammates carried him off the field. A senior, Moran would sit out the remainder of his college career. Cleve told Moran's former Moorhead High School Spuds teammate Pat Hilde to take over passing and kicking duties for the rest of the season.

St. Mary's had played St. John's to a scoreless tie and then enjoyed a bye week before their pending game against the Cobbers. Cleve knew the

Blue and Gold (1933)

Cardinals would hold their ground, led by one of their own, Nicholas J. "Nic" Musty, a three-time letter-winner in football for the Cardinals and a standout at end. The 1929 St. Mary's graduate had taken the head coaching job in 1932 after three seasons as an assistant.

Twenty-two Cobbers, including the injured Moran, departed Moorhead by bus at 9:00 a.m. Friday morning. The team stayed in Minneapolis Friday night and then traveled down to Winona on Saturday morning. A sports editor from the *Concordian* rode along with the team and the newspaper tasked him with sending a play-by-play back to Moorhead using a direct wire. Fans paid 15 cents apiece to sit in the Concordia chapel and listen to the results of each play. When the Cobbers arrived at St. Mary's on November 4, 1933, they found the field in good condition. Winona had escaped the snow and rain that had hit other parts of the region. When the teams took the field, Bob Fritz started at fullback.

In the first quarter, St. Mary's used a quick kick to punt the ball out of bounds at Concordia's 1-yard line. Concordia chose not to attempt a run or pass and instead opted to punt the ball away for better field position. Because the end zone at St. Mary's spanned 2 yards short of regulation, the officials placed the ball 3 yards further from the goal line to give Hilde room to punt. He launched his kick but the Cardinals blocked it and the ball fell back to the 1-yard line where Hilde recovered the ball. The officials ruled that the Cardinals had scored a safety because they now had to move the ball back again 3 yards after the play. Concordia found themselves down 0-2. It was the first time in eight games a team had scored against the Cobbers.

In the second quarter, Concordia tried an aerial attack. Hilde completed 2 passes for 15 yards each but those two passes accounted for the entirety of Concordia's first downs in the first half.

In the second half, Concordia started hot. Fritz smashed past the Cardinals tackles for decent gains while Ralph Miller raced around the ends and Hilde completed passes. Concordia completed 9 of 25 pass attempts for 80 yards in the game. Twice in the second half Concordia moved the ball into St. Mary's territory but missed on field goal attempts. Hilde attempted both placekicks, the first from the 15-yard line, which sailed wide, and the second from the 2-yard line, which the Cardinals blocked. When the final second ticked off the official's watch, St. Mary's walked off victorious 2-0. The Cardinals had defended their turf for the win and had knocked Concordia out of conference title contention.

After the game, Fritz revealed he had injured his face in the first quarter. He hadn't told anyone at the time, but when the team returned to Moorhead an x-ray revealed he had broken his jaw, which sidelined Fritz for the remainder of the season.

* *

Coach Casey Finnegan's North Dakota State football teams had never lost a game to South Dakota, but the season's late autumn snows now threatened to derail his plans. Finnegan had hoped to fill his short week of practices with full-contact scrimmages, but the snow had piled up too deep on Dacotah Field. Instead, he had his players run in sweats and sneakers around the indoor track inside the physical education building, and in the gymnasium they walked through defensive assignments and ran through offensive play execution for passing, spinner plays, and line-bucking plunges. But it wasn't enough. His players needed a true scrimmage to develop the muscle memory needed for timing and execution. Finnegan arranged for his players to stop in Sioux City, Iowa, the day before the game for a real practice on Bass Field at Morningside. They would spend the night there and leave for Vermillion at 9:30 a.m. Saturday morning for the 2:00 p.m. kickoff.

When the 26 Bison players and their coaches emptied the bus and took the field Saturday afternoon, November 11, 1933, they stood on the sideline across from a Coyotes team with six linemen at least 6 feet tall and more than 195 pounds apiece. In an effort to increase fan attendance, South Dakota had reduced ticket prices for the game from $1.10 per person to just 75 cents, but fan enthusiasm had waned and the stands at Inman Field sat nearly empty. When Finnegan clapped his hands for his men to take the field, Herb Peschel started at right tackle, Bud Marquardt started at left end, and Fritz Hanson, even though he felt sick, started at right halfback.

Blue and Gold (1933)

Immediately after the opening kickoff, Wendy Schollander stood at midfield and completed a long pass to Hanson who caught the ball at South Dakota's 10-yard line. Hanson slipped by several potential tacklers and scored a touchdown.

Throughout the remainder of the half, the Coyotes played uninspired football, which confirmed earlier reports that the players continued to demand that their coach Stanley Backman should resign from his position. The school newspaper, the *Volante*, said the squad lacked interest and failed to train, and "men who do not care a whoop about training are wrecking a brilliant team." Meanwhile, the Bison gained considerable ground but failed to score again before the break.

In the second half, the Coyotes keyed on Hanson and stopped him for losses. And then, on offense, South Dakota reached North Dakota State's 7-yard line on a 37-yard run, but officials called the play back on a penalty. In the fourth quarter, after Schollander broke his ankle, Finnegan moved Acey Olson from end to halfback and moved Peschel to end. The Bison drove 58 yards to South Dakota's 2-yard line and then smashed through for a touchdown. Marquardt kicked the extra point and the Bison beat the Coyotes 14-0. North Dakota State had secured second place in the NCC.

In this game, multiple Bison backs gained considerable ground and Marquardt cemented his reputation as the best punter in the NCC. Finnegan had kept Marquardt in the game on most plays.

Afterward, Finnegan told the *Spectrum* he credited the team's esprit de corps on the field for their performance. "Most teams that I have associated with," he said, "usually pat a man on the back and say, 'better luck next time' when the player misses a tackle. But my 1933 crew of outlaws just lights on the player and pans him so much he doesn't dare ever again fall down in his playing assignment." He shared how the linemen routinely tell jokes, mostly puns, at the line of scrimmage.

* *

With Earl Moran and Bob Fritz out for the season, a diminished Concordia squad would face St. Olaf for a share of second place in the MIAC. No one could replace Fritz, especially on defense. To avoid more injuries, Coach Frank Cleve gave his Cobbers the day off on Monday to process their loss to St. Mary's. When they returned to practice on Tuesday, Cleve told them not to dress. Instead, he and Louie Benson assembled the players around the blackboard. They mapped out plays, and later in the week, the men dressed in sweats and sneakers and walked through those plays.

Cleve had watched St. Olaf play Carleton. He felt the Oles had outplayed the Knights and that Carleton had won on one play, a 70-yard punt return for a touchdown. The Oles featured Slippery Syl Saumer who had enrolled at St. Olaf again after a year out of college. Like Fritz at Concordia, Saumer had faced dropping out of school again in 1933 due to the cost of college but St. Olaf figured something out and he remained enrolled and in football.

Only 800 fans braved the cold weather in Northfield on Armistice Day, November 11, 1933, for a game between the black-and-gold Oles and the maroon-and-gold Cobbers. Late in the first quarter, the Cobbers returned a punt to their own 45-yard line. At the end of a long drive, Pat Hilde went over center for a touchdown. The Oles responded with a 70-yard off tackle run for a score.

In the second quarter, St. Olaf returned a punt to Concordia's 30-yard line. After a series of runs, the Oles fullback plunged over from the 3-yard line for a touchdown. Later in the same period, the Oles blocked a Cobber punt and took over at Concordia's 11-yard line. Saumer then slid around left end for a touchdown.

In the third quarter, the Ole backs carried the ball over 100 yards, including on a 97-yard drive. The long advance ended in a fumble and a touchback, however, and St. Olaf failed to cross the goal line for a score. In the fourth quarter, the Oles recovered a Cobbers fumble on Concordia's 25-yard line. Three plays later the Oles ran in a touchdown. Saumer completed a pass for the extra point.

Near the end of the game, the Cobbers took to the air and moved the ball to St. Olaf's 6-yard line where Hilde reached in for the final score. In the end the Cobbers lost the struggle 25-13 and finished the season tied for fourth in the conference

*

Blue and Gold (1933)

After more than a week in bed at St. Luke's Hospital in Moorhead, Bob Fritz returned to school. With wires inside his mouth to keep his jawbones in place, he attended Concordia's annual football banquet where he had to skip the beef tenderloin, mashed potatoes, and pumpkin pie and instead drank a glass of fruit juice and a glass of eggnog.

During the banquet, Cleve recounted the Cobber season, and he noted that in his nine years as Concordia's football coach, only St. Mary's had scored a safety against one of his teams, and they had scored it on the Cobbers' only blocked punt on the season.

With his jaw wired shut, Fritz had an excuse not to give a speech when Cleve announced Fritz had earned all-conference honors at fullback, his third year in a row on the mythical team. Fritz had earned a spot on the all-conference team at fullback in 1931, at halfback in 1932, and at fullback again in 1933. After four seasons at Concordia, including his freshman season in 1929, Fritz would hang up his cleats. He expected he would focus entirely on finishing his studies. However, a few days later, Fritz learned the MIAC had changed its eligibility rules in a way that would allow him to play football one more year at Concordia. Due to the cost of attending school, Fritz had missed several semesters, and the conference had decided that an athlete would remain eligible as long as he had not been in school for more than four full years. Fritz planned to return to play football in 1934.

* *

Frigid weather had forced the Winnipeg Rugby Club to practice indoors. Coach Carl Cronin used the opportunity to step through every play in Winnipeg's game against Regina and to explain the mistakes the Winnipegs had made. He also shared what he knew about the Calgary Altomah Indians, their next opponent. On Armistice Day, the Winnipegs and Indians would play for the WCRFU title and the Hugo Ross Trophy in Winnipeg.

Since 1911, no team from Calgary had won the WCRFU title, but this year, an American, Dave Jowett, who had played college football at Gonzaga University and for the Western Army service team during the

Bob Fritz

Blue and Gold (1933)

Great War, now coached Calgary's entry into the playoffs. The Winnipegs would face another formidable test in their quest to claim the western football title. The Indians would bring 33 men to Winnipeg and a starting line that weighed an average of 200 pounds per man.

Later in the week, the Winnipegs moved their practices outdoors where Greg Kabat worked out the linemen harder than he had all year. He had the halfbacks run plays again and again. Meanwhile, Cronin kept his men guessing until game day about who would start against Calgary.

At 8:00 a.m. on the morning of the game, November 11, 1933, workers at Carruthers Park began to clear snow for the 2:30 p.m. kickoff. With the promise of warmer weather, over 3,000 fans had purchased tickets, but the weather remained icy cold. When fans arrived they wore robes, fur coats, earmuffs, and goloshes and carried blankets to keep warm. And when the players stepped out onto the field they found treacherous footing. Rosy Adelman, the longtime starting center for the Winnipegs, sat out the game in uniform with an injured thumb.

In the first quarter, the Winnipegs activated the scoreboard. First, they blocked a Calgary punt attempt, and then on offense, Cronin and Russ Rebholz moved the ball on option runs. After Cronin completed a short pass to move the ball into field goal range, Kabat split the uprights with his kick. Later in the same period, Kabat attempted another placekick for a field goal but missed the uprights and the ball rolled to the deadline. Officials canceled the rouge because the Winnipegs had not given Calgary's potential returner a 5-yard cushion for his catch.

At halftime, the Lyceum Theater provided musical entertainment while fans passed the hat and collected $310 for Eddie James who had broken his arm during the 1932 season but who still wore a sling. James expected to wear the sling for another six months but hoped to return to the gridiron for the 1934 season.

After Calgary kicked off to start the second half, Rebholz led the team to midfield. He completed a long pass to Cronin, 35 yards through the air, and Cronin, whom the *Winnipeg Tribune* called a "five-foot-seven-inch stick of human dynamite" slid past tacklers and loped 25 more yards for a touchdown. A few minutes later, Cronin intercepted a pass at midfield and weaved his way 50 yards through opponents for another touchdown.

Blue and Gold (1933)

In the fourth quarter, the Winnipegs allowed the Indians to complete four consecutive passes but then forced Calgary to settle for a rouge. Winnipeg beat Calgary 15-1.

When the final gun cracked the cold air, Adelman leapt from the bench. The old Tammany Tiger grabbed the game ball and marched toward the dressing room with his head held high with Winnipeg pride. The team had taken one more step toward the Grey Cup.

Johnny Buss, a sportswriter for the *Winnipeg Tribune*, said he could sum up Winnipeg's success in three words: Cronin, Kabat, and Rebholz. Buss wrote, "This trio of smart backfield gridiron warriors who learned their rugby at universities in the United States led the team to triumph after triumph this season." Meanwhile, the Manitoba student newspaper sang praises for the nine students and alumni who now played for the Winnipegs, which included Cronin, a second-year law student.

*   *

For their final contest of the 1933 season, the North Dakota State Bison would travel over 800 miles for a non-conference game in Oklahoma City. During two days of practice in Fargo ahead of the game, Coach Casey Finnegan decided to keep the mood and the physical demands light. He let each of his players decide how to stay in shape. Some players chose to run on the indoor track while others played basketball in the gymnasium. Still others chose to practice outside and to step through formations.

The Bison had beaten Oklahoma City 27-7 in 1932, but Finnegan knew next to nothing about the Goldbugs in 1933 because Coach Wesley Leonard "Wes" Fry had taken over the reigns. Unlike during past seasons when the Goldbugs had played with power, this year they used speed and deception to score points. Born in Hartley, Iowa, Coach Fry had earned all-conference honors in the Big Ten at fullback for the University of Iowa. He went on to play for Red Grange's New York Yankees in the AFL in 1926 and played one more year with the Yankees in the NFL in 1927. After that, he coached the Classen High School football team in Oklahoma City to a 44-9-1 record over five years before he took over at

Oklahoma City. This year, under Fry, the Goldbugs would enter their game against the Bison with a 5-1 record and one week after losing 39-0 to the University of Tulsa.

Finnegan, Bob Lowe, and 21 Bison players departed Fargo at 8:00 a.m. Wednesday morning and didn't arrive in Oklahoma City until Friday. When they took the practice field that day the southern sun baked their northern hides. Finnegan had told his men to wear track shirts instead of football sweaters.

On the day of the game, November 18, 1933, Bud Marquardt started at left end, Herb Peschel started at right tackle, and Fritz Hanson started at right halfback. Meanwhile, on the Goldbugs sideline, Fry remained upset with his team's performance against Tulsa the week before. He didn't start his regulars in the backfield. He made them sit.

Twice in the first quarter, Hanson slipped past Oklahoma City tacklers and broke loose on runs for the Bison. The first time he broke free from the crowd, he stumbled and fell, and the second time, after weaving his way through a maze of Goldbug tacklers and after running 40 yards downfield, he fell to the ground exhausted before he reached the goal line. Sportswriter Charles Saulsberry for the *Daily Oklahoman* observed, "Feinting, reversing his field, side-stepping and changing gears with the ease of a yet-to-be invented free-wheeling race car, the trim little towhead made them look awkwardly foolish." But the entire Bison squad suffered in the Oklahoma heat.

In the second quarter, after the Bison fumbled the ball on Oklahoma City's 38-yard line, Fry sent in his regulars to see whether they might redeem themselves. On the next play, the Goldbugs backfield completed a 49-yard pass to North Dakota State's 13-yard line. Three plays later, the Goldbugs scored on a run through the line.

In the third quarter, the Bison drove to Oklahoma City's 33-yard line and used a forward pass to Acey Olson, who then lateraled it back to Hanson. The "Blonde Whirlwind of the Plains" then raced the ball to the 10-yard line. Four plays later, the Bison turned the ball over on downs after taking 5 yards in losses.

In the fourth quarter, a Goldbug backfielder broke through the center of the Bison defensive line and raced 51 yards before Hanson took him

Blue and Gold (1933)

down at the 12-yard line. On their next play, the Goldbugs scored on a run around their right end. The Goldbugs later intercepted a pass at midfield and returned it to North Dakota State's 31-yard line. Three plays later, the Goldbugs completed a 19-yard pass for the score. The Goldbugs defeated the Bison 19-0.

Hanson, the "Fargo Express," never did score. He had played while sick against South Dakota, and he continued to feel sick in the game against Oklahoma City. But despite his illness, Hanson pleased the crowd as he frequently reversed his runs across the field. On several occasions, the crowd stood to watch Hanson carry the ball. "Time and again the 145-pound youngster bewildered the Goldbug defense, weaving and twisting his way almost into the clear," wrote sportswriter Norman Smith of the *Oklahoma News*. Eugene Fitzgerald, sportswriter for the *Fargo Forum*, looked at Hanson's antics from a different perspective. "Blocking for Hanson had to be sort of extemporaneous," he said, "as the mite back was running from one side to the other and nobody ever knew where he'd go next."

All season long, Finnegan had had to revamp the Bison backfield, and Hanson stood out as the one regular. Acey Olson, who had never scrimmaged at halfback and who had only played a few snaps at that position against South Dakota, fumbled the ball while playing that role against Oklahoma City. Leo Gerteis, who played as a blocking back in the quarterback position against the Goldbugs, injured his foot and had to come out of the game. Backup fullback Neville Reiners, too, had to leave the game with a cracked rib. The trainer taped him up and Reiners pleaded to be put back in, but Finnegan refused. He'd seen enough injuries for the year.

*

At the end of the 1933 season, both Hanson and North Dakota's Ralph Pierce received honorable mentions to the Associated Press All-America football team.

* *

Blue and Gold (1933)

In previous years, WCRFU champions had to wait a whole month until the unions in the East finished their playoff games. The western entrant then met the eastern representative in the Grey Cup title game. In a change for 1933, the WCRFU champion, the Winnipeg Rugby Club, would compete in a semifinal playoff for the opportunity to play in the Grey Cup championship.

Winnipegs Coach Carl Cronin flew to Hamilton to watch the Toronto Argonauts play the Montreal Winged Wheelers for the IRFU title. The winner would play Winnipeg in a Grey Cup semifinal. Cronin watched as the Argonauts American coach, Lew Hayman, guided the team. Originally from Paterson, New Jersey, Hayman had played football at Syracuse University as an All-American. He moved to Canada in 1932 to work as an assistant coach at the University of Toronto under Warren Stevens, the American who had completed the first touchdown pass in Grey Cup history when his Winged Wheelers beat Regina in 1931. After that win, Hayman took an assistant coach position with the Argonauts, and the Argos made him their head coach in 1933. Hayman brought fellow Syracuse alum Frank Tindall to the Argonauts and also Andy Mullan, a fellow Patersonian who had played for the Paterson Nighthawks in the Eastern Football League.

Cronin watched Hayman's Argonauts beat the Winged Wheelers 15-5. When he returned to Winnipeg, he reported that he believed they had an even chance against the Argonauts, even though the Argonauts fielded a heavier, younger squad than the Winnipegs.

On Thursday morning before the game, 22 Winnipegs players and the team's administrators boarded a train on the Canadian Pacific Railroad headed east through a new blanket of snow. During the trip, Russ Rebholz and two other players fell "train sick" while other players caught colds. Those who traveled well bonded over card games. Lou Mogul declared Greg Kabat to be the world's worst bridge player. In small groups, Cronin led his men in chalk talks to go over the plays that he had observed Toronto run against the Winged Wheelers.

When the team arrived in Toronto they checked into the Royal York Hotel, which claimed to be "the largest and finest hotel in the British Empire" with a giant mezzanine, the Imperial Dining Room, a huge

Blue and Gold (1933)

ballroom, a library with over 12,000 books, and a Canadian Public Radio broadcasting suite on the upper floors. Well-wishers greeted the Winnipegs at the hotel.

Cronin took his men to Maple Leaf Stadium to practice. While Kabat led the linemen and backs through their paces, Rebholz focused on the passing game and the receivers.

On the day of the game, December 2, 1933, the Winnipegs arrived at Varsity Stadium dressed in what the Toronto press described as purple uniforms, while the Argonauts wore their double-blue kits. Approximately 10,000 fans, many inspired by Winnipeg's underdog status (the gamblers favored Toronto 4-to-1) entered the stadium while Winnipeg fans back home listened to the game broadcast on radio station CKY. When the Argonauts emerged from the locker room, they didn't wear socks, and officials discovered the players had smeared their legs with grease, which would make them more difficult to tackle. This caused a 10-minute delay while officials made the Argonauts wipe it all off, an impossible task without solvent. The officials allowed them to play, anyway.

The Winnipegs received the noonday opening kickoff on a slippery field. The sun had melted the ice out of the turf and both clubs would fumble the ball 5 times each during the game.

Late in the first quarter, the Argonauts completed a long pass but the ball-carrier slipped and fell at the 25-yard line. The Argos settled for a rouge. In the second quarter, Toronto missed a 27-yard field goal but scored a rouge on the play. When Winnipeg got the ball back, the Argonauts intercepted a pass attempt. Toronto then drove downfield and scored another rouge on a missed field goal. In the same period, Cronin returned a punt 60 yards but once again Toronto held and forced the Winnipegs to punt.

Late in the second quarter, Kabat shanked a kick from the Winnipeg 15-yard line and it fell into the hands of Mullan who rushed 50 yards down the sideline until Kabat crossed in front of him. Officials awarded Mullan a touchdown, but to nearly everyone in the stadium, Kabat appeared to have forced Mullan out of bounds before he crossed the goal line. The crowd booed the officials while reporters in the press box scratched their heads because they, too, believed Mullan had stepped out of bounds.

In the third quarter, the Argonauts scored another rouge. On Toronto's next possession, they fumbled at their own 10-yard line and Bill Ceretti recovered the ball for the Winnipegs. With opportunity in hand, Kabat carried the ball 4 yards, and then on second down, Cronin tossed a lateral toward Kabat on an option run. An Argonauts player intercepted the toss and raced the opposite direction until Herb Mobberley pulled him down at Winnipeg's 7-yard line. The Winnipegs managed to hold the Argonauts back from the goal line, but the Argos scored another rouge to increase their lead.

The Winnipegs attempted 27 passes against the Argonauts, and at the end of the game, Rebholz completed three consecutive pass attempts. The crowd rose to its feet to watch them fly and after Rebholz went down with a bad leg cramp, they gave him a standing ovation as his comrades carried him off the field. Kabat took over passing duties and managed to hit a receiver in the end zone but the receiver dropped the ball and the Toronto crowd chastised officials for not calling pass interference against Toronto. When Winnipeg took possession of the ball again, they fumbled on an end run and the ball bounced into their own end zone. Three Argonauts and one Winnipegs player leapt onto the ball and Toronto scored a safety. Winnipeg's hopes fell and Toronto won 13-0.

When the final gun sounded, tears of frustration flowed on the Winnipeg bench. They had lost their chance at a championship bout. And while they had made it to the Grey Cup semifinal on stellar play execution, three times they had found themselves within 10 yards or less of the Toronto goal line, and each time they had failed to score due to a mistake. Meanwhile, the Winnipegs had played well on defense. They did not allow any big gains through the line nor did they allow Toronto to block a single punt. Both Kabat and Rebholz had out-punted the opposition. And they even had the opposing home crowd behind them.

Elmer Dulmage, a Canadian Press staff writer, opined that the Winnipegs had "sold" western Canadian football to the East in that game. The Toronto crowd had cheered all afternoon for the Winnipegs, especially when Rebholz unleashed the pass, and they groaned when passes fell incomplete. Eastern sportswriter Edwin Allan said, "For once the west sent down a rugby team that lived up to advance notices" and "the westerners deserved a better fate."

After the game, many Argonauts and Winnipegs players exchanged sweaters in the locker room. In a postgame interview, Cronin shared his opinions about football in Canada. He said he favored Canadian teams playing by American rules, but he liked some of the Canadian rules, too. He was a fan of Lionel Conacher's attempts at mixing the Canadian and American rules for his professional football endeavor in Toronto, and he said he didn't like it when newspapers in the East pointed fingers at Americans like himself and called them undesirable "imports." He said, "Canada has been sending amateur hockey players across to the United States for years, and no effort has been made to treat these players as if they were violating some criminal code of the criminal law, but the inference here in the East seems to be that we Americans are nothing short of crooks."

The Americans on the Winnipeg squad had stolen the hearts of fans in Toronto, but back home, the team struggled. The club had had to borrow money to finance its trip east and had to repay the loans from the 50 percent of gate receipts they had received in Toronto. During the trip, the team had waited to eat its meals at stops along the way instead of eating more expensive meals in the dining car. Joe Ryan had to turn down the Hamilton club's offer to use their field for practices for better secrecy because the team couldn't afford trips from Toronto to Hamilton and back each day. On game day, officials had advised the team to wear cleats suitable for mud, but the Winnipegs only had one set of cleats per player. Edward Armstrong, a sportswriter for the *Winnipeg Free Press*, chastised Winnipeg fans for not supporting the team better during the regular season. "It is a human impossibility," he said, "to finance rugby teams on the net gates in Winnipeg." The club would have a tough time keeping the team together. Kabat needed a job to remain in Canada. A business in Sarnia, Ontario, had offered Rebholz a position with the understanding he would play for the team there. And Cronin, too, had received offers to play elsewhere.

Blue and Gold (1933)

During the 1933 postseason and into the offseason, sportswriters in the West renewed their calls for changes in Canadian football to bring the game more in line with the American code. In the *Winnipeg Free Press*, Bob Priestly called for changes in the rules for blocking. In 1933, Canadian rules didn't allow linemen to block behind the line of scrimmage and they could block no further than 3 yards beyond the line of scrimmage, which created a 3-yard zone of blocking from sideline to sideline. As a result, "linemen charge through the line of scrimmage with such force that often they go beyond the 3-yard line creating interference, and their team is penalized, before they realize they have gone the distance, so it is of little use to an offensive team" to block, he said. Priestly argued the Canadian code should allow blocking anywhere behind the line of scrimmage and up to 5 yards beyond it. He suggested that the efforts to promote professional football in Montreal and Toronto had proven the need for change. The Intercollegiate Rugby Football Union (CIRFU), which tended to be more progressive than the Big Four, agreed. In January 1934, the CIRFU met and proposed rules changes for both blocking and passing. The changes would allow players to block anywhere behind the line of scrimmage and up to 3 yards beyond. They would also remove the penalty for an incomplete pass outside of the end zone.

In February, Dr. E. A. McCusker, a representative from the WCRFU, rose to the position of President of the CRU. Under his leadership, CRU membership considered rules changes to bring the game more in line with the American code. McCusker also told the body that if the CRU did not let the WCRFU host the Grey Cup championship in 1934, the West might see fit to split from the CRU and adopt the American code in its entirety.

The CRU rejected McCusker's push for drastic rules changes but begrudgingly declared that, yes, the WCRFU would host the Grey Cup. If the Eastern contender failed to send its team west, the CRU would award the Grey Cup to the western contender. The CRU intended to alternate the championship game between the East and the West theretofore.

Blue and Gold (1933)

The CRU did adopt some rules changes:

- An expanded blocking zone would include 1 yard behind the line of scrimmage to give backfielders the opportunity to help interfere with defenders who attempt to block punts and to provide more interference on running plays.
- On pass plays, offensive pass interference would force a turnover at the spot of the foul.
- The 2-point safety would count as a 1-point rouge, instead.
- On a kick, if the ball did not strike the ground before it landed beyond the end line, the kicking team would score a rouge but the opposing team would begin with the ball at their own 40-yard line. If the ball landed within the end zone before it exited beyond the end line, the opposing team would begin with the ball at their own 25-yard line.
- Instead of sending individual players to a penalty box on timed penalties for their offenses, which reduced the number of men on the field for the penalized side, officials would impose yardage penalties. However, officials could banish for the rest of the game any player who fought, abused an official, or deliberately caused an injury, and the penalized team could replace that player to avoid fielding a short-handed side.
- Only the referee would carry a whistle. Instead of whistles, the umpire and head linesman would carry horns, which they would sound if a player committed an offense that should not stop play. The referee would have a horn, too, but only his whistle would stop play.

Sportswriters pounced on the whistle-horn rules change. "The business of putting a horn instead of a whistle into official mouths is…likely to meet substantial competition from the sidelines," reported the *Leader-Post*. "Football fans have always had their horns. Now the referee has one, the umpire has one and the head linesman has one… What happens when a spectator toots is not forecast."

The lack of progressive rules changes incensed the West. Bill Lewis, a sportswriter for the *Edmonton Bulletin*, said the changes "failed in every way to give the expected help to the game in the West."

In April, colleges in the East expressed opposition to alternating the Grey Cup game between East and West because they would have a hard time fitting the necessary travel into their schedules.

Meanwhile, in Toronto, Lionel Conacher announced that his Canadian professional football experiment would continue He had rebadged his team as the Wrigley Aromints under the sponsorship of the Wm. Wrigley Jr. Company, the chewing gum maker. Instead of playing in a league, the team would play independently. Conacher said he planned to play his Aromints against teams from Rochester, Buffalo, and Niagara Falls, New York, and he hoped to play night games in Toronto and also Thanksgiving Day and Sunday games in Montreal. Practices would begin in early September and Lionel's brother, Charlie, and also several hockey players and professional wrestlers with football experience, and former Canadian football players, would join him on the Aromints.

Blue and Gold (1933)

CHAPTER 4 - BROWN AND GOLD (1934)

In 1934, the NCAA would update the rules for college football in a way that would open up the game and increase scoring. At Concordia, with new offensive weapons on the team, Bob Fritz would lead the Cobbers in pursuit of another conference title. And at North Dakota State, Fritz Hanson, Herb Peschel, and Bud Marquardt would take on big, new challenges against bigger schools. Neither the Cobbers nor the Bison, however, would lay claim to local supremacy on the gridiron.

Meanwhile, in Winnipeg, the University of Manitoba would resurrect varsity football in unprecedented fashion, while the Winnipeg Rugby Club would struggle to retain its identity as an emerging western powerhouse. In Regina, the Roughriders would fill up their roster with familiar names from the Swede Belt, while in Eastern Canada, Lionel Conacher would bring back his team for another round of pro football in Canada.

* *

In early April 1934, North Dakota State Coach Casey Finnegan put out a notice that all men who planned to participate in spring football practice should obtain their uniforms from the athletic department. He expected 40 players would report. The team would only lose three players to graduation.

Despite a huge cut in the athletics budget, Finnegan had managed to preserve, and in some cases enhance, activities at the school. During the Depression, Finnegan had managed to purchase over $10,000 in equipment and he had established athletic relationships with larger schools, including Midwest, Eastern, and Southern schools. His teams traveled, sometimes long distances, to play games. Finnegan had accomplished all of this by reducing the number of his assistants and by also taking a deep pay cut. He also figured out ways to reduce travel expenses.

At Concordia, four new students with football experience enrolled at the school during spring semester, including two graduates of Crosby-Ironton High School, John Butorac and Mike Chupich, who had played freshman football at Minnesota. The other two, Henry Held and Roy Cleve, Coach Frank Cleve's cousin, had both graduated from Minneapolis South High School and then played football for the successful Minneapolis Flour City amateur park league team. All four men turned out for spring football on April 4, the Wednesday after Easter break.

*

For 1934, the NCAA had once again updated the rules on the field. In an effort to increase scoring, the rulemaking body eliminated penalties for most incomplete forward passes in the following ways:

- On the 100 yards of field between the goal lines, officials would no longer penalize the offense 5 yards for a second, successive incomplete pass.
- In the end zones, officials would no longer always award a touchback to the defense for an incomplete pass.
- Except on fourth down, officials would treat the first incomplete pass thrown over the goal line like an incomplete pass anywhere else on the field.
- On fourth down, or on a successive incomplete pass thrown over the goal line on the same series of downs, officials would continue to award a touchback.

The NCAA expected the rules changes would open up the running game, especially near the goal line, because defenses would have to worry more about pass attempts.

Finally, and perhaps most significantly, the NCAA decided to reduce the circumference of the football by a full inch. Cleve welcomed the change in ball size. "The smaller-sized ball will make forward passing more of a scoring venture than a threat," he said.

For future recruits, Cleve and Finnegan would need to prepare for rules changes at the high school level, too. North Dakota had decided to stop using collegiate rules and instead adopted the official interscholastic football rules of the National Federation of State High School Athletic Associations, the same body of rules students in adjacent Minnesota and South Dakota subscribed to. The federation first published its code in

1932. Similar to the rules for professional football, the federation rules allowed players to throw a pass from anywhere behind the line of scrimmage. Because the NCAA had decided not to follow the federation and pro football's lead, college passers would continue to have to be at least five yards behind the line of scrimmage to throw a pass.

Both Finnegan and Cleve had their work cut out for them.

*

The Bison and Cobbers started practice outdoors on April 9, and good weather followed. The Cobbers would lose nine men to graduation, but Cleve had 35 men show up for spring football. Louie Benson's eyes grew wide at the potential size of his line with Butorac, Chupich, and Roy Cleve in competition for a starting position. He expected they might average 190 pounds per man when they started football again in the fall. In the backfield, Cleve focused on finding someone who could punt and pass to replace the loss of Pat Hilde and Earl Moran. The speedy and elusive Held competed for one of the open backfield spots and, optimistic, Cleve said, "The material this spring is the best I've had to work with since coming to Concordia." At the end of spring football, Cleve named Bob Fritz captain for 1934 and then had the football field dragged and seeded.

On the Bison turf, with most of the team expected to return in the fall, Finnegan made sure his varsity men felt compelled to compete for a starting job against next year's sophomores. Meanwhile, when he wasn't training for and participating in track meets, Bud Marquardt punted long, high spirals in competition with a new guy, Lyle Sturgeon. Fritz Hanson, too, again competed in track.

*   *

During the Canadian football offseason, Manitoba announced the school's varsity team would return to the gridiron in the fall and that the team would play four exhibition games under American collegiate rules. The Bisons would play four different teams from North Dakota colleges, including the North Dakota State School of Science in Wahpeton, Jamestown, Minot State, and the North Dakota freshman team.

Brown and Gold (1934)

To teach the team how to play with American rules, the school hired Walter L. "Wally" Hass, a Holstein, Iowa native who had lettered three years with Minnesota and who had coached a freshman team there. At quarterback, he captained the Golden Gophers in 1932. Hass in turn hired Walter Odhe, also a former Gopher, to be his line coach. Odhe had played end for Minnesota and he claimed to have been the lightest player in Big Ten history to letter at end, at 160 pounds. Odhe had also played outfield on the Minnesota baseball team and graduated alongside Hass in 1932. He went on to coach high school football in Mound, Minnesota, his home town, before Hass called him up to Winnipeg. The university would not pay Odhe to assist, however, and so someone outside official channels had found a way to attract him to Winnipeg to coach. To maintain continuity, Manitoba retained the team's previous coach, Gordon Bowes, and sent him to a coaching school in Minot so that he could assist Hass with the American game.

"Varsity's venture into the realm of international competition is made primarily in the hope of making rugby pay its way," noted sportswriter Ralph Allen in the *Winnipeg Tribune*. "The tie-up with nearby institutions across the border will eliminate heavy travelling expenses, and give the students the kind of football calculated to rouse the old college spirit." Allen also wrote, "The Brown and Gold plans to go in for the American game in no half-hearted manner. Four of its six games will be under the across-the-border rules and practices will be directed accordingly." The Bisons also scheduled two Winnipeg Senior League games against the Winnipeg Rugby Club and they would play those games under the Canadian code. Meanwhile, the university would also field a freshman team to compete against local high school and junior-level teams. Looking ahead, the university leveled and graded a parcel of land at Fort Garry to prepare the grounds for seeding in the spring of 1935. The University planned to erect a fence and a grandstand at the field for gridiron contests.

When Hass opened fall practice at Manitoba, more than 50 students showed up for tryouts.

Meanwhile, the Winnipeg Rugby Club helped to secure a job for Greg Kabat. He found work with San Antonio Gold Mines Limited, which operated a mine near the town of Bissett on the north shore of Rice Lake, northeast of Winnipeg. Russ Rebholz, too, remained in and worked in Winnipeg. The team suffered a huge blow, however, when Coach Carl Cronin accepted a more lucrative employment opportunity in Hamilton, Ontario. In addition, Cronin would join the Hamilton Tigers coaching staff and lead the team in Big Four competition. Sportswriters raced to point out how Hamilton had resisted and chastised the practice of fielding Americans. But now with Cronin, the Tigers would dive head first into the import strategy as they secured the services of Cornell captain Johnny Ferraro, a Buffalo, New York native. Hamilton paid Ferraro $2,000 and found him a job at a hotel.

In response, the Winnipegs decided to pass the clipboard from Cronin to Kabat, the line coach, while Rebholz would continue to coach the backfield. Rebholz had hoped to use Kabat, too, out of the backfield, but he discovered that Kabat had primarily played line in the past because of his near-sightedness—which explained why placeholders always laid a strip of tape on the ground for Kabat before each placekick attempt. Kabat couldn't see the goalposts.

The club used Cronin's departure as a fundraising opportunity: They held a public "informal banquet" at the St. Charles Hotel where Winnipeg fans could wish Cronin all the best in his new adventure. Approximately 80 well-wishers attended.

Cronin's departure set the club's wheels in motion to acquire talent. The team secured the services of John "Jughead" Anderson from Oklahoma City and Bobby Schiller from the University of Wisconsin. When Schiller arrived, he roomed with Manitoba coach Hass to share expenses. The Winnipegs also picked up former players from the Regina Roughriders, including Cliff Roseborough, and also players from the Garrison team in Winnipeg and from the Deer Lodge neighborhood junior team that had competed in the western playoffs in 1933. Winnipeg's Deer Lodge acquisitions included Jeff Nicklin who had played for the Shamrocks junior team before he joined Deer Lodge. In late summer, the Winnipegs also obtained the services of Lynn Patrick, the son of Canadian hockey player Lester "The Silver Fox" Patrick who in 1934 served as manager of the New York Rangers. The elder Patrick had

Brown and Gold (1934)

first gained fame while playing for the Brandon, Manitoba, team in the North West Hockey League.

Alongside Manitoba, the Winnipegs lined up games against American teams, including a club team dubbed the Minnesota All-Stars composed of Gopher alumni letter winners and coached by All-American end Kenneth Haycraft. The Winnipegs also scheduled games against North Dakota and Concordia.

To increase their footprint in Winnipeg, the Winnipeg Rugby Club established and held tryouts for a junior-level team. Rebholz and Kabat would coach the team so that both the junior and senior teams would be "in sync" and so the Winnipegs could draw talent from the juniors.

Meanwhile, Regina, too, continued to fill its roster with Americans, including former North Dakota star Ralph Pierce. They also picked up Paul Kirk, an East Grand Forks, Minnesota, native who had played for Minnesota through 1930. After college, in 1931, Kirk had played for the Minnehahas, a Minneapolis amateur park league team, and then he played for the Minnesota All-Stars in 1931, 1932, and 1933. The Roughriders outbid Winnipeg for the services of Pierce and Kirk. Steve Adkins, an all-conference end, Walter "Oke" Olson, and Bob Walker, all who had played for South Dakota, also joined Regina.

In the East, the Ottawa Rough Riders added Americans Francis "Buddy" Meiers and Bernard McNutt, both from Michigan State University, and also Chris Schearer from the University of Detroit. Montreal added Wes Bacon from Colgate, Carl Palombo from Pennsylvania, and Bill Pendergast from Manhattan College. Hamilton secured the services of Jerry Brock from Cornell and Bus Blum from Colgate. Only one team in the Big Four had a Canadian coach.

Meanwhile, the CIRFU announced its teams would no longer compete for the Grey Cup. The prevailing wisdom held that the colleges could no longer compete with the club teams and their American imports.

According to sportswriter Ralph Allen in the *Winnipeg Tribune*, Canadian football had become "as frank in its shamateurishness as the common decencies permit." He expressed his support for bringing more Americans into Canadian football. "As one more partial to a good football game than a poor football game, I am in favor of the import system," he said. "It would be at best a hazardous business to guess what club introduced the first American to Canadian football; but it would be playing a lead-pipe cinch to guess that whoever was responsible had no thought of the Frankenstein-ish proportions the experiment was to assume under pressure of competition."

As for the rules of the game, "The sentiment in favor of American and against Canadian rules is growing all over Western Canada," Allen said. "It is questionable if there would be any great amount of lamenting if [the Canadian rules] were discarded entirely in favor of the U.S. Intercollegiate code."

* *

When Joe Ryan booked the Minnesota All-Stars to play the Winnipeg Rugby Club at Osborne Stadium, he knew exactly the type of talent his team would face. A Minneapolis park league team, the All-Stars had featured Minnesota alumni since they started playing in 1932.

In the fall of 1932, the All-Stars had dominated their opponents and featured the likes of Jack Manders, Ken Haycraft, and Bobby Marshall. Manders, who last played for the Gophers in 1932, moved on in 1933 to play professional football with the Chicago Bears in the NFL, where he continued to play now in 1934. Marshall, too, had dropped from the squad, but at 54 years old in 1934, who could blame him? Marshall last played for Minnesota in 1906 and had played in the NFL (then the American Professional Football Association) for the Rock Island Independents in 1920 and for the NFL's Duluth Eskimos in 1925. But Haycraft, who last played for Minnesota in 1928, still played for the team, and so did Herb "Chief" Franta, who last played for St. Thomas in 1925; the two men had played together in the NFL for the Minneapolis Red Jackets in 1929 and 1930 and for the Green Bay Packers in 1930. Allen "Tuck" Teeter, who last played at Minnesota in 1931, had also played in the NFL, for the Staten Island Stapletons in 1932.

Under the leadership of Bert Oja, the team's coach and right guard in 1934, the All-Stars continued to field an excellent squad made up of former All-American and All-Conference players. Oja had played for

Brown and Gold (1934)

Minnesota through 1929, and that year, Knute Rockne had named Oja to his All-Nations All-American team at center. The All-Stars also featured former Gophers Fred Just (last played in '25), Paul Berry ('29), Win Brockmeyer, Bill Brownell, Al Krezowski, and Clint Riebeth ('30), Lloyd Stein and John Peter "Pete" Somers ('31), Elmer "Bull" Appman, Jim Dennerly, Mervin Dilner, and Sam Swartz ('32), as well as Slats Stafford (Catholic University '31) and Jim Peterson. And the All-Stars included Johnny Hass, the brother of new Manitoba Coach Wally Hass. Brothers Johnny and Wally had played together at Minnesota before Johnny left the team in 1931 due to debilitating sinus issues. He moved to California to live in a different climate, but in the fall of 1934 he returned to play as a reserve on the All-Stars.

More than 30 players turned out for Winnipeg Rugby Club practices. Crowds sat in the bleachers or stood on the sidelines at Osborne Stadium to watch the team work out. Most came out to see Jughead Anderson in uniform. Under Greg Kabat's direction, the team practiced lining up in a modified Double Wing formation and ran spinner plays, lateral end runs, and halfback option pass plays during a light-contact scrimmage. The Winnipegs practiced until after dark so that the new players could get acquainted to playing under floodlights.

The club had already sold more tickets than expected, and *Winnipeg Tribune* sportswriter Ralph Allen observed that fans had become emotionally invested in the team. "Where a few years ago, most people knew football players only by such vague appellations as 'the fat one' or 'the skinny one,' there are today hundreds of fans who can predict the starting lineup [as] accurately as anyone," he said. The newspapers billed the game as a Big Ten-adjacent rivalry between Winnipeg's Kabat, Russ Rebholz, and Bobby Schiller, all from Wisconsin, and the mostly Minnesota alumni squad, the All-Stars.

Approximately 3,000 fans filled Osborne Stadium on Saturday evening, September 15, 1934, as the Princess Pats played energetic music to get listeners in a festive mood. The near-capacity crowd watched as the Winnipegs took the field in brand-new blue-and-gold uniforms, and when the Minnesota All-Stars ran onto the field Kabat, Rebholz, and Schiller grinned along the sideline as the band played "On Wisconsin," the fight song for the University of Wisconsin Badgers. During a pregame ceremony, Winnipeg's mayor presented the team with the Hugo Ross Trophy for winning the 1933 WCRFU title, and Manitoba Premier John Bracken performed the ceremonial first kick.

Early in the first quarter, the All-Stars entered Winnipeg territory and attempted a field goal, but the ball flew low. In the second quarter, the Winnipegs reached the All-Stars' 12-yard line where Anderson attempted a field goal. His kick flew wide but over the end line for a rouge. Throughout the first half, under Canadian rules, officials inflicted numerous penalties upon the All-Stars, including for scragging (tackling around the neck).

The Princess Pats provided the halftime entertainment, and then the crowd welcomed Wally Hass, the new Manitoba head coach to the field to serve as referee for the second half played under American rules.

In the third quarter, with offensive players able to block downfield under the American code, an All-Stars backfielder broke through the line and raced 41 yards to reach Winnipeg's 12-yard line. The Winnipegs forced a turnover on downs, however, with Kabat hitting the holes for tackles. To end the quarter, the Winnipegs punted the ball, and the All-Stars started the fourth period on Winnipeg's 29-yard line. After Kabat left the game with an injured nose, All-Stars backfielders managed successive runs of 17 and 12 yards, the last on a reverse around left end for a touchdown. Somers scored the extra point for the All-Stars who took a 7-1 lead.

On Winnipeg's next drive, the All-Stars intercepted a pass and returned the ball to Winnipeg's 26-yard line. A few plays later, they reached the goal line, and on the third attempt at the line, the All-Stars plunged over center for the score. Despite the 13-1 deficit, the Winnipegs played hard, and late in the game, Jeff Nicklin recovered a fumble deep in All-Stars territory. Kabat re-entered the game and threw a pass, and then Rebholz took over at fullback. On the 25-yard line, Rebholz attempted a pass into the end zone but an All-Stars defender knocked it down. Rebholz attempted another pass on second down but the ball traveled far beyond all of the receivers. With 20 seconds remaining, Rebholz urged his men to line up quickly at the line of scrimmage and after the snap, Rebholz threw a pass in a high arc down the middle of the field. The pigskin tumbled end-over-end through the air. Lynn Patrick, past the goal line and with nobody nearby, nabbed the ball out of the air. The crowd roared. Time expired and the All-Stars walked away victorious 13-8.

Throughout most of the game the All-Stars had forced the Winnipegs to play within their own territory and prevented the Winnipegs from running the ball for substantial gains. The crowd felt Anderson had disappointed, but he had played with a taped-up ankle, an injury he suffered during practice.

After the game, *Winnipeg Tribune* sportswriter Johnny Buss boldly predicted, "Each year the officials over on this side of the border are gradually adopting the American code of rules and at some future date, not so far distant, a uniform set of rules for both countries will be legislated."

*

After the Winnipegs lost to the All-Stars, Anderson didn't show up at practice. According to reports, Anderson had left Canada for the United States to follow the fortunes of a race horse named Snorky who had raced in Winnipeg all summer. Eddie James returned to practice in Anderson's place after a full season on the sidelines with a broken arm. James had pitched hay and stooks of grain to get back into shape.

In advance of the upcoming game against North Dakota in Grand Forks, the *Grand Forks Herald* declared the Winnipegs "one of the strongest teams in the Dominion and the most American of all rugby outfits." The Winnipegs would bring players who weighed between 160 and 215 pounds while the Sioux players each weighed between 145 and 200 pounds. C.D. Locklin, sportswriter for the *Herald*, attempted to enlighten readers about Canadian football rules and explained, "The Canadians have five men in the backfield, one quarterback and four halfbacks. Don't ask us what the extra man is for."

At North Dakota, Coach Jack West ran his men through a new playbook. During the offseason, West had decided to switch from the Double Wing to the Short Punt formation as the team's base offense. In the new system, West expected to have three players in the backfield who could pass or catch the ball. To prepare for the evening game against the

Winnipegs, West had his men scrimmage for two nights under the floodlights and he devoted their final practice to Canadian-style offensive play with five men in the backfield. The *Herald* reported, "The players had a hilarious time as they opened up with a deluge of lateral and backward passes."

On the day of the game, approximately 40 Winnipeg fans joined more than 30 Winnipegs players on chartered buses for the trip south. Other fans, including cabinet ministers motored down from Winnipeg in their own automobiles. The team left Friday afternoon with plans to return home after the game.

When the Canadians took the field in front of 5,000 fans, Memorial Field's huge arc lights dazzled. Curt Schave, the former Regina Roughrider and returning Sioux product, stood on the grid wearing an official's shirt and a whistle. His experience in both the Canadian and American games provided him with a special niche of knowledge for the contest.

In the first half under Canadian rules, after the Winnipegs discovered the Sioux knew how to pursue option runs, Winnipeg switched to line plunges and passes. Rebholz threw the ball while Schiller ran the ball, including for 32 yards on one carry. North Dakota, meanwhile, used both forward and lateral passes but had a hard time moving the ball. Kabat left the game early with a broken finger.

Rebholz punted the ball to behind North Dakota's goal line where the Sioux returner attempted a forward pass to avoid the rouge. Officials ruled the misstep a safety, a score for the Winnipegs. Later, the Winnipegs drove the ball near to North Dakota's goal line, but the Sioux held, and the Winnipegs kicked to score a rouge. Twice in the second quarter the Sioux marched into Winnipeg territory only to be thwarted first by an interception and second by a fumble. The *Grand Forks Herald* observed, "North Dakota's offense under Canadian rules was ragged until the Sioux dropped any attempt to play rugby. In the second quarter, West's backfield settled down to straight football."

To open the second half, North Dakota forced Winnipeg to punt. The Sioux then made good yardage under the American code with a passing attack and in the running game with good blocking. The Sioux reached

Winnipeg's 3-yard line and then ran off tackle for the score. After a missed extra point, the Sioux led 6-3.

In the fourth quarter, Rebholz completed a 40-yard pass to Patrick and Schiller raced 32 yards on a fake kick, but North Dakota intercepted a long pass attempt and returned the ball to Winnipeg's 44-yard line. With only 3 minutes remaining in the game, a Sioux backfielder ran off left tackle behind good blocking and rushed 32 yards for a touchdown. The Sioux scored the extra point and walked off victorious 13-3.

Throughout the game, Winnipeg used a seven-man defensive line and kept North Dakota to only a few yards over center. *Winnipeg Free Press* sportswriter Edward Armstrong labeled the loss a moral victory for the Winnipegs and he credited the Sioux's performance to West's recruitment. Armstrong said North Dakota's players had come from more states than did all the imports in Canada.

* *

Concordia Coach Frank Cleve kicked up dust as he trotted onto the field for the team's first fall practice. The city had refused to give the college a watering permit and the drought had killed the grass he seeded last spring. Once again, poor field conditions would force the Cobbers to play home games on their rival's grid at Moorhead State.

Cleve needed someone who could pass and kick, and he needed a signal caller. He hoped to find someone to fill those responsibilities amongst the 22 men who showed up for the first day of practice, or maybe he would discover a gem amongst the half dozen or more who might show up a few days later. Cleve tried out John Butorac and Ralph Miller at punter but in the end, he expressed displeasure. "I'm scared to death of this game," he said. "Unless I can get good kicking, and now I don't know where I can, it's going to be too bad for us." Only six lettermen returned to practice and the start of two-a-days. When sportswriter Hank Hurley from the *Fargo Forum* asked what Cleve thought about the situation, Cleve responded, "I don't know where people get the idea that I'm going to have such a wonderful club this year."

In the hot afternoons, Cleve filled practices with light drills and saved conditioning and contact drills for cool evenings. This year, Cleve expected the smaller ball might open up the game and he would field a heavier but faster team than he led in 1933. The line averaged 190 pounds while the backfield averaged 160 pounds per man.

During freshman orientation, Bob Fritz, the 25-year old captain of the football team, gave a speech to beanie-clad youngsters about the need to support the team. He then promptly injured his finger during practice. Cleve feared a break but an x-ray showed the finger intact. Cleve said he would allow Fritz to play in the opening game against North Dakota State.

Bison Coach Casey Finnegan also needed a punter, and his prospects put a smile on his face. Bud Marquardt had filled in for George May in 1933, but now a new kid, a 275-pound freshman tackle from Moorhead High School named Lyle Sturgeon, claimed that he, too, could punt. And boy, could he. With spectators on hand, Finnegan held a punting contest between Sturgeon, May, and Marquardt, and Sturgeon sent every kick high and far. Sure, Marquardt still limped a little from an ankle injury that he had suffered earlier in practice but he had never kicked the ball like Sturgeon did. Finnegan had found his man, but he told Sturgeon that he and Lowe would put him on a special training regimen. He needed to get down to 240 pounds.

With only three lettermen lost to graduation, 26 Bison players showed up for that first day of practice. Finnegan expected that number might grow to as many as 37 over the next few days, up until the first day of classes. He had nine letterman return to play on the line and eight lettermen return to play in the backfield. With Sturgeon at tackle, Finnegan moved Herb Peschel to fill a hole at guard. Marquardt, meanwhile, met competition in a six-foot-five end named Forest Stevens. And everyone on the team grew big smiles when they saw Shifty Gove return to the practice field after he had missed an entire season with a broken leg.

Just days before the Bison-Cobbers game, a stomach bug hit Concordia's camp. Meanwhile, the Bison camp appeared healthy, but Finnegan, bitten by injuries the previous year, said, "Everything looks so rosy that I'm afraid something's going to happen."

Brown and Gold (1934)

On game day, September 21, 1934, the Concordia Cobbers entered flood-lit Dacotah Field wearing brand-new gabardine jerseys in a brighter maroon and gold than previous seasons and with large white numerals on the back and smaller numerals on the front. The players wore maroon trousers with gold stripes along the length of the thigh and wore socks striped in both colors. Two Cobbers played sick with the stomach flu. Fritz started at fullback for Concordia. Peschel started at right guard for North Dakota State but Marquardt, with his sore ankle, did not start. Neither did Fritz Hanson, the 145-pound "Bundle of Chain Lightning" that Finnegan tended to hold back from the initial fray in most games.

Sturgeon kicked off to open the game. Soon after, the Bison defense forced the Cobbers to punt. North Dakota State then executed a long drive to Concordia's 2-yard line, but the Cobbers held. The teams exchanged punts through the rest of the period.

In the second quarter, Concordia took over the ball on downs at their own 32-yard line. Fritz then led the Cobbers on a drive that included four first downs. He completed two forward passes, one lateral, and then he bashed through the line to reach North Dakota State's 12-yard line, where the Bison held.

On Concordia's offense, Henry Held proved effective on reverse runs, and all four of the Cobber newcomers who had previous post-high school football experience—Held, Roy Cleve, Mike Chupich, and Butorac—played well, but Fritz stood out above the rest on both sides of the ball.

Both sides punted frequently and the Cobbers returned few of Sturgeon's high, long kicks.

In the second half, North Dakota State's Erling Schranz returned a punt 35 yards to Concordia's 44-yard line. Wendy Schollander completed a 35-yard pass to Gove to reach Concordia's 9-yard line but then the Cobbers intercepted a lateral pass and took possession of the ball to end the drive. Later in the third quarter, North Dakota State drove all the way to Concordia's 6-yard line, but once again the Cobbers forced a turnover on downs, this time at the 1-yard line. Before the period ended, Schranz suffered an injury and Finnegan sent in Hanson.

Midway through the fourth quarter, Schollander launched a pass to Hanson, "The Bison Meteor." Hanson leapt into the air for the ball and the pigskin bounced off his arms. He managed to pull it in and he raced to Concordia's 48-yard line. Gove then took the ball on a reverse run and angled around right end out of bounds for a first down. On Concordia's 32-yard line, Hanson faked a handoff to Gove and then slanted off right tackle where he twisted his way through the defense to reach the 5-yard line. The Cobbers called a timeout to regroup, and on the next play, Hanson shot off right tackle to reach the 3-yard line. Gove hit the center of the line but the Cobbers stopped him 6 inches short of the score. Finally, Gove crashed into the same spot and into the middle of the scrum and he fell over the goal line for the score.

In the closing minutes, the Cobbers used a passing attack to advance the ball, but Finnegan had employed a six-man Bison line with five men back to cover the pass the entire game. The Bison intercepted Fritz's pass to end the contest and win 6-0.

Both teams executed well and committed few penalties, and while the Bison took home the victory, both the *Fargo Forum* and the *Moorhead Daily News* extolled Frtiz's performance for the Cobbers. Sportswriter Dick Hackenberg said, "Fritz threw passes, skirted the ends, buckled the line, blocked viciously, backed up his own forward wall and made enough tackles for six ball games."

*   *

Wally Hass prepared Manitoba for its first game against the North Dakota State School of Science. After the initial varsity practice, between 30 and 40 men, most former junior-level players, continued to turn out to play. Hass put his men through two-a-days, just like at any successful American institution. And because the team would play under American rules he emphasized learning how to block. As the *Winnipeg Tribune* observed, "None of the prospects have more than a surface knowledge of the game as played under American rules, [but] that's the way the University of Manitoba intends its teams to play rugby henceforth—the American way," which Ralph Allen, sportswriter for the *Tribune*, said "will be a welcome relief from the confusing half-and-half system the [Winnipeg Rugby Club] has been forced to sponsor."

Brown and Gold (1934)

Unfortunately for Hass and his players, Manitoba didn't have facilities or equipment like at American colleges. "Regarding athletics here," wrote the *Winnipeg Manitoban*, "the new rugby mentor's opinion is that we do not take our physical development seriously enough. He stated that in North Dakota there are special gyms and paid coaches who look after the development of students and teach the athletes on the teams all the scientific points of their respective games, thus lessening the number of injuries incurred and increasing the popularity of college athletics."

Undeterred by his primitive surroundings, Hass taught his men the finer points of the Bob Zuppke and Fritz Crisler playbooks, and he answered questions about American rules in a special column in the *Winnipeg Free Press*. At Minnesota, Hass had played under Crisler who now coached Princeton.

After a few weeks of training, the *Tribune* suggested the student athletes appeared inspired, more so than past Manitoba varsity teams. Hass agreed on the point of eagerness. "I think that the team is one of the most willing outfits I have ever seen," he told the *Manitoban*. "If the team shows the same spirit on Saturday as shown in practice, North Dakota [State School of Science] will have a hard game on their hands." Manitoba's roster included Morris "Tubber" Kobrinsky, a chunky, dark-haired man with swift legs and a strong arm. The *Winnipeg Tribune* had dubbed him a "one man team" when he led the YMHA juvenile squad to a 21-12 victory over the Deer Lodge neighborhood team in the juvenile rugby final in 1930.

North Dakota Science held practices before the start of the school year to prepare players for their trip to Winnipeg. Coached by Carl Bute, the Wildcats fielded 35 players, including six letterman, and the linemen averaged 175 pounds while the backfield averaged 165 pounds per man compared to an average weight of 195 pounds on the line and 180 pounds per man in the backfield for Manitoba. Don Nutter, an all-conference halfback from Sydney, Montana, served as the team's captain. William Jones, a Native American from Beulah, North Dakota, worked the trenches at tackle. He led the team in blocking punts. The school's newspaper, the *Dakota Scientist*, assured readers that the Wildcats would have a fighting chance against Manitoba even though the northern school drew athletes from a student body of approximately 2,000 students.

"Although this may seem like a school out of our class, the number of students having high school football training is relatively small," wrote the paper.

In the days before Manitoba's first game, Hass led a pep fest in Convocation Hall on campus. In the *Tribune*, Allen applauded Hass's efforts. "The University of Manitoba has at last gone collegiate," Allen wrote. "The pleasant pyrotechnics associated with the athletic activities of colleges to the right and left and south of us have been rather backward in appearing within the cloisters of Manitoba, but the belated appearance is none the less welcome."

To raise awareness about the first game in Winnipeg history to be played entirely under the American code, the University ran newspaper advertisements with the heading "American Football." Fans could purchase tickets at the university or from the same venues where the Winnipeg Rugby Club sold tickets, including at the cigar stand at the Grain Exchange.

The Wildcats departed Wahpeton on Thursday afternoon and spent the night in Grand Forks where on Friday, they watched North Dakota play Omaha University. After the game, the Wildcats traveled to Winnipeg for their game on Saturday.

While the Wildcats watched the Sioux play the Cardinals in Grand Forks, students in Manitoba held a Rugby Booster Night at Wesley Park. Cheerleaders and a military band greeted students as they arrived in a parade of cars decorated in brown and gold ribbons, pennants, and banners. After Hass introduced a few players, he gave a brief talk and explained that he did not want the players to participate in the chilly evening festivities, not on the night before a game, and so he dismissed them. The other students lit the bonfire, led cheers, and participated in a snake dance.

The Wildcats arrived in Winnipeg on Saturday morning and went for a jog to limber up before the game. Meanwhile, at Hass's request, local high schools postponed their games at Osborne Stadium ahead of Manitoba's home opener. He wanted the rain-soaked turf to be in good shape for his players.

Brown and Gold (1934)

While the Winnipeg Rifles Band played their welcome the Manitoba Bisons took the field on September 29, 1934, in brand-new gold jerseys with brown shoulders and with gold helmets. Manitoba's premiere, John Bracken, watched as his son took the field with the varsity squad for the first varsity game since 1931. On the opposite sideline stood the Wildcats in black jerseys with white shoulders and with red helmets. Students in the crowd wore brown and gold ribbons.

Approximately 1,000 fans watched the teams play on a rain-soaked field in a cold drizzle. Both teams struggled, spattered in mud, while Ryan provided play-by-play over the public address system. Russ Rebholz, Bobby Schiller, and Greg Kabat from the Winnipegs, all Americans, officiated the American game.

In the first quarter, the Wildcats opened with a passing attack, but on a pass attempt from their own 40-yard line, Kobrinsky broke through the right side of the North Dakota Science line and intercepted the ball. He never broke stride and returned the ball 40 yards for a Manitoba touchdown. Through the remainder of the first half, until late in the third quarter, the teams struggled near midfield, but then the Wildcats began a 70-yard scoring drive that included a 27-yard pass to the Manitoba 20-yard line. The Wildcats moved the ball on the ground and on fourth down Nutter scored from less than a yard.

The Wildcats gained the ball back in the fourth quarter and reached Manitoba's 30-yard line. Once again Kobrinsky intercepted a pass to stop the drive. In the final minutes, Manitoba engineered a 53-yard drive that ended on a turnover on downs at North Dakota Science's 12-yard line. The Bisons beat the Wildcats 7-6.

Despite the win, sports pages found reasons to criticize the close finish. "Lack of experience at the American rules [was] reflected in Manitoba's chief weakness, the inability to make full use of opportunities for [blocking]," observed the *Tribune*. The *Manitoban* concurred, "Running interference and blocking are new to the Varsity squad and, consequently, the Wildcats from Wahpeton were superior in this department of the game."

Afterward, both teams attended a tea dance at the Roseland Dance Gardens where the public could pay 25 cents to dance and listen to an 11-piece orchestra. Radio station CJRC broadcast the event.

With the return of football to Manitoba, the student newspaper scolded the student body, which "[had] always complained that it did not wish to support losing teams," observed the *Manitoban*. "The football squad this year seems to be a good one and it certainly deserves the support of the students... There is, of course, a certain financial consideration in bringing teams here from across the border... It has been stated in well-informed circles that football is on trial and that if it does not succeed it will be discontinued as a major sport."

* *

Minnesota Coach Bernie Bierman played up his team's competition. While *Minneapolis Star* sportswriter Bernard Swanson ranked North Dakota State "a minor league foe," Bierman rated the Bison higher than the South Dakota State team the Gophers had beaten 19-16 in 1933. Bierman listed his gripes:

- The Gophers would enjoy only two weeks of practice before they played the Bison.
- Downpours at the old Northrop Field practice grid had prevented the team from a healthy regimen of contact scrimmage. When Fritz Crisler's Gophers team had played the Bison in the second game of a double-header in 1931—the Gophers had beaten Ripon College of Ripon, Wisconsin, 30-0 in the first game—the Gophers walked away victorious but by a slim 13-7 margin.
- He had yet to match up against Bison Coach Casey Finnegan.
- He had sent his backfield coach "Red" Dawson west on a train to watch the Bison play the Cobbers and altogether, things didn't look rosy for Minnesota.

Brown and Gold (1934)

Almost nobody believed Bierman's self-assessment. He had seventeen lettermen return to his squad in 1934, including Francis "Pug" Lund, the team captain who played at left halfback. Lund had rushed for more yards in 1933 than all of the Gophers' opponents combined. Many picked Minnesota to win the Big Ten title or even the national championship in 1934. Most expected the Gophers would beat the Bison by more than four touchdowns.

Finnegan knew he would never match Bierman's credentials. Born in Springfield, Minnesota, Bierman had played high school football in Litchfield, Minnesota, before he starred at halfback for the Golden Gophers from 1913 to 1915. He served as captain of the team in 1915. After graduation, Bierman went on to coach the high school football team in Butte, Montana, to an undefeated season. In 1917, he enlisted as an officer in the U.S. Marine Corps during World War I. When he returned to civilian life in 1919, he coached football at the University of Montana through the 1921 season. In 1922, he coached football at Pillsbury Academy, a prep school in Owatonna, Minnesota, and in 1923 he took the job of assistant coach at Tulane University in New Orleans, Louisiana. Two years later, he served as an assistant coach at Mississippi State University, and then returned to serve as head coach at Tulane from 1927 to 1931. His team competed but lost to the University of Southern California 21-12 in the 1932 Rose Bowl. Bierman had returned to Minnesota in 1932 to coach the Gophers.

In Fargo, Finnegan followed the same tack as Bierman. He said his 1934 squad didn't have the same "bruising strength" of his 1931 team, which had played Minnesota and also held Wisconsin to a 12-7 score that season. Finnegan's current squad had experienced practice limitations. The wet weather had forced the team to practice inside the gymnasium and on the running track. Finnegan expressed concern that without an outdoor scrimmage the team would fail to prepare well enough for the Gophers. Many of his players had caught bad colds. Fortunately, the Bison had already played one game, whereas Minnesota had yet to engage in any combat whatsoever.

In its pre-assessment, the *Minneapolis Tribune* declared the Bison backfield a threat. "The ball carrying troupe includes Fritz Hanson, sensational touchdown runner from Perham, Minn., who weighs only 145 pounds but who was the North Central Conference's most dangerous scoring threat the last two seasons. Finnegan seldom starts Hanson, but the midget tow-head is often inserted at critical junctures of a game." The *Star* also pointed to Bud Marquardt and Herb Peschel as outstanding players. The *Daily Argus-Leader* took a less exuberant approach. "North Dakota State will meet a team which is being rated with the greatest in the country. [The Bison] will have no reason to feel discouraged if they can hold the Gophers below 40 points." North Central Conference teams had played Big Ten teams 20 times since the NCC had organized in 1922, and every time the Big Ten team won. In the *Fargo Forum*, Eugene Fitzgerald said, "Even if the Bison do score once they will accomplish something few teams do against Minnesota."

When Bierman's scout, Dawson, had returned from Fargo, he told Bierman, "Next Saturday, we will see the fastest ball player we probably will see all season" in Hanson. Dawson said when he approached Finnegan after the game against Concordia, Finnegan bragged about his little halfback. He said Hanson had scored a touchdown in every game he played in 1933 despite the fact he never played more than five minutes in a game. Dawson told *Star* sportswriter Bernard Swanson, "If our Gophers give that kid half a chance, he'll get away and they'll have the toughest time catching him [that] they will have all year." He said Finnegan had taught the Bison to execute the Rockne system to perfection. Dawson ranked Peschel, now at 200 pounds, the best lineman on the team.

By Wednesday afternoon, the rains had subsided enough to allow the Bison to practice outdoors, but the team didn't accomplish much in the mud. The Gophers, too, found an opportunity to scrimmage outside.

Finnegan and 30 Bison players departed Fargo for Minneapolis at 4:20 p.m. Thursday afternoon and then checked in late at the Andrews Hotel, the same hotel where Concordia Coach Frank Cleve and his Cobbers stayed during trips to The Twin Cities. On Friday, the team visited Memorial Stadium to practice on the foreign grid and the team finished up just as the Gophers took the field for their own scrimmage. That evening, Finnegan took his entire football team and coaching staff to

Brown and Gold (1934)

watch St. Olaf beat St. Thomas 2-0. The Tommies impressed the Bison with their tackling ability.

Shortly before noon on Saturday, the day of the game, Finnegan's appointed Bison captain, Leonard House, decided to take a nap in his room at the hotel. When the team departed for Memorial Stadium they didn't notice House was not with them. House, the left guard, ran to the stadium and when he arrived, out of breath, he barely had enough time to dress and join his team for the 2:00 p.m. opening kickoff.

Memorial Stadium displayed the game time on an electric clock, a new innovation for the venue. The ticket-takers counted 26,544 fans in the stands, the biggest opening day crowd in Minnesota football history. Radio station WTCN, jointly owned by the *Minneapolis Tribune* and the *St. Paul Dispatch-Pioneer Press*, broadcast the play-by-play, as well as WLB, the University of Minnesota radio station. Reports said Lyle Sturgeon weighed in at 282 pounds for the game and his presence on the field served as a spectacle for the media.

Wendy Schollander returned the opening kickoff 21 yards to North Dakota State's 28-yard line. When the offense lined up for the first play Peschel started at right guard across from a red-headed Gopher named Vern Oech from Beach, North Dakota. Meanwhile, Sturgeon started at left tackle. On defense, Peschel and Sturgeon would switch positions to place Sturgeon's bulk in the center of the line across from Oech. The Bison played strong defense and held the Gophers scoreless through the first quarter, but Minnesota Coach Bierman substituted frequently to keep his men fresh.

In the second quarter, after the Gophers executed a 19-yard run to reach North Dakota State's 27-yard line, the Gophers used both runs and a pass to reach the 1-foot line where the fullback went over for the score. In the same period, the Gophers regained the ball when Lund recovered a bad Bison snap at North Dakota State's 22-yard line. On the next play, Lund scored on a touchdown pass. Later, the Gophers returned a punt, and after a few plays Minnesota unleashed 210-pound reserve fullback named Stanislaus "Stanley" Kostka, a South St. Paul native. Kostka and Hanson had both competed in the state track meet in 1931. Kostka carried the ball over to score for the Gophers and he broke loose again near the

At Minnesota (Minneapolis, Minnesota)

end of the first half and scored a touchdown on a 64-yard run. Kostka took on the role of featured back and in the third quarter, he carried the ball frequently and scored again on a 5-yard run. The Gophers scored yet again when they tackled the Bison kick returner in the end zone for a safety. Five minutes later, the Gophers scored on a 76-yard run.

In the fourth quarter, the Gopher reserve center flubbed the snap and forced Minnesota to attempt a punt from their 4-yard line. Peschel broke through the line, blocked the kick, and fell on the ball beyond the goal line for the score. On Minnesota's next drive the Gophers fumbled and the Bison recovered the ball on Minnesota's 26-yard line. Hanson ran a sweep and completed a pass to the 7-yard line. Hanson then connected with Marquardt on a touchdown pass. The little halfback later left the game with a leg injury.

Minnesota scored again on a 15-yard run. Late in the game, Kostka scored again on a 22-yard run. At the final gun, the new electronic scoreboard read Minnesota 56, North Dakota State 12. Only the 1927 Minnesota squad had scored more points in a game when they beat North Dakota 57-10.

Minnesota rushed for 347 yards in the game and held North Dakota State to just 29 yards rushing. The Bison managed to complete 7 of 13 pass attempts for 58 yards while Minnesota completed 3 of 6 attempts for 52 yards. Throughout the game, Bierman used three different platoons and fielded a total of 37 different players and Minnesota's third-string platoon scored the final two touchdowns against the Bison. Peschel played the entire game without substitution.

After the game, Finnegan said, "I never saw so much man power vested in one team in all my years of football. It didn't seem to make a particle of difference what combination of players Minnesota had on the field, [they] showed tremendous power."

In all, Hanson gained only 11 yards on 5 carries but still he entertained the crowd. "Hanson was outstanding for the visitors," wrote George A. Barton, sportswriter or the *Minneapolis Tribune*. "This fast-stepping and alert little fellow [gave] the Gophers considerable trouble to prevent him from getting away for a touchdown run or two." In the *Forum*, Fitzgerald explained Hanson's efforts differently. "Hanson ran all over the stadium,"

Brown and Gold (1934)

he said, "although he didn't make a lot of ground. But it gave the fans a thrill." In the *Bison* yearbook the students wrote, "The Herd played a great game against the highly rated Minnesota team and the Bison brought due credit to themselves for scoring against the Gophers."

*   *

A cold rain had kept the Dragons indoors, but Moorhead State Coach Sliv Nemzek had grown tired of chalk talks. Despite his team's 19-4 win over Jamestown, he didn't like how his team had performed against the pass in that game. He told his men to suit up. They would go outside for a few minutes to run through formations. Nemzek soon discovered the rain had soaked the grass so much that even walk-throughs proved difficult. He sent his men back inside soaked to the bone.

Meanwhile, indoors at Concordia, half a dozen Cobbers nursed injuries. Coach Frank Cleve welcomed the respite. The Bison had thwarted the Cobbers using a six-man line instead of the usual seven-man front and he needed to give his men the necessary chalk talk about how to get open with more defenders in the defensive secondary.

Later in the week, when the rain subsided Cleve continued to try out punters, including Bob Fritz. Concordia's kicker from the first game, Ralph Miller, had fallen ill with the stomach flu and Cleve needed a replacement. Nemzek, too, took advantage of the lapse in rain. He sent his players outside for a full-contact scrimmage and he focused on defending the option run.

This year, the Cobbers outweighed the Dragons, both on the line and in the backfield, but "as far as I'm concerned, [the game] will be as hard as ever," Fritz told the *Western MiSTiC*. "We're not overconfident a bit, but it's going to be a darn good fight."

The night before the game, students at Moorhead State filled the gymnasium. A pep squad of 17 students led the campus body in a pep fest.

When the Cobbers and Dragons ran onto Memorial Field on September 29, 1934, all of Moorhead knew the score. The Cobbers and Dragons had played a dozen times since 1922 and in 50 percent of those games, the struggle had ended in a scoreless tie, including in three of their last four matchups in 1933, 1931, and 1930. The Dragons had beaten the Cobbers only once, in 1926.

In the first quarter, the Cobbers tried an aerial attack, but when Fritz attempted a pass, the Dragons intercepted and gained possession of the ball at Moorhead State's 35-yard line. Out of the Dragons backfield Vincent Yatchak and Marco Gotta combined for 35 yards on two runs and the Dragons scored a touchdown on a 30-yard pass. In the second quarter, Concordia used the ground game to move the ball on option runs led by Fritz. The Cobbers achieved four consecutive first downs to reach Moorhead State's 4-yard line where Fritz plunged over center for the score. Later in the same period, Fritz led the team from Concordia's 20-yard line to Moorhead State's 9-yard line where, on a hurry up play, Henry Held ran off left end for the touchdown.

In the third quarter, the Dragons tied the score on a flea-flicker pass that resulted in a touchdown. In the fourth quarter, Concordia reached the 9-yard line but lost the ball on downs. The Cobbers later regained the ball and reached the 10-yard line where Held attempted a field goal but missed wide. The game ended in a 13-13 tie.

Concordia had tried but failed in their passing game as the Cobbers completed only 4 of 18 pass attempts with 2 interceptions. Both sides ran the ball well. *Moorhead Daily News* sportswriter Dick Hackenberg said the Dragons backfielders had "turned in spine-tingling performances in advancing the ball" while the Cobbers were "dynamite," "lightning," and "wiry."

*   *

Lionel Conacher and his Wrigley Aromints professional football team started up in Toronto as planned, with promotional help from Leo Dandurand, the managing director for the Montreal Canadiens hockey team. For the 1934 season, Conacher hired Mike Rodden, two-time Grey Cup championship-winning coach with the Hamilton Tigers, to lead the team. Besides Lionel and his brother Charlie, the 25-man Aromints roster included Canadian athletes with experience in multiple amateur and professional sports, including Olympic events, hockey, golf, baseball, wrestling, and Canadian rugby or American intercollegiate football. The few Americans on the team included Ernie "The Beast" Zeller, an All-American wrestler and, in football, a lineman and backfielder who had played for Indiana State University in Terre Haute, Indiana, from 1930 to 1933. The most interesting player on the Aromints, however, was "Hap" Watson, the former first base coach and pitcher for the defunct Toronto Oslers baseball club. Fans knew Watson as the Oslers player who had entertained the crowd between innings by juggling and performing comedy routines. In recent years, Watson had played and performed throughout the United States for the barnstorming American and Canadian Clowns baseball club.

The Aromints opened their independent professional run on October 3, 1934, at Maple Leaf Stadium in Toronto against the Rochester Oxfords, a semi-professional team from the Rochester, New York, sandlot circuit. The Oxfords brought years of football history to the gridiron. In 1929, the Oxfords had played the Buffalo Bisons of the NFL. By 1934, however, the Oxfords fielded a diminished squad.

In front of 3,000 fans, the Oxfords found themselves down 0-10 at the half. Perhaps it took a while for the Oxfords to grasp the modified mixture of American professional and Canadian rules that allowed forward passes from anywhere behind the line of scrimmage and for players to block up to 10 yards beyond the line of scrimmage. Lou Marsh, sportswriter for the *Toronto Daily Star*, said in his opinion, the rules were "what have you" and remained a mystery to most.

In the third quarter, an Oxford backfielder with the last name McQue "ripped through the Toronto line at will" and scored a touchdown and the extra point to close the score 6-10. The Aromints finished strong, however, first by scoring a rouge and later as Lionel Conacher completed a touchdown pass to his brother, Charlie. The Aromints scored the extra point and walked away victorious 17-6.

In the *Toronto Daily Star*, Marsh praised the game for its "sensational long runs" and "astounding forward passes," but he also panned the event. He suggested the Aromints had put on a performance because, throughout the game, Watson's pants "threatened to fall off" and "[his] struggles to keep his jeans on, his shirt down, and his helmet out of his eyes" entertained the crowd.

After the game, the Ottawa Junior City Football League approached Conacher about having the Aromints play a two-game series in Ottawa as a fundraiser for the junior league. Conacher had already scheduled the Aromints to play in Montreal on October 14 and so he offered to play an exhibition game in Ottawa on October 13 with a second game on October 20. Conacher said he would cover the $700 guarantee to bring in a team from Buffalo, New York, and that the Aromints would receive 40 percent of gate receipts.

* *

Even though Fritz Hanson stood atop Coach Casey Finnegan's depth chart in talent, the old coach had kept Hanson on the sideline as a not-so-secret weapon for North Dakota State. Instead, Finnegan started Erling Schranz and he sent in Hanson when the team moved within striking distance of the goal line. To Hanson, "striking distance" meant from anywhere on the field. Nevertheless, Schranz started games, but during practice in the week after the Bison had lost to the Gophers, Schranz revealed he had suffered internal injuries in the home opener against Concordia. He had aggravated the injuries against Minnesota. Finnegan ordered Schranz to the hospital. Wendy Schollander, too, then suffered an injury during practice. Hanson would have to start against St. Thomas.

The Bison and the Tommies tied 7-7 in their 1933 matchup and now St. Thomas would play in Fargo after a 2-0 loss to St. Olaf. The Tommies needed a win, but with three of the team's best players out with injuries, St. Thomas Coach George Barsi would have to tap into his reserves. The student newspaper at St. Thomas, the *Aquin*, reminded its readers that "the 56 to 12 whipping which Finnegan's boys took at the hands of Bernie Bierman's slashing Gophers last Saturday wasn't as derogatory as the score advertises." The purple and gray Tommies would have their hands full.

Barsi, the new head coach at St. Thomas, had taken over the football program from Wilbur Eaton, who had taken over the program from Joe

Brown and Gold (1934)

Boland in 1933. The St. Thomas football program had suffered frequent, sometimes yearly changes at the football head coach position since 1904. Born in Jackson, California, Barsi had played high school basketball and football in Stockton, California, before he went on to play both sports at the University of Santa Clara in California. He served as captain of the Broncos basketball team there and coached the freshman football team to an undefeated season. A year after graduation, in 1931, Barsi took the job as coach of the basketball team and assistant backfield coach for the football team at St. Thomas. Barsi served under Boland who had been the former Santa Clara line coach for football.

After the 1933 season, St. Thomas decided to cut costs. The school dismissed Eaton and hired Barsi to be the head coach for both football and basketball. Meanwhile, Boland had moved from his radio gig at WCCO to become an assistant coach to Elmer Layden at Notre Dame, Boland's alma mater.

Barsi brought 26 players to Fargo for the game played October 5, 1934, at Dacotah Field. Both teams sustained a scoreless first quarter, but in the second period, the North Dakota State line charged a St. Thomas punt and the kick shot low. Lyle Sturgeon recovered the ball. On the next play, Hanson ran the ball 26 yards to St. Thomas' 35-yard line and an unnecessary roughness penalty against the Tommies advanced the ball to the 20-yard line. Hanson then ran near to the sidelines, around the left side of the line, and he reversed his run toward the opposite sideline to gain a total of 16 yards. Bob Erickson, who had filled in for Shifty Gove at fullback, moved the ball 3 yards, and then Hanson scored a touchdown on a 1-yard run through the line on a spinner play. On North Dakota State's next possession, Hanson returned a punt to St. Thomas' 35-yard line. The Bison completed a pass to St. Thomas' 19-yard line and on a spinner play, Hanson zipped to the 5-yard line. Erickson stormed across the goal line for the score.

In the third quarter, Leo Gerteis completed a 31-yard pass, and on the next play, he carried it over for the score. In the fourth quarter, North Dakota State blocked a Tommies punt and recovered the ball on St. Thomas' 4-yard line where the Bison attempted three runs at the line. On fourth down, North Dakota State scored on a pass from Gerteis to an uncontested Bud Marquardt. The Bison beat the Tommies 27-0.

The Bison reached first down 15 times in this game compared to twice for St. Thomas. The Bison didn't play the game without mistakes, however, as they fumbled the ball 7 times and lost 4 to the Tommies. Six different Bison backfielders had run and passed the ball for North Dakota State. *Moorhead Daily News* sportswriter Dick Hackenberg said the Bison had reached first down "almost at will... with little Fritz Hanson's breathtaking, field-reversing runs." The *Spectrum*, too, felt the need to describe Hanson's running in descriptive detail. "In daring fashion, Hanson twisted and scampered over the field," wrote the student newspaper. "Often, when he was seemingly trapped, the fleet half[back] showed he had other plans—and, minus any interference, promptly launched his course in the opposite direction." The *Spectrum* described Hanson's route as a "sparrow trail."

* *

At Manitoba, the student newspaper reported with enthusiasm that the team continued to practice with zeal. "If aggressiveness and a never-say-die spirit have anything to do with the winning of games—and we believe that they have—then the Buffalos [*sic*] should be odds-on favorites against Jamestown," wrote *Manitoban* columnist J.C. Portnuff. The newspaper went on to urge students to turn out to support the team if they hoped to see a future for the sport at the university. Meanwhile, Bisons Coach Wally Hass leveraged the sorority girls at the university to sell tickets. The sorority that sold the most books of season tickets would receive a prize, and the two girls who sold the most tickets would receive a free ride in an airplane over Winnipeg.

On the practice field, Hass concentrated on teaching how to defend against the pass and on offense, he added forward-lateral plays to the playbook. He had been informed that Jamestown employed the Rockne system, a new offensive play style for the young Bisons to defend against. Hass would go head-to-head with Jimmies Coach E.J. Cassell who had coached the team to win the North Dakota College Athletic Conference

Brown and Gold (1934)

title in 1933. Cassell had played football and baseball at Carleton where he captained the grid team as a senior and twice earned all-state honors at halfback. After Cassell graduated in 1925, he went on to serve as athletic director and coach at Olivet College in Olivet, Michigan. In 1929, he took a similar position at Epworth Military Academy in Iowa. He took over at Jamestown in 1930.

Cassell and 22 men, including seven lettermen, arrived in Winnipeg Thursday night before the game. The team stayed at the Fort Garry Hotel while the University of Manitoba staged another pep fest for students.

On Friday morning, October 5, 1934, the Jimmies assembled at Osborne Stadium for practice. Later in the day, in front of 1,000 shivering fans, the Jimmies took the field in orange and black while the Winnipeg Rifles band welcomed everyone to the venue for the game. The Jimmies saw how the Bisons outweighed them in every category. The Bisons averaged 195 pounds on the line, 20 more per man than the Jimmies, and the Bisons averaged 180 pounds in the backfield, 15 more per man. The home team had eight more men in reserve than the visitors.

In the first quarter, Jamestown received the opening kickoff and Coach Hass quickly learned that his pregame intelligence had failed him. The Jimmies did not, in fact, run a Rockne system offense. Instead, they ran plays out of the Warner Double Wing formation. After big gains on two plays the Jimmies lined up at Manitoba's 32-yard line and tried an end around run, which would prove to be the decisive play against the Bisons. Jamestown right end Don Hall raced with the ball around left end and behind great blocking, he ran 32 yards for the score. Five minutes later, the Jimmies completed an 18-yard pass to reach Manitoba's 22-yard line and then ran the same end-around play and Hall scored again.

In the second quarter, the Bisons fumbled and lost the ball at the 50-yard line. The Jimmies reached first down twice on running plays and then Hall caught a pass and the Bisons tackled him at the 1-yard line. A Jamestown halfback then plunged over for the score.

Manitoba received the kickoff to open the second half. Tubber Kobrinsky returned the kick 20 yards from the goal line and in four plays he ran the ball another 30 yards, but Jamestown shut down Manitoba's drive and took possession of the ball. Meanwhile, Jamestown covered a lot of ground as the Jimmies frequently gained 20 yards or more per play. In the third quarter, the Jimmies completed a 22-yard touchdown pass. Late in the game, the Bisons threatened to score when Kobrinsky returned a punt to Jamestown's 30-yard line, but the Jimmies intercepted a pass to shut down the drive and win the game 27-0.

Despite the lopsided loss, Coach Hass expressed satisfaction with his team's performance. He blamed inexperience in blocking and in shedding blocks for the loss, but also speed. The Manitoba student newspaper concurred. "No sooner had Varsity's kicks left Kobrinsky's toe than the whole of the visitors team had formed a well-nigh invincible interference for the receiver. And after interference was gone, sheer speed carried him to huge advantages." *Winnipeg Tribune* Columnist Richard Allen praised Jamestown's execution. "I think Jamestown played the prettiest football these unsophisticated eyes have ever beheld," he said. Afterward, the Bisons held a reception for their vanquishers.

In the ensuing days, sportswriters derided Manitoba's student body. In the *Winnipeg Free Press*, E.A. Armstrong wrote, "The student body should really feel disgraced with the attendance at last night's game. An enrollment of over 3,000 students and not 500 out to cheer their club. Nothing but a disgrace." Amongst the fans who did attend sat Concordia Cobbers coaches and players. Coach Frank Cleve and his men had arrived in Winnipeg earlier in the day and in the coming days they would play the Winnipeg Rugby Club in two games, the first on Saturday, and the second on Monday, Canada's Thanksgiving Day holiday. After the Manitoba game, Cleve told the *Free Press* he felt Manitoba had a good foundation in American football and that, given another year of coaching and practice in the Yankee game, they would match up well with American colleges south of the border. Cleve also praised the play of Kobrinsky.

To prepare for their series in Winnipeg, which the teams would play half-and-half under American and Canadian rules, Cleve had given his starters a rest while he scrimmaged his reserves. He intended to play his starters on Saturday and his reserves on Monday.

In the Winnipegs camp, quarterback Bobby Schiller had left town by plane for Chicago to visit his sick mother. Meanwhile, Eddie "Dynamite" James practiced well, and though he wore a brace on his arm that made it

Brown and Gold (1934)

difficult for him to tuck the ball and he could no longer stiff-arm an opponent and keep the ball secure, he carried the pigskin for long gains. James could no longer lateral the ball effectively. As for coach Greg Kabat, he continued to deal with a fractured hand but expected to play with his hand bandaged. Kabat expected the Cobbers would attack through the air and he welcomed the challenge because it would prepare the Winnipegs for their expected playoff game against the Regina Roughriders. He had a hard time preparing his men for Concordia, however, because torrential rains early in the week had forced the team to practice on the ice rink at the Granite Curling Club.

Two hundred or so miles across an international border separated Winnipeg from Moorhead, which proved difficult for reporters on both ends. While the *Winnipeg Tribune* correctly noted that Cleve was "known to Winnipeg baseball fans as Fargo-Moorhead's second baseman of last year," the *Tribune* misnamed the Cobbers the "Cobblers" and said the team wore "cerise" (reddish pink) instead of maroon with gold. In Moorhead, the *Concordian* student newspaper referred to the Winnipeg team as the "Rough Riders" [Winnipeg's rival] coached by Hass [Manitoba's coach] and with Cronin [who had left for Hamilton] on the team. The Winnipeg papers did do a good job of promoting the game, however. The *Winnipeg Free Press* noted that although Concordia's Bob Fritz weighed 190 pounds, he "travels like a lightweight." The *Tribune* promised that both teams possessed "fast traveling, snaky-hipped ball carriers, ripping, crashing line plungers, true forward passers and sure receivers, so there should be plenty of variety in the attacks made on both north and south goal lines." The *Tribune* justified the Cobbers series of games by saying, "Concordia will present a team that has held the strongest team in the American Northwest, namely North Dakota State, to a 6 to 0 score, and if the 'Pegs can present an offence that can click against this opposition they will have little to worry about in the western playdowns."

Approximately 1,500 fans turned out at Osborne Stadium for the first game on Saturday afternoon, October 6, 1934. The officials for the game included Manitoba coaches Wally Hass and Walter Odhe. In the first quarter, Fritz, at fullback, attempted a long pass for Concordia that fell incomplete but his failed attempt set up the next play. From the same formation, Fritz chose to run the ball, instead, and found a hole off tackle. He ran 51 yards for a touchdown. When Winnipeg regained the ball, the Cobbers intercepted a lateral pass and returned the ball for a touchdown. Before the first quarter ended, Concordia scored again when Fritz carried the ball over center 50 yards near to the goal line. The Cobbers then scored on a line plunge. In the second quarter, Fritz completed a 17-yard touchdown pass to put the Cobbers ahead 26-0. The Winnipegs responded with an aerial attack and Russ Rebholz completed a 37-yard pass to Lynn Patrick in the end zone for a touchdown. Near the end of the first half, Rebholz launched another pass in a long, high arc. The ball traveled 68 yards through the air and Patrick raced under it and caught it with outstretched arms at the 10-yard line. Patrick's inertia carried him the final 10 yards into the end zone for a total gain of 78 yards and a score.

Coach Kabat had decided his reserve players should play the first half under American rules but the reserves had offered only "tissue-paper resistance" to Concordia's offense. The Cobbers, meanwhile, had given the Winnipegs a lesson in blocking, off the line, out of the backfield, and in the open field.

In the third quarter, Rebholz fumbled and lost the ball on a punt return. The Cobbers swept up the bouncing ball and advanced it for a touchdown. Concordia then fumbled a punt return into their own end zone where the Winnipegs leapt on the pigskin for a touchdown. On their next possession, the Winnipegs drove to Concordia's 1-yard line and on third down crashed off tackle for a touchdown to come within one score of the Cobbers. Late in the game, Rebholz attempted more long passes to Patrick but the Cobbers knocked them down and finished the game on top 33-27.

Fritz played the full 60 minutes in this game and won the hearts of fans who saw him as a worthy captain for the Cobbers.

Afterward, Winnipeg newspapers proclaimed the Rebholz-Patrick pass, at 78 yards, to be the longest forward pass completed on the North American continent, longer than the 70-yard pass Harold "Brick" Muller had completed to Brodie Stephens for the University of California, Berkeley, against Ohio State University in the 1921 Rose Bowl.

Brown and Gold (1934)

*

In the second game, played on Thanksgiving Day Monday, October 8, 1934, Concordia wore out its welcome in front of 2,000 fans. In the first quarter, the Cobbers drove from their own 30-yard line and quickly gained four first downs. Fritz completed a 5-yard pass to halfback Henry Held for the first score. On their next possession, the Cobbers reached Winnipeg's 1-yard line just as the quarter ended. After the teams reversed field, Held bounded over the line for another touchdown. When Winnipeg regained the ball, they fumbled and lost possession on their own 40-yard line. Fritz then engineered an advance that included passes and line smashes. The drive ended on a 15-yard halfback run around right end for the score. On their next possession, the Cobbers drove from their own 44-yard line and worked their way downfield on four first downs. At the 5-yard line, the Concordia linemen opened a huge hole and Fritz tiptoed over the goal line for a touchdown. The Cobbers scored the extra point and Concordia finished the first half of the game ahead 26-0.

In the third quarter, the teams played under the Canadian code, and while Concordia racked up penalties, lost yardage, and punted, the Winnipegs gained steam. Winnipeg ran option runs and drove the ball deep into Concordia territory where they attempted a field goal. The pigskin bounced off the upright but fell through for the score. On Winnipeg's next possession Rebholz completed a 40-yard forward pass to Concordia's 5-yard line where James drove through the right side of the line for a touchdown. In the fourth quarter, the Winnipegs regained the ball at Concordia's 29-yard line. Three plays later James smashed through two yards of tacklers for a touchdown, but it wasn't enough. In the end, Concordia won the game 26-16.

The game showed how each team excelled under its own familiar sets of rules. In the first half played under the American code, Concordia dominated while the Winnipegs only possessed the ball long enough to execute 6 plays, including 2 punts and 2 plays that resulted in lost fumbles. Observed the *Winnipeg Tribune*, the Cobbers "chopped through [the] Winnipegs' pitiful attempts at [blocking] with incredulous ease... and when in possession, [Concordia] bowled over opposing tacklers while Fritz and his backfield chums were hippety-hopping down the field for huge gains." In the second half, when the Cobbers could no longer block for their backs just anywhere on the field, the Winnipegs excelled.

Once again, Fritz's generalship impressed Winnipeggers. "In the hero role, [Fritz] stood head and shoulders above any other man on the field," observed sportswriter Bill Metcalfe in the *Winnipeg Free Press*. The *Winnipeg Tribune* concurred:

> "The young men from Moorhead, Minn., with husky, colorful Bob Fritz in full command, trampled through [the] Winnipegs' 6-2-1-2 defence with comparative ease. Fritz, probably the best football player ever seen here was an unusually clever strategist, and while he annoyed the people in the bleachers with the signals he rhymed off, he also had the locals playing Blind Man's Bluff as they expected one play and chased after an entirely different one."

The papers aid James, meanwhile, "seems to have lost some of his dynamite over his long lay off from the gridiron game," observed Ralph Allen in the *Winnipeg Tribune*. James did hit the line hard, however, and had managed to pull in both lateral and forward passes. He was seen "grinning happily through the thick of another football fight," observed Allen.

* *

While Concordia crushed Winnipeg in Winnipeg, Lionel Conacher's Wrigley Aromints played a second game in Toronto, on October 8, 1934, Thanksgiving Day in Canada. The Aromints played a team from Buffalo, New York, that included several players who had played for schools in upstate New York, including Canisius College in Buffalo, Niagara University in Lewiston, Syracuse University, and the University of Buffalo. In the Aromints' second professional football game of the season, both sides put on an aerial show with Buffalo completing 11 of 30 pass attempts and with the Aromints completing 6 of 13. Conacher's

Brown and Gold (1934)

men sped to a 14-0 lead at halftime, and while Buffalo managed to score a touchdown in the second half, the Aromints finished strong to win 19-5. The *Toronto Daily Star* reported that once again, "Neither players nor fans appeared to be the least accustomed to the rules." When Conacher scored a rouge, "the baffled Buffalo team wondered what had happened."

After the game, Dr. M.B. Kinsella, former CRU president, pronounced professional football in Canada dead on arrival. "As for professional football—well, it's just a planned show," he said. "There is no danger of it ever supplanting the amateur game." *Collyer's Eye & Baseball World* viewed things differently. "There are at least 50 American college players now tossing forward passes and showing their wares in Canadian rugby," wrote the *Eye*. "The influx is causing some worry to Canuck coaches as there are just a few of them left."

Just a few days before the Aromints' scheduled game at Lansdowne Park in Ottawa, Ontario, the Ottawa Junior City Football League announced they had to cancel the two-game series featuring the Aromints to make room for other athletic events.

*   *

Bison coaches Casey Finnegan and Bob Lowe had understood how to tame the South Dakota Coyotes, but in 1934, South Dakota fielded an altogether different animal. In June, Coyotes athletic director Stanley Backman, who had lost the confidence of his players, stepped back from his role as head football coach and hired Harry Gamage to lead the them. A 1926 graduate of the University of Illinois, Gamage had played football for the Illini and coached the freshman team there before he took the head coaching job at the University of Kentucky in Lexington, Kentucky, in 1927. During his seven seasons at Kentucky, Gamage led the Wildcats to a 32-25-5 overall record. Gamage signed a three-month initial contract with South Dakota.

The day after North Dakota State's victory over St. Thomas, Finnegan and Lowe had traveled to Vermillion to watch the Coyotes defend their home turf against North Dakota. The Bison mentors watched as the Coyotes used both the Short Punt and regular Long Punt formations to run their plays. Quarterback Chappie O'Connor tossed passes and reeled off gains, including a 50-yard run on the first play of the game. They also watched as the Sioux dropped Coyote backfielders for losses on pass plays.

When Finnegan and Lowe returned to Fargo they had the reserves scrimmage in South Dakota's new offense while varsity defenders focused on getting after the passer. On offense, Finnegan and Lowe figured they could use their Bison ball carriers to run down the clock to keep the Coyotes' offense off the field. After a week of strong practices, Finnegan expressed confidence in his men when he told them, "Those Coyotes better be tough."

Gamage and his team left Vermillion for Fargo on Thursday morning. He brought along 20 players but had to leave O'Connor behind. The NCC had declared O'Connor ineligible to play any more college football. During the summer, O'Connor had played one game with the Sioux Falls Canaries professional baseball team in the Nebraska State League. And Gamage had to say goodbye to another player, Rex Phillips, whom the NCC declared ineligible because, in part, he hadn't enrolled in school.

Both teams practiced under the lights at Dacotah Field on Thursday evening.

North Dakota State opened its first conference game of the season on October 12, 1934. Fans without season tickets paid 75 cents for general admission seating while kids under 14 entered the venue for free with the knothole gang. When the Bison took the field Herb Peschel started at right guard and Fritz Hanson started at right halfback. North Dakota State used just seven plays in the first quarter to score a touchdown. At the end of that drive, Hanson took the ball off right tackle on a spinner play and bounded 15 yards through a broken field to cross the goal line. Later in the same period, Hanson returned a South Dakota punt 47 yards to score. In the second quarter, the Bison drove 65 yards and this time the reserves scored a touchdown on an 8-yard off-tackle run.

At halftime, Finnegan and Lowe took heart in the fact the Bison had dominated in time of possession. Finnegan had substituted backfielders to keep his men fresh and to keep the Coyote defense on its toes.

Brown and Gold (1934)

In the middle of third quarter, the Bison fumbled and lost the ball on their own 42-yard line. The Coyotes then marched to the Bison 1-yard line, but a bad snap bounced the ball wild and the Bison recovered at the 5-yard line. In the fourth quarter, Peschel blocked a punt and the ball rolled out of the end zone to score a safety for the Bison. With 5 seconds remaining in the game Hanson returned a punt 25 yards and the Coyotes tackled him as the final gun sounded. The Bison beat the Coyotes 22-0. Both teams walked toward the field house and the crowd flooded the playing field. The standings showed the Bison atop the NCC tied with the Sioux. North Dakota State had yet to allow an opponent to cross its goal line.

*   *

When St. Olaf beat Concordia in 1933, Slippery Syl Saumer had played a big part in the Oles' victory. Thankfully for Concordia, however, Saumer had graduated and moved on to play in the NFL. The Boston Redskins had initially invited him to their organization, but then he made his way to the Pittsburgh Pirates roster and later to the Cincinnati Reds where Saumer scored a touchdown on a run against the Chicago Bears.

Earlier in the 1934 season, Charles Nadelhoffer had served as Saumer's replacement, but against St. Thomas, Nadelhoffer sustained a broken chest bone, several broken ribs, and internal injuries. He later developed pneumonia.

Concordia Coach Frank Cleve didn't know what to expect. To prepare for the their home stand and first conference game of the season, Cleve sent Louie Benson to Northfield to watch St. Olaf play Macalester to a 7-7 tie. When Benson returned, he warned Cleve and the players about the remaining Oles backfielders whom he compared to Fritz Hanson in their running style, in other words, "small, plenty fast, and tricky" behind a tight, heavy Oles line. The St. Olaf threat included "Pop-eye" Shirley who had zipped out a 70-yard run against the Scots; Abe Fox, "one of the shiftiest open field runners in the conference," according to St. Olaf's *Manitou Messenger* student newspaper; and John Kirkeby, a triple-threat

Brown and Gold (1934)

who had left the game with a hip injury but whom Benson expected might play.

Meanwhile, the *Messenger* understood how Bob Fritz served as the engine for Concordia's football machine. Student sportswriter James Rottsolk wrote, "Fritz' favorite pastime is plowing through opposing linesmen. Occasionally he drops back to whip a pass far down the field to a waiting end, or he may take a jaunt around end now and then."

Both Lutheran colleges, St. Olaf and Concordia, counted themselves as rivals in part because Cleve had starred in the Oles passing game when he played for St. Olaf. In fact, 10 years prior, in 1924, when St. Olaf had come to Moorhead, Cleve helped the Oles defeat the Cobbers 16-0. During that game, St. Olaf had covered 130 yards on the ground but 135 yards through the air. Cleve played right end and scored 1 receiving touchdown. He drop-kicked a point after. The Oles won 16-0.

Cleve said he believed Concordia's wins in Winnipeg had instilled confidence in his men. After a pregame practice on Moorhead State's Memorial Field on Thursday before the game, however, Cleve began to worry about overconfidence. He reminded his men how the Oles had defeated them 25-13 the previous season.

On a hot, summer-like Saturday on October 13, 1934, Concordia met St. Olaf at Memorial Field at Moorhead State, the home grid for the Cobbers in 1934. In the opening period, Concordia used a combination of runs up the middle, runs around the ends, and a couple of passes to march from their own 32-yard line to St. Olaf's 17-yard line where quarterback Hank Held, the recipient on a reverse and lateral, skipped 17 yards through daylight for the touchdown. Later in the first quarter, Concordia recovered a fumble on St. Olaf's 22-yard line. Fritz then completed a pass and carried the ball twice, first over center and then off left tackle, to score a touchdown. Concordia intercepted an Oles pass in the second quarter and returned the ball to the 1-yard line. Fritz then plunged over right guard to score again.

In the third quarter, St. Olaf gained momentum with the forward pass. The Oles achieved three consecutive first downs to reach Concordia's 9-yard line and then scored a touchdown on a sweep around left end. St.

Olaf managed to hold the Cobbers scoreless in the second half, but at the final gun, Concordia won the game 19-7.

After the game, Fritz told Cleve, "After we'd piled up a 19-0 lead, I decided to try out some different plays in the second half," he said. "The ones that worked in the first half were too easy, so I thought I'd experiment with the rest of them." In the *Moorhead Daily News*, Dick Hackenberg observed, "And if that doesn't characterize Fritz to a 'T.' He doesn't like his football too easy. The tougher the going the better he likes it."

* *

Coach Wally Hass worked out his Manitoba Bisons for up to four hours at a stretch. The enthusiastic young men needed to learn how to block, how to shed blocks, and how to tackle. Despite the team's lopsided loss to Jamestown, Hass remained satisfied with his young Canadians. He blamed inexperience, and he reminded Winnipeg's sportswriters that not only did his players need to learn how to play under American rules they needed to forget how to play under Canadian rules, too. In advance of the team's game against the North Dakota freshmen he added a couple of new plays to the offense, but for the most part, he focused on fundamentals.

At North Dakota, freshman team Coach Clem Letich prepared his men to take advantage of the weight difference the Bisons would offer. The Sioux Papooses outweighed the Bisons by 23 pounds per man. Letich expected big Ed Rorvig, North Dakota's 200-pound freshman fullback and former Mayville State Comet who had played in Winnipeg in 1933, to find big holes and plow for yardage. He figured all 24 of his young men would get to play in the upcoming two-game series, which included a game against Manitoba on Saturday afternoon and a game against the Winnipeg Rugby Club on Monday evening.

On Saturday afternoon, October 13, 1934, from the very first play, things didn't look good for Manitoba. The team's star ball-carrier, Tubber Kobrinsky, bobbled the ball on the opening kick return and failed to advance the pigskin. Forced to punt from their own end zone, the Bisons kicked the ball away for field position and North Dakota returned the punt to Manitoba's 35-yard line. Six plays later, the Sioux Papooses opened a big hole at the 8-yard line and scored a touchdown. Rorvig scored the extra point and North Dakota took a 7-0 lead.

From the start, the Sioux Papooses front took charge of the line of scrimmage while North Dakota's backfielders' gained yards as a matter of course. Letich kept his squad fresh and gave every man a chance to play. Manitoba responded with brilliant open-field running by Kobrinsky. The 155-pound Jewish backfielder "staged a one-man battle to keep his team in the running, doing 80 percent of the ball carrying and backing up the line like a Trojan," observed *Grand Forks Herald* sportswriter Fred O'Neil. But the Sioux Papooses forced a punt. Later in the opening period, the Bisons fumbled and lost the ball at their own 25-yard line. The Sioux Papooses then completed a 15-yard pass and two plays later ran around right end for a touchdown.

In the second half, North Dakota moved the ball downfield on a 25-yard run. On a fake kick the Sioux Papooses completed a 25-yard pass and then scored on a 12-yard run. Late in the third quarter, North Dakota blocked a Bisons punt at Manitoba's 15-yard line and the Sioux Papooses drove in for a touchdown. Late in the game, North Dakota blocked another punt and scored on a 25-yard run around end to cinch the game 31-0.

Only once did the Bisons hold their ground inside their own 10-yard line when they stopped the Sioux Papooses at the 5-yard line to gain possession on a turnover on downs.

The Winnipegs players had watched from the stands. Afterwards, they expressed consensus that North Dakota would offer them an even contest. The Sioux Papooses had rushed for 150 yards and completed 4 passes for 100 yards.

Despite Manitoba's losses, Winnipeg sportswriters continued to reprimand the student body for non-attendance. Johnny Buss at the *Winnipeg Tribune* described how the weather at Osborne Stadium that day had greeted him with "a perfect day for rugby" but then he felt surprised to see the stands half empty with the majority of spectators older men instead of students. "There is something wrong somewhere when the

Brown and Gold (1934)

students fail to come out and support their teams," he wrote. Meanwhile, with 1,500 fans in the stands, the *Winnipeg Manitoban* observed how the Bisons had played in front of their largest crowd so far this season.

*

Immediately after Manitoba's loss, Coach Greg Kabat took off his officiating sweater at Osborne Stadium and then he and his Winnipegs suited up and took the field for practice.

New and familiar faces had joined the team. Dave Harding, who now joined the Winnipegs as both a player and as an unofficial coach, had most recently played with the Ottawa Roughriders from 1930 to 1932. Harding had started playing rugby in Petrolia, Ontario, in 1914. A longtime serviceman and RCAF pilot, he later played on a service team in New Zealand. In 1919, he helped to organize the Sarnia Imperials, and he played for Queen's in 1921. Harding played on RCAF teams from 1924 to 1926 and played rugby in England in 1928. In 1929 he played for the Camp Borden military base located approximately 60 miles northwest of Toronto. On the gridiron, Harding eschewed the Winnipegs' shiny gold leather helmet and football pants for a tweed cap with hockey pants and hockey stockings.

Arni Coulter also returned to the Winnipegs.

With the North Dakota-Manitoba game fresh in his head Kabat installed new plays the Winnipegs could use against North Dakota to leverage the running talent of Eddie James.

Two days later on October 15, 1934, when the Winnipegs took the field to play the Sioux Papooses, they met a freshman team that had learned a thing or two about the Canadian game. In the first half played under American rules, North Dakota used seven plays to gain four successive first downs and on the eighth play of the drive, Rorvig ran 8 yards for the score. On their next possession, North Dakota gained 20 yards in field position on Winnipeg penalties, and on a series of runs that exhibited great blocking the Sioux Papooses advanced the ball to Winnipeg's 20-yard line where North Dakota completed a touchdown pass. Rorvig kicked the extra point and North Dakota increased their lead to 13-0. In the final minutes of the half, the Winnipegs returned a punt to midfield,

Brown and Gold (1934)

and after Rebholz ran 15 yards on a fake kick to reach the 35-yard line, he tossed a 35-yard touchdown pass to James.

The teams played the second half under Canadian rules and the Sioux Papooses suffered numerous penalties, which kept Winnipeg in the game. They opened with an exchange of punts, but then North Dakota used the passing game to reach Winnipeg's 40-yard line where the Sioux Papooses kicked to the deadline to score a rouge to go up 14-6. The Winnipegs then reached North Dakota's 30-yard line where Rebholz ran off-tackle. The whistle sounded for offsides against North Dakota but Rebholz continued to run until the Sioux Papooses tackled him at the 1-yard line. By rule, the Winnipegs could choose to decline the penalty and take the yardage, but because the referee had used his whistle instead of his horn to indicate the play should continue, the officials met to discuss the discrepancy. They ruled the Winnipegs should have the ball at the 1-yard line. Two plays later, the Winnipegs plunged for a touchdown and scored the extra point.

On Winnipeg's next drive, North Dakota intercepted a lateral pass and advanced the ball 28 yards for a touchdown. The Winnipegs nearly de-pantsed the runner as they tried to tackle him. Next, the Winnipegs moved the ball to North Dakota's 17-yard line where they scored a rouge. On Winnipeg's next possession, Rebholz completed a 54-yard touchdown pass to Kabat and the Winnipegs scored the extra point to tie the game 20-20. While the clock ticked down, the Sioux Papooses took advantage of Canadian rules to break the tie when they kicked a rouge to go ahead 21-20 to win the game and the series.

After the game, *Winnipeg Free Press* sportswriter Cam McKenzie observed that "the majority of Winnipeg fans seemed tickled to death to see the freshmen win," similar to the way fans in Toronto had responded to the Winnipegs in their game against the Argonauts the year before. Both sets of fans showed more interest in entertainment than in loyalty. The *Dakota Student* newspaper declared the game featured "brilliant aerial attacks by both teams." The Winnipegs had leaned on their passing game as Rebholz completed 5 passes for 30 yards or more. The North Dakota freshmen effectively shut down most of Winnipeg's running game, especially the option run, and the *Winnipeg Tribune* suggested the

Brown and Gold (1934)

Winnipegs had exhibited weakness in the same fashion against Toronto the year before. While Winnipeg's passing game displayed flashes of brilliance, the Winnipegs needed to improve their running game.

* *

The game in Montreal, Quebec, continued as planned for Lionel Conacher's professional football team. At 2:00 p.m. Sunday, October 14, 1934, at De Lorimier Stadium, the Wrigley Aromints met the Tonawanda Pros, another sandlot team from upstate New York. Like in Rochester, the sandlots in Buffalo, New York, and in surrounding communities like Tonawanda produced professional football teams. In 1921, the Tonawanda Kardex had played in the NFL. Like the Rochester Oxfords, this Tonawanda team brought years of football history to the gridiron.

Disappointed fans found out that the main draw for the game, Lionel Conacher, had signed a contract to play for the Montreal Maroons hockey team and did not play.

Tonawanda took an early lead with a rouge and an 80-yard interception return for a touchdown. The Aromints then shut down the Tonawanda running game and forced Tonawanda to use a less-effective passing attack. In the third quarter, the Aromints sprang ahead with two touchdowns by Charlie Conacher, first on an 80-yard run and second on a 60-yard scamper. The Aromints beat the Pros 10-7.

Thus ended Lionel Conacher's experiment with professional football in Canada. Proponents in Western Canada viewed the trial as a success. Bob Elson, a sportswriter for the *Province* in Vancouver, British Columbia, suggested that Canadian football teams in the Big Four, who had suffered from low gate receipts so far in 1934, should field an all-star team and play an exhibition game in Western Canada using the rules the Aromints had introduced.

* *

Prognosticators predicted that either Concordia or St. John's, two teams that would not play each other in 1934, would win the conference title. Coach Frank Cleve felt if his Cobbers could beat Macalester in St. Paul, they could win it all. Macalester had played their first two opponents to a total score of 54-7, including a 47-0 victory over Augsburg where Macalester head coach Al Gowans had to rely on a jury-rigged backfield, with a tackle at fullback and an end at quarterback. Cleve expected three Macalester starters would return to the orange-and-blue lineup on Saturday. Meanwhile, during scrimmages, the Cobbers offense executed plays like a well-oiled machine despite the fact injured right tackle, Roy Cleve, had to watch from the sidelines, a bittersweet event for the coach's cousin. Like quarterback Hank Held, young Cleve had played for Minneapolis South High School and so the game in St. Paul would feel like a homecoming of sorts. Coach Cleve also kept one of his reserve players, the slight and curly haired Art Myrom out of the fray. Myrom had suffered a broken nose against Winnipeg and so Cleve worked him out at placekicker, instead.

Late in the week, fans learned that three ends on the Macalester squad, including the end who had moved to quarterback, had suffered injuries during practice and would not play. The student newspaper at Macalester, the *Mac Weekly*, deemed the Cobbers the "heaviest club in the conference, tackle to tackle" with "a one man steam roller in the crushing [Bob] Fritz."

Concordia's coaches and 24 players boarded the Northern Pacific Railway's Fargonian at 8:00 a.m. Friday. When they stepped onto the grid at Shaw Field at 2:30 p.m. Saturday they stood beneath a steady downpour. Pools of water gathered every few feet and the players knew that soon their cleats would turn the entire field into a bog.

Back in Moorhead, 245 students and faculty had purchased tickets to gather in Concordia's chapel to hear the play-by-play of the game relayed by telegram.

In the first quarter, Concordia blocked a punt and recovered the ball at Macalester's 8-yard line. Officials advanced the ball 5 yards on a penalty and on the next play, Fritz plunged over left tackle for a touchdown. When Fritz, the placeholder, received the snap for the point after attempt, he received a heavy, wet ball covered in mud. And yet Myrom, with his broken nose, kicked the ball straight through the uprights for the extra point. Concordia took a 7-0 lead.

Brown and Gold (1934)

Throughout the game, the small crowd who braved the rain laughed in satisfaction whenever a player fell into a pool of mud.

In the second half, the Scots returned the kickoff to their own 33-yard line. On their first play from scrimmage, a Macalester backfielder skirted left end and then reversed his field twice on his way to score on a 67-yard run. The Scots failed the extra point attempt and Concordia led 7-6. On Macalester's next possession, the Scots fumbled and lost the ball at their own 10-yard line. Fritz then smashed the line four times and went over for the score on the fourth try. Myrom missed the extra point but the Cobbers took a 13-6 lead.

Late in the game, Concordia chose to punt away from their own 9-yard line, but the Scots blocked the kick. The ball rolled into the end zone and the Scots fell on it for a touchdown. Down 13-12, the Scots attempted to kick the point after but the pigskin passed beneath the crossbar. The Cobbers walked away victorious by the score 13-12.

When the Cobbers returned to Moorhead, students with cheerleaders and the pep band gathered at the Northern Pacific depot to greet the team, and Fritz gave a speech.

* *

"[Fritz] Hanson is perhaps the most spectacular back in the conference, being exceptionally fast and shifty," said the *Sioux City Journal*. In advance of North Dakota State's game against Morningside, the *Daily Argus-Leader* suggested the Bison had "probably the finest backfield material in the conference, an offense combining dazzling speed and terrific line plunging [that] should prove to be the deciding factor."

In five seasons, Morningside had never scored against Coach Casey Finnegan's Bison, but the Maroons had beaten every other school in the NCC at least once. This season, Morningside had defeated the defending conference champion, South Dakota State, 13-7. Maroons backfielder Denton Dean now had one more year of experience on the gridiron, and the coach's son, Jason "Saundy" Saunderson Jr., led the team from the quarterback position in the Short Punt formation. He also returned punts.

At Macalester (St. Paul, Minnesota)

To prepare for the Maroons, Finnegan had his men execute and defend the pass in practice. He had Sturgeon, who suffered from an ankle injury, take some time off his legs. Due to a long rainstorm, which had turned the fields in Sioux City into pools of mud, Finnegan agreed to postpone the game until Saturday.

When the Bison boarded the train at noon on Thursday Finnegan took along 25 players. They stayed overnight Thursday in Sioux Falls, and when the team arrived in Sioux City on Friday they suited up for practice only to find the gridiron in a muddy condition, which slowed down Hanson. "I don't know if I'll even start him if it isn't better Saturday," Finnegan told the *Sioux City Journal*. But because the Bison weighed more than the Maroons they would have more leverage. At 282 pounds, Sturgeon would face off against a 170-pound Maroons tackle.

The game kicked off at 8:00 p.m. October 20, 1934, on a rain-soaked field at Stock Yards Park. After Morningside returned the opening kickoff to their own 40-yard line, Dean led the charge. He carried the ball to North Dakota State's 32-yard line and, on the next play, he completed a 32-yard touchdown pass to Saunderson Jr. In the second quarter, Hanson ran over left tackle. He cut back over his right guard and rotated through the Morningside line. He reversed his direction twice and avoided four Maroons tacklers to run 75 yards for a touchdown. When the Maroons regained possession of the pigskin, they responded with an aerial attack and some trickery with the Statue of Liberty play but they did not score again as the half ended in a 6-6 tie.

Midway through third quarter, referee Elmer Smeby raised his hand and cried, "Time out!" He fell to one knee and collapsed into the mud. Finnegan raced onto the field and the spectators fell to a hush. Several Bison players rushed onto the field, too, and they carried Smeby back to the sideline where two physicians had been called from the crowd to examine the man. They called an ambulance. Meanwhile, the other officials shuffled roles and installed an experienced former college football player from the crowd to be head linesmen. They resumed the game but then halted play again as an ambulance entered the grounds and drove up to the North Dakota State bench. They placed Smeby onto a stretcher and drove him away.

Brown and Gold (1934)

Play resumed. The Maroons started a drive but then fumbled and lost the ball on their own 38-yard line. The Bison then drove to the goal line and scored on a line plunge. In the fourth quarter, the Maroons regained momentum when Dean completed a 20-yard pass to North Dakota State's 28-yard line. Two plays later, he ran 17 yards around left end. The Maroons finished the drive with a score on an off-tackle run.

Both teams struggled to break the deadlock. Late in the game, Hanson ran around left end where the Maroons nearly took him down but he shook loose from the line and raced 28 yards to Morningside's 27-yard line. Hanson then ran six more times to reach Morningside's 4-yard line but the Bison turned over the ball on downs. To gain field position, the Maroons responded with a punt, but Hanson fumbled the ball on the return and the Bison recovered at midfield. Undeterred, the Bison switched to the passing game, but Wendy Schollander threw an interception and Morningside marched down the field. Time ran out before the Maroons could score and the game ended in a 12-12 tie.

The Bison had rushed for 214 yards in the game but suffered 55 yards in penalties. As the Bison walked off the field they learned that the referee, Smeby, had passed away from a cerebral hemorrhage.

* *

One day before the first game in the MRFU championship series between the Winnipeg Rugby Club and the University of Manitoba, teams in Western Canada learned that the CRU had met in a special executive meeting where the CRU decided to reverse its decision about the Grey Cup final. The East and West champions would *not* play the Grey Cup game in a western venue as promised. Instead, the teams would play the game in the East. When asked for his opinion about the decision, former CRU president Dr. M. B. Kinsella offered that the game *couldn't* be played in the West because while it was difficult for men in both the East and the West to get away from work for travel, in the East at least they could attract more fans and gate receipts.

In reply, the *Star-Phoenix* in Saskatoon, Saskatchewan, suggested the West should break from the East.

At Morningside (Sioux City, Iowa)

Meanwhile, Manitoba declared five of its Bisons football players ineligible to play because they had not registered for classes and had not paid their fees. The next day, those players showed up for football practice anyway. Coach Wally Hass told the *Winnipeg Tribune* he did not know the players hadn't registered for classes but that two of the players had taken steps to register and he expected the other three would, too. Hass said he started practices over a month before the last day of registration and while he had asked for that information, he had not received it. The day before the university's game against the Winnipegs, the *Winnipeg Manitoban* reported that three of the students had earned eligibility. On the day of the game, however, they did not play.

The Winnipegs met the Bisons at Osborne Stadium on October 20, 1934, in the first of a two-game series to determine the MRFU champion. Despite the fact Manitoba had played using American intercollegiate rules all season, and despite the fact the Winnipegs had also played using American rules for portions of their games, the teams played the MRFU championship game under Canadian rules, a technical requirement for Western playoff competition.

The injury bug bit early and bit hard. After a scoreless first quarter, the Winnipegs charged downfield when Russ Rebholz completed a 28-yard pass. Eddie James then carried the ball to Manitoba's 8-yard line. On the next play, James ran over center and gained 2 yards but he fell onto his harnessed left arm—the same arm that had taken so long to heal—and he broke it in multiple places. Less than two months after he had returned to the gridiron James had injured his arm where it had broken before.

With James out of the game, the Winnipegs switched to an aerial attack while the Bisons improved on the ground. Manitoba's Tubber Kobrinsky continued to display the likeness of a slippery halfback, and the way he ran around the ends "supports the contention that he would be a worthy addition to the Winnipeg [Rugby Club] team," suggested the *Winnipeg Tribune*. Kobrinsky enjoyed runs of 15 and 30 yards but when the half ended, neither team had scored.

The scoreless deadlock continued until the fourth quarter when the Winnipegs put in rested reserves to play against the tired Bisons. Due to player eligibility issues the Manitoba squad had played the game with a

Brown and Gold (1934)

depleted roster, and the Winnipegs took advantage of the situation. The Bisons had started the game with six reserve players but were down to three healthy reserves in the fourth quarter when Rebholz punted to the deadline for a rouge. A few minutes later, he punted into Manitoba's end zone and Dave Harding tackled Kobrinsky behind the goal line for a second rouge.

Unimpressed by the Winnipegs' performance, the crowd turned on them and cheered for the Bisons. But the Winnipegs rallied. When they regained possession of the ball they moved 30 yards on four downs to Manitoba's 5-yard line where Harding cracked the line for a touchdown. In the last minute of the game, Rebholz completed a pass into the end zone for the final score. The Winnipegs beat the Bisons 14-0.

After the game, even though the Winnipegs had practically earned the right to represent the MRFU in the playoffs, few fans believed they had a chance against the Regina Roughriders who had clinched the SRFU title with five consecutive victories. *Tribune* sportswriter Johnny Buss declared, "After Saturday's exhibition against Varsity, the most rabid supporter sadly shook his head and dreaded to think of the forthcoming battle with the Roughriders." The loss of James had diminished hopes for a WCRFU title. Fans later learned that before the game, Winnipeg's trainer had begged James not to play, but James had insisted, for the love of the game.

*

To prepare for the second game in the MRFU title series, the Winnipegs practiced with a more grim and determined attitude. Coach Greg Kabat set strategy aside and used practices to focus on fundamentals. He had his linemen practice blocking while Rebholz had the backfield practice ball-handling. Bobby Schiller returned from his visit home to replace James and to join new arrival Harding in the backfield.

In the Bisons camp, coaches Hass and Walter Odhe hoped their student athletes might clear up registration issues and return to the grid, but even without them, the team displayed confidence. After a strong showing in their loss to the Winnipegs, the team no longer felt like underdogs.

When game day arrived on October 27, 1934, Manitoba had multiple players out injured or ineligible to play. The Bisons would have to play the second game with fewer reserves than the first game. For the second match, Lionel Conacher, in town with the Montreal Maroons for an exhibition hockey series against the New York Rangers, performed the ceremonial first kick.

In the first quarter, Tubber Kobrinsky fielded a Winnipeg missed field goal attempt but then fumbled and lost the ball in the end zone. Herb Mobberley pounced on the pigskin for a touchdown. Early in the second quarter, Kobrinsky fielded a punt in the end zone but Russ Rebholz tackled him behind the goal line to score a rouge for the Winnipegs. On Winnipeg's next possession, Cliff Roseborough plunged twice for a total of 25 yards to reach Manitoba's 35-yard line. The Winnipegs executed a running drop-kick and the Bisons fumbled and lost the ball on their own 10-yard line. Roseborough then carried the ball to the 1-yard line where on the next play, Rebholz ran the ball in for the score.

Throughout the contest, the Winnipegs abandoned the pass and focused on moving the ball with the running game. The team displayed improved execution of the option run. And even with Kabat on the sideline injured the offensive line proved better at blocking.

Manitoba's defense held the Winnipegs scoreless in the third quarter while the Bisons offense twice drove half the length of the field to score, first on a rouge kick by Kobrinsky when the Bisons tackled return man Arni Coulter inside the goal line, and second, on their next possession, Kobrinsky completed a 30-yard pass to Winnipeg's 30-yard line and then completed a 30-yard touchdown pass, but officials called it back because they said Kobrinsky didn't throw the ball from at least 5 yards behind the line of scrimmage. Two plays later, Kobrinsky kicked a field goal. To finish the third period, Rebholz kicked to score a rouge.

In the fourth quarter, the Winnipegs twice advanced the ball to within Manitoba's 20-yard line but were forced to settle for single points on rouge kicks. The third time proved the charm, however. After the Winnipegs intercepted a pass at Manitoba's 20-yard line, Rebholz carried the ball to the 2-yard line. On the next play, Schiller plunged for a touchdown and the Winnipegs beat the Bisons 21-4.

Kobrinsky played the full 60 minutes.

Brown and Gold (1934)

The game helped Kabat determine his final 20-man roster for the WCRFU semifinal. He knew the team would have an uphill battle. The *Winnipeg Free Press* observed that "early in the season all one could hear among the fans was, 'I wouldn't miss that Regina game for anything'" but "now there are many not so sure they will bother making the trip."

In the days after the game, Manitoba forced the resignation of the football team's student manager when they discovered he had overspent the program's budget by over $200 on equipment, perhaps due to a general overzealousness at the school for the football program to succeed. Two days later, the worn-out Bisons played a game against the Deer Lodge neighborhood junior rugby club. Deer Lodge had secured the junior-level title in Manitoba under the tutelage of coach Fred Ritter, an original member of the Regina Roughriders. Ritter had captained and coached Regina when he played from 1910 to 1913 and when the Roughriders had won western titles in 1912 and 1913. The players he coached in Regina included Horace Alvin "Al" Ritchie, the longtime recent coach for the Roughriders. Ritter had left Regina to work as an assistant coach at Princeton and then he returned to Canada to live in Winnipeg. Over the years, Ritter had been involved in Canadian football in Winnipeg, including as a coach for the Manitoba varsity team.

The Bisons beat Deer Lodge handily 14-3 only three days out from their last game of the season against Minot State.

* *

Moorhead Daily News sportswriter Dick Hackenberg noticed that the new rules put in place for the 1934 football season had benefited both offenses and fans. While Concordia, Moorhead State, North Dakota State, and their opponents had racked up an average of 12.8 total points per game in 1933, those same schools and their opponents had scored 29.4 total points per game so far in 1934.

With offensive football top of mind, the citizens of Fargo and Moorhead prepared for another big weekend. The schedules for both Concordia and North Dakota State had aligned so that both schools would once again celebrate homecoming on the same day, and this year both teams had proven themselves contenders for conference titles. North Dakota State would host North Dakota while Concordia would host St. Mary's.

After the 1933 season, St. Mary's head football coach Nic Musty, a St. Mary's alum, announced he would resign his position to study medicine. Whether he went on to study medicine is not clear, but Musty did take a job as an assistant coach under George Barsi at rival St. Thomas. To fill Musty's absence, St. Mary's hired Edward "Moose" Krause, born Edward Kraucuinas, a Chicago native who had enrolled at Notre Dame in 1930. Krause practiced just three weeks under Knute Rockne during spring football in 1931 before Rockne died unexpectedly in a plane crash near Bazaar, Kansas. Three seasons later, as a senior, the 6-foot-3, 220-pound Krause earned All-American honors at tackle. Even before he graduated from Notre Dame in the spring of 1934, Krause accepted the job at St. Mary's to coach football, basketball, and baseball the following year. But before Krause could pick up his whistle and clipboard, he first had to compete alongside other All-American selections in the August 31 Chicago Charities College All-Star Game. He and his fellow collegians played the Chicago Bears to a scoreless tie at Soldier Field during the World's Fair.

At St. Mary's, Krause fielded a Cardinals team that excelled in the passing game. His Cardinals had scored on a touchdown pass on the last play of the game to tie St. John's 6-6. With only 19 players on the varsity squad, Krause's Cardinals lacked depth, but 40 freshmen had turned out to play football for Krause and the future looked bright.

Meanwhile, at Concordia, Coach Frank Cleve didn't know what to take away from his team's performance against Macalester in the mud. "I'm not sure we played badly against Macalester," he said, "because the condition of the field set up an iron-clad alibi for the team." So far in 1934, every opponent had found a way to score against the Cobbers, a worrisome situation for Cleve.

Due to injuries, and to prepare for St. Mary's offense, Cleve shifted some players around. To secure the flanks he moved Bob Fritz to halfback on defense, and to make up for the big fullback's absence in the middle of the formation, Cleve had his defensive center step back and

Brown and Gold (1934)

play as a line backer. As practices progressed, Cleve expressed concern to Hackenberg about the team's lax attitude. They had forgotten their assignments on plays Cleve had installed the week before. Cleve reminded his men how St. Mary's had held them scoreless in 1933 and had beaten them by a safety, which had knocked Concordia out of title contention. He pasted photos of the St. Mary's football squad onto the mirrors in the players' dressing room. By the end of the week, the Cobbers displayed perfect execution with "zip and dash," reported Hackenberg. After all, the Cobbers meant to defend their honor during the school's homecoming celebration, and for Fritz and others, they would play their last home game of their college careers against St. Mary's.

On Friday night before Saturday's game, the Cobbers held a coronation ceremony for their homecoming queen in the gymnasium and then fired up the student body with a pep fest and a bonfire. On Saturday afternoon, the students put on a parade. Floats by the school's eight literary societies, the various royalty, and student organizations traveled down Seventh Street to Center Avenue in Moorhead where the procession crossed the bridge to Fargo to snake through the business section on the North Dakota side.

After the parade, with the number 50 on his jersey, three-time letterman and team captain Bob Fritz took the field in Moorhead for the last time. He smiled as he looked back at the sideline. Cleve had dressed his four biggest freshmen and had them sit on the bench to make it appear as though Concordia had big men in reserve.

At Memorial Field on the Moorhead State campus, the Cobbers emerged hot. In the first quarter, on a punt return, Concordia quarterback Henry Held lateraled to his right halfback, Eddie Dahl, who scooted 47 yards to advance the ball to St. Mary's 20-yard line. On the next play, Held ran around right end for a touchdown. St. Mary's followed with an aerial attack, but Concordia shut them down. In one instance, Held recognized a forward-lateral play in progress and he managed to knock the ball loose from the first receiver's grasp. He tackled the second receiver only a few strides from the line of scrimmage. Held later intercepted a pass and returned it to St. Mary's 28-yard line. A couple of plays later, Fritz stood behind his line and called out to the St. Mary's team, "Try and stop this baby!" and then took the snap and smashed over the line for a touchdown. Still in the first quarter, the Cobbers regained possession of the ball, and reserve backfielder Bobby Holzer swept around end for a 23-yard gain to reach St. Mary's 22-yard line. Three plays later, Fritz scored again on a 3-yard plunge.

In the second quarter, behind by three touchdowns, St. Mary's reached Concordia's 15-yard line but then the Cardinals retreated 25 yards on three plays, including 15 yards on penalties, and had to punt the ball away. Late in the second quarter, the Cobbers blocked a punt that sailed past the deadline to score a safety for Concordia.

In the second half, Dahl scored two touchdowns on punt returns, the first on a 30-yard return and the second on a 55-yard return. Dahl scored the team's final touchdown on a 19-yard end run. When the final gun sounded, the Cobbers walked off victorious over the Cardinals 39-0.

The Cobbers gained 261 yards from scrimmage while the Cardinals gained a net negative 32 yards. After the game, Krause told Cleve the Cobbers were the best team he had ever seen from a small college. The *Minneapolis Tribune* attributed Concordia's win to its "stalwart line" while the student yearbook, the *Cobber*, recalled how the backfielders had been "virtually unstoppable." On defense, the Cobbers shut down the Cardinals' passing game until the final period. Throughout the game, the Cobbers "spilled Redmen backs time and again for great losses," observed the *Tribune*.

During the alumni supper, and later at the reception in the gymnasium, Cobbers fans buzzed. With one conference game remaining, Concordia stood tied for the conference title with St. John's. Throughout the MIAC, fans predicted both St. John's and Concordia might finish the season without a loss and they began to call for a championship playoff game between the two schools. However, after St. John's had severed ties with Concordia near the end of the 1933 season the two institutions had not renewed competition.

Meanwhile, several North Dakota students in town for the Sioux-Bison game who were also Notre Dame fans tracked down Krause for the opportunity to meet him.

Brown and Gold (1934)

* *

During the past five consecutive games, no opponent had crossed North Dakota's goal line, which stood as perhaps the best defensive record in the team's history, according to *Grand Forks Herald* sportswriter C.D. Locklin. Opponents had only made 9 first downs in total against the Sioux, and two opponents, Omaha University and South Dakota State, had failed to make a single first down, not even through penalties. Locklin said, "It takes no football expert to figure that whatever outfit *does* set the Sioux down will have to show an unusual offense."

With Fritz Hanson at halfback, North Dakota State fielded an unusually potent offense. In advance of the Bison-Sioux contest, newspapermen dubbed him "The Main Hope of the Bison," "Perham's Peerless Parcel of Speed and Smoothness," "The Blond Ghost," a "Blond Bit of Dynamite," and a "Towhead Meteor." Sioux Coach Jack West concurred. "He can break up any football game at any time," he said. Tacklers had a hard time wrapping up the short-legged speedster below the waist, which had allowed Hanson to use his legs to escape. "[His] elusiveness is attributed to his exceptional speed and his ability to change his course with little loss of motion," observed Eugene Fitzgerald in the *Fargo Forum*. "Hanson is the type of runner who may be tossed for a 15-yard loss on one run but go for a touchdown on the next play. It is largely a problem of getting him into the open." If he can get past the line of scrimmage, "he is pretty capable of taking care of himself." He continued,

> "Sioux partisans are justified in fearing Hanson. He has more than speed. He has a quick reaction which often permits him to go places where his speed would be of no benefit. He is the one fellow who can wreck the Sioux hopes. The only one who may not feel that he is of so much importance is Little Mel [Hanson] himself. But he'll be in there trying, just as if he did believe it."

To stop Hanson, North Dakota would have to spread out wide on the line of scrimmage with their six-man line, but that would open up holes for Shifty Gove at fullback or for his backup, Bob Erickson. Both Gove and Erickson had proven they could smash the line for yardage. During a week of Bison practices, Coach Casey Finnegan used Erickson up the middle and Hanson around the ends, which proved lethal against the reserves. But in the *Herald*, Locklin predicted the Bison would gain little with Gove or Erickson. "The Bison coaches have had West's team scouted in every game it has played," he said, "so there will likely be few attempts on the part of the [Bison] to make ground through the center of the Nodak line." Instead, "the Bison attack will undoubtedly be a wide open affair," he said, "with forward passing playing a big part, while they attempt to shake Hanson loose." On the Sioux side of the line, Fritz Falgren at end would have to contain Hanson but he would also have to defend against the pass. Meanwhile, on the Bison side, Bud Marquardt would return from injury to play end. And if the Sioux did contain Hanson? "[He] can heave that oval far and accurately and can throw them pretty good on the run," observed Fitzgerald.

The Sioux fielded a strong defense with the smallest number of players in years, 27 in uniform but only 17 without injuries. The Sioux lineup had remained consistent throughout the season and most of the players played the full 60 minutes. The whole situation drove West to express concern about overconfidence in his ranks. "There is a very distinct inclination on the part of the players to regard the game with the Bison as already won," he told the *Herald*. To make matters worse for the Bison, Wendy Schollander had provided the Sioux with a reason to get fired up. He had apparently called the Sioux "daffodils" for their vanity, and in response, Sioux fullback Irving Kupcinet, in his column in the *Dakota Student* sports pages, gave Schollander the nickname "Daffodil." He also suggested the Bison linemen were no match for the Sioux. He compared Lyle Sturgeon, the big Bison tackle, to a real-life Bison ready for slaughter.

To prepare his men for battle, West had his reserves scrimmage against his freshman starters instead of against his freshman second-stringers. The reserves played defense during the entire scrimmage and they played well. The next day, West had his varsity squad concentrate on forward pass plays but they had little success against the reserves. Only Falgren managed to catch a pass and to get past the reserve defensive backs to score a touchdown.

Meanwhile, in Fargo, Coach Finnegan feared the unknown. Yes, the Sioux had begun using a new offensive scheme in 1934 but they had been executing a straightforward set of plays all season. What might be up West's sleeve? It had been two years since the Sioux had beaten the Bison and Finnegan expected the Sioux to take the field with adrenaline. The North Dakota lineup included five of the top 10 scoring players in the conference and both teams still contended for the conference title. If the Sioux came out on top, they would win it all.

In any event, the Bison would bring more depth to the sidelines, with nearly two full squads and with a good replacement at every position. Instead of worry, Finnegan focused on the team's strengths. He knew Sturgeon displayed better kicking abilities than the Sioux, and so he practiced punting. He knew Herb Peschel, a potential all-conference lineman, had been the backbone for the Bison offense, and so he practiced blocking. Late in the week, Finnegan had the Bison scrimmage until long after sunset, and during the scrimmage, Hanson scored touchdowns on a kickoff return, a punt return, and a pass catch. On the other side of the ball, "[Bud] Marquardt's defensive play was the last word," wrote Fitzgerald. The Bison stood ready. The homecoming stand would be the last home game for Hanson, Marquardt, and Peschel during their college careers.

For a $2 fare over 100 students joined the 102-piece University of North Dakota Concert Band and the 35 players and coaches involved in Sioux football on the special Great Northern charter train that departed University Station in Grand Forks at 9:15 a.m. Saturday morning. They expected the train would arrive at 11:00 a.m., and the students could return at 10:00 p.m. Saturday or on any Sunday train at the same rate. The first block of game tickets in Grand Forks had sold out and newspapers in Grand Forks predicted more than 200 students might drive to Fargo for the game. They expected as many as 1,000 Sioux rooters in total would be in the stands, in the band, or on the sidelines.

Before kickoff on October 27, 1934, both bands marched onto Dacotah Field to entertain the crowd of approximately 5,000 fans. A blast of cold northwest wind diminished the official's whistle to start the game. Hanson returned the opening kick 25 yards to North Dakota State's 40-yard line. On the third play from scrimmage, Hanson attempted a pass but Kupcinet intercepted the ball and returned it to North Dakota's 49-yard line. For the remainder of the half, the Bison and the Sioux exchanged punts. The Sioux reached first down seven times during the first half, and the teams spent the majority of their time within North Dakota State territory. The half ended in a 0-0 tie.

During halftime, the bands marched onto the field together and played the "North Dakota Hymn" with music arranged by Dr. C.S. Putnam, the Gold Star Band's director, and also "Americans We."

In the second half, on North Dakota State's first possession in the fourth quarter, Hanson reeled off a 28-yard run that compounded with a penalty against the Sioux to reach North Dakota's 48-yard line. Erickson then exploded over center to reach the 28-yard line, but two plays later the Sioux intercepted Wendy Schollander at their own 18-yard line. The Sioux punted the ball away to gain field position and Hanson returned the pigskin to North Dakota State's 47-yard line. Three plays later, the Bison executed their standby, a forward-lateral, Schollander to Acey Olson to Hanson. Hanson cut through a crowd of tacklers, burst into the open., and raced to the Sioux 5-yard line where, after several tacklers attempted to bring him down he lost his balance and fell to his knees. Three plays later, he shot around left end and stepped over the corner of the end zone for a touchdown.

On the ensuing kickoff, Kupcinet returned the ball 50 yards to North Dakota State's 30-yard line where Schollander took him down. The Bison halted the Sioux advance and forced a turnover on downs. To run out the clock, the Bison ran their fullbacks into the line and when the final gun sounded, the Bison won the game 7-0.

Only the Bison had scored a touchdown against the Sioux so far in 1934 and the Bison had reached first down more times in one game than all of the Sioux's previous opponents combined. The *Herald* credited the Bison line with the victory. "Even in the first half when University was making its headway, A.C. linemen were continually in the Nodak backfield," wrote the *Herald*. "And when University threatened, [the

Bison] tore through at every point to smother the Sioux offense." The *Herald* said the Bison proved "impassable" at the ends and that "Sioux ballcarriers had almost no protection because the line buckled [and] the interference had no time to form."

After the game, the Gold Star Band hosted the University band for a 6:00 p.m. banquet at the Gardner Hotel.

* *

Dick Hackenberg at the *Moorhead Daily News* asked Concordia Coach Frank Cleve what he thought about increased offensive scoring throughout the various regional conferences in 1934. Cleve responded that he believed the NCAA would soon adopt the same rules for the forward pass that both high school and professional teams followed, which allowed the passer to toss the ball from anywhere behind the line of scrimmage instead of from at least 5 yards behind the line. Cleve predicted teams would use the forward pass as their primary offensive play and he said he wouldn't be surprised if most forward passes sailed to receivers just beyond the line of scrimmage instead of farther downfield. He predicted offenses would use more deception and trickery to confuse defenses.

Despite Cleve's enthusiasm for a more unrestricted forward pass, the NCAA refused to adopt any change to the rules out of fear it would turn the game into "a modified form of basketball."

In the meantime, Cleve took his forward pass and 25 players to Sioux Falls to play two-time South Dakota Intercollegiate Conference defending champion Augustana. The Vikings had won 10 straight games and stood atop their conference tied with both Huron University of Huron and Dakota Territorial Normal School of Spearfish, South Dakota. The upcoming game against Concordia would be the first time Augustana would ever play another Lutheran college. Vikings coach Leonard "Lefty" Olson, a 1921 Red Wing, Minnesota, high school graduate who had lettered in football four years at Luther College in Decorah, Iowa, had led a successful Augustana football program since 1931. In advance of their game against Concordia, however, the *Daily Argus-Leader* didn't give

Olson and Augustana much of a chance. The Cobbers fielded a heavier squad with a line that averaged 190 pounds per man and the Vikings had never beaten a Minnesota team. And while the Vikings had only played "ordinary" teams on their schedule, Concordia had played "strong clubs."

When the Cobbers worked out on Augustana's grid the night before the game, the *Argus-Leader* said spectators walked away "impress[ed] with their brawn in both line and backfield positions."

The Vikings and Cobbers kicked off under the lights on November 2, 1934. In the first quarter, the Vikings began a drive on Concordia's 40-yard line but fumbled and lost the ball. Cobbers halfback Eddie Dahl then caught an underhand forward pass and ran 32 yards for a touchdown. In the second quarter, Concordia reached Augustana's 10-yard line on two passes. Quarterback Henry Held hustled 8 more yards. Bob Fritz then smashed the line off-tackle for a touchdown. The Vikings and Cobbers fumbled and lost the ball three more times in this period. When the dust cleared, Fritz completed a 30-yard touchdown pass to increase Concordia's lead.

To open the second half, Augustana received the kickoff. The Vikings returner ran the ball 53 yards to Concordia's 11-yard line. Four plays later they scored on a run. Concordia's final score came after Augustana fumbled and lost the ball at their own 18-yard line with Held scoring on a shovel pass from Fritz. The Cobbers won 26-6.

In the forward passing game, Concordia had completed 11 of 16 pass attempts for 173 yards with 1 interception against the Vikings.

After the game, the Cobbers learned St. Thomas had beaten St. John's 12-0, which meant Concordia controlled its own destiny in its quest to earn an undisputed conference title.

*   *

North Dakota State had beaten Concordia 6-0. The Cobbers then tied Moorhead State 13-13. Now, the Bison would play the Dragons in Moorhead, and Coach Casey Finnegan figured the Dragons posed a sincere challenge for his Bison. "Any club that can score twice on

Concordia under normal weather conditions must have something," he said.

In their last outing, the Dragons had beaten St. Cloud State Teachers College 13-6 in St. Cloud. Moorhead State had won that game without their two star players, fullback Vincent Yatchak and halfback Marco Gotta, whom the NTAC executive committee had declared ineligible to play in conference games. The committee also forced Moorhead State to forfeit the two conference games the men had played in. Yatchak, who averaged nine yards per carry for the Dragons and who could drop-kick field goals from 40 yards had played high school football in Wakefield, Michigan, and then went on to play freshman football for Purdue University in 1933. By conference rule, a student athlete could not engage in conference competition during his first quarter in a new school within the NTAC. Nemzek said he had a letter from Purdue stating Yatchak had withdrawn from the school before he had competed in a game and before he had received any grades. But Yatchak apparently did *not* withdraw from Purdue until December 20, 1933, and he had earned a numeral while on the freshman team. It's not clear whether Yatchak had shared these details with Nemzek. The conference also declared Gotta, who had played high school football in Bessemer, Michigan, ineligible because Gotta had attended Michigan State in 1932 where he received grades and a numeral for freshman football. In 1933, he played for the independent Bessemer Bearcats football team, which newspapers sometimes identified as "amateur" and at other times as "semi-professional." It's also not clear whether Gotta had shared these details with Nemzek.

Of course, Moorhead State's upcoming game against North Dakota State would be a non-conference affair, and so while Nemzek protested the conference ruling he had Yatchak and Gotta suit up and practice for their game against the Bison. Nemzek expected Coach Finnegan would try to stop Yatchak and Gotta and so the Dragons practiced the pass.

The two schools had originally scheduled the game for 2:00 p.m. Saturday but Nemzek and Finnegan moved the game to Friday so that it would not interfere with the expected exodus of fans to Minneapolis to watch the University of Michigan play Minnesota during Minnesota's homecoming. The coaches also moved the time to 3:00 p.m. so that it would not interfere with Friday classes. The game would be the final contest on Moorhead State's schedule and the final time Fritz Hanson, Bud Marquardt, and Herb Peschel would play together in Fargo or Moorhead.

On the night before the game, and after the pep fest at Moorhead State, Dragon rooters carried torches and followed the German Band through the streets of Moorhead and Fargo. They cried, "Down with the Bison!"

On November 2, 1934, at Memorial Field in Moorhead, the Dragons returned the opening kickoff to North Dakota State's 38-yard line. Yatchak then fumbled the ball on a run and Marquardt recovered at North Dakota State's 22-yard line. The Bison gained four consecutive first downs to reach Moorhead State's 2-yard line, but the Dragons held, and after a turnover on downs, Moorhead State punted the ball to gain field position. Twice more in the first quarter and within their own 20-yard line the Dragons fended off the Bison attack.

In the second quarter, the Dragons reached North Dakota State's 22-yard line, but the Bison pushed the Dragons back and took over the ball on downs. The Bison responded with a drive that included five first downs. From Moorhead State's 13-yard line, Hanson retreated 15 yards as he scrambled around the backfield to shake off would-be tacklers and then he threw a wobbly pass off his back foot. Quarterback Leo Gerteis pulled in the pigskin in the end zone for a touchdown. On the kick attempt for the extra point Hanson fielded a bad snap and tried to run it in but the Dragons smothered his advance. The Bison took a 6-0 lead.

In the third quarter, Gotta repeatedly ran the ball to reach North Dakota State's 12-yard line. The Dragons then fumbled and lost the ball to the Bison. After North Dakota State took over, Shifty Gove fumbled a bad pass from center and the Dragons recovered at North Dakota State's 5-yard line. Two plays later, the Dragons scored, and Yatchak scored the point after when he ran off tackle on a fake kick. The Dragons took a 7-6 lead. Later in the same period, with the wind at his back, Yatchak booted an 85-yard punt that soared 70 yards through the air over Hanson's head.

In the fourth quarter, Yatchak attempted a punt from his own 18-yard line, but Peschel rushed in and blocked the kick. He picked up the pigskin

Brown and Gold (1934)

at the 16-yard line and ran into the end zone for the score. Wendy Schollander's attempt to kick the extra point sailed wide but the Bison took a 12-7 lead. On the next Dragons drive, a Bison defender intercepted a pass. As Dragons tacklers descended upon him, he attempted a lateral, but the ball bounced loose and Moorhead State recovered the ball at North Dakota State's 32-yard line. The Dragons then used a trick play with a double lateral and forward pass to reach North Dakota State's 6-yard line. The Bison called time out and the Dragons used the break to strategize. On the next play the Dragons backfielders faked a fumble, and while the Bison scrambled to find the ball, a Dragons ball-carrier found a hole over left guard to score a touchdown. Moorhead State missed the extra point but went ahead 13-12. When the Bison regained the ball with 6 minutes remaining in the game, they took to the air, but the Dragons intercepted a pass to end and win the game 13-12.

The one successful Dragons point after touchdown had been the difference in the game. Fans flooded the field and carried the Dragons to their locker room. The Moorhead State players embraced, laughed, wept, and sang victory songs in the showers. "A great bunch of kids," Nemzek told reporters. "They played ball out there today."

Yatchak and his performance on defense had proved the key to Moorhead State's victory. In the *Fargo Forum*, Eugene Fitzgerald credited Yatchak, who had repeatedly broke through the line and stopped ball-carriers for losses, with preventing four or five Bison touchdowns. The next day, none other than Red Grange talked about Moorhead State's victory over North Dakota State on NBC radio. He said Moorhead State must have "a whale of a team" and he suggested the Dragons should play either the University of Alabama or Southern Methodist University, both powerhouses in 1934, in the inaugural Sugar Bowl in New Orleans. Nemzek indicated to the media that he would consider offers from southern universities to play, but offers never materialized.

Northward, Coach Jack West at North Dakota attempted to arrange a game between the Sioux and the Dragons in Grand Forks on Saturday, November 10, but Nemzek turned down the challenge. He said North Dakota could not offer a large enough financial guarantee and that he wouldn't have enough time to prepare his men for the Sioux. The team

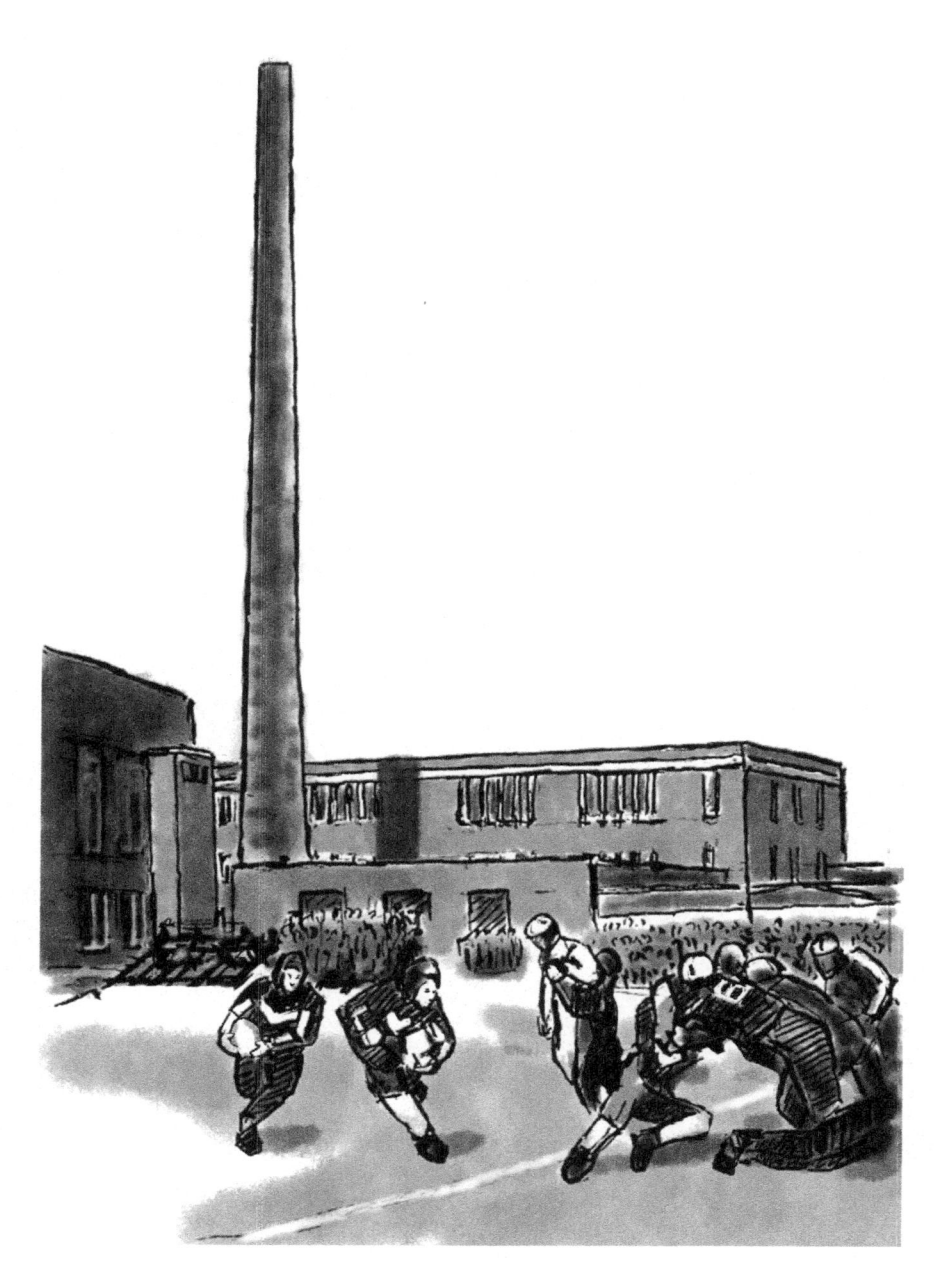

At Moorhead State (Moorhead, Minnesota)

had already turned in their equipment and had stopped training. "Give me another week and a better guarantee and I'll take 'em on," he said. But West couldn't accommodate a later date because the Sioux would soon travel to the East Coast to play.

In the *Moorhead Daily News*, Dick Hackenberg declared the 1934 Moorhead State Dragons would forever be remembered as "the team that beat the Bison," a triumph that cross-town rival Concordia could not claim. Moorhead State had finished the season undefeated—if one ignored the two forfeits, which Nemzek had appealed—and they had tied the Cobbers and defeated the Bison, both title contenders in their respective conferences. The Dragons had outscored their opponents 145-35 in seven games.

A few weeks later, the conference confirmed the executive committee's decision to declare Yatchak and Gotta ineligible in 1934. The Dragons had forfeited two conference games to losses and also sacrificed the conference title. The conference declared both players ineligible until October 12, 1935.

* *

For the first time in four years the Manitoba football team traveled to play a game on the road. Twenty-one players plus the coaches, trainers, managers, and as many as 20 fans left Thursday on a 320-mile bus ride to Minot to play the Minot State Beavers on a Friday night under the lights. With Manitoba's football budget in a deficit, the manager of Canadian-American Bus Lines, a big fan of the school's American football experiment, donated transportation to the team. When the Bisons arrived in Minot, Coach Wally Hass stepped off the bus and told a *Minot Daily News* reporter that "The American game, which is gradually replacing the rugby style of play in Canada, is proving to be popular with fans in the land of the maple leaf. The [WCRFU] is seriously considering adopting American rules for all games. The game on [the American] side is much better from the spectators' viewpoint because of the teamwork it produces." Hass critiqued the lack of blocking in Canadian football rules and the toll it took on runners. "[In Canadian football], the theory is to

Brown and Gold (1934)

toss the ball to someone and then everybody see how hard they can hit him."

To prepare for the invaders and to avoid injury, Minot State avoided rough practices in cold weather. Instead, Coach James W. "J.W." Coleman walked his men through the assignments necessary to defend against the option run, which he expected Manitoba would use from their Canadian football playbook. The Beavers coach since 1927, Coleman had played center and served as team captain in football at the University of Arkansas in Fayetteville from 1917 to 1919, where he earned all-conference honors in 1918 and 1919. Coleman went on to coach at a military school in Tennessee and then at Georgetown College in Georgetown, Kentucky, and the University of Akron in Ohio before he took the job in Minot.

Only a few hundred fans braved the cold on November 2, 1934, to watch the last home game of the season for Minot. The officiating crew included Phat DeFrate, the former Regina Roughrider. In the first quarter, Manitoba played against the wind, and as the teams traded punts, the pigskin remained in Manitoba territory. Late in the period, the Beavers returned a kick 42 yards to Manitoba's 25-yard line. The Bisons held, and Manitoba's Tubber Kobrinsky kicked the ball away for field position. In the second quarter, Beavers quarterback Howard Dunnell ran a sweep to the right and gained 51 yards to reach Manitoba's 12-yard line. Ted Anderson then scored a touchdown for Minot State. Later in the same period, Beavers halfback Melley Johnson, a track star from Kenmare, North Dakota, returned a punt 85 yards for a touchdown behind a wedge formation but officials failed to penalize the Beavers for the illegal play. When Manitoba regained possession they fumbled and lost the ball on Minot State's 45-yard line. The Beavers gave the ball to Johnson again. He hit the line but then cut back and sprinted 55 yards for another touchdown.

In the second half, the Beavers returned Kobrinsky's punt to Manitoba's 40-yard line but the Bisons held them back and forced a turnover on downs. Manitoba then fumbled and lost the ball and the Beavers engineered a 60-yard scoring drive that ended on a 15-yard plunge over center for the score. On the next drive, Manitoba started with the ball at their own 15-yard line and used an aerial attack combined with running plays to reach the 3-yard line. The Beavers held, however, and forced a turnover on downs. On a later possession, Manitoba executed another long drive but then fumbled and lost the ball. On their final possession, Manitoba again approached the Minot goal line but failed to score. The Beavers beat the Bisons 26-0.

Once again, the Bisons struggled with blocking and disarming blocks but they proved effective in the short passing game. Overall, the players were tired because they had played multiple games within a short period of time late in their schedule. The 14-hour bus ride from Winnipeg to Minot further drained their energy.

*

In the wake of the 1934 season, the Manitoba student council, which controlled all revenue and expenses related to student activities, including athletics, looked at the football team's $300 loss on the season and questioned the need for football at the school. The *Manitoban* blamed the weather, low fan support from a "lethargic student body," and overspending for what the student council deemed an unsuccessful season. The team had great coaches in Hass and Walter Odhe who had led the Bisons to one win in the American game and to close games against the Winnipegs. There had been more pep rallies, booster activities, and press coverage than ever before but it all failed to bring in gate receipts. Sportswriter Johnny Buss at the *Winnipeg Free Press* berated the student council's concerns. "Rugby in the university can be made a paying proposition," he said, "but it takes time and also a little money. These battles [over funding] do no good and have a tendency of dividing the factions, with the result the students lose not only their spirit but interest, which results in failure of the athletic projects." The *Manitoban* suggested the school should continue to field a football team that plays by American intercollegiate rules. "The general trend in Western Canada seems to be favorable to the game played south of the border," wrote the editors. "University students and Winnipeg citizens have had numerous opportunities to compare the merits of the two systems of play and... the majority seem to favor the more spectacular, crowd-pleasing style in vogue in the States." Besides, the paper argued, the University of British Columbia, too, had played American football in 1934.

Brown and Gold (1934)

*

In Vancouver, Gordon "Doc" Burke, an American medical doctor who had played high school football in Tacoma, Washington, and then studied medicine at the University of Washington, now coached the University of British Columbia Thunderbirds in Canadian football on a volunteer basis. The school fielded its first "Canadian rugby" (as opposed to "English rugby") team in 1924 and Burke had helped to elevate the program when he became the team's coach in 1925, when the team also played and lost American football contests against the College of Puget Sound (54-0) in Tacoma, Washington, against the University of Washington (27-6) in Seattle, and against the Washington State Normal School at Bellingham (46-6). Burke's blue and gold Thunderbirds competed for fans with the school's English rugby team and Burke had instilled discipline in the players with 6:00 a.m. practices.

Before the 1934 season, with calls throughout Western Canada to adopt American intercollegiate rules for Canadian football, Burke decided his Thunderbirds should once again play American college teams by American rules. The team would also play Canadian club teams by Canadian rules, but Burke desired for his men to play other colleges. The school newspaper, the *Ubyssey* (the acronym U.B.C spelled out as a word) echoed Burke's sentiment. "It is time that this University got out of downtown leagues and started intercollegiate competition," the *Ubyssey* said. "The most logical place to look for this competition is to the south." The *Ubyssey* suggested the school might eventually join the Pacific Coast Conference (PCC) and play college teams from the Pacific Northwest in the United States.

British Columbia played their first game under American rules for 1934 against the last American team it had played in 1925, the Washington State Normal School at Bellingham. The Americans met the Canadians on October 6, 1934, at Athletic Park in Vancouver where a larger-than-normal crowd watched the game. But just like at Manitoba, the student athletes at British Columbia proved slow to adjust to blocking, disarming blocks, and using forward passes. Reserve players scored most of the Bellingham Vikings' points. Thunderbirds fans felt unamused. The *Ubyssey* reported, "By the time the game finished the stands were almost deserted and most of the spectators had either gone home or were down on the sidelines watching the play." The Vikings destroyed the Thunderbirds 44-0.

In response to the loss, some U.B.C. students published a satirical newspaper, the *Canyessey*, which mocked the school's American football ambitions:

> "Why should I, burdened now with too much expense, pay out my hard-earned dimes and quarters to see such fiascos as the late lamented game in which Bellingham Normal, with a third-rate team, beat us so badly that the whole Commerce Faculty sat up all night calculating the final score (finally announcing that it was 44 to 0)?" asked the *Canyessey*. "[Why should I] pay to watch the Americans pile up first down after first down in monotonous succession while the Varsity team, woefully undertrained, stood powerless to halt them, entranced by the invaders' superior technique?"

A follow-up editorial in the *Ubyssey* suggested British Columbia stood to gain little from its American football aspirations:

> "For this college to enter into the sacred circles of the [Pacific Coast Conference], it would have to follow the suit of the American colleges and import players," the newspaper said. "These imported players would be provided with jobs by football mad alumni who wish to see their dear old Alma Mater distinguish itself in athletic arenas. It would be necessary to obtain a coach. Coaches are an expensive item in any college budget. In the United States coaches are so highly paid that in most cases they receive more than the average faculty member."

Nevertheless, Burke stuck to the school's commitments to play American colleges. On November 16, 1934, the Thunderbirds traveled to

Brown and Gold (1934)

Tacoma to play Pacific Lutheran College. The Lutes fielded a heavy, fast, experienced team that used long forward passes to score three touchdowns in the first quarter. Pacific Lutheran beat British Columbia 51-12.

On November 24, 1934, the Thunderbirds hosted the Loggers from the College of Puget Sound. The *Ubyssey* described the game as "a dull and dismal exhibition of brute strength pitted against gallant ignorance." The Loggers used repeated line plunges in a puddle of mud in the rain to score 6 touchdowns and walk away victorious 39-0. "It was rather spectacular to observe three or four or five heroic [Thunderbird] souls tear madly toward yellow shirted opponents and prostrate themselves violently in the mud before them, disappearing in self-raised fountains of inky gumbo," described the *Ubyssey*.

* *

With Eddie James lost to injury, the Winnipegs prepared for the WCRFU semifinal match against the Regina Roughriders. Coach Greg Kabat and the team's manager, Joe Ryan, scouted the Roughriders during Regina's 19-0 win over the Saskatoon Hilltops, where Regina kept its top talent on the sidelines until late in the game, to avoid injuries. Afterward, Kabat decided the team should focus on their passing game for the upcoming struggle, which they had to practice on a snow-covered field. Meanwhile, Ryan shared his thoughts about Regina with the *Winnipeg Free Press*. In his opinion, the Roughriders had a strong line with excellent ends but their American backfielders didn't impress. Both Ralph Pierce and Oke Olson had failed to complete many passes and while Pierce proved a shifty runner, Olson "is no speed demon [and] bucks the line a lot, but not with any particular drive." And Ryan said Paul Kirk "didn't set the world on fire."

In other words, Ryan set the stage for a grudge match.

The *Winnipeg Tribune* suggested that both Regina and Winnipeg fielded strong defenses but the Roughriders held the upper hand on offense with a good passing game. The Winnipegs, meanwhile, suffered from a lack of good receivers and end-runners. Sportswriter Ralph Allen told readers to expect "an aerial fight of punts and passes." Meanwhile, the *Leader-Post* suggested that while Regina played a soft schedule, the Winnipegs enjoyed the benefit of a tough regular season against American teams with heavy linemen. In Lionel Conacher's opinion, from what he had seen of the Winnipegs, they couldn't beat any team in the Big Four.

Meanwhile, in Regina, the Roughriders proved as popular as ever as over 1,000 fans watched them practice each day.

Kabat selected 23 players for the trip. For $8.65 each approximately 100 fans traveled with the team to Regina and back again on the Canadian Pacific Railroad. The rest of Winnipeg would listen to the play-by-play on the radio.

On the day of the WCRFU semifinal, on November 3, 1934, Kabat dressed 20 players. The team's trainer, Billy Hughes, used 500 yards of bandages, 390 yards of tape, and three pounds of cotton on the bodies of the players before, during, and after the game. The team took the field in front of 6,000 fans. On Winnipeg's first drive, Russ Rebholz kicked the ball past the goal line on a rouge attempt but the Winnipegs failed to give the return man a berth on the catch and the rouge failed. On Winnipeg's next drive, Bobby Schiller fumbled and lost the ball at Winnipeg's 35-yard line. Regina speedster Pierce then ran 30 yards around end. On the next play, Olson attempted a rouge but Rebholz caught the ball in front of the deadline and returned it out of the end zone.

On the next Roughrider possession, Pierce gained ground around his ends and Regina reached Winnipeg's 18-yard line. Olson attempted a drop-kick but the Winnipegs got a hand on the kicked ball and it sailed past the goal line where a Winnipeg player caught it. This time, Regina lost the rouge opportunity when they failed to give the return man a berth on the catch.

On Winnipeg's next possession, Rebholz attempted a field goal but the Roughriders blocked the kick. Rebholz picked up the loose pigskin and attempted a drop-kick on the run to score a rouge but Pierce caught the ball past the goal line and zig-zagged 20 yards out of the end zone.

With 10 minutes remaining in the second quarter, Kabat wrenched his knee and had to leave the game. Meanwhile, the Roughriders gained momentum and reached Winnipeg's 3-yard line where they crashed the

Brown and Gold (1934)

line three times in succession. When the official blew his whistle to end the half the ball remained a foot outside the goal line. The teams took the break in a 0-0 tie.

In the second half, the Winnipegs found themselves on the defensive. Twice, Kirk attempted field goals from near Winnipeg's 10-yard line, and twice Winnipeg blocked the kick attempts. Both teams had played conservative football. With 50 minutes of game time behind them, neither team had completed a single forward pass or had attempted an option run. With the score tied 0-0, Regina decided to take to the air. Pierce completed a 20-yard pass to Regina's 40-yard line and then Olson tossed a 40-yard pass to Kirk—the 81st completed pass from Olson to Kirk on the season—to reach Winnipeg's 20-yard line, where Rebholz tackled Kirk. Olson then attempted a rouge. Rebholz picked up the ball in front of the goal line and attempted a return kick on the run, but a Roughrider blocked Rebholz's kick attempt and the ball bounced past the goal line into the end zone. The Roughriders fell on the ball and scored a touchdown.

In the final minutes, officials ejected Kabat from the game for arguing with them about a call. Winnipeg then tried a desperate aerial attack in which Rebholz completed a 40-yard pass, but the Winnipegs failed to score. Meanwhile, Regina scored 2 more points on successful rouge attempts. The Roughriders defeated the Winnipegs 8-0.

During the game, Roughrider fans collected $240 to help support Eddie James in his recovery.

* *

To claim the undisputed MIAC title, Concordia needed to beat or tie Gustavus in St. Peter. A loss would mean St. Thomas could claim the conference title by virtue of the school's win percentage in conference matchups. And while the Cobbers as a team pursued the conference championship, 6-foot, 190-pound "Blasting Bob" Fritz chased a roster spot on the all-conference team for the fourth time in four seasons.

Gustavus hadn't scored a point in conference play and the Cobbers didn't put in much effort during practices, which left Coach Frank Cleve frustrated. He feared his opponent, Coach George Myrum, might have something up his sleeve for his Golden Gusties offense.

The Cobbers departed Thursday for Minneapolis. The schools had originally scheduled the game for Saturday but Minnesota hosted Indiana University that day, and so Cleve and Myrum moved the game to 2:30 p.m. Friday afternoon.

On Friday morning, the Cobbers traveled from Minneapolis to St. Peter. Meanwhile, in Moorhead, boosters set up the chapel at Concordia so that fans could follow the game delivered as play-by-play via telegraph. Fans paid 10 cents each to sit in the pews and pray.

In a cold, northern gale on November 9, 1934, Fritz received the opening kickoff, but the Golden Gusties shrouded his advance and tackled him at Concordia's 8-yard line. The Cobber backfield advanced the ball 23 yards but then chose to punt to gain field position. Gustavus started with the ball at their own 34-yard line but soon chose to punt. The Cobbers then drove from their 22-yard line into Gustavus territory where the teams exchanged fumbles. With Concordia back in possession, quarterback Henry Held ran over right tackle and behind a wall of interference that dispatched all but three would-be tacklers. Held rambled 39 yards and dodged the final three Gusties for the score.

In the second quarter, Concordia continued to move the ball with ease as Fritz helped the team to gain four first downs and 42 yards. He then carried the ball on a 25-yard touchdown run to score. Late in the first half, the Gusties fumbled on a punt return and Concordia recovered the ball at Gustavus's 38-yard line. Once again, Fritz led the drive, and from the 2-yard line he plunged over for the score.

In the second half, to thwart a possible passing threat, Concordia switched from a seven- to a six-man line on defense. By the end of the third quarter, the Cobbers offense reached Gustavus's 1-foot line, but Held fumbled and lost the ball and Gustavus punted the pigskin away for field position. When the Cobbers regained possession at their own 46-yard line, Fritz and his backfield worked together to reach the 6-yard line where Fritz completed a pass to Held for a touchdown. The Cobbers walked off with the 26-0 win and the conference championship.

Brown and Gold (1934)

All seven Concordia starting linemen played the full 60 minutes and the Cobbers gained a total of 359 yards from scrimmage. They had finished 4-0-0 in the conference and outscored opponents 97-19. Concordia won its second conference championship in four years. The *Concordian* observed, "In past seasons, Concordia elevens have been known primarily for their great power. This year, however... [Coach Cleve] dug down into his bag of tricks and came out with a very plentiful assortment of baffling trick plays."

Cleve and his men stayed in Minneapolis Friday night so they could go to Memorial Field on Saturday to watch the Golden Gophers beat the Hoosiers 30-0. After the game, they boarded the Fargonian on the Northern Pacific Railroad line and when they arrived in Moorhead at 11:55 p.m., students, faculty, and the pep band greeted them at the depot. The school arranged for taxis to carry the players and coaches to the dining hall where they held a late-night pep fest celebration. The school held a second pep fest on Monday morning in the chapel where the college president, Moorhead's mayor, the pep band, the pep squad, students, coaches, and players all celebrated the team's championship win. Fritz spoke at both events.

*

Colleges in Fargo and Moorhead routinely filled their athletic rosters with student athletes from mostly small, rural towns, where many of them had never even played football. To mold a competitive team the colleges required good coaches, and North Dakota State, Moorhead State, and Concordia each had great ones. "It's not much of a trick to mold a team out of brilliant material, a wide range of talent that knows fundamentals, that is far advanced in football technique when you take hold of them and begin to whip them into shape as one machine," wrote Dick Hackenberg in the *Moorhead Daily News*. "But it does take coaching to develop youths who have had little training, in some cases none whatever, and build them from these rough parts a fine working, smooth functioning football juggernaut."

Among the star athletes in college football, Bob Fritz had played very little football while in high school in International Falls. But in 1934, after a brilliant career at Concordia, Bill Haman at the *St. Paul Daily News*

At Gustavus (St. Peter, Minnesota)

declared Fritz "the one outstanding player in the state" for his role as captain and signal-caller from the fullback position for Concordia. "Fritz was head and shoulders over any other backfield man in the Minnesota conference," Haman said and he named Fritz to his all-state college football team at fullback. Fritz also earned all-conference honors at fullback on the Associated Press coaches' poll and at quarterback for his signal-calling on the *St. Paul Dispatch-Pioneer Press* all-conference squad. He also received an honorable mention at fullback on the United Press and Associated Press All-America teams. In the *Moorhead Daily News*, Hackenberg eulogized Fritz's career in his daily column:

> "The greatest, most colorful gridiron leader Concordia ever had—dynamiting Bob Fritz, four times all-state back... one year a captain but four years a leader... lover of contact, the more brutal the better. Fritz has made history in the state college conference. Never before, to our knowledge at least, has one man been named all-state so many times—three times on the official coaches' selections, four times on newspaper all-star teams. In the annals of Concordia College, Bob will go down, quite possibly, as the school's football great. In years to come his name will be one to conjure with, at least to future Cobber athletes. Those fortunate enough to have seen this ball carrying demon in action will never forget his battering, bruising charges into the line, his swift, accurate passes... and above all, his love of the game, his characteristic cry, 'Try and stop this baby!' as he hurtled himself through or over opposing forward walls for touchdown and after touchdown. Concordia's second state championship football machine was a remarkably well-coached, smooth functioning combination, [but] on the playing field, however, it was the dynamic leadership of Fritz that spurred them on to resounding victories. Always in a hurry, always an inspiration, a hard-driving master, the Cobber captain should receive a full measure

Brown and Gold (1934)

of credit for Concordia's 1934 success. There were others, of course, who contributed immeasurably... [but] they were dominated by Fritz whose relentless fury must have imparted much to their greatness... There is no denying that Fritz stood out like a lighthouse in a fog on that team, testimony enough to his ability. His leadership was not of the selfish kind. He did not use the play of his mates to his advantage."

Despite a scarlet fever epidemic within the community, Concordia held its MIAC championship victory banquet at the college. At the banquet, Fritz dismissed the laurels he had received. "All-state teams," he said, "are a lot of hooey to my way of thinking. Of course, it's nice to 'make' them, but in my opinion too many good men are left off." He went on to praise the contributions of his individual teammates. He received a gold football to mark the 1934 championship and he earned yet another letter in football. His college football career had now come to an end.

* *

The Dragons left the Bison with more than just injured souls. Over half of North Dakota State's starters suffered an injury that affected his ability to play well or play at all. Fritz Hanson had thrown himself into a tackle on defense and the effort had knocked him out of the game and out of practice for a week. Bud Marquardt suffered a nagging charley horse and the big man, Lyle Sturgeon, could no longer play due to an injury.

The Bison knew the Jackrabbit faithful would turn out in force for their homecoming game in Brookings. A loss to South Dakota State would give the conference title to the Sioux. And Coach Casey Finnegan would have to face a new challenger in Reginald H. "Red" Threlfall, a Massachusetts native who had served as an assistant coach under Cy Kasper for three years. After Kasper resigned on a high note at the end of the Jackrabbits' 1933 championship season, Threlfall took over the reins for 1934. A 1927 graduate of Purdue, Threlfall had played as a lineman for the

Boilermakers. After graduation, he coached at Bates College in Lewiston, Maine, before Kasper called him to South Dakota in 1930.

With two losses in the NCC, the Jackrabbits would play the underdog to the Bison. However, North Dakota State assistant coach Bob Lowe had scouted South Dakota State when they played Dakota Wesleyan University and he recognized the danger posed by a Jackrabbit halfback, "Speedboy" Paul Miller, a track athlete from Platte, South Dakota, who had finished close behind Hanson in spring track meets. Miller had scored 13 touchdowns in six games. South Dakota State's two conference losses stood now as a mirage.

On Friday afternoon, in advance of Saturday's game, the Bison practiced in Brookings. When the game kicked off at 2:00 p.m. Saturday, November 10, 1934, Fay Brown of KFYR radio in Bismarck broadcast the play-by-play and "[gave] KFYR listeners one of his characteristic intimate descriptions of the contest from start to finish," reported the *Bismarck Tribune*. On the opening drive, the Bison fumbled and lost the ball on their own 48-yard line. Two plays later, Miller zig-zagged 47 yards and eluded Hanson, the Bison safety, to score the first touchdown. The Jackrabbits forced the Bison to punt and the kick fell short. South Dakota State then used a series of passes and runs to reach the end zone for a score.

In the second quarter, the Jackrabbits began a drive from their own 38-yard line where Miller raced 32 yards off right end to reach North Dakota State's 30-yard line. Three plays later, Miller slipped across right tackle for a 1-yard touchdown run. Near the end of the first half, the Bison fumbled and lost the ball again near midfield. Five plays later, Miller scored again on an 18-yard run.

In the second half, Miller intercepted a Bison pass at South Dakota State's 38-yard line. Miller then caught a 59-yard touchdown pass to pile on the points. In the fourth quarter, the Bison attempted to punt but fumbled and lost the ball at their own 30-yard line. The Jackrabbits drove in for another Miller touchdown. The Bison limped off the field in a 0-38 loss to the Jackrabbits.

Miller's five touchdowns brought him to 110 points in eight games to lead the nation in scoring. The Jackrabbits handed the NCC title to the

Brown and Gold (1934)

Sioux who finished conference play with a 3-1-0 record and .750 win percentage. The Sioux had outscored conference opponents 51-7. Meanwhile, the Bison finished 2-1-1 with a .667 win percentage while opponents outscored them 50-42.

* *

When 27 Regina Roughriders arrived on a Canadian Pacific Railroad train at 9:00 a.m. Friday morning in Vancouver to play the Meraloma Club for the WCRFU championship title, newspapers on the West Coast didn't treat the Roughriders as rivals but as mercenaries. Sportswriter Bob Elson in the *Province* published the following "old 'collitch' yell" for Regina fans to use at the game:

North Dakota,
South Dakota,
Minnesota, Rah!
Regina, Regina, Ha! Ha! Ha!

One dispatch from Vancouver pointed to the fact the Meralomas didn't have any American imports on their roster. "When a senior Canadian rugby team hasn't an American in the line-up, it's news," said the report, reprinted in the *Winnipeg Tribune*. The Meralomas "are in the embarrassing position of being a wholly Canadian team" and "strangely enough, they are even coached by a Canadian... In any event, the series will be an interesting experiment—an Americanized squad invading the last stronghold of real Canadian rugby." The Meralomas fielded mostly former English-style rugby players who supplied their own uniforms. Originally a swim team, the Mermaid Athletic Club from the Kitsilano area of Vancouver later expanded into other sports and derived the Meraloma name from the slogan "Mermaids, first, last, and always" or [Mer]maids, [al]pha, [om]ega, and [a]lways.

To prepare for the Roughriders, Meralomas Coach Hammie Boucher and his players watched and studied film footage of the Meralomas' victory over the University of Alberta. Thirty players huddled around a

At South Dakota State (Brookings, South Dakota)

small film viewer that offered a screen no more than several inches across. Boucher expressed concern about Regina's passing and kicking game.

When the Roughriders arrived at Athletic Park on Friday to practice the groundskeeper refused to let them onto the rain-saturated field, and so they practiced in a nearby park. Ralph Pierce stood and watched while he nursed torn muscles in his left hip.

On the day of the first game, on Saturday, November 10, 1934, the sunshine over Athletic Park felt welcome to the fans while the Roughriders in red and black boiled. They had worn too many layers. To encourage fans to attend the WCRFU championship series, English rugby clubs in Vancouver had canceled their games. Coupled with good weather and the fact no radio station would broadcast the game, approximately 3,000 fans paid $1 per adult, 50 cents per high school student, and 25 cents per child for the match, which meant the Meralomas collected enough in gate receipts to cover their guarantee for Regina. The Kitsilano Boys Band entertained the crowd as they entered the grounds, and before the 2:30 p.m. kickoff, the public address system announced the arrival of the Meralomas in orange and black.

For the first 20 minutes of the game, despite the wet turf and a slippery ball, the Meralomas had the Roughriders on their heels. The former English rugby players, practiced in lateral passing, executed an effective option run that was "something entirely different from any on the prairies," observed Dave Dryburgh, sportswriter for the *Leader-Post* in Regina. The Roughriders kept the Meralomas out of the end zone, however, and after they figured out how to defend against Vancouver's west-coast offense, the Roughriders offense found momentum. Pierce scored on a 50-yard run before halftime.

Throughout the first half, both teams played clean football with few penalties—so clean, in fact, that "telegraph operators cast dirty looks at newspaper men who kept them busy sending copy," Dryburgh quipped. They wanted to watch the game.

In the second half, Regina remained in control as Oke Olson took to the air and connected with Steve Adkins, his favorite target. Sportswriter Himie Koshevoy in the *Vancouver News-Herald* described Olson as "some huge Martian in his close-fitting leather helmet... a quadruple-threat or

Brown and Gold (1934)

more. He boots the ball far and high, passes with precision, runs a smart twisting course on ball-carrying and can knife through a line on a buck." *Vancouver Sun* sportswriter Hal Straight said Olson, "takes his football so seriously, every time he errs a bit he goes through all the actions of a temperamental prima donna." Sportswriter Jack Patterson in the *Sun* concurred. "He is worth the price of the admission alone to see," he said. The Roughriders scored three more touchdowns and beat the Meralomas 22-2.

Afterward, a cartoon in the sports section of the *Vancouver Sun* depicted Regina as the biblical Goliath. The single-panel comic suggested the Roughriders hailed from "Regina (and points south)." The cartoon also showed a Meraloma player asking a Roughrider, "Well-l-l. How's things in Regina?" and the Roughrider answers, "Search me brother. I'm from Kalamazoo." In Vancouver, the newspapers made sure to identify each U.S. import on the Roughrider roster by the state they had hailed from. In the *Province*, sportswriter Bob Elson said the Roughriders had been "built to order for the Canadian championship" as opposed to "British Columbia's gallant homebrew legion." In the *Sun*, Patterson said Regina's college football players from the States had been "selected for the express purpose of winning a Dominion crown for Regina."

Oke Olson told Straight of the *Sun* that the Roughriders had worked out two to three hours per day and that he sometimes spent up to five hours a day throwing passes to Adkins. The Roughrider passing game had proved effective, he said, because the Meralomas line never charged the passer. Straight quipped, "The passer could lace his shoes up and still get the ball away."

*

On their day off between games, the Vancouver and Regina players spent some casual time together, and players from both teams suggested Ralph Pierce could take the place of any great U.S. college halfback. Pierce, meanwhile, continued to nurse his injury and suggested he might not play on Monday.

But he did play. On Monday evening, November 12, 1934, with an 8:00 p.m. start, in curtains of rain and on a muddy field, Pierce "provided most of the color when he was fielding Meraloma kicks," reported the

Province. "He would take the ball on the dead run, gallop away for 15 and 20 yards at a time, spinning around through or hurdling over Meraloma ends. Just what Mr. Pierce could do on a sunny afternoon, on a dry field when he is feeling right is a picture for your imagination." At most, 500 spectators huddled under the grandstands to avoid the downpour as they watched the mud war on the field and floodlights exploding in the rain. The Roughriders and Meralomas punted the ball 29 times apiece for a total of 58 punts for 2,135 yards. Regina won the game off the feet of Olson's punts and Kirk's placekicks. Kirk sent the pigskin over the crossbar twice and the Roughriders scored 1 rouge while the Melaromas scored 2 to end the game 7-2 in favor of Regina.

In the end, the Meralomas finished their three playoff games, one against Alberta and two against Regina, with a total deficit of $125, not bad for a swim team in rugby pants. In the Province, sportswriter Bob Elson said the Meralomas "can also take pride in their record as a Canadian—with emphasis on the nationality please—football team. Can you field a better, Regina, Winnipeg, et al?"

*

In the week following the Roughriders' victory over the Meralomas, debate raged within the AAUC about whether Canadian football teams should be allowed to import players from the United States. One side argued teams no longer needed Americans to learn the forward pass, and the other side argued the imports had revived interest in the game. "Now that Canadian footballers have the idea of the new forward pass there is not much further need for imports," offered Dr. M. B. Kinsella, former CRU president, to the *Toronto Daily Star*. "Our footballers are as good as the Americans any day of the week." The AAUC determined they would request the CRU to stop the importation of players from the United States.

In Winnipeg, some voices rose up against how Joe Ryan and the Winnipeg Rugby Club had imported players and had pushed for a more American style game. However, Rosy Adelman, the long-time Winnipegs veteran, quieted the opposition. In a column in the *Winnipeg Free Press*, Adelman reminded Winnipegers how before the team had imported talent, both players and fans exhibited low turnout and excitement for the game. He agreed, however, that all teams should cease the practice, but "the only way to stop importation is a mutual agreement between all western teams," he said. "Successful football in Winnipeg is predicated on our ability to beat Regina or furnish them with stiff opposition. The Regina-Winnipeg game is the Yale-Harvard, the Army-Notre Dame, the Minnesota-Michigan game of the prairies. Fans in both cities look to this game as the ultimate deciding factor of whether the season is successful, and whether the game they are watching is worth seeing or not." Adelman argued that no team in Western Canada without imports could compete with teams in the East simply because those teams drew from a larger population of athletes. Universities in the East drew students from all over Canada and those graduates stayed and played for club teams there.

Meanwhile, in his office in the Grain Exchange and with the Winnipegs sidelined for the remainder of the postseason, Ryan continued to think about how to increase fan interest in football. "Joe thinks rugby football 12 months of every year," wrote E.A. Armstrong in his column in the *Winnipeg Free Press*. Ryan sought to combine the Manitoba and Saskatchewan unions into a single interprovincial union. He argued that fans desired more competition between teams in the provinces, and the Winnipegs suffered from a lack of competition in Manitoba. Without such an arrangement, the Winnipegs would have to continue to find opponents in the United States to fill out their schedule.

Voices in Winnipeg argued the city should return to the Winnipeg Senior League model and foster more teams, but Ryan argued for home-and-home games between Regina and Winnipeg and the same for the Saskatchewan and Manitoba university teams. The new interprovincial union would also include club teams from Moose Jaw and Saskatoon.

Both the University of Saskatchewan and the Saskatoon Hilltops agreed to Ryan's plan and schedule. The university, in particular, favored the plan to play home-and-home games against Manitoba and suggested the teams could use a points total basis to determine which college would play Alberta for the Hardy Trophy. The WCRFU might also secure a special rail travel rate for rugby clubs. Regina, however, rejected Ryan's idea. And while the Roughriders agreed home-and-home games between the cities would bring in more gate receipts, Regina did not pursue such an arrangement. The situation would force the Winnipegs to schedule some games against American college teams again in 1935. "It is largely a question of providing enough good football for the Winnipeg customers," observed sportswriter W.G. Allen in the *Winnipeg Free Press*. "As it is now, we have to depend on teams from across the line."

In the *Winnipeg Tribune*, sportswriter Ralph Allen feared the circumstances would compel both the Winnipegs and the Bisons to permanently adopt the full American intercollegiate football code and break away from the rest of the WCRFU. He feared Winnipeg would lose its historical rivalry with Regina and that fan interest would wane.

* *

In 1933, the last time North Dakota State played Oklahoma City, Fritz Hanson had amazed the Okie crowd with his speed and agility, but he had also been sick and had collapsed on runs before he could reach the goal line. The Goldbugs went on to beat the Bison 19-0. The year before, the Bison beat the Goldbugs 27-7 in Fargo when Hanson scored 3 touchdowns against the southerners. Unsurprisingly, the *Daily Oklahoman* described "Hula-Hipped Hanson," the "Fargo Express," as a "one-man team" with, according to the *Oklahoma City Advertiser*, "rubber legs." The Oklahoma City student newspaper *Campus* referred to Hanson as a "bundle of shiftiness." In Fargo, the *Spectrum* responded that Hanson "needs no adjective to describe him to folks in *these* parts" [emphasis added] and that he would "furnish the southern folks with some idea of the top speed of the hardy northern Swedes." Now in 1934, Goldbugs fans felt concerned about Hanson because they mistakenly believed Hanson had scored 2 touchdowns against undefeated Minnesota. In fact, Hanson had scored 1 touchdown on a pass to Bud Marquardt. Now, Hanson suffered from lingering injuries. Coach Casey Finnegan had pulled him from the game against South Dakota State.

In Oklahoma City, the Goldbugs played under their third coach in three years. Their new coach, Stanley L. "Stan" Williamson, a two-time All-American, had played center for the University of Southern California in two Rose Bowl victories in 1930 and 1932. In his final season at USC,

Brown and Gold (1934)

he captained the team in a fourth-quarter rally to defeat Notre Dame 16-14. After college, he went on to coach at Classen High School in Oklahoma City before taking over the Goldbugs in 1934.

After a 26-6 loss to the University of Arizona Wildcats in 1934, the Goldbugs' eighth loss in a row, Williamson had his team focus on stopping the pass, the team's season-long weakness. Against Hanson and the rest of the Bison backfield, Williamson's boys would have to crowd up to the line to stop the run, but he also knew Wendy Schollander could throw bullets. The loss of the Goldbugs' star defensive left end to an injured knee only complicated the situation. On defense for the Bison, Bud Marquardt had played a great game against the Goldbugs in 1933 when "he made one side of the line almost impregnable," observed the *Oklahoma News*.

Early in the week before the game, Oklahoma City president, Dr. Walter Scott Athearn, passed away. Athearn had been a big supporter of the Goldbugs football program and the *Campus* encouraged the team to win one for Athearn. The *Campus* also hoped the southern heat would sap the Bison and that they would "wilt in the sun."

At North Dakota State, multiple injuries meant Finnegan asked his men to perform only light workouts. They practiced the pass, and Hanson, too, tossed the pigskin. The team departed Fargo on Wednesday morning, and Finnegan and his 21 players arrived in Oklahoma City on Thursday. They practiced under the lights Thursday evening.

On November 16, 1934, the northerners and southerners met on the gridiron. For most of the first quarter, the teams kept the ball between the goal lines, but by the end of the first period, North Dakota State had gained momentum. The Bison began a drive at their own 35-yard line, which carried over into the second quarter when Hanson slipped through the line to carry the ball 17 yards for a touchdown. The Bison held the Goldbugs scoreless into the third quarter until the Goldbugs blocked a Bison punt at North Dakota State's 8-yard line. The ball bounced into and out of the end zone for a safety. A few minutes later, the Bison attempted another punt, this time from their own goal line. Again, the Goldbugs blocked it and fell on the ball in the end zone for a touchdown. Late in the third quarter, Hanson intercepted an Oklahoma City pass at the 3-

yard line and returned the ball 97 yards for the score. Oklahoma City attempted a comeback but with 30 seconds remaining in the game, the Goldbugs threw an interception and the Bison won 13-8.

Afterward, one of the officials for the game, Edward Cochrane, told Finnegan that Hanson had exhibited some of the best running he had seen in 1934. As the sports editor for the *Kansas City Journal-Post*, Cochrane had the ear of Grantland Rice, the prolific sportswriter who had taken over for Walter Camp in the selection of All-Americans in football. Cochrane said he would recommend Hanson to the All-America team. Meanwhile, the *Spectrum* complained that the *Dakota Student* at North Dakota had left Hanson off its mythical all-conference eleven. The *Spectrum* also reprinted a letter from sportswriter Hi Doty of the *Campus*. Doty said, "Please do something about Fritz Hanson. Drown him, choke him, decapitate him, it doesn't matter what, but please make sure that he won't be visiting us again. That hula-hipped little devil lost me five dollars last Friday night and, I am positive, shortened my life by at least ten years. Ninety-seven yards. Whew!"

* *

Two weeks after the Manitoba Bisons had finished their schedule, the Saskatchewan Huskies challenged the Bisons to play for the Hardy Cup, the championship trophy for college teams in Western Canada. The Cup had been donated several years before by Evan Hardy, former head of the agricultural engineering department at Saskatchewan. Hardy had played for the team as a faculty member before rules prevented it. In 1934, the Huskies had just reacquired the trophy from Alberta who had acquired it from British Columbia. Manitoba last competed for the trophy in 1931, but lost. To play for the Hardy Cup again, Manitoba would have to find a substitute coach because Wally Hass had already returned home to the United States. The universities scheduled to play the game at Osborne Stadium but Saskatchewan later pulled out of the agreement due to a lack of funds for travel. When Manitoba offered to travel to Saskatchewan to play, instead, Saskatchewan declined. The Bisons felt the Huskies simply feared to defend the trophy.

Brown and Gold (1934)

*   *

Two days after their victory in Oklahoma City, the Bison arrived by train in Lubbock, Texas, to take on the Texas Technical College Matadors. Because they had arrived on Sunday, the Bison would practice at Tech Field for a few days before the game. When Coach Casey Finnegan got off the train the *Lubbock Avalanche-Journal* asked him to describe his team. Finnegan started with his star. "Fritz Hanson, our little halfback, is a great crowd pleaser," he said. "He made a big hit at Minnesota." The Bison had scored 2 touchdowns against Minnesota, the number one team in the country, and Finnegan knew he could name-drop the Golden Gophers to raise interest in the Bison-Matador game. The *Lubbock Morning Avalanche* said Hanson "promises to be the biggest pain in the Tech's neck Friday. A triple-threater, Hanson stars particularly on broken field runs, and his speed carries him to touchdowns enough to make North Dakota State a dangerous opponent on any field." Lubbock High School coach Weldon Chapman had scouted the Bison for Texas Tech when North Dakota State played in Oklahoma City. Chapman told the *Morning Avalanche* that the Matadors "must watch Hanson every minute, or he is sure to be off and away. Once past the line of scrimmage, there's not much that can be done toward halting him. He can shake a mean leg in an open field, stopping and starting, reversing his field, and eluding tacklers like a frightened rabbit." He compared Hanson to Bohn Hilliard at the University of Texas. Hilliard had scored the touchdown that beat Notre Dame earlier that season. But Chapman said Hanson was "even faster and more elusive than Hilliard. If he gets any good blocking at all, he's going to travel." Texas Tech Coach Pete Cawthon used that information to focus his men on stopping the run.

A Houston native, Cawthon had performed as a four-sport athlete when he attended Southwestern University in Georgetown, Texas. After college, he coached high school athletes in Beaumont and at the Terrill School for Boys in Dallas. He coached college athletes at Rice University in Houston and at Austin College in Sherman before he took over the Matadors football program in 1930.

During practices, both teams locked the gates to fans. Early in the week, the Bison complained that the higher altitude in Lubbock made it harder for them to catch their breath. Later in the week, cooler weather descended on Lubbock, which put the Bison in good spirits.

The Bison met the Matadors on November 23, 1934, in a late-season intersectional matchup in front of 3,500 fans. The Matadors scored the first touchdown in the first quarter when their right halfback ran 25 yards and carried two tacklers with him over the goal line. Texas Tech scored a second time on a 90-yard drive that featured an aerial attack and a touchdown pass. Hanson only played 5 minutes in the first half. In the third quarter, Hanson returned a short Matador punt to Texas Tech's 30-yard line. He then carried the ball three times to gain 15 yards, and on the next play, Bud Marquardt caught an 11-yard pass to reach the 4-yard line. On a spinner play, Hanson carried the ball over the goal line for North Dakota State's first touchdown.

The Bison regained possession in the third quarter when Hanson returned a punt to midfield. Hanson and his fullback compatriot, Bob Erickson, alternated runs, and then Hanson carried the ball over from the 1-yard line to tie up the score. In the fourth quarter, the Matadors returned a short punt to North Dakota State's 30-yard line and two plays later, the Matador's scored on a 28-yard touchdown pass. After the Bison returned the kickoff to the 28-yard line, Hanson attempted to run the ball but the Matadors stopped him for a 5-yard loss. North Dakota State then executed the most memorable play of the day when Hanson stood up close behind center, took the snap, and followed Erickson through the line. "The elusive little man wriggled through the line of scrimmage," wrote the *Fargo Forum*. He then "escaped the clutches of Tech's secondary as a greased pig would run through a butter-fingered party of taffy pullers," reported the *Lubbock Morning Avalanche*. "[He] tucked his knees under his chin and the pigskin under his arm and went to the village like a carrier pigeon in a hurry to get home." Hanson ran 77 yards and crossed the goal line with the nearest player 20 yards behind him and the Bison tied up the score 20-20. Late in the game, the Matadors drove into Bison territory but North Dakota State intercepted a pass to regain possession. A few minutes later, the Matadors drove into Bison territory again but the final gun sounded and stranded Texas Tech at North Dakota State's 17-yard line. The game ended in a 20-20 tie.

Throughout the game, Bison receivers dropped passes all over the field, but Hanson, the "will o' wisp," shined. "The tiny Swede from the windswept swales of North Dakota [is] the fastest thing that ever flashed over Texas Tech's turf," reported the *Avalanche*, "and that takes in a lot of territory." In total, the Bison rushed for 264 yards against Texas Tech.

After the game, fans called for Hanson to represent the West at the annual East-West Shrine Game in San Francisco. In the *Bison* annual, editor Cathryn Ray noted Hanson's departure from the college gridiron when she wrote, "The year marked the close of the spectacular four-year career of 'Fritz' Hanson. It was Hanson's unmatched speed that left both the Bison fans and the Herd opponents breathless." Soon after, the Associated Press named Hanson to its Little All-American Team, which the press picked from small colleges throughout the United States. They picked Hanson ahead of Paul Miller of South Dakota State, who received an honorable mention. Hanson also received all-conference honors for 1934, as did Herb Peschel.

*   *

The Regina Roughriders believed their passing game would be the key to beating the Sarnia Imperials in the Grey Cup final. "We know we're the under dogs," Paul Kirk told the *Leader-Post*, "and we firmly believe the first quarter will win the game. And we don't see how they can stop our passing attack." However, as they headed east on the train toward Toronto, they encountered heavy snow and they knew their aerial attack might be in jeopardy.

For the 7th time in 12 years, the Regina Roughriders represented Western Canada to compete for the Grey Cup. They had Americans on their squad, but so did Sarnia who had Ormond Beach from the University of Kansas in Lawrence, Rocky Parsaca from the University of Detroit, and Gil Putnam, also from the state of Michigan. The team's coach, Art Massucci, had been the line coach at Detroit. Although Sarnia had won four straight Ontario Rugby Football Union (ORFU) titles, this would be the team's first berth in the Grey Cup final. The top-scoring teams in Canada, the Roughriders and the Imperials, would enter the game unbeaten and untied.

Over 1,000 fans traveled from the oil town of Sarnia to Varsity Stadium in Toronto. They joined 7,000 more who came from Ontario and further to watch the teams play on a cold Saturday under overcast skies November 24, 1934. A slight wind blew through the Roughriders' red jerseys while Sarnia also wore red, but in a lighter shade.

Sarnia surprised Regina with a tough pass defense, and while the Roughriders also played strong defense against the Imperials, Regina first allowed Sarnia to score 5 points on two rouges and a drop-kick for a field goal. Sarnia moved the ball through the air and reached the goal line where the Imperials scored a touchdown on an option run. Before the half, Regina managed to move the ball into Sarnia territory and Oke Olson scored a rushing touchdown.

In the second half, Regina fumbled a punt return in the end zone and Sarnia recovered the ball for a touchdown. Late in the game, Regina finally managed to move the ball through the air and Olson connected with Steve Adkins for a score. In the end, Sarnia's rouge and field goal kicks made the difference and the Imperials won the Grey Cup 20-12.

After the game, as he removed the tape that held him together, Ralph Pierce told a reporter that for the first time all season, the game program spelled his name correctly. Before the Grey Cup game, even the *Leader-Post* in Regina had insisted on spelling his last name Pearce instead of Pierce. Despite the loss, Pierce had played well. Sarnia offered him and Olson positions with the Imperials, but they chose to stick with Regina.

* *

In November 1934, in a syndicated newspaper article, Benny Friedman, a former two-time All-American from Michigan and a four-time All-Pro in the NFL, declared the forward pass no longer served as a play of last resort. Instead, he said, the play had emerged as the most effective offensive weapon in football, both to defeat the defense, but also to defeat fan boredom. "Intercollegiate football has finally come to the realization that it must sell its product to the public," he said. "The pass is the one great hope of the weaker team. With one perfect toss the little fellow can match the power and drive of the stronger team's running attack. The pass is the 'homerun' play of the game."

But more than just a moonshot, the forward pass offered the offense the opportunity to gain short yardage. By 1934, teams had learned to throw short passes just over the line of scrimmage or out to the flank instead of running the ball. "Of themselves, they gain very little ground," Friedman said of the short passes. "But they open the way to something else." He mentioned all of the trickery coaches had begun to use with lateral and shovel passes in addition to the forward pass. "With the [new rule] allowing the offense to pass over the goal line once without losing possession of the ball, and the coaches all using their ingenuity to take advantage of this new liberty, it would take a book to include all the tricks invented in the first few weeks of this season."

In addition to more forward passes, teams had begun to use multiple formations, even on a single drive. "It was practically unknown to use three or four systems in a single march down the field until the pros started doing it," Friedman said. "Now this is not uncommon," he said, and the philosophy had caught on in the college ranks. "I have not seen the Illinois team of this year," he said, "but last year Zuppke was using practically everything: the Single Wingback; the Double Wingback; the Long and Short Punt formations; and sometimes he was using a balanced line, other times an unbalanced line; to say nothing of one or two innovations he defied you to describe... The selection of a system, of course, depends on the material."

The American game offered strategy and entertainment. In Canada, many voices called for Canadian football to adopt the American code. "The importation of United States stars to this country at a rapid rate has fathered the idea to a great extent," wrote sportswriter Mac Eggleston in the *Star-Phoenix*. However, Eggleston disagreed with the Americanization of the Canadian game. Instead, he pined for an imagined past when teams played for laurels and accolades from those who believed in romantic tales of heroic amateurs, and not for gate receipts. "The United States game is manipulated to provide entertainment for the spectators," Eggleston said.

"It has been realized that in order to get action at the gate, one must give them something for their money, with the result that the game is purely put on for their benefit." Detractors like Eggleston argued that *because* the game entertained it had become a performance, much like the scripted matches in pro wrestling—never mind the fact coaches hid their playbooks and strategies from one another, and gamblers lost their fortunes on predicted outcomes.

In the *Winnipeg Tribune*, sportswriter Ralph Allen said he was all for moving to the American code immediately, "but grave danger lies in that direction unless something close to unanimity is reached," he said. "The experience both of [Manitoba's] Varsity and of the Winnipegs dabbling gingerly with running interference against players trained in its use all their lives proved beyond dispute that there is one feature of American football which cannot be learned overnight." Blocking. He observed that Canadian high school and junior teams must teach the fundamentals of blocking and shedding blocks so that Canadian players will know how to compete in the American game on the college and club teams. In the *Province*, sportswriter Bob Elson called for incremental changes to the Canadian code, in part to stave off full adoption of American intercollegiate rules by colleges in Canada.

During the 1934 western finals, the WCRFU met and adopted a number of rules changes for Western Canada, and the union affirmed the West would play by those rules whether or not the CRU adopted them for all of Canada. The WCRFU changed the rules in the following ways:

- Players could block anywhere behind and up to 5 yards in front of the line of scrimmage.
- Players could pass from anywhere behind the line of scrimmage, on any down, and from anywhere on the field. This new forward pass rule mimicked the rules the NFL had adopted in 1933, which meant Canadian football in the WCRFU had progressively leapfrogged American intercollegiate rules.

Brown and Gold (1934)

- After an opponent scores a touchdown, officials would offer the scored-upon team the choice of whether to kick or receive the ball.
- The new rules would allow for the unlimited substitution of players.
- Officials would use hand signals to communicate all scores and penalties to the sidelines, with signals taken from the American code.

As expected, the CRU flatly rejected the WCRFU's proposed changes. However, after the CRU had promised in 1934 that the Grey Cup would be played in the West but then reneged on that promise, the West no longer believed the CRU had their best interests in mind. Clearly, the CRU favored eastern teams.

The West also requested that the Grey Cup be played as a series of games with both sets of rules, but the request fell on deaf ears. The West would play by their own rules and the East by a different set of rules, and East and West would play for the Grey Cup in the East or in a place selected by CRU executives, and under CRU rules.

CHAPTER 5 - GREY (1935)

In the wake of the 1934 football season Minnesota Coach Bernie Bierman visited Moorhead State. In the auditorium at Weld Hall he projected highlights of the Golden Gophers' national championship season on the silver screen while he described the plays for the audience. Perhaps Bob Fritz, Fritz Hanson, or Herb Peschel sat amongst the 180 people in attendance. Their college football careers had ended and soon their respective colleges would break for the holidays, but sports occupied their minds. Bud Marquardt couldn't attend. He had begun his fourth season of varsity basketball at North Dakota State, and that day he played in Minneapolis against the Gophers. Marquardt had played on two conference championship teams with the Bison in 1932 and 1933.

Early in their college careers, both Marquardt and Hanson had played together on the Bison squad, and Marquardt had played against Fritz in a game against Concordia. Both Hanson and Fritz moved on from college basketball, however. Hanson continued to play hoops in city leagues and in tournaments for his fraternity, Theta Chi, as did Marquardt for Alpha Tau Omega. Marquardt also played against the barnstorming Harlem Globetrotters. Fritz, meanwhile, continued to represent the Minnesota side of the river in exhibition games between local college athletes. He also played hockey for a team called the Eskimos in the Fargo-Moorhead Amateur Hockey League. Hanson, too, played hockey in the Fargo Commercial Hockey League. And Marquardt and Hanson both competed in track and field events in the spring. Meanwhile, Peschel stuck to football. In the summertime Marquardt worked for a power company while Hanson taught swimming lessons. Fritz worked at the sawmill. Soon, they would graduate.

Among these college stars, Fritz stood out as the most likely of the four to play professional football. Hanson had more star power and in the spring, together with Marquardt, he would form an independent basketball team to play exhibition games in the area like so many other college stars of the day. But at 25 years old, Fritz had the most developed body. He was already a full-grown man because he had skipped semesters and had managed to navigate eligibility to play five years of college football, including his freshman season in 1929. His former high school teammate, Bronko Nagurski, was less than nine months older and already, Nagurski had five full seasons of professional football under his belt. Now in his prime, Nagurski had helped the Chicago Bears win two NFL championships. Surely Fritz could find an opportunity to play professional football, even if it meant he had to play in one of the lesser leagues in New York or California, or for one of the many independent teams. More likely, he might find a spot on the Minnesota All-Stars or a similar team, either in Minneapolis, St. Paul, Wisconsin, or Michigan. And besides, the Canadians, too, played football, and his home in International Falls sat across the Rainy River from Fort Frances, Ontario. Already, Fritz had played football in Winnipeg three times.

After the Christmas and New Year's holidays, members of the Winnipeg Rugby Club met in the board room at the Manitoba Wheat Pool to discuss their plans for the 1935 season. They elected Frank Hannibal, an executive with the Canada Company to be president of the club, and they appointed Joe Ryan manager.

Financially, the Winnipeg club had turned a corner from loss to income, but half that income had come from resources other than gate receipts. "It is hard to believe that football, which has such a tremendous appeal in eastern Canada and the United States, should not be able to attract more than 2,000 people in Winnipeg, a city of over 300,000," Armstrong wrote. Only 2,000 spectators had come to watch the Winnipegs play the Minnesota All-Stars in 1934, the club's highest-attended game that season. Crowd sizes had increased, yes, but the club felt the 1935 season would prove critical to the future of football in Winnipeg.

Ryan insisted the club needed to bolster the team with more American imports, and everyone agreed, "even if they have to induce a few Lunds and Kostkas [from the Golden Gophers] to reside in these parts," mused E. A. Armstrong in the *Winnipeg Free Press*. In an effort to increase revenue to cover the cost of American imports the Big Four clubs in the East had discussed a nine-game schedule for each team. In the West, Vancouver, Calgary, and Regina had already introduced themselves to American prospects. Winnipeg needed to do the same. The club members walked away from the meeting "with an unofficial but clearly expressed mandate to build the most powerful team in Manitoba's history," reported the *Winnipeg Tribune*.

Ryan hit the road. The Winnipegs and the Bisons had played a number of teams in the Swede Belt of the United States during the 1933 and 1934 seasons and he had a good idea whom to recruit. It didn't take long.

In early March, Dick Hackenberg told readers in the *Moorhead Daily News* that he had heard a rumor that Fritz had been offered to play football in Winnipeg for the 1935 season. Two weeks later, the *Concordian* repeated the rumor. One month after Hackenberg had spilled the beans the *Winnipeg Tribune* announced that not only Fritz but also Hanson would join the Winnipegs and that Fritz would also serve as coach.

With Fritz's performance with Concordia against the Winnipegs in recent memory, the press in Manitoba gushed. The *Winnipeg Tribune* said Fritz, who "hails from International Falls, the hometown of Bronko Nagurski" is "pals" with Bronko and "the professional ace would very much like to have had Bob with him on the Bruin club next season," suggested the *Winnipeg Free Press*. Fritz has "fine knowledge of the game," the *Tribune* said, and "great qualities of leadership" to coach and play. The *Free Press* said Fritz "will be of inestimable value as a plunger and passer." Fritz and the Cobbers had beaten the Winnipegs twice in 1934 and had lost by only one questionable point in 1933. Ryan also asked Fritz to help him find good players in the United States.

Meanwhile, Hanson, the "flashy triple threat," would join as a player. Ryan had found Hanson at a bar in Dilworth, Minnesota, where Hanson was sitting on top of a piano and sharing a beer with some of his buddies, all football players from North Dakota State. The *Winnipeg Tribune* said, "Hanson has a terrific burst of speed and steps the hundred regularly in nine and four-fifths" and noted that Hanson had scored against Minnesota, the U.S. national champions, and that he had played in two collegiate victories against Ralph Pierce of the Regina Roughriders. "These two speedy boys will meet again no doubt." Hanson had considered playing for an NFL team, but depending on whom you ask, after his mother had discovered a clause in an NFL contract that allowed the team to dismiss him with only 24 hours notice he turned down offers to play for the Brooklyn Dodgers, the New York Giants, and/or the Detroit Lions. With a degree in physical education and a desire to coach, the best job Hanson could find in that category paid $90 per month and so he decided to put his teaching and coaching career on hold to play for Winnipeg. When Hanson arrived in the province Ryan had lined up a job for him as a candy salesman.

In both Fritz and Hanson, Ryan had acquired not only great players but also great marketing material. Behind the scenes, Ryan verbally promised both of the men jobs in Winnipeg plus $900 for Fritz for the season and $125 per game for Hanson. Ryan also gave Fritz an overcoat as a bonus. They had to reside in Winnipeg by September 1 to meet the WCRFU residency rule. Fritz said he would move to Winnipeg in July. He had committed to help coach spring football at Concordia and he still had to complete a two-week stint as a student teacher in Kindred, North Dakota. And he had to graduate. After Fritz moved to Winnipeg, Hanson joined him and they lived together. They paid $35 for room and board at the Balmoral Street rooming house in Winnipeg.

*

Ahti "Bert" Oja was born October 29, 1907, in Eveleth, Minnesota, to Anna M. (Valli) Oja and John Oja who had emigrated from Finland. John moved to the United States in 1896 and Anna in 1902. At the time of his birth, Bert's parents worked at a bakery in Eveleth. Bert grew up with older siblings, Jacob and Ali, and the family later moved to Gilbert, Minnesota, where father John started a farm. Bert lived out his teenage years in Gilbert. After high school, Oja attended and played football, basketball, and competed in track and field at Virginia Junior College in Virginia, Minnesota. He later enrolled at the University of Minnesota where he pursued a Bachelor of Science degree in Education and joined the Alpha Sigma Phi fraternity. In 1927, he played on the freshman football team as an end and earned a numeral. In 1928, Oja joined the Golden Gophers varsity squad as a reserve player and played alongside Bronko Nagurski. In 1929, he started at guard and then moved to center. After graduation in 1930, Oja took a job as the physical education director and assistant coach in football, basketball, and track at duPont Manual Training High School in Louisville, Kentucky. Two years later, he returned to Minnesota where he enrolled in the school of medicine and joined the Delta Sigma Delta fraternity.

Football still coursed through Oja's veins and so in 1932, he joined other former Minnesota football players on the Kunz Oil amateur football team in the Minneapolis park league, which at the time was coached by former Minnesota guard Bob Reihsen. Oja played center for the Kunz Oil club. Because the team included so many former Gophers stars, including the older Kenneth Haycraft but also a concurrent Gopher star, Jack Manders, newspapers referred to the team as Haycraft's Minneapolis All-Stars, Jack Manders' All-Stars, or simply the Minnesota All-Stars. It appears the team would sometimes play exhibition games outside the park league, including games against teams from Duluth, Minnesota, and Ironwood, Michigan.

After the 1932 park league football season, Oja formed a basketball team dubbed Oja's All-Stars made up of mostly former Gophers, including Manders. They competed in the city league in St. Cloud, which also included teams organized under Nagurski's name. The schedule included exhibition games against the New York Nationals and the Harlem Globetrotters.

In the spring of 1933, Oja agreed to play for a Minnesota alumni team against the 1933 Golden Gophers varsity team in a spring game. This team of Minnesota all-stars also played the Chippewa Marines in Chippewa Falls, Wisconsin. In the fall of 1933, Oja took a job as a line coach at Augsburg but he continued to play football with Haycraft's Minnesota All-Stars, including in the first-ever night football game in Minneapolis against the Northern Giants at Nicollet Park.

In 1934, Oja took over as coach of the Minnesota All-Stars and after the All-Stars had beaten the Winnipegs 13-8 in Winnipeg in September, the All-Stars went on to play the Chicago Bears in an exhibition game at Highland Park in St. Paul on November 7. That midweek contest stood between the Bears' regularly scheduled Sunday NFL games. Both Nagurski and Manders, then with the Bears, scored touchdowns for Chicago. Afterward, the Bears thought Oja had coached a bit too aggressively for a midweek exhibition. "Bert Oja, who learned his football under Doc Spears at Minnesota, took the game too seriously to suit the

Grey (1935)

Chicago Bears," wrote sportswriter George A. Barton in the *Minneapolis Tribune*. "The pro champions didn't awe him in the least as he demonstrated by frequently stopping their ball carriers without gain."

Five months later, in April 1935, the Winnipegs announced they had recruited Oja to play and coach on the line for Winnipeg in 1935. Cronin, the former Winnipegs leader, called Oja "the best line coach in the [United States] outside of Hunk Anderson at Notre Dame."

In June, the Winnipegs announced they had secured Tubber Kobrinsky, the University of Manitoba star, to play for the Winnipegs, and that Eddie James, whom everyone expected to retire because of his oft-broken arm, would also return to play in 1935.

*

Early in the basketball season during his senior year at Moorhead High School in 1930, Bud Marquardt and the Spuds had played a double-header in the Moorhead Armory against the Crosby-Ironton Rangers. Opposite Marquardt on the court that day stood Joe Perpich, a tall, muscular, 200-pound center. The two boys elbowed one another and competed for the rebound all game long at the post. In the end, Marquardt scored 16 points on 7 field goals and 2 free throws while Perpich scored 9 points on 3 field goals and 3 free throws. The Spuds beat the Rangers 32-25.

The next spring, Marquardt went on to play in the 1931 Minnesota state high school boy's basketball tournament. Marquardt played three games and scored 41 points—the lead score in the tournament. Officials named Marquardt to the all-state team at center for 1931. A few weeks later, at the end of the school year, Marquardt competed with Perpich again in the regional track meet. They both ran the 120-yard high hurdles where Marquardt took first place in 16.5 seconds and Perpich finished fourth. At the same meet, Hanson met Perpich in the shot put, where Perpich took first and Hanson second. The next year, in 1932, while Marquardt began his college career with Hanson at North Dakota State, Perpich captained his high school team to the state tournament where he played three games and scored 39 points—the lead score in that tournament. Like for Marquardt the year before, officials named Perpich to the all-state team at center. Perpich continued to play basketball at

Crosby-Ironton, but also football. In his senior year, officials named him to the All-Central Minnesota Team at end.

In 1934, after high school, Perpich enrolled at St. Cloud State Teachers College where he played football. From his position at left end he scored multiple touchdowns as a receiver. By midseason he began to punt for the Huskies. The *Daily Times and Daily Journal-Press* observed that Perpich as a punter "was outstanding and would have been a credit to many of the larger college teams." When the Dragons had beaten St. Cloud State in 1934, Perpich had intercepted a lateral pass on St. Cloud's 20-yard line and returned the ball 80 yards for a touchdown. Perpich had also booted long and well-placed kicks in the game.

During basketball season, Perpich had played forward and center for the Huskies. In December 1934, five days short of exactly four years since they first played against each other, Perpich faced Marquardt again on the court. The Bison beat the Huskies 60-39 but this time Perpich scored 11 points on 4 field goals and 3 free throws while Marquardt scored 8 points on 4 field goals. Eight months later, in August 1935, the *Brainerd Daily Dispatch* announced that Perpich would not return to St. Cloud State for his sophomore year. Instead, the 6-foot-3, 200-pound athlete would play both football and basketball in Winnipeg.

Meanwhile, after he graduated from North Dakota State, Marquardt rode freight trains to California where he received a forwarded letter that invited him to Canada to play with the Winnipeg Toilers basketball team. Joe Ryan had gotten to him first, however, with an offer to play football for the Winnipegs.

A few days after Winnipeggers had learned their team had acquired Perpich, the *Winnipeg Tribune* announced that the Winnipegs had also added Marquardt and Peschel to the team. Peschel had enlisted in the U.S. Army after graduation but he got out of his enlistment to play football in Canada, instead. Ryan promised Oja, Perpich, Marquardt, and Peschel jobs in Winnipeg as well as $500 apiece, the same deal Russ Rebholz and Greg Kabat had received. Ryan operated with a $7,400 budget for personnel and a $15,000 budget overall.

Grey (1935)

While Winnipeg filled its roster with imports, both Calgary and Regina scoured the ranks of American college football to find fresh blood. "From Vancouver in the far west to Winnipeg in the east there is a hustle and bustle of activity on the [western] rugby front as the boards of strategy behind the various clubs prepare their squads for the biggest campaign that the west has ever known—a campaign that many hope will bring a national title to the west," observed the *Star-Phoenix*. The three cities of Winnipeg, Regina, and Calgary had begun to build "super-teams," the paper said. And as Harry Randall observed in *Maclean's* magazine, "Last season's activities were only the lull before the storm. Now the West is preparing the big push against the East."

But while Winnipeg had made big announcements about its American acquisitions, both Calgary and Regina remained hush. In Calgary, the Calgary Altomah Athletic Association rugby component reorganized under the local booster's club as the Calgary Rugby Club. They chose the name Bronks, also the nickname of the local senior amateur hockey team in the Southern Alberta Hockey League. Calgary hired Carl Cronin to coach, but not play, and they brought in four or five other American players, including Oran Dover from Washington State College in Pullman and also Chuck McKenna from De La Salle Academy in Chicago. Newspapers speculated they had also acquired players from Washington or Montana.

In Regina, the club convinced its former coach, Al Ritchie, to come out of retirement and return to the Roughriders. The team had acquired American players Elmer Lorentson from Washington State, Chappie O'Connor from South Dakota, Cleon Kohanek from Marshall High School in Minneapolis who had played for the Golden Gophers freshmen team, and Lloyd Connolly who had played for the Flour City team in the Minneapolis park league in 1934 alongside Concordia's Roy Cleve. After the Cobbers had finished their 1934 season, Cleve had rejoined the Flour City roster and Connolly to help them win the league championship.

Canadian football teams in the East had also acquired new American players. In Ottawa, the Rough Riders picked up a player who went by the name of Roy Berry from Tulsa. They also acquired Stan O'Neil from Pittsburgh and Bud Bonar from Notre Dame. Montreal added Bill

McNamara from New York University, Pat Ryan from Manhattan, Bill Shanahan from Pennsylvania, and Leo Bielski and Russ Roach, both from Syracuse.

*

In the eyes of *Winnipeg Tribune* sportswriter Ralph Allen, the University of Manitoba's 1934 season had proven to be the start of something good but only if the school would stand behind the effort. The *Manitoban* expressed the opinion that the school's experiment in American football had been a success and that the program should continue in part because it would cost less to field the football team in 1935 because American schools would return the favor and travel to Winnipeg to play. In March 1935, Manitoba students voted to continue to field a football team but to play against colleges in Western Canada instead of American teams. However, in the next few weeks, the backlash against the team's operating deficit continued, and because the school didn't wish to rely on gate receipts to fund a successful team the school decided to drop varsity football altogether in favor of fielding "interfaculty" teams, whereby students within six different academic departments at the university would play against one another. To assist with the development of the program, both American and Canadian players on the Winnipegs agreed to help coach the various interfaculty teams, but the loss of Manitoba would reduce the number of senior-level teams in Winnipeg to just one, the Winnipegs.

Criticism against the "commercialization" of rugby in Winnipeg continued. Fred Ritter, who had coached the Deer Lodge neighborhood junior team to a Western Canada championship title in 1934 argued against the importation of American athletes. He also argued against the importation of athletes across provincial lines. He knew the Winnipegs needed a senior-level opponent in the MRFU and so he decided to throw his hat into the ring as a coach. In an attempt to prove his points he revived the old Victoria Rugby Club name and stocked the senior-level team with "home town talent only." Ritter told the *Winnipeg Tribune*, "I have given my personal assurance to the men who control the Victoria club franchise that it will be operated on a strictly amateur basis," he said, and the team would publish financial statements as proof. But Ritter himself had been spoilt by the American game. He had played football at Princeton and afterward, before the Great War, he led the Regina Roughriders and recruited two former players from Notre Dame to play for him.

The Victoria Rugby Club, also known as the Winnipeg Victorias or the "Bisons," began operations in 1915 when they took over rugby from the Winnipeg Rowing Club, which had played the game from 1902 to 1914. To regroup, the Victorias immediately dropped from senior-level competition and the club suspended operations during World War I. After the war, the Victorias re-emerged at the senior level and competed against St. John's and Manitoba. In 1924, the Victorias qualified to compete for the Grey Cup but the team never made the trip East. The Victorias suspended operations in 1928. Eight seasons later former Victorias manager, Jim Crossin, the club president in 1935, had kept the organization intact, and he agreed to resurrect the Victorias in part because his son, Bill, would play on the team.

The Winnipegs scheduled a series of three games against the Victorias in 1935, in addition to games against Concordia College, Sarnia, the Minnesota All-Stars, and the North Dakota freshmen.

*

In the fall of 1935, the Winnipegs added more Canadian talent to its roster, including Bryce Gillis, the former Garrison standout and the son of a former Ottawa Rough Riders club executive, Lt. Col. Walter Gillis. The younger Gillis had played for the Riders late during the 1934 season. The Winnipegs also added former Winnipegs junior rugby player Percy Daigle who had played for the senior Winnipegs late in 1934. And they added Les Cohen from the YMHA All-Stars junior club. The Winnipegs also acquired Dick Lane and Eddie Peterman who had played at Manitoba in 1934 and also Marsden "Slush" Harris, a former Toronto Argonauts junior player. Alec Grant, a newcomer, also made the team.

*

By early September 1935, just 10 days before the Winnipeg Rugby Club would host Concordia, Bob Fritz, the "Concordia Cannonball," had his men participate in heavy scrimmages at Osborne Stadium. The normally soft-spoken Fritz, now a coach, let his displeasure fly with choice words. He knew, of course, the kind of talent Frank Cleve and Louie Benson would bring to Winnipeg. He demanded his players expend every ounce of available energy during practice. With five new guys fresh out of American colleges in Fritz, Fritz Hanson, Bud Marquardt, Herb Peschel, and Joe Perpich, with Lane, Peterman, and Tubber Kobrinsky accustomed to training under Wally Hass at Manitoba, and with three more seasoned American veterans in Russ Rebholz, Greg Kabat, and Bert Oja, the updated squad took to regimented practice like fish to water.

In just a handful of seasons, the Winnipegs had evolved from one of several local teams filled with local boys who played Canadian football without the forward pass into the only credible football threat in the province. Manager Joe Ryan had stuffed the roster with Americans, including some of the best players at their level of competition and with the skills necessary to play a game that had evolved in Western Canada into one that more closely resembled the American professional game than the American intercollegiate version. With Ryan at the promotional helm the city had a blue and gold football machine that wore the colors of his beloved Notre Dame, and to onlookers, the team Ryan had assembled looked incredible. The starting lineup included:

End	Joe Perpich, St. Cloud State
Tackle	Lou Mogul, Winnipeg
Guard	Bert Oja, Minnesota (line coach)
Center	Rosy Adelman, Winnipeg
Guard	Eddie Kushner, Winnipeg
Tackle	Herb Peschel, North Dakota State
End	Bud Marquardt, North Dakota State
Flying Wing	Greg Kabat, Wisconsin (captain)
Quarterback	Bob Fritz, Concordia (coach)
Halfback	Fritz Hanson, North Dakota State
Halfback	Russ Rebholz, Wisconsin
Halfback	Tubber Kobrinsky, Manitoba

Grey (1935)

The team had talent for every offensive play. In the ground game, Fritz could hit the line hard while Rebholz, Hanson, and Kobrinsky could race around the ends. Both Rebholz and Fritz could throw the ball well while Marquardt, Perpich, and Hanson had all proven good receivers. Perpich kicked like a veteran and both Rebholz and Gillis also kicked well.

And the team had depth. Gillis, along with Winnipeg veterans Eddie James, Cliff Roseborough, and Dave Harding could plunge the line while Arni Coulter could trace the ends. Daigle and Cohen rounded out the backfield.

At the ends, Winnipeg veterans Jeff Nicklin and Herb Mobberley could catch while Mobberley blocked well. In the middle of the line, Winnipeg veterans Chauncey Dagg, Bill Ceretti, Johnny Christie, Eric Law, Eddie Kushner, and Johnny Patrick filled out the reserves, joined by Lane, Peterman, Harris, and Grant.

With all these men assembled, Ralph Allen, sportswriter for the *Winnipeg Tribune*, looked over the roster and said, "I guess if they don't win the Canadian championship next December, they never will."

The newly adopted rules in the WCRFU would speed up the game, Fritz said, and it would be easier for him to adapt American plays for use in the Canadian game. And Fritz understood his political position, too. "Our success or failure this year will depend in a sense upon the Winnipeg boys playing with us," he told the *Tribune*. "A number of key positions will be filled by players from across the border [from the United States], but particularly in the line, we will stand or fall on the local players."

Two or three hundred fans watched practices each day. "There's many an onlooker who, after witnessing the workouts this week, has left the Stadium muttering to himself that the current crop of athletes playing under the colors of the Winnipeg Rugby club looks to be the sweetest array of porkhide toters ever gathered together in this city," reported the *Winnipeg Tribune*. "From end to end every lineman packs power and weight."

At the new rugby club headquarters in the 11-story Paris building downtown, ticket sellers worked non-stop. Meanwhile, the Commercial Girls' Club of Winnipeg, to help support unemployed women in the community, sold blue and gold ribbons, which Allen of the *Tribune* suggested would be "very handy to have about the home in case somebody accuses you of climbing on the band wagon later in the year when you start boasting about the loyal support you gave the new champions, if any."

For several days the Winnipegs practiced under the floodlights at the stadium to prepare in the trick-light of night to defend against Concordia's passing game. As game day approached, Fritz had his men practice in full equipment and at full speed. The Winnipegs would play the Cobbers in a half-American, half-Canadian game once again. In this half-and-half arrangement, the Cobbers led the series 2-1. Fritz said under Canadian rules he planned to use players more experienced with the Canadian game.

Meanwhile, at Concordia, Coach Frank Cleve had 10 lettermen return to the squad but he had lost three veteran backfielders to graduation, including Fritz. Just a few days before the game in Winnipeg, three new players, all backfield material, including one big fullback and two speedy halfbacks, showed up for practice. All three men had played for St. Paul-Luther College in the Phalen Park neighborhood of St. Paul, Minnesota, but the school had closed when it merged with Wartburg College in Waverly, Iowa. The men had transferred to Concordia and because their school had closed, they stood eligible to play. After one week of practice Cleve, Benson, and 30 Cobbers departed Moorhead on Saturday morning for the evening game. The *Concordian* observed, "It will seem pretty queer to the players who have been used to hearing Bob Fritz urging them on from behind and then to hear him... on the opposition."

*

On game day evening, September 14, 1935, at least 2,500 fans (in some reports 4,000 fans) filled Osborne Stadium, which the *Winnipeg Free Press* declared to be "the most modern stadium in Canada" in part because of the sound system the *Tribune* had sponsored for installation at the venue. The Winnipegs would use the new loudspeakers to explain penalties and other in-game details. On the radio, CJRC and Vic Driver also provided play-by-play for listeners.

The Winnipeg Grenadiers military band entertained the crowd as the Cobbers stepped onto a dry field on a warm evening. At 8:30 p.m., Frank Hannibal, president of the Winnipeg club, opened the game with a

Grey (1935)

ceremonial kick. The Winnipegs started the game with strong defense and twice blocked Concordia punts with Greg Kabat and Bert Oja getting through the line. On the second thwarted kick the Winnipegs recovered the ball at Concordia's 31-yard line. Three plays later, Bob Fritz completed a pass to Fritz Hanson who ran behind Bud Marquardt. The rangy end took out Concordia's fullback and then Hanson danced through a field of tacklers to score the first touchdown.

In the second quarter, Joe Perpich launched a 65-yard punt. Marquardt gunned it down at Concordia's 1-yard line. The Cobbers immediately punted the ball to gain field position and the Winnipegs responded with two first downs. Hanson then carried the ball 15 yards around his right end for the second touchdown.

Late in the first half, Fritz put in the reserves. The Cobbers drove into Winnipeg territory before the half ended.

To open the second half, Concordia received the kickoff and drove into Winnipeg territory but the Winnipegs forced a turnover on downs. Hanson and Cliff Roseborough alternated carries but then the Winnipegs fumbled and lost the ball at Concordia's 25-yard line. Two plays later Tubber Kobrinsky intercepted Concordia's pass attempt and the Winnipegs punted to push the Cobbers back deep into their own territory where Kobrinsky intercepted another pass. He returned the ball 27 yards to Concordia's 1-yard line. On the next play, to open the fourth quarter, Russ Rebholz stepped over the goal line for the third Winnipeg touchdown.

Once again, Fritz put in the reserves. When the Winnipegs regained control of the ball, Eddie James plunged the line for a first down and Kobrinsky scored a rouge. When Concordia got the ball back at their own 25-yard line they punted it away and the Winnipegs began a drive at their own 47-yard line. Three plays later, Kobrinsky completed a 35-yard pass to Mobberley for the team's fourth touchdown.

Late in the game, Fritz put in the reserves one last time and the Cobbers drove to Winnipeg's 2-yard line. Concordia's Henry Held stepped over for a touchdown but the Cobbers had stepped offsides and officials called it back. On the next play, the Cobbers attempted a pass into the end zone but it fell incomplete and Winnipeg took over the ball. The game ended with Winnipeg on top 26-0.

Throughout the game, Fritz's "loud, clear voice [could be] hard all over the field" as he called his signals. Every player on Winnipeg's roster saw action. Hanson, a "Blond Package of Dynamite," stole the show, however, with his two touchdowns, "one in a snaking 12-yard dash down the touchline" and the other "on a 20-yard trip off tackle that pierced Concordia's line like a sabre thrust and left its secondary defence clutching vainly at thin air," rhapsodized the *Winnipeg Evening Tribune*. "The smallest member of the team, Hanson... was the fastest and the shiftiest football player local fans have seen." The *Brandon Daily Sun* described Hanson as "a small, chunky cotton-haired man" who was "Greased Lightning Personified" and who could "elude and shake off would-be tacklers with amazing regularity." On one particular play, the *Sun* observed, Hanson took the ball for a line plunge, but when no hole opened up he reversed his field and the Cobbers chased him 20 yards behind the line of scrimmage. Hanson, "dodging and twisting," eluded them all and when the Cobbers finally tackled him he had gained 10 yards for the Winnipegs. Observed Eugene Fitzgerald in the *Fargo Forum*, "Hanson was every bit as electrifying as he was as a Bison, and already they like him in Winnipeg."

As a team, the Winnipegs had displayed "a show of controlled power that surpassed all expectations" observed the *Winnipeg Evening Tribune*. The Winnipegs "tore Concordia wide asunder" and as *Tribune* sportswriter Allen suggested, "Until the Winnipeg Rugby Club shows of back-pedaling from its first game of the season, you'll have to take Bob Fritz and his riot squad very seriously." He said, "I doubt very much if any starting line-up has ever been assembled in Canada with more all-around power, speed, and snap than the one that Fritz threw at Concordia." It was clear to anyone, he said, how "Oja and Peschel bolstered the line" and "how effectively Marquardt and Perpich patrolled the end." Meanwhile, both Kabat and Rebholz, "now relieved of coaching worries," played their best football.

The Americans, new or established, did not dominate Winnipeg's psyche, however. Kobrinsky, the local boy who had played for both the YMHA juvenile and junior teams and for Manitoba had thrilled fans with his contributions. "Tubber stepped into a tough spot—he was only subbing Hanson—and he delivered," Allen said.

After the Cobbers returned home to Moorhead, "the football boys report[ed] that Fritz looks a lot bigger when he's running the other way," smirked the *Concordian*.

In the crowd on the day of the game sat 45 newspaper boys, all guests of the *Winnipeg Free Press*, including 25 boys from Brandon, Manitoba. Twenty-two of those Brandon boys had witnessed their first-ever game of Canadian football and the *Sun* reported "all were of the opinion that it is a great sport."

*

The very next day, news reverberated throughout the world that the German Reich had enacted the Reich Citizenship Law, which stripped German Jews of their citizenship. In advance of the 1936 Olympic Games, which the Germans would host in Berlin, the Germans had segregated Jewish German athletes, and now they had lost their rights as citizens. But in Canada, the Winnipegs had formed a team of brothers that included four men of Jewish descent, including Rosy Adelman, Tubber Kobrinsky, Eddie Kushner, and Lou Mogul, as well as at least four men of German or part-German descent, including Bob Fritz, Fritz Hanson, Bud Marquardt, and Herb Peschel. While the German Reich actively separated Jews from Germans in Europe, men from both heritages in Winnipeg relied on human brotherhood in their quest for a Grey Cup victory.

* *

In the autumn of 1935, the 1934 Grey Cup champion Sarnia Imperials toured Western Canada. They beat the Vancouver Meralomas 19-2, the Calgary Bronks (twice) 39-0 and 17-2, the Saskatoon Hilltops 19-1, and the Regina Roughriders 4-0. They lost their star halfback, Norm Perry, to injury in Calgary, and they arrived in Winnipeg "train-weary and injury-riddled," according to the *Windsor Star*. Nevertheless, Sarnia had won 14 consecutive games, which tied the Canadian record set by Hamilton in 1930, and they sought their 15th straight win against the Winnipegs. While the defending champion Imperials remained largely intact in terms of personnel from 1934, the Winnipegs had only practiced and played together for two weeks, and no senior-level team in Western Canada had ever beaten an eastern counterpart. Sarnia appeared unstoppable.

Behind closed gates, the Imperials allowed *Winnipeg Free Press* sportswriter E.A. Armstrong to watch them practice. Armstrong reported Sarnia appeared to have perfected the forward pass and they flawlessly executed the lateral pass on the option run, a play that many American college teams had problems with when they played against the Winnipegs during the past two seasons. The Winnipegs had more American collegians on their roster than ever before.

In advance of the contest, Coach Bob Fritz knew the game might become a battle for field position and so he pulled Joe Perpich aside and coached him in punting technique. In short order, Perpich managed to kick the ball higher and farther than ever before. Clearly, Fritz had learned a thing or two from Coach Frank Cleve at Concordia.

Before the game, the Winnipegs held a lunch for the Imperials at Drewry's Banquet Hall where Gordie Patterson, a Sarnia backfielder, recalled how Winnipegs veteran Dave Harding had been "the idol of every 'teen-aged kid in Sarnia" when Harding had played rugby in Ontario, a nod to Harding's abilities, but also to his age.

At Osborne Stadium on September 21, 1935, the Winnipegs wore their big "W" jersey fronts while the Imperials wore three stars, the symbol of the Imperial Oil company. In the first quarter, Sarnia's Bummer Stirling kicked with the wind at his back and Fritz Hanson fumbled the return. Sarnia recovered the ball and a couple of plays later, they settled for a rouge. In the second quarter, Perpich tied up the score 1-1 with a rouge on a 60-yard kick from midfield. In the second half, Hanson returned a Sarnia punt to Sarnia's 20-yard line and the Winnipegs reached Sarnia's 10-yard line, but a penalty forced them back and they had to settle for a rouge on a kick by Russ Rebholz. In the fourth quarter, Winnipeg reached deep into Sarnia territory but turned the ball over on downs at Sarnia's 2-yard line. The teams exchanged kicks and then Eddie Kushner tackled Stirling in Sarnia's end zone for a rouge and the final point. Winnipeg walked off the field victorious 3-1 and the Winnipeg Rugby Club had

Grey (1935)

written itself into the annals of Canadian football history as the first western team to defeat an eastern team, and they did it in dominant fashion with twice as many yards from scrimmage. Afterward, the Winnipegs celebrated the honor alongside the Imperials at Hudson's Bay Grill.

While Perpich had averaged 41 yards on punts for Winnipeg, Bummer Stirling averaged only 31 yards for Sarnia. The Winnipegs had blocked Stirling's kicks 3 times, twice by Mogul and once by Peschel. Perpich, too, blocked one of Stirling's punts but officials called the play back on a penalty. "It wasn't Stirling's fault that he had to get fully half his punts away with a resolute horde of Westerners breathing down his neck," observed Ralph Allen in the *Winnipeg Tribune*. Allen noted how Winnipeg's line had been the difference in the game. "Except for a minor injury to Mogul in the final quarter, the line would have played the full 60 minutes without relief," he said. "And it was still moving at top speed through the final three minutes, which ought to give a fair indication of the team's condition." The *Winnipeg Free Press* joked that the holes the Winnipeg line had opened up for its backfielders were "still there."

After the game, *Leader-Post* sportswriter Dave Dryburgh from Regina already looked ahead to the WCRFU semifinal where he expected a battle between Regina and Winnipeg. He said ticket sales for that game had already taken off. He offered his assessment of the Winnipegs and said above all the new imports stood out, including "Bob Fritz for line plunging, Fritz Hanson for tricky broken field running, [and] Bert Oja, who makes holes in the line in a manner that indicates nobody in the west can give him any lessons on the art." As for Fritz, "[He] is half a team in himself," Dryburgh said. "He calls the signals, throws the short forward passes and does practically all the plunging. Big and powerful, he never tires, and at the close of the game [he] was still calling plays and getting them timed perfectly." Dryburgh said the Winnipegs looked like a team "in midseason form." Rebholz served as the team's main threat for the long ball. "Russ can lay them on a dime from 50 yards and waits plenty long before he lets the ball go."

And while Coach Fritz demonstrated his leadership ability, "the girl friends go for" Hanson, Dryburgh said. In the *Winnipeg Tribune*, Allen

Fritz Hanson

described Hanson's on-field antics. "One picture that stands out vividly in this writer's mind from Saturday's football game," he said, "was the facial expression of a portly Sarnia lineman who, about to make what seemed a certain tackle, saw Hanson flit from his grasp in the mystic fashion of a wary eel." The tackler had "a look of such overwhelming disgust and self doubt." Allen continued. "Hanson has been the sensation of this Winnipeg team," he said. "I have an idea he will continue to bring gasps from his audiences even after they have grown accustomed to him... You can stop one player in most sports by assigning policemen to him but it's a very difficult thing to do in rugby, particularly where the person happens to combine the speed of a 10-second man with a stride that takes him sidewise as rapidly as straight ahead." After only two games, Allen believed the Winnipegs would win the Grey Cup.

*

Before the 1935 season had begun, the WCRFU determined that the SRFU and MRFU champions would play the WCRFU semifinal match on November 2 at Osborne Stadium in Winnipeg. By late September, the Regina Roughriders felt confident they would represent the SRFU in the playoff game but when they learned that the field at Osborne Stadium had a 100-yard grid instead of a 110-yard grid, they objected. At the time, the rulebook stated, "The field shall be 110 yards long by 65 yards wide or as near these dimensions as practicable with the boundaries distinctly marked." The Winnipeg Rugby Club argued that the stadium fell within the rules because of the words "as practicable." It's not clear when stadium officials had set up the grid to be 100 yards instead of 110 yards but the fact Manitoba had played by the American code in 1934, that the Winnipegs had played and would continue to play halves by that code, and that Joe Ryan had pushed for the adoption of the American code all likely had something to do with the setup.

* *

For five seasons, amateur football teams in the "Twin Cities" of Minneapolis and St. Paul, Minnesota, had played one another in a league that evolved into the Twin City Football League, sometimes referred to as "the park league." Over time, several of the teams, including the Minnesota All-Stars had begun to operate semi-professionally. The All-Stars, especially, moved beyond the park league to play against teams in Wisconsin and Michigan and against others, most notably the Winnipeg Rugby Club, the NFL's Chicago Bears, and the St. Louis Gunners, an independent team that finished out the Cincinnati Reds schedule for the NFL in 1934. Now in 1935, teams in Chippewa Falls and La Crosse in Wisconsin and in Ironwood, Michigan, joined teams in the Twin City league to form a new Northwest Football League with two divisions, the Twin City division and the Tri-State division. The All-Stars played alongside the Wisconsin and Michigan teams in the Tri-State division.

The Minnesota All-Stars team that played in the Northwest Football League in 1935 no longer resembled the team that had held the Chicago Bears to a 14-3 margin in 1934. Bert Oja had left the All-Stars to play in Winnipeg but many others had left, too. Only Ken Haycraft, Freddie Just, Jim Dennerly, and Win Brockmeyer remained from the 1934 iteration of the All-Stars. The team had added Art Pharmer to the squad. Pharmer had led the Golden Gophers in rushing in 1929 and then started five games at tailback for the Frankford Yellow Jackets and five games for the Minneapolis Red Jackets in the NFL in 1930, as well as two more games for Frankford in 1931. The All-Stars also added Pete Somers, an International Falls native who had last played for Minnesota in 1931 and who had played against Rebholz in the East-West Shrine Game in 1932. The All-Stars featured "three of the five greatest backs developed at Minnesota in the last 10 years" in Brockmeyer, Pharmer, and Somers, said the *Winnipeg Free Press*. But the All-Stars just didn't live up to expectations. On September 21, the same day the Winnipegs had beaten the Imperials, the Chippewa Falls Marines downed the Minnesota All-Stars 39-0. The diminished All-Stars would travel next to Winnipeg.

In Winnipeg, fans deserved a lot of credit for sticking with their team in 1935. Sure, the Winnipegs now featured great talent and fantastic football feats, but for many, the whole enterprise was a head-scratcher. In the first game of the season, the Winnipegs had played a game with half American intercollegiate and half Canadian football circa 1934 rules to accommodate Concordia's knowledge of the game. Against Sarnia, the

Winnipegs had played a game with CRU rules used by football teams in Eastern Canada in 1935. Next, the Winnipegs would play a game against the Minnesota All-Stars using half American intercollegiate and half WCRFU football rules for 1935.

With the season underway, Joe Ryan continued to recruit Americans to play for the Winnipegs, but he didn't have to go far. At Wesley College in Winnipeg he found Nick Pagones who had quarterbacked the Granville High School Golden Horde to its third consecutive North Eastern New York High School Football League championship in Granville, New York, in 1934. Ryan enlisted Pagones to join the Winnipegs ahead of their game against the All-Stars and Coach Bob Fritz installed him at halfback. Rosy Adelman, Tubber Kobrinsky, Eddie Kushner, and Lou Mogul would all miss the game. Oja moved to center, Bill Ceretti took his place, and Slush Harris stepped in at left tackle.

For the second time in as many seasons, on September 28, 1935, the All-Stars played the Winnipegs at Osborne Stadium. In the first quarter, the Winnipegs turned on the excitement when "Hurricane Fritz Hanson" intercepted a pass on Winnipeg's 40-yard line and returned the ball to the All-Stars' 39-yard line. On the next play, Hanson ran off left end for 15 yards. Russ Rebholz then completed a 21-yard pass to Joe Perpich to reach the All-Stars' 3-yard line. Hanson plunged over for a touchdown.

On Winnipeg's next possession, on third down with the ball at Winnipeg's own 45-yard line, Hanson ran to his left. He dodged multiple tackles and the fans rose to their feet and cheered as he raced down the sideline to the 10-yard line. It appeared that All-Stars defender Somers would push him out of bounds at the 10, but at the last second Rebholz threw a block on Somers and Hanson cut back to his right and outran his pursuers. Hanson crossed the goal line "with tacklers strewn all over the place," observed Cam McKenzie in the *Winnipeg Free Press*. At the end of the first half, Somers led the All-Stars to three successive first downs to reach Winnipeg's 4-yard line. Three hard plunges later, the All-Stars scored and Somers scored the extra point to close out the half. The teams finished play under American rules with the Winnipegs ahead 14-7.

The Winnipeg reserves open the second half under the new WCRFU football rules. Eddie James and Cliff Roseborough carried the ball and

Grey (1935)

reached near to the All-Stars' goal line. The All-Stars held, however, and gained possession of the ball at their own 3-yard line on a turnover on downs. The All-Stars then managed to move the ball to their own 30-yard line where they fumbled and Herb Mobberley recovered for the home team. The Winnipegs then took advantage of the new WCRFU pro-style forward pass rule when Arni Coulter took the snap and ran around the end on what appeared to be a run. He stopped short of the line of scrimmage and completed a 15-yard forward pass to Eddie "Dynamite Kid" James who ran the remaining 15 yards for the score. James thrilled again in the fourth quarter when he intercepted a pass. Bryce Gillis then booted a long punt and the Winnipegs tackled an All-Stars running back in the end zone to score a safety. Late in the game, Haycraft completed a long pass to reach near to Winnipeg's goal line and then he hit the line three times and scored on the third plunge. Haycraft's efforts were too little, too late, however, as the Winnipegs beat the All-Stars 22-13.

Injuries piled up for the Winnipegs in this game. Coach Fritz kept "Darting Fritz Hanson," the "greatest running halfback ever seen in these parts," out of the action in the second half, which disappointed the crowd, but James provided good entertainment in his place. Every man on the Winnipegs played in the game, and the reserves stayed in most of the second half. As a result, the game "did not hold the sustained interest of the crowd because it always seemed too easy for Winnipegs who won pretty well as they pleased despite the fact four of their best men were on the sidelines," wrote McKenzie in the *Free Press*. After the game, a member of the Minnesota All-Stars told E.A. Armstrong of the *Free Press* that the Winnipegs had the best line they'd ever seen and "What a man that Hanson is! The way you fellows started out had us gasping." During halftime, "Goldie" Smith, a scout for the Detroit Red Wings in attendance, had asked members of the press, "Is Hanson a hockey player, too?"

*   *

The upcoming three-game series between the Winnipeg Rugby Club and the Victoria Rugby Club had evolved into a battle of ideals. Victorias

Coach Fred Ritter saw the games as a struggle that would pit Canadians against Americans and true amateurs against paid amateurs. Meanwhile, some Victoria players might have seen the games as a grudge match. The men who tried out for the team included at least 10 former Winnipegs, including Ace Bailey, Percy Campbell, Cam Doherty, Alf McLaughlin, Tommy Miller, Bill Nairn, Steve Olander, Art Raven, Harvey Russell, and Bev Stewart. Both Olander and McLaughlin had played on the 1932 St. John's team. Other players saw the resurrected Victorias as an opportunity to play at the senior level for the first time. Former Deer Lodge and Winnipegs juniors Bill Crossin, Bill Hicks, Jimmie Lightfoot, Dave Morris, Bert Nelson, and Carl Schultz tried out for the team. Bob Leckle, who had played for Manitoba in 1934, also went out for the team.

When the starters for the Winnipegs and the Victorias stepped out onto the field for game one of the series on October 5, 1935, the Victorias starting lineup included four former Winnipegs.

In the first quarter, Fritz Hanson returned a punt by Olander, former Winnipeg reserve, but then fumbled and lost the ball when the Victorias tackled him in Winnipeg territory. The Victorias attempted to move the ball on the ground but three plays later they settled for a field goal. After an exchange of kicks, Lou Mogul recovered a Victorias fumble on Victoria's 5-yard line. Bob Fritz hit the line twice and scored a touchdown. Late in the first period, Greg Kabat suffered a deep cut above his eye and broke his cheekbone when he tackled Olander on the run at halfback. They carried Kabat directly to the hospital.

In the second quarter, Hanson gained on end runs of 15 and 25 yards. Mogul then shifted to end and Fritz connected with him on a forward pass to the 5-yard line. The Winnipegs hit the center of the line twice, and on the third try, Hanson slid to his left and scored a touchdown. After an exchange of kicks, the Winnipegs gained possession at their own 40-yard line. Russ Rebholz completed a 50-yard touchdown pass to Joe Perpich.

In the second half, Rebholz completed passes to Perpich and Tubber Kobrinsky. Hanson then carried the ball to Victoria's 13-yard line and on the following play Rebholz slipped through the middle of the line to reach the 1-yard line. On the next snap, he plunged over for the score.

Grey (1935)

In the final quarter, the Winnipegs reached deep into their playbook and attempted long forward passes. Three times Bud Marquardt dropped bombs launched by Rebholz. Late in the game, the Victorias fired up their own aerial attack but fumbled the ball. Rebholz picked it up, slipped past would-be tacklers, and ran 55 yards to score a touchdown as officials blew the final whistle. The Winnipegs beat the Victorias 29-3.

Throughout the game, when the Victorias hit the line, they bounced back, "as though they had hit the Woolworth building," quipped the *Lethbridge Herald*. The newspaper said Hanson was "hell on wheels" and "his deceptiveness, his amazing speed and ability to change pace are uncanny. He can go into high from a standing start so fast that it leaves you gasping." The *Herald* described Bert Oja as a "flaxen-haired giant."

Despite Perpich's stellar past performances, Steve Olander for the Victorias outkicked him in this game. Doctors predicted Kabat would miss ten days of football because of his injury.

When the Winnipegs hit the showers, Fritz complained to his men about a lack of conditioning.

*   *

The Winnipeg Rugby Club's second game against the Victoria Rugby Club would determine whether the Winnipegs would win the MRFU title or whether a third game would determine the champion. Greg Kabat would sit out the game with his broken cheekbone. Both Johnny Christie and Johnny Patrick would sub for him on the line. Tubber Kobrinsky would also miss the game and compete instead for the medical school's interfaculty team at Manitoba. To give Herb Peschel's hamstring a rest, Coach Bob Fritz planned to play Dick Lane in place of Peschel. He also planned to use Eddie James and Cliff Roseborough out of the backfield.

Kabat sat on the bench at Osborne Stadium in street clothes on October 12, 1935, as he watched his blue and gold Winnipegs take the field to play the red and white Victorias. In the first quarter, Hanson ran back Steve Olander's punt to Victoria's 32-yard line. On the next play, he ran around left end for 27 yards. Fritz completed the drive when he charged the line for a touchdown. Four minutes into the game, the

Winnipegs regained possession of the ball and Hanson ran off tackle for 16 yards. He twisted his ankle on the play and left the field for the remainder of the game.

In the second quarter, penalties against the Victorias and a Russ Rebholz run moved the ball to Victoria's 25-yard line. On the next play, rookie Nick Pagones ran for 15 yards. Fritz then missed on a pass to Joe Perpich but he connected with Perpich on the next play for a touchdown. On the next possession, the Winnipegs backed the Victorias up to their own 8-yard line where former Winnipeg reserve Alf McLaughlin faked a kick. He carried the ball 30 yards before Pagones ran him out of bounds. When the Winnipegs regained possession of the ball, they took to the air, and Fritz gained a total of 40 yards on two pass completions, first to Pagones and second to Rebholz. The Winnipegs finished the drive on the ground when Fritz smashed over the goal line from 4 yards for a touchdown.

At halftime, MRFU president Stan Pepler gave out three footballs to fans in the children's section.

In the third quarter, the Victorias held the Winnipegs near to Winnipeg's goal line. When Rebholz punted the ball away for field position the Victorias partially blocked and recovered the ball at Winnipeg's 14-yard line. The Winnipegs stopped the Victorias and forced a turnover on downs. Perpich attempted a punt but he shanked it and gave Victoria possession of the ball at Winnipeg's 18-yard line. James, upset, slugged an opponent. Officials ejected him from the game and assessed the Winnipegs a 10-yard penalty. The Victorias attempted two runs and a pass from the 8-yard line but turned over the ball on downs. In response, Rebholz connected with Perpich on a long pass to midfield, and the Winnipegs continued the drive on the legs of Fritz. The Victorias intercepted a Rebholz pass attempt only to fumble and lose the ball on their own 40-yard line. The Winnipegs gained more yards but turned the ball over on downs when Pagones took the ball on an end run and then threw it out of bounds. Lou Mogul hobbled off the field with a bruised hip.

As the third quarter ended, Bert Oja blocked a punt and Jeff Nicklin recovered the ball. The Winnipegs drove to Victoria's 12-yard line where

Grey (1935)

Rebholz connected with Perpich in the middle of the end zone for a touchdown. In the final minutes, the Victorias took to the air but Pagones intercepted a pass. Fritz then ran for 25 yards to Victoria's 26-yard line. He scored the last touchdown on a 9-yard run that ended with a leap and a somersault for a 29-0 win over the Victorias. He injured his hamstring on the play.

The Winnipegs suffered over 100 yards in penalties in this game, mostly for offsides. Emotions flew. Not only did the officials eject James but also Slush Harris for the Winnipegs and Ace Bailey for the Victorias, for slugging. During the contest, Rebholz had wrenched his left leg but finished the game. The Winnipegs had earned the MRFU title for the third year in a row but the Victorias didn't allow them to walk away unscathed.

After the game, the Winnipegs received an invitation from the New York Giants to play an exhibition game at the Polo Grounds in New York on November 10. However, the Winnipegs expected to play in the WCRFU final on November 9 and so they turned down the offer.

* *

With the MRFU title locked up, newspapers in Winnipeg had little to say about the scheduled third game between the Winnipeg Rugby Club and the Victoria Rugby Club. Coach Bob Fritz had decided to make Rosy Adelman the coach for the upcoming game and for the most part, the reserves would play. He figured the Winnipegs would benefit from experienced reserve players down the line. He also called up Bernie Olander from the junior Winnipegs to punt.

With the knowledge that most of the Americans would not play, the *Winnipeg Tribune* suggested the game might provide "a more interesting struggle than the two previous games." On the line, Jeff Nicklin and Herb Mobberley would start at ends while Slush Harris, Bill Ceretti, Adelman, Johnny Christie, and Dick Lane would fill the middle. Arni Coulter would start at quarterback with Eddie James and Tubber Kobrinsky halfbacks, Russ Rebholz at fullback, and Cliff Roseborough at flying wing.

To many observers, the first two games had proven the Fred Ritters of the world wrong. The Canadian game could no longer pretend to be an amateur game played only by Canadians. The tide had turned and to succeed, a team needed a whole platoon of paid Americans on the field.

Or did it?

In the final game of the MRFU championship series on October 19, 1935, the Victorias took an early lead in the first quarter when Rebholz failed to return Steve Olander's punt out of the end zone. The Victorias scored a rouge to go ahead 1-0. Later, Rebholz punted the ball and Alf McLaughlin fumbled on Victoria's 5-yard line where Adelman recovered the ball. Three plays later, Coulter crossed the goal line for the score. Before the first quarter ended, Rebholz split the uprights for a field goal from the 25-yard line. The Winnipegs quickly reclaimed the pigskin and after several first down runs through the line, Rebholz completed a 20-yard pass to Bud Marquardt to reach Victoria's 20-yard line. James then split the line and ran 20 yards for the score. Three minutes later, with Fritz out of the province, Coulter called an option run, which Fritz had yet to call in 1935. The Winnipegs ran the option from Coulter to Dave Harding to Nick Pagones for a 26-yard stretch to reach near Victoria's goal line. On the next play, Pagones charged in off tackle for the score.

In the second quarter, reserve center Eric Law knocked himself unconscious when he tackled Olander, injuring Olander's leg. The Winnipegs carried Law off the field and Olander limped off. Neither player returned.

The Victorias kicked off to open the second half and Coulter returned the ball 50 yards to Victoria's 28-yard line. James and Roseborough then alternated runs and James scored again on the run. Coulter attempted a field goal from the 15-yard line and scored a rouge when the Victorias failed to return the ball out of the end zone. Later, the Winnipegs drove again into Victoria territory and after Kobrinsky reached the 5-yard line, Roseborough stepped across for the score.

The Winnipegs never let up. Late in the game, Kobrinsky completed a 45-yard pass to Joe Perpich to reach Victoria's 28-yard line. On the next play, Rebholz bobbled the snap and chased the ball back to midfield where he turned back around and launched a pass to James who stepped into the end zone for the score. In the final minute of the game, James wrenched his knee and had to be carried off the field.

Grey (1935)

The Winnipegs, heavy with reserves, had trounced the Victorias 39-1 and proved the team didn't need their key American players to beat the Victorias. "The amazing James was the dynamite kid of old," observed the *Winnipeg Tribune* and noted that whenever James carried the ball, he covered 5 yards or more. And "little Arni Coulter, filling the quarterback shoes of Coach Bob Fritz called almost every play in the Winnipegs' repertoire, and in most cases they were well executed," observed Cam McKenzie for the *Winnipeg Free Press*. Ralph Allen of the *Winnipeg Tribune* quipped, "After watching the strange contradiction of a football team that can show a 50 percent improvement when stripped of half its power, I have decided that my All-American board of strategy for 1935 will consist of one coach, one psycho-analyst and one hypnotist.

"I am convinced," he continued, "[the Winnipegs] will not only defeat the Roughriders, but—Regina papers please copy—defeat the Hell out of them."

Fritz, Fritz Hanson, Greg Kabat, and Bert Oja all learned about Winnipeg's victory from a distance. They had traveled to Saskatoon to scout the Roughriders.

*   *

In 1935, the complexion of the North Dakota freshman football team changed considerably. Coach Jack West had recruited 10 players with all-state honors from the region, including one Native American and one Black player. In both North Dakota and Manitoba, those changes provoked curiosity in the newspapers. The upgraded Sioux freshman team included a halfback by the name of Dog Eagle, a Native American from Linton, North Dakota, a town near the Standing Rock Indian Reservation and the home for a portion of the Lakota or "Sioux" people. A multi-sport athlete, Dog Eagle had starred on Linton's football, basketball, and track teams. In football, he received an honorable mention at end on North Dakota's all-state team in 1933. In 1934, he won the 220-yard low hurdles and took second in shot put at the Central North Dakota track meet. In advance of the game between the Winnipegs and the North Dakota freshman, the *Winnipeg Free Press* pointed to Dog Eagle as a "feature" of the team. The *Bismarck Tribune* exclaimed that the North Dakota football team finally had "a real Sioux" on the squad. The *Tribune* also proclaimed that "no Indian ever had been a member of any North Dakota football squad" until that year. It's not clear whether the newspaper meant the University of North Dakota or North Dakota in general, but in short order, a *Tribune* reader, Fred Sleight of New England, North Dakota, informed the paper that North Dakota Agricultural College had once had a Native American player on the team named Byron Wilde. The team captain, Wilde had run better and scored more touchdowns than anyone else on the team. Sleight had played tackle with the fleet-footed halfback and he shared how Wilde, at 160 pounds, had led North Dakota Agricultural College to beat North Dakota by a wide margin. Mr. Sleight, or the *Tribune*, got some of the details wrong, however, including the score, the date, the year, and where they played the game, but indeed, Byron Wilde did play halfback and he served as team captain when North Dakota Agricultural College beat North Dakota 47-0 on November 8, 1902. A member of the Arikara Nation in North Dakota, Wilde had attended preparatory school at Carlisle from 1896 until 1899. He left the school the same year Pop Warner had arrived to coach the football team. Wilde enrolled at North Dakota Agricultural College in 1900 and played and captained both the football and baseball teams. In 1903, he returned home to Elbowoods, North Dakota, where he worked as a blacksmith, farmed 240 acres, and raised three orphan children.

A Black player, Horace W. "Hoss" Johnson, had also joined North Dakota's upgraded freshman team. Johnson had come to North Dakota from Cheyenne, Wyoming. It's not clear whether Johnson had played football prior to enrolling at North Dakota.

*

North Dakota freshman team coach Clem Letich and his North Dakota freshmen Sioux Papooses arrived at Osborne Stadium at noon on October 24, 1935, and found beautiful autumn temperatures over a slippery field from snow that had melted and then froze. Winnipeg Rugby Club Coach Bob Fritz suggested the slippery field would be good for the Winnipegs because they hadn't been tested yet on that type of surface. The teams would play the first half of the game under American

Grey (1935)

intercollegiate rules and the second half under WCRFU football rules. The teams played on Thanksgiving Day, which had been moved to October 24 so that the holiday would not interfere with the October 14 general election.

When the teams kicked off at 2:30 p.m., Bert Oja sat out the game while Greg Kabat played with a rubber guard over his fractured cheekbone. Tacklers seemed to bounce off veteran halfback and Winnipeg native Eddie James as he returned the opening kickoff 65 yards along the sideline to North Dakota's 30-yard line. On the first play from scrimmage, James carried the ball another 12 yards. Four plays later, on the sixth play of the game and on fourth down, Tubber Kobrinsky kicked a field goal to put the Winnipegs on the scoreboard.

After Winnipeg regained the ball, the Sioux Papooses forced them to punt and North Dakota partially blocked Joe Perpich's kick. The Papooses then gained 28 yards on an end run and eventually reached Winnipeg's 8-yard line. The Winnipegs held. Arni Coulter intercepted a pass and the Winnipegs immediately punted the ball away for field position. North Dakota punted right back but Rosy Adelman blocked the kick and recovered the fumble to give Winnipeg the ball. Russ Rebholz then completed a 17-yard pass to Bud Marquardt. On the next play, with Fritz as the lead blocker, Fritz Hanson, the "Blond Whirlwind," ran through a big hole between left tackle and end. He ran 25 yards to cross the goal line for the score. "Not a man even came close to touching the 'Peg speedster" and "[fans] made whoopee and roared," said the *Winnipeg Free Press*.

In the second quarter, Winnipeg backed up North Dakota near to its own end zone and the Sioux Papooses chose to punt. Surrounded by would-be tacklers, Hanson received the kick at Winnipeg's 40-yard line. Fritz blocked three North Dakota players out of the way for Hanson and the speedy little halfback broke away to his left. He outran two safeties and reached the goal line on a 60-yard touchdown run. In the *Winnipeg Free Press*, sportswriter E.A. Armstrong declared the run "the finest trip ever made in pursuit of a major score on a local gridiron," not because of Hanson's running, but because of Fritz's blocking. All around, sportswriters commented on how the American rules, which allowed for blocking anywhere on the field, increased the game's excitement for fans. Near the end of the first half, the Sioux Papooses kicked a 55-yard punt to Winnipeg's goal line where Kobrinsky attempted to pick up the ball and return it, but he fumbled. North Dakota recovered the pigskin in the end zone for a touchdown.

In the second half, under WCRFU rules, the game slowed down, and the Winnipegs used "many weird formations," observed *Winnipeg Free Press* sportswriter E.A. Armstrong. He blamed the presence of scouts from Regina and figured Fritz had chosen not to reveal the Winnipegs' game plan to future opponents. Fritz also chose to play his backfield reserves for most offensive plays. Late in the second half, for the first time, Fritz called an option run. On laterals from Fritz to Kabat to Hanson the Winnipegs reached North Dakota's 5-yard line. A few plays later Fritz charged the line to score.

Late in the game, North Dakota ran 50 yards on an option run to Winnipeg's 10-yard line where Winnipeg stopped their advance. North Dakota settled for a rouge. The Winnipegs beat the Sioux Papooses 23-7.

Because Hoss Johnson for North Dakota had managed to knock down or intercept Winnipeg's pass attempts, the Winnipegs had a difficult time with their passing game. Meanwhile, North Dakota used the option run frequently throughout the game but Winnipeg's Marquardt and Dick Lane "refused to give ground on any occasion," Armstong said.

After the game, *Winnipeg Tribune* sportswriter Ralph Allen declared the 1935 edition of the Winnipegs had proven that Canadian football should adopt the American code.

> "After many years spent in the half-world between major and minor sports, in the west at least, rugby football has definitely graduated to the status of a big league enterprise. This is due almost wholly to the influence of certain estimable young men from across the line to whom we refer as 'imports.' They are better football players than our Canadian football players and the public, by its increased patronage, recognizes them as such. My proposition is that their football game is also

better than our football game, and that the public is beginning to recognize that, too. I submit that it will not necessarily be a sign of weakness in the rule makers if they decide to give the public what it wants."

Allen said any doubts whether the Canadian game should include the forward pass should be put to rest. "Now, honestly, gentlemen," he wrote, "how many one-dollar bills would you spend on football during the course of next season if the forward pass were suddenly abolished from the game? The forward pass is one feature that originated across the line and improved our game—shall we say—100 percent."

The impending game against Regina "has roused this city to an unprecedented feverish pitch," Armstrong reported. "So much so, few tickets are left."

* *

When the North Dakota freshman team returned to Grand Forks, Bob Fritz followed close behind. He continued southward to Moorhead and on Saturday, October 26, he participated in Concordia's homecoming festivities. He watched the Cobbers beat Augustana 13-6. When Fritz returned to Winnipeg to prepare the Winnipeg Rugby Club for the WCRFU semifinal game against the Regina Roughriders, the management at Osborne Stadium had spread seven tons of straw across the field to protect it from the elements. Meanwhile, to meet demand, the stadium's box office had sent additional tickets to Regina. In short order, all 500 tickets for Reginans sold out. The stadium's management placed benches in front of the bleachers to accommodate an additional 400 fans and then three days before the game, they closed the box office because they had no more tickets to sell.

When the Roughriders arrived on the eastbound Canadian Pacific Railway train on Friday evening Coach Al Ritchie and his 22 men exhibited a "supremely confident attitude" as they stepped off the train onto the platform. In the chilly weather, Ritchie held his signature coonskin coat draped over his arm as he spoke to the newspapermen gathered there. He declared the new WCRFU rules had proven to be the best way to play the game in Canada because the fans felt more entertained and it offered teams more strategy. "*We* have the game out here," he said, and he disparaged the rules still in force in the East. When asked how he felt about the strength of the Winnipegs, he said, "If the Winnipegs are as good as they're said to be, that would make it about even, wouldn't it?" Winnipeg had beaten Sarnia, and Sarnia had beaten Regina, but in total for the season, Regina had scored more points and had fewer points scored against them. Had either team played stiff competition outside of Sarnia? Debatable. However, no one could refute the truth that both teams fielded more Americans than Canadians in their starting lineups. In total, the Roughriders had eight Americans and the Winnipegs had nine. Both teams reported their squads healthy and injury free save for the Roughriders' reserve halfback, Samuel "Moose" Stinson. After the impromptu press conference, Ritchie and the Roughriders checked in to the Royal Alexandra Hotel, a Canadian Pacific Railway property.

On Saturday morning, Roughriders fans arrived by train, and by game time on November 2, 1935, oddsmakers believed more money had been wagered on the game than on any previous game played in Western Canada.

Tales of impropriety circulated. Before the game, Winnipeg had sent $50 to the Saskatoon Hilltop Football Club and because officials in Saskatoon had been selected to choose officials for the WCRFU semifinal, conspiracy theorists in Regina believed Winnipeg had attempted to influence those selections. Winnipeg communicated they had sent the $50 to help Saskatoon assuage the monetary loss they realized when they hosted Sarnia during the Imperials' fall tour through the West. When the WCRFU finally announced the names of the officials, they included Angie Mitchell, the former Roughriders star and rumored successor to Al Ritchie. In the *Winnipeg Tribune,* Johnny Buss complained about the selections.

Coach Bob Fritz ignored the buzz and accusations. He focused on football, and he knew he would need help. He talked to Bert Oja who enticed Pete Somers of the Minnesota All-Stars to travel up to Winnipeg to coach from the bench while Fritz called plays on the field. During practices, Fritz focused on pass defense and pass offense. On the day of the game, he dressed 28 players. He didn't announce the starting lineup until game time. Cliff Roseborough would play in his 68th consecutive game, a streak that began in 1929.

When the Winnipegs and Roughriders took the field at Osborne Stadium on a cold, windy afternoon in front of 7,000 fans, the Roughriders, in black and red, sought to capture their 17th western title in 22 years. Fritz Hanson received the opening kickoff for the Winnipegs but the Roughriders ran him out of bounds at Winnipeg's 10-yard line. Both teams then played strong defense and forced an exchange of multiple punts. Winnipeg finally moved the ball when Fritz completed two passes, one to Joe Perpich and another to Bud Marquardt, to reach Regina's 20-yard line. Fritz then stabbed Marquardt for another 15 yards to reach the 5-yard line. Three plays later, Hanson, the Winnipegs' "Mighty Atom," took the snap from well behind the line, and with Russ Rebholz in the lead he raced outside right end where Rebholz blocked a man to the outside. Hanson slipped between Paul Kirk and another Regina tackler to cross the goal line for the score. In the *Winnipeg Free Press*, E.A. Armstrong said Hanson "showed he had all the virtues of a great ball carrier by his instinctive running, photographic eyes, and lightning reflexes. He moved around for that touchdown faster than Santa Claus."

On Regina's next possession, Rebholz intercepted an Oke Olson pass attempt and then Oja punted the ball. The Roughriders caught and fumbled the ball at their own 6-yard line where Lou Mogul jumped on it to give possession to the Winnipegs. Fritz then tossed a pass to Marquardt but Kirk knocked it down. On the next play, Rebholz launched the ball in a high arc toward Eddie James who stood in the end zone near the deadline between Ralph Pierce and Kirk. James managed to pull it down and score just 2 minutes after the team's first touchdown. The Winnipegs scored the extra point and after only 9 minutes of game time, Regina trailed 0-12. In the *Free Press*, Armstrong observed the Winnipegs had "unloos[ed] a wide open, reckless attack before many of the customers had even found their seats."

In the second quarter, Fritz injured his leg when he ran out of bounds and crashed into the press box. Arni Coulter substituted. Both James and Hanson rushed for long distances, but penalties and turnovers reversed their gains. Hanson injured his leg and Tubber Kobrinsky took his place. A moment before halftime, Regina's Olson punted from Winnipeg's 45-yard line and the ball hit the cross bar and fell past the deadline for a rouge. The teams broke for the half with the score Regina 1, Winnipeg 12.

In the second half, Fritz re-entered the game and returned the opening kickoff to Winnipeg's 25-yard line. Gains and punts filled the third quarter while the Roughriders emerged from their slumber. Pierce tore up the field and twice the Roughriders enjoyed a first down within Winnipeg's 10-yard line, but twice the Winnipegs rebuffed and forced a turnover on downs. In the fourth quarter, Greg Kabat punted the ball and Pierce returned it to Regina's 48-yard line. On the next play, Pierce attempted a forward pass but Oja intercepted the ball and ran it back to Winnipeg's 40-yard line. James then carried the ball twice for a total of 8 yards, and Rebholz kicked the ball from placement to the deadline for a rouge. With one minute remaining in the game, the timekeeper handed his watch to the referee and the Roughriders started their final drive with the ball at their own 25-yard line. Regina took to the air. The crowd cheered for the forward pass as Olson completed a 26-yard pass to Kirk to Regina's 49-yard line. Olson then completed a 34-yard pass to Lloyd Connolly to reach Winnipeg's 15-yard line. Connolly caught the ball despite the fact Kabat had tipped the pass on its way. On the third play of the drive, Olson tossed another pass, tipped by Fritz this time, which connected with Pierce for a 15-yard touchdown pass. Regina had scored too little, too late, and Winnipeg won 13-6.

While Regina had completed 5 of 17 pass attempts for 129 yards with 3 interceptions, the Winnipegs had dominated the ground game with 141 yards rushing compared to Regina's 56. Overall, the Winnipeg line had proven to be a tough barrier. As Dave Dryburgh summed it up in the *Leader-Post*, "Winnipeg's wing line, backed up by a quick-thinking, hard-charging secondary defense, was too strong! There you have the whole story of the west's major football game of 1935." The Roughriders had

Grey (1935)

only managed to score a touchdown when they took to the air late in the game, but before then, Regina had completed only two of fourteen pass attempts. In the *Tribune*, Buss complained the Winnipegs had played safe football and should have increased their lead to prove they could contend with the East. Dryburgh said, "They looked like a pro football team, these Winnipegs." Behind the scenes, too, Winnipeg may have *spent* like a pro team. "Somebody in Winnipeg said, 'We can't lose,'" wrote Dryburgh. "The inside story as we got it is that they couldn't *afford* to lose."

After the game, the Winnipegs roared and celebrated in their dressing room. It didn't take long for the mob of spectators to break down the barriers and rush in to celebrate with them. Every man reached to shake the hand of Coach Fritz who appeared relieved to have thrown off the yoke of the Winnipeg-Regina spectacle, while others just stood in awe of "Dynamite Kid" James and his immaculate recovery from injury after injury. Longtime fans congratulated Rosy Adelman on the victory while Rosy smiled in agony as trainer Billy Hughes dressed his injured right leg. Meanwhile, Hanson heaped high praise on his former collegiate opponent, Pierce. And Oja, the former Golden Gopher who had coached the Winnipeg line through two goal-line stands treated the victory as just another big game. He looked ahead. The crowd parted as Regina's Coach Ritchie walked into the dressing room. He congratulated the Winnipegs on their victory and declared they had proven to be the best football club the West had ever witnessed. He then spoke personally with James, his former player, and shared his pleasure that James had healed and returned to the grid.

Meanwhile, in the Regina dressing room, the boys remained quiet, but satisfied. They had put up a good fight but they knew that Winnipeg had a hell of a team and that Winnipeg represented the West.

Before they departed their dressing room, the Winnipegs learned that Carl Cronin, the former Winnipegs leader, had coached his Calgary Bronks to a 14-0 victory over the Vancover Meralomas on an ice-covered field in Calgary in the other WCRFU semifinal game. The Bronks and Winnipegs would play for the Western championship in Winnipeg.

Afterward, the team celebrated at the Adelman home, through the evening and into the night.

* *

The Metropolitan Theatre in Winnipeg, with seating for 2,500 people in its main auditorium and mezzanine, showed a news reel on Wednesday that included highlights and many crowd scenes from the Winnipeg-Regina game. The reel also included one hundred feet of film with images from the Winnipeg-Sarnia game. The Winnipeg Rugby Club had taken hold of the community's consciousness.

Oddsmakers believed Winnipeg would beat Calgary in the WCRFU championship. In the East, when fans talked about football in the West they only talked about Winnipeg. They hoped to see the blue and gold play in the Grey Cup championship game.

Meanwhile, Winnipeg's players practiced in sub-zero temperatures on the straw-covered field at Osborne Stadium. Russ Rebholz and Rosy Adelman, both injured, watched from the sidelines but Greg Kabat, who had a minor operation on his cheekbone after the game against the Roughriders, practiced with the others.

Coach Bob Fritz knew little about Calgary's offense. He had heard rumors they had a strong line. He worried about field conditions and fumbles and he channeled Concordia Coach Frank Cleve when he told E.A. Armstrong in the *Winnipeg Free Press* that he would not suffer overconfidence. He would sit any man who didn't work hard in practice. "Our fixture on Saturday is now more important than the one against Regina," he said, "and believe me, there is to be no let-up."

At their final practice before the game, Tubber Kobrinsky, the medical student, lightened the mood when he shared how he had performed his first operation. He had removed ingrown toenails from a patient. Bert Oja, the dentist, joked how he used his smashmouth tactics on the line to generate new customers.

The Calgary Bronks, too, practiced in sub-zero temperatures on their home turf. After they arrived in Winnipeg on Friday morning, they practiced in the straw behind closed gates at Osborne Stadium.

As of Friday evening, the box office had sold only $1,000 in tickets. The Winnipeg Rugby Club owed Calgary a $1,031 guarantee. The club

Grey (1935)

needed good attendance to cover the guarantee and to finance a trip east for the Grey Cup game. Club executives felt concerned about the club's solvency. The city's interest in football had climaxed with the Winnipeg-Regina rivalry game, and so club executives put out a plea to fans through Armstrong in the *Free Press*. It didn't help that the 1935 WCRFU playoffs imparted a little déjà vu. Just like in 1933 when the Winnipegs had advanced to the Grey Cup semifinal game in Toronto, the team had to first beat Regina and Calgary in Winnipeg. Winnipeg had played Calgary during a blizzard in 1933, and in 1935 the forecast called for the same weather. Off the field both fan complacency and the weather worked against the Winnipegs.

On November 9, 1935, the rebranded Calgary Bronks met the Winnipegs in the WCRFU final for the Hugo Ross Trophy and for the opportunity to represent the West in the Grey Cup. In a 2:30 p.m. start, the players shuffled onto a slippery field with blowing snow in front of 1,500 fans. Meanwhile, folks at home listened to the play-by-play on radio station CKX, which broadcast the game with a 100-watt transmitter. Carl Cronin, the man who had led the Winnipegs to victory *against* Calgary in 1933 now stood with the opposition, but only as a coach. Cronin did play in a couple of exhibition games against Regina earlier in the year, but against the Winnipegs, he would have to resist the impulse to take the field and carry the pigskin himself. Under blizzard conditions, both teams plodded along the grid with plunges and off-tackle runs.

Ten minutes into the game the Winnipegs finally marched into Calgary territory but the Bronks held and forced a punt. Greg Kabat stood at midfield and shanked the ball to the left where it bounced once before the Bronks attempted to field it. As a Calgary player grabbed for the pigskin a Winnipeg player tackled him and the referee blew his whistle. The players didn't hear the whistle and the ball popped loose. Bud Marquardt leapt into 2 inches of snow to recover the loose ball. The umpire, who also did not hear the referee's whistle, awarded the ball to Winnipeg. The officials consulted and they awarded the ball to Winnipeg at Calgary's 5-yard line. On the next play, Russ Rebholz ran off tackle and through a big hole for the score.

For the remainder of the game, the Winnipeg offense plunged or quick-kicked while Calgary responded in-kind with runs and punts. Four times Winnipeg's defensive line blocked Calgary's punt attempts. Four times Winnipeg fumbled the ball and four times Calgary recovered it. Calgary fumbled and lost the ball twice. Rebholz, Kabat, Bob Fritz, and Fritz Hanson handled most of the carries for Winnipeg while Calgary featured Chuck McKenna, the prep school kid from Chicago, out of the backfield. Washington State product Oran Dover didn't play that day for Calgary due to injuries. In all, the Winnipegs gained 179 yards on the ground compared to Calgary's 41. The starters played most of the 60 minutes. Kabat scored Winnipeg's final point on a rouge and Winnipeg beat Calgary 7-0. The Winnipegs had won the Hugo Ross Trophy and had earned the opportunity to play in the Grey Cup championship game.

After the game, in the Winnipegs dressing room, Fritz signed autographs, but many fans had left the stadium disappointed the Winnipegs had failed to score more points. Rosy Adelman rebuffed the idea that the Winnipegs could have increased the margin. "Don't ever think those fellows weren't plenty tough," he told Armstrong of the *Free Press*. "They had a ball club and a sweet ball club." Meanwhile, Hanson said he never knew a man who tackled harder than Calgary's Bill Currie, a bank clerk from Lethbridge, Alberta.

In Calgary's dressing room, Johnny Buss from the *Winnipeg Tribune* asked Cronin about the Winnipegs. "Bob Fritz, Greg Kabat, and Russ Rebholz are plenty tough for any club," Cronin said, "and this lad Hanson is a son of a buck."

In the evening, the Winnipegs hosted Calgary for dinner at the St. Regis Hotel where WCRFU officials awarded the Hugo Ross Trophy to Winnipeg, only the fourth time a Winnipeg team had held the trophy, first in 1924 by the Winnipeg Victorias, then in 1925 by the Winnipeg Tammany Tigers, and most recently in 1933 by the Winnipeg Rugby Club.

*

On the day of the WCRFU championship, both before and after the game, WCRFU executives met at the Royal Alexandra hotel to discuss business. The WCRFU decided they would send a large delegation to the annual CRU meeting in February where they would demand the West be given the opportunity to host the Grey Cup in alternating years. Otherwise, the WCRFU would withdraw from the CRU.

Meanwhile, in late November 1935, the AAUC suspended all members of the Ottawa Rough Riders team because the AAUC had learned the team's American backfielder, Roy Berry, was actually Bohn Hilliard from the University of Texas and that Hilliard had also played professional baseball that summer for the Boston Red Sox affiliate in the West Dixie League. Hilliard (or "Berry") had already exited Canada, immediately after Ottawa's game against the Argonauts on November 16. The AAUC said Hilliard had assumed the identity of Roy "Skeeter" Berry, the University of Tulsa football star. Ottawa's suspension put all Big Four teams in jeopardy because they had played against Ottawa, but the AAUC allowed Hamilton to move forward in the playoffs.

* *

The Minto Armoury for the volunteer militia in Winnipeg provided a warm, open indoor space for the Winnipegs to practice, but the paved floor proved difficult for a good scrimmage. As in past years, the western entrant for the Grey Cup would have to wait out the playoffs in the East, and this year, the Winnipegs refused to play a Grey Cup semifinal match against the ORFU champion. After all, they had earned the right to represent the West in the Grey Cup. The last time the Winnipegs had agreed to play in a Grey Cup semifinal, in 1933, the team had lost to Toronto. As a result, two Eastern teams played for the Grey Cup in the final and the Winnipegs had financed a fruitless trip East. Now in 1935, unable to convince the railroad to allow the Winnipegs to pay travel expenses against future Grey Cup gate receipts, club president Frank Hannibal and John T. Boyd, president and general manager of Shea's Brewery in Winnipeg, secured a $1,500 loan together to fund this year's trip.

The University of Toronto offered to play Winnipeg in an exhibition game, but the Winnipegs turned down the offer in favor of an exhibition game against Assumption College of the University of Western Ontario in Windsor, Ontario, across the Detroit River from Detroit, Michigan.

The Winnipegs would practice for the Grey Cup at University of Detroit Stadium, the home of the university's Titans and also the Detroit Lions of the NFL. Assumption College would use the exhibition game as a fundraiser for the Windsor Lions Club to benefit the blind.

On November 27, 1935, several hundred fans, including Winnipeg's mayor and Manitoba's premier, gathered at the Canadian National Railway depot at 6:00 p.m. to wish the team well. Some fans carried signs, and Rosy Adelman grabbed a sign from a fan that read, "Winnipeg Wants that Championship!" He took the sign with him onto the train. Twenty-four players plus the executives and a handful of fans and local sportswriters headed East. On the train that evening, the team played bridge and poker while Adelman, Bob Fritz, and Joe Perpich entertained everyone with their harmonies. Trainer Billy Hughes ensured the players hit the sack by 10:00 p.m.

When the team arrived in Toronto they switched trains. Joe Ryan left the depot long enough to meet with CRU officials and he pushed them to hold the Grey Cup final at Varsity Stadium in Toronto, a neutral venue with the potential for more earnings in gate receipts. Bert Oja and Pete Somers remained in Toronto to watch Hamilton play Sarnia in the Eastern final while the remainder of the team took the final leg to Detroit. The Winnipegs checked in at Webster Hall, a 12-story "stag hotel" with 800 rooms, two coffee shops, and a 100,000-gallon indoor pool in the basement. The team held its first practice on Friday afternoon on a field covered in ice and snow. After Hamilton beat Sarnia, Oja and Somers traveled to Detroit to join the rest of the team. The Winnipegs would play Hamilton for the Grey Cup.

On Sunday, with 12,000 other fans, the Winnipegs watched the Detroit Lions play the Brooklyn Dodgers in sub-zero temperatures. The Winnipegs rooted for Brooklyn because Stan Kostka from Minnesota now played for the Dodgers, and while most NFL players received approximately $50 per game, Kostka had received $5,000 for the season with a $500 signing bonus to become the highest-paid player in the NFL. At the start of the fourth quarter, the Lions led the Dodgers 12-0 and the Lions had the ball. Fritz and the others watched as Detroit tailback Glenn Presnell lined up as a flanker back on the left side of the formation. At fullback, Ace Gutowsky took the snap. Gutowsky performed a pump fake toward Presnell and Dodgers defenders momentarily bit on the fake. Gutowsky then tucked the ball and ran while Presnell took off running. The defenders pursued Gutowsky, but before he crossed the line of scrimmage he stopped and launched a pass to Presnell who caught the ball and carried the pigskin into the end zone. Impressed, Coach Fritz sat down that night and added a similar play to the Winnipeg playbook. He would have to wait to put it into practice, however, because the next day, the Winnipegs would cross the Detroit River to play Assumption.

*

The Winnipeg Rugby Club met the Purples of the Assumption College of the University of Western Ontario at Kennedy Collegiate Institute Stadium in Windsor on December 2, 1935. The Purples team of 27 players included both current and former Assumption players and also players from the Windsor-Walkerville Technical School football team, which had won the Western Ontario Secondary School Association championship in 1935. The tech school boys featured Mike Hedgewick, a halfback with explosive speed who had won medals in the broad jump and 100-yard dash. The roster also included a lineman, Trip Trepanier. Coached by Rev. W.P. "Willie" McGee, Assumption competed in the Michigan-Ontario Collegiate Conference and played under American intercollegiate rules. The Purples had finished their 1935 season 2-3-1 with wins over the Detroit Institute of Technology and the Lawrence Institute of Technology, both in Detroit, and the Purples roster included several student athletes from the United States. Assumption's student newspaper, *Purple & White*, said the American half of the game would "give no advantage to [Assumption], however, for many of the players on the Winnipeg team are former stars from several American universities."

In front of approximately 100 spectators, which included sportswriters and Hamilton coach Fred Veale and his star player, Johnny Ferraro, the Winnipegs played a half-and-half game under American intercollegiate rules and CRU football rules. Fritz Hanson's pretty blonde sister, Esther, an enthusiastic football fan, also watched the game. She had traveled east to join her brother for the exhibition and for the Grey Cup game.

In the first quarter under American rules, on fourth down the ambidextrous Fritz used his left arm to complete a pass to Fritz Hanson in the end zone for the score. In the second quarter, Fritz put in the reserves and his backup, Arni Coulter, but neither team scored before the half. The teams didn't take a break, however. Instead, they switched sides and added a player to each squad to continue play under CRU rules.

In the third quarter, Fritz threw a pass to Perpich who stood near the goal line amidst four Assumption defenders. Perpich caught the 30-yard toss and fell over the goal line to score. In the fourth quarter, Lou Mogul blocked an Assumption punt from Assumption's 30-yard line. The Winnipegs recovered the ball on Assumption's 5-yard line. On the next play, Fritz lateraled to Russ Rebholz who ran around right end for a touchdown.

In their first game of the season outside of Winnipeg, the Winnipegs looked terrible. With Coulter in for Fritz, Coulter called a new play that involved a fake plunge and a lateral pass. Fritz barked at Coulter for calling that play with scouts in attendance. Overall, the Winnipegs were "woefully rusty," reported Ralph Allen in the *Winnipeg Tribune*. "Plays didn't click," he said. "Tackling was away off. Pass defense was disorganized" and "coming out of huddles, players straggled dispiritedly to their posts." On a hard, slippery field, Fritz called only simple plays to avoid injuries. Nevertheless, the Winnipegs beat Assumption 17-0.

During the game, Allen had overheard Veale and Ferraro tut-tut what they had seen. Later, Veale acknowledged that the Winnipegs hadn't played serious football against Assumption. For their part, the Winnipegs said they felt disorganized and that it had taken them a while to execute plays well. Explained Fritz, "It was the first real scrimmage we have had since we won the western championship a month ago from Calgary and we found we need work. Boy, how we need work. We're going to be a different team when we run into Hamilton Saturday, I'll tell you that much."

Before the Winnipegs returned to Detroit, they joined their Assumption foes for a banquet at the Prince Edward Hotel in Windsor, sponsored by the Walkerdale Dairies. The next day, the team toured the General Motors proving grounds and factory, 40 miles outside of Detroit.

Grey (1935)

They enjoyed lunch with GM executives, but after they left, they focused on football and Fritz's new play.

*

While the Winnipegs prepared for the Grey Cup, the Winnipeg Rugby Club executive committee sent its past president, Barry Bain, to Toronto to meet with CRU officials at the Royal York hotel. Bain asked again for the Grey Cup to be moved to Toronto and that the one western official on the crew be named referee. The CRU held firm on the venue and rejected the officiating request on the grounds the West had adopted its own rules in 1935. The CRU told Bain that Hamilton only had to claim the Grey Cup to have it because the West had played by its own rules. Hamilton, however, did not wish to claim the Cup without a game but said if the CRU did move the game from Hamilton they would claim it without a contest; and besides, the CRU constitution stated the game must be played in the eastern champion's venue if an eastern team had won the Grey Cup the previous year. The CRU would only change the venue if it proved inadequate, as was the case for Sarnia in 1934. The CRU had enacted the venue rule in 1934 but only after its past president, Dr. E. A. McCusker, a western representative, had turned over the reins to the organization's newly elected president, John Degruchy, an eastern representative. It didn't matter to the CRU that teams in the East had flouted the CRU constitution when they held playoff games through the end of November, two weeks later than the rules allowed, in the quest for profits at the gate. The Big Four had taken an extra week while the ORFU had taken two extra weeks to decide their champions.

In the *Winnipeg Tribune*, Ralph Allen wrote, "The uncompromising reaffirmation of the CRU's attitude toward the upstarts of its hinterland will almost certainly hasten that worthy body's demise." Once again, he suggested the WCRFU might break away from the CRU. Meanwhile, Joe Ryan told *Windsor Star* sports editor Vern DeGeer that if Winnipeg lost the Grey Cup it would be the last time Winnipeg would play for the trophy. The West had been more progressive and had adopted the brand of football fans enjoyed, he said, and teams in the West had grown tired of having the East dictate what happens in Canadian football. But if Winnipeg won, of course, they would defend the title. Rumors flew that

Winnipeg intended to win the cup, bring it home, and keep it in Winnipeg. Meanwhile, the ORFU, too, complained the Big Four had too much control over the CRU, and with the CIRFU out of Grey Cup competition it seemed inevitable the CRU might disband after 1935.

After Bain departed Toronto, the CRU announced Winnipeg had agreed to play Hamilton in Hamilton. And after Ryan pushed some more by telephone, the CRU announced that the western and eastern members of the officiating crew would alternate at referee and they had appointed a head linesman from the CIRFU instead of from the Big Four.

* *

When the Winnipegs returned to practice, snow had fallen and helped to soften the surface of the field at University of Detroit Stadium. Coach Bob Fritz, however, didn't practice. During the exhibition game he had wrenched his arm on a line plunge and he injured his wrist, but he didn't say anything to trainer Billy Hughes until the next day when his hand had swollen so that he couldn't move his fingers. Concerned, Hughes contacted Dr. William E. Keane, the team physician for both the Detroit Tigers baseball and Detroit Lions football teams. Keane took four separate x-rays and determined Fritz had sprained the wrist but Hughes would have to tape it. Fritz told Hughes no matter what, he would play. He told the press that even if he couldn't play he had full confidence in Arni Coulter as a signal-caller.

Meanwhile, Bud Marquardt had developed a bad cold while Slush Harris suffered a stomach malady.

The soft snow proved better for practice, but when the Winnipegs had chosen to work out in Detroit ahead of the Grey Cup they had hoped to escape the wintry weather. Less than a block from their hotel they discovered Wayne State University had a gymnasium adjacent to Kelsey Field. The athletic director there had coached both Russ Rebholz and Greg Kabat on the freshman team at Wisconsin. In short order, the Winnipegs moved their practices to Kelsey Field and inside to the gymnasium where the athletic director lay down 20 mats to cushion their falls. Hundreds of students watched as the Winnipegs practiced blocking

Grey (1935)

and tackling. Afterward, Rosy Adelman said he'd never had a better workout. Meanwhile, outdoors on Kelsey Field, Fritz called Joe Perpich aside and coached him again on his punting technique. Hamilton had an excellent kicking game and the Winnipegs needed to try to match it or get through Hamilton's line to block the Tigers' punts. Perpich nursed a hamstring injury and hadn't punted in the exhibition game against Assumption. But at Kelsey field that day, Perpich displayed his finest punting yet, even with a wet ball.

For the remainder of the week, the Winnipegs practiced at Wayne. Fritz installed new formations, practiced the option run, and worked on the new play he had put together after the Lions game. At their final practice both Fritz and Rebholz coached out of uniform. Fritz's wrist had nearly healed but he didn't want to reinjure it. Rebholz suffered from nagging knee injuries that required heavy taping. He needed a break.

On Thursday before the game, ticket-sellers in Hamilton reported brisk sales and that fans had expressed a desire to see a Grey Cup game filled with forward passes, with Johnny Ferraro tossing the ball for the Tigers, with Fritz tossing short passes with either arm, and with Rebholz and Kabat tossing long passes for the Winnipegs. Perhaps the ticket-sellers only claimed they had sold a lot of tickets to generate more interest in the game. When G. Sydney Halter, the treasurer for the Winnipeg Rugby Club, stopped in at the sporting goods store in Hamilton to see how ticket sales had progressed, only a few tickets had been sold. Hamilton club executives at the store assured him that more would sell by morning. Meanwhile, a policeman knocked on the door to interrupt their conversation. They let him in and the Hamilton executives introduced the officer as one of the Tigers' linemen. He would work the night shift and then after just a few winks, he would play in the Grey Cup. Hamilton's confidence made Halter's head spin.

On Thursday night in Detroit, the Winnipegs watched the Boston Bruins play the Detroit Red Wings at Olympia Stadium. Afterward, Joe Ryan read the weather forecast for Hamilton, which said "milder and cloudy." He told the press, "that's all we want—warmer weather. Give us traction and we'll beat those Tigers by two or three touchdowns. We were worried about the frozen ground but if it gets milder, the Tigers will never stop our running attack."

On Friday, the team departed Detroit at 4:00 p.m. and arrived in Hamilton shortly after 9:00 p.m. that evening. They took the long walk together from the Canadian National Railway depot to the Royal Connaught Hotel with its marble-floored bathrooms. Hotel staff showered them with telegrams from Winnipeggers who wished them well. Billy Hughes told the press the players seemed grouchy. A good thing, he said. They had Tigers to tame.

Meanwhile, two trains filled with fans arrived from Toronto.

*

When the 1935 season began, the Hamilton Tigers had gotten off to a slow start, but Johnny Ferraro, the team's on-field coach and quarterback had turned the Tigers into a powerful force. Hamilton had built their team around Brian "Old Man of the Mountain" Timmis, a native of Winnipeg who went on to play in Regina and Ottawa before Hamilton. As a fullback he smashed through his opponents.

In the playoffs, the Tigers had first defeated Queen's at Kingston 44-4, despite the fact the CIRFU had withdrawn from competition for the Grey Cup. Queen's insisted that they should compete in the playoffs and so Hamilton swept them aside. In their next game, Hamilton defeated Sarnia 22-3. Bert Oja, who scouted that game provided the Tigers with motivation when he told the press afterward that he felt disappointed because "the Tigers didn't show any attacking strength from scrimmage." He said, "We think our line is as strong as any and certainly, it won't give way before the Tigers. We have a better forward pass defense than Sarnia had Saturday and I think the Tiger tacklers will have trouble bringing down Fritz Hanson and Russ Rebholz." The Winnipegs outweighed the Tigers 17 pounds per man on the line. Oja admitted, however, that Ferraro looked great as both a pass thrower and pass defender and as an open-field runner. The press asked Fritz, too, about Hamilton and he said he believed Perpich would prove the better punter and that the Winnipegs had better return men. At the ends, the Winnipegs towered over their opponents and Fritz figured because they had managed to contain Ralph Pierce in the Regina game they could contain the Tigers backfield just as well. As for Hamilton's containment strategy, Elmer Dulmage in the *Lethbridge Herald* offered advice, "They say when Hanson shakes himself loose, you just walk in front of the goalposts to get ready for the place-kick after touchdown."

The press asked the Sarnia Imperials, who had lost to both teams, to offer their analysis, and the players said they believed the Winnipegs tackled harder, passed better, and had the best runner in Hanson, but Hamilton would win because the Tigers had beaten the Imperials by more points. Ormond Beach declared Oja to be the best lineman in Canada. Even Johnny Buss in the *Winnipeg Tribune* predicted Hamilton would win because the Winnipegs had suffered "four weeks of idleness," but most of all, he blamed the "inferiority complex" western teams carried with them eastward. Buss seemed to have forgotten, however, that the Winnipegs included nine Americans, some from college programs that had been the best in their conferences. Most of them had played on a bigger stage. The Americans did *not* have an inferiority complex.

Earlier in the week, oddsmakers gave Hamilton 5-3 odds. Later in the week, they gave Hamilton 3-1, 2-1, and 3-2 odds to win the game. The odds never swung in Winnipeg's favor.

The night before the game, with his wrist submerged in steaming hot water, Coach Fritz, the "Concordia Cannonader," told Ralph Allen of the *Winnipeg Tribune* that he, Bert Oja, and Pete Somers had discussed game strategy "at least a dozen times." He said they had modified their line play to ensure they wouldn't gain penalties for illegal blocks under CRU rules and he said Somers would watch the linemen from the sidelines. "And you can put it in the book," he said, "that any one of them who isn't busting in there—on kicks especially—will be hauled to the bench pronto." Fritz believed he had devised a defense to counter everything, but he expressed concern about kicking. He said if Perpich would perform at his best, they would do well. He hoped for a good field, too, or at least good footing. He said, "I'm confident that, if we go out there and play the kind of football we can play, we'll take them." He promised he would not play conservative on a lead.

*

Early the next morning on the day of the game, December 7, 1935, rain fell and froze when it hit the ground. It covered the pavement in Hamilton with a coat of ice and encased the field at the Hamilton Amateur Athletic Association Grounds. Groundskeepers scrambled to spread and rake several tons of sand over the grid. A cold mist filled the air in above-freezing temperatures.

The Winnipegs had received a lot of telegrams but when the telegram boy approached Fritz Hanson directly in the dressing room before the game, he smiled. He read the message, and just like before every game he had played at North Dakota State or in Winnipeg, he tucked the message into his shoe. His mother, Bertha, had wished him luck.

When fans arrived at the stadium, Manitoba Premier John Bracken and Winnipeg Mayor John Queen joined hundreds of fans from throughout western Canada. They sat with the Winnipeggers dressed in blue and gold in their own reserved section. Some Winnipeg fans had arrived by cattle train because they couldn't afford the more expensive passenger fare.

More reporters stuffed the press box than in recent memory. Shag Shaughnessy, the play-by-play announcer, and a field reporter with a sideline microphone prepared to call the game over radio stations CKY and CJRC, the very first national broadcast for a Grey Cup game. In International Falls, Minnesota, where listeners might have tuned in from across the border, readers opened the *Daily Journal* to read that "A football game of unusual interest will be played this afternoon" and that not Bronko Nagurski, but Bob Fritz, had reached the big stage, and another local boy, Pete Somers, had joined Fritz on the sidelines.

In his final pregame speech, Hamilton Coach Fred Veale warned his men about the Winnipegs. He told them to look out for... practically all of them. The Hamilton Camels club band greeted the Hamilton players with "Hold That Tiger" as the team took the field under a steady drizzle.

In Winnipeg, listeners heard only music as they waited for the Grey Cup broadcast to cut in.

Winnipeg chose to kick to open the game. In front of 6,405 fans the Winnipegs lined up for an onside kick but Bert Oja sent the ball to Hamilton's 15-yard line where it bounced in front of Hamilton's Jack Craig. When Craig didn't pounce, Hamilton's Jim Smiley fielded the ball,

Grey (1935)

instead, but Herb Peschel snatched it out of Smiley's hands to gain possession for Winnipeg. Bob Fritz then smashed the line three times but Hamilton forced a turnover on downs.

On first down for Hamilton, Huck Welch punted the ball away. Hanson, the "Baby-faced Streak of Lightning," returned the ball to Hamilton's 23-yard line. Two plays later, Fritz unleashed the play he had drawn up after the Detroit Lions game. He faked an end run and then floated a pass to Bud Marquardt on the other side of the field. Marquardt caught the ball as he stepped into the end zone for a touchdown. Greg Kabat missed the point after but Winnipeg went ahead 5-0. Only 5 minutes of game time had elapsed and the astonished Hamilton crowd generated an uproar.

Newspapermen at the *Winnipeg Free Press* only heard music on the radio. The Grey Cup broadcast still had not cut in, but then they watched as news of the first touchdown came across the wire. Immediately, they phoned their friends and word spread throughout Winnipeg.

Hamilton chose to kick instead of receive, and Fritz returned Johnny Ferraro's kick 30 yards to Winnipeg's 41-yard line. On second down, Joe Perpich surprised Hamilton with a quick kick and Welch fielded the ball at Hamilton's 19-yard line. Oja tackled him and Welch injured his hip, sending him to the bench with a limp. Fritz patted Welch on the back as he left the field. The Winnipegs had taken out the highest-scoring player in the East.

Finally, radio stations in Winnipeg had picked up the Grey Cup signal and listeners in the city heard Shaughnessy share the score. The Winnipegs had already gone ahead by a touchdown! Now all fans in front of their radios in Winnipeg sat on edge with excitement.

On offense, Hamilton used Smiley around the ends, Brian Timmis up the middle, and Ferraro off tackle while the Winnipegs used Kabat up the middle. Ferraro also attempted long and short passes, but to no avail. Frank Turville and Russ Rebholz punted in a back-and-forth affair, most of the time within Winnipeg territory. The Tigers managed to reach Winnipeg's 20-yard line where Turville kicked a field goal to close the score 5-3.

At Hamilton, Ontario

After an exchange of kicks, Rebholz fielded Turville's punt and lateraled to Hanson. The crowd rose to its feet as the "Blonde Ghost of Winnipeg" ran 45 yards along the sideline. The Winnipegs then used the option run to gain some ground but the back-and-forth kick-and-return game continued. During the melee, Oja charged through the line. He wrapped up Ferraro twice and his second tackle jarred the ball loose, but the Tigers recovered. Turville punted the ball out of bounds at Winnipeg's 52-yard line and then Hanson and Fritz found holes to reach Hamilton's 43. Rebholz completed a 38-yard pass to Perpich to reach the 5-yard line as the quarter ended.

To start the second quarter, on first-and-goal, Hanson lateraled to Eddie James who lost his balance and lost 5 yards. Rebholz then ran for 3 yards and officials called roughing against the Tigers and moved the ball to Hamilton's 4-yard line. Kabat attempted a field goal, but the ball sailed wide. Turville retrieved and kicked the ball out of Hamilton's end zone. Hanson fielded the oval at Hamilton's 33-yard line.

Once again, Fritz called a variation of the play he had drawn up after the Detroit Lions game. On first down, Fritz lateraled to Rebholz who faked an end run. Rebholz faded back 15 yards and threw a pass 21 yards through the air to Kabat. With only one would-be tackler to beat Kabat finished a 33-yard touchdown catch. Hanson kicked the extra point to put Winnipeg up 11-3.

The back-and-forth continued, and at one point Lou Mogul and Peschel charged through the line and together sacked Ferraro for a 12-yard loss. After an exchange of kicks, on second down Kabat kicked the ball away from Winnipeg's 19-yard line, and Turville kicked it back past the goal line. Hanson caught the ball in the end zone and the Tigers ran him out of bounds to score a rouge. Winnipegs 11, Hamilton 4.

With the ball on their own 25-yard line, Hanson found 6 yards and James ran for 2. Kabat punted. Wilf Paterson caught the ball and lateraled to Turville who returned it to midfield. The Tigers tried a run and then Ferraro threw an incomplete pass, and so Turville punted the ball from midfield. Hanson, the "King of the Prairie Gridders," caught the ball at Winnipeg's 10-yard line and started running. "Hanson's marvelous change of pace had Tiger tacklers bewildered," reported Elmer Dulmage in the

Grey (1935)

Lethbridge Herald. Hanson ran the ball 52 yards to Hamilton's 48-yard line. Kabat used a quick kick to send the ball to Hamilton's 8-yard line. James injured his ankle on the play.

The Tigers gained 10 yards on a penalty against Winnipeg and then Welch, back in the game, punted the ball away. Hanson, the "Minnesota Mercury," returned the ball 20 yards. Kabat plunged for 6 and Fritz charged for 5 to reach Hamilton's 40-yard line. Hanson ran around the end for a 10-yard gain and officials penalized Hamilton 15 yards for roughing on the tackle. Fritz smashed the line twice to move the ball in line with the goal posts and Kabat attempted a field goal. Once again, Kabat's kick flew wide but it reached the deadline for a rouge to put Winnipeg ahead 12-4. With the ball on their own 25-yard line, Ferraro attempted a forward pass. Oja intercepted the ball and ran it back to the line of scrimmage. Rebholz, too, threw an interception. The teams exchanged kicks to end the half.

Halter watched as the Tigers lineman who had worked the night shift dragged his way to the dressing room.

At halftime, fights broke out in the crowd over bets that had been placed. A newspaperman found Joe Ryan and asked, "Well it looks like you've got this Grey Cup thing in the bag. What are your team's plans for the future?" Ryan, bitter from his constant struggle with the CRU, replied, "I'll tell you what we're going to do. We're going to take the Grey Cup back home and dump it right in the middle of the Red River."

Meanwhile, in the Winnipegs dressing room, Fritz and Oja discussed strategy with the players, but Hanson slept. As Fritz later told the *Winnipeg Tribune*, "Fritzie simply leaned back in the dressing room and picked himself off a good forty winks. That's how much he had his wind up."

In the third quarter, Rebholz returned the opening kickoff to Winnipeg's 20-yard line. Fritz fumbled and lost the ball on the first play. In short order, the Winnipegs no longer appeared destined to win. Hamilton ran twice for 3- and 5-yard gains. On the second run, Oja tackled high, which would have incurred a 15-yard penalty, but because the officials couldn't apply the full yardage they sent Oja to the penalty box for 3 minutes. On the next play, with 11 Winnipegs against 12 Tigers, Fritz called for four line backers but Paterson ran through the hole where

Oja would have stood to score a touchdown. Turville missed the extra point attempt and Hamilton closed the score with Winnipeg ahead 12-9.

The Winnipegs chose to kick instead of receive. Paterson fumbled and lost the ball on the return. Hanson ran for 5 yards and then Kabat attempted to punt the ball but the Tigers blocked the kick and recovered the pigskin at Winnipeg's 28-yard line. Ferraro threw an incomplete pass and then tried a 40-yard field goal but the ball hit the crossbar. The Winnipegs then chased down Smiley for a 20-yard loss on an end run. Turville punted and Rebholz returned the ball to the 24-yard line. Kabat ran for 2 yards and then punted the ball away. Smiley returned the ball 26 yards to Winnipeg's 30-yard line and then Turville punted the ball to score a rouge to bring the score to 12-10 in favor of Winnipeg.

The Winnipegs started with the ball at their own 25-yard line where Fritz plunged for 4 yards. Kabat then punted the ball away and it rolled to Hamilton's 45-yard line. The Winnipegs tackled Turville on the return.

Welch came back into the game. He kicked a short punt to Winnipeg's 35-yard line where the ball bounced into Hanson's arms. Hanson paused. The three Tigers tacklers who had formed a triangle around him to stop his advance also paused to avoid a potential penalty. By rule, they had to give him five yards leeway until he caught the ball. And then, as Ralph Allen in the *Winnipeg Tribune* described it, Hanson "shot like a frightened bullet straight ahead." One account said Hanson juked to his left and spun to evade the middle tackler. Dulmage contended, "The wisp of a man hadn't dodged that scattered group. He had merely slipped through it at a speed the Hamilton Tigers never had had to contend with." He bolted straight ahead as the Tigers "clutched with desperation" but "felt nothing but the whistling wind." As E.A. Armstrong in the *Winnipeg Free Press* described, "He travelled straight down the center of the field not deviating a single foot." Or as Dulmage described, "The shadow darted straight downfield within reach of another half-dozen players. It was flying now and still nothing had touched it." On the radio, Shag Shaughnessy said, "Watch that little son of a gun go!" Dulmage wrote, "He was traveling faster than any football player in Canada ever travelled... like a fleeting shadow in the dusk of late afternoon." With 35 yards left to go, only Winnipeg players stood in Hanson's way. They "cheerfully moved out of his way" and Kabat followed close behind. As Vern DeGeer in the *Windsor Star* described it, Hanson "responded to the silent urging of a mother's message" inside his shoe as he completed his 75-yard touchdown run. No one had laid a hand on him and from the sidelines, the Hamilton players on the field appeared dumbstruck. The whole scene looked as if an official had blown his whistle to call the play dead but really Hanson had made everyone else appear motionless. And then "the crowd realized it had seen a play the like of which it never would see again," Dulmage said. "That crowd had *lived*. It stood up to a man and cheered the greatest ball-carrier it ever saw."

Rebholz kicked the extra point and the Winnipegs increased their lead to 18-10.

Shaugnessy told Armstrong of the *Free Press* that he had never seen a more amazing run in his 34 years of football. In the eyes of many, Dulmage said, Hanson's run "finally broke every eastern hope of turning back this Manitoba assault." But the Tigers still had more fight in them.

Hamilton chose to kick instead of receive. After Winnipeg could gain only a yard, Kabat punted the ball to Hamilton's 40-yard line to start the fourth quarter. Welch fielded the ball and kicked it back on the run. Hanson caught the ball and the "Blond Bomber" returned it 35 yards and left "three tacklers stretched out" on the field. More back-and-forth ensued. At one point the Tigers tried an option run but Perpich tackled Turville for a 5-yard loss. Hamilton tried an aerial attack but had to punt the ball away and Hanson returned the ball 25 yards to Hamilton's 52-yard line.

Late in the fourth quarter, Hamilton had Winnipeg pinned back at their own 10-yard line. Fritz fumbled but recovered the ball on a rushing attempt and the Winnipegs chose to punt the ball away. The snap flew low at Kabat's feet in the end zone where he jumped on the ball to take a safety. The scoreboard declared Winnipeg 18, Hamilton 12 with 3 minutes remaining in the game.

The Winnipegs started with the ball on their own 25-yard line, where Kabat punted the ball away. The Tigers received the ball at the Winnipeg 43-yard line. Every fan in the stands stood to watch Hamilton's march, and many pushed their way close to the edge of the playing field. The waning light under sheets of rain made it difficult to recognize the players.

Arni Coulter entered the game to replace Fritz on defense and he knocked down Ferraro's pass attempt. The Tigers then gained 11 yards on an option run to reach Winnipeg's 32-yard line. Ferraro passed again and this time he connected on a 27-yard pass to Paterson to reach Winnipeg's 5-yard line.

At this point, fans who huddled around their radios in Winnipeg heard Shaughnessy's voice replaced by music. One can only imagine how they stomped in frustration or fiddled with the dial.

Meanwhile, on the field, Smiley failed to cross the line of scrimmage on an end run. With the game clock ticking down, Hamilton decided to attempt a running kick into the end zone with the hope that the Tigers might recover the ball for a touchdown. On Paterson's first try, Rosy Adelman blocked the kick, but the Tigers recovered at the 15-yard line. Paterson tried the running kick again, and according to Dulmage, "while 9,000 wild-eyed spectators roared in a frenzy of excitement... little Fritz Hanson, greatest running halfback ever to play football in this sector, snatched an onside kick and carried it safely out." Hanson wriggled through his tacklers and fell into the slush. The referee blew his whistle. In the final moment, Hanson held the ball. The Winnipegs had won the Grey Cup, beating the Tigers 18-12.

On the radio in Winnipeg, Shaugnessy's voice returned. He announced that the Winnipegs had won the game.

Winnipeggers took to the streets in celebration. Fans crowded restaurants and dance halls. Orchestras dedicated songs to the Winnipegs and crowds punctuated their festivities with cheers.

In Hamilton, the Hamilton Camels club band took the field and played "Red River Valley."

For the first time in Grey Cup history, a western team had claimed the trophy. The Winnipegs celebrated as they ran off the field into the dressing room where the Tigers congratulated them and foes exchanged sweaters. Hanson's sister Esther pushed through the throng and she gave him a hug and a kiss and said, "You played a great game, honey." Hanson demurred. It had been a team effort. When reporters asked Hanson about

Grey (1935)

his 75-yard touchdown run, he blushed and said he'd been surprised himself. "It looked as though those three Hamilton tacklers had me covered," he told the *Winnipeg Tribune*, "but I took a chance with the unexpected. I guessed they were looking for me to try and sidestep them. Instead, I ran straight ahead and they were momentarily caught off balance. By the time they realized it, I was in the clear." Besides, he said, "a slippery field always gives the advantage to the ball carrier. He knows where he's going; they don't." Hanson admitted he never worried about the outcome. "Even when we were trying to work out plays under difficult conditions at Detroit, I felt our power would carry us through against Hamilton."

Meanwhile, Adelman sat in silence. He could hardly believe that after 17 years on the gridiron he had played with a team that had won the Grey Cup. He thought about when he and the Winnipeg Tammany Tigers had lost the Grey Cup a decade ago and how sportswriters in the East panned the club as "a bunch of intermediates." Adelman had carried that with him all the way to Hamilton.

When the Winnipegs boarded the bus for the hotel, Fritz counted heads. He proclaimed the game had been "the biggest kick of my life" and everyone agreed, even the Americans who had played in big games in front of crowds much larger than Hamilton's. As the bus lurched forward, Fritz said, with tongue in cheek, "Okay, fellows. You can all have a bottle of beer tonight." They all laughed. Fritz didn't have any more say in the matter. Perhaps they suggested Slush Harris should buy the first round. While in Toronto, Harris had placed a $20 bet that the Winnipegs would win. He would collect $150 when he returned home. As they stepped off the bus, the team heard music inside the hotel. The Hamilton Camels club band greeted them in the lobby and Winnipeg fans applauded their arrival.

Inside his hotel room, Hanson hadn't even finished his post-game shower when he heard a knock at the door. His roommate, Fritz, called for him and so Hanson wrapped in a towel and stepped out of the shower. Scouts from at least three teams in Ontario and Quebec stood in the room. They made offers to Hanson and Fritz to play for them in 1936. The same scouts had visited Mogul, Rebholz, and Oja, too.

The Winnipegs hadn't earned enough from gate receipts to pay the hotel bill and so a club executive paid the bill for the team. In total, the club had lost $1,800 on the trip and they still had to make it home.

As they waited in the lobby for the bus to take them to the train station, Fritz stood and grinned. He asked the newspapermen, "What do you think of us now?" When Hanson appeared relieved to step onto the bus, Fritz explained, "The kid doesn't like people to make a fuss over him. He's ready to find a hole and crawl into it."

At the train station, reporters asked Ryan about the trophy. He said CRU officials claimed they didn't know where it had been stashed. As he climbed aboard the homebound train, Ryan grinned and said, "It's probably down in Sarnia. We don't care very much if we ever get it, but I suppose it'll come along later."

In International Falls, the newspaper noted how Fritz had seldom called for himself to carry the ball. And "particularly in the matter of generalship, he was an outstanding figure." As DeGeer in the *Windsor Star* suggested, Fritz had "literally dazzled the Tigers with a crossword puzzle of plays." In fact, the 1935 Winnipegs playbook only contained about two dozen plays.

Dulmage of the *Lethbridge Herald* noted the strengths of the Winnipegs when he described their "towering, impregnable" line led by Oja and their "well-equipped backfield that carried every attack weapon except the punt." As for Hanson, "Fritzie's twinkling toes were the deciding factor," and with that, Dulmage had given Hanson his enduring nickname "Twinkle Toes." In Winnipeg, Allen had dubbed Hanson "The Golden Ghost."

Hanson had proven to be the key ingredient that helped Winnipeg overcome its perceived kicking handicap. During the first two-thirds of the game, the Winnipegs had leaned on Rebholz and Kabat for punts. Before the game, Fritz and Oja had been concerned that Perpich, just a kid by comparison, didn't have enough big-game experience to do well, but when they did finally give him punting duties he kicked better than the others. His first three punts averaged 55 yards. In total, he averaged 45 yards on five punts.

Grey (1935)

Throughout the game, both teams had kicked often for field position and they chose to kick instead of receive after an opponent scored. Winnipeg's line had forced both Welch and Turville to get their punts away fast and their kicks traveled for shorter-than-normal distances. Tigers tacklers couldn't get downfield fast enough. When Hanson caught the ball on the return he made up for lost field position with large gains in the open. He tallied returns of 75, 52, and 45 yards and three or more for at least 25 yards apiece. After his 75-yard touchdown return, the Tigers had started aiming their punts toward Rebholz, instead, but Rebholz just fielded them and lateraled them across the grid to Hanson. In total, Hanson had gained 334 yards on punt returns under Canadian rules with no blockers in the open field. Tigers fans complained that Welch and Turville should have kicked their punts out of bounds to keep them away from Hanson.

According to the *Globe and Mail*, Hanson "represented the difference between victory and defeat. Even brilliant Tiger tacklers... were completely baffled by this tricky little fellow. He caught faultlessly as well as recklessly and was good for a gain every time he got possession of the ball. He ran the ends with telling effect, he threw passes, and he also took timeout to plunge for good gains... He did things that were all wrong, according to Canadian football ethics, and yet he got away with it. For instance, he would run back and then march for long distances." As Dulmage described, Tigers tacklers "flung themselves in his path—or what looked to be his path. They snatched at his slender ankles and nearly always missed." The *Globe and Mail* talked to some former Tigers players "and they all agreed that the Winnipegs are one of the strongest teams they have ever seen... they voted unanimously that Hanson was the best player seen in the country since the era of Lionel Conacher."

"What they will always remember is Fritz Hanson," Dulmage wrote in the *Lethbridge Herald*. He said the game became "an episode of deathless football history only because Hanson was in the game. He wrote the story of this battle with his flying feet in slippery mud that wasn't designed for ball-carrying."

Hanson had scored only 1 touchdown. The Detroit Lions-inspired plays led to 2 more. Fritz revealed to the press that he had drawn up the

Fritz Hanson

plays and the team had practiced them only the week before. In the *Winnipeg Free Press*, Armstrong said those plays had made the Tigers "look like novices."

To Dulmage, the fighting Tigers had looked desperate. Winnipeg had forced them to play catch-up football the entire game. Hamilton's backfielders had had trouble getting past Marquardt and Perpich who forced them back inside into the arms of tacklers. Ferraro struggled to complete passes and in the third quarter, all four of his forward pass attempts fell incomplete. "So perfect was [the Winnipeg] aerial defense that five times Ferraro deliberately threw the ball to an open point on the field," observed the *Globe and Mail*. "Every eligible receiver was covered and Winnipeg's advance guard was rushing down on him." The Winnipegs had sacked Ferraro twice. Armstrong in the *Winnipeg Free Press* observed, "Our big, willing line poured through to torment their backs, harass their kickers, and hurry their passers. The defense was soundly conceived and brilliantly executed." The Winnipegs played a 6-3-1-2 defense against the Tigers, which Hamilton had not played against. On the line, Oja watched plays develop and then charged in to tackle the ball carrier. He said because he had scouted Hamilton, he anticipated their plays well, especially in the second half.

The Winnipegs had suffered a number of penalties, most often because they violated blocking restrictions. And throughout the game, Oja pulled from his guard position to block for a backfielder, an illegal move, according to one sportswriter, but the officials had failed to penalize him for the infraction.

A United Press correspondent from the United States, Henry McLemore, had attended the game. In his opinion, the Canadian football game he witnessed, played by CRU rules, "is a much more vivid spectacle than our game." He said, "the Canadian variety places a much higher premium on individual effort. This is especially true of the backfield men. The very fact that Canadian football rules forbids running interference makes the ball carrier develop initiative, not to mention all manner of cunning with which to elude tacklers." Of course, Hanson's performance dazzled McLemore, but he overlooked the fact Hanson had honed his skills playing American intercollegiate football, not Canadian ball. But

Grey (1935)

then McLemore did make a clever observation when he said, "I think Americans would like the Canadian rule on punts, too. Up here, opposing players must not approach within 5 yards of a safety man until the ball has settled in his arms. This makes for a run back of some sort on every kick and it's something to see when a twisting, dodging back attempts to elude a horseshoe of tacklers who have gathered about him as the ball descends." Hanson's unique skill set suited the Canadian return game perfectly. McLemore said he had talked to several of the American players before the game and they all said the Canadian game was more fun to play than the American game. Somers, too, expressed preference for the Canadian game because of its playoff system, which the American professional game lacked. But even though the Americans preferred the Canadian game overall they much preferred the WCRFU version of the rules, which allowed for more blocking.

All of Western Canada identified with the Winnipegs in their victory. Dryburgh in the *Leader-Post* succinctly stated, "The west's greatest ambition in sport has been realized." In the East, sportswriters praised Winnipeg's victory. Edwin Allan of the *Toronto Mail and Empire* said Canadian football had benefitted from the western win. When easterners complained about the Americans on Winnipeg's team, Lou Marsh in the *Toronto Star* told readers, "Quit howling. The better team won a great game." In the *Winnipeg Free Press*, W.G. Allen remarked, "We can imagine how the western lads on the NHL teams have been rubbing it into their eastern confreres."

The *Winnipeg Free Press* published a poem in homage to the Winnipegs.

Out where the flashing Hanson dashes,
Out where the Ed James and Kabat crashes,
Out where Bob Fritz directs the play,
Out where Oja knocks them the other way,
Out where the Grey Cup is come to stay,
That's where the West begins.

* *

During the trip home, the Winnipegs received congratulatory telegraphs from all over Canada, both on their train stops along the way and at home. At their first stop in Toronto the Winnipegs made a deal with the Royal York Hotel. The players slept four together at $3 per room.

On the last leg of the trip from Toronto to Winnipeg, the players felt exhausted, but elated. On Tuesday morning, as the train reached Dugald, a few miles east of Winnipeg, three airplanes from the No. 12 Cooperation Squadron of the Royal Canadian Air Force at Stevenson Field approached overhead. The pilots performed a flyover just a couple hundred feet above the team's Pullman car and the players rushed to the windows to watch. The planes circled the train as they escorted the Winnipegs to the station.

At the Canadian National Railway train station in Winnipeg, the station manager had roped off the center of the depot from the streetside to the trackside doors and had erected a raised platform near the street entrance. He had also decorated the building in blue and gold streamers. In below-zero temperature, women from the Girls Commercial Club sold blue and gold ribbons to the gathering crowd of 1,500 fans, most of whom wore blue and gold. They packed every inch of the depot. Some blew big, brass horns.

After the train pulled in at 8:45 a.m., the team waited nearly 10 minutes to disembark. The crowd grew anxious. And then, policemen opened the trackside doors. They held back the crowd as the players stepped off the train and into the rotunda. A 10-foot sign on the balcony above the opposite wall read, "Well Done Winnipegs!" in gold letters on black. The Grenadier Guards band played "Hail, Hail, the Gang's All Here." Rosy Adelman stepped off the train first. He smiled and waved a blue and gold sweater in one hand and he raised a sign in his other hand, the same sign he had grabbed from the crowd when he left Winnipeg to travel east. The sign, which originally said, "Winnipeg Wants that Championship!" had the word "Wants" crossed out. Adelman had replaced "Wants" with "Has." The crowd cheered their old champion. Behind Adelman, Coach Bob Fritz, who had injured his foot during the game, stepped off the train with his hoof in a bedroom slipper. And then someone yelled, "There's Hanson!" and the crowd erupted in cheers as shorter onlookers stood on their tiptoes to see Fritz Hanson emerge from the train.

Grey (1935)

As the players walked between the ropes through the depot to the street and up onto the platform, the policemen held back the crowd, but fans swarmed in upon the players as they descended the platform to get into cars. The automobiles joined a parade of decorated trucks. One of the trucks played circus music on an electric calliope. The parade then proceeded on a route through the city, and along the way the masses cheered. Every business with a flag had it flying. Most businesses had closed their doors for the morning hours. The procession delivered the players to Eaton's Department Store in Winnipeg where they took the elevators to the 7th floor and to the Spanish Coffee Court. Over breakfast, several dignitaries gave speeches. When Coach Fritz rose to speak the crowd sang "See Him Smiling" with the concluding words "Ain't He Handsome?" Fritz blushed and raised his wound-dressed hand in front of his scarred face. Adelman, too, spoke to the guests. "I was numbed after the game," he said. "The further I got from Hamilton, the better I felt. Maybe in a few days I'll be able to collect myself and tell you how I feel. [But] I'll tell you one thing—if God were to strike me down this moment, I think my life would not have been lived in vain." The crowd gave him a standing ovation. When the crowd asked for Hanson to speak, he simply stood and replied, "There's been so much said, and it has been so well said, I shall not occupy your time further," and he sat down, bashful.

After breakfast, the players and executives proceeded to the Grain Exchange where two large banners, one on each side of the street, said "Grain Exchange Welcomes Champions." They proceeded onto the trading floor where the grain market had ceased trading for 20 minutes while hundreds of employees at the Exchange cheered and greeted the men. After the cheers died down, Adelman made his entrance. He carried his sign but also a Hamilton Tigers sweater. He threw the sweater at his feet in the center of the trading floor and stomped all over it. The crowd erupted.

The Winnipeg Kiwanis Club then hosted the players for lunch at the Royal Alexandra hotel.

At 8:30 p.m. that evening, approximately 2,000 Winnipeggers paid 50 cents apiece to attend a reception and fundraiser event for the Winnipeg Rugby Club at the Winnipeg Auditorium. As many as 40 sports organizations throughout Winnipeg had hung their banners inside for the event and Isadore Leavitt and his 12-piece band entertained the crowd while they waited for the Winnipegs. At 9:30 p.m., to the crowd's delight, stage hands pulled aside a big blue curtain to reveal the Winnipeg players on the stage. When Fritz stepped forward to give a speech the crowd rose into a cheer of "Bob Fritz for mayor!" He thanked everyone and finished by thanking "every little kid on the street who feels proud of his hometown team." Adelman then introduced the members of the Winnipegs and he shared a little story about each one. Only Slush Harris, Bert Oja, and Johnny Patrick did not attend the event. Perhaps Harris had stayed home in Toronto and Oja had traveled home to Minnesota. After introductions, the team together sang a song they had written for the occasion. Before Adelman dismissed the team from the stage, the Harmony Lane Quartet sang a new song for the men, "The Blue and Gold," which CKF radio organist Alan Caron wrote for the team after their victory. The players then mingled and danced with fans and enjoyed vaudeville acts during intermissions.

A few days later, Dean S. J. Hedelund, the rector at Saint John the Divine Episcopal Church in Moorhead, entered the offices of the *Moorhead Daily News*. He carried with him a copy of the *Winnipeg Evening Tribune* and handed it to Dick Hackenberg. Winnipeg had gone nuts, he said, over the local boys from Fargo and Moorhead. He said Winnipeggers now regarded them as citizens.

Celebrations continued. On Thursday night, the Winnipegs were recognized at a junior hockey game at the Winnipeg Amphitheatre, and on Saturday night they attended a $1 per person dinner and dance at the Fort Garry Hotel where Hanson sang "Footloose and Fancy Free" for attendees. The city and the province also recognized the players with special honors at official events.

An administrator from St. Mary's College in Morago, California, reached out to WCRFU executives and asked for help to arrange a Christmas Day football game in San Francisco between the Winnipegs and St. Mary's. The St. Mary's Gaels had risen to prominence in recent years under coach Edward "Slip" Madigan, a former Notre Dame player who had played for Rockne. St. Mary's attracted as many as 80,000

Grey (1935)

spectators to watch their games in Kezar Stadium and trainloads of fans often followed the team to away games. The WCRFU sent back contact information for Joe Ryan and while the Winnipegs awaited a formal invitation, Vancouver invited the team to play a warm-up game in Athletic Park against an all-star team from the area. Ryan wouldn't commit to the Vancouver invitation without a formal invitation from St. Mary's in California. The games never came to fruition.

Meanwhile, Hanson autographed, dated, and donated his shoes from the Grey Cup game to the Winnipeg Tribune Empty Stocking Fund. Hudson's Bay Company put the shoes on display in the sporting goods department and the *Winnipeg Tribune* put a call out for bids. John T. Boyd, who had helped the Winnipegs cover Grey Cup expenses, paid $125 for the shoes. Meanwhile, in Hamilton, the player who had traded for Hanson's sweater raffled it off for approximately the same amount for a charity there.

On December 23, the Grey Cup trophy finally arrived in Winnipeg. The Club had no official club facility and so Ryan kept it in his office.

The Grey Cup Trophy

AFTERWORD

In 1935, the Canadian Press named four Winnipegs to the All-Canadian team, including Hanson at halfback, Fritz at quarterback, Oja at guard, and Bud Marquardt at end. Hanson came in 2nd place in voting for Canada's Most Outstanding Athlete of 1935. The Associated Press listed Hanson's efforts in the Grey Cup game versus Hamilton as "the best individual achievement in Canadian sport" for 1935.

In the wake of Winnipeg's Grey Cup victory for the West, Calgary, Regina, and Winnipeg agreed to form a new Western Interprovincial Football Union (WIFU) for 1936. Calgary would also retain membership in the ARFU.

Meanwhile, at their annual meeting, the Canadian Rugby Union (CRU) adopted a new residence rule that required a player to reside in Canada for at least one year prior to October 1 of the current season, otherwise the player could not play in games that mattered in union standings within the CRU. The CRU allowed Americans still resident as of Mach 1, 1936, to continue to play. The CRU hoped the new rule would limit the number of American imports in Canadian football and thereby reduce professionalism and the cost of fielding a competitive team. Joe Ryan argued for a one-year suspension of the rule to give Eastern teams time to secure some American players for themselves because he feared the teams would raid the Winnipegs for talent, but the CRU dismissed his concerns. At the same meeting the CRU also refused to play the Grey Cup in the West because Eastern teams did not want to play in late-November weather in the West.

When the 1936 Grey Cup rolled around, the Regina Roughriders stood as the western contender but due to the new residency rule the Roughriders had five ineligible American players on their roster. The Roughriders declined to play for the Grey Cup and once again two Eastern teams played for the trophy.

Contests between teams in Western Canada and college teams south of the border continued. In 1936, Winnipeg played North Dakota State in Winnipeg. Before that game, when Coach Casey Finnegan saw the Canadian regulation field 65 yards wide, he complained. "I coached [Fritz]

Afterword

Hanson for four years," he said. "Do you think I'm going to let you turn him loose on a 10-acre farm?" Joe Ryan had sawdust laid down to shorten the width to 50 yards, over 3 yards shorter than the regulation width for American football fields. Winnipeg went on to beat the Bison anyway, 33-13. Winnipeg also played Concordia College in Winnipeg in 1936 and beat them 21-19.

Winnipeg hosted Concordia again in 1937 and beat them 14-0. They also beat the University of North Dakota in Winnipeg 10-8.

In 1938, North Dakota returned the favor and beat Winnipeg 21-7, while Winnipeg beat North Dakota State in Winnipeg 16-1. Meanwhile, Concordia beat the Calgary Bronks 7-6 and lost to the Regina Roughriders 24-7.

In 1940, Winnipeg beat Concordia 38-7.

After 1940, the cross-border battles cooled down but continued as late as the 1948 season when Concordia beat the University of Manitoba 52-0 in Moorhead.

*

The *Winnipeg Evening Tribune* first called the Winnipeg team the "Blue Bombers" on September 5, 1936, when the newspaper wrote, "Coach Bob Fritz is sure his Blue Bombers will start their 1936 campaign—a campaign which he fondly hopes will lead to another National crown—with victory over the [Calgary Bronks]." *Tribune* sportswriter Johnny Buss used the nickname again in his "An Earful" column on September 9. Bob Priestly repeated the name on October 14 in the *Winnipeg Free Press*.

As of 2021, Winnipeg has competed for the Grey Cup 29 times, first as the Winnipeg Tammany Tigers in 1925, twice during wartime (1942, 1943) as the Winnipeg Royal Canadian Air Force (RCAF) Bombers service team, and 26 times as the Winnipeg Blue Bombers. Winnipeg first won the Grey Cup in 1935 and has since won the Cup a total of 12 times, the last time in 2021.

Winnipeg competed for the Grey Cup in 1925, 1935, 1937-1939, 1941-1943, 1945-1947, 1950, 1953, 1957-1959, 1961-1962, 1965, 1984, 1988, 1990, 1992-1993, 2001, 2007, 2011, 2019, and 2021.

Winnipeg won the Grey Cup in 1935, 1939, 1941, 1958-1959, 1961-1962, 1984, 1988, 1990, 2019, and 2021.

Afterword

The 1935 Winnipegs (now the "Blue Bombers")

Americans from Fargo-Moorhead Colleges
Bob Fritz
Melvin "Fritz" Hanson
Wilbur "Bud" Marquardt
Herb Peschel

Americans from Other Colleges and Prep Schools
Greg Kabat
Ahti "Bert" Oja
Nick Pagones
Joe Perpich
Russ Rebholz

Canadians
Lou "Rosy" Adelman
Bill Ceretti
Johnny Christie
Arni Coulter
Dave Harding
Marsden "Slush" Harris
Eddie James
Morris "Tubber" Kobrinsky
Eddie Kushner
Dick Lane
Eric Law
Herb Mobberley
Lou Mogul (b. Louis Mogulovsky)
Jeff Nicklin
Johnny Patrick
Cliff Roseborough

Manager, Joe Ryan

Afterword

Bob Fritz was inducted into the Concordia College Athletic Hall of Fame in 1987. He played and coached for the Winnipeg Rugby Club (1935-1937), the Edmonton Eskimos (1938-1939), and the Winnipeg RCAF Bombers. He also served in the U.S. Navy. He attended graduate school at the University of Minnesota and coached at the University of Alberta (1940-1941). Fritz worked as a radio announcer at CJCA in Edmonton and had a daily program on the Canadian Broadcasting Corporation. He later returned to the United States where he worked as a backfield coach at Concordia College in the late 1940s and early 1950s. After football, Fritz went into the sporting goods business. In 1954, he opened Bob Fritz Sporting Goods in Fargo.

In 1939, **Melvin "Fritz" Hanson** won the Lionel Conacher Award, which is awarded to the Canadian male athlete of the year. He was inducted into the Canadian Football Hall of Fame in 1963, the North Dakota State University Athletic Hall of Fame in 1972, the Manitoba Sports Hall of Fame in 1980, the Winnipeg Blue Bombers Hall of Fame in 1984, and the Canada Sports Hall of Fame in 1987. The Blue Bombers inducted Hanson into their Ring of Honour in 2018. He played for the Winnipeg Rugby Club (1935-1946) and the Calgary Stampeders (1947-1948). He served in the Winnipeg Light Infantry in the Canadian Army (1942-1945). Hanson continued to live in Canada and later worked in the insurance industry while coaching high school and junior football in his spare time.

Wilbur "Bud" Marquardt was inducted into the North Dakota State University Athletic Hall of Fame in 1974, the Winnipeg Blue Bombers Hall of Fame in 1984, and the Manitoba Sports Hall of Fame in 2004. He played for the Winnipeg Rugby Club (1935-1941). He also played basketball for the Winnipeg Toilers. He continued to live in Canada and worked for the Hudson's Bay Company until his retirement.

Herb Peschel was inducted into the North Dakota State University Athletic Hall of Fame in 1976 and the Winnipeg Blue Bombers Hall of Fame in 1987. He played for the Winnipeg Rugby Club (1935-1941). After football, he returned to the United States to live in Breckenridge, Minnesota. He served in the U.S. Army (1942-1947).

Afterword

Greg Kabat was inducted into the Canadian Football Hall of Fame in 1966, the Winnipeg Blue Bombers Hall of Fame in 1984, the University of Wisconsin Athletic Hall of Fame in 1995, and the Vancouver College Hall of Honour in 2000. He played for the Winnipeg Rugby Club (1933-1940) and coached the Vancouver Grizzlies (1941). He went on to coach at Vancouver College preparatory school in Vancouver, British Columbia, and at the University of British Columbia.

Ahti "Bert" Oja played for the Winnipeg Rugby Club (1935-1937). After football, he opened a dental practice in Winnipeg. The Blue Bombers have an award named after Oja, the Dr. Bert Oja Memorial Trophy, which they award annually to the club's most valuable offensive lineman.

Nick Pagones played for the Winnipeg Rugby Club (1935). Afterward, he attended and played football at St. Bonaventure University in Allegany, New York. He later taught adult elementary education at Great Meadow Correctional Institution in Comstock, New York.

Joe Perpich was inducted into the Crosby-Ironton Athletic Hall of Fame in 1995. He played for the Winnipeg Rugby Club (1935-1936) and the Edmonton Eskimos (1938). He also played for the Winnipeg Toilers basketball team alongside Marquardt.

Russ Rebholz was inducted into the Canadian Football Hall of Fame in 1963, the Winnipeg Blue Bombers Hall of Fame in 1984, and the University of Wisconsin Athletic Hall of Fame in 2000. He played for St. John's Rugby Football Club (1932) and the Winnipeg Rugby Club (1933-1938). He later coached at high schools in Stevens Point, Racine, and Rio, Wisconsin. He also served as the head basketball coach at the University of Wisconsin-Milwaukee (1952-1963).

Lou "Rosy" Adelman was inducted into the Winnipeg Blue Bombers Hall of Fame in 1984. He played for the Winnipeg Tammany Tigers (1924-1929) and the Winnipeg Rugby Club (1930-1937, 1941).

Bill Ceretti was inducted into the Winnipeg Blue Bombers Hall of Fame in 1985 and the Manitoba Sports Hall of Fame in 2004. He played for St. John's Rugby Football Club (1932) and the Winnipeg Rugby Club (1933-1949).

Johnny Christie played for the Winnipeg Rugby Club (1930-1935).

Afterword

Arni Coulter played for the Winnipeg Rugby Club (1931-1937).

Dave Harding played for the Ottawa Roughriders (1930-1932), the Winnipeg Rugby Club (1934-1935), and for Toronto Balmy Beach (1936).

Marsden "Slush" Harris played for the Winnipeg Rugby Club (1935, 1937).

Eddie James was inducted into the Canadian Football Hall of Fame in 1963, the Winnipeg Blue Bombers Hall of Fame in 1984, and the Manitoba Sports Hall of Fame in 2004. He played for the Regina Roughriders (1928-1931), St. John's Rugby Football Club (1930, 1932), and the Winnipeg Rugby Club (1935). His son, Gerry James, played running back for the Winnipeg Blue Bombers (1952-1955, 1957-1962) and the Saskatchewan Roughriders (1964) and joined his father in the Canadian Football Hall of Fame in 1981.

Morris "Tubber" Kobrinsky played for the Winnipeg Rugby Club (1935-1937). He went on to work as a family physician. He later drowned during a hunting trip.

Eddie Kushner played for the St. John's Rugby Football Club (1932) and for the Winnipeg Rugby Club (1933-1939).

Dick Lane played for the Winnipeg Rugby Club (1932-1936).

Eric Law played for the St. John's Rugby Football Club (1932) and the Winnipeg Rugby Club (1933-1935). He went on to coach the St. John's Roamers junior team.

Herb Mobberley played for the St. John's Rugby Football Club (1931-1932) and the Winnipeg Rugby Club (1933-1939).

Lou Mogul (b. Louis Mogulovsky) was inducted into the Winnipeg Blue Bombers Hall of Fame in 1984. He played for the Winnipeg Rugby Club (1932-1942). During World War II, he played for the Winnipeg United Services team and was the line coach for the Winnipeg RCAF Bombers. He later played for the Montreal Alouettes (1946) and the Edmonton Eskimos (1949). After football, he sold stocks and bonds.

Jeff Nicklin was inducted into the Winnipeg Blue Bombers Hall of Fame in 1984 and the Manitoba Sports Hall of Fame in 2004. He played for the Winnipeg Rugby Club (1934-1940). Lt. Col. Nicklin commanded the 1st Canadian Parachute Battalion in the Royal Canadian Infantry Corps during World War II. He was killed in action. The CFL has an award named after Nicklin, the Jeff Nicklin Memorial Trophy, awarded annually to the most outstanding player in the league's West division.

Johnny Patrick played for the Regina Roughriders (1931), St. John's Rugby Football Club (1932), and the Winnipeg Rugby Club (1935).

Cliff Roseborough was inducted into the Winnipeg Blue Bombers Hall of Fame in 1985 and the Manitoba Sports Hall of Fame in 2004. He played for the Saskatoon Quakers (1931), Regina Roughriders (1932-1933), and the Winnipeg Rugby Club (1934-1942).

Joe Ryan was inducted into the Canadian Football Hall of Fame in 1968, the Manitoba Sports Hall of Fame in 1982, and the Winnipeg Blue Bombers Hall of Fame in 1984. He served as an executive for the Winnipeg Rugby Club (1931-1941), Montreal Alouettes (1946-1949), and Edmonton Eskimos (1960-1964). His teams contended for the Grey Cup seven times and won four.

*

South Dakota State College Coach **Red Threlfall** went on to coach the Winnipeg Rugby Club (1938-1945) and led them to two Grey Cup championships in 1939 and 1941. North Dakota Coach **Jack West** also went on to coach Winnipeg (1946-1948).

Stan Kostka, the Minnesota Golden Gophers fullback who ran over the North Dakota State Bison in 1934, caused quite a stir when he signed with the Brooklyn Dodgers in the NFL in 1935. That's because Kostka had forced NFL teams into a bidding war for his services. Therefore, in 1936, the NFL instituted its annual NFL Draft. Kostka later coached the North Dakota State Bison in 1941. He then served in the U.S. Navy during World War II and returned to coach the Bison in 1946 and 1947. He later purchased a sporting goods store in Fargo and renamed it Stan Kostka Sporting Goods.

Afterword

"Hanson, then, it was, and Hanson it shall be even unto the childrens' children of all this astonished section, so long as they talk of football." - Ralph Allen, *Winnipeg Tribune*

APPENDIX – SEASON RECORDS

Concordia College 1931 Results

9-18	Concordia	0	@	North Dakota State	19
10-3	Concordia	26	@	Hibbing	6
10-10	Concordia	18	@	Macalester	0
10-17	Concordia	0	vs.	Moorhead State	0
10-31	Concordia	29	vs.	St. John's	0
11-7	Concordia	41	vs.	Gustavus	6
11-14	Concordia	7	@	St. Thomas	0
11-21	Concordia	6	@	St. Olaf	21

Concordia College 1932 Results

9-23	Concordia	0	vs.	North Dakota State	6
10-1	Concordia	20	@	Moorhead State	6
10-8	Concordia	13	vs.	St. Olaf	7
10-15	Concordia	7	@	Macalester	7
10-22	Concordia	12	vs.	St. Thomas	18
10-29	Concordia	0	@	St. John's	0
11-5	Concordia	0	@	Gustavus	0

Concordia College 1933 Results

9-22	Concordia	0	@	North Dakota State	0
9-30	Concordia	0	vs.	Moorhead State	0
10-7	Concordia	0	vs.	Gustavus	0
10-14	Concordia	26	vs.	Macalester	0
10-21	Concordia	13	@	Winnipeg Rugby Club	14
10-28	Concordia	6	vs.	St. John's	0
11-4	Concordia	0	@	St. Mary's	2
11-11	Concordia	13	@	St. Olaf	25

Appendix – Season Records

Concordia College 1934 Results

9-21	Concordia	0	@	North Dakota State	6
9-29	Concordia	13	@	Moorhead State	13
10-6	Concordia	33	@	Winnipeg Rugby Club	27
10-8	Concordia	26	@	Winnipeg Rugby Club	16
10-13	Concordia	19	vs.	St. Olaf	7
10-20	Concordia	13	@	Macalester	12
10-27	Concordia	39	vs.	St. Mary's	0
11-2	Concordia	26	@	Augustana	6
11-9	Concordia	26	@	Gustavus	0

North Dakota Agricultural College 1932 Results

9-23	North Dakota State	6	vs.	Concordia	0
9-30	North Dakota State	18	vs.	South Dakota	8
10-8	North Dakota State	12	@	South Dakota State	6
10-14	North Dakota State	27	vs.	Oklahoma City	7
10-22	North Dakota State	7	vs.	North Dakota	6
10-29	North Dakota State	24	vs.	Moorhead State	0
11-4	North Dakota State	0	@	George Washington	20
11-12	North Dakota State	0	@	Army	52
11-24	North Dakota State	20	@	Morningside	0

North Dakota Agricultural College 1933 Results

9-22	North Dakota State	0	vs.	Concordia	0
9-29	North Dakota State	7	vs.	St. Thomas	7
10-6	North Dakota State	7	vs.	Morningside	0
10-14	North Dakota State	7	vs.	South Dakota State	13
10-21	North Dakota State	0	@	Superior State	0
10-28	North Dakota State	7	@	North Dakota	7
11-4	North Dakota State	20	@	Moorhead State	0
11-11	North Dakota State	14	@	South Dakota	0
11-18	North Dakota State	0	@	Oklahoma City	19

Appendix – Season Records

North Dakota Agricultural College 1934 Results

9-21	North Dakota State	6	vs.	Concordia	0
9-29	North Dakota State	12	@	Minnesota	52
10-5	North Dakota State	27	vs.	St. Thomas	0
10-12	North Dakota State	22	vs.	South Dakota	0
10-20	North Dakota State	12	@	Morningside	12
10-27	North Dakota State	7	vs.	North Dakota	0
11-2	North Dakota State	12	@	Moorhead State	13
11-10	North Dakota State	0	@	South Dakota State	38
11-16	North Dakota State	13	@	Oklahoma City	8
11-23	North Dakota State	20	@	Texas Tech	20

Winnipeg Rugby Club 1935 Results

9-14	Winnipegs	26	vs.	Concordia	0
9-21	Winnipegs	3	vs.	Sarnia	1
9-28	Winnipegs	21	vs.	Minnesota All-Stars	13
10-5	Winnipegs	29	vs.	Winnipeg Victorias	3
10-12	Winnipegs	29	vs.	Winnipeg Victorias	0
10-19	Winnipegs	39	vs.	Winnipeg Victorias	1
10-24	Winnipegs	26	vs.	North Dakota Sioux Papooses	7
11-2	Winnipegs	13	vs.	Regina Roughriders	6
11-9	Winnipegs	7	vs.	Calgary Bronks	0
12-2	Winnipegs	17	@	Assumption	0
12-7	Winnipegs	18	@	Hamilton Tigers	12

Appendix – Season Records

RESEARCH NOTES

The information in this book has been gleaned from approximately 2,300 individual sources, mostly articles from daily newspapers and student newspapers, but also from many other sources. I owe a great debt to sportswriters in Fargo, North Dakota, Moorhead, Minnesota, and Winnipeg, Manitoba, as well as sportswriters throughout the United States and Canada for their devotion to sharing more than just the results of football games. In particular, the work of Dick Hackenberg in the *Moorhead Daily News*, Ralph Allen in the *Winnipeg Tribune*, Edward A. Armstrong in the *Winnipeg Free Press*, and Eugene Fitzgerald in the *Fargo Forum* stand above the rest as valuable sources of information. Other major sources of information include sportswriters Johnny Buss and Paul E. Warburg in the *Winnipeg Tribune*, W.G. Allen, Campbell McKenzie, and Maurice Smith in the *Winnipeg Free Press*, and Hank Hurley and Marvin Quinn in the *Fargo Forum*. Other sportswriters worth mentioning include Everett Wallum and Walt McGrath in the *Spectrum*, Vern DeGeer in the *Windsor Star*, Dave Dryburgh in the *Leader-Post*, Bob Elson in the *Province*, C.D. Locklin in the *Grand Forks Herald*, Elmer Dulmage in the *Lethbridge Herald*, Ralph Wilson in the *Calgary Herald*, Bernard Swanson in the *Minneapolis Star*, George A. Barton in the *Minneapolis Tribune*, and Ed Steinbrenner in the *Sioux City Journal*.

Newspapers did not include a byline with every article and so it's worth noting that I gleaned most of the information for this book from the *Fargo Forum*, *Moorhead Daily News*, *Winnipeg Free Press*, and *Winnipeg Tribune* daily newspapers and also the *Concordian*, *Spectrum*, *Western MiSTiC*, and *Winnipeg Manitoban* student newspapers.

I viewed the majority of newspaper articles for this book using the services NewspaperArchive.com and Newspapers.com. I gleaned information from the *Toronto Daily Star* through the Toronto public library's digital archive, from the *Concordian* through the digital resources provided by the Concordia College Archives, and from the *Western MiSTiC* through the digital resources provided by the Minnesota State University Moorhead Archives.

Research Notes

Because the *Fargo Forum* is not available in a digital format, I accessed articles from that newspaper by viewing microfilm. The North Dakota State University Archives provided the space and equipment for me to view microfilm, where I also viewed microfilm obtained from the State Historical Society of North Dakota, especially for articles from the *Dakota Student*, *Grand Forks Herald*, and *Minot Daily News*. I visited the Minnesota Historical Society to view microfilm for Minnesota newspapers that have not yet been made available in a digital format.

Most colleges and universities now provide access to digital archives, which oftentimes include scanned images of student newspapers and college yearbooks. I gained access to some college yearbooks through Ancestry.com where I also viewed other historical records, including census records, international border crossing records, birth and death records, obituaries, and more.

Both the NDSU and Concordia archives provided access to physical media, especially college yearbooks but other materials, as well. When I could not access physical media at some colleges and universities, librarians at those institutions found and scanned information for me from student newspapers and college yearbooks. The Bronko Nagurski Museum in International Falls found and provided some information for this book.

Sports information departments at various colleges and universities routinely publish media guides, which have been a great resource, and the North Dakota State Athletics Department, especially, helped me to clear up a key mystery for this book. I also gleaned information from Sports Reference LLC and their *Pro Football Reference* web site. Frank Cosentino's book *Canadian Football: The Grey Cup Years* provided valuable information about Canadian football's past, which pointed me in the right direction for further research.

I leveraged many other resources, including some books and many credible web sites, too numerous to mention individually.

It's worth noting that sports-writing before and during the early 1930s provided different, less exact information than it does today, especially in terms of statistics. Sportswriters and team statisticians had no film to watch later to double-check observed yardage gained, and while one source might give a runner 2 yards on a play, another source might give 3 yards. Observers typically rounded up for their own players and rounded down for opposing players. Depending on weather and field conditions, the disparity between observed yardages might be wider. Whenever possible, I deferred to using information from sources local to the home team.

Also, because the forward pass was relatively new in importance, some observers awarded the entire distance of a pass from where the passer stood behind the line of scrimmage to where the receiver caught the ball, while others awarded the distance of the pass from the line of scrimmage to the receiver. Some tacked on the receiver's yards gained after the catch, but not all observers awarded that yardage. Some broke down a pass into pass yardage and run yardage. Modern practice awards the distance of the pass from the line of scrimmage and includes the yards gained after the catch. Whenever possible, I share passing yardage gained using the modern practice.

Sometimes, accounts of the same game in different newspapers awarded touchdowns and other scores to different players. Accuracy depended on knowing who was whom and being able to read numbers on jerseys, if they had them at all and if they were clean, and if the players wore their correct numbers. In these situations, I deferred to using information from sources local to the home team.

In rare instances, newspapers shared the events of a game that were recorded second-hand from firsthand observers who relied on memory, which is very fragile.

A key observation I can share about newspapers and statistics is that early on when football was primarily a running game, most articles only mentioned the final score, starting lineups with last names, and how many first downs each team gained. As football progressed to include more of the passing game, fans grew more interested in the game, and newspaper articles began to share more statistics.

In Winnipeg, the Winnipeg Rugby Club played several half-and-half games using American intercollegiate rules in the first half of a game and Canadian rules in the second half of a game, or vice-versa. Sometimes,

Research Notes

but not always, the scorekeepers awarded teams more points than they had earned while playing under Canadian rules in those games.

Most early newspaper accounts only mentioned the most significant plays from a game, but some newspapers published play-by-play accounts.

-R. C. Christiansen

BIBLIOGRAPHY

3Down Staff. "A Look at the Early History of the CFL." 3DownNation. July 12, 2020. Accessed May 28, 2021. https://3downnation.com/2020/07/12/early-history-of-the-canadian-football-league/

A&E Television Networks, LLC. "The Roaring Twenties." History.com. March 11, 2021. Accessed December 6, 2021. https://www.history.com/topics/roaring-twenties/roaring-twenties-history

A&E Television Networks, LLC. "Stock Market Crash of 1929." History.com. April 27, 2021. Accessed December 6, 2021. https://www.history.com/topics/great-depression/1929-stock-market-crash

Abbott, J.C. "The Porter and the Pass Catcher: Uncovering the Black Football Trailblazers Canada Forgot." 3DownNation. February 27, 2021. Accessed November 1, 2021. https://3downnation.com/2021/02/27/the-porter-and-the-pass-catcher-uncovering-the-black-football-trailblazers-canada-forgot/

Abilene Morning News. 1934. "In the Grid Camps." Abilene Morning News, November 20:2.

Aho, Eino. 1934. "Mighty Dragons Repulse North Dakota State." Western MiSTiC, November 9:1.

Albert Lea Evening Tribune. 1932. "Bisons Take Easy Win from South Rival." Albert Lea Evening Tribune, October 15:6.

Alegi, Peter Christopher, Bernard Joy, Richard C. Giulianotti, Jack Rollin, and Eric Weil. 2020. Football. January 22. Accessed March 18, 2020. https://www.britannica.com/sports/football-soccer.

Allen, Ralph and Johnny Buss. 1934. "Punters Welcome Thoroughbreds Back to Polo Today." Winnipeg Tribune, June 16:19.

Allen, Ralph. 1932. "Regina Roughriders Sweep St. John's from Title Trail." Winnipeg Evening Tribune, November 7:16.

———. 1932. "Senior Rugby League Increased to 4 Teams." Winnipeg Evening Tribune, August 26:10.

———. 1932. "St. John's Gridders Blank Regina Roughriders in Exhibition Clash." Winnipeg Tribune, September 5:2.

———. 1932. "St. John's Gridders Hand Regina Roughriders Severe Trouncing." Winnipeg Tribune, September 6:12.

———. 1933. "West's Misplay Jinx Stops Great Winnipeg Team." Winnipeg Tribune, December 4:10.

———. 1934. "One Man's Opinion." Winnipeg Tribune, October 23:11.

———. 1934. "One Man's Opinion." Winnipeg Tribune, November 1:15.

———. 1934. "One Man's Opinion." Winnipeg Tribune, November 5:15.

———. 1934. "One Man's Opinion." Winnipeg Tribune, November 10:23.

———. 1934. "One Man's Opinion." Winnipeg Tribune, November 13:11.

———. 1934. "One Man's Opinion." Winnipeg Tribune, November 23:19.

———. 1934. "One Man's Opinion." Winnipeg Tribune, October 6:19.

———. 1934. "One Man's Opinion." Winnipeg Tribune, October 2:11.

———. 1934. "One Man's Opinion." Winnipeg Tribune, October 9:15.

———. 1934. "One Man's Opinion." Winnipeg Tribune, October 16:15.

———. 1934. "One Man's Opinion." Winnipeg Tribune, October 23:11.

———. 1934. "One Man's Opinion." Winnipeg Tribune, September 8:19.

———. 1934. "One Man's Opinion." Winnipeg Tribune, September 15:27.

———. 1934. "One Man's Opinion." Winnipeg Tribune, September 27:13.

———. 1934. "Sentiment Grows in Favor of American Grid Rules." Winnipeg Tribune, August 18:21.

———. 1934. "Winnipeg and Regina Split Playoff Rugby Battles." Winnipeg Tribune, November 5:14.

———. 1934. "Winnipeg Rugby Club Report Received with Calm." Winnipeg Tribune, August 11:19.

———. 1935. "Eastern Clubs Seek Winnipeg Rugby Stars." Winnipeg Tribune, December 9:14.

———. 1935. "Edict Would Have Given Tigers Crown." Winnipeg Tribune, December 4:12.

———. 1935. "Final Practice Puts 'Pegs in Top Shape." Winnipeg Tribune, December 6:1.

———. 1935. "Fritz Suffers Arm Injury--C.R.U. Nearly Halted 'Pegs." Winnipeg Tribune, December 4:12.

———. 1935. "Ice-Encrusted Field to Handicap Players in Final Rugby Tilt." Winnipeg Tribune, December 7:1.

———. 1935. "One Man's Opinion." Winnipeg Tribune, December 6:19.

———. 1935. "One Man's Opinion." Winnipeg Tribune, December 13:19.

———. 1935. "One Man's Opinion." Winnipeg Tribune, July 27:23.

———. 1935. "One Man's Opinion." Winnipeg Tribune, November 4:12.

———. 1935. "One Man's Opinion." Winnipeg Tribune, November 11:13.

———. 1935. "One Man's Opinion." Winnipeg Tribune, November 6:13.

———. 1935. "One Man's Opinion." Winnipeg Tribune, November 25:11.

———. 1935. "One Man's Opinion." Winnipeg Tribune, October 21:13.

———. 1935. "One Man's Opinion." Winnipeg Tribune, October 25:15.

———. 1935. "One Man's Opinion." Winnipeg Tribune, October 31:15.

———. 1935. "One Man's Opinion." Winnipeg Tribune, September 16:11.

———. 1935. "One Man's Opinion." Winnipeg Tribune, September 23:13.

———. 1935. "Winnipeg Club Regains Western Grid Championship." Winnipeg Tribune, November 11:12.

———. 1935. "Winnipegs Give Sluggish Display against Windsor." Winnipeg Tribune, December 3:12.

———. 1935. "Winnipegs Shatter Lengthy Eastern Rugby Reign." Winnipeg Tribune, December 9:14,18.

Allen, W.G. 1933. "Snapshots on Sport." Winnipeg Tribune, November 4:25.

———. 1933. "Snapshots on Sport." Winnipeg Tribune, November 11:31.

———. 1933. "Snapshots on Sport." Winnipeg Tribune, December 2:24.

———. 1934. "Snapshots on Sport." Winnipeg Tribune, November 3:25.

———. 1935. "Snapshots on Sport." Winnipeg Tribune, September 27:16.

———. 1935. "Snapshots on Sport." Winnipeg Free Press, December 6:13.

———. 1935. "Snapshots on Sport." Winnipeg Free Press, December 10:14.

———. 1935. "Snapshots on Sport." Winnipeg Free Press, November 9:25.

———. 1935. "Snapshots on Sport." Winnipeg Free Press, November 6:15.

———. 1935. "Snapshots on Sport." Winnipeg Free Press, October 5:27-28.

———. 1935. "Snapshots on Sport." Winnipeg Free Press, October 26:25.

———. 1935. "Snapshots on Sport." Winnipeg Free Press, October 30:14.

———. 1937. "Snap Shots on Sport." Winnipeg Free Press, September 1:19.

Amarillo Globe-Times. 1970. "Wes Fry, Former Coach, Succumbs." Amarillo Globe-Times, November 12:15.

American-Israeli Cooperative Enterprise. "The Nuremberg Laws: The Reich Citizenship Law." Jewish Virtual Library. 2021. Accessed September 28, 2021. https://www.jewishvirtuallibrary.org/the-reich-citizenship-law

Ancestry.com. 1910 United States Federal Census. Lehi: Ancestry.com Operations Inc., 2006.

———.. 1900 United States Federal Census. Provo: Ancestry.com Operations Inc., 2004

———.. 1910 United States Federal Census. Lehi: Ancestry.com Operations Inc., 2006

———.. 1920 United States Federal Census. Provo: Ancestry.com Operations, Inc., 2010.

———.. 1930 United States Federal Census. Provo: Ancestry.com Operations, Inc., 2002.

Bibliography

———.. 1940 United States Federal Census. Provo: Ancestry.com Operations Inc., 2012

———.. Minnesota, Birth Index, 1900-1934. Provo: Ancestry.com Operations Inc., 2015

———.. Minnesota, Territorial and State Censuses, 1849-1905. Provo: Ancestry.com Operations Inc., 2007

———.. North Dakota, U.S., Select County Marriage Records, 1872-2017. Lehi: Ancestry.com Operations, Inc., 2016

———.. U.S. WWII Draft Cards Young Men, 1940-1947. Lehi: Ancestry.com Operations Inc., 2010.

———.. U.S., Border Crossings from Canada to U.S., 1895-1960. Lehi: Ancestry.com Operations, Inc., 2010.

———.. U.S., Department of Veteran Affairs BIRLS Death File, 1850-2010. Provo: Ancestry.com Operations, Inc. 2011.

———.. U.S., School Yearbooks, 1900-1999. Provo: Ancestry.com Operations Inc., 2010.

Aquin. 1934. "Vikings Defeat Tommies 2 to 0." Aquin, October 5:1.

Armstrong, Edward A. 1933. "A Few Punts on 'Pegs-Argo Game." Winnipeg Free Press, December 4:2.

———. 1933. "Overlooking the Local Rugby Situation." Winnipeg Tribune, December 9:29-30.

———.. 1933. "'Pegs Impressive in Defeat." Winnipeg Free Press, December 4:1.

———. 1934. "In the Realm of Sport." Winnipeg Free Press, May 9:16.

———. 1934. "In the Realm of Sport." Winnipeg Free Press, October 6:23.

———. 1934. "In the Realm of Sport." Winnipeg Free Press, November 16:16.

———. 1934. "In the Realm of Sport." Winnipeg Free Press, November 21:15-16.

———. 1934. "In the Realm of Sport." Winnipeg Free Press, November 22:18.

———. 1934. "In the Realm of Sport." Winnipeg Free Press, February 21:16.

———. 1934. "Winnipeg Downed by N. Dakota 13 to 3." Winnipeg Free Press, September 22:23.

———. 1935. "Assumption Game Serves Purpose; Bewilders Scouts." Winnipeg Free Press, December 4:10.

———. 1935. "Hanson's Name Is Toast of East after Brilliant Performance of Saturday." Winnipeg Free Press, December 9:12.

———. 1935. "In the Realm of Sport." Winnipeg Free Press, January 9:12.

———. 1935. "In the Realm of Sport." Winnipeg Free Press, September 21:25.

———. 1935. "In the Realm of Sport." Winnipeg Free Press, September 30:14.

———. 1935. "In the Realm of Sport." Winnipeg Free Press, September 26:14.

———. 1935. "In the Realm of Sport." Winnipeg Free Press, September 27:16.

———. 1935. "In the Realm of Sport." Winnipeg Free Press, October 18:18.

———. 1935. "In the Realm of Sport." Winnipeg Free Press, October 29:14.

———. 1935. "In the Realm of Sport." Winnipeg Free Press, October 30:14.

———. 1935. "In the Realm of Sport." Winnipeg Free Press, November 11:6.

———. 1935. "In the Realm of Sport." Winnipeg Free Press, November 9:25.

———. 1935. "In the Realm of Sport." Winnipeg Free Press, November 6:14.

———. 1935. "In the Realm of Sport." Winnipeg Free Press, November 27:14.

———. 1935. "'Pegs Plan to 'Get Jump' on Hamilton at Start." Winnipeg Free Press, December 7:1.

———. 1935. "'Pegs Score Seventh Straight Win—Sarnia Imperials Bump Balmy Beach." Winnipeg Free Press, October 25:16.

———. 1935. "Renewed Enthusiasm in Camp Following Two Stiff Practices." Winnipeg Free Press, December 6:13.

———. 1935. "Western Rugby Champs Speed East Hopeful of Winning Dominion Title." Winnipeg Free Press, November 29:16.

———. 1935. "Winnipeg Rugby Club Scores 13-6 Victory over Regina Roughriders; Calgary Next." Winnipeg Free Press, November 4:1,14.

———. 1935. "Winnipegs Leave for East Wednesday--Ottawa Branch Precipitates Furore." Winnipeg Free Press, November 22:16.

Asheville Citizen-Times. 1970. "S.G. Backman, Soldier and Educator, Dies." Asheville Citizen-Times, March 27:20.

Ashley, James D. 1934. "Augustana Beaten 26 to 6 by Concordia College." Daily Argus-Leader, November 3:11.

Augustana Mirror. 1934. "Cobblers Pass 26-6 Victory over Vikings." Augustana Mirror, November 23:4.

———. 1934. "Cobblers, Vikings to Meet in Inter-Conference Tilt." Augustana Mirror, October 31:4.

Barr, A.F. "Biddy". 1932. "Canadian Forward Pass Is Still in Infancy." Winnipeg Tribune, November 11:13.

Barton, George A. 1927. "Watching the Sport Show Through the Referee's Eyes." Minneapolis Sunday Tribune, October 23:38.

———. 1934. "Gophers Crush North Dakota State, 56-12." Minneapolis Tribune, September 30:20.

———. 1934. "Sportographs." Minneapolis Tribune, November 9:28.

Batesel, Paul. "Luther Seminary/St. Paul-Luther College." LostColleges.com. N.D. Accessed September 28, 2021. https://www.lostcolleges.com/luther-seminary

Batte, James. 1925. "Boys' Basketball: 1924-1925." In The Northern Light, 56.

Baumgartner, Stan. 1933. "Just a Moment." Philadelphia Inquirer, October 24:16.

Becker, John Emil. "The History of the Minnesota Intercollegiate Athletic Conference, 1920-1970." PhD diss. The Ohio State University, 1971. Pages 49-50.

Beebe, Bob. 1931. "Buffalo Upsets Moorhead in State Cage Feature." Minneapolis Tribune, March 27:22.

———. 1934. "Concordia Noses Out Macalester in Mud Battle, 13-12." Minneapolis Tribune, October 21:16.

Beitsch, Rebecca. "In 1930, UND changed nicknames quietly." Bismarck Tribune. March 14, 2011. Accessed July 21, 2021. https://bismarcktribune.com/news/local/in-1930-und-changed-nicknames-quietly/article_8bc121f0-4e70-11e0-a2ff-001cc4c03286.html

Bessemer Herald. 1932. "Gotta Gets Frosh Grid Award at State." Bessemer Herald, December 2:5.

Bismarck Tribune. 1929. "Moorhead Eleven Laments Loss of Regular Linemen." Bismarck Tribune, August 30:12.

———.. 1931. "Bismarck, Fargo Each Qualify 4 in Meet Semi-Finals." Bismarck Tribune, May 9:1,7.

———.. 1931. "Bison Yearlings Turn Back Nodak Freshmen 26 to 6." Bismarck Tribune, November 7:28.

———.. 1931. "Stubborn Cobbers Defeated by Bison at Fargo, 19 to 0." Bismarck Tribune, September 19:28.

———.. 1931. "University Frosh Beaten by Rivals." Bismarck Tribune, October 17:17.

———.. 1931. "One Record Falls in Qualifying Rounds of Annual May Festival." Bismarck Tribune, May 9:10.

———.. 1932. "29 Bison Grid Stars Leave for Brookings." Bismarck Tribune, October 7:19.

———.. 1932. "Bison and Nodaks Win Opening Games." Bismarck Tribune, September 24:11.

———.. 1932. "Bison Football Team Scores 7 to 6 Victory Over Nodak Machine." Bismarck Tribune, October 24:11.

———. 1932. "Bison Loom as Threat in North Central after Beating Rabbits 12-6." Bismarck Tribune, October 10:11.

———.. 1932. "Bison Preparing for Jackrabbits." Bismarck Tribune, October 3:7.

———. 1932. "Bison Score Brilliant 27 to 7 Gridiron Victory over Oklahoma City U." Bismarck Tribune, October 15:12.

———. 1932. "Bison to Battle South Dakota State." Bismarck Tribune, October 7:19.

———.. 1932. "Bison Will Have Speed Merchant." Bismarck Tribune, September 17:12.

———.. 1932. "Bison Work Satisfactory As Nodak Go Approaches." Bismarck Tribune, October 19:6.

———.. 1932. "Census of Bison Grid Stars Shows Various Occupations." Bismarck Tribune, July 28:16.

———.. 1932. "Expect Big Year for Bison Grid Captain." Bismarck Tribune, September 15:10.

———. 1932. "George Washington Trounces North Dakota State 20-0." Bismarck Tribune, November 5:16.

———. 1932. "N.D.A.C. Gridiron Squad Will Leave Tonight for East." Bismarck Tribune, November 1:16.

———.. 1932. "Optimism Prevails at Camp of Nodaks." Bismarck Tribune, October 19:6.

352

Bibliography

———. 1932. "Prospects Bright for Strong Bison Football Machine." Bismarck Tribune, September 30:16.

———. 1932. "West Will Take No Chance on Further Injury to Regulars." Bismarck Tribune, October 20:15.

———. 1933. "Bison and Nodaks Battle to 7-7 Tie in Traditional Tilt." Bismarck Tribune, October 30:12.

———. 1933. "Bison Land Second Place in North Central Loop by Crushing Coyotes." Bismarck Tribune, November 13:12.

———. 1933. "Bison Slight Favorites to Defeat Nodaks Saturday." Bismarck Tribune, October 25:11.

———. 1933. "Bison, Seeking Second Place in Conference, Leave for Vermillion." Bismarck Tribune, November 9:20.

———. 1933. "Cobbers, Johnnies Fight Over Officials." Bismarck Tribune, November 3:16.

———. 1933. "Court Champions of North Central Conference." Bismarck Tribune, March 14:6.

———. 1933. "Dakotans Mentioned." Bismarck Tribune, December 2:15.

———. 1933. "Former Cobber Star Will Coach Nodaks." Bismarck Tribune, April 14:11.

———. 1933. "Hanson Leads North Dakota State Bison to 7-0 Win over Morningside." Bismarck Tribune, October 9:11.

———. 1933. "Nodaks Await Bison with Lineup Riddled by Injuries." Bismarck Tribune, October 27:15.

———. 1933. "Nodaks Will Get Plenty of Rest Before Tilt with Bison Saturday." Bismarck Tribune, October 25:11.

———. 1933. "Nodaks Will Outweigh Bison Tuesday." Bismarck Tribune, May 20:11.

———. 1933. "North Dakota State and Concordia Elevens Battle to Scoreiess Tie." September 23:12.

———. 1933. "North Dakota State and St. Thomas Elevens Battle in 7 to 7 Deadlock." Bismarck Tribune, September 30:12.

———. 1933. "Oklahoma City's Goldbugs Defeat Bison by 19 to 0." Bismarck Tribune, November 19:6.

———. 1933. "'Red' Grange Will Be Minot Fair Attraction." Bismarck Tribune, June 14:11.

———. 1933. "Three Jamestown Men Honored on Coaches' All-State Grid Eleven." Bismarck Tribune, December 12:14.

———. 1933. "Underdog Bison Hope for Victory Despite South Dakota State Jinx." Bismarck Tribune, October 14:12.

———. 1934. "Big Ten Favorites Ready for Bison." Bismarck Tribune, September 29:31.

———. 1934. "Bison Candidates Get Initial Workout." Bismarck Tribune, September 6:6.

———. 1934. "Bison Down Sioux, 7-0, at Homecoming." Bismarck Tribune, October 29.

———. 1934. "Bison Triumph over Cobbers, 6-0, to Open Fall Campaign." Bismarck Tribune, September 22:12.

———. 1934. "Cobbers, Gusties Will Battle for Loop Title." Bismarck Tribune, November 5:12.

———. 1934. "Gophers Set for Game with Bison." Bismarck Tribune, September 27:16.

———. 1934. "KFYR to Broadcast Bison-Rabbit Game." Bismarck Tribune, November 3:4.

———. 1934. "Minot Teachers Defeat Manitoba." Bismarck Tribune, November 3:16.

———. 1934. "Only Three Lettermen Missing As Bison Call Roll." Bismarck Tribune, August 31:7.

———. 1934. "St. Mary's of Bismarck Third in Central North Dakota Track Meet." Bismarck Tribune, April 23:11.

———. 1935. "Fibs, Facts, and Fancies." Bismarck Tribune, September 21:5.

———. 1935. "Fibs, Facts, and Fancies." Bismarck Tribune, September 28:6.

———. 1958. "Veteran NDAC Coach Casey Finnegan Dies." Bismarck Tribune, December 29:14.

———. 1991. "Thomas Kasper." Bismarck Tribune, December 30:9.

Bison Illustrated. "History Lesson from Henry L. Bolley." Bison Illustrated, September 3, 2014. Accessed May 11, 2021. https://www.bisonillustrated.com/history-lesson-henry-l-bolley/

Blanchard, Don. 1965. "Twinkle Toes' Liked Playing 60 Minutes." Winnipeg Free Press, September 18:62.

Board of Regents of the University of Wisconsin System. "Russ Rebholz." UW Athletic Hall of Fame. 2021. Accessed May 28, 2021. https://uwbadgers.com/honors/uw-athletic-hall-of-fame/russ-rebholz/182

———. "Greg Kabat." UW Athletic Hall of Fame. 2021. Accessed June 19, 2021. https://uwbadgers.com/honors/uw-athletic-hall-of-fame/greg-kabat/112

———. "Ted Whereatt." UW Athletic Hall of Fame. 2021. Accessed July 16, 2021. https://www.uwsuper.edu/alumni/halloffame/ted-whereatt_hof541565

———. "Howard Buck." UW Athletic Hall of Fame. 2021. Accessed June 22, 2021.

Board of Regents of the University of Wisconsin System. UW Athletic Hall of Fame. 2021. Accessed December 9, 2021. https://uwbadgers.com/honors/uw-athletic-hall-of-fame

Boston Globe. 1933. "Bone Crushers Victors over Medford A.A., 14-0." Boston Globe, November 27:8.

———. 1933. "Two Games for Lowell Fans." Boston Globe, October 14:7.

———. 1977. "Robert McCoy, 71." Boston Globe, March 10:20.

———. 1933. "Big Shakeup Reported in Pere Marquettes." Boston Globe, October 10:22.

Brainerd Daily Dispatch. "Perpich, Range Star, to Winnipeg for Cage, Rugby." Brainerd Daily Dispatch, August 12:7.

———. 1930. "Brainerd, C.-I., Staples, Wadena, Play Here Tonight: Advocates Competitive Bidding for Athletes." Brainerd Daily Dispatch, March 7:5.

———. 1931. "Warriors Defeat Rangers; Become District Champs." Brainerd Daily Dispatch, March 17:4.

———. 1931. [No Heading]. Brainerd Daily Dispatch, March 12:1.

———. 1933. "Perpich Leads Team Scoring in Rough Contest." Brainerd Daily Dispatch, December 21:11.

Brand, Werner. 1933. "Coach Cleve Issues Call for Spring Football." Concordian, March 24:3.

Brandon Daily Sun. 1935. "Changes Urged in Rugby Code for the Year." Brandon Daily Sun, February 23:16.

———. 1935. "Eastern Rugby Teams Already Making Overtures to Stars on Winnipegs Champion Squad." Brandon Daily Sun, December 9:4.

———. 1935. "Rugby Radio." Brandon Daily Sun, November 8:4.

———. 1935. "Will Broadcast Final Rugby Game between Tigers and Winnipegs." Brandon Daily Sun, December 6:3.

———. 1935. "Winnipeg Rugby Squad Defeated Regina 'Riders." Brandon Daily Sun, November 4:4.

———. 1935. "Winnipegs Have Trouble Beating Calgary Bronks." Brandon Daily Sun, November 11:3.

———. 1935. "Winnipegs Start Rugby Season in Winning Form." Brandon Daily Sun, September 16:3.

Bridgeport Telegram. 1954. "Col. Ralph Sasse Dies." Bridgeport Telegram, October 17:21.

Britannica, T. Editors of Encyclopaedia. "Pop Warner." Encyclopedia Britannica, September 3, 2021. https://www.britannica.com/biography/Pop-Warner.

Britz, Kevin. "Of Football and Frontiers: The Meaning of Bronko Nagurski." Journal of Sports History. University of Illinois Press. Vol. 20, No. 2 (Summer 1993), p. 103.

Brooke, George H. 1906. "How to Play Football under the New Rules." New York Daily Tribune, September 23:8.

Brown University Library. Remembering Brown Sports: Items from the Edward North Robinson Collection of Brown Athletics. 2002. Accessed July 15, 2021. https://library.brown.edu/exhibits/archive/sports/between_printable.html

Brown, Denny. 1935. "Rambling over the Dial." Winnipeg Tribune, September 14:27.

Burrell, Jackie and Marcus Thompson II. 2004. "St. Mary's Dissolves Football Program." Contra Costa Times, March 4.

Buss, Johnny and Ralph Allen. 1934. "Hamilton Tigers Lining Up Powerful Rugby Squad." Winnipeg Tribune, June 8:11.

Buss, Johnny. 1931. "St. John's Blank 'Pegs 2-0 on Greasy Gridiron." Winnipeg Tribune, September 21:14.

———. 1931. "St. John's Stage Last Quarter Rally to Down Varsity." Winnipeg Tribune, October 5:15.

———. 1932. "An Earful with Johnny Buss." Winnipeg Tribune, November 11:13.

———. 1932. "An Earful with Johnny Buss." Winnipeg Tribune, November 7:17.

———. 1932. "Garrison Rugby Team Drops Opening Game, 26 to 6." Winnipeg Tribune, September 26:12.

———. 1932. "St. John's Extended to Avert Defeat against Winnipegs." Winnipeg Tribune, October 17:18.

———. 1932. "St. John's Retain Manitoba Rugby Championship." Winnipeg Tribune, October 20:16.

———. 1933. "An Earful with Johnny Buss." Winnipeg Tribune, November 13:15.

———. 1934. "Injuries Mar Winnipegs' Defeat by North Dakota 'U'." Winnipeg Tribune, September 22:20.

Bibliography

———. 1934. "One Man's Opinion." Winnipeg Tribune, November 2:19.
———. 1934. "One Man's Opinion." Winnipeg Tribune, August 29:11.
———. 1934. "One Man's Opinion." Winnipeg Tribune, November 3:19.
———. 1934. "One Man's Opinion." Winnipeg Tribune, October 1:11.
———. 1934. "One Man's Opinion." Winnipeg Tribune, October 8:11.
———. 1934. "One Man's Opinion." Winnipeg Tribune, October 15:13.
———. 1934. "One Man's Opinion." Winnipeg Tribune, October 22:5.
———. 1934. "One Man's Opinion." Winnipeg Tribune, September 17:14.
———. 1935. "One Man's Opinion." Winnipeg Tribune, September 19:13.
———. 1935. "One Man's Opinion." Winnipeg Tribune, April 25:11.
———. 1935. "One Man's Opinion." Winnipeg Tribune, August 9:11.
———. 1935. "One Man's Opinion." Winnipeg Tribune, December 7:28.
———. 1935. "One Man's Opinion." Winnipeg Tribune, December 28:26.
———. 1935. "One Man's Opinion." Winnipeg Tribune, November 5:15.
———. 1935. "One Man's Opinion." Winnipeg Tribune, November 1:14.
———. 1935. "Referee's Decision Led to 'Pegs Lone Touchdown." Winnipeg Tribune, November 11:12.
———. 1936. "An Earful." Winnipeg Evening Tribune, September 9:6.
Calgary Herald. 1929. "Ruling Given by Officials on New Play." Calgary Herald, September 28:6.
———. 1930. "Two Trophies Won Outright in Marathon." Calgary Herald, December 8:8.
———. 1933. "Juniors Will Test Senior Club." Calgary Herald, September 12:7.
———. 1934. "Confident 'Riders." Calgary Herald, November 9:7.
———. 1934. "West Given Grid Final Next Season." Calgary Herald, February 26:7.
———. 1935. "Senior Altomah Rugby Club Will Meet Tomorrow." Calgary Herald, January 19:6.
———. 1965. "Football Was Fun in Marquardt's Era." Calgary Herald, November 30:18.
Callan. 1934. "Meraloma Nemesis." Vancouver Sun, November 12:12.
Cameron Sun. 1963. "'Twas Forty Years Ago." Cameron Sun, December 3:6.
———. 1967. "Noted Coach Dies in Home Here." Cameron Sun, February 23:1.
Cameron, Linda A. "For Minnesota Farmers, the Roaring Twenties Were Anything But." MinnPost, January 8, 2018. Accessed March 6, 2020. https://www.minnpost.com/mnopedia/2018/01/minnesota-farmers-roaring-twenties-were-anything/
Campus. 1932. "Bugs Receive 27-7 Defeat at Fargo." Campus, October 21:4.
———. 1933. "Football Schedule." Campus, November 17:4.
———. 1934. "Bugs Outplay Bison but Go Down, 13 to 8." Campus, November 28:4.
———. 1934. "Fargo Express.'" Campus November 16:4.
———. 1934. "North Dakota's Bison Battle Hard-Pressed Bugs Here Today." Campus, November 16:4.
Canada's Sports Hall of Fame. "Eddie James." Canada's Sports Hall of Fame. 2021. Accessed May 27, 2021. https://www.sportshall.ca/hall-of-famers/hall-of-famers-search.html?proID=210&lang=EN
———. "Fritz Hanson." Canada's Sports Hall of Fame. 2021. Accessed October 26, 2021. https://www.sportshall.ca/hall-of-famers/hall-of-famers-search.html?proID=226&catID=all&lang=EN
Canadian Football Hall of Fame. "Brian Timmis." Class of 1963. 2020. Accessed October 7, 2021. https://cfhof.ca/members/brian-timmis/
———. "Grey Cup Winners." Canadian Football Hall of Fame. 2021. Accessed May 26, 2021. https://cfhof.ca/grey-cup-winners/

———. "Melvin 'Fritz' Hanson." Class of 1963. 2021. Accessed October 26, 2021. https://cfhof.ca/members/melvin-fritz-hanson/
———. "Michael J. Rodden." Class of 1964. 2021. Accessed August 29, 2021. https://cfhof.ca/members/michael-j-rodden/
———. Grey Cup Winners. 2020. Accessed July 26, 2021. https://cfhof.ca/grey-cup-winners/
Canadian Football Review. 1951. "Hanson... Hall of Fame Candidate." Canadian Football Review, pages 21-22.
Canadian Pacific Broadcasts. The Band of Princess Patricia's Canadian Light Infantry. Archive.org. Accessed August 6, 2021. https://ia903107.us.archive.org/7/items/162037415823/162037415823.pdf
Canadian Press. "Professor Discovers Piece of Sports History in Storage Room." Archive.org. 2009. Accessed September 20, 2021. https://web.archive.org/web/20090323143313/http://www.tsn.ca:80/cis/story/?id=253731
———. 1933. "Toronto, Montreal to Have Pro Rugby Football this Fall."
Hamilton Spectator. 2018. "Past Winners Have Been…" Hamilton Spectator, December 28.
Carroll, Dink. 1938. "Football Town." Maclean's, October 15:19,45.
Carroll, J. M. "Red Grange." Encyclopedia Britannica, June 9, 2021. https://www.britannica.com/biography/Red-Grange.
Carter, Adam. "Resurgent Royal Connaught Proving Downtown Hamilton's Comeback Is Real." CBC Radio Canada. January 22, 2018. Accessed October 8, 2021. https://www.cbc.ca/news/canada/hamilton/royal-connaught-1.4498366
Cedar Rapids Gazette. 1945. "Jack West Resigns as North Dakota U. Athletic Director." Cedar Rapids Gazette, November 25:29.
Cederberg, Ernest. 1933. "Cobbers Drop Final Game Before Mighty Ole Eleven." The Concordian, November 24:3.
———. 1933. "Gustavus, Concordia Play Scoreless Gridiron Battle." Concordian, October 20:3.
Celizic, Mike. 1992. "Notre Dame Loses a Friend." Record, December 13:145.
CFL Enterprises LP. "Bud Marquardt." Winnipeg Football Club Hall of Fame. 2021. Accessed October 26, 2021. https://www.bluebombers.com/2017/04/10/bud-marquardt/
———. "Fritz Hanson." Winnipeg Football Club Hall of Fame. 2021. Accessed October 26, 2021. https://www.bluebombers.com/2018/09/18/ring-honour-inductee-fritz-hanson/
———. "Herb Peschel." Winnipeg Football Club Hall of Fame. 2021. Accessed October 26, 2021. https://www.bluebombers.com/2017/04/25/herb-peschel/
———. "Leland 'Tote' Mitchell." Winnipeg Blue Bombers. 2021. Accessed October 25, 2021. https://www.bluebombers.com/leland-tote-mitchell/
———. 11 Sips from the Cup. Winnipeg Blue Bombers. Accessed April 5, 2021. https://www.bluebombers.com/grey-cups/
CFL.CA Staff. "1931 - Montreal Winged Wheelers 22, Regina Roughriders 0." Canadian Football League, 2021. Accessed May 28, 2021. https://www.cfl.ca/2005/10/05/grey_cup_memories__1931/
———. "1934 - Sarnia Imperials 20, Regina Roughriders 12." Grey Cup Memories. October 8, 2005. Accessed September 14, 2021. https://www.cfl.ca/2005/10/08/grey_cup_memories__1934/
CFLapedia. "Lou Mogul." The Encyclopedia of CFL History. 2021. Accessed October 12, 2021. https://www.cflapedia.com/Players/m/mogul_lou.htm
CFLdb. "Winnipeg Victorias." CFLdb Statistics. 2021. Accessed September 30, 2021. https://stats.cfldb.ca/team/winnipeg-victorias/
Charlotte Observer. 1917. "Dakotans Swamped Fifty-Eighth, 45 to 0." Charlotte Observer, November 15:11.
Cherney, Bruce. 2007. "Cross-border football rivalry--Shamrocks played University of North Dakota in 1903." November 2. Accessed March 12, 2020. https://www.winnipegrealestatenews.com/publications/real-estate-news/727
Chicago Tribune. 1931. "Capt. Backman to Coach South Dakota Grid Squad." Chicago Tribune, March 8:30.

354

Bibliography

———. 1967. "Ex-Grange Teammate, Green, Dies." Chicago Tribune, May 13:54.

Chippewa Herald-Telegram. 1933. "Minnesota U All-Stars Battle Chippewa Marines Here Sunday." Chippewa Herald-Telegram, September 19:7.

———. 1935. "Chippewa Marines Rout Haycraft's All-Stars 39 to 0." Chippewa Herald-Telegram, September 23:5.

———. 1935. "Expect Large Crowd at Marines and All-Stars Battle Here on Sunday." Chippewa Herald-Telegram, September 21:1.

Club de hockey Canadien, Inc. Jos Cattarinich (1909-1910). Our History. 2008. Accessed June 18, 2021. http://ourhistory.canadiens.com/gm/Jos-Cattarinich

Coe College. "Homecoming." Coe College: The First Hundred Years. 2006. Accessed May 19, 2021. http://www.public.coe.edu/historyweb/athletics_traditions_and_rivalries_homecoming.htm

Coleman, Jim. 1975. "Jim Coleman." Medicine Hat News, August 22:9.

———. 1979. "Joe 'Tiger' Ryan: End of line for Blue Bombers and Als founder." Ottawa Citizen, June 8:26.

———. 1994. "Imports pay duty: Americans have 63 years of starring history in Canadian game." The Province, November 27:67

———. 1996. "Facts & Arguments: Lives Lived." Globe and Mail, April 12.

Colgate University Athletics. Leonard D. Macaluso. Hall of Honor. 2021. Accessed July 14, 2021. https://gocolgateraiders.com/honors/hall-of-honor/leonard-d-macaluso/42

Collegian Reporter. 1933. "M.S. Gridders Bow to North Dakota State." Collegian Reporters, October 11:3.

———. 1934. "Maroons Hopeful for Win over Bison." Collegian Reporter, October 19:3.

Collyer's Eye and the Baseball World. 1932. "Professional Rugby Expected to Oust Amateur Game for Montreal." Collyer's Eye and the Baseball World, December 17:8.

———. 1934. "Canadian Notes." Collyer's Eye & Baseball World, September 29:5.

Concordia College Archives. "Frank Cleve (b. 1899 - d. 1970)." Concordia Memory Project, accessed July 9, 2020. http://concordiamemoryproject.concordiacollegearchives.org/exhibits/show/concordia-greats/athletics/frank-cleve

———. 2017. "Pioneering the Pigskin:' The Founders of Concordia Football. November. Accessed February 5, 2020. http://concordiacollegearchives.weebly.com/pioneering-the-pigskin-the-founders-of-concordia-football.html.

Concordia College. "Frank Cleve." Cobber. Moorhead: Concordia College, 1935. Page 176.

———. "Robert F. Fritz." Concordia College Athletic Hall of Fame. Moorhead: Concordia College, October 17, 1987.

———. "Stand Up and Cheer." Lyrics. 2020. Accessed July 13, 2021. https://www.concordiacollege.edu/alumni/homecoming/lyrics/

———. "The Championship Campaign." In Cobber, 189-192. Moorhead: Concordia College, 1932.

———. Concordia College Athletic Hall of Fame: Frank I. Cleve. Moorhead, Minnesota: Concordia College, 1989.

———. Concordia College Athletic Hall of Fame: Robert F. Fritz. Moorhead, Minnesota: Concordia College, 1987.

Concordia Memory Project. "Frank Cleve (b. 1899 - d. 1970)." Concordia Memory Project. Accessed July 9, 2020. http://concordiamemoryproject.concordiacollegearchives.org/exhibits/show/concordia-greats/athletics/frank-cleve

Concordian. 1929. "Our Faculty One by One." Concordian, March 15:2.

———. 1929. "Our Faculty One by One." Concordian, March 15:2.

———. 1929. "Our Faculty One by One." Concordian, March 15:2.

———. 1929. "Cleve's Men Prepare for Bison Go Sept. 28th." Concordian, September 19:3

———. 1929. "Cobber Frosh Make 20 First Downs to Trim Morris Aggies." Concordian, November 7:3.

———. 1929. "First Year Rule Goes Into Effect." Concordian, September 19:3.

———. 1929. "Frosh Drive Hard to Beat Moorhead Team." Concordian, October 26:5.

———. 1931. "1931 Champions." Concordian, November 20:2.

———. 1931. "Aggies Win Opener from Concordia 19-0." The Concordian, September 25: 3.

———. 1931. "Bit of Action at Macalester." The Concordian, October 16: 3.

———. 1931. "Champs Lose First Conference Battle." Concordian, December 4: 3.

———. 1931. "Clevemen Receive All-Conference Recognition." Concordian, December 4: 3.

———. 1931. "Cobbers and Dragons Battle to Scoreless Tie in Grid Contest." Concordian, October 30: 5.

———. 1931. "Cobbers Defeat Tommies to Win State Grid Title." Concordian, November 20: 1.

———. 1931. "Cobbers Primed for Fire of Starting Gun in State Title Race." Concordian, October 9:3.

———. 1931. "Cobbers Romp Over Hibbing Junior College 26-6." The Concordian, October 9: 3.

———. 1931. "Cobbers Stay on Top by Drubbing Johnnies 29-0." Concordian, November 6: 3.

———. 1931. "Cobbers Stay on Top by Drubbing Johnnies 29-0." Concordian, November 6: 3.

———. 1931. "Cobbers-Gusties to Scrap in High School Gym." Concordian, January 16:3.

———. 1931. "Concordia Crushes Gustavus with Powerful Attack, 41-6." Concordian, November 20:3.

———. 1931. "Concordia Lettermen Hold Annual Reunion During Homecoming" Concordian, November 6: 3.

———. 1931. "Concordia Shows Power in First Loop Game." The Concordian, October 16: 3.

———. 1931. "Football Champions Receive Much Praise at Chapel Exercises." Concordian, November 20:1.

———. 1931. "Cobber Football Schedule." Concordian, September 25:3.

———. 1932. "Clevemen Meet Tommies in Homecoming Contest." Concordian, October 22:5.

———. 1932. "Clevemen Open State Race against Oles Tomorrow." Concordian, October 7:3.

———. 1932. "Clevemen Open State Race against Oles Tomorrow." Concordian, October 7:3.

———. 1932. "Coach Cleve Issues Call for Spring Football." Concordian, April 1:3.

———. 1932. "Cobbers Battle Champs to Scoreless Deadlock." The Concordian, November 4: 3.

———. 1932. "Cobbers Smash Way to 20-6 Conquest of Peds." Concordian, October 7:3.

———. 1932. "Cobs Fight Gusties to Scoreless Tie in Last Game." The Concordian, November 18: 3.

———. 1932. "Concordia Wins From Ole Squad by 13 to 7 Score." Concordian, October 22:5.

———. 1932. "Conference Coaches and Directors Meet." Concordian, April 1:3.

———. 1932. "Figenshaw, Fritz Are Placed on All-State Eleven." The Concordian, December 2: 3.

———. 1932. "Figenshaw, Fritz Named All-State." The Concordian, November 18: 3.

———. 1932. "Gridmen Show Promise of Another Tough Squad." Concordian, April 15:3.

———. 1932. "Powerful Team Promised as Squad Breaks Camp." Concordian, April 29:3.

———. 1932. "Tommies Beat Cobbers; Smash Hopes for Title." The Concordian, November 4:3.

———. 1933. "Bison Speedster." Concordian, September 22:3.

———. 1933. "Canadian Team Defeats Cobbers in Rugby-Football." Concordian, October 28:5.

———. 1933. "Cleve and Sattre Attend Meetings." Concordian, April 7:3.

———. 1933. "Cobbers to Meet St. Mary's Team." Concordian, October 28:5.

———. 1933. "Cobs Beat Johnnies, Lose to St. Mary's Eleven: St. John's Cuts Sport Relations with Concordia." Concordian, November 10:3.

———. 1933. "Cobs Clash with Johnnies in Homecoming Tilt." Concordian, October 28:5.

———. 1933. "Concordia Will Engage Winnipeg Team in Rugby-Football Saturday." Concordian, October 20:8.

———. 1933. "Depleted Cob Squad Faces Oles in Finale." Concordian, November 10:3.

———. 1933. "Freshmen Here Receive Three Day Orientation." The Concordian, September 22:1.

———. 1933. "Fritz to Have Chance for Place on Fourth All-Conference Team." Concordian, December 8:3.

———. 1933. "Gustavus Takes Conference Title." Concordian, November 24:3.

355

Bibliography

———. 1933. "Powerful Team Promised As Squad Breaks Camp." Concordian, May 6:3.

———. 1933. "Prizes Awarded to Football Men." The Concordian, May 29: 3.

———. 1933. "Snow Brings Halt to Spring Football Practice." Concordian, April 7:3.

———. 1933. "Ten Seniors Play Last Home Game." Concordian, October 28:5.

———. 1934. "1934 All Conference Teams." Concordian, November 23:3.

———. 1934. "Bison Get Edge on Cobbers with 6 to 0 Victory." Concordian, September 28:3.

———. 1934. "Clevemen Meet Oles in First Conference Game." Concordian, October 12:3.

———. 1934. "Cob Field Is Left Lonely This Year." Concordian, September 21:3.

———. 1934. "Cobber Gridders to Don New Uniforms." Concordian, September 21:3.

———. 1934. "Cobber Statistics." Concordian, November 2:3.

———. 1934. "Cobbers and Dragons Fight to 13 to 13 Deadlock on Ped Field." Concordian, October 5:3.

———. 1934. "Cobbers Begin Season against Bison on Friday." Concordian, September 14:8.

———. 1934. "Cobbers Down Gusties to Win State Title: Clevemen Take Championship of State Conference." Concordian, November 10:1,4.

———. 1934. "Cobbers Lead Conference with Grid Victory: Cobbers Are Tied with St. John's for First Place." Concordian, November 2:3.

———. 1934. "Cobbers Meet Augustana College in Game Tonight." Concordian, November 2:3.

———. 1934. "Cobbers Meet Redmen in Homecoming Game." Concordian, October 27:5.

———. 1934. "Cobbers Open Season in Tilt with Bison Tonight." Concordian, September 21:3.

———. 1934. "Cobbers Score 13 to 12 Victory Over Macalester." Concordian, October 27:5.

———. 1934. "Cobbers Score 26 to 6 Victory over Augustana." Concordian, November 10:3.

———. 1934. "Cobs Go North to Play Two Games at Winnipeg." Concordian, October 5:3.

———. 1934. "Cobs, Dragons Tangle for City Title Saturday." Concordian, September 28:3.

———. 1934. "Conference Doings." Concordian, November 2:3.

———. 1934. "Conference Doings." Concordian, November 10:9.

———. 1934. "Conference Doings." Concordian, October 27:5.

———. 1934. "Conference Doings." Concordian, October 5:3.

———. 1934. "Conference Doings." Concordian, October 5:3.

———. 1934. "Conference Doings." Concordian, September 14:8.

———. 1934. "Conference Doings." Concordian, September 21:3.

———. 1934. "Conference Doings." Concordian, September 28:3.

———. 1934. "Enrollment Is Maintained at Last Year's Level as 44th Year Opens: Orientation Program Is Given for Freshman Before Start of School." Concordian, September 14:1.

———. 1934. "Enthusiastic Student Body Honors Team." Concordian, November 16:1.

———. 1934. "Faculty, Students Will Greet 1934 Football Champions at Two Pepfests." Concordian, November 10:1.

———. 1934. "Fritz Mentioned on All-American." Concordian, December 7:1.

———. 1934. "Fritz Places on All State Team." Concordian, November 23:1.

———. 1934. "Game with Gusties Changed to Friday." Concordian, November 2:3.

———. 1934. "Gridders End First Week of Fall Practice." Concordian, September 14:8.

———. 1934. "Kobber Kernels." Concordian, May 11:3.

———. 1934. "Minnesota College Conference." Concordian, November 16:3.

———. 1934. "Ole Midgarden Is Named Captain of 1935 Grid Team." Concordian, November 23:3.

———. 1934. "Roster of 1934 Conference Champions." Concordian, November 10:3.

———. 1934. "Six Seniors Play Last Home Game." Concordian, October 27:5.

———. 1934. "Supporters Send Team to Victory." Concordian, October 27:5.

———. 1935. "Bob Fritz Signs to Play Rugby with Canadians." Concordian, April 12:3.

———. 1935. "Clevemen to Invade Canada in Opener Saturday." Concordian, September 13:3.

———. 1935. "Cobber Grid Squad Is Rounding into Shape." Concordian, May 10:3.

———. 1935. "Cobs Down Auggies in Initial Victory." Concordian, November 1:3.

———. 1935. "Forty Gridders Respond to Call for Fall Practice." Concordian, September 13:3.

———. 1935. "Fritz Considers Offer to Play in Canada." Concordian, March 22:7.

———. 1935. "Kobber Kernels." Concordian, September 13:3.

———. 1935. "Over Two Hundred Alumni Return to Alma Mater for Homecoming." Concordian, November 1:4.

———. 1935. "Students Continue Practice Teaching." Concordian, May 24:4.

———. 1935. "Through the Monocle." Concordian, September 20:2.

Connolly, Bob. 1933. "Spectrum Sport Speculations." Spectrum, November 17:3.

———. 1933. "Spectrum Sport Speculation." Spectrum, September 22:3.

———. 1933. "Spectrum Sport Speculations." Spectrum, September 29:3.

Cornell College. "Alan Gowans." Hall of Fame. 2021. Accessed May 17, 2021. https://www.cornellrams.com/halloffame/ID/16

Cornell University Library. "Arpeako Meat Products." Digital Collections. 2020. Accessed July 12, 2021. https://digital.library.cornell.edu/catalog/ss:19343301

Cosentino, Frank. 1969. Canadian Football: The Grey Cup Years. Toronto: The Musson Book Company Limited, 13-19, 24, 29-30, 35-36, 39, 40, 43, 47-50, 53-57, 59, 61-63, 85-86, 89, 91-92, 94-108.

Courier-Journal. 1994. "Harry Gamage, 94, UK Football Coach from 1927-33, Dies." Courier-Journal, August 24:11.

Crosby-Ironton High School. C-I Athletic Hall of Fame. 2021. Accessed December 9, 2021. https://www.ci-rangers.org/page/3020

Cullum, Dick. 1970. "Dick Cullum." Minneapolis Star Tribune, August 16:40.

Cunnion, Don. 1937. "The Sports Periscope." Post-Star, September 21:10.

Daily Argus-Leader. 1933. "Heavyweight Group in U. Squad Grows." Daily Argus-Leader, September 19:5.

———. 1930. "Former Purdue Athlete to Be Kasper's Aide." Daily Argus-Leader, June 11:9.

———. 1932. "Backs to Be First to Get Attention in Bison Training." Daily Argus-Leader, August 25:10.

———. 1932. "Bison May Show Strength in Tilt with West Point." Daily Argus-Leader, November 10:9.

———. 1932. "Bison Schedule Tough; But Team May Be Greatest." Daily Argus-Leader, January 9:3.

———. 1933. "Coyotes, Rabbits to Attack N.D. Teams." Daily Argus-Leader, October 9:5.

———. 1933. "N.D. Ags Win over Maroons." Daily Argus-Leader, October 8:8.

———. 1933. "North Dakota 'U' Beats Winnipeg." Daily Argus-Leader, September 24:9.

———. 1933. "North Dakota University, Bisons Play Tie Game." Daily Argus-Leader, October 29:9.

———. 1933. "Rabbits Unseat Bisons As Conference Rulers." Daily Argus-Leader, October 15:8.

———. 1933. "State College Coaches Scheme to Crack Strong Defense Shown by North Dakota Ags." Daily Argus-Leader, October 10:9.

———. 1934. "Bison Depending on Stellar Backs to Win N.C. Title." Daily Argus-Leader, October 18:11.

———. 1934. "Concordia Team Here Tonight; Preps Meet Central at Sioux City." Daily Argus-Leader, November 2:13.

———. 1934. "Coyotes to Play North Dakota Ags Tomorrow Night." Daily Argus-Leader, October 11:9.

———. 1934. "Creighton, Iowa Next Foes for State and U." Daily Argus-Leader, September 24:3.

———. 1934. "Dethroned Rabbits Threaten N.D. State's Hold on Lead." Daily Argus-Leader, November 5:9.

———. 1934. "Flickertails Win Conference Opener from South Dakota." Daily Argus-Leader, October 7:9.

———. 1934. "Gamage Revamps S.D. Attack for Bison Tilt." Daily Argus-Leader, October 11:9.

———. 1934. "O'Connor, University Backfield Man, Also Declared Ineligible." Daily Argus-Leader, October 8:3.

356

Bibliography

———. 1934. "Rabbits' Coach Foresees Strong Team If Doubtful Spots Can Be Bolstered." Daily Argus-Leader, August 8:5.

———. 1934. "Rabbits Have Best Lineup Set for Bison." Daily Argus-Leader, November 8:9.

———. 1934. "State College Stops Title-Bound Bison, 38 to 0." Daily Argus-Leader, November 11:9.

———. 1934. "University Defeated 22 to 0 by N.D. State." Daily Argus-Leader, October 13:3.

———. 1971. "Elsewhere." Daily Argus-Leader, February 19:2.

Daily Globe. 1933. "Bessemer Bearcats Hold Get-Together." Daily Globe, August 12:2.

———. 1933. "Bessemer Bearcats Start Grid Drills Next Week." Daily Globe, August 11:7.

———. 1933. "Odanah Indians to Open Grid Season." Daily Globe, September 5:7.

———. 1933. "Wins Purdue Grid Letter." Daily Globe, December 22:10.

———. 1934. "Vincent Yatchak, Gotta Are Declared Ineligible." Daily Globe, October 20:7.

Daily Gopher. "The NFL Draft Exists Because of a Minnesota Football Star." Daily Gopher. April 27, 2017. Accessed December 6, 2021. https://www.thedailygopher.com/2017/4/27/15453054/nfl-draft-minnesota-football-philadelphia-eagles-stan-kostka

Daily Journal. 1963. "What They'll Shoot At." The Daily Journal, May 18:5.

Daily Oklahoman. 1934. "Bugs Stopped by Nodaks in 13 to 8 Game." Daily Oklahoman, November 17:12.

———. 1934. "Bugs Tackle Star Who Scored on Minnesota." Daily Oklahoman, November 13:14.

———. 1965. "Stan Williamson Services Today." Daily Oklahoman, August 19:27.

Daily Plainsman. 1932. "University Gridders Demand Backman's Removal." Daily Plainsman, October 14:9.

Daily Province. 1929. "Forward Pass Will Be Given Trial in West." Daily Province, June 18:10.

Daily Times and Daily Journal-Press 1928. "Results Shown in Spring work of Grid Squad." Daily Times and Daily Journal-Press, April 5:9.

———. 1929. "Football Fans Watch Coming Session at 'U.'" Daily Times and Daily Journal-Press, August 29:17.

———. 1929. "Moorhead to Enter Nat'l Cage Tourney at Chicago." Daily Times and Daily Journal-Press, March 26:10.

———. 1930. "Moorhead Squad Has Few Elders." Daily Times and Daily Journal-Press, September 5:20.

———. 1931. "West High Cops First Place by Less than One Point." Daily Times and Daily Journal-Press, June 8:13.

———. 1932. "Conference to View Games of Week in State." St. Cloud Daily Times and Daily Journal-Press, October 5:13.

———. 1932. "Three Johnnies Are Honored by League Coaches." St. Cloud Daily Times and Daily Journal-Press, November 21:13.

———. 1933. "Bert Oja's Quint Plays at St. Cloud." Daily Times and Daily Journal-Press, January 20:12.

———. 1933. "Concordia Defeats St. Johns to Dim Championship Hopes." Daily Times and Daily Journal-Press, October 30:10.

———. 1933. "Neil of Tech and Neis of Cathedral Place on All-Central State Team." Daily Times and Daily Journal-Press, November 23:16.

———. 1933. "Tech Plays Brilliantly but Loses to Crosby-Ironton by 27-25 Count." Daily Times and Daily Journal-Press, February 18:14.

———. 1933. "St. Cloud Athletic Club Takes Over City Basketball for 1933." Daily Times and Daily Journal-Press, January 11:5.

———. 1934. "Defense Holds Hard Smashing Backs in Check." Daily Times and Daily Journal-Press, October 27:8.

———. 1934. "North Dakota State Wallops Peds--Tech Easy Victor over Little Falls." Daily Times and Daily Journal-Press, December 15:9.

———. 1934. "Peds Defeat Bemidji, 19 to 7 - Cathedral Loses to De La Salle, 7 to 6." Daily Times and Daily Journal-Press, October 15:9.

———. 1934. "Virginia Will Open Schedule on Home Court." Daily Times and Daily Journal-Press, November 10:10.

———. 1934. "St. Cloud Teachers Bow to Stevens Point, 7 to 6, in Opening Contest." Daily Times and Daily Journal-Press, September 24:10.

———. 1934. "St. Johns Presents Snappy Offense to Outplay St. Cloud Peds, 19 to 0." Daily Times and Daily Journal-Press, October 1:12.

———. 1935. "Swamp Upstate Peds by 38-16 Win Saturday." Daily Times and Daily Journal-Press, January 31:8.

———. 1950. "Joseph Benda, St. John's Coach, Dies at Home." Daily Times and Daily Journal-Press, June 21:1.

Dakota Scientist. 1934. "Wildcats Open Season with U. of Manitoba." Dakota Scientist, September 27:1.

Dakota Student. 1931. "Baby Bison Wallop Sioux Frosh 26 to 6." Dakota Student, November 10:3.

———. 1931. "Frosh Seeking Revenge on Bison Tonight." Dakota Student, November 4:3.

———. 1931. "Papooses Set for Annual Classic with A.C. Baby Bison Here Tonight." Dakota Student, October 14:3.

———. 1932. "Bill Mjogdalen Playing on Canada Rugby Team." Dakota Student, November 3:3.

———. 1932. "Freshman Gridders Hang Up Uniforms." Dakota Student, November 3:3.

———. 1932. "Grid Classic to Draw 400 Nodak Followers." Dakota Student, October 21:1.

———. 1932. "Nodak Frosh Will Battle Canadian Rugby Team Today." Dakota Student, November 11:3.

———. 1932. "Nodaks Battle Jackrabbit Gridders Tonight." Dakota Student, October 28:3.

———. 1932. "Nodaks Invade Fargo October 22." Dakota Student, October 14:5.

———. 1932. "Sioux Frosh Meet Manitoba Rugby Squad Saturday." Dakota Student, October 28:3.

———. 1932. "Sioux Open Loop Schedule with A.C. Saturday." Dakota Student, October 21:3.

———. 1933. "Coach West Makes Changes in Lineup for Bison Battle." Dakota Student, October 27:1.

———. 1933. "Grid Schedule to Start on Saturday." Dakota Student, September 22:3.

———. 1933. "Sioux Gridders to Leave Today." Dakota Student, September 22:4.

———. 1933. "Sioux, Bison Teams Battle to 7-7 Impasse." Dakota Student, October 31:3.

———. 1933. "Sioux, Winnipeg Football Clubs Guests at Banquet." Dakota Student, September 25:3.

———. 1933. "U-A.C. Clash Tomorrow." Dakota Student, October 27:1.

———. 1934. "Fans Board Special to Fargo." Dakota Student, October 26:1.

———. 1934. "Freshmen Eleven to Play Canadians." Dakota Student, October 12:3.

———. 1934. "Frosh Trim Winnipeg, 21-20." Dakota Student, October 16:1.

———. 1934. "Special Train to Take Rooters to A.C. Saturday." Dakota Student, October 23:1.

———. 1934. "Yearlings down Manitoba U, 31-0." Dakota Student, October 16:3.

———. 1935. "Baby Sioux Defeated." Dakota Student, October 25:1.

Danbom, David B. Going It Alone: Fargo Grapples with the Great Depression. St. Paul: Minnesota Historical Society Press, 2005. Pages 11, 207.

Davis, Dick. 1934. "Dick's Dibs." Mac Weekly, October 18:3.

Dayton Beach Morning Journal. 1963. "Pete Cawthon Dead at 64." Daytona Beach Morning Journal, January 1:15.

DeGeer, Vern. 1933. "From Another Angle." Gazette, November 18:21.

———. 1933. "Sport Gossip." Windsor Star, December 6:25.

———. 1933. "Sport Gossip." Windsor Star, November 27:21.

———. 1935. "Bad Weather for Classic." Windsor Star, December 7:19.

———. 1935. "East Seeks Winnipeg Stars As They Win Grid Title." Windsor Star, December 9:21.

———. 1935. "Sport Gossip." Windsor Star, December 2:24.

———. 1935. "Sport Gossip." Windsor Star, September 23:9.

———. 1935. "Winnipegs Trim Assumption College 17-0 in Exhibition." Windsor Star, December 3:23.

———. 1950. "From Another Angle." Gazette, November 18:21.

———. 1950. "From Another Angle." Gazette, September 9:21.

Democrat and Chronicle. 1933. "Arpeakos Thrill Crowd of 10,000 with 18-15 Victory over Toronto Chefs." Democrat and Chronicle, October 10:17.

———. 1933. "Conacher and Toronto Chefs Face Arpeakos Tonight on Stadium Gridiron." Democrat and Chronicle, October 13:28.

Bibliography

———. 1933. "New Football Club Lists Spring Work." Democrat and Chronicle, April 29:15.

———. 1933. "Swarthout Leads Chefs to Victory." Democrat and Chronicle, October 22:30.

———. 1933. "Toronto Chefs Fall to Arpeakos for Second Time in Night Fray, 12-6." Democrat and Chronicle, October 14:14.

———. 1933. "Toronto Hopes to Reverse Tables on Arpeako's Squad." Democrat and Chronicle, October 12:18.

Department of Canadian Heritage. "Thanksgiving and Remembrance Day." Canadian Heritage. November 17, 2008. Accessed October 2, 2021. https://web.archive.org/web/20110504081116/http://www.pch.gc.ca/pgm/ceem-cced/jfa-ha/action-eng.cfm

Des Moines Register. 1928. "Gowans Sees Des Moines U. 100% Better." Des Moines Register, September 28:15.

———. 1932. "North Dakota State Keeps Circuit Record Clean by Tripping Morningside, 20-0." Des Moines Register, November 25:6.

———. 1933. "Sophomore Guides Morningside to 13-7 Grid Victory." Des Moines Register, September 30:6.

———. 1947. "Here's How to Watch That Football Game." Des Moines Register, October 3:1.

———. 1950. "Saunderson, Morningside, Dies at 63." Des Moines Register, February 17:15.

Des Moines Tribune. 1926. "Tigers Fit for Grid Game with Beavers." Des Moines Tribune, October 1:26.

Dickinson College. "Byron Wilde Student File." Carlisle Indian School Digital Resource Center. 2021. Accessed October 1, 2021. https://carlisleindian.dickinson.edu/student_files/byron-wilde-student-file

Diedrich, Dr. J.W. 1920. "High School Football in Minnesota." Bemidji Daily Pioneer, September 15:3.

Doty, Hi. 1934. "N. Dakota Bisons Meet OCU Tonight." Oklahoma City Advertiser, November 16:1.

———. 1934. "Sports Hi Spots." Campus, November 16:4.

Doyle, Joe. 1992. "Krause Was Truly 'Mr. Notre Dame.'" South Bend Tribune, December 12:2.

Dryburgh, Dave. 1931. "In Winnipeg Tunics, Roughriders Compile Club's Record Score." Leader-Post, November 9:9.

———. 1932. "Regina Team Still Strong." Star-Phoenix, August 31:12.

———. 1932. "Roughriders Beat Calgary 30 to 2, Maroons Beat Calgary Juniors 17-8." Leader-Post, November 11:1.

———. 1934. "Along the Sport Byways." Leader-Post, November 5:16.

———. 1934. "Kirk Completes Pass to Put Reginans in Scoring Mood—Lydiard Gets the Touchdown." Leader-Post, November 5:16.

———. 1934. "Last-Half Attack Gives 'Riders 22-2 Win over Meralomas." Leader-Post, November 12:16.

———. 1934. "Pearce May Not See Much Action in Today's Rugby Tilt." Leader-Post, November 10:16.

———. 1934. "Regina Best Go Begging before Game." Leader-Post, November 24:1.

———. 1934. "'Riders Play on Slippery Field." Leader-Post, November 10:1.

———. 1934. "'Riders Weakened." Leader-Post, November 12:16.

———. 1934. "Sarnia Wins Rugby Final 20-12--Roughrider Fumbles Prove Costly." Leader-Post, November 24:1.

———. 1934. "Snow, Snow and Then More Snow All That Roughriders Can See." Leader-Post, November 22:1.

———. 1935. "Along the Sport Byways with Dave Dryburgh." Leader-Post, December 9:16.

———. 1935. "The West Arrives!" Leader-Post, September 23:16.

———. 1935. "We Lost..." Leader-Post, November 4:16.

———. 1935. "Winnipeg Scores 13-6 Victory as Defense Balks 'Riders." Leader-Post, November 4:16-17.

Duffy, Bernard J. 1934. "Ed Krause Makes Favorable Impression on His First Visit to St. Mary's College." Winona Daily News, April 3:9.

Dulmage, Elmer. 1932. "Hamilton Tigers Crush Regina Rough Riders 25-6." Windsor Star, December 5:19.

———. 1933. "Argonauts Eliminate Winnipeg 13-0 in Semi-Finals for Canadian Rugby Title before 12,000 Fans." Lethbridge Herald, December 4:8.

———. 1933. "Rebholz Convinces Eastern Grid Fans He Is One of the Greatest Halves in Canada." Winnipeg Tribune, December 4:20.

———.. 1935. "Fritz Hanson's Amazing Run." Lethbridge Herald, December 10:10.

———.. 1935. "Name Ottawans on All-Canada Team." Ottawa Citizen, December 10:11.

———.. 1935. "'Pegs Bring Rugby Title to West." Winnipeg Free Press, December 9:1.

———.. 1935. "'Pegs Place Punting Load on Joe Perpich." Lethbridge Herald, December 4:12.

———.. 1935. "Smashing Attack Humbles Eastern Champions 18-12." Lethbridge Herald, December 7:1.

———.. 1935. "Winnipegs Defeat Assumption, 17-0, But Critic Is Left Cold." Winnipeg Free Press, December 3:12.

Dumsday, William H. 1935. "East Seeks Winnipeg Stars." Lethbridge Herald, December 9:26.

———. 1935. "Keen on Ab Box." Ottawa Citizen, December 10:11.

Dunnell, Milt. 1987. "How the West Broke the Cup Sound Barrier." Toronto Star, November 29.

Dypwick, Otis. 1931. "Concordia Eleven Crushes Macalester, 18 to 0." Minneapolis Sunday Tribune, October 11:18.

———. 1931. "Cinder Title Won by West." Minneapolis Sunday Tribune, June 7:19,21.

E.C.J. 1934. "Kobber Kernels." Concordian, November 10:3.

———. 1934. "Kobber Kernels." Concordian, September 21:3.

———. 1934. "Kobber Kernels." Concordian, September 28:3.

Eads, W.J. 1932. "Cadets Take to Air and Score Eight Times on Bison in 52-0 Win." Fargo Forum, November 13.

Edmonton Journal. 1922. "Title of Eskimo Rugby Team Changed to Edmonton Elks." Edmonton Journal, October 17:16.

———. 1930. "Modified Forward Pass for Canadian Football Is Finally Agreed to." Edmonton Journal, July 7:7.

———. 1966. "Ex-Football Great, Lou Mogul, Dies." Edmonton Journal, January 4:7.

Eggleston, Mac. 1934. "Meandering with Mac." Star-Phoenix, November 7:14.

Eikleberry, Sarah J. "A 'Chief' Year for the 'Iowa Braves': Mayes McLain and Native American (Mis)appropriation at the State University of Iowa." The Annals of Iowa 70 (2011), 111-131.

Elson, Bob. 1934. "On the Sport Front." Province, November 9:24.

———. 1934. "On the Sport Front." Province, November 13:14.

———. 1934. "On the Sport Front." Province, November 7:20.

———. 1934. "On the Sport Front." Province, October 19:26.

———. 1934. "Regina Pass Attack Crushes Meralomas." Province, November 12:12.

Encyclopedia.com. "Hall, Halsey 1898-1977." Contemporary Authors. Encyclopedia.com. 2021. Accessed January 14, 2021. https://www.encyclopedia.com/arts/educational-magazines/hall-halsey-1898-1977

Enfield Athletic Hall of Fame. Enfield Athletic Hall of Fame Class of 2001. Accessed July 15, 2021. http://www.enfieldathletichof.org/2001-2/

Entertainment Guide. Early College Football in Northfield, 1918-1950. Entertainment Guide. Accessed February 26, 2021. https://entertainmentguidemn.com/early-college-football-in-northfield-1918-1950/

Eriksmoen, Curtis. 1997. "Once the highest-paid player in the NFL, Fargoan later coach the Bison." Forum of Fargo-Moorhead, February 3.

Eriksmoen, Curtis. 2019. "Eriksmoen: Youngest North American Coach to Win National Championship Became Fargo Businessman." The Forum of Fargo-Moorhead, July 20.

Evanson, Edmonde. 1934. "Spring Football Practise Begins This Week." Concordian, April 18:3.

Evening Huronite. 1932. "Sophomore Halfback Scores Twice as North Dakota Aggies Win Over Coyotes, 18-8, in Night Grid Game." Evening Huronite, October 1:9.

Fairmont Royal York. History. 2021. Accessed July 29, 2021. http://thefairmontroyalyork.com/history

Fargo Forum. 1932. "Aerial Battle on Concordia Field Looms." Fargo Forum, October 21:1.

———. 1932. "Army Eases Up against Bison in Tilt Today." Fargo Forum, November 12:5.

———. 1932. "Army Team Trounces Bison Gridders." Fargo Forum, November 12:1.

———. 1932. "Bison Off for Trip into East." Fargo Forum, November 1.

———. 1932. "Bison, 25 Others Unbeaten on Grid." Fargo Forum, October 24.

———. 1932. "Bring on Army, Is Bison's Cry after Setback." Fargo Forum, November 5:5.

Bibliography

———. 1932. "Cleve Considered for Wisconsin Job." Fargo Forum, November 22:10.

———. 1932. "Cobbers Drill for Encounter with St. John's." Fargo Forum, October 25:7.

———. 1932. "Cobbers Oppose Hibbing Eleven." Fargo Forum, November 7:11.

———. 1932. "Cobbers to Have Little Practice for Last Game." Fargo Forum, November 10:10.

———. 1932. "Colonials Win from Bison by Tally of 20-0." Fargo Forum, November 5:5.

———. 1932. "Dance Casino." Fargo Forum, October 21:19.

———. 1932. "Dragons See Victory, Cobbers Unimpressive." Fargo Forum, November 3:8.

———. 1932. "Fast Field Promised Bison, Sioux." Fargo Forum, October 21:1.

———. 1932. "Football Sketches." Fargo Forum, October 21:13.

———. 1932. "Four Bison on Scribes' Team." Fargo Forum, November 23:8.

———. 1932. "Fritz Hanson Measures Up to Expectations of Bison. Fargo Forum, October 1:5.

———. 1932. "Gridmen Reach Capital Today." Fargo Forum, November 3:1.

———. 1932. "Herd Works in Washington for Crucial Tilt." Fargo Forum, November 4:10.

———. 1932. "Ideal Weather Promised for Bison-Army Contest." Fargo Forum, November 12:10.

———. 1932. "Introducing New Bison." Fargo Forum, September 21:7.

———. 1932. "Jahr and Meyers of Bison on All-Conference Eleven." Fargo Forum, November 18:10.

———. 1932. "New York Biggest Thrill for Bison." Fargo Forum, November 8:9.

———. 1932. "Passing Hurts Bison Eleven." Fargo Forum, November 13.

———. 1932. "Snow Puts Quietus on Football Contests in This Section." Fargo Forum, November 11:11.

———. 1932. "The Old Army Game' Known to Lowe and Finnegan of Bison." Fargo Forum, November 11:10.

———. 1933. "A.C. Orders Fair Weather As Last Touch on Homecoming." Fargo Forum, October 13:1.

———. 1933. "A.C. Outlines Program for Homecoming Event Oct. 14." Fargo Forum, October 5:1.

———. 1933. "Bison Eleven Drills Lightly for Final Game." Fargo Forum, November 14:10.

———. 1933. "Bison Eleven Leaves Today." Fargo Forum, November 15:8.

———. 1933. "Bison Finish Preparations for Superior." Fargo Forum, October 19:12.

———. 1933. "Bison Oppose Maroons in Feature Night Tilt." Fargo Forum, October 7:5.

———. 1933. "Bison Reserves Employ Warner Style to Gain." Fargo Forum, October 18:8.

———. 1933. "Bison Varsity Stops Frosh." Fargo Forum, October 5:10.

———. 1933. "Bison, Cobbers Ready for Opening Grid Setto Today." Fargo Forum, September 22:12.

———. 1933. "Bob Fritz Lost to Cobbers for Rest of Year." Fargo Forum, November 6:8.

———. 1933. "Committee Adopts Two Changes in 1933 Regulations." Fargo Forum, February 13:3.

———. 1933. "Dragon Work Hard in Preparation for Bison." Fargo Forum, November 1:9.

———. 1933. "Dragons Brave Cold Weather for Grid Work." Fargo Forum, November 8:10.

———. 1933. "Fargoans Prepare to See Football Classic in Grand Forks." Fargo Forum, October 27:1.

———. 1933. "F-M Grid Trio Playing Today; Others Get Set." Fargo Forum, October 6:12.

———. 1933. "Homecoming Air Rules As A.C. Battles S.D. State." Fargo Forum, October 14:1.

———. 1933. "Injury Bugaboo in Mac Camp Lessened." Fargo Forum, October 11:10.

———. 1933. "Nodak Star to Start Contest Against Bison." Fargo Forum, October 27:1.

———. 1933. "Oklahoma City Favored over Bison Eleven." Fargo Forum, November 18:6.

———. 1933. "Sioux Line Up Under Stadium for Practice." Fargo Forum, October 27:1.

———. 1933. "St. John's U, Ired at Officials, Cancels All Games with Concordia." Fargo Forum, November 3:1.

———. 1934. "A.C. Likely to Have Full Power for Game with Tommies Friday." Fargo Forum, November 1:8.

———. 1934. "Bison Expect Hard Fight Friday after Seeing Tommies in Action." Fargo Forum, November 2:8.

———. 1934. "Bison Head for Texas After Hanson's Runs Beat Bugs." Fargo Forum, November 17:7.

———. 1934. "Bison Line Reserves Worry; 6 Cobbers Out." Fargo Forum, September 25:8.

———. 1934. "Bison Oppose Bugs Tonight." Fargo Forum, November 16:12.

———. 1934. "Bison Tie Texas Tech, 20-20, as Sioux Upset Colonials, 7-0." Fargo Forum, November 24:7.

———. 1934. "Cleve and Cobbers Work Optimistically for Oles." Fargo Forum, October 11:14.

———. 1934. "Cobbers Keep League Lead." Fargo Forum, October 22:8.

———. 1934. "Cobbers Triumph over Augustana College, 26 to 6." Fargo Forum, November 3:8.

———. 1934. "Concordia Not at High Peak." Fargo Forum, October 12:14.

———. 1934. "Coronation Is Opening Event at Concordia Fest Tonight." Fargo Forum, October 26:1-2.

———. 1934. "First A.C. Team Learned How to Give and Lots about 'Taking It' on Gridiron Way Back in 1893." Fargo Forum, October 26:1-2.

———. 1934. "Injured Ole Stars Set for Cobbers." Fargo Forum, October 11:14.

———. 1934. "Sioux Eleven Beats Winnipeg All-Stars, 13-3." Fargo Forum, September 22:7.

———. 1934. "Sioux Meet Aggies at Fargo Next Saturday." Fargo Forum, October 21:11.

———. 1934. "Two Concordia Stars Picked." Fargo Forum, November 18:7.

———. 1934. "University Has Only 17 Ready to Go Saturday." Fargo Forum, October 24:10.

Fitzgerald, Eugene. "Bison, Nodaks Turn Attention to Annual Grid Game." Fargo Forum, October 17:7.

———. "Strong Yearling Teams Vie in Prehomecoming Tilt." Fargo Forum, October 12:16.

———. 1932. "22 Southwest Huskies Here to Uphold Grid Prestige." Fargo Forum, October 14:12.

———. 1932. "57-Yard Run Puts A.C. Ahead." Fargo Forum, October 22:1.

———. 1932. "Bison and Cobbers Introduce 1932 Football Tonight." Fargo Forum, September 23:11.

———. 1932. "Bison Eleven Forced Inside by Cold Wave." Fargo Forum, November 17:16.

———. 1932. "Bison Eleven Sent Through Tough Workout." Fargo Forum, October 28:14.

———. 1932. "Bison Finish Grid Workout." Fargo Forum, November 22:10.

———. 1932. "Bison Get Set for Intensive Grid Sessions." Fargo Forum, October 12:7.

———. 1932. "Bison Off on Eastern Trip." Fargo Forum, November 2:9.

———. 1932. "Bison Prepare for Hard Part of Grid Card." Fargo Forum, October 11:8.

———. 1932. "Bison Squad Is Scrimmaged in Tuesday Drill." Fargo Forum, October 26:8.

———. 1932. "Bison Team to Work Hard for Game Saturday." Fargo Forum, October 4:7.

———. 1932. "Bison Welcome Warm Weather for Iowa Drill." Fargo Forum, November 24:10.

———. 1932. "Bison, Dragons Work Indoors on Wednesday." Fargo Forum, October 27:19.

———. 1932. "Fine Running Backs Present Problem to Finnegan." Fargo Forum, October 19:9.

———. 1932. "Finnegan Continues Optimistic Outlook." Fargo Forum, October 6:11.

———. 1932. "Finnegan Fears Maroon Game Thanksgiving Day." Fargo Forum, November 15:8.

———. 1932. "Finnegan Has More Optimism at Bison Drill." Fargo Forum, November 18:10.

———. 1932. "Finnegan Pleased with Working of Bison Line." Fargo Forum, October 5:9.

———. 1932. "Finnegan, Lowe Stress Blocking and Tackling in Bison Grid Workout." Fargo Forum, September 27:8.

———. 1932. "Goldbugs and Bison Put on Great Offensive Grid Show." Fargo Forum, October 15:5.

———. 1932. "Grid Clientele Sees Strongest Cobber Team in Opener." Fargo Forum, September 24:5.

Bibliography

———. 1932. "Hanson on Spot as Bison Face Coyotes." Fargo Forum, September 30:11.
———. 1932. "Herd Eleven Triumphs over Maroons, 20-0." Fargo Forum, November 25:8.
———. 1932. "Important Matters Confront Bison Coaching Staff." Fargo Forum, October 13:11.
———. 1932. "Injuries Fail to Show Up in Bison's Camp." Fargo Forum, October 25:7.
———. 1932. "New Plays Are Handed out to Both Elevens." Fargo Forum, October 18:7.
———. 1932. "The Sport Whirligig." Fargo Forum, November 1:9.
———. 1932. "The Sport Whirligig." Fargo Forum, November 14:7.
———. 1932. "The Sport Whirligig." Fargo Forum, November 15:8.
———. 1932. "The Sport Whirligig." Fargo Forum, November 7:11.
———. 1932. "The Sport Whirligig." Fargo Forum, October 24.
———. 1932. "The Sport Whirligig." Fargo Forum, October 27:19.
———. 1932. "The Sport Whirligig." Fargo Forum, October 31:9.
———. 1932. "Tough Part of Bison Grid Practice Sessions Is at End." Fargo Forum, October 20:13.
———. 1933. "Bison Clash with Tough Coyote Grid Team Today." Fargo Forum, November 11:6.
———. 1933. "Bison Defense Strong in Wednesday Workout. Fargo Forum, October 26:14.
———. 1933. "Bison Forward Wall Makes Casey Finnegan Optimistic." Fargo Forum, October 11:10.
———. 1933. "Bison Get Ready This Week for Final Grid Tilt." Fargo Forum, November 13:8.
———. 1933. "Bison May Take to Air in Game with Dragons." Fargo Forum, November 3:12.
———. 1933. "Bison Plan to Fight Maroons with Aerials." Fargo Forum, October 3:8.
———. 1933. "Bison Please Coaches in Workout; Four of Sioux Regulars Are Hurt." Fargo Forum, October 25:10.
———. 1933. "Bison Practice Behind Closed Gates This Week." Fargo Forum, October 23:13.
———. 1933. "Bison Resume Grid Rivalry with Tommies." Fargo Forum, September 29:11.
———. 1933. "Bison, Dragon Regulars Are Given Rest Monday by Finnegan, Nemzek." Fargo Forum, October 31:10.
———. 1933. "Cobbers To Be More Advanced Than Bison for Opener." Fargo Forum, September 13:11.
———. 1933. "Concordia Looks Hopefully Toward Successful Season." Fargo Forum, September 22:5.
———. 1933. "Erling Schranz Promising As Replacement." Fargo Forum, September 21:11.
———. 1933. "Finnegan Is Not Taking Sioux Defeat Seriously." Fargo Forum, October 24:8.
———. 1933. "Finnegan Places Hopes for Win in 'Hopped Up' Bison." Fargo Forum, October 13:12.
———. 1933. "Finnegan Trifle More Optimistic About Friday Game." Fargo Forum, September 19:9.
———. 1933. "Gerteis, Schranz and May Please Finnegan." Fargo Forum, October 4:10.
———. 1933. "Herd Off to Circuit Test with Coyotes." Fargo Forum, November 9:12.
———. 1933. "Injuries Keep Regulars on Sidelines at N.D.A.C." Fargo Forum, October 10:10.
———. 1933. "Injury Jinx Not Expected to Handicap Local Elevens." Fargo Forum, September 26:8.
———. 1933. "Keeping in Line." Fargo Forum, November 2:14.
———. 1933. "Keeping In Line." Fargo Forum, November 13:8.
———. 1933. "Keeping in Line." Fargo Forum, November 21:9.
———. 1933. "Keeping in Line." Fargo Forum, October 10:10.
———. 1933. "Keeping in Line." Fargo Forum, October 12:16.
———. 1933. "Keeping in Line." Fargo Forum, October 13:12.
———. 1933. "Keeping in Line." Fargo Forum, October 27:11.
———. 1933. "Keeping in Line." Fargo Forum, October 31:10.
———. 1933. "Keeping in Line." Fargo Forum, September 20:13.
———. 1933. "Lack of Outside Work Worries Bison Mentor." Fargo Forum, November 7:8.
———. 1933. "Local Colleges Get Set for Loop Tilts." Fargo Forum, October 2:8.
———. 1933. "Nemzek Takes Passing Role in Grid Drill." Fargo Forum, November 2:14.
———. 1933. "One Task Faces Finnegan and Lowe But It's a Tough One." Fargo Forum, September 20:13.
———. 1933. "Reserves Have Bulk of Burden against Frosh." Fargo Forum, September 27:10.
———. 1933. "Three Fargo-Moorhead Grid Tilts Postponed." Fargo Forum, November 4:6.
———. 1933. Bison and Tommies Battle to 7-7 Tie." Fargo Forum, September 30:5.
———. 1934. "Bison and Cobbers Stake Conference Title Hopes." Fargo Forum, November 5:8.
———. 1934. "Bison and Nodaks Favored in N.C.I. Grid Tilts Today." Fargo Forum, October 12:14.
———. 1934. "Bison and Sioux Again Dominate North Central Race." Fargo Forum, October 13:9.
———. 1934. "Bison Expect Manpower Will Win for Them." Fargo Forum, October 17:12.
———. 1934. "Bison Gridders Defeat Concordia 6-0; Midgets Tie with Detroit Lakes." Fargo Forum, September 22:7.
———. 1934. "Bison Gridmen Sent through Tough Session." Fargo Forum, November 6:10.
———. 1934. "Bison Line Reserves Worry; Cobbers Out." Fargo Forum, September 25:8.
———. 1934. "Bison Make Progress Readying for Coyotes." Fargo Forum, October 10:8.
———. 1934. "Bison Now Favored in North Central Conference Race." Fargo Forum, October 29:10.
———. 1934. "Bison Picked to Defeat Sioux in Game Here Saturday." Fargo Forum, October 26:14.
———. 1934. "Bison Primp Offensive Show for Coyotes Here." Fargo Forum, October 9:8.
———. 1934. "Bison Starting Lineup for Sioux Tilt Taking Form." Fargo Forum, October 24:10.
———. 1934. "Concordia Wins Conference Title with 26-0 Conquest of Gustavus." Fargo Forum, November 10:8.
———. 1934. "Crippled Bison Team May Face S.D. Bunnies." Fargo Forum, November 8:16.
———. 1934. "Dragons Score 13-12 Victory against Bison." Fargo Forum, November 3:8.
———. 1934. "Finnegan, Lowe Select 21 Gridders for Trip." Fargo Forum, November 14:10.
———. 1934. "Herd Polishes Strong Offense in Final Drill." Fargo Forum, October 18:14.
———. 1934. "Herd Prepared for Big Game with Gophers." Fargo Forum, September 29:7.
———. 1934. "Keeping in Line." Fargo Forum, November 5:8.
———. 1934. "Keeping in Line." Fargo Forum, November 6:10.
———. 1934. "Keeping in Line." Fargo Forum, November 21:10.
———. 1934. "Keeping in Line." Fargo Forum, November 28:8.
———. 1934. "Keeping in Line." Fargo Forum, October 1:8.
———. 1934. "Keeping in Line." Fargo Forum, October 24:10.
———. 1934. "Keeping in Line." Fargo Forum, October 25:22.
———. 1934. "Keeping in Line." Fargo Forum, September 28:12.
———. 1934. "Light Work Order of Day in Bison Camp." Fargo Forum, November 13:8.
———. 1934. "Local Gridiron Contingents in Outside Drills." Fargo Forum, September 27:22.
———. 1934. "Shakeup in Bison Lineup for Sioux Game Is Sighted." Fargo Forum, October 27:10.
———. 1934. "Sioux Win N.C.I. Football Title in Weird Race." Fargo Forum, November 12:8.
———. 1934. "Sturgeon's Kicking May Lessen N.D. Defensive Power." Fargo Forum, October 25:22.
———. 1934. "'Those Coyotes Better Be Tough,' Says Finnegan As Bison Get Set." Fargo Forum, October 11:14.
———. 1934. "Varies Bison Attack Planned for Maroons." Fargo Forum, October 16:10.
———. 1934. "Weather Raising Havoc with Grid Coaches in Fargo and Moorhead." Fargo Forum, September 26:10.
———. 1935. "Winnipeg Rugby Club Wins over Concordia, 26 to 0." Fargo Forum, September 15:16.
Forman, Chandler. 1931. "17 Gopher Lettermen Will Report Tuesday." Minneapolis Sunday Tribune, September 13:4.
———. 1934. "Gophers Make Season's Debut against Bison Today." Minneapolis Tribune, September 29:19.
Fort Garry Hotel. Hotel History. Accessed July 27, 2021. https://www.fortgarryhotel.com/winnipeg-hotel-history/#3
Fort Worth Star-Telegram. 1933. "To Study Sports." Forth Worth Star-Telegram, January 30:14.
Fouquerel-Skoe, Louise, Terry Kreps, and Elizabeth Routzahn. "Bishop Whipple: Decolonizing and Indigenizing Concordia." Cordopedia, 2021. Accessed June 7, 2021. http://cordopedia.concordiacollegearchives.org/content/bishop-whipple-decolonizing-and-indigenizing-concordia
Frayne, Trent. 1949. "Halfbacks, Greenbacks and Red Ink." Maclean's, October 15.

Bibliography

———. 1990. "After 55 Years, Cup Still On: Fritz Hanson's Feat Gave National Prominence to Game." Globe and Mail, November 24.

Frederikson, Donald R., Ed. 1933. The Bison 1934. Fargo: North Dakota State College.

French, Chuck. 1932. "Bison Defeat Nodaks in Homecoming Clash to Take State Title." Spectrum, October 28:3.

———. 1932. "Finnegan Has Strong Gridiron Aggregation for Year's Schedule." Spectrum, September 16:3.

———. 1932. "Fritz Hanson Stars as Bison Conquer Coyote Team." Spectrum, October 4:3.

Fridlund, Carl. 1934. "Grange Commends Dragons' Record in Radio Review." Western MiSTiC, November 9:3.

Friedman, Benny. 1934. "Forward Pass Now Is Most Effective Football Weapon, Benny Friedman Points Out." Fargo Forum, November 12:8.

———. 1934. "Grid's Styles Determined by System's Wins." Fargo Forum, November 13:8.

G.W.L. 1934. "Rugby: 1934." Winnipeg Manitoban, November 9:2.

Gazette. 1933. "5,000 Look On As Mount Royals Win Pro Grid Opener." Gazette, October 16:15.

———. 1933. "Aerial Duel Looms in Pro Encounters." Gazette, October 20:14.

———. 1933. "Chefs Beat Buffalo." Gazette, October 23:17.

———. 1933. "Four Officials to Handle Grid Tilt." Gazette, October 12:12.

———. 1933. "Mount Royals and Arrows to Clash." Gazette, October 14:14.

———. 1933. "Mount Royals in Second Straight Triumph by 14-0." Gazette, October 23:17.

———. 1933. "Mount Royals to Be Here Tomorrow." Gazette, October 13:15.

———. 1933. "No More Pro Grid Tilts Carded Here." Gazette, October 27:15.

———. 1933. "Pro Grid League Being Organized." Gazette, October 26:12.

———. 1933. "Red Moore Likely to Sign with Pros." Gazette, October 11:14.

———. 1933. "Ryan Langmard to Aid Mount Royals." Gazette, October 21:14.

———. 1933. "Trojans Signed to Face Local Eleven." Gazette, October 18:12.

———. 1934. "Aromints to Face Tonawandas' Team." Gazette, October 13:4.

———. 1934. "Aromints Triumph over Tonawandas." Gazette, October 15:14.

———. 1934. "Buffalo Grid Team to Face Aromints." Gazette, October 6:15.

———. 1934. "C.R.U. Rules Safety Touch Will Count Only One Point in Future." Gazette, February 26:18.

———. 1934. "Conacher's Squad to Play on Sunday." Gazette, October 12:12.

———. 1934. "Conacher's Team Wins." October 4:14.

———. 1934. "Football Game Is On." Gazette, October 9:17.

———. 1934. "Pro-Football." Gazette, October 13:14.

———. 1934. "Strong Half Line on Toronto Team." Gazette, October 11:16.

———. 1934. "Toronto Beats Buffalo, 19-5." Gazette, October 9:17.

———. 1935. "Bonar, of Notre Dame, New Ottawa Quarter." Gazette, August 24:14.

———. 1935. "C.R.U. Adds Weight to Check Imports." Gazette, March 2:16.

———. 1942. "Bombers Are Slight Favorites to Trim R.C.A.F. Hurricanes." Gazette, December 5: 16.

Gibbon, Guy. "Sioux." Encyclopedia of the Great Plains. University of Nebraska-Lincoln. 2011. Accessed July 21, 2021.

Gibson, Dick. 1929. "What's What in Sport According to Dick Gibson." Windsor Star, February 14:22.

Gilhooly, Walter J. 1930. "Bring on the Forward Pass." Ottawa Journal, November 8:25.

———. 1934. "In the Realm of Sport." Ottawa Journal, November 15:26.

Giloy, Ellen. 2007-2008 Minnesota State High School League Yearbook & Record Book. Brooklyn Center: Minnesota State High School League, 2008. Page 329.

Globe and Mail. 1935. "Winnipegs Defeat Hamilton for Canadian Football Title." Globe and Mail, December 7.

Goplen, Orville. 1936. "Bison Oppose Powerful Winnipeggers Saturday." Spectrum, September 25:3.

Gordon, Aaron. Did Football Cause 20 Deaths in 1905? Re-Investigating a Serial Killer. Deadspin. 22 January 2014. Accessed 29 June 2021. https://deadspin.com/did-football-cause-20-deaths-in-1905-re-investigating-1506758181

Gould, Alan. 1932. "Drastic Changes in Football Code." News and Observer, February 16:8.

Government of Alberta. "William Freeman 'Deacon' White." Provincial Archives of Alberta. 2021. Accessed July 28, 2021. https://hermis.alberta.ca/paa/PhotoGalleryDetails.aspx?CollectionID=2&DeptID=1&ObjectID=A7286

Government of Canada. "The Winnipeg Grenadiers." Canada.ca. November 20, 2018. Accessed September 28, 2021. https://www.canada.ca/en/department-national-defence/services/military-history/history-heritage/official-military-history-lineages/lineages/infantry-regiments/winnipeg-grenadiers.html

Gragg, Amy. "E.J. Cassell." Carleton 'C' Club. April 12, 2021. Accessed August 19, 2021. https://www.carleton.edu/c-club/hall-of-fame/year/1914-1929/e-cassell/

Graham, Jack. 1960. "Brutal, Massed Play Marked Early Football." Yale Daily News, October 29:2.

Grand Forks Herald. "Big Nine' Conference Is Organized at St. Paul Meet Monday; Function in Fall." Grand Forks Herald, February 21:8.

———. 1916. "N.D. Guardsmen Title Holders." Grand Forks Herald, December 19:2.

———. 1932. "Bison-Sioux Football Game Draws Army of Fans." Grand Forks Herald, October 21:12.

———. 1932. "Finnegan Optimistic over Tilt with Sioux Saturday." Grand Forks Herald, October 18:7.

———. 1932. "Nodaks' Hopes for Victory over Bison Rise." Grand Forks Herald, October 19:18.

———. 1932. "Nodaks Take Lead as Pierce Runs 28 Yards for First Touchdown." Grand Forks Herald, October 22:1.

———. 1932. "Sioux Face Opening of Conference Schedule." Grand Forks Herald, October 17:2.

———. 1932. "Sioux Take Last Drill Today for Bison Clash." Grand Forks Herald, October 21:2.

———. 1932. "Thousand Rooters Accompany Nodak Gridders to Fargo." Grand Forks Herald, October 22:1.

———. 1932. "University Has Big Edge in Long Football Rivalry with A.C. Teams." Grand Forks Herald, October 18:6.

———. 1932. "West Calls Off Scrimmages Rest of Week." Grand Forks Herald, October 20:6.

———. 1933. "5,000 Attend Homecoming Football Struggle." Grand Forks Herald, October 28:1-2.

———. 1933. "Aggies Heartened by Showing in Scrimmage." Grand Forks Herald, October 25:7.

———. 1933. "Armory Dance, Reunions Close Sioux Homecoming." Grand Forks Herald, October 29:1.

———. 1933. "Bison Full of Confidence in First Workout." Grand Forks Herald, October 24:7.

———. 1933. "Bison to Invade Memorial Stadium Saturday." Grand Forks Herald, October 22:11.

———. 1933. "Dinner Tonight Starts Annual Sioux Festival." Grand Forks Herald, Octobers 27:1.

———. 1933. "First Signs of Ability Shown by Nodak Team." Grand Forks Herald, September 19:10.

———. 1933. "Little Work for Sioux Grid Squad This Week." Grand Forks Herald, October 23:9.

———. 1933. "Nodak Grid Team Opens at Winnipeg." Grand Forks Herald, November 23:2.

———. 1933. "Nodaks and Bison Battle to 7-7 Tie." Grand Forks Herald, October 29:1.

———. 1933. "Nodaks and Bison in Annual Football Game Today." Grand Forks Herald, October 28:2.

———. 1933. "Old Grads to Visit University Campus for Homecoming This Week." Grand Forks Herald, October 22:8.

———. 1933. "Pierce Likely to Start Game Against Bison." Grand Forks Herald, October 27:9.

———. 1933. "Sioux Gridders Leave Today for Opening Contest." Grand Forks Herald, September 22:9.

———. 1933. "West Would Have Annual Mix with Winnipeg Club." Grand Forks Herald, September 25:2.

———. 1934. "Bison Hopes Rise as Team Shows Power." Grand Forks Herald, October 25:8.

———. 1934. "Bison Offense Reaches High Point of Season." Grand Forks Herald, October 24:8.

Bibliography

———. 1934. "Frosh Take Second Win in Winnipeg." Grand Forks Herald, October 16:6.

———. 1934. "Here's How Bison Upset Sioux 7 to 0." Grand Forks Herald, October 28:12,18.

———. 1934. "Sioux and Bison Scoreless at Half." Grand Forks Herald, October 27:1.

———. 1934. "Sioux Defense Rated As Better than Aggies'." Grand Forks Herald, October 25:8.

———. 1934. "Sioux Open Season against Winnipeg Tonight." Grand Forks Herald, September 21:9.

———. 1934. "Sioux Open Season Friday Against Winnipeg All-Stars." Grand Forks Herald, September 16:13.

———. 1934. "Sioux Out to Continue Campaign of Revenge." Grand Forks Herald, October 23:6.

———. 1934. "Sioux Polishing Up Their Offense for Friday Game." Grand Forks Herald, September 18:6.

———. 1934. "Sioux Yearlings Play Manitoba Gridders Today." Grand Forks Herald, October 13:2.

———. 1934. "Well-Balanced Winnipeg Eleven Will Face Sioux." Grand Forks Herald, September 19:10.

———. 1934. "West Worries about Overconfidence on Team." Grand Forks Herald, October 22:7.

———. 1935. "Winnipegs Beat Sioux Frosh, 23-7." Grand Forks Herald, October 25:10.

Greater Northwest Football Association. Multnomah Amateur Athletic Club "Winged M's" (1891-1939). 2008. Accessed June 3, 2021. https://www.gnfafootball.org/MAAC.htm

Griffith, Major John L. 1933. "Grid Sport Is Still Able to Support Self." Fargo Forum, January 3:9.

Grinaker, Vernon Finn. "Concordia Men's Sports - The First One Hundred Years." Concordia College Athletics. 2021. Accessed January 29, 2021. http://dept.cord.edu/sports/sportsbackup/finn/index.html

Grinois, Walt. 1934. "Sports Shorts." Daily Times, September 14:13.

———. 1934. "Sports Shorts." Daily Times and Daily Journal, October 30:9.

Grohnke, Jack. 1932. "Bison Defeat Dragons in Hard Fought Game Yesterday Afternoon." Spectrum, May 3:3.

Grouse, S. Thom. 1931. "Four Cobbers Placed on United Press All-Loop Team." Moorhead Daily News, November 24:4.

Gustavian Weekly. 1931. "Concordia Trims Gustavus to Keep Record Spotless." Gustavian Weekly, November 10:4.

———. 1932. "Cobbers Battle Gusties to Scoreless Tie Saturday, 0-0." Gustavian Weekly, November 8:4.

———. 1932. "Strong Concordia Cobbers Opponents in Annual Homecoming Grid Classic." Gustavian Weekly, November 1:1.

———. 1933. "Cleve-men Set for Ebonite Onslaught in Opening Loop Tangle." Gustavian Weekly, October 3:4.

———. 1933. "Gallopers Battle Cobbers to Scoreless Deadlock." October 10:4.

———. 1933. "Myrum's Shrouds Tie Carls in Debut, 13-13." Gustavian Weekly, October 3:4.

———. 1934. "Fritz Leads Cobbers to 26-0 Win for State Championship." Gustavian Weekly, November 13:4.

———. 1934. "Gustavus Gridders Menace Concordia Title Drive Friday." Gustavian Weekly, November 6:4.

Gustavus Adolphus College. 2019. Gustavus 2019 Media Guide: Football. Accessed February 20, 2021. https://athletics.blog.gustavus.edu/files/2019/09/2019-Football-Media-GuideSeason.pdf

H.M.J. 1933. "Kobber Kernels." Concordian, October 6.

———. 1933. "Kobber Kernels." The Concordian, December 20:3.

Hackenberg, Dick. 1931. "Aberdeen Normal is Dragon Homecoming Foe Saturday." Moorhead Daily News, October 19:4.

———. 1931. "Cleve Sees Hard Fought Battle with Gusties Tomorrow." Moorhead Daily News, November 6:4.

———. 1931. "Coaches Name Starters in Tomorrow's Battle." Moorhead Daily News, October 16:4.

———. 1931. "Cobber Eleven Shows Spirit in Clash with Reserves." Moorhead Daily News, November 19:4.

———. 1931. "Cobber-Gustavus Vies with Dragon-Bison Tilt Saturday." Moorhead Daily News, November 2:4.

———. 1931. "Cobbers, Dragons Clash in Gridiron Classic Saturday." Moorhead Daily News, October 12:4.

———. 1931. "Conference Title in Balance As Cobbers Meet Tommies." Moorhead Daily News, November 13:4.

———. 1931. "Don Anderson to Start at Guard; Lysacker, Tackle." Moorhead Daily News, October 30:4.

———. 1931. "First Loop Game May Decide Fate of Local Outfit." Moorhead Daily News, October 6:4.

———. 1931. "'Four Norsemen' Intact as Cobbers Leave for St. Olaf." Moorhead Daily News, November 20:4.

———. 1931. "Problem Confronts Cleve As Hilde Bids for Place Among 'Four Norsemen.'" Moorhead Daily News, November 9:4.

———. 1931. "St. John's Star Is Chief Topic of Cobber Camp Talk." Moorhead Daily News, October 29:4.

———. 1931. "Both Elevens in Good Physical Condition for First Contest Tonight." Moorhead Daily News, September 18:4.

———. 1931. "Cleve Announces Starting Lineup for Clash with Bison: Cobbers Practice under Big Lights in Fargo Tonight." Moorhead Daily News, September 17:4.

———. 1931. "Please Note…" Moorhead Daily News, September 18:4.

———. 1932. "Bison Improved; Cobbers, Dragons Set; Holzer Lost." Moorhead Daily News, September 29:4.

———. 1932. "Bison Set for Stubborn Dragon Invasion." Moorhead Daily News, October 28:4.

———. 1932. "Cleve Orders Twice-a-Day Football Drills." Moorhead Daily News, September 8:4.

———. 1932. "Cleve Says Mac Contest Cobbers' Toughest Tilt." Moorhead Daily News, October 14:4.

———. 1932. "Cleve Stresses Tackling; Nemzek Directs Dragons." Moorhead Daily News, October 12:4.

———. 1932. "Cleve Will Try to Out-Do Newby Saturday." Moorhead Daily News, October 6:4.

———. 1932. "Coaches Cleve and Nemzek Drop a Few Remarks 'in Passing.'" Moorhead Daily News, September 28:4.

———. 1932. "Cobbers Await Tommy Onslaught Saturday." Moorhead Daily News, October 21:4.

———. 1932. "Cobbers Must Win Every Remaining Game." Moorhead Daily News, October 17:4.

———. 1932. "Cobbers Ready for Ole Invasion Saturday." Moorhead Daily News, October 7:4.

———. 1932. "Cobbers Vicious in Stopping Tommy Plays." Moorhead Daily News, October 19:4.

———. 1932. "Cobbers Well on Way to Second Grid Title." Moorhead Daily News, October 10:4-5.

———. 1932. "Cobbers, Dragons Exhibit Power in Grid Openers." Moorhead Daily News, September 24:4.

———. 1932. "Cobbers, Dragons Start Grid Wars Friday." Moorhead Daily News, September 17:4.

———. 1932. "Dethroned Cobbers Can Yet Achieve Glory." Moorhead Daily News, October 24:4.

———. 1932. "Dragons, Bison Show Class in Spring Grid Exhibition." Moorhead Daily News, May 3:4.

———. 1932. "Dragons, Cobbers to Begin Spring Grid Drills Monday." Moorhead Daily News, April 9:4.

———. 1932. "Fans See Break in Cobber-Dragon Deadlock." Moorhead Daily News, September 26:4.

———. 1932. "Finnegan to Pit Veterans Against Cobbers." Moorhead Daily News, September 21:4.

———. 1932. "Flashy Freshman Backs Stand Out in Cobber Grid Drills." Moorhead Daily News, April 23:4.

———. 1932. "Hilde and Otteson May Be Kept Out of St. Olaf Game." Moorhead Daily News, October 3:4.

———. 1932. "Otteson to Captain 1933 Cobber Eleven." Moorhead Daily News, December 1:4.

———. 1932. "Please Note…" Moorhead Daily News, November 2:4.

———. 1932. "Please Note…" Moorhead Daily News, November 7:4.

———. 1932. "Please Note…" Moorhead Daily News, October 10:4.

———. 1933. "Please Note…" Moorhead Daily News, October 17:4.

———. 1932. "Please Note…" Moorhead Daily News, October 28:4.

———. 1932. "Please Note…" Moorhead Daily News, October 31:4.

———. 1932. "Please Note…" Moorhead Daily News, September 13:4.

———. 1932. "Please Note…" Moorhead Daily News, September 12:4.

———. 1932. "Please Note…" Moorhead Daily News, September 13:4.

———. 1932. "Please Note…" Moorhead Daily News, September 27:4.

362

Bibliography

———. 1932. "Pre-Season Football Grind Reaches Climax." Moorhead Daily News, September 20:4.

———. 1932. "Spuds Lose Holzer for Opening Grid Tilt." Moorhead Daily News, September 15:4.

———. 1933. "1933 Cobber-Dragon Tilt Looms As Classic." Moorhead Daily News, September 25:4.

———. 1933. "Bison May Be Measuring Rod for Minnesota Champions." Moorhead Daily News, September 30:4.

———. 1933. "Bob Fritz to Enroll at Teachers College." Moorhead Daily News, February 23:4.

———. 1933. "Cleve Sees Toughest Test in St. John's." Moorhead Daily News, October 23:4.

———. 1933. "Cobber President Awaits 'Specific Reasons' for Rift." Moorhead Daily News, November 4:4.

———. 1933. "Cobbers Knock at Loop Throne Room Door." Moorhead Daily News, October 30:4.

———. 1933. "Cobbers Point for St. John's Here Oct. 28." Moorhead Daily News, October 16:4.

———. 1933. "Cobbers, Dragons Await Kickoff Saturday." Moorhead Daily News, September 29:4.

———. 1933. "Cobbers, Dragons Launch Drills for Annual Clash." Moorhead Daily News, September 26:4.

———. 1933. "Cobbers Under Full Steam for Mac Battle."

———. 1933. "College Coaches Plot to Break Tie Jinx." Moorhead Daily News, October 2:4.

———. 1933. "Dragons Card Bison for Grid Homecoming." Moorhead Daily News, February 20:4.

———. 1933. "Dragons Roar Defiance to Bison Invaders." Moorhead Daily News, November 3:4.

———. 1933. "Dragons Seek First Victory in Friday Tilt." Moorhead Daily News, October 12:4.

———. 1933. "Dragons, Cobbers Stress Offense in Drills." Moorhead Daily News, September 27:4.

———. 1933. "Dragons, Cobbers Trail Opponents at Half-Time." Moorhead Daily News, November 4:1.

———. 1933. "Gustavus 'Black Horde' Threatens Cobber Hopes." Moorhead Daily News, October 3:4.

———. 1933. "Hanna Musters Weight for Heavy Lakers." Moorhead Daily News, October 11:4.

———. 1933. "Hanna Shifts Spud Lineup for Wahpeton." Moorhead Daily News, October 18:4.

———. 1933. "Local Gridders End Schedules This Week." Moorhead Daily News, November 6:4.

———. 1933. "Loss of Gove Hard Blow to Bison Hopes." Moorhead Daily News, September 20:4.

———. 1933. "Macs Strengthened for Concordia Battle." Moorhead Daily News, October 10:4.

———. 1933. "Moorhead Elevens Polish Play for Openers Next Week." Moorhead Daily News, September 16:4.

———. 1933. "Moorhead's Football Camps to Begin Drills Next Week." Moorhead Daily News, September 2:4.

———. 1933. "Nemzek Perfects New Plays for Bison Tilt." Moorhead Daily News, November 2:4.

———. 1933. "Please Note.." Moorhead Daily News, November 2:4.

———. 1933. "Please Note..." Moorhead Daily News, December 5:4.

———. 1933. "Please Note..." Moorhead Daily News, March 8:4.

———. 1933. "Please Note..." Moorhead Daily News, November 4:4.

———. 1933. "Please Note..." Moorhead Daily News, November 27:4.

———. 1933. "Please Note..." Moorhead Daily News, October 3:4.

———. 1933. "Please Note..." Moorhead Daily News, October 9:4.

———. 1933. "Please Note..." Moorhead Daily News, October 10:4.

———. 1933. "Please Note..." Moorhead Daily News, October 19:4.

———. 1933. "Please Note..." Moorhead Daily News, October 26:4.

———. 1933. "Please Note..." Moorhead Daily News, September 16:4.

———. 1933. "Please Note..." Moorhead Daily News, September 21:4.

———. 1933. "Relief in Sight for Scoreless Cobbers." Moorhead Daily News, October 9:4.

———. 1933. "Rival Coaches Apply Polish for City Clash." Moorhead Daily News, September 28:4.

———. 1933. "Scoreless Tie Ends Bison Football Rule Over Cobbers." Moorhead Daily News, September 23:4.

———. 1933. "Spud-Midget Tilt Carded for Moorhead." Moorhead Daily News, October 24:4.

———. 1933. "Three Moorhead Football 'Factories' Hum with Activity." Moorhead Daily News, September 9:4.

———. 1934. "Bison Rout Is Biggest Gopher Score in 7 Years." Moorhead Daily News, October 1:4.

———. 1934. "Bison Stampede to 27-0 Triumph over St. Thomas." Moorhead Daily News, October 6:4.

———. 1934. "Bob Fritz Named Captain of Cobber Grid Machine." Moorhead Daily News, April 14:4.

———. 1934. "Cleve Picks Likely Lineup for Bison Game." Moorhead Daily News, September 20:4.

———. 1934. "Cleve Seeks Stronger Defense to Halt Tricky St. Mary's Machine." Moorhead Daily News, October 23:4.

———. 1934. "Cobbers Exhibit Power Despite Bison Triumph." Moorhead Daily News, September 22:4.

———. 1934. "Cobbers Inaugurate Title Play Tomorrow." Moorhead Daily News, October 12:4.

———. 1934. "Cobbers on Last Lap of Campaign for 1934 Title." Moorhead Daily News, November 8:4.

———. 1934. "Cobbers Stake Title Hopes Against Redmen." Moorhead Daily News, October 26:4.

———. 1934. "Cobbers, Bison Clash in Football Debut Tonight." Moorhead Daily News, September 21:4.

———. 1934. "Cobbers, Dragons Appear Headed for Titles in Respective Loops." Moorhead Daily News, October 15:4.

———. 1934. "Cobbers, Dragons Show Offensive Strength in Tie." Moorhead Daily News, October 1:4.

———. 1934. "Concordia Closes Spring Football Grind Tomorrow." Moorhead Daily News, April 26:4.

———. 1934. "Dragon-Bison Clash Climaxes Great Season." Moorhead Daily News, November 1:4.

———. 1934. "Dragons Soar to Immortality with Victory over Bison." Moorhead Daily News, November 3:4-5.

———. 1934. "Dragons, Bison May Use Aerial Maneuvers." Moorhead Daily News, October 30:4.

———. 1934. "Dragons, Cobbers Await Kickoff Saturday." Moorhead Daily News, September 28:4.

———. 1934. "Eddie Dahl Comes into His Own as Cobbers Continue on Title Quest." Moorhead Daily News, October 29:4.

———. 1934. "Flashy Dragons Open Loop Campaign against Winona Teachers Tomorrow." Moorhead Daily News, October 5:4.

———. 1934. "Fritz and Held Pace Cleve Machine in 26 to 0 Rout of Valiant Gusties." Moorhead Daily News, November 10:4.

———. 1934. "Indifference of Cobbers Worries Coaches." Moorhead Daily News, October 24:4.

———. 1934. "Local Grid Spotlight Focuses on Dragon-Bison Battle Next Saturday." Moorhead Daily News, October 27:4.

———. 1934. "Macs, Cadets Hold Key to State Grid Race." Moorhead Daily News, October 17:4.

———. 1934. "Myrom's Kick May Save Title for Cobbers." Moorhead Daily News, October 22:4.

———. 1934. "Nemzek Turns Down Game with Sioux." Moorhead Daily News, November 7:4.

———. 1934. "Please Note..." Moorhead Daily News, December 4:4.

———. 1934. "Please Note..." Moorhead Daily News, November 2:4.

———. 1934. "Please Note..." Moorhead Daily News, November 12:4.

———. 1934. "Please Note..." Moorhead Daily News, November 13:4.

———. 1934. "Please Note..." Moorhead Daily News, November 22:4.

———. 1934. "Please Note..." Moorhead Daily News, November 23:4.

———. 1934. "Please Note..." Moorhead Daily News, November 27:4.

———. 1934. "Please Note..." Moorhead Daily News, October 19:4.

———. 1934. "Please Note..." Moorhead Daily News, October 22:4.

———. 1934. "Please Note..." Moorhead Daily News, October 25:4.

———. 1934. "Please Note..." Moorhead Daily News, October 29:4.

Bibliography

———. 1934. "Please Note..." Moorhead Daily News, October 22:4.

———. 1934. "Please Note..." Moorhead Daily News, October 29:4.

———. 1934. "Please Note..." Moorhead Daily News, October 30:4.

———. 1934. "Schranz Lost to Bison for Tommy Game Tomorrow." Moorhead Daily News, October 4:4.

———. 1934. "Spuds Hope to Even Score with Wahpeton." Moorhead Daily News, October 18:4.

———. 1934. "Spuds, Midgets Set for Prep Grid Classic." September 27:4.

———. 1934. "Tommies Blast St. John's Title Hopes." Moorhead Daily News, November 5:4.

———. 1934. "Undefeated Dragons Favored over Bemidji." Moorhead Daily News, October 19:4.

———. 1935. "Bison Cop Intercity Title in Beating Dragons, 46-24." Moorhead Daily News, February 27:4.

———. 1935. "Please Note..." Moorhead Daily News, December 13:4.

———. 1935. "Please Note..." Moorhead Daily News, March 5:4.

Haman, Bill. 1932. "Fritz, Figenshaw Again Named All-State." Moorhead Daily News, November 17:4.

———. 1934. "Fritz, Midgarden, Butorac Capture All-State Berths." Moorhead Daily News, November 22:4.

Hamilton Spectator. 1926. "Large Crowd Greatly Enthused by Pro Struggle." Hamilton Spectator, November 9.

Harris, Lester O. 1934. "Bison Alone Unbeaten in Conference." Sioux City Journal, October 30:11.

———. 1934. "North Central Crown Will Be Up for Decision." Sioux City Journal, November 5:7.

Herald and Review. 1933. "Carleton Coach to be Knox Prof." Herald and Review, April 1:1923.

———. 1933. "Jackson Named Track Coach." Herald and Review, April 14:5.

Historic Detroit. "Mackenzie Hall." HistoricDetroit.org. 2021. Accessed October 6, 2021. https://historicdetroit.com/buildings/mackenzie-hall

Hockey Hall of Fame and Museum. "Lester Patrick." Player Inductees. 2021. Accessed August 6, 2021. https://www.hhof.com/HonouredMembers/MemberDetails.html?type=Player&mem=p194704

HockeyDB.com. "Calgary Bronks Statistics and History [S-AHL]." The Internet Hockey Database. 2021. Accessed September 24, 2021. https://www.hockeydb.com/stte/calgary-bronks-9270.html

Holland, George. 1930. "Spuds Show Flash in Winning 32-25 from Northerns." Moorhead Daily News, December 20:4.

Hollywood Chamber of Commerce. "Grantland Rice." Hollywood Walk of Fame. 2021. Accessed September 20, 2021. https://walkoffame.com/grantland-rice/

Honolulu Star-Bulletin. 1927. "Dakota Team Leaves Today for Mainland." Honolulu Star-Bulletin, January 5:22.

Hopkins, Jim. 1933. "News and Views." Oklahoma News, November 14:7.

Humber, William and Eves Raja. "The Baseball Tradition in Western Canada." Society for American Baseball Research. 1982. Accessed July 28, 2021. https://sabr.org/journal/article/the-baseball-tradition-in-western-canada/

Hurley, Hank. 1933. "Cobbers Study Rugby Rules for Contest Saturday." Fargo Forum, October 16:8.

———. 1933. "Earl Moran Not Available for St. John's Grid Game." Fargo Forum, October 25:10.

———. 1933. "Frank Cleve Expects Win Over Macalester Saturday." Fargo Forum, October 11:10.

———. 1934. "34 Gridders Report to Nemzek for Work at Moorhead Teachers College." Fargo Forum, September 7:12.

———. 1934. "Bison Gridders Impressive in Practice Work." Fargo Forum, September 13:12.

———. 1934. "Bison Make Progress Readying for Coyotes." Fargo Forum, October 10:8.

———. 1934. "Bison Varsity Enjoys Success Against Tommy Plays." Fargo Forum, October 3:10.

———. 1934. "Cleve Has Hopes for Cobbers in Title Bid." Fargo Forum, October 16:10.

———. 1934. "Cleve Seeks Changed Attitude for Cobbers in Conference Title Fight." Fargo Forum, October 25:22.

———. 1934. "Cleve Sounds Warning Note for Concordia." October 26:14.

———. 1934. "Cleve Warns Gridders Going to Get Tougher." Fargo Forum, September 8:5.

———. 1934. "Return of Gove Brings Smile to Finnegan's Face." Fargo Forum, September 12:12.

———. 1934. "Weather Raising Havoc with Grid Coaches in Fargo and Moorhead." Fargo Forum, September 26:10.

Huron Evening Huronite. 1933. "Cut Admission for Coyote-Bison Tilt." Huron Evening Huronite, November 8:9.

———. 1933. "Jackrabbits Return to Work for N.D. Teams after Week of Rest." Huron Evening Huronite, October 10:9.

———. 1933. "State Is Prepared for North Dakota Hobo Day Invasion." October 18:9.

IMDb.com, Inc. Rackety Rax (1932). IMDb.com. 2021. Accessed July 20, 2021. https://www.imdb.com/title/tt0023367/plotsummary

Indiana State University. 1934. "Ernie Zeller." Hall of Fame. 2021. Accessed August 29, 2021. https://gosycamores.com/honors/hall-of-fame/ernie-zeller/47

International Falls Daily Journal. 1929. "Record Travel U.S. to Canada." International Falls Daily Journal, September 18:1.

———. 1935. "Bob Fritz Leads Winnipegs to Canadian Rugby Title." International Falls Daily Journal, December 9:9.

———. 1935. "Fritz Leads 'Pegs in Quest of Title Today." International Falls Daily Journal, December 7:3.

International Olympic Committee. Los Angeles 1932. 2021. Accessed March 7, 2021. https://www.olympic.org/los-angeles-1932

Iowa City Daily Iowan. 1933. "Sodaks Fall before North Dakota State." Iowa City Daily Iowan, November 12:7.

Ironwood Daily Globe. 1934. "College Stars Coming Sunday." Ironwood Daily Globe, October 23:7.

Ithaca Journal. 1935. "Rules Makers Fail to Make Major Change." Ithaca Journal, February 19:10.

J.F.P. 1929. "Tigers Show Eskimos How." Calgary Herald, September 23:7.

J.M. Smucker Company. "About Us." Crosse & Blackwell. Accessed July 12, 2021. https://www.crosseandblackwell.com/about-us

Jackrabbit Sports Information Service. 2014 South Dakota State University Football Media Guide. Brookings: South Dakota State University. 2014. Page 124.

———. Jacks Football 1988. Brookings: South Dakota State University, 1988. Page 45.

Jahr, Merlyn. 1933. "Spring Football Practice Begins Monday." Spectrum, April 13:3.

Jamestown Sun. 1934. "Jimmies Outclass Manitoba 27 to 0." Jamestown Sun, October 6:6.

Johnson, Carvel. 1933. "Cobs Fight City Rivals to Scoreless Deadlocks." Concordian, October 6.

———. 1934. "Grid Rules Are Changed to Aid Offensive Team." Concordian, May 25:3.

Johnson, Charles. 1922. "Ticket Scalpers Grab Seats for Gopher Battle." Minneapolis Daily Star, October 31:8.

———. 1931. "Crisler Loses Speedy Reserve Back on Eve of Homecoming Tilt." Minneapolis Star, October 30:30.

Johnson, Harlowe. 1933. "Cobs Are Scored On for First Time in Eight Contests." Concordian, November 10:3.

———. 1933. "Fighting Cobs Overwhelm Macs in 26-0 Victory." Concordian, October 20:3.

Jose, Colin. "Manitoba: The Early Years." Canadian Soccer History. 2015. Accessed July 26, 2021. http://www.canadiansoccerhistory.com/Manitoba/Manitoba-%20The%20Early%20Years.html

Kansas City Star. 1925. "Twelve Letter Men Report." Kansas City Star, September 22:18.

Kearney, Jim. 1966. "Jim Kearney." Vancouver Sun, January 6:22.

Kelly, Graham. 1980. "Graham Kelly." Medicine Hat News, November 21:13.

Kenney, Kirk. 2020. "U-T Sports for Kids: NFL Draft Inspired 85 Years Ago by Bidding War for Minnesota Back." San Diego Union-Tribune, April 19.

Keyser, Tom. 1996. "Hanson Leaves Indelible Stamp on Community." Calgary Herald, February 15.

Knox College. Knox College Football Record Book. Galesburg, Illinois, 2019. Page 10.

Korstad, K. Robert, Ed. The Cobber 1935. Moorhead: Concordia College, 1935.

Koshevoy, Himie. 1934. "Olson Passes Riders to 22-2 Triumph over Meralomas." Vancouver News-Herald, November 12:3.

Bibliography

Kryk, John. "Why American Football Added A 4th Down." Toronto Sun, February 2, 2012. Accessed May 28, 2021. https://torontosun.com/2012/02/02/college-football-a-different-game-century-ago

Kunkel, Robert Scott. 1934. "Sioux Sport Slants." Dakota Student, October 30:3.

Kupcinet, Irving. 1933. "Sioux Sport Slants. "Dakota Student, October 31:3.

———. 1933. "Sioux Sport Slants." Dakota Student, October 27:5.

———. 1933. "Sioux Sport Slants." Dakota Student, September 25:3.

———. 1934. "Sioux Sport Slants." Dakota Student, October 26:3-4.

La Crosse Tribune. 1970. "Ted Whereatt Dies at 69." La Crosse Tribune, June 2:11.

Larson, Cal. 1934. "Eaton, Barsi to Lose Jobs, Report Says." Minneapolis Tribune, February 11:13.

Lawrence Daily Journal-World. 1934. "Will Aid Waldorf." Lawrence Daily Journal-World, March 26:10.

Leader-Post. 1930. "Intercollegiate Rugby Moguls Want to Use Forward Pass." Leader-Post, March 4:12.

———. 1932. "Along the Sport Byways." Leader-Post, September 20:10.

———. 1932. "American Rugby Thursday." Leader-Post, September 20:10.

———. 1932. "Carl Cronin, a Knute Rockne Product, Primes Winnipegs to Shatter Hopes of St. John's in Western Rugby Campaign." Leader-Post, August 30:8.

———. 1932. "Former Reginans in Eastern Canada Resent Prominence Given 'Americans' on Roughrider Rugby Lineup of 1932." Leader-Post, December 15:13.

———. 1932. "Homecoming of 'Riders Proves Success." Leader-Post, September 23:14.

———. 1932. "International Rugby." Leader-Post, September 22:15.

———. 1932. "International Rugby." Leader-Post, September 23:15.

———. 1932. "Minot Favors Aerial Attack." Leader-Post, September 21:10.

———. 1932. "Professional Rugby League Planned in East." Leader-Post, December 10:11.

———. 1932. "Regina Breaks Even in Weekend Rugby." Leader-Post, September 26:10.

———. 1932. "Riders to Make Home Debut Tonight." Leader-Post, September 22:14.

———. 1932. "Roughriders Triumph Over St. John's by Score 9 to 1." Leader-Post, November 5:1.

———. 1932. "Weakened Team Faces Maroons." Leader-Post, September 17:11.

———. 1933. "Along the Sport Byways." Leader-Post, November 6:12.

———. 1933. "Riders Will Tackle Minot." Leader-Post, September 23:10.

———. 1933. "Winnipegs Write 'Finis to 'Rider Reign with 11-1 Victory." Leader-Post, November 6:12.

———. 1934. "Canada's Highest Scoring Teams Meet in Final Saturday." Leader-Post, November 23:24.

———. 1934. "Carl Cronin Deserts Winnipeg Rugby Team." Leader-Post, May 1:16.

———. 1934. "Ex-Minnesota Star Last Recruit for Roughriders." Leader-Post, September 1:16.

———. 1934. "Forward Pass Rule Altered." Leader-Post, November 12:16.

———. 1934. "Imperials Have Assortment of Attacks to Fit Weather." Leader-Post, November 22:19.

———. 1934. "New Roughriders." Leader-Post, September 17:16.

———. 1934. "Phat' Defrate." Leader-Post, November 3:16.

———. 1934. "Rugby Refs to Carry Horns." Leader-Post, September 18:17.

———. 1934. "Statistics on Rugby Battle." Leader-Post, November 5:16.

———. 1934. "Weekend at a Glance." Leader-Post, October 22:16.

———. 1934. [No headline.] Leader-Post, October 3:21.

———. 1935. "Bronks Win by 14-point Margin." Leader-Post, November 4:16.

———. 1935. "Dynamite Kid to Return!" Leader-Post, June 8:16.

———. 1935. "Winnipeg Stars on Injured List." Leader-Post, October 14:17.

———. 1935. "Winnipegs Hit Wintry Weather." Leader-Post, December 2:20.

———. 1935. "Winnipegs in Easy Triumph." Leader-Post, October 21:17.

———. 1935. "Winnipegs Lose Star Lineman as Greg Kabat Hurt." Leader-Post, October 7:16.

———. 1935. "Winnipegs May Get Offer to Play in 'Frisco." Leader-Post, December 9:1.

———. 1935. "Winnipegs Trim Minnesotans." Leader-Post, September 30:17.

Leah, Vince. 1943. "From the Sidelines." Winnipeg Tribune, December 1:14.

———. 1958. "Yussel Set a Non-Stop Talking Record." Winnipeg Tribune, June 6:22.

———. 1963. "Another Member for the Alumni." Winnipeg Tribune, January 14:14.

———. 1988. "West Beats East." Winnipeg Free Press, November 27:44.

Lee, Hans. 1934. "Cobbers Lead Conference with Grid Victory: Cobbers Win Over St. Mary's Redmen, 39 to 0." Concordian, November 2:3.

Lefebvre, Jim. "Philly 'Will Be Bonkers' for Irish-Temple Tilt." Forever Irish: Celebrating the Heritage of Notre Dame Football. October 26, 2015. Accessed February 25, 2021. http://ndfootballhistory.com/philly-will-be-bonkers-for-irish-temple-tilt

Lethbridge Herald. 1931. "Hamilton's Mighty Tiger Squad Bite Dust Before Onslaught of Montreal's Winged Wheelers." Lethbridge Herald, November 2:11.

———. 1934. "Roughriders Get New Players for Current Season." Lethbridge Herald, August 7:10.

———. 1935. "Calgary and Winnipeg in Western Final." Lethbridge Herald, November 4:10.

———. 1935. "Cardiac Disturbances Being Predicted for Saturday at 'Riders and Winnipegs Clash." Lethbridge Herald, October 30:10.

———. 1935. "Champion Rugby Squad Is Wildly Welcomed Home." Lethbridge Herald, December 10:5.

———. 1935. "Coach Carl Cronin Busily Whipping Conglomeration of Grid Material into Hoped-for Rugby Champions." Lethbridge Herald, August 30:5.

———. 1935. "More Work for Winnipegs." Lethbridge Herald, December 3:10.

———. 1935. "Sport Chatter." Lethbridge Herald, October 15:10.

———. 1935. "Statistical Account of Winnipegs-Hamilton Epic." Lethbridge Herald, December 9:26.

———. 1935. "Winnipeg Defeats Sarnia Imperials 3-1." Lethbridge Herald, September 23:10.

———. 1935. "Winnipegs Return without Grey Cup." Lethbridge Herald, December 9:26.

Lewis, Bill. 1934. "Pats and Pans." Edmonton Bulletin, March 1:14.

Library of Congress. NCAA and the Movement to Reform College Football: Topics in Chronicling America. 2021. Accessed June 29, 2021. https://guides.loc.gov/chronicling-america-ncaa-college-football-reform

Lileks, James. "The Andrews." The Lost Hotels of Minneapolis. Accessed February 25, 2021. http://www.lileks.com/mpls/hotels/andrews/index.html

Lincoln Star. 1934. "Minnesota Wins 56-12 Game over North Dakotans." Lincoln Star, September 30:5.

Lincoln Sunday Star. 1923. "Dakota Leaguers Report to Links." Lincoln Sunday Star, July 22:9.

Lind, Bob. "Lind: Readers miss cafes, prices of yesteryear." Entertainment. INFORUM.com. March 16, 2009. Accessed July 22, 2021. https://www.inforum.com/entertainment/2887514-lind-readers-miss-cafes-prices-yesteryear

Locklin, C.D. 1932. "Bison Halt Long Nodak Winning Streak by 7-6 Victory." Grand Forks Herald, October 23:1,11.

———. 1933. "Looking through the Knothole." Grand Forks Herald, October 25:7.

———. 1933. "Looking through the Knothole." Grand Forks Herald, October 24:7.

———. 1934. "Inspired Bison Upset Sioux, 7 to 0." Grand Forks Herald, October 28:1,12.

———. 1934. "Looking through the Knothole." Grand Forks Herald, September 19:10.

———. 1934. "Looking through the Knothole." Grand Forks Herald, October 22:7.

Bibliography

———. 1934. "Looking through the Knothole." Grand Forks Herald, October 23:6.

———. 1934. "Looking through the Knothole." Grand Forks Herald, October 25:8.

———. 1934. "West Hopeful as Sioux Beat Winnipeg by 13-3." Grand Forks Herald, September 22:2.

Los Angeles Times. 1965. "Stan Williamson, Former USC Football Star, Dies." Los Angeles Times, August 18:32.

———. 1970. "Col. Stanley G. Backman, 84." Los Angeles Times, March 28:29.

Lowell Sun. 1933. "Bone Crushers Throw Indians." Lowell Sun, November 13:13.

———. 1933. "Lo, the Poor Indians--Face Wrestlers' Team Sunday." Lowell Sun, November 9:32.

———. 1933. "Lowell Indians Stack Up Against All-Wrestler Football Team Here Tomorrow." Lowell Sun, November 11:32.

Lubbock Avalanche-Journal. 1934. "North Dakota State Bisons Arrive Today." Lubbock Avalanche-Journal, November 18:15.

———. 1934. "Friday Battle May Be Closer than Expected." Lubbock Morning Avalanche, November 22:5.

———. 1934. "Matadors and Bisons Drill on Same Field; Westerners Are in Better Spirits." Lubbock Morning Avalanche, November 20:2.

———. 1934. "North Dakota State Gridders Show More Speed in Second Workout Here for Matadors; Tech Smooths Attack." Lubbock Morning Avalanche, November 21:2.

Lyone. 1934. "Down the Bison Trail." Winnipeg Manitoban, October 10:3.

Mac Weekly. 1931. "League Schedule Begins with Tilt against Cobbers." Mac Weekly, October 8:4.

———. 1931. "Macmen Bow to Superior Cobber Team, 18-0." Mac Weekly, October 15:4.

———. 1932. "Gowans' Men Hold Favored Cobbers to Draw." Mac Weekly, October 20:1,3.

———. 1932. "Mac to Meet '31 Conference Champs Saturday." Mac Weekly, October 13:3.

———. 1933. "Battered Mac Team to Meet Concordia." Mac Weekly, October 12:3.

———. 1933. "Cobbers Down Macs 26 to 0 Saturday." Mac Weekly, October 19:3.

———. 1934. "Macs Face Big Test in Cob Battle." Mac Weekly, October 18:3.

Mackenzie, Cam. 1934. "The World of Sport." Winnipeg Free Press, September 22:23.

Mackintosh, George. 1934. "Sporting Periscope." Edmonton Journal, September 18:8.

Mackintosh, George. 1948. "The Sporting Periscope." Edmonton Journal, October 22: 10.

Manitoba Baseball Hall of Fame. "Manitoba Baseball in the Thirties." Honouring Our Pioneers, 2021. Accessed May 29, 2021. https://mbhof.ca/pioneers/

Manitoba Free Press. 1892. "A Rugby Union: Footballers organize a rugby association for the province." Manitoba Free Press, February 24:5.

Manitoba Historical Society. "Historic Sites of Manitoba: Paris Building (259 Portage Avenue, Winnipeg)." Manitoba Historical Society. 2021. Accessed September 28, 2021. http://www.mhs.mb.ca/docs/sites/parisbuilding.shtml

———. "Historic Sites of Manitoba: Royal Alexandra Hotel / Canadian Club of Winnipeg War Memorial (Higgins Avenue, Winnipeg)" Manitoba Historical Society. July 30, 2021. Accessed October 3, 2021. http://www.mhs.mb.ca/docs/sites/royalalexandrahotel.shtml

———. 1935. "Historic Sites of Manitoba: Metropolitan Theatre (281 Donald Street, Winnipeg)." Manitoba Historical Society. January 26, 2020. Accessed October 6, 2021. http://www.mhs.mb.ca/docs/sites/metropolitantheatre.shtml

Manitoba Rugby Hall of Fame. "Winnipeg Blue Bombers." Manitoba Rugby Hall of Fame. 2021. Accessed October 13, 2021. http://www.manitobarugbyhalloffame.com/winnipeg-blue-bombers.html

Manitoba Science, Technology, Energy and Mines. "San Antonio Mine." 2002. Accessed August 5, 2021. https://www.gov.mb.ca/iem/min-ed/mbhistory/mininv/273.htm

Manitoba Sports Hall of Fame. "Bud Marquardt." Honored Members Database. 2021. Accessed October 26, 2021. http://honouredmembers.sportmanitoba.ca/inductee.php?id=280

———. "Frank J. Hannibal." Honored Members Database. 2021. Accessed September 22, 2021. http://honouredmembers.sportmanitoba.ca/inductee.php?id=266

———. "Fritz Hanson 'The Golden Ghost' 'Twinkletoes'." Honored Members Database. 2021. Accessed October 26, 2021. http://honouredmembers.sportmanitoba.ca/inductee.php?id=7

Manitou Messenger. 1924. "Improved Ole Team Defeats Concordia Here Saturday, 16-0." Manitou Messenger, October 7:1.

———. 1931. "Vikings Smash Cobbers 21-6 in Final Thriller." Manitou Messenger, November 24:4.

———. 1932. "Cobbers Turn Back Ademen 13-7 Saturday." Manitou Messenger, October 11:4.

———. 1933. "Eastern School Follows Viking Athletic Events." Manitou Messenger, November 21:4.

Manitowoc Herald Times. 1933. "Superior Men Tie N. Dakota." Manitowoc Herald Times, October 21:12.

Marlborough Hotel. Our Winnipeg Canada Hotel History. 2021. Accessed July 19, 2021. http://www.themarlborough.ca/history-en.html

Marsh, James H. "Lionel Conacher." The Canadian Encyclopedia. November 20, 2017. Accessed November 5, 2021. https://www.thecanadianencyclopedia.ca/en/article/lionel-conacher

Marsh, Lou. 1934. "Conny's Collection Conquer Grid Rivals from Rochester." Toronto Daily Star, October 4:16.

Matheson, Jack. 2000. "They Played, Then Stayed." Winnipeg Free Press, June 10:F6.

Mayville State University. "Ed Rorvig." Hall of Fame. 2021. Accessed October 21, 2021. https://msucomets.com/honors/hall-of-fame/ed-rorvig/83

———. Lewy Lee. Hall of Fame. 2021. Accessed June 23, 2021. https://msucomets.com/honors/hall-of-fame/lewy-lee/64

McGrath, Walt. 1934. "Bison Meet First Conference Foe Tomorrow." Spectrum, January 19:1.

———. 1934. "Brookings Game to Decide NCC Title." Spectrum, November 9:5.

———. 1934. "Decrease in Funds Fails to Reduce Athletic Standard." Spectrum, May 4:4.

———. 1934. "Spectrum Sport Speculations." Spectrum, April 20:4.

———. 1935. "Spectrum Sport Speculations." Spectrum, October 11:12.

McKenzie, Cam. 1931. "Record Crowd Sees Colorful and Exciting Senior Rugby Match." Winnipeg Free Press, October 5:17.

———. 1931. "St. John's Grid Club Has Had Long Career." Winnipeg Free Press, October 31:21.

———. 1932. "Garrison Goes Down to 26-6 Defeat in First Grid Battle." Winnipeg Free Press, September 26:7.

———. 1932. "Johnians Take Opening Senior Rugby Football Game." Winnipeg Free Press, September 19:8.

———. 1932. "St. John's Roll Up 36-1 Score Against Garrison." Winnipeg Free Press, September 29:17.

———. 1933. "Winnipeg Teams Reach Finals." Winnipeg Tribune, November 6:1.

———. 1934. "Locals Disappointing When Defeated by Score of 21-20." Winnipeg Free Press, October 16:16.

———. 1934. "North Dakota Freshmen Score 31-0 Win over Varsity." Winnipeg Free Press, October 15:16.

———. 1934. "University of Manitoba Gridders Make Impressive Debut." Winnipeg Free Press, October 1:8.

———. 1934. "Winnipegs Are Defeated by Minnesota All-Stars, 13 to 8." Winnipeg Free Press, September 17:8.

———. 1935. "After the Ball Was Over'." Winnipeg Free Press, November 4:13.

———. 1935. "Carl Cronin Heaps Praise on Starry 'Peg Halfback." Winnipeg Free Press, November 11:6.

———. 1935. "Minnesota Stars Crushed by 'Pegs--Sarnia Trounces Western Mustangs." Winnipeg Free Press, September 30:14.

———. 1935. "Roughriders Here for Battle." Winnipeg Free Press, November 2:25.

———. 1935. "Victorias Provide Courageous Display When Beaten by 'Pegs 29-3." Winnipeg Free Press, October 7:15.

———. 1935. "Weakened Winnipegs Uncover Class--Toronto Grid Clubs Going Strong." Winnipeg Free Press, October 21:12.

Bibliography

———. 1935. "Winnipegs Make an Impressive Debut--Sarnia Held to 4-0 at Regina." *Winnipeg Free Press*, September 16:12.

McLemore, Henry. 1935. "Canadian Rugby Better than American Game McLemore Discovers." *International Falls Daily Journal*, December 9:9.

McNamara, Jim. 1934. "Purple Pennings." *Aquin*, October 5:7.

McQuilkin, Scott A., and Ronald A. Smith. "The Rise and Fall of the Flying Wedge: Football's Most Controversial Play." *Journal of Sport History* 20, no. 1 (1993): 57–64. http://www.jstor.org/stable/43610431.

Meraloma Rugby Club. "Meraloma Club History." *Meraloma Rugby Club*. 2021. Accessed September 16, 2021. https://www.meralomarugby.com/club-history

Metcalfe, Bill. 1934. "Winnipegs Rally in Last Half but Lose to Concordia 26-16." *Winnipeg Free Press*, October 9:13.

Miami Daily News Record. 1933. "Goldbugs Sting North Dakotans in 19-to-0 Fray." *Miami Daily News Record*, November 19:4.

Milazzo, Brit. 1934. "World's Imaging Centre Captures North America's Largest Sports Market." *Bleacher Report*. 2021. Accessed August 28, 2021. https://bleacherreport.com/articles/152509-worlds-imaging-centre-captures-north-americas-largest-sports-market

Minneapolis Daily Star. 1927. "Dr. Spears Marooned at Jordan as His Men Pick Gibson as Captain." *Minneapolis Daily Star*, December 8:12.

Minneapolis Morning Tribune. 1927. "Gophers' Last Week of Practice Begins Today." *Minneapolis Morning Tribune*, September 26:9.

———. 1928. "Arsenault and Callendar, Gopher Sophomore Backs, Ineligible for Season." *Minneapolis Morning Tribune*, October 4:21.

———. 1928. "Gophers Given Thorough Defensive Workout Against Hawkeye Plays." *Minneapolis Morning Tribune*, October 24:16.

———. 1929. "Perham Drubs Detroit Lakes." *Minneapolis Morning Tribune*, October 26: 29.

Minneapolis Star Tribune. 1987. "Wally Hass, Former Gopher Football Star, Carleton Coach, Dies." *Minneapolis Star Tribune*, September 15:26.

Minneapolis Star. 1929. "Cobber Practice Slowed by Cold Weather." September 18: 18.

———. 1929. "Hendricks, Moorhead to Compete in State Floor Tourney." *Minneapolis Star*, March 18:16.

———. 1929. "May Be Spears' Regular Center." *Minneapolis Star*, September 26:18.

———. 1930. "Bert Oja, Gopher Grid Luminary Lands Louisville Coaching Berth." *Minneapolis Star*, May 13:13.

———. 1931. "All-Stars to Drill Sunday." *Minneapolis Star*, November 21:8.

———. 1931. "Concordia Places Four Men on Star Team." *Minneapolis Star*, November 21:9.

———. 1931. "Injuries Hit Cobber Camp." *Minneapolis Sunday Tribune*, November 17:12.

———. 1931. "Michaelson, Promising Glencoe Gridder, Goes to South Dakota School." *Minneapolis Star*, September 16:14.

———. 1931. "Star Halfback Works Out in Signal Drill." *Minneapolis Star*, October 29:18.

———. 1932. "Bert Oja Back at U to Continue Medical Work." *Minneapolis Star*, September 30:23.

———. 1932. "Bob Reihsen Named Coach of Kunz Football Squad." *Minneapolis Star*, September 6:13.

———. 1932. "Haycraft Team Plays Lidberg Eleven Nov. 24." *Minneapolis Star*, November 3:14.

———. 1932. "John Chommie, Belluzo also Will Enroll." *Minneapolis Star*, March 21:12.

———. 1932. "Manders Makes Last Grid Stand." *Minneapolis Star*, December 1:15.

———. 1932. "Manders Stars Challenge for Twin City Title." *Minneapolis Star*, November 28:13.

———. 1932. "Oja, Another Former Gopher, Joins Kunz'." *Minneapolis Star*, October 22:14.

———. 1932. [No Heading]. *Minneapolis Star*, March 16:14.

———. 1933. "Bert Oja Signed as Augsburg Line Coach." *Minneapolis Star*, September 19:12.

———. 1933. "Earl Jackson Gets Post at Fergus Falls High." *Minneapolis Star*, September 1:22.

———. 1933. "Gopher All-Stars to Play Under Lights Here Thursday." *Minneapolis Star*, October 2:13.

———. 1933. "Gopher Grads to Use Spears-Crisler Style against Gopher Regulars." *Minneapolis Star*, April 15:2.

———. 1933. "Nic Musty Signs as Coach at St. Mary's." *Minneapolis Star*, June 6:17.

———. 1933. "Robinson Gets 17 Players for Football Tilt." *Minneapolis Star*, April 15:1.

———. 1933. "Saumer Eligible for St. Olaf Next Fall; Newby Is Ruled Out." *Minneapolis Star*, May 29:8.

———. 1934. "East Sides and Jerseys Offer Park Threats." *Minneapolis Star*, October 22:14.

———. 1934. "Macs Suffer Serious Blow; Venzke Is Out." *Minneapolis Star*, October 17:17.

———. 1934. "Macs, Cobbers Battle in Big Tilt in Midway." *Minneapolis Star*, October 19:25.

———. 1934. "Three Injured Macs Return." *Minneapolis Star*, October 16:14.

———. 1934. "Wally Hass Leaves Tonight to Become Manitoba Head Man." *Minneapolis Star*, August 27:12.

———. 1934. "Wally Hass Starts as Manitoba Coach without Man Who Has Played Yankee Sport; Premier's Son on Grid Squad." *Minneapolis Star*, September 18:10.

———. 1934. "Wally Hass to Manitoba 'U'." *Minneapolis Star*, August 6:11.

———. 1935. "Twin City, Tri-State Grid Loops Merge for Inter-Division Games." *Minneapolis Star*, August 20:15.

Minneapolis Sunday Tribune. 1926. "N.D. Coach Lays Claim to Invention of 'Huddle.'" *Minneapolis Sunday Tribune*, February 14:37.

———. 1928. "Gopher Summary." *Minneapolis Sunday Tribune*, October 21:36.

———. 1928. "Heroes of Gophers' Great Triumph." *Minneapolis Sunday Tribune*, November 25:23.

———. 1929. "15 Moorhead Prep Gridders Get Letters." *Minneapolis Sunday Tribune*, November 17:28.

———. 1929. "Gophers Engage in Strenuous Scrimmage." *Minneapolis Sunday Tribune*, September 22: 23.

———. 1930. "Close Successful Grid Season." *Minneapolis Sunday Tribune*, November 30:27.

———. 1930. "Up They Jump for Tipoff in State Title Cage Battle." *Minneapolis Sunday Tribune*, March 30:21.

———. 1931. "Bits of Action and Stars of State Prep Track Meet." *Minneapolis Sunday Tribune*, June 7:19.

———. 1931. "Cobbers and Tommies Top All-Conference Eleven." *Minneapolis Sunday Tribune*, November 29:26.

———. 1931. "Cobbers Whip Gusties, 41-6, to Keep Loop Mark Clear." *Minneapolis Sunday Tribune*, November 8:4.

———. 1931. "Frank Cleve's Powerful Cobbers Eye State College Title." *Minneapolis Sunday Tribune*, October 11:18.

———. 1931. "St. John's Stuns St. Olaf Squad with 13 to 0 Upset." *Minneapolis Sunday Tribune*, October 25:18.

Minneapolis Tribune. "Cobbers Defeat Oles in Fiercely Waged Battle, 13-7." *Minneapolis Tribune*, October 9:16.

———. 1927. "Savage Has Made Unusual Record as Coach at Hibbing." *Minneapolis Tribune*, January 2:38.

———. 1930. "Gophers Hang Up Grid Togs; 1931 Prospects Are Bright." *Minneapolis Tribune*, November 24:9.

———. 1931. "Bits of Action and Stars of State Prep Track Meet." *Minneapolis Tribune*, June 7:19.

———. 1931. "Cobbers Romp over Hibbing Jrs., 26-6." *Minneapolis Tribune*, October 4:19.

———. 1931. "Hibbing Junior College Hopes for Title Team." *Minneapolis Tribune*, August 30:31.

———. 1931. "Who's Who in Gopher Football." *Minneapolis Tribune*, October 28:12.

———. 1932. "Bison Wallop Oklahoma City by 27-7 Score." *Minneapolis Tribune*, October 15:21.

———. 1932. "Bison Win Bitter 12-6 Game from S.D. State."

———. 1932. "Cleve Boasts Big, Fast Cobber Squad." *Minneapolis Tribune*, September 11:21.

———. 1932. "Cobbers Open on Thursday." *Minneapolis Tribune*, September 4:15.

———. 1932. "Cobbers Win over Moorhead." *Minneapolis Tribune*, October 2:19.

———. 1932. "Fighting Macalester Team Holds Concordia to 7-7 Tie." *Minneapolis Tribune*, October 16:19.

———. 1932. "Fritz Cobbers' 'Key' Gridder: Ambidextrous Punter, Passer Is Star of Concordia College Eleven." *Minneapolis Tribune*, October 12: 21.

———. 1932. "Fumble Gives Bison 7 to 6 Victory Over North Dakota 'U.'" *Minneapolis Tribune*, October 23:14.

———. 1932. "Jack Manders Leads All-Stars to 12-6 Win." *Minneapolis Tribune*, December 5:12.

Bibliography

———. 1932. "Raferts and Aces Struggle Today." Minneapolis Tribune, November 29:25.

———. 1932. "Raferts and Ewalds Stake Records Today." Minneapolis Tribune, October 23:17.

———. 1932. "State College Squads Start." Minneapolis Tribune, September 11:21.

———. 1933. "Bison Defeat Dragon Team By 20-0 Score." Minneapolis Tribune, November 5:23.

———. 1933. "Bison Start Building New Grid Machine." Minneapolis Tribune, September 10:17.

———. 1933. "Cobbers Show Pep in Drills." Minneapolis Tribune, September 10: 15.

———. 1933. "Gustie Eleven Will Engage Cobber Team." Minneapolis Tribune, October 1:17.

———. 1933. "Moorhead Peds Tie Concordia." Minneapolis Tribune, October 1:16.

———. 1933. "Quarterback Big Need of Bison Squad." Minneapolis Tribune, September 17:18.

———. 1933. "Redmen Ruin Cobbers' Chance to Share Title, 2-0." Minneapolis Tribune, November 5:24.

———. 1933. "St. John's Severs Athletic Relations with Concordia; Cage Tilts Cancelled." Minneapolis Tribune, November 4:21.

———. 1933. "Tie Games Muddle State College Race." Minneapolis Tribune, October 24:15.

———. 1933. "Wilbur Eaton Appointed St. Thomas Grid Coach." Minneapolis Tribune, August 13:13.

———. 1933. "Winnipeg Rugby Defeats Cobbers." Minneapolis Tribune, October 22:17.

———. 1934. "Bears Score 14 to 3 Victory over Gopher All-Stars." Minneapolis Tribune, November 8:18.

———. 1934. "Bison Defeat Cobbers 6-0, in the Opener." Minneapolis Tribune, September 22:20.

———. 1934. "Bison Defeat N.D.U. for Lead in Conference." Minneapolis Tribune, October 28:15.

———. 1934. "Cobbers Down Winnipeg 33-27." Minneapolis Tribune, October 7:20.

———. 1934. "Concordia Smothers Gustavus 26 to 0, and Wins Title." Minneapolis Tribune, November 10:19.

———. 1934. "Concordia Trounces St. Olaf in Conference Opener, 19-7." Minneapolis Tribune, October 14:18.

———. 1934. "Dragons Play Cobber Team to 13-13 Tie." Minneapolis Tribune, September 30:18.

———. 1934. "Flour City Eleven That Retained Its Twin City Grid Title." Minneapolis Tribune, November 30:20.

———. 1934. "Macs and Tommies Hold Key to State Conference Title." Minneapolis Tribune, October 17:17.

———. 1934. "N.D. Bison Trample St. Thomas Eleven under 27 to 0 Avalanche." Minneapolis Tribune, October 6:19.

———. 1934. "Rampaging Cobbers Wallop St. Mary's Eleven, 39-0." Minneapolis Tribune, October 28:12.

———. 1934. "S.D. State Ruins Bison Title Hopes by 38-0 Win." November 11:15.

———. 1934. "Tommies See Little Chance Against Bison." Minneapolis Tribune, October 5:31.

———. 1934. "University Station and WTCN to Join in Grid Broadcast." Minneapolis Tribune, September 22:1.

———. 1934. "Veteran Bison Team Will Face Gophers." Minneapolis Tribune, September 23:21.

Minnesota Historical Society. 1965. "Center Avenue, Moorhead." Collections Online. Accessed February 17, 2021. http://collections.mnhs.org/cms/display.php?irn=10462966

Minnesota Intercollegiate Athletic Conference. "MIAC Football Recordbook." The Official Site of the Minnesota Intercollegiate Athletic Conference. Accessed February 16, 2021. https://www.miacathletics.com/about/honor_history/records/archives/fball-archive

Minnesota Prep Track. 2017. "MSHSL State Meet." Minnesota Prep Track & Field and Cross Country. Accessed October 22, 2019. http://www.mnpreptrack.com/MSHSL%20State%20results/1930%20MSHSL%20State%20T&F.pdf

Minnesota State University Moorhead. "Football Year by Year." MSUM Dragons. Accessed February 17, 2021. https://www.msumdragons.com/documents/2018/8/13//Football_Year_by_Year.pdf?id=3708

Minot Daily News. 1931. "All Star Aggregation Is Named to Oppose Beavers in Charity Grid Contest." Minot Daily News, October 28:6.

———. 1931. "All Star Grid Squad to Practice Sunday." Minot Daily News, October 31:7.

———. 1931. "All Star Gridders Hold Night Workout." Minot Daily News, November 3:8.

———. 1931. "Beavers and All Stars Clash in Charity Grid Game This Evening." Minot Daily News, November 11:6.

———. 1931. "Beavers and All Stars Clash Wednesday Night in Charity Grid Game." Minot Daily News, November 9:6.

———. 1931. "Hey, Kids!" Minot Daily news, November 11:6.

———. 1931. "Minot Beavers Defeat All Stars, 6 to 0, in Charity Grid Contest." Minot Daily News, November 12:8.

———. 1931. "Red Jarrett Will Feature All Star Lineup in Game with Beavers." Minot Daily News, November 10:6.

———. 1931. "You Want to See Jarrett in Action." Minot Daily News, November 10:8.

———. 1932. "Beavers Beat Panthers by Touchdown Margin." Minot Daily News, November 5:10.

———. 1932. "College and Panthers to Play on Weekend." Minot Daily News, November 1:6.

———. 1932. "Minot Independents to Play Regina Pats." Minot Daily News, September 19:5.

———. 1932. "Regina Wins Second Game from Panthers." Minot Daily News, September 26:5.

———. 1934. "Beaver Gridders End Home Season with 26-0 Victory over Manitoba University." Minot Daily News, November 3:8.

———. 1934. "Minot Beaver Gridders Clash with Manitobans in Game Tonight." Minot Daily News, November 2:6.

———. 1934. "Minot Grid Teams Prepare for Tilts Friday, Saturday." Minot Daily News, November 1:8.

———. 1934. "Three Minot Teams Active on Home Field This Week." Minot Daily News, October 31:6.

Mitchell Evening Republican. 1928. "Kasper Favored for West's Post." Mitchell Evening Republican, April 13:2.

Moorhead Daily News. 1928. "12 Cagers on Hanna's 1928 M.H.S. Squad." Moorhead Daily News, November 17.

———. 1928. "Spud Lineup Shifted for Fergus Game." Moorhead Daily News, December 7.

———. 1929. "22 Workout at Concordia on Tuesday." Moorhead Daily News, September 11:11.

———. 1929. "Social Notes." Moorhead Daily News, December 16:4.

———. 1929. "Cobbers Drill Against Auggie Plays." Moorhead Daily News, October 16:3.

———. 1929. "Legion Nine Seek Games with Fargo." Moorhead Daily News, June 26:3.

———. 1930. "KGFK to Have Studio in Comstock Hotel." Moorhead Daily News, April 3:1.

———. 1930. "Moorhead High is Defeated 19-6 by Perham Gridsters." Moorhead Daily News, September 22:4.

———. 1930. "Schranz, Wilbur Marquardt Will Head Spud Teams." Moorhead Daily News, May 27:4.

———. 1931. "18 Cobbers Get Gold Footballs." Moorhead Daily News, December 15:4.

———. 1931. "Bison Boxing Season Begins." Moorhead Daily News, February 2:4.

———. 1931. "Cobber Athletes Get Week's Rest before Cage Call." Moorhead Daily News, November 23:4.

———. 1931. "Cobber-Gustavus Views with Dragon-Bison Tilt Saturday." Moorhead Daily News, November 3:4.

———. 1931. "Cobbers Anxious to Retain Clean Slate in Ole Mix." Moorhead Daily News, November 17:4.

———. 1931. "Cobbers Battle Johnnies Today." Moorhead Daily News, October 31:4.

———. 1931. "Cobbers Drill to Halt Tommy Pass Offense Saturday." Moorhead Daily News, November 11:4.

———. 1931. "Cobbers Prepare for Crucial Tilt with St. John's." Moorhead Daily News, October 28:6.

———. 1931. "Cobbers Prepare for Macalester; Beat Hibbing 26-6." Moorhead Daily News, October 5:4.

———. 1931. "Cobbers Will Try Stopping Gusties' Formations Today." Moorhead Daily News, November 4:4.

———. 1931. "Cobbers, Dragons Given New Plays for Crucial Tilt." Moorhead Daily News, October 13:4.

———. 1931. "Concordia Fights for Grid Title on Wet, Soggy Field." Moorhead Daily News, November 14:1.

———. 1931. "Concordia Gophers Beat Flickers 30-20." Moorhead Daily News, November 27:4.

———. 1931. "F-M Comets to Play Lakes Six." Moorhead Daily News, December 21:4.

368

Bibliography

———. 1931. "Football Results." *Moorhead Daily News*, November 9:4.

———. 1931. "Freshman to Aid Cobbers in Dragon Battle Friday." *Moorhead Daily News*, December 26:4.

———. 1931. "Fritz and Renne May Not Start Against Oles Saturday." *Moorhead Daily News*, November 18:4.

———. 1931. "Marquardt, Hanson Star in Baby Bison Triumph." *Moorhead Daily News*, November 7:4.

———. 1931. "Shipp Rejoins Cobber 'Four Norsemen' Group." *Moorhead Daily News*, October 27:4.

———. 1931. "St. Olaf Leads Cobbers 21 to 0 at End of Half." *Moorhead Daily News*, November 21:1.

———. 1931. "The Starting Lineups." *Moorhead Daily News*, October 16:4.

———. 1931. "Bud Marquardt Named Center on All-State Team." *Moorhead Daily News*, March 30:4.

———. 1931. "Concordia Prepares for Bison Clash Friday Eve; Dragons Fight for Posts." *Moorhead Daily News*, September 14:4.

———. 1931. "Dilworth Outscores Perham Cagers 34-28." *Moorhead Daily News*, January 17:4.

———. 1931. "Moorhead Schools Launch Their 1931 Football Campaigns." *Moorhead Daily News*, September 9:4.

———. 1931. "Record Broken as Crosby-Ironton Is Region Champion." *Moorhead Daily News*, May 25.

———. 1931. "Region Track and Field Meet Opens at M.S.T.C. Today." *Moorhead Daily News*, May 23:4.

———. 1931. "Spuds Collect 72 Points to Triumph in District Meet." *Moorhead Daily News*, May 18:4.

———. 1932. "Army Favorite to Beat Bison." *Moorhead Daily News*, November 12:4.

———. 1932. "Bison Basketeers Prepare for Trip during Holidays." *Moorhead Daily News*, November 26:4.

———. 1932. "Bison May Open Up against Bugs." *Moorhead Daily News*, October 12:4.

———. 1932. "Bison Varsity in Secret Drill for University Game." *Moorhead Daily News*, October 19:4.

———. 1932. "Bison Will Speed East with Great Season's Record." *Moorhead Daily News*, November 1:4.

———. 1932. "Buffalo Captain Lost for Season." *Moorhead Daily News*, October 10:4-5.

———. 1932. "Cleve to Object to Grid Rulings." *Moorhead Daily News*, March 16:4.

———. 1932. "Cobber Squad Leaves for Tough St. John's Battle." *Moorhead Daily News*, October 28:4.

———. 1932. "Cobber-Dragon Clash to Feature Card Next Week." *Moorhead Daily News*, September 24:4.

———. 1932. "Cobbers Lead Dragons 7 to 0 at End of First Quarter in Grid Clash." *Moorhead Daily News*, October 1:1.

———. 1932. "Cobbers, St. Olaf Tied 7 to 7 at Half Period." *Moorhead Daily News*, October 8:1.

———. 1932. "Finnegan Applies Polish to Bison for Nodak Battle." *Moorhead Daily News*, October 21:4.

———. 1932. "Finnegan Wants to Score on Army." *Moorhead Daily News*, November 12:4.

———. 1932. "Football Camps Hum as First Clashes Approach." *Moorhead Daily News*, September 19:4.

———. 1932. "Gold Bugs Due to Arrive Today for Bison Tilt Friday." *Moorhead Daily News*, October 13:4.

———. 1932. "Hanson and Bison Crush Oklahoma City 'U' 27-7." *Moorhead Daily News*, October 15:4.

———. 1932. "Hanson Returns Kickoff for Score as Bison Win." *Moorhead Daily News*, November 25:4.

———. 1932. "Hilde Ready for Macalester Tilt." *Moorhead Daily News*, October 13:4.

———. 1932. "Ice Carnival of '83 Gave Birth to Competitive Idea." *Moorhead Daily News*, November 21:1933.

———. 1932. "Johnny Goal Line Still Uncrossed; Tie Cobbers 0 to 0." *Moorhead Daily News*, October 31:4.

———. 1932. "Moorhead Faces Determined Tommies." *Moorhead Daily News*, October 22:1.

———. 1932. "N.R. Nelson Named Member of Legion Executive Group." *Moorhead Daily News*, January 14:1.

———. 1932. "North Dakota State Ends Cobber Cage Supremacy after Two Years, 39 to 23." *Moorhead Daily News*, December 10:4.

———. 1932. "Three Workouts Daily for Bison." *Moorhead Daily News*, September 13:4.

———. 1932. "Undisputed Loop Grid Title Looms for Bison Eleven." *Moorhead Daily News*, October 24:4.

———. 1932. "Week of Intense Workouts Facing Grid Candidates." *Moorhead Daily News*, September 12:4.

———. 1933. "17 Given Letters at Annual Cobber Football Banquet." *Moorhead Daily News*, November 23:4.

———. 1933. "Alexandria Girls to Drill at Game." *Moorhead Daily News*, August 14:3.

———. 1933. "Bison Face Morningside Beneath Lights Tonight." *Moorhead Daily News*, October 7:4.

———. 1933. "Bison Given Edge in Nodak Contest." *Moorhead Daily News*, October 24:4.

———. 1933. "Bison, Sioux in 40th Grid Battle." *Moorhead Daily News*, October 27:4.

———. 1933. "Bison-Nodak Battle May Be Hanson-Pierce Duel." *Moorhead Daily News*, October 23:4.

———. 1933. "Broken Jaw Puts Fritz 'On Bench' at Grid Banquet." *Moorhead Daily News*, November 23:4.

———. 1933. "Brothers, Cousins Face One Another in Dragon Battle." *Moorhead Daily News*, November 3:4.

———. 1933. "Cleve to Select 22 Men for Trip to Winona Friday." *Moorhead Daily News*, November 2:4.

———. 1933. "Cobber Grid List Now Over Forty." *Moorhead Daily News*, September 11:4.

———. 1933. "Cobbers Wind Up Intensive Drills for 'Black Horde.'" *Moorhead Daily News*, October 5:4.

———. 1933. "Concordia Aerial Offense Groomed for Johnny Game." *Moorhead Daily News*, October 26:4.

———. 1933. "Concordia, Johnnies Are Scoreless at Half Time." *Moorhead Daily News*, October 28:1.

———. 1933. "Dragon Mentor's Biggest Worry Is Overhead Attack." *Moorhead Daily News*, November 1:4.

———. 1933. "Dragon-N.D. State Homecoming Tilt Feature of Week." *Moorhead Daily News*, October 28:1.

———. 1933. "Dragons Prepare for Bison after Loss to Bemidji." *Moorhead Daily News*, October 30:4.

———. 1933. "Earl Moran Lost to Cobber Eleven for Rest of Year." *Moorhead Daily News*, November 3:4.

———. 1933. "Eddie Dahl May Get His 'Chance' in Saturday Tilt." *Moorhead Daily News*, November 7:4.

———. 1933. "Finnegan Ready for Bison Grind." *Moorhead Daily News*, September 9:4.

———. 1933. "Football Armies Ready to Move on Foreign Enemies." *Moorhead Daily News*, October 19:4.

———. 1933. "Frank Cleve Wins Title in 72-hole Tournament." *Moorhead Daily News*, October 2:4.

———. 1933. "Heavy Snow Here Impedes Traffic; More Is Forecast." *Moorhead Daily News*, November 4:4.

———. 1933. "Johnny Team Weighs 17 Pounds Over One Ton!" *Moorhead Daily News*, October 27:4.

———. 1933. "Menacing Gusties Face Cobbers Tomorrow." *Moorhead Daily News*, October 6:4.

———. 1933. "Moorhead Squads Break Camp for Final Grid Games." *Moorhead Daily News*, November 9:4.

———. 1933. "Moran Is Cast in Spectator Role." *Moorhead Daily News*, October 27:4.

———. 1933. "Nemzek Seeks Defense against Bison Aerials." *Moorhead Daily News*, October 31:4.

———. 1933. "Nodaks Beat Bison 19-7 in Grid Tilt." *Moorhead Daily News*, May 25:4.

———. 1933. "Oles Ready for Cobber Invasion." *Moorhead Daily News*, November 8:4.

———. 1933. "Program Carried Out Despite Acts of Mother Nature." *Moorhead Daily News*, November 4:4.

———. 1933. "Roy Platt Lost to Bison Squad." *Moorhead Daily News*, October 12:4.

———. 1933. "St. John's Cuts Athletic Relations with Cobbers." *Moorhead Daily News*, November 3:4.

———. 1933. "St. Thomas Faces N.D. State Eleven in Fargo Tonight." *Moorhead Daily News*, September 29:4.

———. 1933. "Uncrossed Johnny Goal Line Worry to Cleve, Benson." *Moorhead Daily News*, October 25:4.

———. 1934. "Alumni Watch Team in Action." *Moorhead Daily News*, December 17:3.

———. 1934. "Augustana to be Cobbers' '35 Homecoming Opponent." *Moorhead Daily News*, December 18:4.

———. 1934. "Bierman Rates Bison Tough; Admits Gophers Hard to Beat." *Moorhead Daily News*, September 6:4.

———. 1934. "Bison Herd Leaves for Maroon Battle." *Moorhead Daily News*, October 18:4.

———. 1934. "Bison Herd Roars Defiance to N.C. after 22 to 0 Win." *Moorhead Daily News*, October 13:4.

369

Bibliography

———. 1934. "Bison Launch Loop Grind against Coyotes Tonight." Moorhead Daily News, October 12:4.

———. 1934. "Bison Return to Conference Peak." Moorhead Daily News, October 29:4.

———. 1934. "Bison Thundering Southward Today." Moorhead Daily News, November 14:4.

———. 1934. "Chisholm Lost to Dragons; Cobbers Test Oles' Plays." Moorhead Daily News, October 10:4.

———. 1934. "Cleve, Nemzek Chafe As Rain Thwarts Grid Plans.' Moorhead Daily News, September 25:4.

———. 1934. "Coaches Like Looks of Spring Grid Crop." Moorhead Daily News, April 11:4.

———. 1934. "Cobber 'Victory Dinner' to Be Held as Promised." Moorhead Daily News, November 21:4.

———. 1934. "Cobber-Dragon, Spud-Fargo Tilts to Feature Week." Moorhead Daily News, September 24:4.

———. 1934. "Cobber-Ole, Spud-Laker Tilts Feature Grid Card." Moorhead Daily News, October 6:4.

———. 1934. "Cobbers Defeat Rugby Club, 26-16." Moorhead Daily News, October 9:4.

———. 1934. "Cobbers Entrain for Mac Contest." Moorhead Daily News, October 19:4.

———. 1934. "Cobbers Exhibit New Vigor; Cleve Some Heartened." Moorhead Daily News, October 25:4.

———. 1934. "Cobbers Favored in Today's Game." Moorhead Daily News, November 9:4.

———. 1934. "Cobs Play Twice on Winnipeg Grid." Moorhead Daily News, October 3:4.

———. 1934. "Collegiate Grid Camps Speed Up as Openers Near." Moorhead Daily News, September 17:4.

———. 1934. "Concordia Homecoming Battle Tops Grid Card." Moorhead Daily News, October 20:4.

———. 1934. "Dragon Alumni in for Read Gridiron Show Saturday." Moorhead Daily News, October 16:4.

———. 1934. "Dragon-Winona Loop Tiff Tops Next Week's Card." Moorhead Daily News, September 29:4.

———. 1934. "Get Wire Report on Cobber Game." Moorhead Daily News, November 7:4.

———. 1934. "Hanna Whips Spuds into Form for Season Opener." Moorhead Daily News, September 12:4.

———. 1934. "Injured Oles Are Ready for Cobs." Moorhead Daily News, October 10:4.

———. 1934. "Mobilization of Grid Candidates Completed Today." Moorhead Daily News, September 7:4.

———. 1934. "One Week Left of Spring Football; Coaches Pleased." Moorhead Daily News, April 21:4.

———. 1934. "Promising New Athletes Attending Local Colleges." Moorhead Daily News, March 15:4.

———. 1934. "Statistics Show Decisiveness of Cobber Triumph." Moorhead Daily News, November 10:4.

———. 1934. "Strong Men Weep in Dragon Locker Room after Game." Moorhead Daily News, November 3:4.

———. 1934. "Three Grid Rule Changes to Aid Offense." Moorhead Daily News, February 12:4.

———. 1935. "St. Paul Pigskin Toters Strengthen Cob Backfield." Moorhead Daily News, September 13:4.

Morneau, Ed. 1935. "Sport Broadcasting." Purple & White, December 2:5.

Morrison, Jim. "The Early History of Football's Forward Pass." Smithsonian Magazine, December 28, 2010. Accessed May 28, 2021. https://www.smithsonianmag.com/history/the-early-history-of-footballs-forward-pass-78015237/

Mullin, Jim. 2011. "Mullin: Changing the Game - the Ratio." CFL.ca. February 11, 2011. Accessed May 10, 2021. https://www.cfl.ca/2011/02/11/mullin-changing-the-game-the-ratio/

National Football Foundation & College Hall of Fame, Inc. "Harold 'Brick' Muller." Hall of Fame. 2021. Accessed August 24, 2021. https://footballfoundation.org/hof_search.aspx?hof=1406

National Football League Football Operations. Bent But Not Broken. National Football League. 2021. Accessed June 17, 2021. https://operations.nfl.com/the-rules/evolution-of-the-nfl-rules/

National Wrestling Hall of Fame. "Earl McCready." National Wrestling Hall of Fame. 2021. Accessed July 15, 2021. https://nwhof.org/hall_of_fame/bio_by_name/earl-mccready

Nauright, John. 2018. Rugby. June 28. Accessed March 18, 2020. https://www.britannica.com/sports/rugby

Neil, Edward J. 1934. "Among Few Small Colleges Can Be Found All-Star Grid Team to Rival Best in Land." Butte Montana Standard, December 4:20.

Nelson, Paul. Ade Heads Ole Athletic Program. East View Information Services. Accessed February 26, 2021. https://stolaf.eastview.com/browse/doc/45945409

New York Times. "World's Biggest Hotel Opens Today." New York Times, January 25:9.

———. 1974. "Joseph A. Savoldi of Notre Dame, 65. New York Times, January 26:34.

News Journal. 1954. "Colonel Sasse Dies at Home." News Journal, October 16:1.

News. 1977. "Bernie Bierman, 83, Famed Football Coach." News, March 9:53.

Nichols, Jane, Ed. The 1935 Bison. Fargo: North Dakota State College, 1934.

North Dakota Legislative Council. "Constitution." North Dakota Legislative Branch. 2021. Accessed May 21, 2021. https://www.legis.nd.gov/constitution

North Dakota State Athletics. "Alex 'Sliv' Nemzek." Bison Athletic Hall of Fame. Accessed February 17, 2021.https://gobison.com/honors/bison-athletic-hall-of-fame/alex-sliv-nemzek/240

———. "All-Americans." Bison Football 2007. Fargo: North Dakota State University, 2007. Pages 98, 101.

———. "All-Time Coach Records." 2013 Bison Football, 2013:152.

———. "Dr. C.S. Putnam." Bison Athletic Hall of Fame. 2021. Accessed September 7, 2021. https://gobison.com/honors/bison-athletic-hall-of-fame/dr-cs-putnam/207

———. "Herb Peschel." Bison Athletic Hall of Fame. 2021. Accessed October 26, 2021. https://gobison.com/honors/bison-athletic-hall-of-fame/herb-peschel/210

———. "Melvin 'Fritz' Hanson." Bison Athletic Hall of Fame. 2021. Accessed October 26, 2021. https://gobison.com/honors/bison-athletic-hall-of-fame/melvin-fritz-hanson/250

———. "W.P. 'Bud' Marquardt." Bison Athletic Hall of Fame. 2021. Accessed October 26, 2021. https://gobison.com/honors/bison-athletic-hall-of-fame/w-p-bud-marquardt/225

———. 2013 Bison Football. Fargo: North Dakota State University, 2013. Page 156.

North Dakota State School of Science. Agawasie 1935. Wahpeton, North Dakota: North Dakota State School of Science, 1935. Page 86.

North Dakota State University Libraries. "Fargo College Sports." Fargo, North Dakota: Its History and Images. 2021. Accessed July 20, 2021. https://library.ndsu.edu/fargo-history/?q=content/fargo-college-sports

———. "Good Samaritan Institute." Fargo, North Dakota: Its History and Images. 2021. Accessed July 20, 2021. https://library.ndsu.edu/fargo-history/?q=content/good-samaritan-institute

———. "The Closing of Fargo College." Fargo, North Dakota: Its History and Images. 2021. Accessed July 20, 2021. https://library.ndsu.edu/fargo-history/?q=content/closing-fargo-college

———. 1925. "Aerial View of Campus." Fargo, North Dakota: Its History and Images. Accessed August 27, 2020. https://library.ndsu.edu/fargo-history/?q=content/aerial-view-campus

———. State (Towne) Theater. Fargo, North Dakota: Its History and Images. NDSU Archives. Accessed June 2, 2021. https://library.ndsu.edu/fargo-history/?q=content/state-towne-theater

Oakland Tribune. 1931. "George Barsi May Coach St. Thomas." Oakland Tribune, July 30:24.

Office of Registration and Records. Fargo, North Dakota: North Dakota State University.

Oklahoma Daily. 1921. "Pixlee May Take Intramural Work." Oklahoma Daily, January 7:4.

Oklahoma News. 1934. "Bugs Even with North Dakota in Football Series." Oklahoma News, November 13:7.

———. 1934. "Gold Bugs Concentrate on Defense; Comets Hold Speed Tests." Oklahoma News, November 15:7.

———. 1934. "North Dakota State Favored over Goldbugs Tonight." Oklahoma News, November 15:9.

Bibliography

Olson, Gail. 1933. "Oles Smother Cobs 25-12 Saturday." Manitou Messenger, November 14:4.

Olympic Channel Services S.L. Charles William Strack.

O'Neil, Freddie. 1933. "North Dakota Beats Winnipeg All-Stars by 20-12 Score." Grand Forks Herald, September 24:10.

———. 1934. "University Frosh Defeat Manitoba Gridders, 31 to 0." Grand Forks Herald, October 14:10.

Ontario Sports Hall of Fame. "Lew Hayman." Ontario Sport Legends Hall of Fame Inc. 2020. Accessed July 28, 2021. https://oshof.ca/index.php/honoured-members/item/36-lew-hayman

Ontario Sports Legends Hall of Fame Inc. Charlie Conacher. Ontario Sports Hall of Fame. 2020. Accessed July 13, 2021. https://oshof.ca/index.php/honoured-members/item/123-charlie-conacher

Oregon Daily Journal. 1913. "Missouri Fullback to Join Multnomah."

Ottawa Citizen. 1902. "Sporting." Ottawa Citizen, June 12:6.

———. 1930. "Forward Pass Is Approved by Big Four." Ottawa Citizen, December 22:10.

———. 1931. "Canadian Rugby Union Commission Approves Adoption of Forward Pass." Ottawa Citizen, March 2:11.

———. 1932. "Rough Riders Leave for Hamilton for Important Game with Bengals." Ottawa Citizen, October 15:12.

———. 1933. "Lionel Conacher Is Outstanding Although Chefs Lose to Rochester." Ottawa Citizen, October 10:10.

———. 1934. "Pros Not Coming Here on Saturday." Ottawa Citizen, October 10:11.

Ottawa Journal. 1934. "Aromints to Play Buffalo Pros Here." Ottawa Journal, October 8:10.

———. 1934. "Colleges Opposed to C.R.U. Ruling." Ottawa Journal, April 11:16.

———. 1934. "East Is Awarded Canadian Final." Ottawa Journal, October 19:23.

———. 1934. "To Enforce Rule on Match Penalty." Ottawa Journal, September 25:14.

———. 1935. "Ottawa Branch of A.A.U. of C. Discusses Berry Case." Ottawa Journal, November 19:19.

———. 1935. "Rough Riders and Montreal in First Big Four Game Today." Ottawa Journal, September 21:36.

Overby, Kermit. 1931. "Clevemen Meet Johnnies in Tomorrow's Games." Concordian, October 30:5.

Oxford University Press. "soccer, n.". OED Online. Oxford University Press. March 2020. Accessed March 18, 2020. https://www.oed.com/view/Entry/183733?redirectedFrom=soccer

Paine, Denia. 1932. "Saturday's Game Thrilling Event to Both Colleges." Western MiSTiC, October 7:1.

Parris, Collier. 1934. "North Dakotans Tie Tech, 2020; Lubbock Westerners Hold Pampa, 6 to 13." Lubbock Morning Avalanche, November 24:2.

Patterson, J.R. Representing the Newest of New Trains: The North Coast Limited. J.R. Patterson, City Passenger Agent, Northern Pacific Railway, Detroit, Michigan. Accessed February 25, 2021. http://streamlinermemories.info/NP/NP30Patterson.pdf

Patterson, Jack. 1934. "Meralomas Battle Gamely But Regina's Riders Know Too Many Football Tricks." Vancouver Sun, November 12:12.

———. 1934. "Riders Knock Off Meralomas in Final Game, 7 to 2." Vancouver Sun, November 13:10.

Peet, William. 1924. "Carnegie Squad Gets Stiff Scrimmage Upon Arrival at Penn State." Pittsburgh Post, November 7:11.

Peptomist. 1930. "Whereatt to Assume New Coaching Duties at State February 1." Peptomist, January 21:1.

———. 1933. "Peds hold Bison to Scoreless Tie." Peptomist, October 26:5.

Perham Enterprise Bulletin. 1935. "Fans Go Wild As Hanson Runs Hamilton Ragged in Title Game Victory." Perham Enterprise-Bulletin, December 12:1.

Petritz, Joseph S., Ed. 1931 Official Football Review, Rockne Memorial Edition. South Bend, Indiana: University of Notre Dame.

Plummer, Kevin. "Historicist: Going Pro." Torontoist. April 5, 2014. Accessed August 29, 2021. https://torontoist.com/2014/04/historicist-going-pro/

Portnuff, J.C. 1934. "Down the Bison Trail." Winnipeg Manitoban, October 30:3.

———. 1934. "Down the Bison Trail." Winnipeg Manitoban, October 5:3.

———. "Down the Bison Trail." Winnipeg Manitoban, November 6:3.

Post-Star. 1959. "Attend Convention." Post-Star, May 26:3.

PrestoSports.com. "Football." North Central Conference. Accessed May 19, 2021. https://d2o2figo6ddd0g.cloudfront.net/0/5/ylha4dr4qqgm3/08football.pdf

Priestly, Bob. 1933. "Rugby Rambles." Winnipeg Free Press, November 9:20.

———. 1934. "N. Dakota Freshmen vs. Winnipeg Rugby Club." Winnipeg Free Press, October 17:17.

———. 1934. "Winnipegs and Concordia Provide Thrilling Exhibition." Winnipeg Free Press, October 8:14.

———. 1936. "Last Minute Kick to Deadline Gives Winnipegs a 6-6 Tie at Regina." Winnipeg Free Press, October 5:14.

Pro Football Archives. "1923 Rochester Jeffersons (NFL)." Pro Football Archives. Accessed May 10, 2021. https://www.profootballarchives.com/1923nflroc.html

———. "Tom Kasper." Pro Football Archives. Accessed May 10, 2021. https://www.profootballarchives.com/playerk/kasp00400.html

———. 1924 Boston Pere Marquette. Pro Football Archives. 2021. Accessed July 17, 2021. https://www.profootballarchives.com/1924pere.html

———. 1925 Boston Pere Marquette. Pro Football Archives. 2021. Accessed July 17, 2021. https://www.profootballarchives.com/1925bosp.html

———. 1927 Pere Marquette. Pro Football Archives. 2021. Accessed July 17, 2021. https://www.profootballarchives.com/1927pere.html

———. 1928 Pere Marquette Knights of Columbus. Pro Football Archives. 2021. Accessed July 17, 2021. https://www.profootballarchives.com/1928pere.html

———. 1928 Providence Steam Roller (NFL). Pro Football Archives. 2021. Accessed July 17, 2021. https://www.profootballarchives.com/1928nflpro.html

———. 1929 Buffalo Bisons (NFL). Pro Football Archives. 2021. Accessed August 28, 2021. https://www.profootballarchives.com/1929nflbuf.html

———. 1931 Pere Marquette. Pro Football Archives. 2021. Accessed July 17, 2021. https://www.profootballarchives.com/1931pere.html

———. 1932 Paterson Nighthawks (EFL). Pro Football Archives. 2021. Accessed July 28, 2021. https://www.profootballarchives.com/1932eflpat.html

Pro Football Hall of Fame. "Changing the Rules Archived." Pro Football Hall of Fame, December 2, 2011. Accessed November 10, 2021. https://www.profootballhof.com/news/changing-the-rules-archived2/

Province. 1933. "The Yardstick." Province, October 2:8.

———. 1934. "Deficit $125." Province, November 13:14.

———. 1934. "Meraloma Lateral Passing Baffled Reginan Defense for Awhile." Province, November 12:12.

———. 1934. "Regina Roughriders vs. Meralomas." Province, November 9:20.

———. 1934. "Riders Fail to Cross Meralomas Line." Province, November 13:14.

———. 1934. "The Yardstick." Province, November 13:14.

Provo Evening Herald. 1932. "Spinner Play Explained by NEA Service Artist, Krenz." Provo Evening Herald, September 30:5.

Purple & White. 1935. "Assumption Footballers Play Winnipeg To-Day!" Purple & White, December 2:1.

Quinn, Marvin. 1932. "Bison Cast Optimistic Eyes to U Tilt as They Ponder 27-7 Win." Fargo Forum, October 15:1.

———. 1932. "Cleve Attempts to Fortify Concordia's Left Flank." Fargo Forum, October 7:13.

———. 1932. "Cobbers Impressively Smash St. Thomas Plays." Fargo Forum, October 20:13.

———. 1932. "Cobbers Prepared to 'Shoot Works' against St. Olaf." Fargo Forum, October 5:9.

———. 1932. "Cobbers Stop Tommy Plays Used by Frosh." Fargo Forum, October 19:9.

———. 1932. "Dragon and Cobber Backs to Be Ready." Fargo Forum, October 21:13.

———. 1932. "Nemzek to Save His Regulars in Game with A.C." Fargo Forum, October 26:8.

———. 1932. "Oklahomans Come As Big Test to Bison Eleven." Fargo Forum, October 14:1,10.

371

Bibliography

———. 1932. "Three Dragon Frosh to Face Bison at Start." Fargo Forum, October 28:14.

———. 1934. "Aerial Plays Feature Bison's Grid Practice." Fargo Forum, September 18:8.

———. 1934. "Bison Grind Out 27-0 Victory over Tommies." Fargo Forum, October 6:7.

———. 1934. "Bison, Cobbers Complete Hard Training Grind." Fargo Forum, September 18:10.

———. 1934. "North Dakota High Schools Adopt New Football Rules." Fargo Forum, September 13:12.

Railway Age. 1934. [No heading.] Railway Age, July 7:14.

Randall, Harry. 1935. "Will the West Kick Through?" Maclean's, September 15.

Rapid City Journal. 1934. "Harry Gamage, Illinois Star, Has Good Record." Rapid City Journal, June 13:6.

Ray, Cathryn, Ed. The 1936 Bison. Fargo: North Dakota Agricultural College, 1935.

Ray, Kenneth, ed. Gopher. Minneapolis: University of Minnesota, 1935, pp. 186-187.

Records of the Selective Service System, 147; Box: 146. 2011. "WWII Draft Registration Cards for Minnesota, 10/16/1940-03/31/1947." The National Archives of St. Louis, St. Louis, MO.

Records of the Selective Service System, 147; Box: 46. 2011. "WWII Draft Registration Cards for Minnesota, 10/16/1940-03/31/1947." The National Archives of St. Louis, St. Louis, MO.

Records of the Selective Service System, 147; Box: 86. 2011. "WWII Draft Registration Cards for Minnesota, 10/16/1940-03/31/1947." The National Archives of St. Louis, St. Louis, MO.

Remis, Leonard. 1931. "Sport Chatter." Winnipeg Manitoban, September 29:4.

Reno Gazette-Journal. 1936. "University Coach of Track Named by Regents." Reno Gazette-Journal, February 4:12.

Retyi, Richards. "U-M's Shotgun Offense is Older than the Winged Helmets Themselves." MGoBlue.com. 2021. Accessed July 20, 2021. https://mgoblue.com/news/2010/11/9/U_M_s_Shotgun_Offense_is_Older_than_the_Winged_Helmets_Themselves.aspx

Revsine, Dave. 2014. The Opening Kickoff: The Tumultuous Birth of a Football Nation. Guilford: Lyons Press, 24, 26-28.

Riddell, Walt. 1934. "On the Sport Spot!" Star-Phoenix, November 28:15.

———. 1935. "On the Sport Spot!" Star-Phoenix, September 11:11.

———. 1935. "On the Sport Spot!" Star-Phoenix, November 6:15.

Riggle, Alma E. 1932. "Even Dogs Have Swell Time with 'Knotholers' at Grid Contest." Fargo Forum, October 15:1.

Roberts, Kate. 2007. Minnesota 150: The People, Places, and Things that Shape Our State. Minnesota Historical Society, 130.

Roberts, Kate. 2007. Minnesota 150: The People, Places, and Things that Shape Our State. Minnesota Historical Society, 130.

Robinson, Elwyn B. History of North Dakota. Open Educational Resources. Grand Forks, North Dakota: University of North Dakota, 2017. Pages 397-398, 405.

Rockwell, Tod. 1935. "Detroit Team Assured of Tie for Grid Title." Detroit Free Press, December 2:15.

———. 1935. "Lions Swamp Dodgers, 28 to 0, to Lead Western Division." Detroit Free Press, December 2:15.

Rolfsrud, Erling Nicolai, The Cobber Chronicle, (Brainerd, Minnesota, Lakeland Press 1966), 208.

Rottsolk, James. 1934. "'Stop Fritz' Is Battle Cry of Ademen as They Prepare for Cobber Camp Invasion." Manitou Messenger, October 10:4.

Rovnak, Paul and Ryan Tibbits, Eds. Minnesota Football 2020 Media Guide. University of Minnesota, 2020. Page 127.

Rowan, Web. 1934. "Dragons, Cobbers to Decide City Feud in Encounter Tomorrow." Western MiSTiC, September 28:1.

Rudick, Irvin. 1931. "Concordia Wins Title, Beating Tommies, 7-0." Minneapolis Sunday Tribune, November 15:23.

———. 1934. "Gopher Man Power, Blocking Amaze Finnegan, Bison Coach." Minneapolis Tribune, September 30:20.

Sacramento Bee. 1934. "Value of Forward Pass Is Increased Through Football Rule Changes." Sacramento Bee, February 12:14.

Sanders, Carol. "Trophy Namesake a Cut Above." Canadian Football League. November 9, 2007. Accessed December 6, 2021. https://www.cfl.ca/2007/11/09/trophy_namesake_a_cut_above/

Sanderson, J.F. 1935. "New Coach, New Players for Ottawas." Edmonton Journa, September 20:6.

Santa Clara University. "George Barsi '30." Bronco Bench Foundation. 2021. Accessed August 15, 2021. https://www.scu.edu/athletics/broncobench/hall-of-fame/hall-of-fame-inductees/barsi-george/

Santa Cruz Sentinel. 1989. "George A. Barsi." Santa Cruz Sentinel, August 27:21.

Saulsberry, Charles. 1933. "Bugs Batter North Dakota for 19-0 Win." Daily Oklahoman, November 19:23.

Saunders, Tom and Maurice Smith. 1984. "Grey Cup Fever Echoes Epochal 1935 Triumph." Winnipeg Free Press, November 17:69.

Sawatzky, Roland. "Football in Winnipeg." Manitoba Museum. January 18, 2021. Accessed May 25, 2021. https://manitobamuseum.ca/football-in-winnipeg/

Saylor, Roger B. May 1997. "North Dakota Football." College Football Historical Society Newsletter, Vol. 10, No. 3, Page 14.

Schmidt, Raymond. Shaping College Football: The Transformation of an American Sport, 1919-1930. Syracuse, NY: Syracuse University Press, 2007. Page 87.

Schonberger, Bob. 1932. "Sioux Sport Slants." Dakota Student, October 28:3.

Scrantonian Tribune. 1954. "Ex-Army Coach Ralph Sasse Dies." Scrantonian Tribune, October 17:51.

Severson, Walter. 1933. "Conference Chatter." Western MiSTiC, November 3:4.

Shafer, Maine. 1934. "Spectrum Sport Speculations." Spectrum, November 23:5.

Shields, Clem. 1934. "Weekly Whirligig." Winnipeg Free Press, November 17:25.

Sigurdson, Hal. 1991. "'Twinkletoes' Hanson Original Model." Winnipeg Free Press, November 24:C22.

Sinclair, Chris. "Winnipeg Victorias." The Encyclopedia of CFL History. N.D. Accessed September 30, 2021. https://www.cflapedia.com/teams/winnipeg_victorias.php

Sioux City Journal. 1933. "Maroons to Rest Before Bison Game." Sioux City Journal, October 6:15.

———. 1933. "Nodaks to End Southern Road Jaunt Tonight." Sioux City Journal, February 13:7.

———. 1933. "North Dakota State Bison Drive to Win over Moorhead, 20-0." Sioux City Journal, November 5:13.

———. 1933. "Plenty of Ball Toters on Hand." Sioux City Journal, April 4:9.

———. 1934. "Maroons to Play Bison Tonight." Sioux City Journal, October 20:15.

———. 1934. "On the Grid Camps." Sioux City Journal, October 17:13.

———. 1950. "Illness Fatal to Saunderson." Sioux City Journal, February 17:1,10.

———. 1957. "Famed Grid Coach West Dies at 67." Sioux City Journal, October 31:22.

———. 1994. "USD Win Leader Gamage Dies in Arizona." Sioux City Journal, August 24:15.

Slade, Daryl. 1993. "Handing Out the Jeff Nicklin Trophy Showed Fritz Hanson That the Memories Linger." Calgary Herald, November 24.

Smith, Maurice. 1934. "Winnipegs Make Farewell Appearance on Local Gridiron." Winnipeg Free Press, October 29:16.

———. 1959. "Time Out with Maurice Smith." Winnipeg Free Press, March 28:47.

———. 1971. "Time Out with Maurice Smith." Winnipeg Free Press, February 18:49.

———. 1972. "Time Out with Maurice Smith." Winnipeg Free Press, April 22.

———. 1979. "Ryan's Niche in Football Hall of Fame Assured." Winnipeg Free Press, June 4:68.

Smith, Norman. 1933. "Bugs Down N. Dakota." Oklahoma News, November 19:11.

Sorensen, Harley. 1977. "Gophers Legend Bernie Bierman dies." Minneapolis Star Tribune, March 9:1,6.

South Bend Tribune. 1992. "Edward W. Krause." South Bend Tribune, December 12:5.

South Dakota Sports Hall of Fame. "Leonard 'Lefty' Olson." South Dakota Sports Hall of Fame. 2021 Accessed September 10, 2021. https://www.sdshof.com/inductees/leonard-lefty-olson/

Bibliography

South Dakota Sports Hall of Fame. "Steve Adkins." South Dakota Sports Hall of Fame. 2021. Accessed August 6, 2021. https://www.sdshof.com/inductees/steve-adkins/

Spaulding, Bill. 1933. "Three Systems Being Used in Football Today." Fargo Forum, October 25:10.

Spectrum. 1922. "A.C. Athletics to Be Known As Bissons." Spectrum, March 3:3.

———. 1926. "Alumni Want 'North Dakota State College.'" Spectrum, December 10:1,4.

———. 1930. "Six Seniors Turn In Football Togs for Last Time at State." Spectrum, November 25:2.

———. 1931. "Baby Bison Batter Sioux Papooses in Spectacular Game." Spectrum, November 10:3.

———. 1931. "Baby Bison Buffet Sioux Papooses for Record Win Friday." The Spectrum, October 20:3.

———. 1931. "Baby Bison Prepare for University Game." The Spectrum, October 2: 3.

———. 1931. "Bison Yearling to Oppose University Freshmen Friday." The Spectrum, November 6: 3.

———. 1931. "Frosh Offer Severe Opposition to 'U.'" Spectrum, October 16:3.

———. 1931. "Pledges Total 204 at Services Monday." The Spectrum, October 6: 3.

———. 1931. "Strong Frosh Squad Plays Moorhead Team." Spectrum, December 11.

———. 1931. "Varsity Team Makes Good Showing Friday in Exhibition Game." Spectrum, November 24:3.

———. 1931. "Fargo High Takes First in Prep Track Meet." Spectrum, May 12:3.

———. 1931. The Spectrum, October 6: 3.

———. 1932. "Alumni and Student Body Join Today in Parade and Celebration." Spectrum, October 22:1.

———. 1932. "Bison Beat Moorhead Teachers College in Game on Muddy Field." Spectrum, November 1:3.

———. 1932. "Bison Begin Conference Race Tonight on Home Field." Spectrum, September 30:1.

———. 1932. "Bison Defeat Maroons to Keep Conference Record Unblemished." Spectrum, November 29:3.

———. 1932. "Bison Football Men Are Injured in Final Home Game Saturday." Spectrum, November 1:3.

———. 1932. "Bison Gridders Begin Scrimmage Work This Week in Grid Sessions." Spectrum, April 19:3.

———. 1932. "Bison Gridders Begin Spring Sessions with Scrimmage Monday." Spectrum, April 8:3.

———. 1932. "Bison Meet Moorhead State Teachers Team Tomorrow Afternoon." Spectrum, October 28:1.

———. 1932. "Bison Oppose Dragons in First Spring Tilt on Local Field Today." Spectrum, April 29:3.

———. 1932. "Bison Snatch Season Opener from Veteran Cobber Football Team." Spectrum, September 27:3.

———. 1932. "Bison Team Loses Unbeaten Status at Capital City Last Saturday." Spectrum, November 11:3.

———. 1932. "Casey Finnegan, Bob Lowe Coach Football Team for Fourth Year." Spectrum, October 22:4.

———. 1932. "Eastern Games Rival Bison-Sioux Fray for Fan Interest." Spectrum, October 22:4.

———. 1932. "Ends Play Major Part in Spring Competition at Bison Grid Camp." Spectrum, April 26:3.

———. 1932. "Finnegan Looks Forward to Successful Grid Season." Spectrum, June 3:3.

———. 1932. "Football Candidates Complete Ten Spring Practice Sessions." Spectrum, April 22:3.

———. 1932. "Football Practice to Begin Next Week." Spectrum, April 1:3.

———. 1932. "Homecoming Program Scores Huge Success in Minds of Alumni." Spectrum, October 28:1.

———. 1932. "Injuries May Keep Gridders from Game." Spectrum, September 27:3.

———. 1932. "North Central Athletic Committee Convenes in Windy City This Week." Spectrum, December 2:3.

———. 1932. "Oklahoma City Squad Opposes Bison Oct. 14." Spectrum, October 7:3.

———. 1932. "Oklahoma City Team Plays Bison Friday." Spectrum, October 11:3.

———. 1932. "Photography Staff of 1933 Bison Takes Pictures of Parade." Spectrum, October 22:3.

———. 1932. "Pictures Are Taken of Bison Homecoming." Spectrum, November 1:3.

———. 1932. "Record Crowd Expected at Climax Game." Spectrum, October 18:3.

———. 1932. "S.C. Alumni in East Have Planned Details for Bison Welcome." Spectrum, November 1:3.

———. 1932. "Schoenfelder Makes Army Trip." Spectrum, October 28:2.

———. 1932. "Sophomores Take leading Role in Goldbug Defeat." Spectrum, October 18:3.

———. 1932. "South Dakota Bunnies Stand in Bison's Way for Conference Title." Spectrum, October 7:3.

———. 1932. "State College Grad Plays on Rugby Team." Spectrum, November 11:3.

———. 1932. "State College Grid Team Return from Trip East Yesterday." Spectrum, November 15:3.

———. 1932. "State College Team Now Primed to Turn Homecoming Status." Spectrum, October 22:1.

———. 1932. "State Retains Conference Lead By Beating Bunnies." Spectrum, October 11:3.

———. 1932. "Strong Oklahoma City Team Opposes Bison Tonight." Spectrum, October 14:1.

———. 1932. "Thanksgiving Game Is Final Appearance of Year for Champions." Spectrum, November 22:3.

———. 1932. "Three Fraternities Enter Teams in City Basketball Tourney." Spectrum, March 8:3.

———. 1932. "Two Major Tourneys Face Bison Fighters at Start of Season." Spectrum, November 24:3.

———. 1932. "Unconquered Bison Leave for Contests in Eastern States." Spectrum, November 1:3.

———. 1932. "University Brings Its Entire Concert Band to Bison-Sioux Fray." Spectrum, October 22:3.

———. 1932. "University Editor Attends Homecoming." Spectrum, October 22:1.

———. 1932. "Valuable Advertising." Spectrum, September 27:2.

———. 1933. "535 Students Apply for Work." Spectrum, September 22:1.

———. 1933. "Bison and Sioux Meet in Spring Gridiron Contest." Spectrum, May 19:3.

———. 1933. "Bison Defeat South Dakota U to Place Second in Standings." Spectrum, November 17:3.

———. 1933. "Bison Face Formidable St. Thomas Squad Tonight." Spectrum, September 29:3.

———. 1933. "Bison Football Candidates Getting Workout Twice Daily." Spectrum, September 15:3.

———. 1933. "Bison Meet Concordia College Cobbers in Season's Opener." Spectrum, August 25:3.

———. 1933. "Bison Play Last Conference Game Tomorrow." Spectrum, November 10:3.

———. 1933. "Bison Pucksters Win Two Games in League to Keep Clean Slate." Spectrum, January 20:3.

———. 1933. "Bison Show Power in Fight with University Sioux." Spectrum, November 3:3.

———. 1933. "Bison Will Meet Oklahoma Goldbugs, Closing Season." Spectrum, November 17:3.

———. 1933. "Bison-Cobbers Battle to Scoreless Tie in Initial Football Game Friday." Spectrum, September 29:3.

———. 1933. "Coaches Pleased with Showing of Charges." Spectrum, April 28:3.

———. 1933. "College Track Team Enters Moorhead Meet." Spectrum, May 12:3.

———. 1933. "Distinguished Action Wins Finnegan Medal from War Department." Spectrum, August 25:3.

———. 1933. "Football Season Opens with Contest Tonight." Spectrum, September 22:1.

———. 1933. "Football Squad Is Divided for Yellow and Green Contest." Spectrum, May 12:3.

———. 1933. "Forty-Two Football Men Receive Awards." Spectrum, February 3:3.

———. 1933. "'Fritz' Hanson Meets Red Grange at Fair." Spectrum, August 25:3.

———. 1933. "Gala Homecoming Features NRA." Spectrum, October 13:1.

———. 1933. "NDSC Eleven Meets Wisconsin Teachers' in Contest Tonight." Spectrum, October 20:3.

———. 1933. "Next Year's Football Schedule Is Announced by Casey Finnegan." Spectrum, April 7:3.

———. 1933. "On, Bison." Spectrum, August 25:3.

———. 1933. "Plans Laid for Homecoming Oct. 14." Spectrum, October 6:1.

———. 1933. "Power, Speed Expected from 1933 Backfield." Spectrum, May 12:3.

———. 1933. "Sioux Win from Bison in Spring Contest 19 to 7." Spectrum, May 26:3.

Bibliography

———. 1933. "South Dakota State Spoils Bison Homecoming." Spectrum, October 20:3.
———. 1933. "Sport Shots." Spectrum, April 21:3.
———. 1933. "Sport Shots." Spectrum, April 7:3.
———. 1933. "Sport Shots." Spectrum, May 19:3.
———. 1933. "State College Faces First Conference Foe Saturday." Spectrum, October 6:3.
———. 1933. "Team Song." Spectrum, August 25:3.
———. 1933. "Tommies Drill Under Floodlights Last Night." Spectrum, September 29:3.
———. 1933. "Track Squad Takes 12 Firsts at Moorhead." Spectrum, May 19:3.
———. 1933. "Veteran Ends Shift Positions on 1933 Team." Spectrum, May 5:3.
———. 1933. "Xmas Gifts." Spectrum, December 15:3.
———. 1933. "Yellow and Green." Spectrum, August 25:3.
———. 1933. [No heading.] Spectrum, November 3:3.
———. 1934. "21 Bison Invade Southern Grid Camps." Spectrum, November 16:5.
———. 1934. "Bison Vanquished by Gopher Eleven." Spectrum, October 5:5.
———. 1934. "Bunnies Smother Herd 38-0 to Give N.C.C. Title Away." Spectrum, November 16:5-6.
———. 1934. "Dragons Upset Favored Bison in 13-12 Win." Spectrum, November 9:5.
———. 1934. "Finnegan and Lowe Register Optimism over Grid Charges." Spectrum, April 27:6.
———. 1934. "Hanson Places on Little All-America Football Eleven." Spectrum, December 14:21.
———. 1934. "Herd Impressive as South Dakota Is Trounced 22-0." Spectrum, October 19:5.
———. 1934. "Herd to Face Strong Maroon Team Saturday." Spectrum, October 19:5.
———. 1934. "Keen Competition Predicted for 1935 Grid Championship." Spectrum, April 13:6.
———. 1934. "Maroons Lower Bison Hopes as 12-12 Tie Mars Record." Spectrum, October 26:13.
———. 1934. "Reserve Strength Factor in 27-0 Victory for Herd." Spectrum, October 12:5-6.
———. 1934. "Sioux-Bison Encounter Is Gala Day Highlight." Spectrum, October 26:13.
———. 1934. "Spectrum Sport Speculations." Spectrum, April 13:6.
———. 1934. "Spring Football Starts Next Week." Spectrum, April 6:4.
———. 1934. "Stubborn Tommies to Engage Bison Gridders Here Tonight." Spectrum, October 5:5.
———. 1936. "Winnipeggers, Former Bison, Victors, 33-13." Spectrum, October 2:3.
———. 1938. "Breaks Count As Blue Bombers Best Thundering Herd." Spectrum, October 7:4.
Spokane Chronicle. 1933. "Flashy, Powerful Backfield Greets Phelan for Husky Prospects This Year." Spokane Chronicle, September 9:8.
Sports Reference LLC. "1931 Minnesota Golden Gophers Stats." Sports Reference College Football. 2021. Accessed August 13, 2021. https://www.sports-reference.com/cfb/schools/minnesota/1931.html
———. "1933 Fargo-Moorhead Twins." Baseball Reference. 2021. Accessed July 30, 2021. https://www.baseball-reference.com/register/team.cgi?id=b39ab175
———. "Louis Benson." Baseball Reference. 2021. Accessed July 19, 2021. https://www.baseball-reference.com/register/player.fcgi?id=benson002lou
———. "1926 Louisville Colonels Starters, Rosters, & Players." Pro Football Reference. Accessed May 11, 2021. https://www.pro-football-reference.com/teams/lou/1926_roster.htm
———. "1926 NFL Standings & Team Stats." Pro Football Reference. Accessed May 11, 2021. https://www.pro-football-reference.com/years/1926/
———. "1931 Chicago Bears Game Log." Pro Football Reference. Accessed February 25, 2021. https://www.pro-football-reference.com/teams/chi/1931/gamelog/
———. "1932 George Washington Colonials Schedule and Results." 2021. Accessed June 3, 2021.
———. "1934 Cincinnati Reds Statistics & Players." Pro Football Reference. 2021. Accessed August 15, 2021. https://www.pro-football-reference.com/teams/red/1934.htm

———. "1934 Pittsburgh Pirates Statistics & Players." Pro Football Reference. 2021. Accessed August 15, 2021. https://www.pro-football-reference.com/teams/pit/1934.htm
———. "1935 Brooklyn Dodgers Starters, Roster, & Players." Pro Football Reference. 2021. Accessed October 6, 2021. https://www.pro-football-reference.com/teams/bkn/1935_roster.htm
———. "1935 Detroit Lions Statistics & Players." Pro Football Reference. 2021. Accessed October 6, 2021. https://www.pro-football-reference.com/teams/det/1935.htm
———. "1935 West Dixie League." Baseball Reference. 2021. Accessed October 6, 2021. https://www.baseball-reference.com/register/league.cgi?id=ea0bed85
———. "Al Teeter." Pro Football Reference. 2021. Accessed August 6, 2021. https://www.pro-football-reference.com/players/T/TeetAl20.htm
———. "Art Pharmer." Pro Football Reference. 2021. Accessed September 29, 2021. https://www.pro-football-reference.com/players/P/PharAr20.htm
———. "Bahn Hilliard." Baseball Reference. 2021. Accessed October 6, 2021. https://www.baseball-reference.com/register/player.fcgi?id=hillia001bah
———. "Benny Friedman." Pro Football Reference. 2021. Accessed September 17, 2021. https://www.pro-football-reference.com/players/F/FrieBe20.htm
———. "Beny Friedman." Sports Reference. 2021. Accessed September 17, 2021. https://www.sports-reference.com/cfb/players/benny-friedman-1.html
———. "Bobby Marshall." Pro Football Reference. 2021. Accessed August 6, 2021. https://www.pro-football-reference.com/players/M/MarsBo20.htm
———. "Charlie Strack." Pro Football Reference. 2021. Accessed July 15, 2021. https://www.pro-football-reference.com/players/S/StraCh20.htm
———. "Fargo-Moorhead Twins." Baseball Reference. 2021. Accessed July 30, 2021. https://www.baseball-reference.com/bullpen/Fargo-Moorhead_Twins
———. "Frank Cleve." Baseball Reference. 2020. Accessed July 9, 2020. https://www.baseball-reference.com/register/player.fcgi?id=cleve-001fra
———. "Griffith Stadium." Baseball Reference. 2021. Accessed June 4, 2021. https://www.baseball-reference.com/bullpen/Griffith_Stadium
———. "Herb Franta." Pro Football Reference. 2021. Accessed August 6, 2021. https://www.pro-football-reference.com/players/F/FranCh20.htm
———. "Jack Manders." Pro Football Reference. 2021. Accessed August 6, 2021. https://www.pro-football-reference.com/players/M/MandJa20.htm
———. "Jack Spellman." Pro Football Reference. 2021. Accessed July 15, 2021. https://www.pro-football-reference.com/players/S/SpelJa20.htm
———. "Joe Savoldi." Pro Football Reference. 2021. Accessed June 19, 2021. https://www.pro-football-reference.com/players/S/SavoJo20.htm
———. "Ken Haycraft." Pro Football Reference. 2021. Accessed August 6, 2021. https://www.pro-football-reference.com/players/H/HaycKe20.htm
———. "Mayes McLain." Pro Football Reference. 2021. Accessed July 13, 2021. https://www.pro-football-reference.com/players/M/McLaCh20.htm
———. "Pete Saumer." Pro Football Reference. 2021. Accessed August 15, 2021. https://www.pro-football-reference.com/players/S/SaumPe20.htm
———. "Shag Shaughnessy." Baseball Reference. 2021. Accessed June 27, 2021. https://www.baseball-reference.com/s/shaugsh01.shtml
———. "Tony Siano." Pro Football Reference. 2021. Accessed July 15, 2021. https://www.pro-football-reference.com/players/S/SianTo20.htm
———. "Vee Green." Pro Football Reference. Accessed May 11, 2021. https://www.pro-football-reference.com/players/G/GreeVe20.htm
———. "Wes Fry." Pro Football Reference. 2021. Accessed August 1, 2021. https://www.pro-football-reference.com/players/F/FryxWe20.htm
St. John's Record. 1931. "Powerful Cobbers Stop Johnnies 29-0." St. John's Record, November 5:6.
———. 1931. "St. John's to Play Concordia Saturday." October 29:6.

Bibliography

———. 1932. "Johnnies Assure Crown by Tying Cobbers 0-0." St. John's Record, November 3:1.

———. 1933. "First Touchdown Is Called on Johnnies in Thirteen Games." St. John's Record, November 2:1.

St. John's University Athletics. "Saint John's Football All-Time Season Results." Football. Accessed February 18, 2021. https://gojohnnies.com/documents/2009/1/19/All-time%20Season-by-Season%20Results.pdf?id=201

St. Louis Daily Globe-Democrat. 1934. "Gunners Trample over Minnesota Stars, 54-6." St. Louis Daily Globe-Democrat, November 5:10.

St. Olaf Athletics. "Frank I. Cleve." Hall of Fame. Accessed March 2, 2021. https://athletics.stolaf.edu/honors/hall-of-fame/frank-i-cleve/12

———. All-Time Coaches. St. Olaf Athletics. Accessed February 26, 2021. https://athletics.stolaf.edu/sports/2016/1/18/FB_011816064 0.aspx

St. Olaf College. 2020. "Frank I. Cleve." Accessed July 9, 2020. https://athletics.stolaf.edu/hof.aspx?hof=12

———. Football All-Time Records. Accessed April 12, 2021. https://athletics.stolaf.edu/alltime.aspx?path=football

Standring Rock Sioux Tribe. "History." Standing Rock Sioux Tribe. 2021. Accessed October 1, 2021. https://www.standingrock.org/about/history/

Star Tribune. 2020. State Champions. Accessed April 29, 2020. https://www.mnbasketballhub.com/state-champions.

Star-Phoenix. 1927. "North Dakota Outclasses Manitoba." September 26:9.

———. 1927. "Paisley Is Assisting Americans." September 20:11.

———. 1930. "Canadian Rugby Union Abolishes Forward Pass." Saskatoon Star-Phoenix, February 24:10.

———. 1931. "New Canadian Forward Pass Rules Are Announced." Star-Phoenix, May 19:7.

———. 1931. "Rugby Season to Open Here Tomorrow." Star-Phoenix, September 25:17.

———. 1932. "On the Sport Spot!" Star-Phoenix, September 21:11.

———. 1932. "On the Sport Spot!" Star-Phoenix, December 13:11.

———. 1932. "Riders to Winnipeg." Star-Phoenix, August 30:5.

———. 1932. "Rugby Schedules." Star-Phoenix, August 31:13.

———. 1933. "Riders Unleash Power to Top Millers." Star-Phoenix, October 30:6.

———. 1934. "A.A.U. Against Importing Grid Stars." Star-Phoenix, November 17:11.

———. 1934. "Favor New Rugby Rules." Star-Phoenix, February 17:15.

———. 1934. "Northern Teams in Favor of Proposed Rugby Loop." Star-Phoenix, November 17:11.

———. 1934. "On the Sport Spot!" Star-Phoenix, September 18:10.

———. 1934. "On the Sport Spot!" Star-Phoenix, October 20:13.

———. 1934. "On the Sport Spot!" Star-Phoenix, October 23:11.

———. 1934. "On the Sport Spot!" Star-Phoenix, May 2:15.

———. 1934. "Suggest Interprovincial Rugby Union in West." Star-Phoenix, November 16:22.

———. 1934. "Winnipeg Rugby Club Loses Services of Cronin." Star-Phoenix, May 2:14.

———. 1935. "Pegs Take No Action." Star-Phoenix, December 11:14.

———. 1935. "To Calgary." Star-Phoenix, May 11:14.

———. 1935. "Western Grid Teams Prepare for Season." Star-Phoenix, August 1:16.

———. 1957. "Jack West Dies at Grand Forks." Star-Phoenix, October 30:22.

Stats Crew. "1933 Northern League Standings." Minor League Baseball. 2021. Accessed July 30, 2021. https://www.statscrew.com/minorbaseball/standings/l-NORL1/y-1933

Steinbrenner, Ed. 1934. "Death Stalks Field as Morningside Ties Bison." Sioux City Journal, October 21:19.d

———. 1934. "Morningside Upsets Heavy Jackrabbits, 13 to 7." Sioux City Journal, October 7:23.

———. 1934. "Saunderson, Jr., on Injured List." Sioux City Journal, October 11:13.

Straight, Hal. 1934. "Meraloma Moans." Vancouver Sun, November 12:12.

———. 1934. "Moving Pictures May Aid Lomas in Regina Battle." Vancouver Sun, November 9:16.

Sunday Star. 1935. "Tops Canadian Feats." Sunday Star, December 29:22.

Sunday Times Democrat. 1933. "Goldbugs Stage Last Half Rally." Sunday Times Democrat, November 19:9.

Swanson, Bernard. 1934. "Clarkson Leaps Class Room Barrier, Report." Minneapolis Star, September 8:16.

———. 1934. "Coach Taking No Chances of Opening Upset." Minneapolis Star, September 21:22.

———. 1934. "Gophers Will See Real Speed Merchant Saturday, Red Dawson Reports." Minneapolis Star, September 24:12.

Tacoma Daily Ledger. 1907. "University of Washington News." Tacoma Daily Ledger, September 22:10.

Tait, Ed. "Bombers Quest through the Decades: 1930s." Canadian Football League. 2021. Accessed May 25, 2021. https://www.cfl.ca/2020/09/15/bombers-quest-decades-1930s/

———. "Ring of Honour Inductee | Fritz Hanson." Ring of Honour. 2021. Accessed October 26, 2021. https://www.bluebombers.com/2018/09/18/ring-honour-inductee-fritz-hanson/

Taylor, Scott. 1984. "Memories Linger for Football Greats." Winnipeg Free Press, September 13:60.

Thoden, Tom. "Inman Field and Stadium." Tour of the University of South Dakota's Historic Buildings. Vermillion: Pressing Matters Printing, 2014. Page 20.

Thomas, Rod. 1937. "Pixlee Strategy Apt to Splash Color on Colonial-Tide Tussle." Evening Star, October 21:47.

Thompson, Jimmy. 1929. "Rugby Twins." Winnipeg Free Press, October 2:13.

Tiller, Carl. 1932. "Cobber Squad Totals 54; Dragons Given Scrimmage." Moorhead Daily News, September 14:6.

———. 1933. "Classy Yearlings Impress Cleve in Opening Grid Grind." Moorhead Daily News, May 4:4.

———. 1933. "Cleve Calls Cobber Grid Candidates; Four Weeks of Spring Work Planned." Moorhead Daily News, March 29:4.

———. 1933. "Cobbers Wind Up Spring Football; Results Praised." Moorhead Daily News, May 6:4.

Tomahawk. 1929. "'Bibber' McCoy Faces Malciewicz Here Tonight." Tomahawk, January 22:1.

Toronto Daily Star. 1934. "Conacher to Play Against Rochester." Toronto Daily Star, October 2:8.

———. 1934. "Conny and His Pros Take Buffalo Easily." Toronto Daily News, October 9:10.

———. 1934. "Pro. Football Tonight." Toronto Daily Star, October 3:12.

———. 1934. "U.S. Imports Will Decline Argo Official Believes." Toronto Daily Star, October 11:16.

Traill County Tribune. 1933. "Rugby Rules Prove Too Much for Comets." Traill Country Tribune, October 5:2.

Tulip, Tony. 1931. "Touchdown and Tackle." Concordian, October 16: 3.

———. 1931. "Touchdown and Tackle." The Concordian, October 30:5.

———. 1931. "Touchdown and Tackle." The Concordian, September 25: 3.

Tybor, Joseph. 1992. "A Notre Dame Legend Gets a Loving Farewell." Chicago Tribune, December 16:61.

Ubyssey. 1925. "American Ruggers Score First Try." Ubyssey, November 17:4.

———. 1925. "Canadian Rugby Showing Action." Ubyssey, September 29:4.

———. 1925. "Puget Sound Carries Off Honors in Weekend Game." Ubyssey, October 13:1.

———. 1925. "Sporting Comment." Ubyssey, September 23:4.

———. 1925. "U.B.C. Plays Good Game Against Washington." Ubyssey, November 3:1.

———. 1934. "American Code Something New." Ubyssey, October 2:4.

———. 1934. "Gridmen Take 51-12 Licking." Ubyssey, November 20:4.

———. 1934. "Inter-collegiate American Rugby Series Starts Saturday Game Between University of B.C. and Washington State Normal." Ubyssey, October 5:4.

———. 1934. "Intercollegiate Rugby Game Subject of Pep Meet Friday." Ubyssey, October 9:1.

———. 1934. "Major Sport Executives Optimistic." Ubyssey, September 28:4.

———. 1934. "Rugby Team Travels." Ubyssey, November 16:4.

———. 1934. "Should the Inter-collegiate Rugby Series Be Continued." Ubyssey, November 9:4.

Bibliography

———. 1934. "Sportorial." Ubyssey, October 2:4.

———. 1934. "Sportorial." Ubyssey, October 9:4.

———. 1934. "Varsity Loses First Game of American Rugby Series." Ubyssey, October 9:4.

UND Athletic Communications. 2019 Media Guide. Grand Forks: University of North Dakota, 2019. Pages 99, 105, 107, 109, 111-113, 115-116, 118, 175.

———. 2021 University of North Dakota Football Media Guide. Grand Forks: University of North Dakota, 2021. Page 98.

United States Holocaust Memorial Museum. "The Nazi Olympics Berlin 1936." United States Holocaust Memorial Museum. July 28, 2021. Accessed September 28, 2021. https://encyclopedia.ushmm.org/content/en/article/the-nazi-olympics-berlin-1936

United States Military Academy. Howitzer. New York: West Point, 1933. Page 160, 262, 297.

University Hatchet. 1932. "Colonials End Bison Winning Streak, Score 20-0. University Hatchet, November 8:3.

———. 1932. "Undefeated North Dakota State Next Foe." University Hatchet, November 1:3.

University of British Columbia. "Gordon 'Doc' Burke." UBC Sports Hall of Fame. 2021. Accessed September 12, 2021. https://gothunderbirds.ca/honors/ubc-sports-hall-of-fame/gordon-doc-burke/44

University of Detroit Mercy Athletics. Detroit Mercy Titans. 2021. Accessed October 6, 2021. https://detroittitans.com/

University of Minnesota Athletics. "Black History Month: Bobby Marshall." University of Minnesota Athletics. 2021. Accessed August 6, 2021. https://gophersports.com/news/2021/2/1/football-black-history-month-bobby-marshall.aspx

———. "Ken Haycraft." 'M' Club Hall of Fame. 2021. Accessed August 6, 2021. https://gophersports.com/sports/2018/5/21/sports-m-club-spec-rel-hof-haycraft-html.aspx

———. 1931 Football Schedule. University of Minnesota Athletics. 2021. Accessed August 5, 2021. https://gophersports.com/sports/football/schedule/1931

University of Minnesota. Minnesota Football 2020 Media Guide. Minneapolis: University of Minnesota, 2020. Page 124.

University of North Dakota Athletics. "Hall of Fame - 1979 Inductees." North Dakota Fighting Hawks. 2018. Accessed October 1, 2021. https://fightinghawks.com/sports/2007/1/20/750091.aspx

University of North Dakota. UND Football Team: Lewis (Lewy) Lee. Scholarly Commons. 2021. Accessed June 23, 2021. https://commons.und.edu/und-athletics/55/

University of Notre Dame. "The Last Flight of Knute Rockne." 125 Moments. 2021. Accessed September 5, 2021. https://125.nd.edu/moments/the-last-flight-of-knute-rockne/

University of South Dakota. "Year-by-Year Results." 2020-21 Coyote Football Media Guide. Vermillion: University of South Dakota, 2020. Page 49.

University of St. Thomas. "Pride & Passion: St. Thomas Football 2018." ISSUU, 2018. Accessed October 6, 2021. https://issuu.com/universityofst.thomas/docs/0573_18_ath_football_media_guide_p9

———. 2016 St. Thomas Football. St. Paul: University of St. Thomas, 2016. Page 40.

University of Texas at Austin Athletics. "Bohn Hilliard." Hall of Honor. 2021. Accessed September 20, 2021. https://texassports.com/hof.aspx?hof=656

Vancouver News-Herald. 1934. "English Ruggers Are Urged to See West Grid Finals." Vancouver News-Herald, November 9:3.

———. 1934. "Riders Arrive Today for Series." Vancouver News-Herald, November 9:3.

———. 1934. "Riders' Passing Attack May Be Feature Today in Opening Grid Contest." Vancouver News-Herald, November 10:3.

Vancouver College. "Hall of Honour Inductees to Date." Hall of Honour. 2021. Accessed December 9, 2021. https://www.vc.bc.ca/alumni/alumni-events/hall-of-honour/hall-of-honour-inductees

Vanstone, Rob. "Grandson of Inaugural Coach Makes Historic Trip." CFL.ca. 2007. Accessed September 27, 2021. https://www.cfl.ca/2007/06/23/grandson_of_inaugural_coach_makes_historic_trip/

Veterans Affairs Canada. "Lieutenant Colonel Jeff Albert Nicklin." Canadian Virtual War Museum. September 22, 2021. Accessed December 6, 2021. https://www.veterans.gc.ca/eng/remembrance/memorials/canadian-virtual-war-memorial/detail/2232299

Victoria Daily Colonist. 1935. "Winnipegs Surprise by Victory of Tigers." Victoria Daily Colonist, December 8:18.

Victoria Daily Times. 1930. "Tigers Will Still Oppose Forward Pass." Victoria Daily Times, October 8:6.

———. 1935. "Hamilton Tigers Slight Favorites." Victoria Daily Times, December 5:13.

Virtual Museum of Canada. "From Rugby to Football: The History of Canadian Football." Community Stories. 2021. Accessed May 25, 2021. https://www.communitystories.ca/v1/pm_v2.php?ex=00000785&pg=1

Vogel, Mark. The Bison of 1933. Fargo: The Junior Class of North Dakota State College, 1932.

W.E.B. 1933. "Kobber Kernels." Concordian, April 7:3.

Wahpeton High School. The Wopanin. Wahpeton: Wahpeton High School, 1931.

Wallum, Everett. 1931. "Between Halves." Spectrum, November 10:3.

———. 1931. "Between Halves." The Spectrum, November 6: 3.

———. 1932. "Between Halves." Spectrum, April 29:3.

———. 1932. "Between Halves." Spectrum, October 11:2.

———. 1932. "Between Halves." Spectrum, October 14:3.

———. 1932. "Between Halves." Spectrum, October 22:5.

———. 1932. "Between Halves." Spectrum, October 7:3.

———. 1932. "Between Halves." Spectrum, September 30:3.

Wangstad, Andy. "Roosevelt Hall of Fame." Minneapolis Roosevelt High School Reunion in Arizona. Accessed May 17, 2021. https://www.rhs-az.com/app/download/4021713/2016-Hall-of-Fame-Inductees-1.pdf

Warburg, Paul E. 1931. "Varsity Clinches Honors—Regina Smothers St. John's." Winnipeg Tribune, November 9:10.

———. 1931. "The Sport Whirl." Winnipeg Tribune, November 11:12.

———. 1932. "St. Johns Open Senior Rugby League Campaign with 15-1 Win." Winnipeg Tribune, September 19:12.

———. 1932. "St. John's Rugby Team Conquers Winnipegs, 26 to 0." Winnipeg Tribune, October 3:13.

———. 1932. "The Sport Whirl by Paul E. Warburg, Sports Editor." Winnipeg Evening Tribune, August 26:10.

———. 1932. "Winnipegs Come from Behind to Defeat Garrison." Winnipeg Tribune, October 11:12.

Ward County Independent. 1931. "College Beats All Stars 6-0." Ward County Independent, November 12:2.

———. 1933. "Minot Fair Ahead of 1932 Exposition in Receipts, Attendance." Ward County Independent, July 6:1.

Weekly Spectrum. 1919. Weekly Spectrum, October 23:4.

———. 1922. "Move to Change Name Gaining Momentum." Weekly Spectrum, April 21:3.

———. 1922. "Test Ballot Proves Strong Sentiment for Change of Name." Weekly Spectrum, March 31:1.

Western MiSTiC. 1932. "Cobbers Overcome Fighting Dragons in Hard Battle." Western MiSTiC, October 7:4.

———. 1932. "Dragon Gridders Break Even in Two Encounters." Western MiSTiC, November 4:4.

———. 1932. "Dragon-Cobber Football Game Week's Classic." Western MiSTiC, September 30:1.

———. 1932. "Conference Chatter." Western MiSTiC, October 7:4.

———. 1933. "Bemidji Makes Safety to Upset Dragons on Snow-Covered Gridiron." Western MiSTiC, November 3:1.

———. 1933. "Combined Dragon and Gold Star Bands to Play at Football Game." Western MiSTiC, November 3:1.

———. 1933. "Dragons Are Conceded Good Chance to Upset Bison Here Tomorrow." Western MiSTiC, November 3:1.

———. 1933. "Dragons Dragnet." Western MiSTiC, November 3:1.

———. 1933. "Dragons Will Test Offensive Power Against Highly-Touted Cobber Team in Traditional Grid Classic Tomorrow on Concordia Field." Western MiSTiC, September 29:1.

———. 1933. "Homecoming Calendar." Western MiSTiC, November 3:1.

———. 1933. "North Dakota Bison Defeat Dragons 20-0." Western MiSTiC, November 10:4.

———. 1933. "Pep Fest Held Last Night at Weld Hall for Concordia Game." Western MiSTiC, September 29:1.

———. 1933. "Snowstorm Salutes Homecoming Alumni; Unique in History." Western MiSTiC, November 10:1.

Bibliography

———. 1933. "Stage Set for Return of Dragon Alumni to Biggest Homecoming." Western MiSTiC, November 3:1.

———. 1934. "'Down with Bison,' Dragons' War Cry in Torchlight Parade." Western MiSTiC, November 9:1.

———. 1934. "Former Grid Star Recounts Victory Over Bison in 1901." Western MiSTiC, November 9:1.

———. 1934. "Pep Rally Held for Dragon-Cobber Game." Western MiSTiC, September 28:1.

———. 1934. "Spectacular Struggle Results in Deadlock." Western MiSTiC, October 5:4.

Westminster College Athletics. Football Records. Westminster College. 2021. Accessed June 3, 2021. http://wcbluejays.com/sports/fball/2019-20/files/Football_Records_updated_March_2020.pdf

Wheeler, Thomas J. 1932. "Hamilton Defeats Roughriders 25-6." Leader-Post, December 3:1.

Willis, Chris. Red Grange: The Life and Legacy of the NFL's First Superstar. London: Rowman & Littlefield Publishers, 2019.

Wilson, Ralph. 1933. "Sport-O-Scope: Candid Comment by Ralph Wilson." Calgary Herald, May 2:6.

———. 1933. "Sport-O-Scope: Candid Comment by Ralph Wilson." Calgary Herald, August 9:6.

———. 1933. "Sport-O-Scope: Candid Comment by Ralph Wilson." Calgary Herald, September 30:6.

———. 1935. "Sport-o-scope." Calgary Herald, January 14:6.

Windsor Star. 1933. "Argonauts and Winnipegs Ready for Gridiron Classic." Windsor Star, December 1:27.

———. 1933. "Savoldi to Play with Montreal Pro Gridders." Windsor Star, October 4:21.

———. 1933. "Toronto Pro Grid Team Romps to 18-0 Victory over Buffalo." Windsor Star, October 23:20.

———. 1934. "From Cornell to Hamilton." Windsor Star, August 24:23.

———. 1934. "Imperials Happy over Victory." Windsor Star, November 26:20.

———. 1934. "Three Veterans, Two Recruits with Sarnia Imperials." Windsor Star, August 27:20.

———. 1935. "Bohn Hilliard Confesses: Ottawa Executive Cleared." Windsor Star, May 5:26.

———. 1935. "Detroit Lions' Special Brings Title to 'Pegs." Windsor Star, December 9:21.

———. 1935. "Hamilton Becomes Real Jungle." Windsor Star, December 9:21.

———. 1935. "How Grid History Was Made." Windsor Star, December 9:21.

———. 1935. "Joe Ryan Will Guard Grey Cup." Windsor Star, December 24:19.

———. 1935. "'Peg Contingent Is Banqueted." Windsor Star, December 3:24.

———. 1935. "Reigning Champs of Senior Wossa Football Realm." Windsor Star, December 13:35.

———. 1935. "Rites Set for Priest." Windsor Star, November 17:5.

———. 1935. "Sarnia Grid Team Loses." Windsor Star, September 23:20.

———. 1952. "Letourneau Dies, Aged 84." Windsor Star, April 30:36.

———. 1957. "Trip Trepanier Quits Grid." Windsor Star, July 22:3.

Windsor/Essex County Sports Hall of Fame. "Mike Hedgewick." Class of 1989. 2021. Accessed October 7, 2021. http://wecshof.com/inductees/mike-hedgewick/

Winnipeg Evening Tribune. 1932. "Eight Roughriders on All-Western Rugby Team." Winnipeg Evening Tribune, November 30:17.

———. 1934. "Banished 'U' Gridders Continue to Attend Practices." Winnipeg Evening Tribune, October 17:14.

———. 1934. "Deer Lodge Lifts Prairie Junior Championship." Winnipeg Evening Tribune, November 12:14.

———. 1935. "Winnipegs Crush Concordia, 26-0, in First Game." Winnipeg Evening Tribune, September 16:10, 17.

———. 1936. "Winnipegs All Set to Open Campaign." September 5:21.

Winnipeg Free Press. 1926. "M'Gill Bears 'Varsity 7-3; Senators Win." Winnipeg Free Press, October 11:17.

———. 1929. "St. John's Evens Senior Rugby Series with 11-2 Victory." Winnipeg Free Press, September 30:7.

———. 1930. "Winnipegs Determined to Halt March of St. John's Rugby Team." Winnipeg Free Press, September 27:28.

———. 1931. "Big Crowd Sees Winnipegs Defeat 'Varsity Squad, 10-2." Winnipeg Free Press, October 19:9.

———. 1931. "Champion Native Sons Defeat Hebrews in Thrilling Display." Winnipeg Free Press, September 28:7.

———. 1931. "Junior Champs Triumph Again." Winnipeg Free Press, October 9:8.

———. 1931. "Senior Game at Wesley Stadium." Winnipeg Free Press, October 12:6.

———. 1931. "St. John's Club Makes Effort to Get Coulter." Winnipeg Free Press, October 29:16.

———. 1931. "St. John's Conclude League Schedule with 8-2 Victory." Winnipeg Free Press, November 2:18.

———. 1931. "St. John's Continue Winning Streak Defeating Winnipegs." Winnipeg Free Press, October 13:17.

———. 1932. "'Be One of the 5,000' Is Slogan of Regina Rugby Fans." Winnipeg Free Press, November 4:6.

———. 1932. "Famed Roughriders Lose to St. John's, 4 to 0." Winnipeg Free Press, September 5:5.

———. 1932. "Garrison and 'Peg Gridders Battle Today." Winnipeg Free Press, September 24:25.

———. 1932. "Gridiron Gossip." Winnipeg Free Press, September 12:8.

———. 1932. "How They Will Line Up for Tonight's Big Game." Winnipeg Free Press, September 17:23.

———. 1932. "How They Will Line Up This Afternoon." Winnipeg Free Press, October 1:22.

———. 1932. "Johnians Are Prepared for Roughriders Tonight." Winnipeg Free Press, September 3:25.

———. 1932. "Johnians to Throw Remodeled Forward Wall against 'Pegs on Wesley Park Gridiron Today." Winnipeg Free Press, October 15:39.

———. 1932. "North Dakota Frosh Will Play Here on Friday and Saturday." Winnipeg Free Press, November 8:14.

———. 1932. "Powerful Local Senior Grid Squads Open Season Saturday." Winnipeg Free Press, September 15:19.

———. 1932. "'Riders Entrain for Title Game." Winnipeg Free Press, December 2:16.

———. 1932. "Senior and Junior Rugby Teams Prepare." Winnipeg Free Press, September 10:23.

———. 1932. "Senior Rugby Title-Chase Starts Tonight." Winnipeg Free Press, September 17:23.

———. 1932. "St. John's and Garrison Ready for Tomorrow." Winnipeg Free Press, September 27:6.

———. 1933. "Challenging Winnipegs Well-Balanced Team." Winnipeg Free Press, December 2:23-24.

———. 1933. "N.D. Teachers' College Gridders Trounced." Winnipeg Free Press, October 2:17.

———. 1933. "North Dakota Club Arrives for Game This Afternoon." Winnipeg Free Press, September 30:28.

———. 1933. "North Dakota 'U' Brings Fine Team Here for Struggle Today with Winnipeg's Fast Gridders." Winnipeg Free Press, September 23:23.

———. 1933. "'Red Grange' of Northwest Will Perform Here Saturday." Winnipeg Free Press, October 20:6.

———. 1933. "Regina Roughriders Favored to Win Here on Saturday." Winnipeg Tribune, October 31:18.

———. 1933. "Running Attack Will Feature Winnipegs Game with Nodaks." Winnipeg Free Press, September 22:8.

———. 1933. "Senior Rugby League Prepares for Autumn Campaign." Winnipeg Free Press, June 13:8.

———. 1933. "Strong Rugby Club to Face 'Pegs Today." Winnipeg Free Press, October 21:25.

———. 1933. "The Game of the Season!" Winnipeg Tribune, November 3:17.

———. 1933. "Toronto Begins to Respect Winnipegs." Winnipeg Free Press, December 2:23.

———. 1933. "Toronto Sports Writers Not Backward in Eulogizing 'Pegs." Winnipeg Tribune, December 5:15.

———. 1933. "Will the Winnipegs Continue Winning Form of Last Week?" Winnipeg Free Press, November 10:16.

———. 1933. "Winnipeg Club Is Ready for S. Dakota at Osborne Stadium." Winnipeg Free Press, October 14:21.

———. 1933. "Winnipeg Teams in Rugby Spotlight Today." Winnipeg Tribune, November 4:25.

———. 1933. "Winnipegs All Set for Major Test Today." Winnipeg Free Press, November 11:31.

———. 1933. "Winnipegs Down University of South Dakota, 21 to 5." Winnipeg Free Press, October 16:16.

———. 1933. "Winnipegs Entrain for Game in Toronto on Saturday." Winnipeg Free Press, November 29:15.

———. 1933. "Winnipegs Go East Tonight to Meet Argonauts." Winnipeg Free Press, November 28:17.

———. 1933. "Winnipegs Make Fine Showing Against Nodaks." Winnipeg Free Press, September 25:17.

Bibliography

———. 1933. "Winnipegs Not Taking Calgary Altomahs Lightly." Winnipeg Tribune, November 8:17.

———. 1933. "Winnipegs on Edge for Grid Game with Argos on Saturday." Winnipeg Free Press, November 30:21.

———. 1933. "Winnipegs Win Muddy Grid Battle from Concordia, 14-13." Winnipeg Free Press, October 23:17.

———. 1933. "Winnipegs, Western Senior Grid Champs, Going East Tomorrow." Winnipeg Free Press, November 27:14.

———. 1933. "Winnipeg-Toronto Rugby Game Today Will Be Broadcast." Winnipeg Free Press, December 2:3.

———. 1933. "Would Make Sweeping Changes in Rugby Football Rules." Winnipeg Free Press, April 11:9.

———. 1934. "Coach Greg Kabat Selects His Team for Game with Regina." Winnipeg Free Press, November 1:16.

———. 1934. "Concordia Comes Here for Games Next Weekend." Winnipeg Free Press, October 2:17.

———. 1934. "Concordia Will Bring Powerful Squad to City." Winnipeg Free Press, October 4:18.

———. 1934. "Expect Battle of Winglines in Regina-Winnipeg Game." Winnipeg Free Press, October 23:16.

———. 1934. "James Returns to 'Peg Line-Up." Winnipeg Free Press, September 20:22.

———. 1934. "Jewish Aggregation Is Made Favorite to Beat Deer Lodge." Winnipeg Free Press, November 16:16.

———. 1934. "Kabat Will coach Winnipegs." Winnipeg Free Press, August 11:21.

———. 1934. "Kinsemen Bringing Strong Team Here to Meet Lodgers." Winnipeg Free Press, November 8:20.

———. 1934. "New Talent for Ottawa Rough Riders in Grid Race." Winnipeg Free Press, September 20:22.

———. 1934. "Number of Fans to Accompany 'Pegs to Grand Forks Friday." Winnipeg Free Press, September 17:8.

———. 1934. "'Pegs Make Last Appearance Here This Afternoon." Winnipeg Free Press, October 27:23.

———. 1934. "Rugby Football." Winnipeg Free Press, October 4:19.

———. 1934. "Some Rules of American Football Explained." Winnipeg Free Press, September 14:16.

———. 1934. "Varsity All Set for Football Battle Today." Winnipeg Free Press, September 29:25.

———. 1934. "Varsity Faces Powerful Opposition at Osborne Tonight." Winnipeg Free Press, October 5:17.

———. 1934. "Varsity Fumbles Aid Minot Team." Winnipeg Free Press, September 12:25.

———. 1934. "Varsity Prepares for Game Friday with Jamestown." Winnipeg Free Press, October 2:18.

———. 1934. "Varsity Primed for Game this Afternoon." Winnipeg Free Press, October 13:23.

———. 1934. "Winnipeg Juniors to Drill This Weekend." Winnipeg Free Press, May 23:18.

———. 1934. "Winnipeg Rugby Club to Organize Junior Team." Winnipeg Free Press, May 21:18.

———. 1934. "Winnipegs and Varsity Play Against Saturday." Winnipeg Free Press, October 25:16.

———. 1934. "Winnipegs Have Strong Squad Ready for Clash with Classy University of Minnesota Club." Winnipeg Free Press, September 15:25.

———. 1934. "Winnipegs Meet Concordia Gridders Tonight." Winnipeg Free Press, October 6:23.

———. 1934. "Winnipegs Play Varsity Squad This Afternoon." Winnipeg Free Press, October 20:27.

———. 1934. "Winnipegs Put Through Strenuous Floodlight Practice." Winnipeg Tribune, September 13:17.

———. 1935. "Aerial Pass Attack Expected to Play Leading Role in Game." Winnipeg Free Press, December 6:13.

———. 1935. "Big Welcome Is Ready for Grid Champs." Winnipeg Free Press, December 10:1.

———. 1935. "Bob Fritz to Coach 'Pegs Rugby Squad Next Fall." Winnipeg Free Press, April 6:26.

———. 1935. "Bryce Gillis." Winnipeg Free Press, September 5:15.

———. 1935. "C.R.F.U. to Decide Monday Where Grid Final Will Be Played." Winnipeg Free Press, December 2:14.

———. 1935. "C.R.U. Is Not Interested in Western Rules." Winnipeg Free Press, February 25:15.

———. 1935. "Coach Bob Fritz Names Squad Which Will Carry Winnipeg Colors East." Winnipeg Free Press, November 23:25.

———. 1935. "Coach Bob Fritz Points His Men for Western Canada Rugby Football Final." Winnipeg Free Press, November 6:14.

———. 1935. "Earlier Play-Off Dates and Constitutional Guarantees Will Be Demanded at Meeting." Winnipeg Free Press, November 11:6.

———. 1935. "Figuratively Speaking." Winnipeg Free Press, September 23:12.

———. 1935. "Figuratively Speaking." Winnipeg Free Press, December 9:13.

———. 1935. "Hats Off to the Winnipegs." Winnipeg Free Press, November 4:9.

———. 1935. "Joe Perpich Pleases Coach with His Long-Distance Punting in Final Drill." Winnipeg Free Press, September 20:17.

———. 1935. "Many Rooters for Winnipegs." Winnipeg Free Press, December 6:13.

———. 1935. "Minnesota All-Stars Are Next Obstacle for 'Pegs." Winnipeg Free Press, September 24:14.

———. 1935. "Monster Reception Is Being Arranged for New Rugby Champs." Winnipeg Free Press, December 9:1.

———. 1935. "New Quarterback with Winnipegs." Winnipeg Free Press, September 24:14.

———. 1935. "New Rugby Champions Likely to Be Invited to Play Game in California Christmas Day." Winnipeg Free Press, December 10:13.

———. 1935. "Quarter by Quarter on 'Pegs-Hamilton Battle." Winnipeg Free Press, December 9:13.

———. 1935. "Regina Expects Victory over Winnipeg Saturday." Winnipeg Free Press, October 30:14.

———. 1935. "Rousing Send-Off Assured Winnipegs--15,000 May Witness Eastern Final." Winnipeg Free Press, November 27:14.

———. 1935. "Rugby Final Will Be Played at Hamilton; 'Pegs Accept Edict." Winnipeg Free Press, December 3:12.

———. 1935. "Sarnia-Winnipeg Game at Osborne Holds Interest in Rugby Across Canada." Winnipeg Free Press, September 21:25.

———. 1935. "Suspend All Players Who Played in Big Four Loop." Winnipeg Free Press, November 22:16.

———. 1935. "'Toba Will Not Try for Grid Title Again if Unsuccessful Saturday." Winnipeg Free Press, December 4:10.

———. 1935. "Tumultuous Scenes Mark Return of Winnipegs, Canadian Grid Champs." Winnipeg Free Press, December 11:13.

———. 1935. "Vic Seniors Expect to Give Winnipegs Stiff Argument on Saturday." Winnipeg Free Press, October 11:20.

———. 1935. "Vic Seniors Make Debut against 'Pegs Saturday." Winnipeg Free Press, October 1:17.

———. 1935. "West Fans in East Chorus Hope Winnipegs Will Win Rugby Honors Today." Winnipeg Free Press, December 7:22.

———. 1935. "Western Grid Finalists Set." Winnipeg Free Press, November 9:25.

———. 1935. "When Winnipegs Marched to Victory over Regina 'Riders." Winnipeg Free Press, November 5:6.

———. 1935. "Winnipeg Rugby Club Faces Difficult Assignment at Osborne Stadium." Winnipeg Free Press, September 28:30.

———. 1935. "Winnipeg Rugby Club Holds Heavy Work-out on Tuesday." Winnipeg Free Press, September 4:14.

———. 1935. "Winnipegs All Set for North Dakota Freshmen." Winnipeg Free Press, October 24:15.

———. 1935. "Winnipegs are Impressive in Last Heavy Scrimmage." Winnipeg Free Press, September 11:16.

———. 1935. "Winnipegs Are Seen in Stiff Drill Wednesday." Winnipeg Free Press, September 12:15.

———. 1935. "Winnipegs Cheered by Discovery Fritz' Wrist not Broken." Winnipeg Free Press, December 5:1.

———. 1935. "Winnipeg's Grid Machine Ready for Concordia at Osborne Saturday Night." Winnipeg Free Press, September 14:25.

———. 1935. "Winnipegs Will Be at Full Strength--Professional Clubs Are Impressive." Winnipeg Free Press, October 23:14.

———. 1935. [No Heading]. Winnipeg Free Press, September 24:15.

Winnipeg Manitoban. 1930. "Varsity Grads Star in Hamilton Tiger vs. Winnipeg All-Star Rugby Encounter." Winnipeg Manitoban, September 23:4.

———. 1931. "Brown and Gold Take On St. John's This Saturday." Winnipeg Manitoban, September 29:4.

Bibliography

———. 1931. "Varsity Seniors Trimmed by Winnipegs 10-2." Winnipeg Manitoban, October 20:1.
———. 1931. "Varsity Triumphs Against Old Boys 26-16." Winnipeg Manitoban, September 29:1.
———. 1931. "Varsity, 'Pegs, St. John's Form Senior League." Winnipeg Manitoban, September 22:4.
———. 1932. "Y.M.H.A. and 'Pegs Draw, 2-2." Winnipeg Manitoban, October 12:3.
———. 1933. "Ex-'U' Stars with 'Pegs Express 'Die-for-Dear-Old-Rutgers' Spirit." Winnipeg Manitoban, November 3:3.
———. 1933. "Position of Athletics." Winnipeg Manitoban, October 20:2.
———. 1933. "Protests Omission of Cronin from List of Students with 'Pegs." Winnipeg Manitoban, November 14:3.
———. 1933. "Strong Deer Lodgers Vanquish Varsity in Important Contest." Winnipeg Manitoban, October 6:3.
———. 1933. "Varsity Students and Alumni Are Prominent on Roster of Western Champs." Winnipeg Manitoban, November 14:3.
———. 1934. "Brown and Gold Rugby Squad Will Travel to Minot for Game Friday." Winnipeg Manitoban, October 26:3.
———. 1934. "Buffaloes Go Down to Defeat at Hands of Jamestown College." Winnipeg Manitoban, October 10:3.
———. 1934. "Buffaloes Play Smart Rugby But Drop Game." Winnipeg Manitoban, October 30:3.
———. 1934. "Down the Bison Trail." Winnipeg Manitoban, October 2:3.
———. 1934. "Extra: Varsity Football Squad Must Drop Ineligibles." Winnipeg Manitoban, October 16:1.
———. 1934. "Fete for Dakotans Arranged." Winnipeg Manitoban, September 28:1.
———. 1934. "Grant Longhurst Resigns as Football Manager." Winnipeg Manitoban, October 30:1.
———. 1934. "Hass Coached Buffaloes Win Opening Game." Winnipeg Manitoban, October 2:3.
———. 1934. "Hilarity Reigns around Bonfire on Booster Night." Winnipeg Manitoban, October 2:1.
———. 1934. "Intercollegiate Rugby Resumed." Winnipeg Manitoban, September 28:1.
———. 1934. "North Dakota Freshmen Defeat Varsity Bisons." Winnipeg Manitoban, October 16:3.
———. 1934. "North Dakota Freshmen Play Bisons Saturday." Winnipeg Manitoban, October 10:3.
———. 1934. "Prices Reduced for Rugby Tickets." Winnipeg Manitoban, October 2:1.
———. 1934. "Rival Captain." Winnipeg Manitoban, September 28:1.
———. 1934. "Rugby Game Cancelled." Winnipeg Manitoban, November 16:1.
———. 1934. "Stadium Progress Is Reported at Meeting of U.M.S.U. Council." Winnipeg Manitoban, September 28:1.
———. 1934. "Star Player." Winnipeg Manitoban, September 28:1.
———. 1934. "Three Rugby Players to Register." Winnipeg Manitoban, October 19:1.
———. 1934. "To Boost Football Tonight." Winnipeg Manitoban, September 28:1.
———. 1934. "University of Saskatchewan May Meet Bisons." Winnipeg Manitoban, November 13:1.
———. 1934. "Varsity Bisons Play Powerful Winnipegs Tomorrow." Winnipeg Manitoban, October 19:1.
———. 1934. "Varsity Bisons Tackle Jamestown Tonight." Winnipeg Manitoban, October 5:3.
———. 1934. "Varsity Engage Winnipegs for Title Tomorrow." Winnipeg Manitoban, October 26:3.
———. 1934. "Varsity Gridders Brilliant against Winnipegs." Winnipeg Manitoban, October 23:3.
———. 1934. "Varsity Play Minot Tonite." Winnipeg Manitoban, November 2:3.
———. 1934. "Varsity Scores 14-3 Win over Deer Lodge in Final Home Game." Winnipeg Manitoban, November 2:3.
———. 1934. "Varsity's New Rugby Coach." Winnipeg Manitoban, September 28:1.
———. 1934. "Walter Ohde, Varsity Line Coach, Has Enviable Record." Winnipeg Manitoban, October 5:3.
———. 1935. "Editorialettes." Winnipeg Manitoban, September 27:2.
———. 1935. "Interfaculty Rugby Will Be Inaugurated with a Six Team League to Commence on Saturday, October Fifth, at Fort Garry." Winnipeg Manitoban, September 25:3.

———. 1935. "Questionnaire Results Compiled." Winnipeg Manitoban, March 15:1.
———. 1935. "Rugby--New Style." Winnipeg Manitoban, September 27:2.
Winnipeg Tribune. "Proposed Trip Is Called Off: Winnipeg Rugby Football Club Will Not Play in Grand Forks This Season." Winnipeg Tribune, October 29: 8.
———. 1903. "Shamrocks Had Small Part of Score." Winnipeg Tribune, November 3: 8.
———. 1904. "Will Play at Grand Forks: Winnipeg Rugby Club Accepts Challenge of North Dakota University." Winnipeg Tribune, October 8: 8.
———. 1905. "Picked Team Will Play: Cracks of Winnipeg Rugbyists to Meet University of North Dakota Eleven." November 1:8.
———. 1905. "Sporting Snap-Shots." Winnipeg Tribune, September 26:6.
———. 1907. "Sport Nuggets." Winnipeg Tribune, November 16:6.
———. 1929. "Tigers Triumph in City Rugby Championship Struggle." Winnipeg Tribune, October 21:14.
———. 1930. "Juvenile Rugby Honors to Rest with Hebrews." Winnipeg Tribune, November 10:12.
———. 1930. "'Pegs Bow to Champion St. John's Team 7 to 3." Winnipeg Tribune, September 15:14.
———. 1930. "Three Teams Will Make Up Senior Rugby League Here." Winnipeg Tribune, May 15:16.
———. 1931. "Looking Over High School Athletics." Winnipeg Tribune, October 6:15.
———. 1931. "Manitoba Varsity and Roughriders Remain Undefeated." Winnipeg Tribune, November 12:12.
———. 1931. "New City Grid League Formed." Winnipeg Tribune, August 29:17.
———. 1931. "Rugby Follower Avers Officials Too Strict." Winnipeg Tribune, November 17:13.
———. 1931. "St. John's Prove Too Good for 'Peg Gridders." Winnipeg Tribune, October 13:19.
———. 1931. "West Will Be Scene of Many Crucial Rugby Games." Winnipeg Tribune, November 6:18.
———. 1932. "Big Grid Game at Wesley Called Off." Winnipeg Tribune, October 29:20.
———. 1932. "Both 'Pegs and Saints Will Play Nodak Team." Winnipeg Tribune, November 8:13.
———. 1932. "Change in Plans for North Dakota Game." Winnipeg Tribune, November 9:26.
———. 1932. "Cronin Drills 'Pegs in Legal Interference." Winnipeg Tribune, November 10:12.
———. 1932. "Garrison Senior Gridders Battle Winnipegs Today." Winnipeg Tribune, October 10:11.
———. 1932. "Important Senior and Junior Rugby Matches Today." Winnipeg Tribune, September 24:22.
———. 1932. "Innovations for 1932 Rugby." Winnipeg Tribune, August 27:16.
———. 1932. "New Varsity Grid Coach Is Well Equipped." Winnipeg Tribune, September 8:12.
———. 1932. "North Dakota Frosh to Play St. John's Team." Winnipeg Tribune, October 25:15.
———. 1932. "Roughriders and St. John's Launch Rugby Season at Osborne Stadium." Winnipeg Tribune, September 3:19.
———. 1932. "Rugby Classic Played at Wesley Tomorrow." Winnipeg Tribune, October 21:15.
———. 1932. "Rugby Football." Winnipeg Tribune, November 10:13.
———. 1932. "Rugby Games Billed for Wesley Park Called Off." Winnipeg Tribune, November 11:12.
———. 1932. "Rugby Holds Spotlight in Sport." Winnipeg Tribune, September 26:12.
———. 1932. "Rugby." Winnipeg Tribune, September 2:16.
———. 1932. "Saints Will Receive Stiff Test Saturday." Winnipeg Tribune, October 27:16.
———. 1932. "Senior Rugby Chariot Starts Next Saturday." Winnipeg Tribune, September 15:17.
———. 1932. "Senior Rugby Crown within Saints' Grasp." Winnipeg Tribune, October 19:16.
———. 1932. "Senior Rugby." Winnipeg Tribune, September 15:16.
———. 1932. "St. John's Conquers 'Pegs in Final Encounter." Winnipeg Tribune, October 24:14.
———. 1932. "St. John's Juggernaut Attack Routes Garrison, 36-1." Winnipeg Tribune, September 29:13.

Bibliography

———. 1932. "St. John's Ready for Go with Roughriders." Winnipeg Tribune, September 1:10.

———. 1932. "Surprises Abundant as Eastern Rugby Opens." Winnipeg Tribune, October 10:11.

———. 1932. "Wanted 1,500 Boys." Winnipeg Tribune, September 23:16.

———. 1932. "Western Canada Intercollegiate Sport Suspended." Winnipeg Tribune, September 10:20.

———. 1932. "Winnipegs Take Over Juniors." Winnipeg Tribune, September 21:14.

———. 1932. "Winnipegs Will Send Fast Backfield Against Saints." Winnipeg Tribune, September 30:18.

———. 1933. "5 Dead; Three Dying in Toilers' Crash." Winnipeg Tribune, March 31:1.

———. 1933. "Army Favored to Win Rugby Game Saturday." Winnipeg Tribune, October 6:21.

———. 1933. "Booster Rugby." Winnipeg Tribune, October 27:20.

———. 1933. "Cronin in Optimistic Mood as 'Pegs Head Eastward." Winnipeg Tribune, November 28:13.

———. 1933. "Cronin Wants More Players." Winnipeg Tribune, September 7:17.

———. 1933. "Gridiron Test Here Today." Winnipeg Tribune, September 30:21.

———. 1933. "Manitoba Rugby Union Urges Sweeping Rule Changes." Winnipeg Tribune, April 11:15.

———. 1933. "Nodak Game Saturday Fires Rugby Interest." Winnipeg Tribune, September 22:17.

———. 1933. "Nodak Teachers Bring Light, Speedy Squad." Winnipeg Tribune, September 29:18.

———. 1933. "Pegs Leave for East on Tuesday with 22 Players." Winnipeg Tribune, November 27:12.

———. 1933. "Pegs Look Weak in Beating Juniors, 9 to 0." Winnipeg Tribune, October 30:15.

———. 1933. "Pegs Ready for Garrison." Winnipeg Tribune, October 9:12.

———. 1933. "Pegs Train for Week-End Tilts." Winnipeg Tribune, October 3:13.

———. 1933. "Power Vs. Speed in Senior Rugby Opener." Winnipeg Tribune, September 16:21.

———. 1933. "Pro. Rugby Is Mooted in East." Winnipeg Tribune, July 25:10.

———. 1933. "Rugby League Starts Advance Ticket Sale." Winnipeg Tribune, August 24:12.

———. 1933. "Schedule for Senior Rugby Loop Announced." Winnipeg Tribune, September 15:17.

———. 1933. "Shamrock Team Triumphs over Garrison Again." Winnipeg Tribune, October 9:13.

———. 1933. "Shamrocks Upset Army in Senior Grid Opener." Winnipeg Tribune, September 19:16.

———. 1933. "Soldiers Play Winnipeg Team This Evening." Winnipeg Tribune, September 27:14.

———. 1933. "Two Teams Likely to Make Up Senior Rugby League." Winnipeg Tribune, June 13:13.

———. 1933. "Van Vliet Sends Army into Action Tonight." Winnipeg Tribune, September 18:14.

———. 1933. "'Varsity Gridders Will Play 'Pegs Saturday." Winnipeg Tribune, October 26:12.

———. 1933. "Wanted 2,000 Boys." Winnipeg Tribune, October 5:15.

———. 1933. "Weather Man Fails to Stop Today's Game." Winnipeg Tribune, October 21:23.

———. 1933. "West Declares Sioux in Shape." Winnipeg Tribune, September 23:21.

———. 1933. "Winnipeg and Calgary Divide Western Rugby Titles." Winnipeg Tribune, November 13:14.

———. 1933. "Winnipeg Club Lines Up Powerful Gridiron Team." Winnipeg Tribune, August 12:20-21.

———. 1933. "Winnipegs and Garrison Rout North Dakota Teachers." Winnipeg Tribune, October 2:11.

———. 1933. "Winnipegs Defeat Garrisons, 33-6, in Senior Rugby." Winnipeg Tribune, September 28:13.

———. 1933. "Winnipegs Do Well in Game with North Dakota." Winnipeg Tribune, September 25:12.

———. 1933. "Winnipegs Face Powerful Opposition Tomorrow." Winnipeg Tribune, October 20:18.

———. 1933. "Winnipegs Hold Initial Workout at Carruthers." Winnipeg Tribune, October 31:14.

———. 1933. "Winnipegs May Extend South Dakota Gridders." Winnipeg Tribune, October 13:22.

———. 1933. "Winnipegs Nose-out Concordia College, 14 to 13." Winnipeg Tribune, October 23:12.

———. 1933. "Winnipegs Uncover Spectacular Passing Attack." Winnipeg Tribune, October 10:10.

———. 1933. [Damaged Headline: "...ota Under Canadian Rules."] Winnipeg Tribune, October 16:12.

———. 1934. "American Football." Winnipeg Tribune, September 28:17.

———. 1934. "Banished 'U' Gridders Continue to Attend Practices." Winnipeg Tribune, October 17:14.

———. 1934. "Broken Arm Forces Eddie James Out of Rugby Again." Winnipeg Tribune, October 22:4.

———. 1934. "College Gridders Open Season at Stadium Today." Winnipeg Tribune, September 29:22.

———. 1934. "Conacher to Kick Off in Saturday Game." Winnipeg Tribune, October 26:19.

———. 1934. "Concordia Rated Above 1933 Eleven." Winnipeg Tribune, October 4:12.

———. 1934. "Concordia Sweeps Series with Winnipegs." Winnipeg Tribune, October 9:14-15.

———. 1934. "Cronin Guest of Grid Supporters Before Departure." Winnipeg Tribune, May 5:20.

———. 1934. "Excursion to Regina." Winnipeg Tribune, October 27:21.

———. 1934. "Former Garrison Player with Ottawa 'Riders." Winnipeg Tribune, October 24:15.

———. 1934. "Forward Pass Will Be Major Item with 'Pegs." Winnipeg Tribune, September 11:14.

———. 1934. "Injuries Mar Winnipegs' Defeat by North Dakota 'U.'" Winnipeg Tribune, September 22:20.

———. 1934. "Johnny Ferraro Named Hamilton Rugby Coach." Winnipeg Tribune, August 15:11.

———. 1934. "Kobrinsky's 40-yard Run Gives Varsity Victory." Winnipeg Tribune, October 1:10.

———. 1934. "Large Squad Trains Under New University Grid Coach." Winnipeg Tribune, September 8:18.

———. 1934. "Last-Minute Touch Climaxes 'Pegs' Losing Debut." Winnipeg Tribune, September 17:14.

———. 1934. "Lineup and Summary." Winnipeg Tribune, October 25:13.

———. 1934. "Meralomas and 'Riders Retain Championships." Winnipeg Tribune, October 22:4.

———. 1934. "Minnesota 'U' Rugby Squad to Play Here." Winnipeg Tribune, September 8:19.

———. 1934. "Minot Gridders Rout Varsity." Winnipeg Tribune, November 3:18.

———. 1934. "North Dakota Freshmen Here This Weekend." Winnipeg Tribune, October 12:16.

———. 1934. "Peg Gridders Show Improvement." Winnipeg Tribune, October 29:15.

———. 1934. "'Pegs Present Squad Shows Unusual Class." Winnipeg Tribune, September 13:14.

———. 1934. "Pegs to Make Their Last Local Appearance Today." Winnipeg Tribune, October 27:20.

———. 1934. "Rugby Shows Wide Influence of U.S. Leaders." Winnipeg Tribune, November 24:20.

———. 1934. "Senior Grid Final at Coast Today." Winnipeg Tribune, November 10:23.

———. 1934. "Smart Jamestown Team Trims Varsity." Winnipeg Tribune, October 6:19.

———. 1934. "'U' Gridders Learning Fast." Winnipeg Tribune, September 13:14.

———. 1934. "University Arranges New Rugby Football Campaign." Winnipeg Tribune, April 7:24.

———. 1934. "Varsity Adds Two New Plays." Winnipeg Tribune, October 11:13.

———. 1934. "Varsity Coach Works on Line for Saturday." Winnipeg Tribune, October 10:12.

———. 1934. "Varsity Grid Lineup to Remain Unchanged." Winnipeg Tribune, October 4:13.

———. 1934. "Varsity Meets Jamestown Tonight." Winnipeg Tribune, October 5:16.

———. 1934. "Varsity Trounced by North Dakota Freshmen." Winnipeg Tribune, October 15:12.

———. 1934. "Winnipeg Passing Attack Fails to Avert Defeat." Winnipeg Tribune, October 16:14.

———. 1934. "Winnipeg Rugby Club to Have Powerful Team." Winnipeg Tribune, May 3:15.

———. 1934. "Winnipegs Drop Thrill-Packed Game to Concordia, 33-27." Winnipeg Tribune, October 8:10-11.

———. 1934. "Winnipegs Face First Test of 1934 Tonight." Winnipeg Tribune, September 15:26.

Bibliography

———. 1934. "Winnipegs Meet Strong Concordia Team Today." Winnipeg Tribune, October 6:18.
———. 1934. "Winnipegs Open Grid Season at Forks Tonight." Winnipeg Tribune, September 21:16.
———. 1934. "Winnipegs Prepare for Dual Concordia Duel." Winnipeg Tribune, September 29:22.
———. 1934. "Work of 'Peg Backfield Shows New Scoring Power." Winnipeg Tribune, October 5:16.
———. 1934. "Y.M.H.A. Stars Ready for Deer Lodge Squad." Winnipeg Tribune, November 16:19.
———. 1934." United College Notes." Winnipeg Tribune, September 29:30.
———. 1935. "A.A.U. Plans Investigation of Roy Berry." Winnipeg Tribune, November 20:14.
———. 1935. "Bob Fritz to Coach Winnipegs." Winnipeg Tribune, April 5:14.
———. 1935. "Boyd's $125 Bid Wins Boots, Aids Stocking Fun." Winnipeg Tribune, December 24:1.
———. 1935. "Citizens Jam Auditorium to Pay Tribune to Members of Triumphant Rugby Team." Winnipeg Tribune, December 11:3.
———. 1935. "Civic Celebration of 'Peg Victory Planned." Winnipeg Tribune, December 9:17.
———. 1935. "Cobbers Boast Passing Attack." Winnipeg Tribune, September 9:16.
———. 1935. "Eastern Scribes Pay Tribute to 'Pegs." Winnipeg Tribune, December 9:16,18.
———. 1935. "Frank Hannibal Heads Winnipeg Rugby Club." Winnipeg Tribune, January 14:10.
———. 1935. "Granville, N.Y., Youth Out with Winnipegs." Winnipeg Tribune, September 24:11.
———. 1935. "Hamilton's Conquered Tigers Admit New Champions Were Better Team." Winnipeg Tribune, December 9:14.
———. 1935. "Hanson Gives Famous Boots to Stocking Fund." Winnipeg Tribune, December 11:1.
———. 1935. "Hanson Runner-Up to Canada's Outstanding Athlete." Winnipeg Tribune, December 24:12.
———. 1935. "Highlights in Welcome for Rugby Heroes." December 10:1,4.
———. 1935. "Large Crowd Gives Squad Fine Send-Off." Winnipeg Tribune, November 28:15.
———. 1935. "March to the Title." Winnipeg Tribune, December 9:16.
———. 1935. "Minnesota All-Stars Are Bringing Strong Wingline." Winnipeg Tribune, September 27:18.
———. 1935. "'Pegs on Way East for Rugby Final." Winnipeg Tribune, November 28:15.
———. 1935. "'Pegs Ready for Cobbers." Winnipeg Tribune, September 10:16.
———. 1935. "Pegs to Play in Final." Winnipeg Tribune, November 18:14.
———. 1935. "Ritchie Reluctant to Express Opinion on Regina-Winnipeg Game." Winnipeg Tribune, November 2:29.
———. 1935. "Roaring Welcome Is Planned for Title-winning Winnipegs." Winnipeg Tribune, December 9:1.
———. 1935. "Rugby Football Season Opens Tonight." Winnipeg Tribune, September 14:29.
———. 1935. "Rugby Football." Winnipeg Tribune, October 4:14.
———. 1935. "Sarnia Imps Pick Hamilton to Win." Winnipeg Tribune, December 5:15.
———. 1935. "Statistics of the Game." Winnipeg Tribune, November 11:12.
———. 1935. "Ten All-State High School Players on Nodak Squad." Winnipeg Tribune, October 23:12.
———. 1935. "The Weather Was the Same." Winnipeg Tribune, November 1:21.
———. 1935. "Tiger-Killers Given Thunderous Welcome." Winnipeg Tribune, December 10:1,4.
———. 1935. "Tigers Are Favored to Retain Grey Cup." Winnipeg Tribune, December 6:19.
———. 1935. "Vics to Meet Weekend Winnipeg Team Saturday." Winnipeg Tribune, October 18:20.
———. 1935. "Victoria Senior Grid Team to Operate." Winnipeg Tribune, February 12:11.
———. 1935. "Winnipeg Rugby Club Favors More Reinforcements." Winnipeg Tribune, January 9:12.
———. 1935. "Winnipeg Wildly Excited over Triumph at Hamilton." Winnipeg Tribune, December 9:17.
———. 1935. "Winnipegs Coast to 21-13 Victory over Minnesota Team." Winnipeg Tribune, September 30:12.
———. 1935. "Winnipegs Hold All-Stars in Great Respect." Winnipeg Tribune, September 25:15.
———. 1935. "Winnipegs Ready for Game Saturday." Winnipeg Tribune, November 1:14.
———. 1935. "Winnipegs Rout North Dakota Frosh." Winnipeg Tribune, October 25:15.
———. 1935. "Winnipegs Take Form after Hard Drilling." Winnipeg Tribune, September 7:35.
———. 1935. "Winnipegs to Leave for Detroit Next Wednesday." Winnipeg Tribune, November 22:14.
———. 1935. "Winnipegs Trim Vics 29-0 to Take Provincial Title." Winnipeg Tribune, October 14:10.
———. 1935. "Winnipegs, Minus Seven Regulars, Crush Victorias, 39-1." Winnipeg Tribune, October 21:12.
———. 1965. "It Was Jazz, Depression, and the Dusters... Rough, Lean Unselfish Years." Winnipeg Tribune, April 6:A8.
Winona Daily News. 1932. "George Davies of Winona Named Forward on All-State Cage Team." Winona Daily News, March 21:9.
———. 1932. "Nic Musty Appointed Head Football Coach at St. Mary's." Winona Daily News, December 31:13.
———. 1933. "St. Mary's Knocks Concordia Out of Conference Lead." Winona Daily News, November 6:8.
———. 1934. "Musty Resigns as Coach at St. Mary's to Take Up Study of Medicine." Winona Daily News, March 16:11.
———. 1934. "Redmen to Clash with Cobbers at Moorhead Field." Winona Daily News, October 22:10.
———. 1992. "Ex-SMC Coach Krause Dies." Winona Daily News, December 12:9.
Wright Funeral Home. Robert F. Fritz. Moorhead: Wright Funeral Home.
Zukerman, Earl. 2012. THIS DATE IN HISTORY: First football game was May 14, 1874. May 14. Accessed March 18, 2020. https://www.mcgill.ca/channels/news/date-history-first-football-game-was-may-14-1874-106694.
Zuppke, Robert C. Football Technique and Tactics. Champaign, Illinois: Baily and Himes, Publishers, 1924.

Bibliography

ABOUT THE AUTHOR

R. C. Christiansen is an educator with a Master of Fine Arts in Creative Writing from Minnesota State University Moorhead. He is a member of the Professional Football Researchers Association and has more than 30 years experience as a journalist, technical writer, creative writer, editor, and publisher.

Made in the USA
Las Vegas, NV
01 January 2023